末帝宝鉴

The Last Emperor's Collection

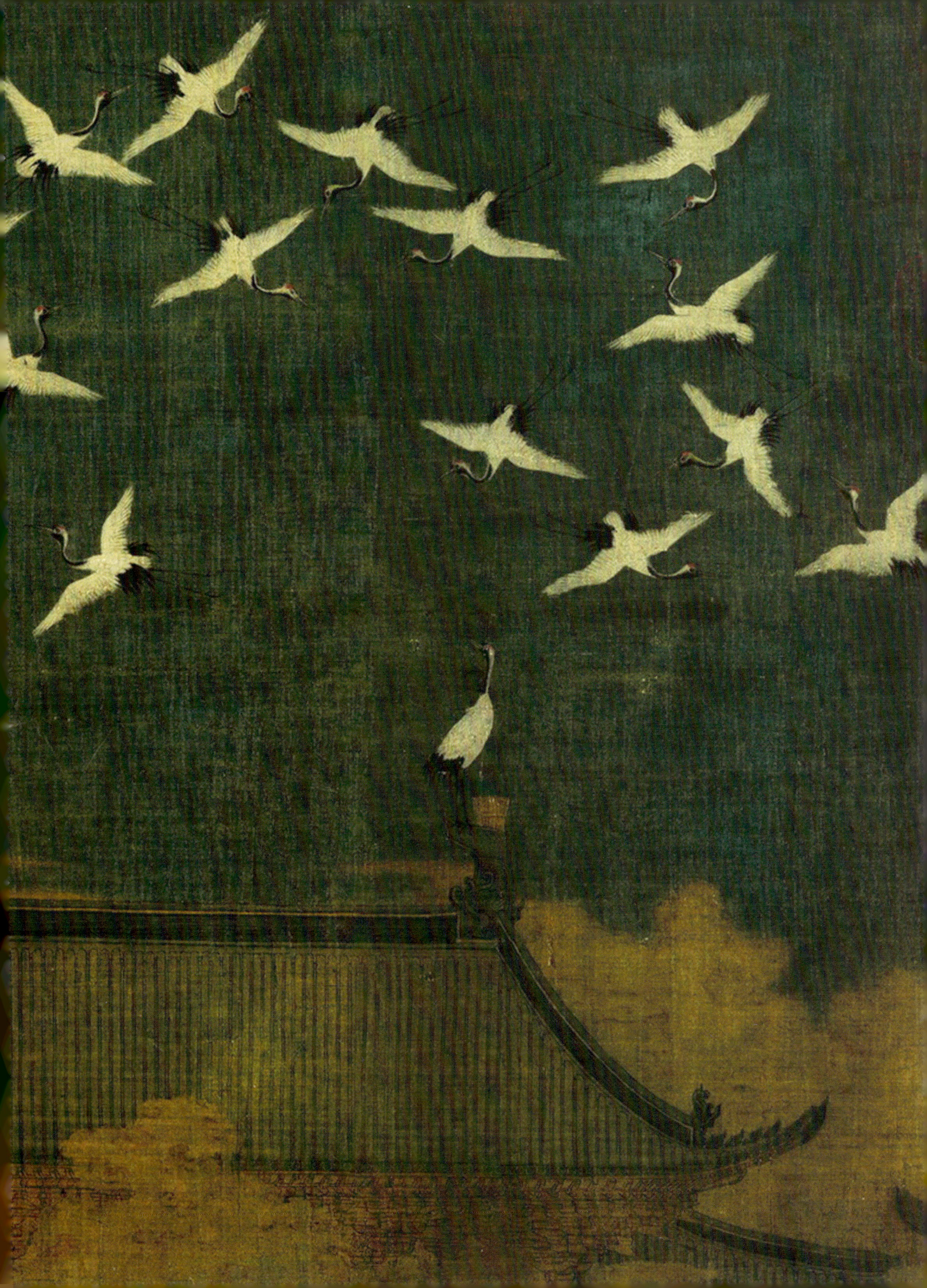

The Last Emperor's Collection

Masterpieces of Painting and Calligraphy from the Liaoning Provincial Museum

Willow Weilan Hai Chang
Yang Renkai
David Ake Sensabaugh

With contributions from Huang Weili, Cary Liu, and Joseph Scheier-Dolberg

Edited by J. May Lee Barrett

China Institute Gallery
China Institute
New York
2008

Distributed by Art Media Resources, Ltd

東坡記游
元豐六年十月十二日夜解衣
欲睡月色入戶欣然起行念

末帝宝鉴

辽宁省博物馆藏
清宫散佚明清书画

海蔚蓝
杨仁恺
江文苇

并包括黄伟利、刘怡玮、
史耀华的文章

华美协进社中国美术馆
纽约， 2008

This catalogue was published to accompany the exhibition
The Last Emperor's Collection: Masterpieces of Painting and Calligraphy from the Liaoning Provincial Museum
Organized by the China Institute Gallery in collaboration with the Liaoning Provincial Museum
and dedicated to the memory of Mr. Yang Renkai.

该图录为配合"末帝宝鉴：辽宁省博物馆藏清宫散佚明清书画"展而出版。
该展览由华美协进社中国美术馆与辽宁省博物馆联合组展。
谨以此展献给杨仁恺先生。

The exhibition will be presented at the following locations:

China Institute Gallery	华美协进社中国美术馆
125 East 65th Street	纽约市东 65 街125号
New York, NY 10065	纽约州，邮编10065
212-744-8181	电话：212-744-8181
September 25–December 14, 2008	展览日期：2008年9月25日至12月14日
Taft Museum of Art	泰夫特艺术博物馆
316 Pike Street	派克街316号
Cincinnati, OH 45202	辛辛纳提，俄亥俄州，邮编45202
513-684-4513	电话：513-684-4513
May 29–August 2, 2009	展览日期：2009年5月29日至8月2日

Library of Congress Control Number:	2008921860
ISBN-10:	0-9774054-3-5
ISBN-13:	978-0-9774054-3-5
General Editor and Project Director: Willow Weilan Hai Chang	主编暨艺术总监：海蔚蓝
English Editor: J. May Lee Barrett	英文编辑：钟美梨
Chinese Editor: Zhou Xiaolu	中文编辑：周晓陆
Translators: David Huiwei Shen, Mansheng Wang, and Ling-Yi Chien	翻译：沈慧伟， 王满晟， 简菱仪
Catalogue Designer: Peter Lukic	图录设计：鲁克彼得
Exhibition Designer: Perry Hu	展览设计：胡维智
Photos courtesy of the Liaoning Provincial Museum unless otherwise indicated	图片如未注明，则均由辽宁省博物馆提供
Printed by Pressroom Printer and Designer, Hong Kong	

Chinese is romanized in the *pinyin* system throughout the text and bibliography
except for the names of Chinese authors writing in Western languages.
Chinese terms cited in Western-language titles remain in their
original form and have not been converted.

图录中所有中文皆以罗马拼音为准。
以外国文字为准的中国作者名字或其他名称则
一概按照原文未作转换。

Cover illustration (section, cat. no. 3)
Zhu Zhanji (Emperor Xuanzong, 1399–1435)
Ten- Thousand -Year- Old Pine Tree, 1431
Handscroll, ink on paper

封面（局部，图录第 3 号）
朱瞻基（宣宗，1399–1435）
万年松图， 1431
手卷，水墨纸本

Half title page: Seal of the last emperor, Puyi (Xuantong yulan zhibao [square/relief])
Frontispiece opposite English title page: Detail of fig. 8 on p. 11
Frontispiece opposite Chinese title page: Detail of cat. no. 6
Last page: Seal of the Qianlong emperor (Yizisun [square/intaglio])

To all those whose passion for art
has promoted its practice and preservation

谨以此展览图录献给所有热爱艺术的人们

Contents
目录

Sponsors of the Exhibition

展览赞助者

*This catalogue, the exhibition, and its related programming have been made possible in part through the generous support of the following**

Patrons

Fidelity Foundation

National Endowment for the Arts

Leaders

Asian Cultural Council

The Blakemore Foundation

Mary Lawrence Porter

Argie and Oscar Tang

Mary and James G. Wallach Foundation

Laurie and David Y. Ying

Contributors

Dr. Young Yang Chung

Carolyn Hsu-Balcer and René Balcer

John R. and Lynne W. Doss

William W. Karatz

Supporters

John R. and Julia B. Curtis
Winnie and Michael Feng
Nancy and Hart Fessenden
Agnes Gund
Angela H. King
Theresa M. Reilly
Jeannette N. Rider
Marie-Hélène Weill
J and H Weldon Foundation,
in honor of Willow Weilan Hai Chang

Individuals

Susan Beningson and Steve Arons,
in memory of Renee Beningson
Dr. Richard and Ruth Dickes
Ta Chun Hsu
Robert W. Lyons, M.D.
Gerard M. Meistrell
Howard and Mary Ann Rogers
Mei Wu Stanton
Denis C. and Kathleen Yang
Robert P. and Barbara Youngman

We are also grateful for the continuing support to China Institute Gallery from China Institute's Friends of the Gallery.

*At the time of printing

Message from the Chair of the Board of Trustees and the President of China Institute

Painting and calligraphy, long considered the best artistic and cultural achievements of Chinese culture, are two of China's most recognizable art forms. Their prominence today is due not only to the gifted artists who created these works of art, but also the passionate connoisseurs who collected, recorded, and preserved them over the course of centuries. China Institute Gallery is proud to present *The Last Emperor's Collection: Masterpieces of Painting and Calligraphy from the Liaoning Provincial Museum,* one of the first major explorations of the history of collecting by China's rulers. Drawing from a group of paintings and calligraphy that had been collected by Chinese emperors, the exhibition is unique in revealing the lives of the artworks and how emperors of China sought to preserve and protect Chinese tradition. It reflects upon the many intricate and, indeed, intimate relationships between art and rulers, scholars and people. Though numerous dynasties have risen and fallen throughout Chinese history, the desire to study, appreciate, and conserve Chinese culture continues today.

China Institute is very fortunate to collaborate with the Liaoning Provincial Museum on this exhibition and fully-illustrated bilingual catalogue. By exhibiting the Liaoning Provincial Museum's masterpieces from the imperial collection, some of which will be on view in America for the first time at China Institute Gallery, it is our shared hope to bring a new appreciation for Chinese painting and calligraphy not only as an art form but also in the context of cultural and political history, with which they were indubitably intertwined. This partnership between Chinese and American scholars is proof of how shared cross-cultural perspectives can lead to greater cultural understanding.

The curators of this exhibition, Willow Weilan Hai Chang, the Director of China Institute Gallery, the late Yang Renkai, the former Honorable Director of the Liaoning Provincial Museum, and Dr. David Ake Sensabaugh, the Ruth and Bruce Dayton Curator of Asian Art at the Yale University Art Gallery, are respected scholars of Chinese painting. They have each published significant research in the area of Chinese art history and have made new contributions to this understudied subject of the imperial collection. We are grateful to them for their dedication and commitment to the project. We would like to thank all the participants of this project, who, under the leadership of Ms. Hai Chang and with the support of dedicated gallery staff, have helped bring every element of this project together seamlessly.

We extend our gratitude to the Liaoning Provincial Museum for sharing the desire to make these masterpieces available to the American audience and for entrusting our gallery to exhibit them. This project would not have gone forward without the assistance of the Liaoning Provincial Cultural Bureau on the Chinese side and the support of the members of China Institute's Board of Trustees, our Gallery Committee, and the Sponsors of the Exhibition, as well as the continuing support of our loyal Friends of the Gallery, on the American side. Our sincere gratitude goes to all of them.

Virginia A. Kamsky
Chair, Board of Trustees

Sara Judge McCalpin
President

致　辞

书法与绘画，一直被公认为中国文化中最有代表性的两种艺术形式。它们的突出成就，不仅属于那些创作出艺术作品的杰出艺术家，同时也属于那些收藏、记录与保存它们的执着的鉴赏家。此次，华美协进社中国美术馆非常荣幸地展出《末帝宝鉴：辽宁省博物馆藏清宫散佚明清书画》的展览，这是在美国探讨中国宫廷收藏史的首举。这些曾为中国皇帝们收藏的书画作品，独特地显示出艺术作品的生命力，以及中国皇帝们寻求保存与承袭中国传统的迫切需求，反映了艺术与社会、以及各阶层人们之间错综复杂而又十分紧密的关系。尽管中国历史上经历了许多朝代的兴衰更替，但这种对中国文化的研究、对书画的鉴赏与保存的热情一直延续到了今天。

我们很荣幸得以与辽宁省博物馆合作举办这次展览，并一起制作双语的展览图录。辽宁省博物馆的馆藏佳作多来自宫廷收藏，有些作品将是第一次在美国展示，我们希望这次展览能给观众带来鉴赏中国书画的全新感受。书法与绘画不仅是艺术，而且与政治和文化密切相关，并有着不可置疑的交融性。这次中美两国学者的合作，证明跨文化视角的交流与共享，可以引导我们更全面地增进对文化的理解。

该展览的策划人为华美协进社中国美术馆的馆长海蔚蓝、辽宁省博物馆的前荣誉馆长杨仁凯、以及耶鲁大学艺术馆亚洲艺术部主任江文苇博士。他们是中国艺术领域中有见解的学者，各自都曾发表过重要的研究成果，此次又对宫廷收藏这个课题作出了前卫的探讨。我们感谢他们在这个研究课题中所做的贡献，并感谢这个项目的所有参与者，感谢海蔚蓝馆长的领导及馆员们的辛勤工作，环环相扣，成功地完成了这一项目。

我们要特别感谢辽宁省博物馆对我中国美术馆的信任，并慷慨将其珍藏与美国公众分享，亦对支持这个项目的辽宁省文化局致谢。借此机会，我们也对华美协进社董事会、艺术委员会、展览赞助者及我中国美术馆之友的竭诚支持，表示衷心地感谢，并对所有关怀这一项目的人们致以最诚挚的谢意。

华美协进社董事长　甘维珍
华美协进社社长　江芷若

Foreword

With its long, continuous history and wide-ranging influence, painting and calligraphy are the most characteristic art forms of Chinese traditional culture. After thousands of years of evolution and vicissitudes, the ancient works of Chinese painting and calligraphy that have come down to us embody the thought, wisdom, and feelings of the Chinese people. They are not only the cultural wealth of the Chinese people, but also the cultural heritage of humankind.

The period of transition from the Ming to the Qing dynasty in the late fourteenth century is an important stage in the development of Chinese painting and calligraphy: a wide range of subjects and styles were explored and many famous artists emerged. People, from the emperor at the top to commoners at the bottom, actively practiced the art of painting and calligraphy. That these arts had spread through the court and among the populace shows how they had become popular and flourished. This exhibition focuses on works of painting and calligraphy by Ming and Qing dynasty masters that represent the styles and artistic levels in that period.

Owing to the serious attention and initiative of the feudal emperors in ancient China, famous works of painting and calligraphy that were handed down through generations were recorded by the internal affairs department of the imperial court. The Qianlong period (1736–95) of the Qing dynasty assembled the last major collection of ancient Chinese painting and calligraphy masterpieces. Greatly treasured, most of the works in this exhibition are from this former collection of the Qing imperial court.

The Liaoning Provincial Museum, founded in 1949, is a large-scale historical and art museum in China with a rich collection of cultural relics and works of fine art, as well as an integrated administrative system. Outstanding among its assemblage of superior and refined objects, this collection of ancient Chinese painting and calligraphy has especially profound characteristics and influence.

This exhibition marks the first time that masterpieces of painting and calligraphy from the Liaoning Provincial Museum will be shown in the United States. We thank China Institute for its invitation and the China Institute Gallery for its hard work in putting together the exhibition and catalogue. It is our hope that this exhibition will encourage further appreciation and understanding of traditional Chinese painting and calligraphy among American audiences. We wish this exhibition complete success!

Ma Baojie
Director
Liaoning Provincial Museum
June 2008

前　言

书法和绘画是中华民族传统文化最具特色的艺术品类，源远流长，影响广泛。千百年来历经沧桑变幻而传世的中国古代书画作品，凝聚着中华民族的思想、智慧和情感，是中华民族的文化财富，是人类的文化遗产。

十四世纪后的明清时代是中国书画艺术发展的重要阶段，题材广泛，风格多样，名家辈出。上至皇帝，下至平民，积极参与书画创作，书画艺术已波及到宫廷和民间，呈现出全面普及的繁盛局面。本次展览集中了明清时代各类名家书画作品，代表着明清时期书画艺术的风格和水平。

在中国古代，由于封建帝王的重视和倡导，传世的历代书画精品多收藏于宫廷内府。清代乾隆年间（公元1736－1795年），实现了中国古代书画精品的最后一次大集中。本次展览的展品多为清代宫廷旧藏，弥足珍视。

辽宁省博物馆是1949年建立的中国大型历史艺术博物馆，馆藏文物数量丰富，体系完整，品质精良，精品荟萃，其中尤以中国古代书画作品的收藏最具特色和影响。

本次展览为辽宁省博物馆馆藏书画精品首次赴美展出。感谢华美协进社的盛邀和中国美术馆同仁的辛勤努力，愿展览能为美国朋友观赏和认知中国传统书画提供契机和载体。预祝展览圆满成功！

中国辽宁省博物馆馆长 马宝杰
二〇〇八年六月

Preface

The word "emperor" (*tianzi*, or "son of heaven") that I often heard as a child would be used by my grandmother, mumbling in her Wu dialect accent, on two occasions. When she wanted to express the uncertainty of social or political changes, she would say, "one group of officials accompanies one dynasty's Son of Heaven" (*yichao tianzi, yichao chen*). But when describing something with great distance, she would always say, "the sky is as high as the emperor is far away" (*tian gao huangdi yuan*). Thus, I had the impression that emperors are always changeable and unreachably distant.

Emperors, of course, were indeed changeable throughout Chinese history; there are around 350 emperors from the first, Qin Shihuangdi (Ying Zheng; r. 221–210 BCE), to the last, Puyi (r. 1909–11). They were also distant, extremely removed from the common people and ensconced within secure, walled palaces—such as the Forbidden City. However, through the use of one item, the light-weight Chinese brush, Chinese cultural achievements endured through the vicissitudes of dynastic change and the distance between emperor and commoner diminished. Just as the Great Wall is the symbol of China as a nation, the brushwork in calligraphy and painting scrolls is emblematic of Chinese culture. In the use of brushwork, the creating of paintings and calligraphy, critiques of the artwork, and in collecting, emperor and commoner are placed on a level playing field with the same scale used for measuring intelligence, sentiments, skill at observation, creative strength, aesthetic sense, and learning.

This exhibition at the China Institute Gallery consists of twenty-four paintings which were recorded in the imperial catalogue *Shiqu baoji* and viewed by the Qianlong emperor (Hongli; r. 1736–95) and his successors, who left their seals as evidence of their connoisseurship. Among these works, *Copying Huaisu's "Thousand-Character Essay"* was executed by the Qianlong emperor himself in 1770. The calligraphy in wild cursive script, done with brush and ink on Chinese rice paper, is 683 cm long and could well be one of the emperor's calligraphic exercises, which he practiced often. Another imperial work of art is the Ming dynasty emperor Xuanzong's (Zhu Zhanji; r. 1426–35) *Ten-Thousand-Year-Old Pine Tree*, painted with brush and ink on Chinese rice paper in 1431. The scroll, 453 cm in length, was a special gift for the emperor's mother to celebrate her birthday. These artworks created by or touched by the emperors can now be viewed by the public. Reflecting on them, one feels like time is frozen and the emperors no longer distant.

The conception of this exhibition, with its emphasis on the emperors, came about quite fortuitously. In March 2005, when Shengyang was still cold from the tail end of winter, I visited the honorable director of the Liaoning Provincial Museum, Mr. Yang Renkai, at his home. I had known him for over a decade and hoped to organize an exhibition on the Neolithic Hongshan culture, known mostly for its jade objects. When I presented him with the catalogue *Passion for the Mountains: Seventeenth Century Landscape Paintings from the Nanjing Museum*, the first international exhibition that I had organized and curated for the China Institute Gallery, he quickly flipped through the pages, his eyes glittering, and burst out in an enthusiastic voice, "You did a great show for Nanjing! Why don't you do one for us?" I was stunned, and blood rushed to my head: everyone knows that his museum's collection of painting and calligraphy is one of the best in China and world renowned as well. On the next day, I was accompanied by Mr. Yang while viewing their exhibition "Selected Masterpieces from the Jin-Tang to Ming-Qing Dynasties," which had quite a numbers of work by emperors. That night I couldn't sleep, but stayed awake thinking of a possible theme for an exhibition. Then in one exciting moment it clicked—the theme and the structure of the exhibition came to me. Next morning, I proposed the title "The Emperor's Collection" for an exhibition on the theme of the imperial collection's history and its management system, an understudied subject; it would include the last emperor's dispersal of the artworks, Mr. Yang's specialization, illustrated through examples from the museum's collection. Mr. Yang immediately slapped the arm of the couch with excitement and shouted "Bravo!" In the following months, we worked on the exhibition proposal and submitted it to the China Institute Gallery Committee. That moment is still vivid in my memory; as soon as they saw the proposal and examples of the artwork, some of the committee members said, "Sign the contract with them (Liaoning Provincial Museum) immediately!" We are also fortunate to have Dr. David Ake Sensabaugh, the Ruth and Bruce Dayton Curator of Asian Art at the Yale University Art Gallery, join Mr. Yang and I as co-curators; it was he who suggested adding the word "Last" to the title, thus focusing on the last emperor.

For the past three years and more, the team worked diligently to make this exhibition and catalogue a reality. I must, first of all, express my gratitude to the sponsors who generously provided funding for this exhibition, especially the Blakemore Foundation which has given us their continuing support, and to individual donors for their generosity, especially Laurie and David Ying, who encouraged me from the very beginning of this project. My sincerest gratitude is extended to the loyal Friends of the Gallery, whose support is like an endless spring of energy for this gallery. I also thank the Gallery Committee and the Trustees of China Institute, both led by Virginia Kamsky, for their support.

Mr. Yang Renkai, who passed away last January, will never be forgotten. Without him, there would have been no exhibition. For this reason, we dedicate the exhibition to his memory. We are also indebted to the director of the Liaoning Provincial Museum Ma Baojie and especially to their deputy director, Ms. Liu Ning, who was consistently helpful, responding to all our various requests from large to small in a professional manner. We thank them and the rest of the museum staff for their assistance over the past few years.

My heartfelt thanks also goes to all the people who worked on this project. I am indebted to Mr. Yang Renkai and David Ake Sensabaugh for their essays and catalogue entries; to Mr. Huang Weili of the Liaoning Provincial Museum, Cary Liu, Curator of Asian Art at the Princeton University Art Museum, and Joseph Scheier-Dolberg, Research Fellow at the Boston Museum of Fine Arts, for their contributions to the catalogue; and to J. May Lee Barrett, who edited the volume, made many knowledgeable suggestions, and compiled the chronology and bibliography. My sincere gratitude is extended to David Huiwei Shen, Mansheng Wang, and Ling-yi Chien for their great translation work, jumping between two languages; to Professor Jonathan Chaves, for his guidance and timely help in translating the ancient poems. This beautiful bilingual exhibition catalogue, as well as its maps, was designed by Peter Lukic, who had to endure our difficult production schedule. Perry Hu's talented installation work brought the exhibition to life, while Nicole Straus and Margery Newman stirred the public's interest. On the Chinese side, I also thank Professor Zhou Xiaolu for editing and Zhao Haimeng for proofreading the Chinese text in response to our rush requests; Mr. Liang Baiquan, the former director of the Nanjing Museum, and Professor Zhao Yuze assisted in checking various references and provided many useful suggestions.

I am also grateful to the gallery staff, Sara Tam, Caroline Antonelli, and Yue Ma, for their diligent work and completion of many meticulous tasks. Separate thanks to Donna Thomas and her Development Department staff for their assistance in raising funds for this exhibition and to France Pepper for arranging an exciting symposium. My sincere gratitude goes to the President of China Institute, Sara Judge McCalpin, for her understanding and support of the Gallery's exhibitions. Finally, from the bottom of my heart, I am grateful for the support of my husband Jerry Chang and my children John and Jeffrey, as I often ignored them while working on this project over the past few years. Although there is no room to mention the names of all the people who helped with and supported this project and the Gallery, I am ever grateful and indebted to them. The readers' enjoyment of this exhibition and the catalogue will be our great reward.

Willow Weilan Hai Chang
Director
China Institute Gallery
Co-curator and Project Director
of the exhibition

序

我小时候，常在两种场合,听到我的亲娘,用那吴侬软语喃喃地说起“皇帝”这个字眼 — 当她形容社会上和政治上的变迁时，她总爱说：“一朝天子一朝臣”；而当她形容远得不可企及的事情时，她总爱说：“天高皇帝远”。所以我的印象中，皇帝总是变来变去的，皇帝也总是永远够不着的。

皇帝当然是变来变去的，中国历史上从秦始皇帝嬴政（在位公元前221-210年）开始到末代皇帝溥仪（在位1909-1911年），大约总有三百五十个左右的皇帝吧。皇帝当然也是够不着的，深秘的宫墙，例如紫禁城，严严实实地隔绝着他们。可是，一支小而轻的中国毛笔，却可以把上下几千年的皇帝们联结在一起，也可以把皇帝和平民之间的距离拉近。一如长城是中国的象征，用毛笔创作而后装成卷轴的书画，亦堪称中国文化的象征。使用毛笔，创作书画、品评书画、鉴藏书画，在此衡量智慧、才情、观察力、创造力、鉴赏力和学识的平台上，天子与平民同在一杆称上。作为文化遗产，中国书画也成为文化血脉代代相传的载体，并为有识之皇帝用来作为强化皇权的工具。

华美协进社中国美术馆的这一展览，包括了24件为清代皇家书画著录《石渠宝笈》所记录的作品，所有的作品都曾为乾隆皇帝弘历（在位1736-1795年）和他后继的一些皇帝所鉴赏，并有钤印为证。其中包括，乾隆皇帝本人的书法作品“临怀素的千字文”，作于1770年，大约是皇帝日常的书法练习，在宣纸上用毛笔书就的草书，有683厘米长。另一件皇帝的作品，则为明宣宗朱瞻基（在位1426-1435年）于1431年所作的“万年松图”，也是用毛笔和水墨在宣纸上的作品，有453厘米长，那是宣宗皇帝为敬贺母亲生日的特殊礼物。这些曾为皇帝们亲手创作和展玩过的作品，现在能够为大众所浏览，抚今追昔，感觉上，时空凝固了，皇帝们也不再遥远了。

这个展览的形成和对皇帝们的关注，纯属偶然。2005年3月，北国的沈阳依旧寒冷。我试图组织一个新石器时代的以玉器著名的红山文化展，因而前去拜访相识了十多年的杨仁恺先生，他是辽宁省博物馆的荣誉馆长。到了他家，我拿出了一本《故山青：南京博物院藏十七世纪山水画》的展览图录送给他，那是我美术馆的第一个原创的并由我策划的国际展览。他接过去，翻了一遍，抬起眼来，目光闪闪，但有点儿嗔怪地道：你给南博做这么好的展览，为什么不给我们做一个啊？！我大吃一惊，热血涌上脑门，谁都知道辽宁省博物馆的书画收藏是全国顶尖的，也是世界著名的啊。第二天，杨老亲自陪我看馆里的展览，真巧，他们正在展出晋唐至明清的精品书画，有许多皇帝们的作品和藏品。那晚，我简直无法入睡，心里盘算着展览的主题，怎样从一个前人所未及或涉及不多的角度来介绍。第二天，我将展览的设想告诉了杨老，展览的题目是“帝王宝鉴”，主题是皇家书画收藏史和管理体系，并包括杨老可信手拈来的由末帝溥仪散佚的清宫书画的历史，通过馆藏品来做介绍。杨老仔细地听了，我话音未落，他就拍着沙发扶手叫好。以后的几个月里，我们一起整了个展览申请报告。当我向华美协进社中国美术馆的艺术委员会呈交这个报告时，那一瞬间还历历在目，有的委员立即叫道：赶快跟他们（辽博）签合同！我们很荣幸，也能够邀请到耶鲁大学艺术馆亚洲艺术部主任江文苇博士，和杨仁恺先生与我一起，作为展览的共同策展人，他很快建议将展览题目定在末代皇帝。

在过去的三年多里，大家都为展览和图录的各项工作勤恳地努力，值此即将大功告成之际，我首先要向展览的赞助者致以深切的谢意，特别感谢贝莱克莫基金会多年来的不断支持，感谢赵应美玉夫妇自项目伊始便给与的鼓励和赞助。对所有支持我美术馆的忠诚的朋友们，我不胜感谢。我并感谢由甘维珍女士领导的华美协进社董事会和艺术委员会的支持。

我无法忘怀杨仁恺先生，他虽已在今年一月仙逝，但没有他便没有这一展览，我们愿籍此展览来纪念他。我也要感谢辽宁省博物馆马宝杰馆长的支持，特别感谢刘宁副馆长，几年来，事无巨细，她从头到尾都兢兢业业地给与帮助。借此机会，我也要向辽宁省博物馆各位给与协助的同仁们致谢。

我深切地感谢参与这个项目并作出了各自贡献的人们：感谢杨仁恺先生和江文苇博士为展览图录撰写的论文和书画条目；感谢辽宁省博物馆的黄伟利先生、普林斯顿大学艺术博物馆的刘怡玮博士和波士顿美术馆的史耀华先生，他们的撰稿丰富了展览图录的内容。我很感谢钟美梨一如既往的优秀的编辑；胡维智充满创意的展览设计；彼得。鲁克精美的展览图录设计；妮可尔。斯祚丝和玛吉瑞。纽曼将展览推介给公众的努力；沈慧伟、王满晟和简菱仪的优秀的翻译；齐皎翰教授神速的译诗和指点；周晓陆教授及时的中文编辑和赵海萌的中文校对，以及前南京博物院院长梁白泉先生审阅我的中文稿后所提出的建议和补充资料，和赵宇泽教授为查核资料所作的工作。

我很感谢我美术馆的同仁谭蔚、安若兰和马玥为展览的各项事务所作的辛勤劳动，并感谢在汤东娜领导下的发展部为该展览募捐的各项努力，亦感谢胡斐兰筹划的展览研讨会。对华美协进社的社长江芷若的理解和支持，我深表谢意。最后，我衷心感谢我的先生张晓军、我的孩子张静山和张海青的支持，在过去的几年里，我常常为了这一展览而忽略了他们。对所有关怀和支持这一展览和我美术馆的朋友们，尽管我不能一一提及你们的名字，我的内心永远满怀感激。但愿你们能欣赏这一展览和图录，那将是对我们的莫大激励。

华美协进社中国美术馆 馆长
展览共同策划人暨艺术总监　海蔚蓝
二〇〇八年八月八日

Chronology of Imperial China and Major Imperial Collectors and Artist-Patrons
中国历史年表及皇家主要艺术鉴藏者一览表

秦朝 QIN	221–206 BCE	Qin Shihuangdi (Ying Zheng; r. 221–210 BCE) 秦始皇帝嬴政
汉朝 HAN	206 BCE–220 CE	Wudi (Liu Che; r. 141–87 BCE) 武帝刘彻 Yuandi (Liu Shi; r. 48–33 BCE) 元帝刘奭
六朝 SIX DYNASTIES	222–589	
三国 THREE KINGDOMS	220–265	
魏 Wei	220–265	
蜀汉 Shu Han	221–263	
吴 Wu	222–263	
晋朝 JIN DYNASTY	265–420	
西晋 Western Jin	265–317	
东晋 Eastern Jin	317–420	Huan Xuan (r. 403–404), usurper 桓玄 (篡位者)
南朝 SOUTHERN DYNASTIES		
刘宋 Liu Song	420–479	Wudi (Liu Yu; r. 420–22) 武帝刘裕 Mingdi (Liu Yu; r. 465–72) 明帝刘彧
南齊 Southern Qi	479–502	Gaodi (Xiao Daochen; r. 479–82) 高帝萧道成
梁 Liang	502–557	Wudi (Xiao Yan; r. 464–549) 梁武帝萧衍 Yuandi (Xiao Yi; r. 552–55) 梁元帝萧绎
陳 Chen	557–589	
北朝 NORTHERN DYNASTIES		
北魏 Northern Wei	386–534	
東魏 Eastern Wei	534–550	
北齊 Northern Qi	550–577	
西魏 Western Wei	535–556	
北周 Northern Zhou	557–581	
隋朝 SUI DYNASTY	581–618	Wendi (Yang Jian; r. 581–604) 文帝杨坚
唐朝 TANG DYNASTY	618–907	Taizong (Li Shimin; r. 626–49) 太宗李世民

五代十国 FIVE DYNASTIES AND TEN KINGDOMS	907–960	
南唐 Southern Tang	937–975	Houzhu (Li Yu; r. 961–75) 李后主李煜
宋朝 SONG DYNASTY	960–1279	
北宋 Northern Song	960–1127	Taizong (Zhao Guangyi; r. 960–76) 太宗赵光义 Renzong (Zhao Zhen; r. 1023–63) 仁宗趙禎 Huizong (Zhao Ji; r. 1100–25) 徽宗赵佶
南宋 Southern Song	1127–1279	Gaozong (Zhao Gou; r. 1127–63) 高宗赵构
金朝 JIN DYNASTY	1115–1234	Zhangzong (Wanyan Jing; r. 1190–1208) 章宗完颜璟
元朝 YUAN DYNASTY	1279–1368	Wenzong (Tugh Temür; r. 1328–32) 文宗图帖睦尔 Princess Sengge Ragi (ca. 1283–1331) 皇姊大长公主祥哥剌吉
明朝 MING DYNASTY	1368–1644	Xuanzong (Zhu Zhanji; r. 1426–35) 宣宗朱瞻基
清朝 QING DYNASTY	1644–1911	Shunzhi (Fulin; r. 1644–1661) 順治皇帝福临 Kangxi (Xuanye; r. 1662–1722) 康熙皇帝玄烨 Yongzheng (Yinzhen; r. 1723–35) 雍正皇帝胤禛 Qianlong (Hongli; r. 1736–95) 乾隆皇帝弘历 Jiaqing (r. 1796–1820) 嘉庆皇帝顒琰 Xuantong (Puyi: r. 1909–11)* 宣统皇帝溥仪

* Puyi was forced to abdicate in February of 1912, but continued to use the Xuantong reign name until he was evicted from the Forbidden City in 1924.

末帝溥仪于1912年2月逊位后仍留居清宫，并沿用宣统年号直至1924年被赶出紫禁城。

MAPS 地图

The Forbidden City

紫禁城示意图

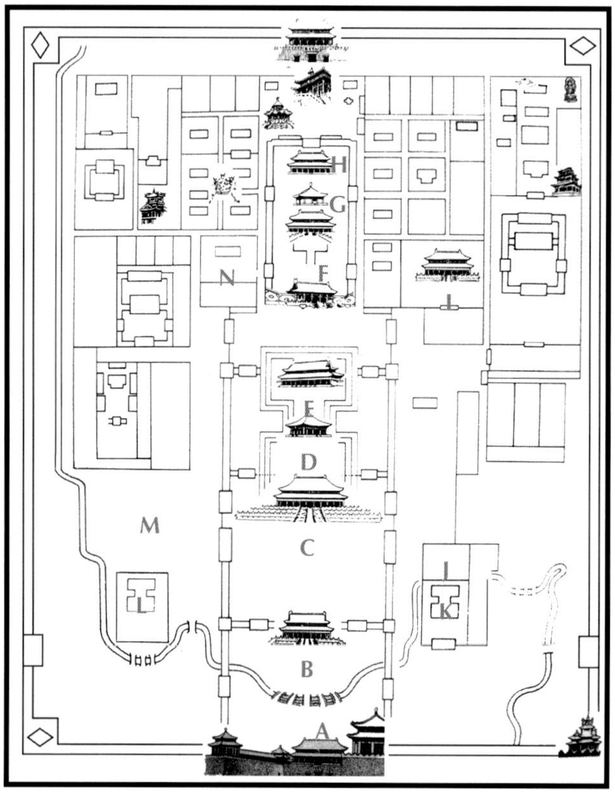

A. Wu Men (Meridian Gate 午門)
B. Taihe Men (Gate of Supreme Harmony 太和门)
C. Taihe Dian (Hall of Supreme Harmony 太和殿)
D. Zhonghe Dian (Hall of Central Harmony 中和殿)
E. Baohe Dian (Hall of Preserving Harmony 保和殿)
F. Qianqing Gong (Palace of Heavenly Purity 乾清宫)
G. Jiaotai Dian (Hall of Union 交泰殿)
H. Kunning Gong (Palace of Earthly Tranquility 坤宁宫)
I. Fengxian Dian (Hall of Serving the Ancestors 奉先殿)
J. Wenyuan Ge (Imperial Library 文渊阁)
K. Wenhua Dian (Cultural Splendor Hall 文华殿)
L. Wuying Dian (Military Heroism Hall 武英殿)
M. Neiwufu (Management Authority of Internal Affairs 内务府)
N. Yangxin Dian (Hall of Mental Cultivation 养心殿)

Puyi's Travel and Escape Routes
溥仪出逃及被俘押解路线图

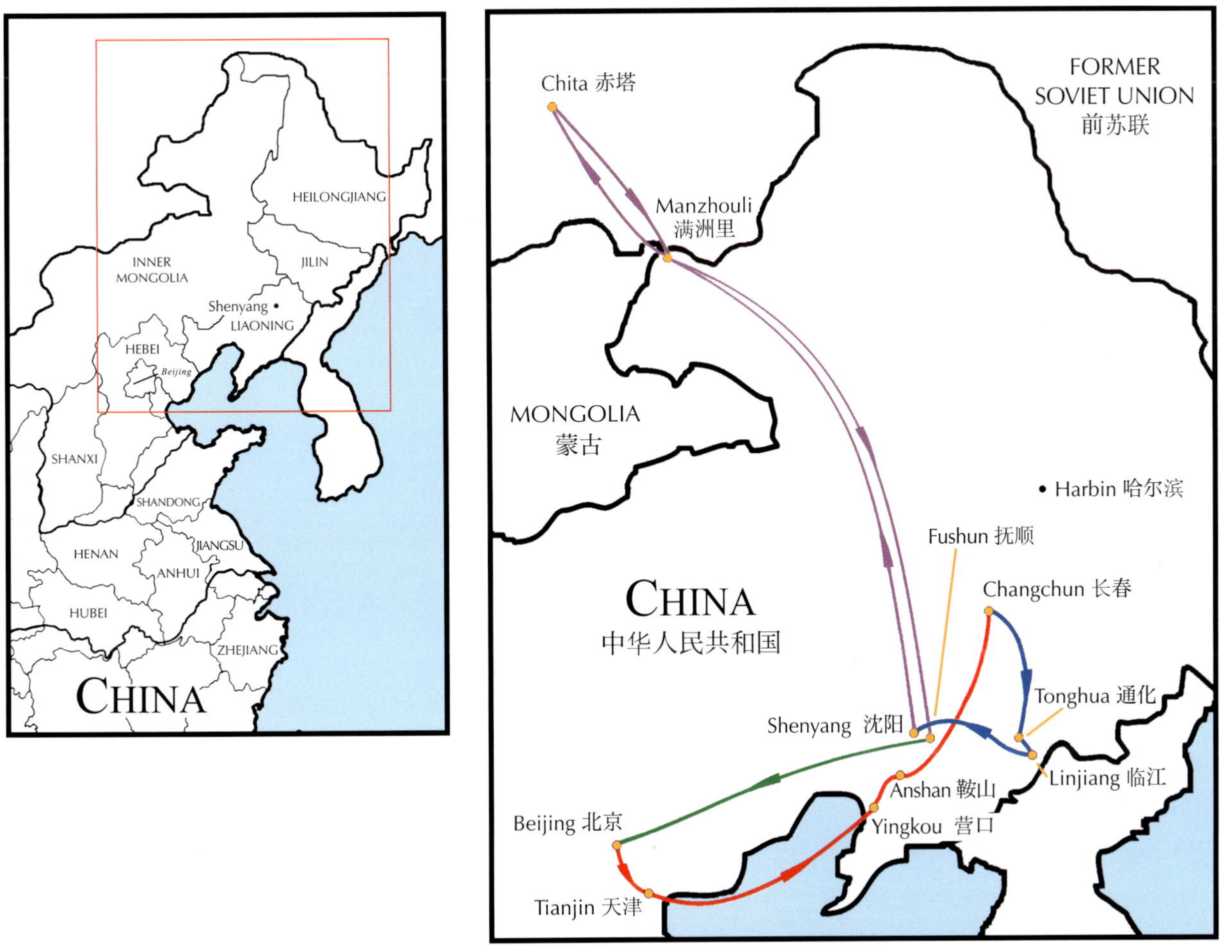

Beijing → Tianjin 北京 — 天津	from the palace to Tianjin 出宫到天津
Tianjin → Changchun 天津 — 长春	route to Changchun to serve as puppet emperor of Manchukuo 赴长春任伪满州国皇帝路线
Changchun → Shenyang 长春 — 沈阳	escape route 逃跑路线
Shenyang → Fushun 沈阳 — 抚顺	route as prisoner under escort 被俘押解路线
Fushun → Beijing 抚顺 — 北京	return to the capital after release 释放返京

THE STORY BEHIND THE LAST EMPEROR'S DISPERSAL OF THE IMPERIAL PAINTING AND CALLIGRAPHY COLLECTION

Yang Renkai

1. The Great Assembly of Painting and Calligraphy Masterpieces at the Qing Imperial Court

Between the Manchu penetration of the Great Wall and their final downfall, the Qing dynasty lasted 267 years and had a total of nine emperors. Among them, the Qianlong emperor (Hongli) was the one most particularly interested in the art of painting and calligraphy. During his sixty-year reign (1736–95), almost all extant works by significant artists of the past had ended up in the court collection. Although there were acquisitions by the imperial court in the reigns that followed, none was to compare with those made during the Qianlong period.

From the ninth to tenth year of the Qianlong period (1744–45), a team of scholars led by Zhang Zhao, Liang Shizheng, and Dong Bangda conducted an identification and appraisal project, the first such attempt to sort through and categorize the vast amount of paintings and calligraphy in the imperial collection. At the time, works relating to religious subjects were compiled into the *Midian zhulin* (Pearl forest of the Secret Hall). A second identification and categorization project, led by Wang Jie, Dong Gao, and others, lasted from the fifty-sixth year of Qianlong (1791) into the fifty-eighth year and resulted in the forty-volume supplement *Midian zhulin Shiqu baoji* (Pearl forest of the Secret Hall and Treasured boxes of the Stone Channel). The third such project was carried out in 1815 (20th year of Jiaqing) with Ying He and Hu Jing in charge. More volumes were added, resulting in the third compilation of the *Midian zhulin Shiqu baoji.*

2. The Illicit Removal of National Treasures from the Forbidden City by Puyi, the Last Emperor

Consistent efforts in conservation and compilation left most works of the imperial collection in clean, fair, and well-preserved conditions except for damage due to occasional fires inside the court, such as the big fire at the Jiaotai Dian hall inside Qianqing Gong palace in the second year of Jiaqing (1797), tenth month (fig.1). The calligraphy work *Wansui Tongtian [reign period, 696–97] Model-book* (*Wansui tongtian tie*)—currently in the collection of the Liaoning Provincial

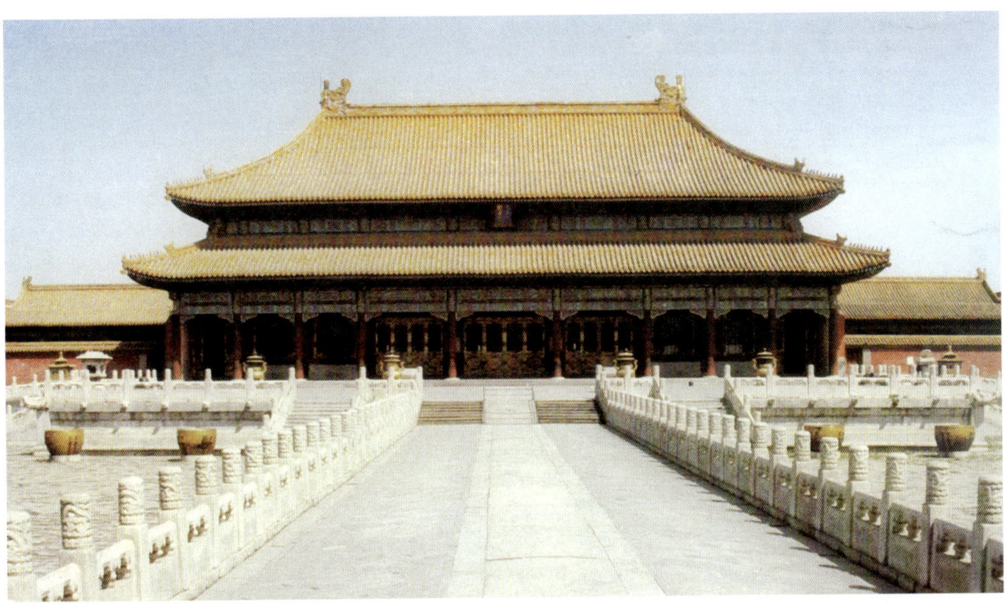

Fig. 1. View of the Qianqing Gong palace, Beijing
北京乾清宫

Museum—has clear indications of burn marks. It was initially damaged in a fire at Hua Xia's Zhenshang Zhai (Studio of True Appreciation) in Wuxi, where it was stored during the second half of the Ming dynasty. Judging from the current condition of the mounting, however, most of the damage must have come from the later fire at the Qianqing Gong palace.

During the Jiaqing reign, an increasing number of works in the court collection began to be used as royal bestowments from the emperor to princes and high ranking officials. Among the pieces awarded to Prince Cheng (also known as Yongxing) were the *Pingfu tie* (currently in the Palace Museum, Beijing) by Lu Ji, a great literary man of the Wei and Jin dynasties, and the horse painting *Night-Shining White* (*Zhaoye bai*), attributed to Han Gan of the Tang. After the Daoguang reign, such royal awards increased. One bestowment awarded to Prince Gong (also known as Yixin) included such works as *Five-colored Parakeet* (*Wuse yingwu tu*) by Emperor Huizong (Zhao Ji) of the Song and *Nine Dragons* (*Jiu long tu*) by Chen Rong; both works are currently in the collection of the Museum of Fine Arts, Boston (see pp. 329-31).

After the 1911 Revolution, the abdicated last emperor, Puyi, continued to live inside the palace for another eleven years. During that period, he took full advantage of the "Articles of Favorable Treatment of the Qing Royal Family" extended to him by the Beiyang government, purloining large quantities of property from the court—including more than a thousand works of painting and calligraphy from various dynasties—and smuggling them out of the Forbidden City. On September 4, 1922,[1] after careful planning with his staff, Puyi began to first steal the precious and rare books of the Song and Yuan dynasties by awarding "gifts" to the royal brothers Pujie and Pujia, who had been routinely allowed to enter the court to keep the emperor company during his morning study sessions. Then, bundle after bundle of rare books were removed from the Forbidden City. Wrapped up in yellow silk cloth, the rare books were approximately the same size as the textbooks the royal Pu brothers were using everyday; therefore no suspicion was raised among the guards of the "Inner City Garrison" under the commands of Capital Area Garrison Commander Wang Huaiqing and Infantry General Nie Xianfan.

Feeling secure after a trial period, Puyi and his men began to remove large quantities of painting and calligraphy masterpieces of the Jin, Tang, and successive dynasties from the imperial palace beginning on November 16, 1922. At first these "gifts" were awarded once every several days, and each time ten or over a dozen books were given away. One bestowment could amount to 35 pieces as gift-giving became more frequent, increasing in quantity each time. According to the figures provided by the Qing Royal Estates Management Committee, the total number of items purloined reached 1,285 handscrolls and 68 albums by January 28, 1923. The above figures were based on calculations by the committee after the July 31, 1925 discovery of the "List of items awarded to Pujie" and "List of items received." When we conducted our sorting and counting process after 1949, however, we gradually came to the realization that the actual number of pieces exceeded the above figures, and some national treasures of the Sui, Tang, Song, and Yuan dynasties were not even registered on the lists. The numerous occurrences of "awarding of gifts" had basically plundered the Qing court of all the valuable scrolls in its original collection. As for albums, only a limited number was left at court. Just as Puyi and his associates were planning to remove more mounted scrolls, war broke out between the Zhili and Northern armies, changing the situation drastically. At the end of October 1924, General Feng Yuxiang of the Zhili Army marched into Beijing and put President Cao Kun—who was elected into office through bribery—under house arrest inside the Yanqing Lou tower, located behind Wuying Dian palace. He also declared a "cease fire" throughout the rest of China. On November 5, newly appointed garrison commander Lu Zhonglin and the police chief, Zhang Bi, led twenty soldiers armed with pistols into the palace and evicted Puyi along with his pathetic courtiers from the Forbidden City.

3. Sale of National Treasures in Tianjin as a Means of Sustenance

The artifacts removed from the palace by the royal Pu brothers included paintings, calligraphy, antique books, and jewelry; these were all brought into the Residence of Prince Chun, which belonged to Puyi's father, Zaifeng. After the illicit removal operation, the brothers made contact with Sun Baoqi, chief administrator of the National Tax Bureau, by sending Pujie to meet with the chief through persons related by marriage; from the chief they obtained permits of exemption from examination and taxation. Thereafter, they crated the treasures into some seventy to eighty big containers and shipped them via railroad to a Western style mansion that had been purchased in the British Concession in Tianjin. After Puyi was expelled from the palace, he first stayed at the Residence of Prince Chun and shortly afterwards sought refuge at the Japanese Embassy. He then slipped into Tianjin on

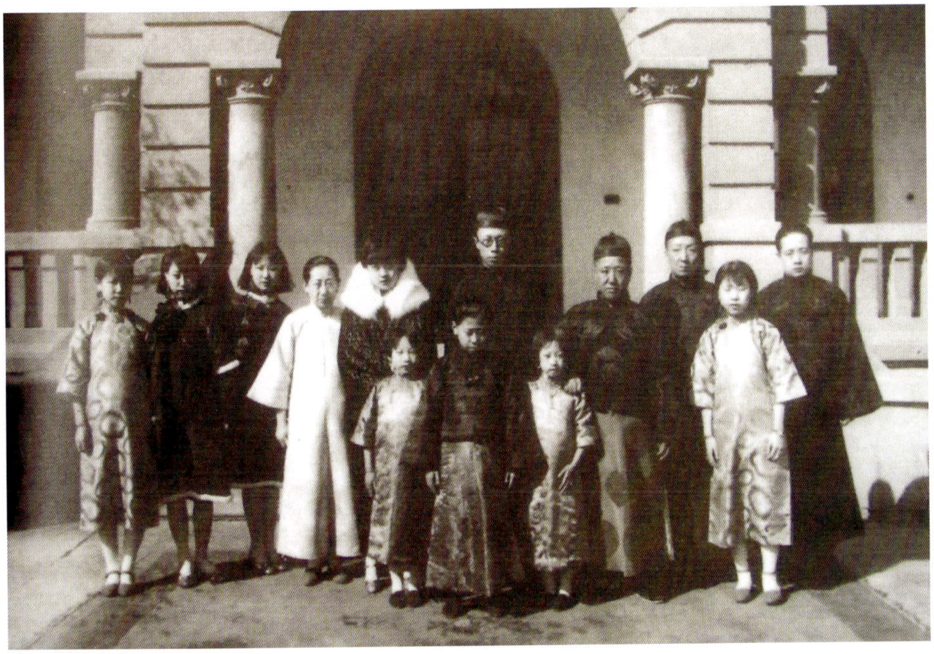

Fig. 2. The last emperor, Puyi, at the Zhang Yuan residence, Tianjin, ca. 1925
溥仪在天津张园

February 23, 1925, and settled into the Zhang Yuan garden, located in the Japanese Concession (fig. 2). While in Tianjin, Puyi set up a "mini court," assembling a so-called Administrative Office of the Qing Imperial Court in his enclave.

Although a hefty annual subsidy of four million silver dollars was granted by the Republican government to the abdicated emperor Puyi and his remaining staff, it was still far from enough to cover their huge expenses. They then came up with the idea of making money from the model calligraphy and famous paintings of the various dynasties that they had smuggled out of the palace. Through introductions by antique dealers and people of various backgrounds, they found buyers, mostly foreigners, and started dealings which were handled by old courtiers such as Chen Baochen, Baoxi, and Zheng Xiaoxu. It remains a mystery as to how many pieces of important painting and calligraphy were sold by Puyi during his several-year stay in Tianjin because many of these deals were not recorded.

According to Mr. Wang Qingxiang in "On This Day of August Fifteenth," a chapter from his *Wei man xiao chaoting fumie ji* (Downfall of the puppet court of Manchukuo), Puyi "awarded" an assortment of painting and calligraphy to one of his agents by the name of Liu Junye, the nephew of Chen Baochen, and the "gifts" included such handscrolls as *Emperors of Previous Dynasties* (*Lidai diwang tu*) and *Emperor Taizong Receiving the Tibetan Envoy* (*Bunian tu*), both by Yan Liben of the Tang; *Fairy Maidens in a Grand Garden* (*Langyuan nüxian tu*) by Ruan Gao; and a Song dynasty rubbing, the *Dingwu [period] version of "Preface to Poems Composed at the Orchid Pavilion"* (*Dingwu lantingxu taben*). Among the above items, *Emperors of Previous Dynasties* found its way to the USA through undisclosed channels and ended up in the collection of the Museum of Fine Arts, Boston (see pp. 42-43). Fortunately however, the owner of the other two scrolls, *Emperor Taizong Receiving the Tibetan Envoy* and *Fairy Maidens in a Grand Garden*, did not sell them to foreigners but brought them back to Fujian as a dowry for his daughter's marriage. They were then donated to the People's government after 1949 and are currently in the collection of the Palace Museum, Beijing.

The following dealings were documented in Hu Siyuan's *Zhilu riji* (Diary of Zhilu), a manuscript now in the Liaoning Provincial Library:

> On the 18th day of the 3rd month in the *xinwei* year [1931], hand-written Order from His Majesty Puyi: "Former English tutor to the empress, Isabel Ingram, brought in an American claiming to be a museum staff member in his country to view the court collection. Twelve items were selected for purchase, among which three were instructed to be pulled from the sale due to drastic differences in reaching an agreement in price. The English tutor was on the verge of crying, her hands shaking during repeated bargaining. Knowing that there was no use insisting, she said that the rest of nine items must go at the counter-offer prices. So the deal was cut in haste. During a check-off later, it was

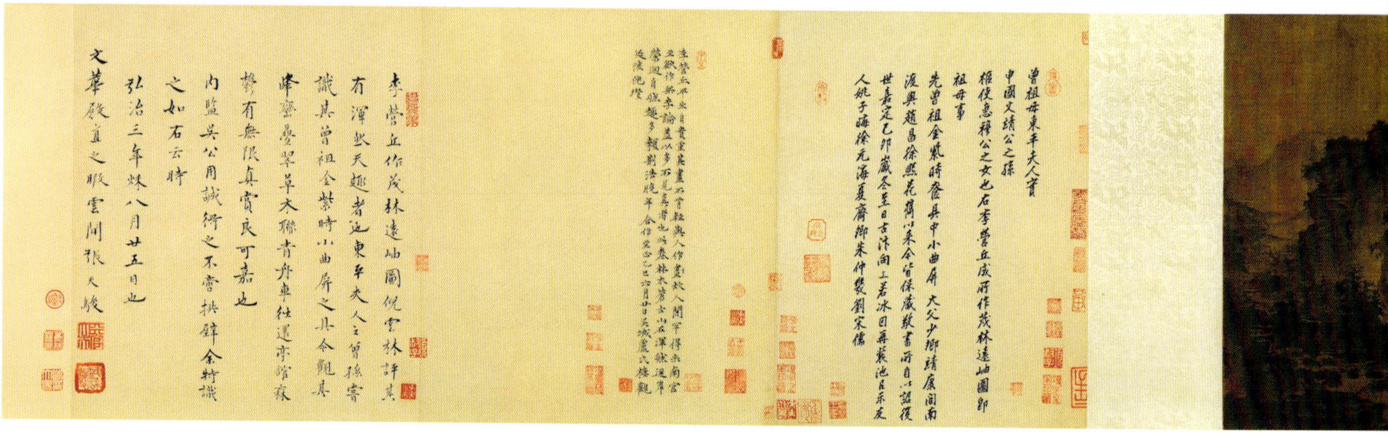

Fig. 3. Li Cheng (919–ca. 967), *Lush Forest and Distant Hills.* Handscroll. Ink on silk. Liaoning Provincial Museum
北宋，李成，茂林远岫图，手卷，绢本水墨，辽宁省博物馆

found that an extra item had been taken and that the sale prices were less than ten percent of the initial asking prices. What was odd was that when the buyer came, we initially wanted Chen Zengshou to negotiate with him; but Tutor Ingram insisted that Chen's presence was not necessary so as to avoid possible conflicts. This had apparently been planned. Now someone has been sent to find that American, and reports came that the buyer had left for Beijing with the purchased scrolls. The tutor was found again but we were bluntly told that once a price agreement has been reached, there are no withdrawals or regrets, and further talks were angrily rejected. Yesterday, Lu Yutong and Qi Jizhong were sent into Beijing to pursue further negotiations with said American. It is uncertain whether they'd succeed. Discussions are needed for planning recovery efforts. Waiting for results."

It is really an annoying situation as I kneel reading the above. We are fortunate that the items on which price agreements could not be reached were not handed over, except for the extra one which had been taken. There is enough reason to take it back and say it's not for sale. However, it is uncertain if that American is going to show up or, worse, if any dealings would be denied. We did not obtain any receipts from that person and therefore the matter is going to be hard to deal with. [We] should consult a lawyer…

(The 19th.) Order from His Majesty [Puyi]: "Lu Yutong arrived in Beijing, met with the American at the International Hotel (Liuguo fandian), and argued for an extended time. Finally the return of the five pricier items and the one extra item taken was agreed to. The buyer can keep the rest of the four pieces at the original sale prices… Someone needs to be sent from the Japanese commander's office to escort the returned pieces as a safety measure. Waiting for results."

A paper record listing the items returned and sold has been furnished, and I saw that the [amount for the] sold pieces was not that far from the original asking price, so it was agreeable. Items returned included two pieces by Li Cheng, one by Yan Wengui, and two scrolls by anonymous Song artists, for which we originally asked over 300,000 but were counter offered less than 20,000. Fortunately they are back now; otherwise it would have been a tremendous swindle, and we could have been totally screwed.

The entry on the sixth day of the fourth month in the *Zhilu riji* records the following: "handed over the written order of the 28th to Zhu Yifan [and] learned that the Japanese Embassy had safely escorted the return of the six scrolls *Wintry Forest* (*Han lin tu*), *Lush Forest and Distant Hills* (*Mao lin yuan xiu tu*) (fig. 3), *Valley Breeze* (*Xi feng tu*), *Sheep Herding* (*Muyang tu*), *Illustration of the Odes of Bin* (*Bin feng tu*), and a flower painting—all items returned safely."

The information documented above provides us not only with the details of a deal in which Puyi got swindled but also proof that he sold off treasures in the collection of the Qing court to foreigners. What a shame!

Fortunately, Li Cheng's surviving masterpiece *Lush Forest and Distant Hills* and the *Wintry Forest* attributed to him are now kept in the Liaoning Provincial Museum; the *Valley Breeze* by Yan Wengui is now in the collection of the Palace Museum, Beijing; and the unsigned *Illustration of the Odes of Bin* by an anonymous Song artist has been located at an auction overseas.

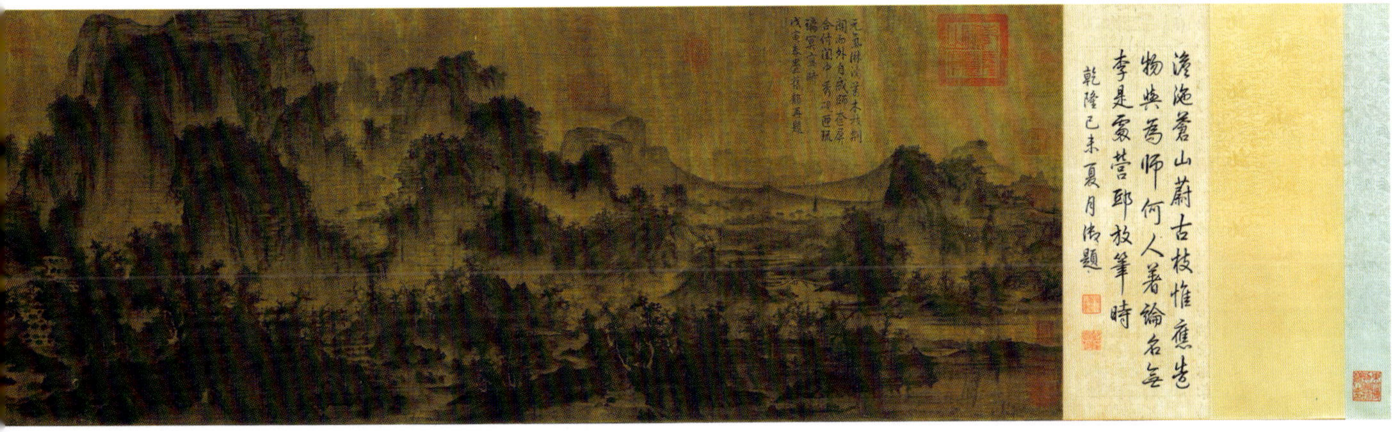

4. The Pillage of the Manchukuo "Imperial Palace" in Changchun

After the "9-18 Incident," the Japanese military created Manchukuo, a puppet regime in Changchun. In October of 1931, under the control of Doihara Kenji and accompanied by Zheng Xiaoxu, Zheng's son, and some Japanese agents, Puyi, disguised as a Japanese military officer, boarded the Awaji Maru, a Japanese commercial ship, and landed at Yingkou. He then stayed at Tanggangzi near Anshan for a period of time. In April of the next year, he and the entire crew moved into the Manchukuo "imperial palace" in Changchun (which by then was being called Xinjing, "the New Capital").

Along his escape route from the Japanese Concession in Tianjin, Puyi had to pass through territories controlled by the Republican army; therefore, he could only carry with him a limited number of jade objects during his escape, leaving large quantities of court treasures in Tianjin ready for shipping at a later date. According to memoirs revealed in early 1952 by Yan Zhenwen, who was left behind to take care of the treasures stored in Tianjin, the items moved from the Zhang Garden to the Jin Garden included the following:

- 30 crates of painting and calligraphy handscrolls (approximately 1,300 pieces)
- 4 crates of albums (a total of 40 pieces)
- 1 crate of mounted hanging scrolls (21 pieces)
- 31 crates of books printed in the Song and Yuan dynasties (200 sets of books)
- 3 crates of palace-printed books (an unknown number of sets)
- 2 large money chests, containing 2 leather cases and more than 30 small hand-carried money cases (19 shipped to Changchun and the rest remained in Tianjin)

After Puyi was enthroned as puppet emperor of the Manchukuo regime, Lieutenant General Yoshioka Yasunori of the Japanese Guandong Army, who was assigned to watch over him, had the national treasures moved from Tianjin to the "imperial palace" in Changchun. Among these treasures, the classic books and works of painting and calligraphy were stored in crates on the ground floor of the east room of the library building known as the "Small White House" in the East Courtyard of the "imperial palace," where they remained in storage for the next thirteen years (fig. 4).

Catastrophic damage to the treasures took place when Manchukuo collapsed. On August 10, 1945, Otezō Yamada, general commander of the Japanese Guandong Army made a

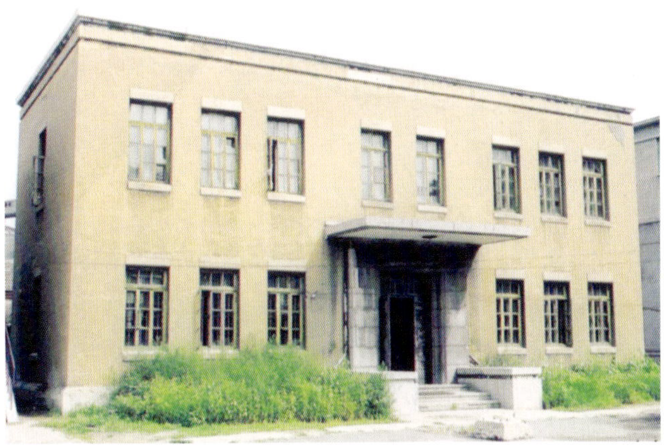

Fig. 4. The Small White House where Puyi had stored the imperial paintings and calligraphy from the 1930s to 1940s, in the Manchukuo "Imperial Palace," Changchun, Jilin Province
坐落在吉林省长春市伪皇宫的"小白楼"，曾为溥仪在三、四十年代存放清宫书画之处

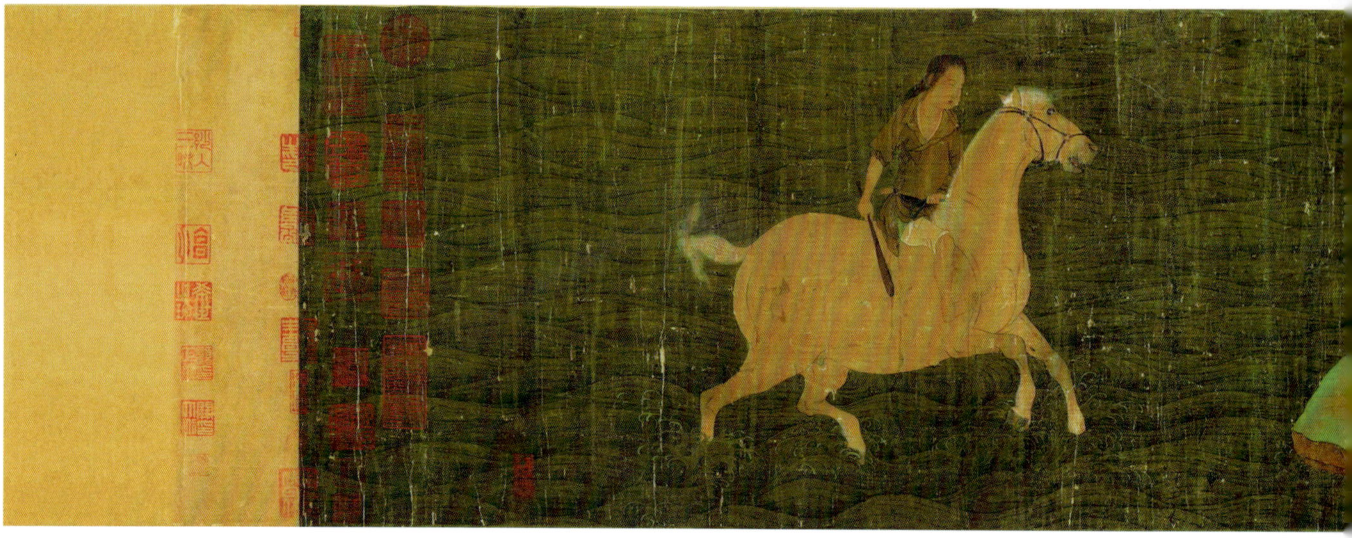

Fig. 5. Attrib. Han Gan (act. 8th century), *Heavenly Steed*, Northern Song (960–1126). Handscroll. Color on silk. Liaoning Provincial Museum
北宋，传唐代韩干，神骏图，手卷，绢本设色，辽宁省博物馆

surprise announcement that the capital of Manchukuo would be moved to Tonghua. At this point, Puyi fled in panic, taking with him about one hundred of the best paintings and calligraphy from the Jin, Tang, Song, and Yuan dynasties, along with some jade objects and jewelry. After the Japanese army pulled out of the "imperial palace," it was left to be guarded by Chinese troops belonging to the puppet regime of Manchukuo. These soldiers began to steal items that were light and easy to take out.

One day, a "Manchukuo soldier" passing by on duty peeped into the window of the Small White House and saw many wooden crates stacked up in piles, so he broke into the house through the window. Upon breaking open one of the crates he found many small wooden boxes stacked inside. He went on to open some of the boxes and found the contents wrapped in patterned yellow-ground silk twill with white undersides. Unveiling the contents, he found rolled-up scrolls mounted with a protective flap of colored brocade and fastened by jade pins with gold inlaid characters. This soldier picked a few scrolls and brought them back to the guard booth. After his superior, Platoon Leader He, saw these, they started to remove the items while trying not to disclose the discovery. However, more and more "Manchukuo soldiers" learned about the secret. Some of these soldiers had some high school education or might have worked as elementary school art teachers; they were delighted with the loot. As a result, the pilfering became outright robbery and ended up as a chaotic pillage.

In the struggle, some of the masterpieces were seriously damaged. For example, the *Three Horses* (*San ma tu*) by Li Gonglin, a master painter of the Northern Song, was split into at least three sections (now stored in separate locations, at the Palace Museum in Beijing and in a private Hong Kong collection). Mi Fu's highly acclaimed surviving masterpiece *Six Poems on Shaoxi Creek* (*Shaoxi shi liu shou*), written on *chengxintang* paper—currently in the collection of the Palace Museum, Beijing—was torn into many pieces during the flight. Some works, such as the ink original of *Ji shi tie*, a calligraphy model-book by Yu Shinan of the early Tang dynasty, were permanently ruined and lost. This frenzied plundering continued until there was nothing left to snatch. Soon after the disaster, the spoils from the Manchukuo "imperial palace" in Changchun began to surface on the market; these works of art from various dynasties were referred to as "goods from the Northeast" and became hot commodities sought after by important military and civil officials, connoisseurs, collectors, foreign art dealers, and antique shops in the northeastern cities of Beijing, Changchun, Shenyang, and Tianjin. Some of these items spread throughout the rest of China and overseas as profiteering and reselling activities increased.

During his flight to the city of Tonghua, Puyi and his motorcade of sixty vehicles stopped briefly on August 14 at Dalizigou, or Chestnut Creek, a town along the upper reaches of the Yalu River on the Sino-Korean border, to evaluate the situation. By that time the currency of the Manchukuo puppet regime had lost its circulatory value, so that they had to cheaply trade the jewelry and valuable artwork that they were carrying with them for the daily necessities of the entire entourage. Some

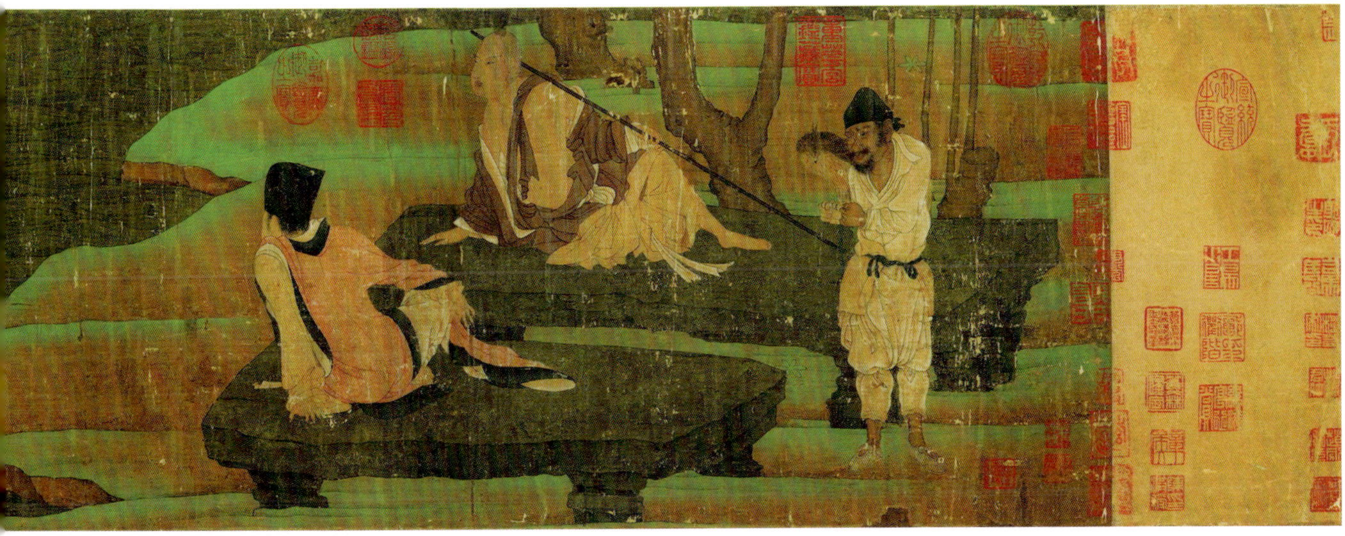

of the works of art recovered during the Land Reform Movement [1950–52] were discovered in that area. These works include a horse painting, *Heavenly Steed* (*Shenjun tu;* fig. 5), by Han Gan of the Tang and *New Moon over Boat among Lotus* (*Lian zhou xinyue tu*), attributed to Zhao Boju of the early Song (both currently in the Liaoning Provincial Museum), as well as the Yuan dynasty master Zhao Mengfu's *Water Village* (*Shuicun tu*), which was acquired in the 1960s by the Baoguzhai antique shop in Beijing's Liulichang art and antique district and is currently in the Palace Museum, Beijing.

On August 17, Puyi and his entourage switched over to a train and headed towards Linjiang, in present-day Jilin Province. Before their departure, they distributed the treasures among the individuals traveling together and left behind whatever they could not carry to be stored with the local gentry, whom they had bribed. On the evening of August 18, Puyi left the complex in Linjiang and fled to Shenyang. Puyi and his fellow travelers, a group of eight, were captured on August 19 by the Soviet Red Army at Shenyang's Dongta Airfield as they were trying to board a military plane headed for Japan. Li Jinming and Xu Fengshan of the First Regiment of the United Allies for a Democratic Northeast learned about the situation upon arrival, and they started working immediately through persuasion and confiscation to recover most of the items Puyi had left with the local gentry at their residences. They then handed the treasures over to higher authorities in their own troops for protection. Included among the treasures were works of painting and calligraphy of various dynasties that had been brought out of the Manchukuo "imperial palace" in Changchun.

5. Salvation and Preservation Efforts after the Establishment of the People's Republic of China

After the 1948 liberation of the entire Northeast (Manchuria) by the People's Liberation Army, the People's Government of the Northeastern Provinces set up an institution in Harbin called the Northeastern Committee for the Management of Cultural Relics, which was responsible for gathering the art treasures from the Qing imperial court that were captured or confiscated by the troops during the war. The Committee had these treasures stored temporarily at the People's Bank of the Northeast in Changchun. In November of that year, the Committee moved from Harbin to Shenyang and began preparations for setting up the Museum of the Northeast, using as a base the existing National Museum of Shenyang, which had had nothing substantial in terms of collections or administration up to that point. (The Museum of the Northeast opened its doors on July 7, 1949 but changed its name to the Liaoning Provincial Museum in 1959 (fig. 6), coinciding with the disassembly of the Northeastern Bureau [of the Chinese Communist Party].)

In the fall of 1950, under the instructions of Mr. Chen Yun, the art treasures from the Qing imperial court in temporary storage at the People's Bank of the Northeast were moved into the Museum of the Northeast. At that time, I was hired as a research fellow at the Ministry of Culture under the Northeastern Bureau. I plunged into work for the protection of antiques and building of the museum. Faced with the enormous amount of antiques transferred from the People's Bank of the Northeast, as well as objects at the warehouse of a museum yet to be staffed, strengthened, and institutionalized, we started working right

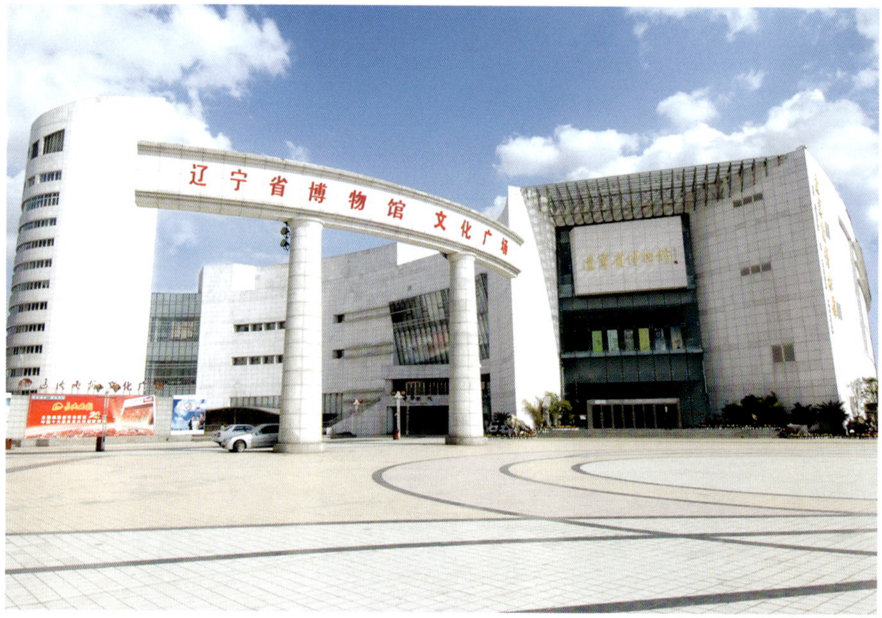

Fig. 6. Exterior view of the Liaoning Provincial Museum
辽宁省博物馆

away, going through piles upon piles of antiques in an attempt to sort out the real gems from the rest.

After going through an initial identification process, examining about 150 works of art from the Qing court one piece at a time, we were ecstatic with joy to find that more than half of the items were extremely valuable works of the past and that some were the only surviving works of certain artists or were simply priceless; only a few were fakes that got mixed in with the authentic artwork.

In calligraphy, the well-documented Jin dynasty ink original of *Eulogy for Cao E* (*Cao E leici*), a piece written in small standard script, was rediscovered (fig. 7). Many colophons and comments had been inscribed on it by renowned connoisseurs from the Southern dynasties through the Tang and Song dynasties, and it had been highly acclaimed in dozens of historical texts. Thanks to its survival, we are now able to see a real example of the kind of writing style prevalent during the transition period before standard script in Chinese writing was firmly established.

There were also two works of ink calligraphy by Ouyang Xun of the Tang dynasty. Of the two, the *Thousand-Character Essay* (*Qian zi wen*) has room for different opinions about authenticity due to the consideration that it was created when the author was of a young age. The second work, *Confucius Predicting Death in a Dream* (*Meng dian tie*), however, has been unanimously acknowledged as an absolutely authentic Ouyang ink original. Ouyang enjoyed using historical events and stories as subjects for calligraphy. His extant works, such as the *Zhang Han Biography* (*Zhang Han tie*) and *Dialogue between Confucius and the Student Bu Shang* (*Bu Shang tie*), all deal with historical events and stories. Among the three works mentioned, *Confucius Predicting Death in a Dream* is the only ink original created during his old age and has long been regarded by the art world and museums as a national treasure and a pinnacle of ink work.

By the high Tang dynasty, cursive script (*caoshu*) reached a climax with the splendid achievements of such artists as Zhang Xu, who was active during the Kaiyuan period (714–41) and created a style of calligraphy which came to be known as "wild grass" (*kuangcao*). In *Four Classic Poems* (*Gushi si tie*), Zhang Xu's only surviving original, the power and level of sophistication of the mad grass style is clearly demonstrated. Another work, titled *On the Art of Calligraphy* (*Lun shu tie*), is an ink original by the monk Huaisu (active during the middle of the second half of the Tang dynasty), whose calligraphy shows a direct line of descent from that of Zhang Xu. Among the Song dynasty ink originals recovered, there were as many as three works by Zhao Ji, Emperor Huizong of the Song, alone. Among them was his *Thousand-Character Essay in Cursive Script* (*Caoshu qian zi wen*), an 11.72-meter-long scroll, done on pristine paper in excellent ink. A wonderful demonstration of Huizong's expressiveness in brushwork, this truly best represents his achievement in the cursive style. Thus, major and monumental works of Chinese calligraphy created in the sixteen hundred years since the Jin dynasty had resurfaced and were finally ready to gleam like gems at the Museum of the Northeast.

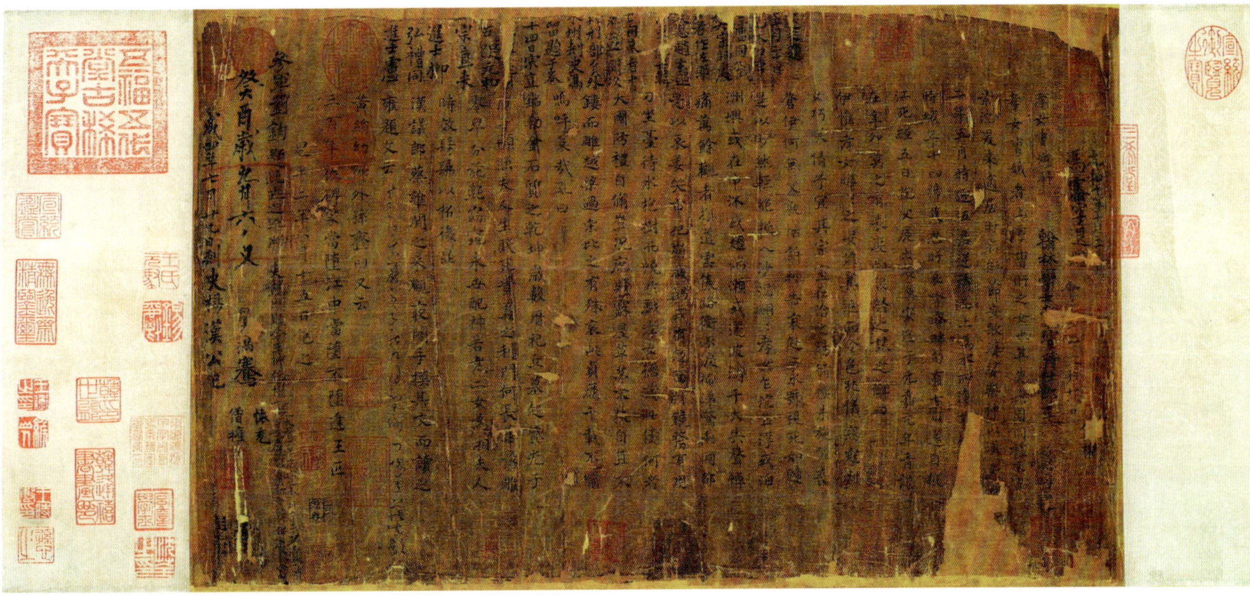

Fig. 7. Attrib. Wang Xizhi (ca. 303–ca. 361), *Eulogy for Cao E*, Jin dynasty (265–420). Handscroll. Ink on silk. Liaoning Provincial Museum
晋，传王羲之，曹娥诔辞, 手卷，绢本水墨，辽宁省博物馆

Although the number of paintings transferred to the Museum of the Northeast was fewer than that of calligraphy, they included extremely important works that are nothing less than national treasures. Among them are the following:

- *Nymph of the Luo River* (*Luo shen fu*), the most faithful extant copy of the original by Gu Kaizhi of the Eastern Jin dynasty
- *Xiao Yi Acquires the Orchid Pavilion Manuscript* (*Xiao Yi zhuan lanting tu*), attributed to Yan Liben of the early Tang
- *Court Ladies Adorned with Flowers* (*Zan hua shinü tu*) by the high Tang court artist Zhou Fang, vividly reflecting the prevailing customs of the Tang dynasty Zhenyuan era
- *Awaiting the Ferry at the Foot of the Mountains in Summer* (*Xia jing shankou dai du tu*) by master painter Dong Yuan, who pioneered and established the Southern School of landscape and also served as a minister to the court of the Southern Tang kingdom during the Five Dynasties period
- *Studies of Birds and Insects from Life* (*Xiesheng zhen qin tu*), the only surviving original by Huang Quan, head painter at the court of the Western Shu kingdom
- *Lush Forest and Distant Hills* (*Mao lin yuan xiu tu*) by the pioneering landscape artist Li Cheng of the Northern Song
- *Horse herding after Wei Yan* (*Mo Wei Yan mufang tu*) by master figure painter Li Gonglin of the Northern Song
- *Auspicious Cranes* (*Rui he tu*) by Zhao Ji, Emperor Huizong of the Song (fig. 8)

All the above items are extremely rare and important works of art. More surprising, however, was the discovery of the original *Life along the River on the Eve of the Qingming Festival* (*Qingming shanghe tu*) by Zhang Zeduan of the Northern Song. There, among the three works bearing the same title, was the real one, a veritable miracle! When this painting was published in 1954 and made its premiere in the *Weida zuguo yishu tulu* (Catalogue of our homeland's great art), it stunned the public. Later, when it was sent to a show at the Palace Museum in Beijing, it captivated the attention of the nation and became known worldwide.

In January of 1952, officers of the Changchun Public Security Bureau discovered during routine investigations that some residents and former antique shop owners had paintings and calligraphy from the Manchukuo "imperial palace" in their homes. Based on this information, a special task team was formed to deal with the recovery of these works. Along with Mr. Zhao Qi (who was later transferred to Beijing University), I was appointed by the Ministry of Culture of the Northeast to get to the bottom of things. I headed for Changchun immediately, and, starting with the clues from the cases handled by the Security Bureau, I gradually learned the details of events prior to the collapse of Puyi's puppet regime. Finally, I was able to unravel the mystery surrounding the pillage of treasures stored at the Small

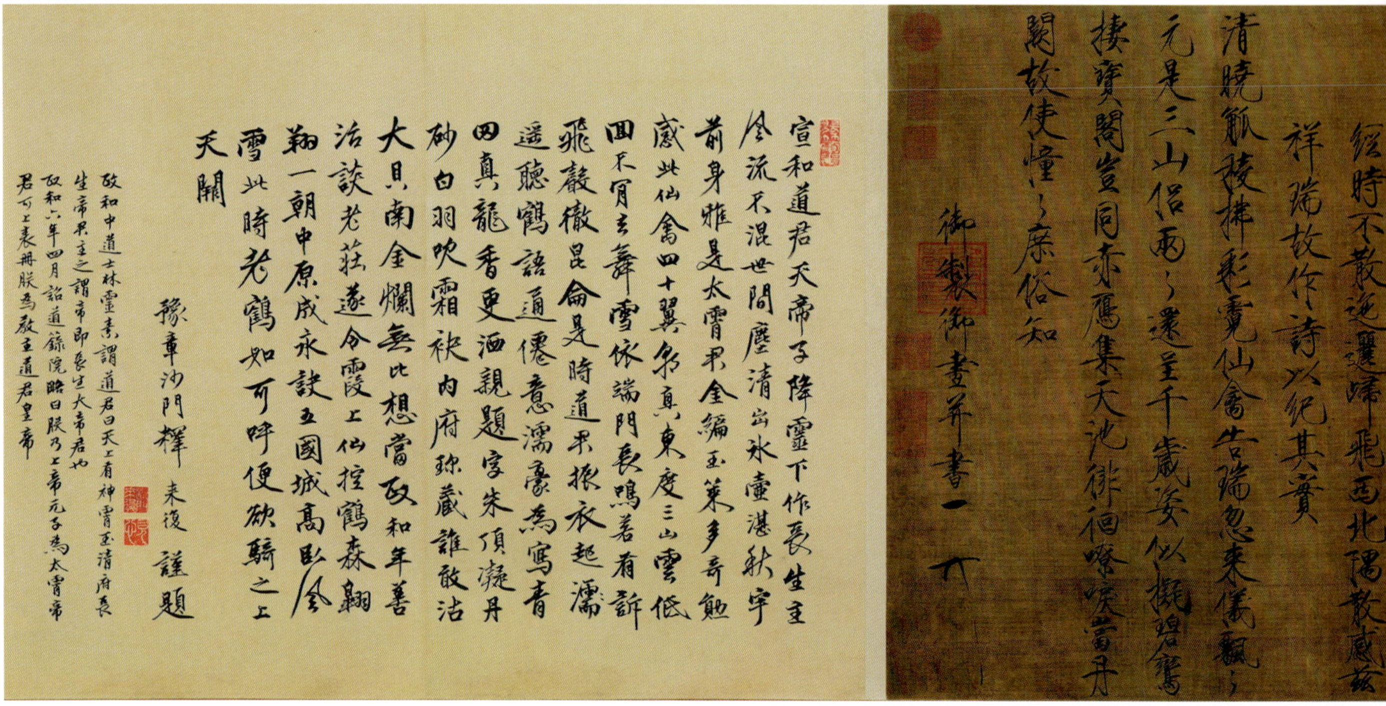

White House in the "imperial palace" and how they were dispersed after being plundered. After formulating policies and establishing rewards for recovery, we started with the individual soldiers who had taken part in the pillage. The recovery operations were intense and complicated as we jumped right in, extending our search areas from Changchun to as far as Beijing, Tianjin, and all across the northeastern territories. We kept working day and night, and in less than two months we were able to recover nearly two hundred national treasures of painting and calligraphy from the Jin, Tang, Song, and Yuan dynasties.

Among these recovered works, the following are exceptionally rare masterpieces: *Studies of Butterflies from Life* (*Xiesheng jiadie tu*) by Zhao Chang, the great flower painter of the Northern Song; *Sparrows in Winter* (*Han que tu*) by Cui Bai of the mid-Northern Song; and *Plum Blossoms in Snow* (*Xue mei tu*) by Yang Wujiu, a pioneering artist of plum painting during the early Southern Song dynasty. These recovered items were handed over to the Palace Museum in Beijing to replenish its collection of important works of painting and calligraphy, which had been terribly depleted by repeated removals. The arrival of these masterpieces was instrumental in the opening of the Gallery of Paintings at the Palace Museum.

During preparations for the opening of the Gallery of Paintings at the Palace Museum, the Museum of the Northeast sent four major treasures to support the opening exhibition: *Studies of Birds and Insects from Life* by Huang Quan of the Five Dynasties period and *Horse Herding after Wei Yan* by Li Gonglin, *Life along the River on the Eve of the Qingming Festival* by Zhang Zeduan, and *Landscape in Autumn* (*Jiangshan qiuse tu*) by Zhao Boju of the Song dynasty. These pieces were later transferred over. With the full support of art circles, cultural institutions, and other museums, the Gallery of Paintings at the Palace Museum in Beijing formally opened its doors on October 1, 1954, to coincide with the celebration of the fifth anniversary of the founding of the People's Republic.

After the tasks of sorting and searching for the artwork missing from the former "imperial palace" in Changchun came to a conclusion, recovery efforts continued uninterrupted and some important items were found. For example, one day in April of 1964 a young man from Harbin brought a bundle of stuff wrapped in cloth to the Rongbaozhai retail store in Beijing, saying that he had some old works of art to sell. When the store clerk opened the cloth wrapper, there was just a pile of paper bits and fragments inside. But the collection seals of the Qing court on some of the fragments caught the clerk's attention. I happened to be a guest at the store on that day and was invited to join in the identification. As we carefully put the little pieces together, we were astonished to find that in the pile there were in fact a

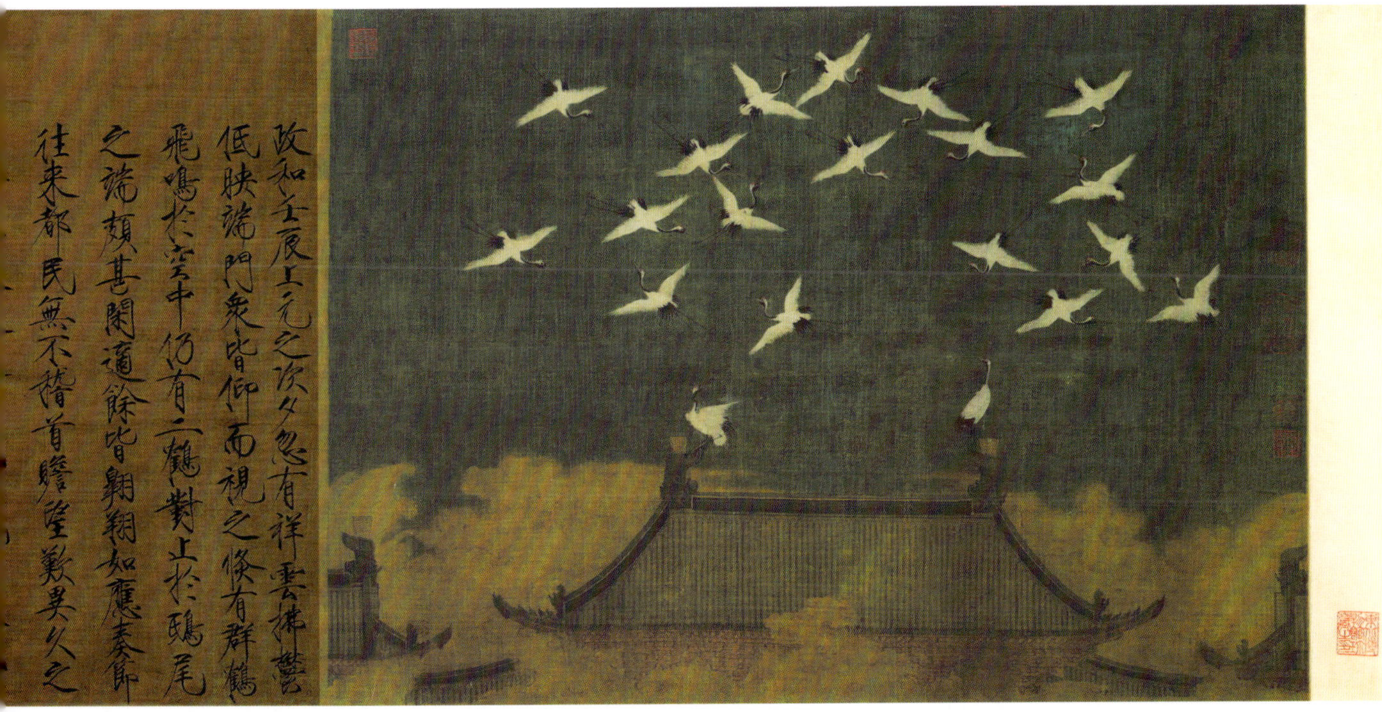

Fig. 8. Zhao Ji (Emperor Huizong; 1082–1135), Auspicious Cranes (*Rui he tu*). Handscroll. Color on silk. Liaoning Provincial Museum
北宋，宋徽宗赵佶，瑞鹤图，手卷，绢本设色，辽宁省博物馆

total of thirty-seven valuable works of art that were from the Manchukuo "imperial palace." Among them was the *Six Poems on Shaoxi Creek*, representing the best of the Northern Song master calligrapher Mi Fu. The same young man from Harbin came again the following year with another pile of paper fragments, from which we retrieved at least twenty important works, including the *Two Letters* (*Er zha tie*) by the famed literary giant Fan Zhongyan of the Northern Song.

To answer to my responsibility and conscience as a museum worker, I started collecting information from all available sources with the goal of finding the whereabouts of the important works of painting and calligraphy throughout history that are extant today and understanding their historical and artistic value. Since then, I have never stopped working on this project, keeping at it even during the troubled years of the Cultural Revolution when I was sent to live in a remote mountain village. After China's reform and open door policy was put in force, opportunities of visiting abroad and exchange activities gradually increased. I was able to see a lot and learn a great deal of information from the many museums and related institutions in Europe, America, and Japan, as well as from private individuals, with important works in their collections. This has enabled me to sort out the facts and form a general idea of the whereabouts of the paintings and calligraphy previously in the collection of the Qing imperial court. As a result of some thirty years of search and research, I was able to compile a book titled *Guobao chenfu lu—Gugong sanyi shuhua jianwen kaolue* (The loss and recovery of national treasures: Stories of the missing artwork from the Forbidden City) that deals exclusively with the subject, concluding my work of forty years in this area. It also serves as a report to those people both in China and abroad who care about the current whereabouts of all the works of art that Puyi hauled out of the Forbidden City.

Translated by David Huiwei Shen

1. Palace records of these gifts were dated according to the traditional lunar calendar, and the year given was in the Xuantong reign, as if Puyi had never abdicated. For the purpose of the English essays in this publication, these dates have been converted to the Gregorian calendar. — ed.

末帝散佚书画始末

杨仁恺

一、历代法书名画在清宫内府的大集中

自清王朝入关到覆灭的267年中，一共经历了九位君王，其中讲求书画艺术的，首推乾隆皇帝弘历。在他统治的六十年里（1736－1795年），全国传世的名迹基本上都已进入清宫，随后历朝虽有积累，但已经不能与乾隆朝相比。

乾隆九年（1744年）到乾隆十年，由张照、梁诗正、董邦达等主持，清宫进行了第一次鉴定、整理活动，其中，有关涉及宗教之书画入《秘殿珠林》，编成《石渠宝笈。秘殿珠林》初编四十四卷。从乾隆五十六年（1791年）春开始，由王杰、董诰诸人负责，进行了第二次鉴定、整理活动，直到乾隆五十八年始告完成。编成《石渠宝笈·秘殿珠林》续编四十卷。清嘉庆二十年（1815年），由英和、胡敬诸人负责，进行了第三次鉴定、整理活动，编成《石渠宝笈·秘殿珠林》三编若干卷。

二、末代皇帝溥仪盗运国宝出宫

内府书画经过一再整理，眉目清晰，宫中庋藏情况一向良好。只是历次火灾，特别是嘉庆二年（1797年）十月乾清宫交泰殿大火，可能对宫中书画多少有所波及，如现藏于于辽宁省博物馆的《万岁通天帖》，就有明显的火烧痕迹，此帖在明中后期藏于无锡华氏的真赏斋时曾遇大火，但从装裱现状考察，仍以乾清宫火灾劫余的可能性较大。

嘉庆年间（1796－1820年），皇帝用宫中所藏法书名画颁赐亲王和大臣多了起来。如颁赐成亲王永瑆的那一部分中，有两晋大文学家陆机的《平复帖》（现藏于北京故宫博物院）和传为唐人韩干的《照夜白图》。道光以后，赏赐有增无已，仅颁赐恭亲王奕訢的一笔中，就有宋徽宗赵佶的《五色鹦鹉图》、陈容的《九龙图》（现均藏于美国波士顿美术博物馆）等剧迹。

辛亥革命以后，逊位末帝溥仪在居宫的十一年中，利用北洋政府给予的“清室优待条件”作庇护，大肆窃取宫中财物，历代法书名画被盗运出宫达千余件之巨。经过“小朝廷”的周密策划，从1922年7月13日起，溥仪从珍贵的宋、元版善本书下手，趁溥杰、溥佳二人每天上午进宫陪其读书之机，以“赏赐”其弟为名，一个包袱接着一个包袱地运出紫禁城。善本书与溥杰兄弟平时随带的课本表面上大小一致，用黄缎包袱裹起来，不致引起京畿卫戍司令王怀庆、步军统领聂宪藩所属“内城守备队”值勤士兵的疑窦。

经过一段时间的试探，见时机成熟，溥仪等人从1922年9月28日开始，将大批晋唐以来法书名画盗运出宫，先是几天“赏”一次，每次10卷或10册，随后几乎逐日“赏赐”，数量渐增，高峰时一次就“赏”35件，至1922年12月12日止，总共盗出历代书画手卷1285件，册页68件之多。这是国民政府 “清室善后委员会”根据1925年7月31日发现“赏溥杰单”和“收到单”后所统计的数字。但是1949年后，当我们在清理的过程中，逐渐发现事实上不仅此数，还有不少隋、唐、宋、元的国宝名品根本没有登记到清单上。经过连续不断的“赏赐”，清宫原藏书画卷子，已基本被洗劫一空，至于册子，所留者亦极为有限。当他们按计划向宫外搬动画轴的时候，直奉战争使时局发生了骤变。1924年10月底，直系的冯玉祥将军发动“北京政变”，幽禁了贿选大总统曹琨，通电全国“停止内战”。11月5日，新任卫戍总司令鹿钟麟和警察总监张璧率二十名短抢手，进入紫禁城，撵走了溥仪和他的“小朝廷”。

三、在天津变卖国宝支撑门面

溥杰兄弟从宫中运出的书画、古籍和珠宝，均携到了溥仪之父载沣的醇王府中。当他们停止直接从宫中盗运以后，由溥杰出面，通过姻亲关系，找到当时的全国税收督办孙宝琦，获得了免验、免税护照。随后，他们便将宫中的宝物装为七八十口大箱，通过铁路运抵在天津英租界事先买好的洋房中。溥仪被逐出宫后，先回到醇王府，不久即躲进了日本驻华公使馆中，1925年2月23日，偷偷地潜到天津，在日租界张园安顿下来。溥仪在天津成立了所谓“清室办事处”，又形成一个“小朝廷”。

尽管他们当时得到民国政府每年拨给逊位末帝溥仪四百万元的巨额费用，但仍满足不了巨大惊人的开销，于是竟把生财的念头转到了盗运出宫的历代法书名画上，由旧臣陈宝琛、宝熙、郑孝胥等人经手，通过古董商等各种人物搭桥介绍卖出，卖主多为外国人。溥仪在天津的几年中，究竟卖出多少件法书名画，无案可稽，难以查清具体数目。

据王庆祥先生撰《伪满小朝廷覆灭记》书中《八·一

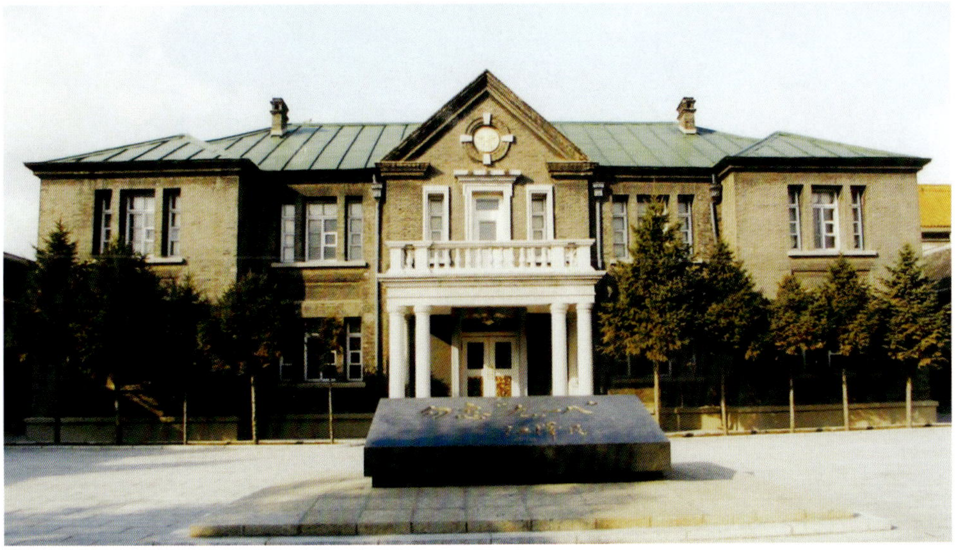

图一.坐落在吉林省长春市的满洲国伪皇宫之一景。
Part of the Manchukuo "imperial palace" in Changchun, Jilin Province

五这一天》一文中所述，溥仪在天津时曾"赏赐"经手人，即陈宝琛的外甥刘骏业一批书画，其中有唐人阎立本的《历代帝王图》卷、《步辇图》卷、五代阮郜的《阆苑女仙图》卷以及宋拓《定武兰亭序拓本》卷等。《历代帝王图》不知通过什么途径流的美国，现藏波士顿美术博物馆，所幸后来保管《步辇图》、《阆苑女仙图》的主人，没有转售与外国人，而是做为女儿的嫁妆带到福建，1949年以后捐献给了人民政府，现藏于北京故宫博物院。

又据胡嗣瑗《直庐日记》手稿（辽宁省图书馆藏）记，辛未（1931年）三月十八日溥仪"手敕"："承谕：'有前充皇后英文教习兰菘（音译）引一美国人自称为该国博物馆员者，来看内藏书画，检购十二件，内有三件因谐价相去大远，命其剔去，但教习遽手颤欲泣，争执再三，既知未可终强，则谓其余九件非一律听其买去不可，匆匆划出价码而去。后查视竟多取去一件，所划之价与原拟数目不及十分之一。最可怪者，当其来时，本欲叫陈曾寿与之面议，任教习固请不必来，免生冲突云云，显有他意。随派人往觅该美人，则谓已携所购画卷赴京，及觅到该教习，竟谓价经说定，不能翻悔，一气驳回。昨已派鲁郁彤及内侍齐继忠追踪入京向美人交涉，不知能得手否?可再筹议补救。等因'。伏阅不胜忧懑。好在议价未交，渠又多取一件而去，论理尽可索回原物不买，但恐彼美人匿不出面，或竟无理狡赖，我未取有其人收据，交涉不免棘手，当出于律师谋之……。（十九日）承谕：'鲁郁彤到京，与该美人见于六国饭店，辩论颇久，始允将重价者五件，多取者一件，如数交出，余四件须如原议与之，……拟嘱日司令部派人代送较为稳便。等因'。並出示交回及留售各件清单一纸，窃见所留者售价与拟价相差无几，自可照允。交回者为李成两卷，燕文贵一卷，宋人无名氏两卷，原拟价三十万元以外，所还不及二万，幸已索回，否则遭此巨骗，处置极难矣"。《直庐日记》四月初六日又记："交下朱益藩二十八日手函，知日使馆代运回画卷，计《寒林图》、《茂林远岫图》、《谿风图》、《牧羊图》、《豳风图》、《花卉》凡六件，均已交到不误……。"这段资料不仅道出了溥仪上当受骗的过程，而且还证实了他们向外国人出售清宫藏宝的史实，令人为之齿寒。

所幸李成的传世杰作《茂林远岫图》、传为李成的《寒林图》现珍藏在辽宁省博物馆，传为燕文贵的《谿风图》现珍藏在北京故宫博物院，宋人无款的《豳风图》已在海外的拍卖中有了音信。

四、发生在长春伪皇宫的浩劫

"九•一八"事变以后，日本军国主义分子在长春制造了"满洲国"伪政权。1931年10月，经土肥原贤二操纵，在郑孝胥父子和日本间谍们陪同下，溥仪乔装成日本军人模样，乘日本"淡路丸"号商船到达营口，在鞍山附近汤岗子住了一段时间。次年4月，全班人马进入长春（时已改称"新京"）伪皇宫（图一）。

从天津日租界潜逃时，必须经过当时国民军的辖区，所以溥仪随身只能携带少量的玉器，至于大批宫中珍宝只能置津待运。据当时在津专门管理这批珍宝的严振文在1952年初回忆：由张园迁入静园的法书名画手卷约30箱，内装1300件；法书名画册页4箱，内装计40件；书画挂轴1箱，内装21件；宋、元版书三十一箱，内装200部；殿版书3箱，内装部册不详；大金库2个，内装皮匣2个、小金库手提箱30余个（运往长春十九个，余留津）。

溥仪充任伪满洲国傀儡皇帝后，负责监管伪皇帝的日本关东军司令部中将吉岗安直，将暂存在天津的国宝偷运到了

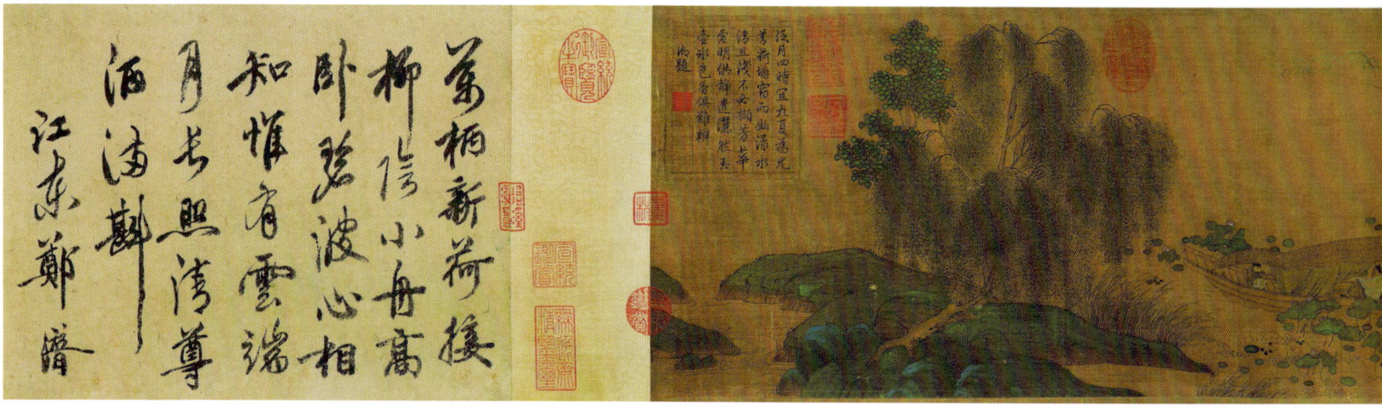

图二. 元，传赵伯驹（活动于1127–1162），莲舟新月图，手卷，绢本设色，辽宁省博物馆。
Attrib. Zhao Boju (act. 1127–62), *New Moon over Boat among Lotus*, Yuan dynasty. Handscroll. Color on Silk. Liaoning Provincial Museum

长春伪皇宫。其中古籍和书画部分，整箱置于伪宫东院的图书楼楼下东间，在这座时称“小白楼”中，沉寂了13年。

浩劫发生在伪满洲国倒台之际。1945年8月10日，在日本关东军司令小田乙三突然宣布伪满洲国都迁往通化后，溥仪携带百余件晋、唐、宋、元法书名画和明清书画精品及一批珠宝玉翠仓惶出逃。日军撤出以后，伪皇宫随即改由“满洲国”伪军把守，他们开始将轻便的财物盗出。

一天，一个值班的伪“国兵”路过“小白楼”，从窗外窥见里面许多木箱叠在一起，于是破窗而入，砸开大木箱后，发现重叠更多的小木匣，开匣后再打开黄地白里的花绫包袱皮，见画卷包首的色锦及刻字填金的玉别子。此“国兵”顺手拿了几卷回到值班室。排长何某见后，便将这一发现隐瞒起来，并开始盗运。可是，越来越多的“国兵”获知内情，其中有些念过国高或当过小学美术教员的“国兵”，尤见猎心喜。于是，由暗偷到明取，直到哄抢。

争夺中，有些名迹被严重破坏，如北宋大家李公麟的《三马图》（现分藏于北京故宫博物院和香港私人处）至少被撕裂为三截；米芾书于澄心堂纸上的传世名迹《苕溪诗六首》（现藏于北京故宫博物院）被撕抢为碎片；有些被毁得竟不能再现人间，如初唐虞世南的《积时帖》墨本。这次疯狂的掠夺，直至瓜分殆尽为止。不久以后，从长春伪皇宫散佚出来的历代法书名画便被称为“东北货”，成为军政要员、文物鉴藏者、外国古董客以及北平、长春、沈阳、天津等城市古玩文物店的攫取目标，并随着愈演愈烈倒卖活动，而流向国内外各地。

逃往通化途中的溥仪，一行60辆大车，于8月14日走到中朝边境鸭绿江上流的大栗子沟时，暂停下来观望时局之变。其时，伪满洲国货币已失去流通价值，只能用携带的珠宝和名贵书画，以低廉的价格换取一行人的生活用品。后来在土改运动中发现的原题名为唐韩干作《神骏图》、传为南宋初期赵伯驹作《莲舟新月图》（图二）（现均藏于辽宁省博物馆）以及六十年代北京琉璃厂宝古斋购得的元赵孟頫《水村图》（现藏于北京故宫博物院）等卷，都是在当地出来的。

8月17日，溥仪等人改乘火车移向临江（今属吉林省），行前将随带之书画珍宝除分散于随行人员外，还买通当地士绅，存放了剩余部分。8月18日晚，溥仪离临江公寓，逃往沈阳。8月19日，溥仪一行八人在沈阳东塔机场企图乘军用飞机逃往日本时，被苏联红军截获。随后赶到的东北民主联军第一团李金明、许凤山得知情况后，迅速做工作收缴了溥仪存放在乡绅家中的大部分物品，并缴上级部队保护起来，其中也包括从长春伪皇宫携带出来的历代法书名画。

五、中华人民共和国成立以后的拯救与保护工作

1948年间东北被解放军解放以后，东北人民政府在哈尔滨成立了东北文物管理委员会。东北文物管理委员会将战时部队收缴的清宫原藏书画珍宝集中起来，暂时存放在了位于长春的东北人民银行。同年11月，东北文物管理委员会由哈尔滨迁至沈阳，在原国立沈阳博物院的空架子基础上，积极筹建起东北博物馆（1949年7月7日正式对外开放，1959年东北局撤销，遂易名为辽宁省博物馆）。

1950年秋，经陈云先生亲自批示，暂存于东北人民银行的清宫原藏书画珍宝一并转入东北博物馆珍藏。那时，我以应聘为东北局文化部的研究员的身份，全身心的投入到了文物博物馆的事业中。面对从东北人民银行拨交过来的，堆放在尚未健全的博物馆库房中的文物，良莠杂存、

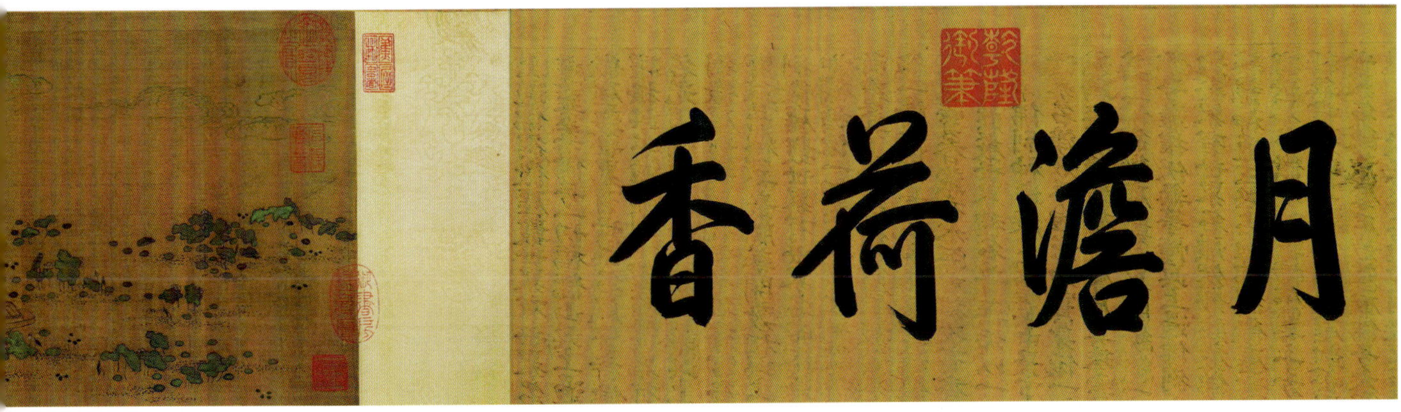

玉石不分的状况，我们立即开始了紧张的整理工作。

经过对其中150件左右清宫原藏书画的逐一鉴定，从中的发现令人惊讶和兴奋，因为，除了少量混进的伪赝品之外，其中多半数以上都是极为珍贵的法书名画，更不乏孤本或精绝之宝。例如在法书中，晋人书《曹娥诔辞》墨迹，是具有明确年代的小楷书，经南朝、唐、宋以下知名鉴藏家的题识和品评，推崇备至，几十种文献著录，流传有绪，使我们能够看到在我国楷书最后奠定格局之际的过渡面貌。唐代欧阳询的墨迹有两卷，《千字文》因其早年作品的缘故，有些不同的看法，而《梦奠帖》(图三)却是大家一致公认的欧阳氏书法真迹，欧阳氏平生喜用史事入书，世传《张翰帖》、《卜商帖》等均属所书史事帖范畴，仅此帖为三帖中唯一的晚年真迹，被文博界视之为国宝墨皇。我国草书发展到盛唐之际，达到辉煌的境界，唐开元（714－741年）时的大书法家张旭，即为我国狂草书的开派人物，而《古诗四帖》为其唯一的传世孤本，充分体现狂草书的艺术成就。《论书帖》则是中晚唐僧人怀素的墨迹，他的书法从张旭的狂草书中直接继承过来。宋人墨迹中，仅宋徽宗赵佶的行草作品，就有三件之多，其中《草书千字文》卷长达11.72米，纸精墨妙，信笔狂书，诚乃赵氏草法的代表作。自晋代以来一千六百余年传下来的赫赫名迹，如我国书法艺术宝库中的一颗颗明珠，终在东北博物馆重新发出了灿烂的光芒。

同批拨入东北博物馆的绘画作品，较书法数量少些，但却不乏珍贵至极的国之重宝。其中有：东晋顾恺之画作最为忠实的摹本《洛神赋》卷，传为初唐时阎立本所作《萧翼赚兰亭图》卷，盛唐时宫廷画家周昉所作的具体而生动反映唐贞元年间社会风尚的《簪花仕女图》卷，五代时南唐副史、江南山水画开派宗匠董源所作的《夏景山口待渡图》卷，西蜀画院首领黄筌的传世孤本《写生珍禽图》，北宋初期的开派画家李成所作的《茂林远岫图》卷，北宋名家李公麟作的《牧韦偃牧放图》卷，宋徽宗赵佶所作的《瑞鹤图》卷，均为稀有的传世珍宝。在三件同名为《清明上河图》的画作中，北宋张择端的真迹竟奇迹般地出现了，此图于1954年编入《伟大祖国艺术图录》，名声大噪，后又送北京故宫博物院展出，遂不胫而走，轰动全国，风靡世界。

1952年1月初，长春市公安局在办案过程中，发现某些居民及前古玩店主家中存有伪皇宫散佚出来的书画。据此，东北文化部当即决定由我和图书馆的赵琦先生（不久赵琦又被调往北京大学）组成的清查组，彻底清理此事。我立即赶赴到长春，从公安局查办案件涉及的问题入手，逐渐深入到溥仪伪政权倒台时的具体细节，终于大体上掌握了国宝在伪皇宫小白楼中被洗劫的过程及长期流动的线索。制定了相关的政策和奖励办法以后，即从参与分夺国宝的国兵们开始，进入了紧张而繁琐的征缴工作。搜索范围从长春顺延到北京、天津及东北各地，夜以继日地工作，在不到两个月的时间内，即从所有的线索及相关人士手中，陆续追回晋、唐、宋、元及历代书画国宝近二百件。其中，传为北宋早期花卉大家赵昌的《写生蛱蝶图》卷，北宋中期名家崔白的《寒雀图》卷，南宋初期梅花开派大家杨无咎的《雪梅图》等等，都是传世稀有的名迹。征集起来的这批历代书画，经东北博物馆转交予北京故宫博物院，以充实其由于屡次外迁而造成的书画精品方面的空白，这对故宫博物院绘画馆的开馆，起到了决定性的作用。

在故宫博物院绘画馆紧张筹备的阶段，东北博物馆又将原藏之五代黄筌《写生珍禽图》、宋李公麟《摩韦偃牧放图》、张择端《清明上河图》、赵伯驹《江山秋色图》等四件重宝借予一并展出，后来又办了转拨手续。在各有关文博界单位的大力支援下，1954年10月1日建国五周年大庆之际，北京故宫博物院绘画馆正式开放。

在集中清理、征集了大批长春伪皇宫散佚出来的历代法书名画以后，有关的征集工作一直在不间断地进行着，发现了一些重宝。例如，1964年4月的一天，一个哈尔滨青年带着一个布包来到北京荣宝斋门市，说有旧书画要出售，当店员打开布包时，里面是一堆碎纸片，但纸片上的清宫收藏印，引起了他的重视。当时我正在该店做客，遂应邀予以鉴定，当我们耐心地将碎片一一缀合以后，不想从中竟发现了37件伪皇宫流散之名贵书画，其中就有北宋大书法家米芾代表作《苕溪诗》。这个哈尔滨青年，次年，又送来一堆碎片，从中又发现了20件重要作品，其中就有北宋大名鼎鼎范仲淹所书的《二札帖》。这前后两次的重大发现，均进一步充实了北京故宫博物院的书画收藏。

与此同时，本着博物馆工作者的职责和良知，我开始多方搜集相关资料，目标就是要将已散佚的历代法书名画查个水落石出，并要弄清其历史和艺术价值。此后，这项工作就再也没有间断过，即使在“文革”的灾难中，被赶到偏远的山村中，也在继续。改革开放以后，随着出访交流的逐渐增多，在欧美、日本等许多藏有重要作品国家的博物馆等相关机构和个人手中，我看到或得到很多极其重要的珍品及信息，使得清宫散佚书画目前的下落及各自的归属，能够屡清一个基本的眉目。因此，历经三十余年的搜索研究，终于撰成了《国宝沉浮录—故宫散佚书画见闻考略》这样一部专业著作，总算将这四十年来在这方面所作的工作，作一番交代，以便国内外关心溥仪运出的清宫原藏全部作品下落的人们，对此有所了解。

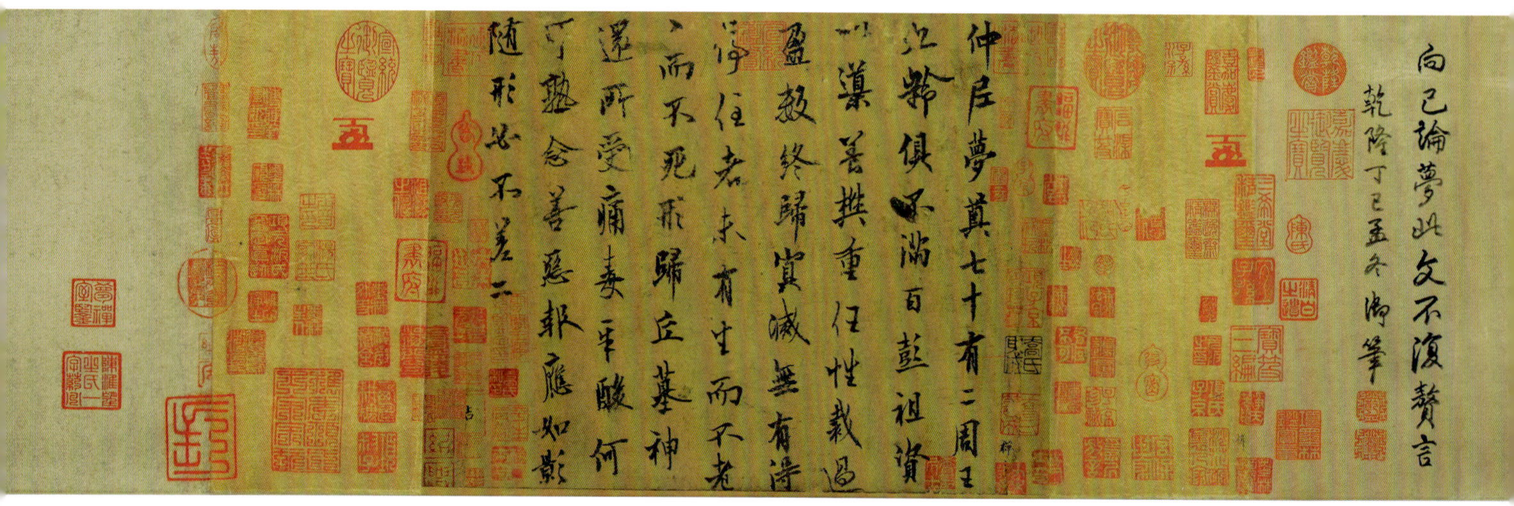

图三. 唐，欧阳询（557–641）行书仲尼梦奠帖，手卷，纸本水墨，辽宁省博物馆

Ouyang Xun (557–641), *Confucius Predicting Death in a Dream*. Handscroll. Ink on Paper. Liaoning Provincial Museum

Suitable for Sons and Grandsons
The Qing Emperors and the Imperial Collection of Calligraphy and Painting

David Ake Sensabaugh

Puyi (1906–1967) ascended the Dragon Throne in December of 1908 following the death of his uncle the Guangxu emperor a month earlier. He was not quite three years old at the time, and his reign as the Xuantong emperor proved to be short. With the revolution of 1911 led by Sun Yat-sen (1866–1925) and the founding of the Republic of China, he was forced to abdicate in February of 1912. He became the last emperor of China, the last Manchu ruler of the Qing dynasty, and the last emperor to inherit the vast collections of art assembled in the Beijing palaces.

Under the "Articles of Favorable Treatment of the Emperor of the Great Qing after his Abdication," Puyi continued to live in the Forbidden City until November of 1924 when he was expelled from the palaces by the warlord Feng Yuxiang (1882–1948).[1] During those years, he came to see the collections—particularly the holdings of calligraphy and painting—as a form of security for his future. He and his younger brother Pujie (1907–1994) contrived to smuggle over a thousand scrolls out of the palace before 1924.[2] These scrolls were soon sent to the foreign concessions in Tianjin for safekeeping and were later taken to Manchukuo when Puyi became head of state in 1932 and the Kangde emperor in 1934. At the end of the war with Japan in 1945 and amidst the chaos of civil war, this collection was dispersed. Only in the early 1950s after the founding of the People's Republic of China were the scrolls reassembled to form the basis of what is now the calligraphy and painting collection of the Liaoning Provincial Museum.[3] The survival of this part of the Qing imperial collections during the twentieth century, as related by Yang Renkai's essay in this publication, is a remarkable story. Why the scrolls were in the palace in the first place and the role of the Qing emperors, Puyi's predecessors, in amassing such a vast collection is the story told below.

Calligraphy and painting as works of art only gradually came to be considered the most important parts of a ruler's collection.[4] In antiquity it had been the Nine Tripods (*jiuding*) and the charts and records (*tuji*) that were at the heart of a ruler's possessions. They were the treasures (*bao*) that conferred legitimacy on a ruler. They had a magical aura (*ling*) about them: the Nine Tripods were said to have been cast by the mythical Emperor Yu and to have descended from him to the Xia and Shang kings and then to the Zhou kings. When the First Emperor of Qin (Qin Shihuangdi; r. 221–210 BCE) failed in 219 BCE to recover them from a river, it was considered an ill omen for his rule, and indeed the Qin dynasty (221–206 BCE) was short lived. Zhang Yanyuan (b. ca. 815), writing in the ninth century, associated this same magical aura with the charts and records that were recovered from the Qin palaces by the officials of the first Han emperor, Liu Bang (r. 206–195 BCE).[5] It was their ownership that conferred legitimacy to rule; without them, however, he could not have ruled effectively. These objects were like a tally that the ruler matched with Heaven once the Mandate of Heaven had been conferred on him, and they were kept carefully guarded within the precincts of the palace in "secret boxes" (*miji*). They were the ruler's viscera (*zang*) that must be collected (*cang*) in order to enable him to rule. Once the magical associations of the early *lingbao* began to be transferred to works of art, it was the power of these works to confer legitimacy that became foremost in the amassing of works of art in the palace. Such objects acted as a guarantee of the legitimate political and cultural tradition.

The transition from magico-religious objects to works of art collected for aesthetic reasons happened during the centuries from the end of the Han dynasty (206 BCE–220 CE) to the founding of the Sui dynasty in 589. This happened first with respect to calligraphy and then to painting. In the thousand years following the Sui, great collections of calligraphy and painting were assembled in the palaces only to be dispersed during times of imperial weakness or at the end of a dynasty.[6] The Tang emperor Taizong (r. 626–649) assembled one of the largest collections, particularly of calligraphy, in the seventh century. After the rebellion of An Lushan in the mid-eighth century, however, many of these works left the palace or simply disappeared. During the Song dynasty collections were again assembled, culminating under Emperor Huizong (r. 1101–1125) at the end of the Northern Song (960–1126). Many works that had been assembled and catalogued under Huizong were once again lost when the Jin overran the Song capital at Kaifeng and took the retired emperor into captivity. Southern Song (1127–1279) collections were in turn lost when Hangzhou fell to the Mongols in the 1270s. The Mongols established their capital in the north, at Dadu, on the site of the present Beijing. Members of the Mongol imperial family were collectors, notably Princess Sengge Ragi and Emperor Wenzong (r. 1328–1332),[7] and works from their collections passed into the Ming imperial collection, which was assembled first in Nanjing and then in Beijing after the Yongle emperor (r. 1403–1424) moved the capital back to the north in 1421. None of the later Ming emperors are noted as collectors, although they patronized court artists and thus added to the palace collections. The period from the late sixteenth to early seventeenth century was one of weakness for the Ming, and many important works appear to have found their way out of the palace collection. This was the situation when the Manchus arrived in Beijing in 1644.

The Early Qing Emperors: Shunzhi and Kangxi

The Manchus, who had been a rising military power on the northeast borders of the Ming empire, had already established a state on the Chinese model when their troops were invited to help drive out rebels from Beijing. After relieving the city, they found a chaotic situation: a looted city and a government without a head, the Ming emperor having committed suicide as the rebels under Li Zicheng approached the capital. The rebels were driven out, and the Manchus, who stayed as occupiers, extended their conquest over most of China during the next several years. The imperial palaces, which were at the center of the city, had been partially burned and looted. But what remained of their collections of calligraphy and painting now functioned to legitimize Manchu rule in China.[8]

Shunzhi (r. 1644–1661), the first Manchu emperor of China, was a boy at the time of the conquest, and the country was ruled through regents during his minority. Throughout his reign the Manchus were faced with the military issues of extending their rule and bringing order to the land that they had conquered. There was probably little thought given to the works of art in their possession, although their Chinese advisors would certainly have recognized the value of calligraphy and painting scrolls as symbols of the Manchus' right to rule. Scrolls were given as gifts to generals and high officials but there is little evidence for collecting activities during the Shunzhi reign beyond paintings executed by the emperor himself.[9]

The situation may have changed only slightly when Prince Xuanye (1654–1722) ascended to the throne in 1661 as the Kangxi emperor after the early death of his father from smallpox.[10] He, too, was a boy, not yet seven, when he became emperor, and there were four regents in charge of the court until 1669. During the early years of the Kangxi reign, the fight to counter claimants to the Ming throne continued and was followed by the suppression of the Rebellion of the Three Feudatories, a rebellion led by three Chinese generals who had been awarded with princedoms in the south and southwest for their contributions to the conquest effort. It was not until in the early 1680s that the last of the Ming pretenders was killed, the Rebellion of the Three Feudatories was suppressed, and all of the former Ming realm came under Manchu control. Given the military and political situation during the first two decades of the Kangxi reign there was again little time for collecting calligraphy and painting despite the young emperor's interest in calligraphy.

During the latter part of his reign, however, the Kangxi emperor sought to engage the Chinese cultural world, and the palace collection of calligraphy and painting began to grow through his patronage of the arts. Painters along with other artisans had studios in the Ruyiguan workshop of the Qixiang Gong palace.[11] Official portraits for ritual uses as well as informal portraits and depictions of life in the palaces were executed by these anonymous artists. Those known to us by name, such as Jiao Bingzhen and his student Leng Mei (ca. 1670–after 1742), executed paintings employing Western techniques of perspective and shading. High officials who also painted, like Wang Yuanqi (1642–1715) and Jiang Tingxi (1669–1732), were important in shaping the landscape painting and bird-and-flower painting of the later Kangxi reign. Wang Yuanqi was the grandson of Wang Shimin (1592–1680), a painter and collector who had studied under Dong Qichang (1555–1636). Wang Yuanqi followed in the tradition initiated by Dong that came to be called the Orthodox School (*zhengpai*) during the seventeenth century. He brought this type of painting, favored by the educated Chinese elite, into the palace and made it a part of court painting. Jiang Tingxi, after obtaining his *juren* degree in 1699, started as a painter at court before advancing in his bureaucratic career. Paintings by Wang and Jiang went directly into the palace collection, and the Kangxi emperor is known to have inscribed works by Jiang Tingxi. The emperor also inscribed works by the Manchu painter Heyi and by Gao Qipei (1660–1734), works which also entered the palace collection.[12] By far the greatest painting project of the Kangxi court was initiated after the Kangxi emperor began making inspection tours to the south. He made a total of six tours during his reign, beginning in 1684; these grand gestures were intended to display the power of the Manchus to the southern populace. It was after the second southern inspection tour (1689) that a series of great handscrolls were planned. They were executed under the direction of Wang Hui (1632–1717), another painter of the Orthodox School, who had positioned himself to receive the appointment.[13] Through this project the Kangxi emperor literally took pictorial possession of the heartland of Chinese culture.

Literary projects, such as the compilation of the *Kangxi zidian* (Character dictionary of the Kangxi reign period) and the *Peiwen yunfu* (Rhyme treasury from the Studio of Pendant Literature), a phrase-dictionary, were also a means of taking possession of Chinese culture. They were commissioned by the emperor and took a number of years and the efforts of many scholars to complete. Even if the emperor was not actively collecting antique works of calligraphy and painting, he could still command the historical texts relating to them. In 1705 he commissioned Wang Yuanqi to serve along with four other scholars as editors of the *Peiwenzhai shuhuapu* (Calligraphy and painting compendium of the Studio of Pendant Literature). This work in one hundred fascicles was completed in 1708 and remains an important reference source to this day. These literary projects were perhaps closer to the Kangxi emperor's heart than his patronage of painters or his collecting activities. In an informal portrait painted by a court artist, Kangxi had himself portrayed in the role of a scholar surrounded by books rather than by paintings or objects. The books are depicted using Western perspective, demonstrating the influence of Kangxi's broad intellectual curiosity on the work of court artists (fig. 1).

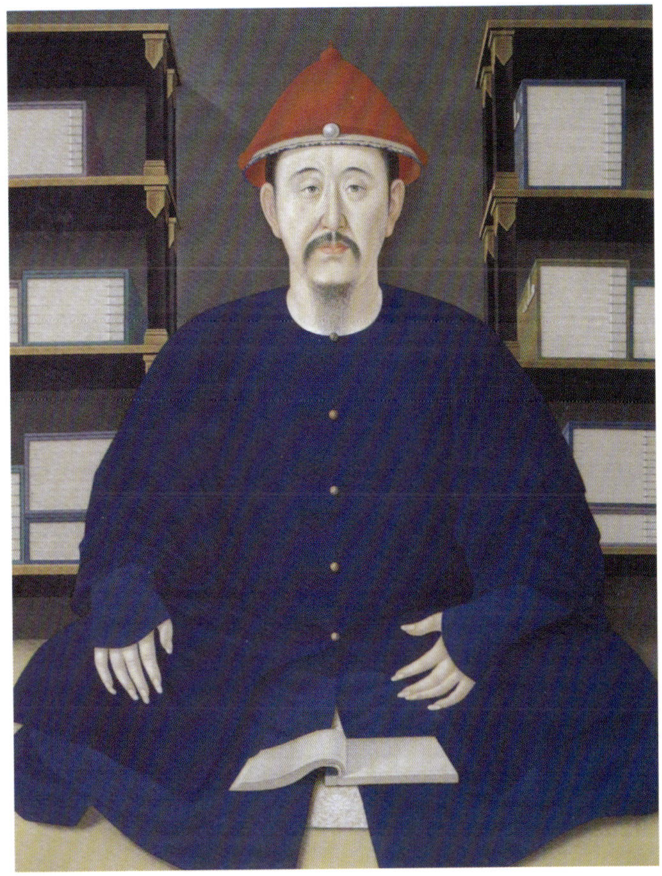

Fig. 1. Anonymous court artists 佚名（宫廷画家）,
The Kangxi Emperor Reading 康熙读书图, 17th–18th century.
Hanging scroll. Ink and color on silk, 138 x 106.5 cm.
Palace Museum, Beijing (GU6411)

Private Collections and the Shaping of Imperial Taste

Outside the palace during both the Shunzhi and Kangxi reigns, there was considerable activity in collecting calligraphy and painting, and the taste of the collectors and the shape of their collections clearly informed subsequent imperial collecting. It is thus worth noting a number of these collectors. In the decades after the Manchu conquest important private collections were formed by high officials such as Sun Chengze (1593–1675) and Liang Qingbiao (1620–1691).[14] Both Sun and Liang had been serving in the Ming government at the time of the conquest, and both remained in Beijing during the brief regime of Li Zicheng before going over to the Manchu side. Sun Chengze, who had been a metropolitan censor, was given this same position under the Manchus and rose to become senior vice-president of the Board of Civil Offices in 1652. Two years later he was caught up in court politics and permanently relieved of office. In retirement he devoted himself to study and in 1660 wrote *Gengzi xiaoxiaji* (Notes to idle away the summer of the *gengzi* year), in which he made notes on the paintings in his own collection as well as on those that he had seen in other collections. Although he did not record the particulars of each painting, he left an important record of his research and connoisseurship. Liang Qingbiao left no catalogue of his collection, but judging from surviving works with his seals on them he had a very large collection that included many now famous Northern and Southern Song and Yuan dynasty paintings. He was highly esteemed as a collector by his contemporaries, and many of the early paintings from his collection found their way into the palace. Less is known of his life than that of Sun Chengze. He served the short-lived regime of Li Zicheng before joining the Manchus and, through a long career under both the Shunzhi and Kangxi emperors, rose at the end to be grand academician (*daxueshi*) in the Hall for the Preservation of Harmony (Baohedian). He appears to have left his collection to his descendants, who subsequently dispersed it. Quite a number of works from his collection, including Tang Yin's *Master Wuyang in Self-Cultivation* (cat. no. 10), later found there way into the palace collection.

Other somewhat younger Chinese connoisseurs with direct connections to the court, like Song Luo (1634–1713),[15] Geng Zhaozhong (1640–1686),[16] and Gao Shiqi (1645–1703),[17] as well as the Manchu official and collector Songgotu (d. 1703),[18] built their collections primarily during the Kangxi reign. Song Luo's father, Song Quan (1598–1652), had been governor of the metropolitan district around Beijing at the time of the conquest. He surrendered to the Manchus and was reappointed to his former position. Before his death in 1652 he rose to be a grand secretary and grand guardian of the heir apparent. Through his father's position, the young Song Luo came to the attention first of the Shunzhi emperor and then of the Kangxi emperor. He served with distinction as governor of Jiangxi and Jiangsu provinces and became wealthy enough to entertain the Kangxi emperor during the southern inspection tours of 1699, 1703, and 1705. He was well known as a poet and patron and built a collection of calligraphy and painting while serving in his governorships. His seals appear on a number of important paintings that later entered the palace collection.

Geng Zhaozhong's family had been in service to the Manchus since before the conquest and was part of the Plain Yellow Banner. His father, Geng Jimao (d. 1671), served the Manchus with distinction during the conquest. As a consequence of his father's service, Geng Zhaozhong was married to an imperial princess. Although his older brother was one of the three generals who led the Rebellion of the Three Feudatories in the south and was subsequently executed, he maintained favor as the consort of a princess and managed to build an important collection which included *Waiting for the Ferry at the Mouth of the Summer Mountains* (*Xiajing shankou dadu tu*), a scroll thought to be by the tenth-century master Dong Yuan (d. 962) and one of the scrolls taken by Puyi to Manchuria.

Gao Shiqi rose from humble origins to become a secretary and confidant of the Kangxi emperor without ever obtaining an advanced degree. He amassed considerable wealth, and although he was several times accused of bribery, he managed throughout to maintain his personal relationship with the emperor. In 1693, during a period when he was out of office, he completed *Jiangcun xiaoxialu* (*Jiangcun's Record of Whiling Away the Summer*), a catalogue of the calligraphy and paintings that he had seen in the previous three years. He appears to have been the first to record all the particulars of the scrolls—measurements, media, signatures, seals, and inscriptions—but he did not follow Sun Chengze in making comments on individual works. Gao Shiqi also left lists of calligraphy and paintings by category. It is interesting to note that those works categorized as to be given to the throne or to be given as presents to others are consistently the least expensive items in the list. The most valuable paintings are categorized as to be kept forever. For someone who is considered to have advised the Kangxi emperor on matters of calligraphy and painting, he appears to have put self interest ahead of his loyalty. A large portion of Gao's collection was eventually acquired by the palace.

Among the Manchus at court, Songgotu was one of the most important collectors. He was uncle of the empress and great uncle of the heir apparent Yinreng which made him very influential at court but also brought about his downfall during the struggles among the sons of the Kangxi emperor over issues of succession. He had amassed great wealth, which he used to build a collection of ancient bronze vessels, calligraphy, and painting. Famous works from his collection also found their way into the palace collection.

One more collector—the youngest of the group and one who remained active well into the eighteenth century—deserves to be mentioned: An Qi (1683–ca. 1744), a salt merchant from a Korean family that had been bondservants to the Manchus since before the conquest.[19] As a young man An Qi was able to see works still owned by the families of Liang Qingbiao and Geng Zhaozhong, and in 1715 he met with Wang Hui and viewed a famous painting attributed by Dong Qichang to the early Song dynasty monk painter Juran. That same year Wang Hui added the landscape elements to a portrait of An Qi seated in a garden surrounded by paintings.[20] Because the An family had made their fortune through the salt trade, An Qi was able to acquire some of the most famous paintings of the age. He left a

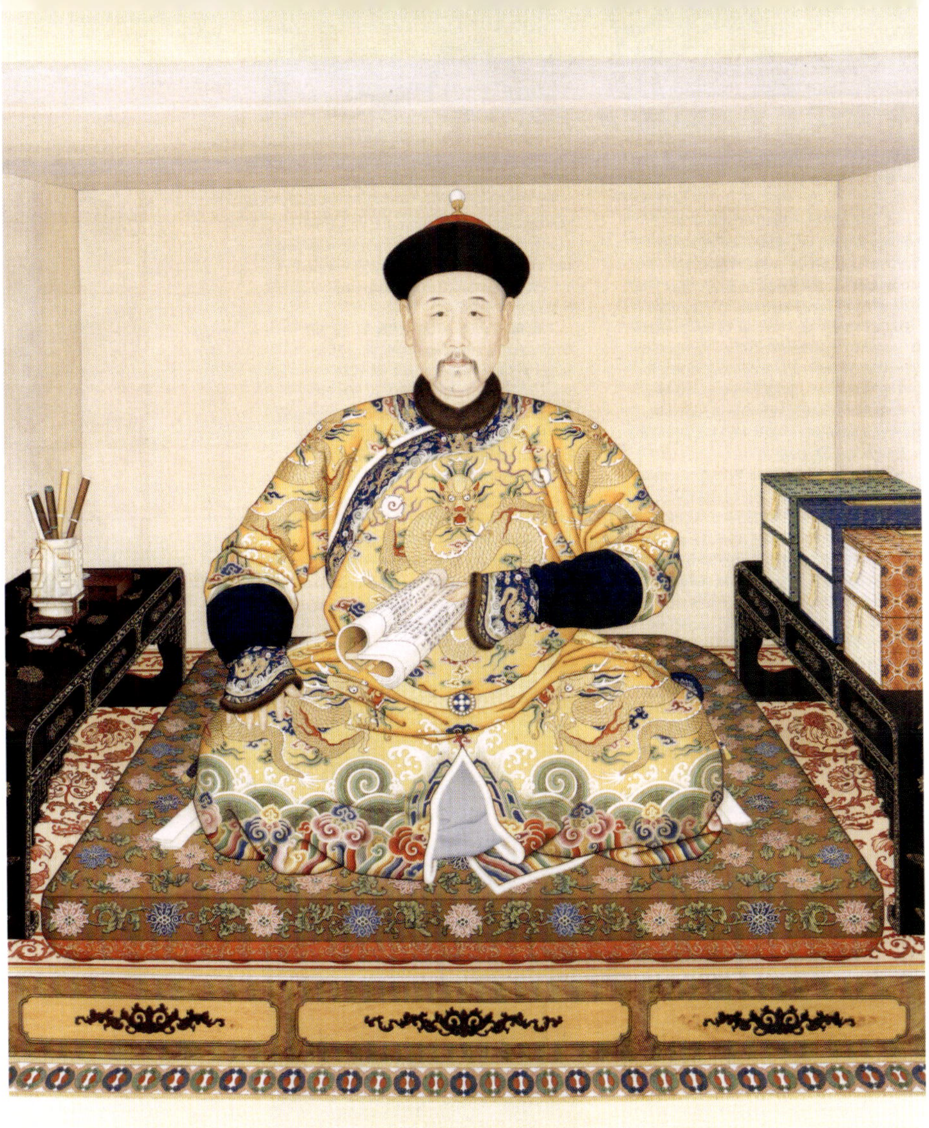

Fig. 2. Anonymous court artists 佚名（宫廷画家）, *Portrait of the Yongzheng Emperor Reading a Book* 雍正读书像图, 1722–35. Hanging scroll. Ink and color on silk, 171.3 x 156.5 cm. Palace Museum, Beijing (GU6446)

record—*Moyuan huiguan*—of the calligraphy and painting that he considered it his fate to have seen and owned. In it he followed Gao Shiqi's example in recording measurements, media, signatures, seals, and inscriptions along with his own sometimes very acute comments.

The Yongzheng Reign

Upon the death of the Kangxi emperor in December of 1722, his fourth son, Yinzhen (1678–1735), ascended the throne as the Yongzheng emperor (r. 1723–35).[21] There had been a struggle among the princes for the succession, and throughout his reign the Yongzheng emperor remained suspicious of the other princes, depriving them of their power to control the bannermen allotted to them as retainers. Through these means the emperor further concentrated power in his own hands. He was an able and conscientious ruler who sought to enforce the laws and to end the corruption that had increased during the later years of his father's reign. In doing so he laid the foundations for the prosperity of the next reign, that of his son the Qianlong emperor (r. 1736–95).

Little is known of Yongzheng's activities as a collector of calligraphy and painting, except that he did patronize the court painters and thus, like his father, augmented the palace collections. This was true even before he became emperor, when he had himself and his wife depicted as peasants engaged in tilling and weaving. The resulting album, although not seen outside the court, was like propaganda for the future ruler, showing his concern for the common people.[22] After he became emperor, Yongzheng commissioned long handscrolls that documented events during his reign, similar to the southern inspection tour scrolls of his father.[23] A number of smaller-scale albums show him in various roles, as if in costume. Like the album depicting him engaged in tilling and weaving, these images show him as if he were the master of all roles.[24] In one full portrait image (fig. 2), he had himself depicted in his study reading: he is holding a book, and there are books on the shelves to either side. But even though he was an accomplished calligrapher, he did not choose to have himself portrayed as a cultured literatus in the same way that his father did in his informal portrait (fig. 1). These paintings are evidence of the high level of refinement that court painting attained during Yongzheng's reign. His real contribution to the arts, however, lay in his patronage of ceramics, which likewise attained a high level of refinement rarely seen in later reigns. Selections from the palace collections of antiquities and ceramics were illustrated in several long handscrolls; the choices of objects appear to reflect his personal taste and confirm his interest in the ceramic arts.[25]

The Qianlong Reign

Hongli (1711–1799), the fourth son of the Yongzheng emperor, succeeded to the throne in October of 1735 under the reign title Qianlong.[26] His sixty-year reign was an age of prosperity and territorial expansion and saw the true growth of the palace calligraphy and painting collection. During the early years of his reign, he built upon the foundations laid by his father, further centralizing power in the throne at the expense of the princes. It was only in the middle years of his reign that a trend towards luxuriousness set in, culminating in rampant corruption during his final years. Despite the brilliance of Qianlong's reign, his successors did not inherit an empire with the same solid foundations that he had inherited in 1735.

The Qianlong emperor was aware, more so than his predecessors, of the legitimizing function of the palace art collections. He saw himself in the role of emperor-collector on the model of Tang Taizong and Song Huizong, assembling works in the palace that would buttress the Manchu claim to be the legitimate holders of the Mandate of Heaven. He was always conscious, however, not to allow himself to be seen as too involved with art and inattentive to government, a criticism that historians had aimed at Song Huizong. He had begun collecting as a prince and continued on a grander scale once he became emperor. Famous works that had been in the great private collections in the seventeenth and early eighteenth century were now acquired, and in many cases reacquired, by the palace. A major purchase of a thousand scrolls from the collections of Gao Shiqi and An Qi was completed in 1746 with the help of his brother-in-law Fuheng. Other famous scrolls came as gifts to the emperor. For instance, Shen Deqian (1673–1769), a high official as well as a prominent poet, presented him with Zhang Zeduan's *Spring Festival Along the River* (*Qingming shanghe tu*), a painting that was later taken out of the palace by Puyi.

The palace collections of calligraphy and painting had

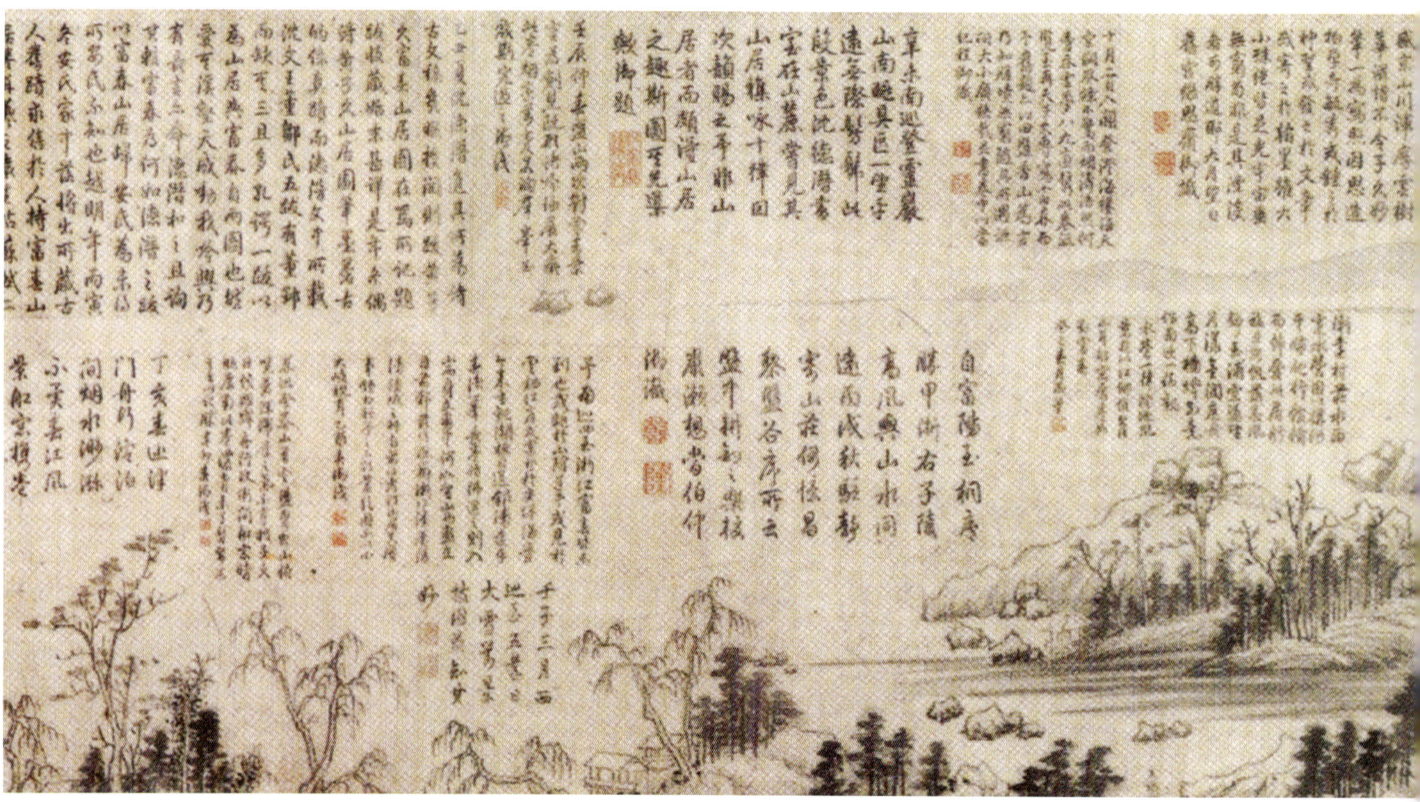

grown to such an extent that the Qianlong emperor, after nine years on the throne, felt it was necessary to inventory them, and in January of 1744 he commissioned a catalogue of the Buddhist and Daoist calligraphy and paintings kept in the palaces. The catalogue, called *Midian zhulin* (Pearl forest of the Secret Hall) after the Secret Hall of the Han dynasty emperor Wudi (r. 141–87 BCE), included 271 works and was completed during the summer. In the spring of 1744, while work was advancing on the *Midian zhulin*, Qianlong commissioned a catalogue of the secular calligraphy and paintings in the collection. This part of the inventory was called *Shiqu baoji* (Treasured boxes of the Stone Channel) in reference to the Han dynasty Stone Channel Pavilion where the first Han emperor, Liu Bang, had kept the charts and records taken from the Qin palace. The inventory took a year and a half to complete; it was presented to the throne in the fall of 1745 and included 1,774 works. The editorial board was under the direction of Zhang Zhao (1691–1745), a scholar who shared the emperor's interest in calligraphy, particularly that of the Song dynasty masters and Dong Qichang (see cat. no. 19). Working alongside Zhang were four other scholars all of whom held various high positions at court. Since the catalogue was an inventory, the calligraphy and paintings were listed according to the palace buildings where they were stored. Each work was ranked as either superior or secondary, and for all superior works, full catalogue information was given using the private catalogues of the seventeenth century, particularly those of Sun Chengze and Gao Shiqi, as models.

By 1791 the number of calligraphic works and paintings added to the collection—more than half of them works by court artists and by the emperor himself—necessitated a supplement (*xubian*) to both the *Midian zhulin* and *Shiqu baoji*. These were completed and presented to the throne in 1793. The organizational principles were the same, but the works were no longer ranked as either superior or secondary. All works were given thorough treatment. After the death of the Qianlong emperor in 1799, his son the Jiaqing emperor (r. 1796–1820) felt that yet a further inventory was necessary, and in 1815 he commissioned a third series (*sanbian*) for both *Midian zhulin*

Fig. 3. Attributed to Huang Gongwang (1269–1354) 传黄公望, *Dwelling in the Fuchun Mountains* 富春山居图, Ziming version 子明本, 1336 (probably 16th–17th century). Handscroll (section). Ink on paper, 33 x 589.2 cm. National Palace Museum, Taipei (古畫甲01.09.01017)

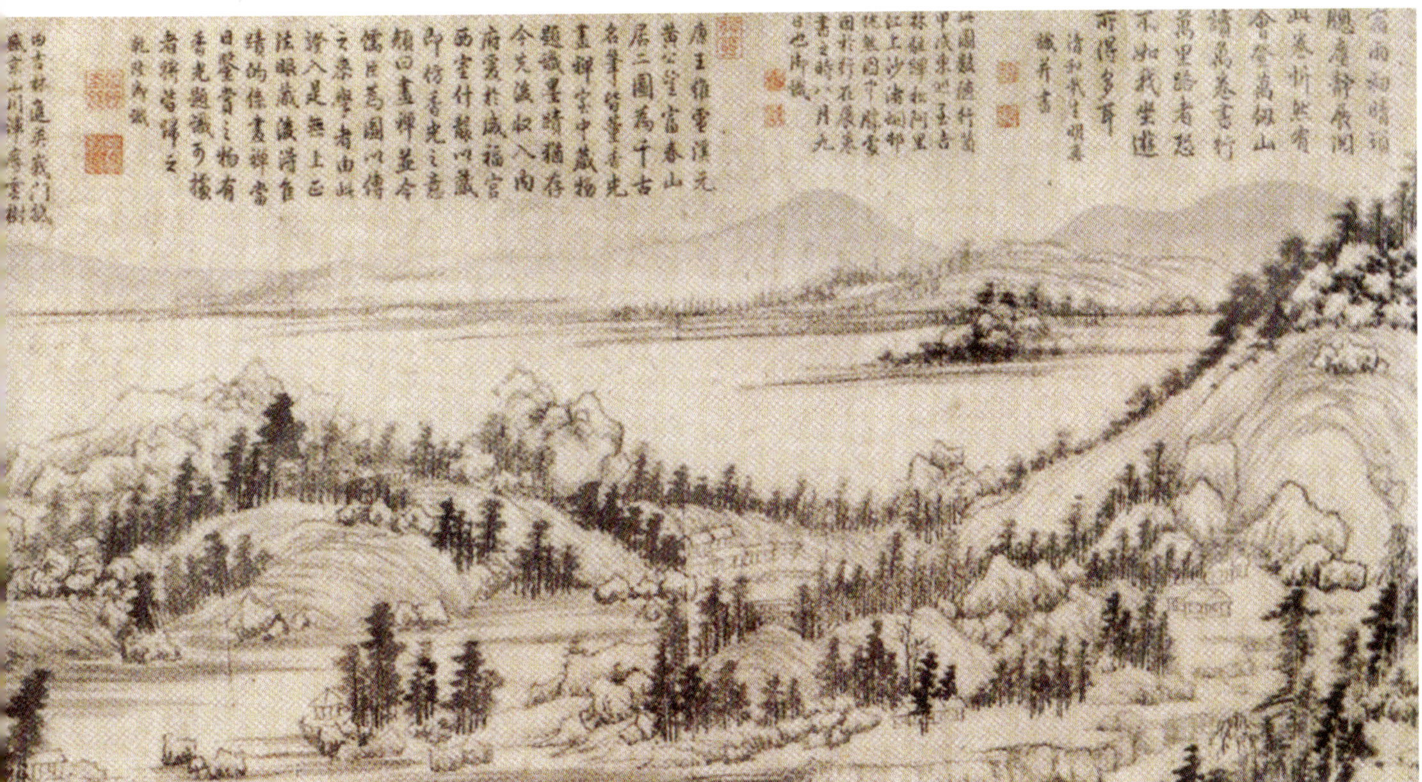

and *Shiqu baoji*. This series was completed in the following year. Without the Qianlong emperor looking over their shoulders, the editors were able to complete their task with greater efficiency.

Throughout his reign the Qianlong emperor was personally involved with the collection. He worked closely with the editors of his catalogues, conducted his own research on the calligraphy and paintings, and wrote numerous inscriptions and colophons for the works.[27] He avidly sought out famous examples of calligraphy as the highest of art forms. Qianlong was especially keen on seeing that major works of the canonical tradition of Wang Xizhi (ca. 303–ca. 361) and his son Wang Xianzhi (344–388) entered the collection. He achieved this with the acquisition of works by the two Wangs and by Wang Xizhi's nephew Wang Xun (350–401). The emperor called them the "Three Rarities" (*sanxi*) and named his studio after them, the Hall of the Three Rarities (Sanxitang).[28] In 1749 he commissioned *Sanxitang fatie* (Calligraphy models in the Hall of the Three Rarities), a compendium of rubbings reproducing 340 works of calligraphy by 135 calligraphers from the third to the early seventeenth century. Through such a project he demonstrated his command of Chinese culture and thereby reassured the educated elite that the values embodied in the works of the past were being preserved and transmitted to future generations. Although aimed at his own descendants, his seal legend which reads "yizisun," or "suitable for sons and grandsons"—adapted from a seal of Geng Zhaozhong—conveyed this idea. He saw himself as the guardian of Chinese tradition.

The Qianlong emperor's personal attachment to the scrolls in his collection can be seen in his inscriptions on two works by the fourteenth-century masters Huang Gongwang (1269–1354) and Ni Zan (1306–1374). Following the writings of Dong Qichang and the Ming period canonization of Huang Gongwang, Wu Zhen (1280–1354), Ni Zan, and Wang Meng (ca. 1308–1385) as the "Four Great Masters of the Yuan," he assembled as many of the famous works of these four artists for the palace as was possible. One scroll by Huang Gongwang that was very famous in the Ming period and had increased in fame during the seventeenth century was *Dwelling in the Fuchun Mountains* (*Fuchun shanju tu*). The scroll had been owned by Shen Zhou (1427–1509), and upon seeing the painting, Dong Qichang pronounced his judgment in an inscription written on the mounting at the beginning of the scroll. He exclaimed: "This is my teacher! This is my teacher!"

In 1745 the palace acquired the coveted scroll; Huang Gongwang's inscription at the end of the scroll names the recipient as Ziming.[29] Qianlong and his advisors determined that this was the famous Huang Gongwang scroll owned by Shen Zhou and seen by Dong Qichang, and they immediately catalogued it in *Shiqu baoji*. The following year, however, a similar scroll dedicated not to Ziming but to a Wuyong was purchased.[30] The acquisition of the Wuyong version raised the question of authenticity, and the emperor consulted with his advisor Liang Shizheng (1697–1763), who had been one of the editors of *Shiqu baoji*. They determined that the first decision had been correct, and the Ziming version thus became the object of the emperor's obsessive attention.

Between 1746 and 1795, Qianlong wrote a total of fifty-six inscriptions on the surface of the Ziming version, filling almost every blank space available (fig. 3).[31] He took the painting with him on his travels, and when he was inspired he would inscribe it and record the circumstances. Most of these inscriptions are poems, but there are also some prose accounts. In one of the accounts he discussed the relationship of the Ziming version to the Wuyong version. For the Qianlong emperor, the scroll was a lifelong companion. Perhaps only towards the end of his life did he inscribe the beginning of the scroll with the following line: "From now on I will only unroll and enjoy the scroll and not inscribe it further." With his inscriptions, the Qianlong emperor had completely transformed the appearance of the scroll, providing visible evidence of his rightful role as emperor. The Wuyong version, although acquired in 1746, was not catalogued until the third series of *Shiqu baoji*. At that time, the editor Hu Jing (1769–1845) could question the authenticity of the Ziming scroll.[32] This would not have happened while the Qianlong emperor was still alive.

Ni Zan's *Lion Grove Picture* (*Shizilin tu*; fig. 4) had also been very famous throughout the seventeenth century. This artist's reputation as a refined scholar had risen very high by the end of the Ming dynasty, and the sparseness of his compositions and his dry linear style became an ideal followed by many seventeenth-century painters. The *Lion Grove Picture* was particularly well-known as one of only a few handscrolls by Ni Zan. Acquired by the palace before 1744 and catalogued in *Shiqu baoji*, it had been in the collections of Sun Chengze and Gao Shiqi.[33] Sun had included it in his catalogue and had described in detail the circumstances of his acquisition of the scroll.[34] It had been brought to the north as war booty by soldiers after the Manchu forces had taken Nanjing. Because there were Southern Ming reign dates and a colophon by Ma Shiying (1591–1646), a notorious official of the Southern Ming court, attached to the scroll, all of the colophons had been cut off. When Sun obtained it, the scroll was ragged at both ends but the painting was not damaged. In early 1654 he had it remounted and recorded the circumstances. The Qianlong emperor had the scroll remounted again, provided it a frontispiece, and wrote a poetic inscription on the mounting preceding the painting. In his poem he wondered whether the Lion Grove still existed.

Over the course of his reign he inscribed the surface of the painting six times and wrote another inscription on the mounting following the painting. These inscriptions record his interactions with the painting. In 1757, on his second southern inspection tour, he visited Suzhou and found that the Lion Grove still existed, although it was now owned by a Huang family and no longer called the Lion Grove. He was delighted because the painting served to make the identification of the existing garden possible, and he ordered the scroll to be brought from Beijing so that he could record his discovery on the painting and correct his earlier poem. In 1762, on his third southern tour, he again had the scroll brought to Suzhou when he visited the garden, and he made a copy of the scroll. He repeated his visit on the 1765 southern tour, his fourth, and compared his earlier copy with the original scroll; he inscribed both scrolls during his visit. The Qianlong emperor's interest in the Lion Grove, both as a painting and as a garden, became so intense that he had the garden replicated in Beijing and Chengde. In 1774, after the completion of the garden at Chengde, he made another copy of the painting and once again inscribed the surface of the original to record the event. His final inscription on the surface of the painting was in 1784, during his sixth southern tour. In it he wanted to correct the then popular misconception that the Lion Grove had been Ni Zan's own retreat. He pointed out that the Lion Grove had been established as a monk's retreat and that this was clear from the dedication of the scroll to the monk Ruhai. He had his court scholars attach the fruits of their historical research in colophons following the painting. As with his inscriptions on the Ziming version of *Dwelling in the Fuchun Mountains*, Qianlong transformed the appearance of the Ni Zan scroll and in the process strengthened his image as emperor.

The emperor also acquired two versions of the poet and painter Xu Ben's (1335–1380) twelve views of the Lion Grove retreat. One was in album format and the other a handscroll.[35] He determined that the album was authentic and the handscroll a copy, and he accordingly had the copy declared an anonymous Ming work. When he acquired Du Qiong's (1396–1474) 1468 depiction of the Lion Grove, Qianlong noted that the artist's inscription stated that he was making his image after Xu Ben. The emperor, who had both Ni Zan's scroll and Xu Ben's album in his collection, recognized that Du Qiong's painting resembled that of Ni rather than Xu. In 1771 and 1772 he wrote three inscriptions on the surface of Du Qiong's painting, and in one of the 1772 inscriptions he tried to reconcile the differences raised by the visual evidence: although Du Qiong may have been inspired by Xu Ben's twelve views, he was executing a single image and thus could not get away from Ni Zan's original conception.[36]

The concern with historical accuracy seen in Qianlong's last inscription on the *Lion Grove Picture* and his use of empirical evidence when discussing Du Qiong was indicative of his training as an historian in the methods of evidential research, or *kaozheng* scholarship, which was at the core of the intellectual concerns of the eighteenth century.[37] His own concern for historical accuracy is seen in many inscriptions. When, for instance, he came into possession of a large colored landscape attributed to the tenth-century painter Dong Yuan that had been in the collection of Dong Qichang, he reinterpreted the subject matter based on textual research.[38] Dong Qichang had investigated the subject of the painting and had come to the conclusion that Dong Yuan might have painted it for the Song emperor Taizu (r. 960–976) when Taizu came to Nanjing after the fall of the Southern Tang state, where Dong Yuan had been a court painter. The connoisseur Zhang Chou (1577–1643) had offered another interpretation. He saw the subject as related to the inauguration ceremony for Song Taizu's ascent to the throne. The Qianlong emperor criticized both interpretations and offered his own view: the painting depicted an ancient praying-for-rain ceremony. Based on a careful study of earlier texts, Qianlong pointed out that neither Dong Qichang's nor Zhang Chou's interpretations were verifiable. He found that Song Taizu had not gone to Nanjing, the Southern Tang capital, to receive the Southern Tang ruler's surrender; nor could Dong Yuan have gone to the new Song capital at Kaifeng when Taizu became emperor, because the Southern Tang had not yet surrendered to the Song. Once he had thus refuted both Dong Qichang's and Zhang Chou's views on the subject matter, Qianlong searched through ancient texts and decided that the true subject of the painting must be a praying-for-rain ceremony found in the *Zuozhuan* (Zuo commentary). In such inscriptions his method of research clearly followed the evidential scholarship of *kaozheng* studies and showed him to be a master of careful

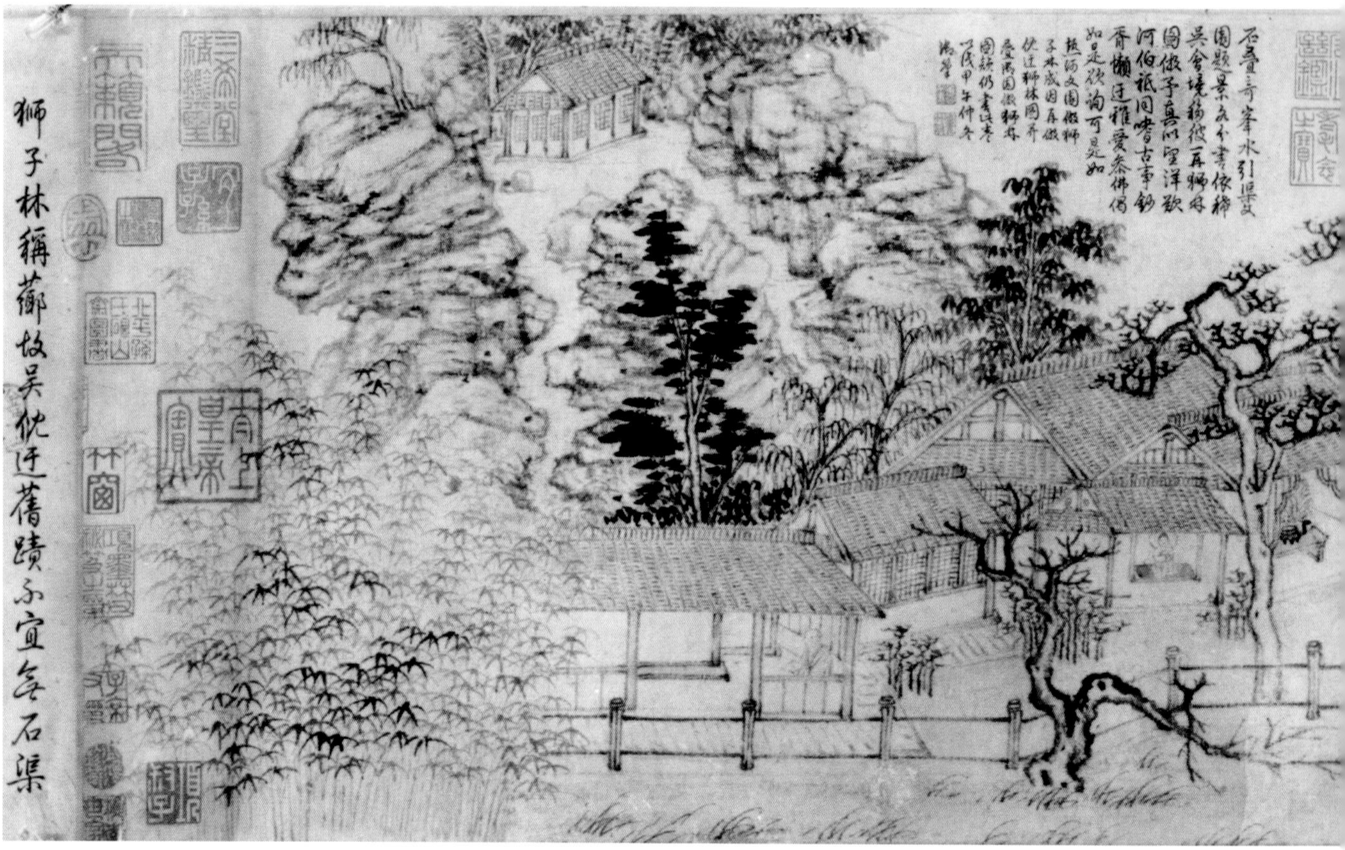

textual research, once again fashioning an image of himself that demonstrated his proper place as ruler of China.

The Qianlong emperor's textual and philologically based connoisseurship further led him to see the paintings in the collection in political terms. In 1746 he had written a colophon for the Song painter Li Di's *Herding Rams* (*Mudi tu*).[39] He identified the subject matter of the scroll as the story of Su Wu, a Han dynasty official who had been captured by the Xiongnu and held in captivity for nineteen years. During his years of detainment Su had married and made a living by herding sheep and goats, but he had remained loyal to the Han. The emperor ordered his court scholars to contribute colophons on the loyalty of Su Wu and changed the title of the painting to *Loyalty to the Han under an Icy Sky* (*Bingtian Han jie*). He wrote the four characters as the frontispiece.

In 1788 he wrote another colophon for the scroll, this time a discussion of Su Wu and his own military commander Yang Zhongying, who had been captured by the Burmese during the disastrous campaign against Burma in the 1760s. He placed Yang higher than Su in terms of absolute loyalty: Yang had not married, had not worn Burmese clothes, and had not lost his pride in being a Qing soldier. When Yang returned to Beijing after twenty-one years as a prisoner, the emperor welcomed him as a hero. In the years prior to Yang's return the emperor had been engaged with issues of loyalty. In *Erchen zhuan* (Lives of twice-serving ministers), he had criticized the former Ming officials who had surrendered to the Manchus and who had contributed to the success of the conquest. He condemned them as traitors. His colophon on Yang's loyalty was written in this context and in the context of the literary inquisition against writings deemed disloyal to the Qing.[40] Thus his colophon became part of a discourse on absolute loyalty to Manchu rule, and through it the emperor once again asserted the power and authority of his rulership.

The Qianlong reign represented the high point for the amassing of art within the Qing palace. In this period, the greatest collection of calligraphy and painting ever assembled was used to support the authority of the Manchu rulers and to guarantee the legitimacy of their rule. When the Qianlong emperor had himself portrayed by his court painters Giuseppe Castiglione (Lang Shining; 1688–1766) and Ding Guanpeng (active 1726–1770) seated in a garden enjoying paintings and surrounded by antiquities, he made

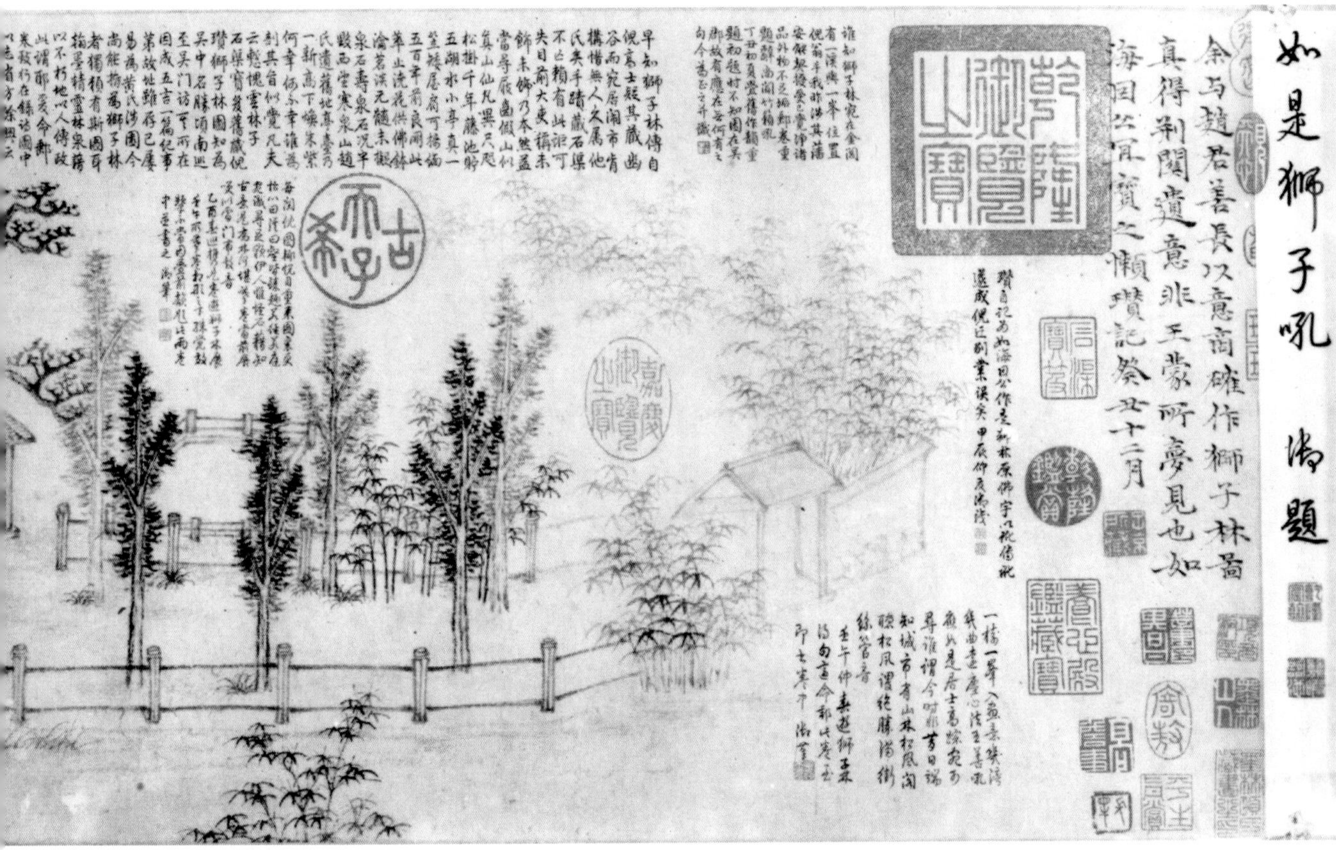

Fig. 4. Attributed to Ni Zan (1306–1374) and Zhao Yuan (fl. 1350–75) 传倪瓒和赵原, The Lion Grove 狮子林图, 1374 (probably 16th–17th century). Handscroll. Ink on paper, 30 x 100 cm. Palace Museum, Beijing (XN 146662). Photograph courtesy of Xu Bangda

the point that it was he who possessed the Chinese past (fig. 5). The Manchus' Great Enterprise (*daye*) to rule China had become under the Qianlong emperor a great cultural enterprise.

The Last Emperors

Although the Jiaqing reign saw the completion of the third series of the imperial catalogues, *Midian zhulin sanbian* and *Shiqu baoji sanbian*, in 1816 under the editorship of Hu Jing (1769–1845), the reign nevertheless marked the beginning of the decline of the imperial collections of calligraphy and painting. Many works began to be given to princes, eunuchs, and high officials and thus left the palace. Yongxing (1752–1823), the first Prince Cheng (Cheng qinwang), for instance, was given Lu Ji's (261–303) *Pingfu tie*, one of the earliest calligraphic works in the collection, and *Night-Shining White* (*Zhaoye bai*), a handscroll attributed to Han Gan of the Tang dynasty.[41] This practice continued under the Daoguang emperor (r. 1821–50) and during the remaining reigns. Yixin (1833–1898), Prince Gong (Gong qinwang), was presented with Song Huizong's *Five-colored Parakeet* (*Wuse yingwu tu*) and Chen Rong's *Nine Dragons* (*Jiu long tu*).[42] The Jiaqing emperor followed his father in placing seals on the calligraphy and paintings in the collection, but none of the other nineteenth-century emperors did so. After the Jiaqing emperor, only the Xuantong emperor, Puyi, placed seals on the scrolls in the imperial collection.

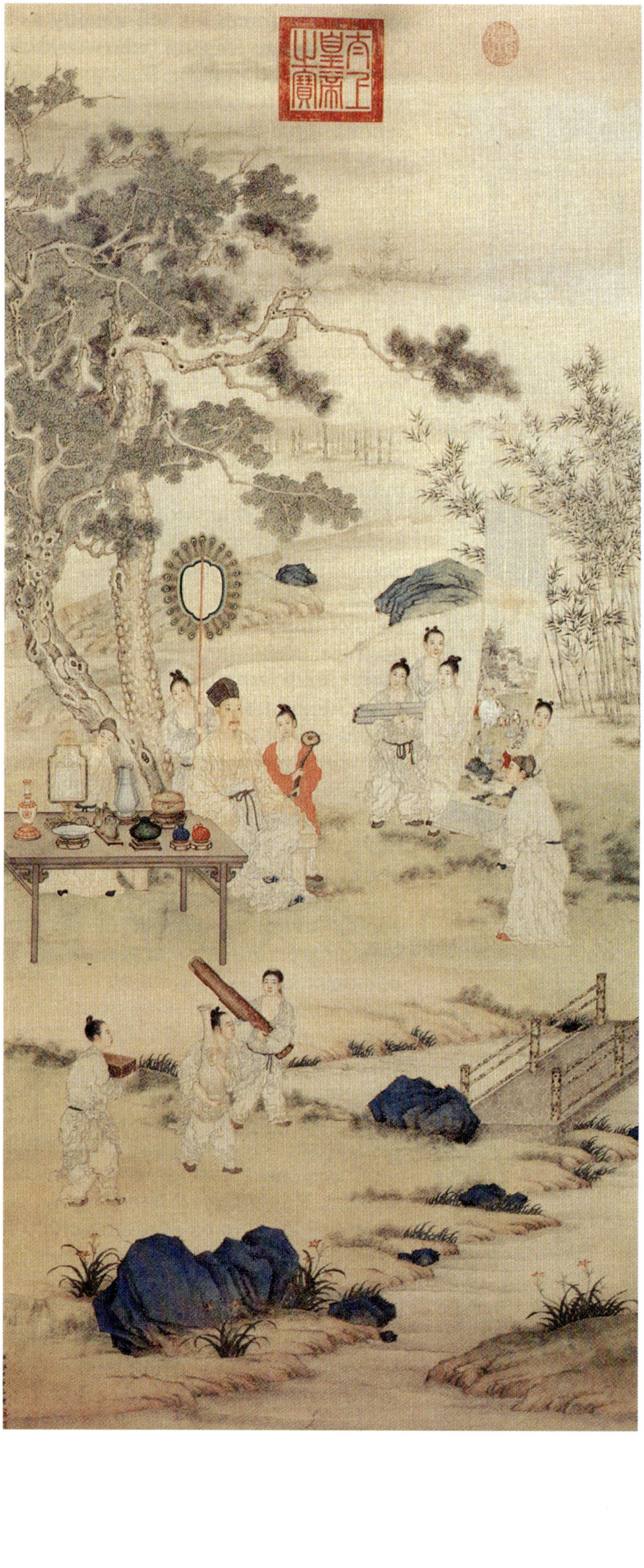

Fig. 5. Giuseppe Castiglione (Lang Shining, 1688–1766) and Ding Guanpeng (fl. 1738–68) 朗世宁和丁观鹏, *The Qianlong Emperor as a Chinese Connoisseur Viewing Paintings* 乾隆观画图, ca. 1746–50. Hanging scroll. Ink and color on paper, 136.4 x 62 cm. Palace Museum, Beijing (GU5366)

Coda

With the fall of the Qing dynasty in 1911, the centuries-old way in which the collection of calligraphy and painting was thought of changed, but the memory of its function as a symbol of legitimization remained. Although Puyi had thought to provide for himself by smuggling works out of the Forbidden City, he nevertheless kept most of the calligraphy and paintings with him and took them to Manchukuo when he became ruler there. The calligraphy and paintings remaining in the palaces in Beijing after he left in 1924 came to be seen as national treasures (*guobao*), as did the entirety of the palace collections.[43] As the possibility of war with Japan became more acute, the government of the Republic of China deemed these collections important enough to the Republic to have shipped the cream of the collections to southwest China to prevent them from falling into the hands of the Japanese. After the conclusion of the Second World War the collections were brought to Nanjing, the Nationalist capital, as if to legitimize the regime. They remained in Nanjing until defeat in the civil war seemed imminent and the decision was made to choose the most important works for secret shipment to Taiwan, where the Nationalist government soon retreated. These collections now form the basis of the National Palace Museum in Taipei. In the early years of the People's Republic of China, the calligraphy and paintings dispersed from the old imperial collections along with the works taken to Manchuria by Puyi were actively searched out and brought back to the palaces in Beijing or collected for what is now the Liaoning Provincial Museum. As national treasures, they too served to legitimize the new government. They are still works "suitable for sons and grandsons."

Notes

1. Puyi's life in the Forbidden City is recounted by his tutor Reginald F. Johnston in *Twilight in the Forbidden City* (New York: D. Appleton-Century Company, 1934).
2. See Puyi, *From Emperor to Citizen: The Autobiography of Aisin-Gioro Pu Yi*, translated with new general and chapter introductions by W. J. F. Jenner (Oxford: Oxford University Press, 1987), pp. 128–29.
3. See Yang Renkai, *Guobao chenfu lu—Gugong sanyi shuhua jianwen kaolue* [Record of the vicissitudes of national treasures: A brief account of what is known of the calligraphy and paintings dispersed from the former palace] (Shanghai: Shanghai renmin meishu chubanshe, 1991), for a history of the calligraphy and paintings taken from the palace by Puyi. See also Jeannette Shambaugh Elliott and David Shambaugh, *The Odyssey of China's Imperial Art Treasures* (Seattle and London: University of Washington Press, 2005).
4. The following account relies on Lothar Ledderose, "Some Observations on the Imperial Art Collection in China," *Transactions of the Oriental Ceramic Society* 43 (1978/79): 35–46. For the Nine Tripods, see K. C. Chang, *Art, Myth, and Ritual: The Path to Political Authority in Ancient China* (Cambridge, MA: Harvard University Press, 1983), particularly pp. 95–97.
5. Zhang Yanyuan, *Lidai minghua ji* [Record of famous painters of successive dynasties], translated by William R. B. Acker, *Some T'ang and Pre-T'ang Texts on Chinese Painting* (Leiden: E. J. Brill, 1954), pp. 75–80.
6. For the history of palace collections in general and collections of calligraphy and painting in particular, see Yang, *Guobao chenfu lu*, pp. 1–15; Elliott and Shambaugh, *Odyssey*, pp. 3–47; and Chang Lin-sheng, "The National Palace Museum: A History of the Collection," in *Possessing the Past: Treasures from the National Palace Museum, Taipei*, ed. Wen C. Fong and James C. Y. Watt (New York: The Metropolitan Museum of Art, 1996), pp. 3–25.
7. See Shen C. Y. Fu, "Princess Sengge Ragi: Collector of Painting and Calligraphy," in *Flowering in the Shadows: Women in the History of Chinese and Japanese Painting*, ed. Marsha Weidner (Honolulu: University of Hawaii Press, 1990), pp. 55–80; and Marsha Weidner, "Aspects of Painting and Patronage at the Mongol Court, 1260–1368," in *Artists and Patrons: Some Social and Economic Aspects of Chinese Painting*, ed. Chu-tsing Li (Lawrence: Kress Foundation Department of Art History, University of Kansas, 1989), pp. 37–59.
8. The rise of the Manchus and the fall of Beijing are treated in a number of sources. See in particular Frederick Wakeman, Jr., *The Great Enterprise: The Manchu Reconstruction of Imperial Order in Seventeenth-Century China* (Berkeley: University of California Press, 1985).
9. Nineteen paintings by Qing Shizu, the Shunzhi emperor, are recorded in the first series of the imperial catalogues *Midian zhulin* [Pearl forest of the Secret Hall] and *Shiqu baoji* [Treasured boxes of the Stone Channel], completed in 1745 and reprinted in combined form as *Midian zhulin Shiqu baoji hebian*, 12 vols. (Shanghai: Shanghai shuju, 1988); see vol. 1, pp. 9–10, and vol. 2, pp. 257–58. For an illustration, see *Gugong shuhua tulu* [Illustrated catalogue of calligraphy and painting in the National Palace Museum], vol. 10 (Taipei: National Palace Museum, 1992), pp. 7–8.

10. On the Kangxi emperor and his reign, see Jonathan D. Spence, *Emperor of China: Self-Portrait of K'ang-hsi* (New York: Knopf, 1974). Kangxi is one of the subjects at the focus of the exhibition catalogue *China: The Three Emperors, 1662–1795*, ed. Evelyn S. Rawski and Jessica Rawson (London: Royal Academy of Arts, 2005); see Evelyn S. Rawski, "The 'Prosperous Age': China in the Kangxi, Yongzheng, and Qianlong Reigns," pp. 22–40, and Regina Krahl, "The Kangxi Emperor: Horseman, Man of Letters, Man of Science," pp. 208–39.

11. See Fang Chao-ying, "Hsüan-yeh," in *Eminent Chinese of the Ch'ing Period*, ed. Arthur W. Hummel (Washington: U. S. Government Printing Office, 1943), pp. 327–31. For an overview of Qing court painting, see Nie Chongzheng, "Qing Dynasty Court Painting," in *China: The Three Emperors*), pp. 76–115.

12. For paintings inscribed by the Kangxi emperor, see *Shiqu baoji* (1745) in *Midian zhulin Shiqu baoji hebian*, vol. 1, pp. 406, 451–2, 672, 675, and vol. 2, pp. 786, 813–15, 1164.

13. See Chin-sung Chang, "Mountains and Rivers, Pure and Splendid: Wang Hui (1632–1717) and the Making of Landscape Panoramas in Early Qing China" (PhD diss., Yale University, 2004), and Maxwell K. Hearn, "Document and Portrait: the Southern Tour Paintings of Kangxi and Qianlong," in *Chinese Painting under the Qianlong Emperor*, ed. Ju-hsi Chou and Claudia Brown, Phoebus 6, no. 1 (Tempe: Arizona State University, 1988), pp. 91–131.

14. For Sun Chengze, see Dean R. Wickes, "Sun Ch'eng-tse," in *Eminent Chinese* (see note 11), pp. 669–70; Xie Wei, *Zhongguo huaxue zhuzuo kaolu* [Catalogue of writings on Chinese painting] (Shanghai: Shanghai shuhua chubanshe, 1998), pp. 434–35; and Hin-cheung Lovell, *An Annotated Bibliography of Chinese Painting Catalogues and Related Texts* (Ann Arbor: Center for Chinese Studies, The University of Michigan, 1973), pp. 34–35. For Liang Qingbiao, see Sherman E. Lee and Wai-kam Ho, "The Nature and Significance of the Collection of Liang Ch'ing-piao," in *Zhongyang yanjiu yuan guoji Hanxue huiyi lunwenji* [International Conference on Sinology] (Taipei: Zhongyang yanjiu yuan, 1981), pp. 102–57.

15. For Song Luo and his father Song Quan, see Tu Lien-che, "Sung Lao" and "Sung Ch'uan," in *Eminent Chinese* (see note 11), pp. 688–90.

16. See Thomas Lawton, "Notes on Keng Chao-chung," in *The Translation of Art: Essays on Chinese Painting and Poetry*, Renditions Special Art Issue, ed. James C. Y. Watt (Hong Kong: Center for Translation Projects, The Chinese University of Hong Kong, 1976), pp. 144–51.

17. See Fang Chao-ying, "Kao Shih-ch'i," in *Eminent Chinese* (see note 11), pp. 413–15; Xie, *Zhongguo huaxue*, pp. 478–80; and Lovell, *Annotated Bibliography*, pp. 38–41.

18. See Fang Chao-ying, "Songgotu," in *Eminent Chinese* (see note 11), pp. 663–66.

19. See Fang Chao-ying, "An Ch'i," in *Eminent Chinese* (see note 11), pp. 11–13, and Thomas Lawton, "The Mo-yuan hui-kuan by An Ch'i," in *Qingzhu Jiang Fucong xiansheng qishisui lunwenji* [Symposium in honor of Dr. Chiang Fu-tsung on his seventieth birthday] (Taipei: Gugong bowuyuan, 1969), pp. 13–35.

20. The painting is now in the collection of the Cleveland Museum of Art. See *Eight Dynasties of Chinese Painting: The Collections of the Nelson Gallery-Atkins Museum, Kansas City, and The Cleveland Museum of Art* (Cleveland: The Cleveland Museum of Art, 1980), pp. 351–52.

21. For the Yongzheng emperor, see Fang Chao-ying, "Yin-chen," in *Eminent Chinese* (see note 11), pp. 915–20, and Regina Krahl, "The Yongzheng Emperor: Art Collector and Patron," in *China: The Three Emperors*), pp. 240–45. The tenor of the Yongzheng reign is beautifully evoked in Jonathan D. Spence, *Treason by the Book* (New York: Viking Penguin, 2001).

22. See Nie Chongzheng, ed., *Qingdai gongting huihua* [Qing dynasty court paintings] (Shanghai: Shanghai kexue jishu chubanshe, 1999), no. 11, pp. 74–90.

23. See Nie, *Qingdai gongting huihua*, no. 14, pp. 101–3, and no. 15, pp. 104–5; and *China: The Three Emperors*, pp. 126–27.

24. See Nie, *Qingdai gongting huihua*, no. 16, pp. 106–11, and no. 18, pp. 118–23; *China: The Three Emperors*, pp. 248–49; and Wu Hung, "Emperor's Masquerade—'Costume Portraits' of Yongzheng and Qianlong," *Orientations* 26, no. 7 (July/August 1995): 25–41.

25. Two handscrolls are presently in London, one in the collection of the Percival David Foundation for Chinese Art and the other in the Victoria and Albert Museum. See *China: The Three Emperors*, pp. 252–55.

26. There is considerable literature on the Qianlong emperor and his reign. See in particular Fang Chao-ying, "Hung-li," in *Eminent Chinese* (see note 11), pp. 369–73; Harold L. Kahn, *Monarchy in the Emperor's Eyes: Image and Reality in the Ch'ien-lung Reign* (Cambridge, MA: Harvard University Press, 1971); Ju-hsi Chou and Claudia Brown, *The Elegant Brush: Chinese Painting Under the Qianlong Emperor, 1735–1795* (Phoenix: Phoenix Art Museum, 1985); *Qianlong huangdi de wenhua daye/Emperor Ch'ien-lung's Grand Cultural Enterprise* (Taipei: Guoli gugong bowuyuan, 2002); Zhang Hongxing, *The Qianlong Emperor: Treasures from the Forbidden City* (Edinburgh: National Museums of Scotland, 2002); Patricia Berger, *Empire of Emptiness: Buddhist Art and Political Authority in Qing China* (Honolulu: University of Hawaii Press, 2003); Chuimei Ho and Bennet Bronson, *Splendors of China's Forbidden City: The Glorious Reign of Emperor Qianlong* (London: Merrell; Chicago: The Field Museum, 2004); Gerald Holzwarth, "The Qianlong Emperor as Patron and the Formation of the Collections of the Palace Museum, Beijing," and Jessica Rawson, "The Qianlong Emperor: Virtue and the Possession of Antiquity," in *China: The Three Emperors*, pp. 41–53 and pp. 270–75, respectively.

27. For a discussion of the Qianlong emperor as connoisseur, see Kohara Hironobu, "The Qianlong Emperor's Skill in the Connoisseurship of Chinese Painting," in *Chinese Painting Under the Qianlong Emperor* (see note 13), pp. 56–73.

28. On the choice of the name and its multiple meanings, see Holzwarth, "The Qianlong Emperor as Patron," pp. 44–45.

29. For documentation of the scroll dedicated to Ziming, see *Gugong shujhua tulu*, vol. 17 (1998), pp. 281–88.

30. For documentation of the scroll dedicated to Wuyong, see *Gugong shuhua tulu*, vol. 17, pp. 289–98.

31. See the discussion of the Ziming version in *Qianlong huangdi de wenhua daye*, pp. 80–81.

32. See *Shiqu baoji sanbian* in *Midian zhulin Shiqu baoji hebian*, vol. 9, pp. 518–22, and *Gugong shuhua tulu*, vol. 17, p. 296.

33. See *Shiqu baoji* in *Midian zhulin Shiqu baoji hebian*, vol. 1, p. 593, and Zhang Hongxing, *The Qianlong Emperor*, pp. 94–95.

34. Sun Chengze, *Gengzi xiaoxia ji* (1660; reprint, Taipei: Hanhua, 1971), 2.9a–10a, pp. 95–97.

35. The album was recorded in *Shiqu baoji xubian*. See *Gugong shuhua tulu*, vol. 22 (2003), pp. 148–53. The handscroll was not catalogued until the third series of the imperial catalogue. See *Shiqu baoji sanbian* in *Midian zhulin Shiqu baoji hebian*, vol. 12, pp. 4413–14.

36. For the Du Qiong scroll and its documentation, see *Gugong shuhua tulu*, vol. 6 (1991), pp. 137–38.

37. For a discussion of evidential scholarship during the Qianlong reign, see Benjamin A. Elman, *From Philosophy to Philology: Intellectual and Social Aspects of Change in Late Imperial China* (Cambridge, MA: Council on East Asian Studies, Harvard University, 1984), and R. Kent Guy, *The Emperor's Four Treasuries: Scholars and the State in the late Ch'ien-lung Era* (Cambridge, MA: Harvard University Press, 1987).

38. The painting, known as *Longsu jiaomin tu* or *Residents of the Capital City*, was catalogued in *Shiqu baoji xubian*. See *Gugong shuhua tulu*, vol. 1 (1989), pp. 77–80. The subject matter remains enigmatic. For a discussion, see Qi Gong, "Dong Yuan *Longsu jiaomin tu*" [Dong Yuan's painting of "Residents of the Capital City"], *Meishu jia* [Artist], no. 5 (1978): 50–51.

39. See *Gugong shuhua tulu*, vol. 16 (1997), pp. 157–60, and the discussion in *Qianlong huangdi de wenhua daye*, p. 77.

40. See Pamela Kyle Crossley, *The Translucent Mirror: History and Identity in Qing Imperial Ideology* (Berkeley and Los Angeles: University of California Press, 1999), pp. 290–96, and L. Carrington Goodrich, *The Literary Inquisition of Ch'ien-lung* (Baltimore, MD: Waverly Press, 1935).

41. See Yang, *Guobao chenfu lu*, p. 56. Lu Ji's calligraphy is now in the Palace Museum, Beijing, while Han Gan's *Night-Shining White* went first into the collection of Sir Percival David and then to the Metropolitan Museum of Art, New York.

42. Both paintings are now in the Museum of Fine Arts, Boston.

43. On the early history of the palace collections and the concept of "National Treasures," see Chu-tsing Li, "Recent History of the Palace Collection," *Archives of the Chinese Art Society of America* 12 (1958): 61–75, and Elliott and Shambaugh, *Odyssey*, chapter 3.

宜子孙
清朝皇帝与其宫廷书画收藏

江文葦

1908年十二月，在叔父光绪帝去世一个月后，溥仪(1906–1967)登上了皇帝的龙椅宝座。当时还不到三岁的他，只做了短短几年的的宣统皇帝。1911年，孙逸仙(1866–1925)领导革命并建立了中华民国，溥仪被迫于翌年1912年二月宣布退位。他是满清逊帝，大清皇朝的最后一个统治者，也是继承北京皇城里无数珍贵收藏的最后一个皇帝。

依《清帝退位優待條件》条款的规定，溥仪仍得以继续住在紫禁城里。直到1924年十一月时，才被军阀冯玉祥(1882–1948)[1]逐出皇宫。在那几年间，溥仪认定皇宫里的种种收藏 — 尤其是书画藏品 — 将成为他未来安全的最佳保障。他与弟弟溥杰(1907–1994)谋划，在1924年前，将一千多件卷轴陆续盗运出宫[2]。这些卷轴旋即被送到天津的租借地保管。1932年溥仪到满洲国，并于1934年登极为康德皇帝时，将它们一并带到了长春。1945年中日战争结束时，这批书画在内战的一片混乱中，一件件地流失了。直到1950年代中国人民共和国成立之后，这些前清收藏才又被集结起来，成为今天辽宁省博物馆的基本馆藏[3]。杨仁恺在他的著作中，描述了这些清宫书画收藏在二十世纪前半期，历经辗转流离、劫后余生的故事。它们最初如何进入内府、如何被一一纳入宫中庞大的收藏、与溥仪前历代清帝们所扮演的角色，其种种过程与历史背景，将在此文中详细交待。

书画作品成为统治者最重视的收藏，有一个逐渐发展的过程[4]。在古代，九鼎与图籍是帝王所欲收集和占有的重心。它们被认为是赋予统治者政治合法性的宝物，带有灵性。九鼎相传是神话中的玉帝所铸，并由他传给夏商朝的帝王，然后传递到周朝各王。公元前219年，秦始皇（公元前221–210年在位）在泗水江中打捞沉没的九鼎无功而还，人们认为这是他政权的一大噩兆。果然，秦朝(公元前221–206)只持续了一段相当短暂的时间。九世纪时，张彦远(生于约815)在其著作中，亦以相同的神秘口吻，提及汉朝开国皇帝汉高祖刘邦(公元前206–195在位)的将士在秦皇宫中寻得图籍一事[5]。可见，占有这些国之重宝，就是拥有了统治天下的绝对合法权的象征。没有它们，刘邦将无法合法地治国，成为一统天下的帝王。这些物品，是统治者拥有受天承命之天意的重要筹码，因此均深藏于宫中禁区的内府。因其如此重要一如统治者之“脏（藏，发音为 zang）”，就必须“藏(发音为cang)”而宝之，以其为天命之象征，助统治者掌握王权。其后，此对“灵宝”之物的联系，逐渐地转移至艺术品，使统治者将集结大批艺术品于宫中的收藏能力,视为确保政权的最高要务，事实上，艺术品的收藏，确实成为统治者拥有政治与正统文化权威的最高保证。

从政治化神教物品到以艺术为艺术而收藏，此态度的变迁，发生在汉朝末年(公元前206–公元220年)到公元589年隋朝开国的这段时期。先由书法艺术开始，之后延及绘画。隋朝之后的几千年间，书画杰作均不断地汇集于宫中，直至帝国衰落或王朝覆灭，才散失各处[6]。唐太宗(626–649在位)拥有七世纪时最丰富的收藏，其中以书法作品冠绝古今。八世纪中期安禄山之乱后，大部分作品或流出宫中，或不知所终。宋朝时期，北宋(960–1126)的最后一个皇帝徽宗(1101–1125年在位)重振宫中收藏。许多珍品虽得以在徽宗时编入皇家目录，但在金兵攻入首都开封、擒获徽钦二宗时，再一次地流失。南宋(1127–1279)时期的收藏，则在杭州于1270年间落入蒙古人手中而散失。蒙古建都于北方的大都（即今天的北京），并建立元朝。蒙古皇室成员多为收藏家，最知名的是鲁国大长公主祥哥剌吉（约1282-1332）与文宗帖睦尔(1328–1332在位)[7]。他们二人的收藏后来被明朝宫廷接收，原本收在南京宫中，后在永乐皇帝(1403–1424在位)于1421年将国都迁往北方时，再被带回北京。永乐之后的明朝皇帝，虽继续画院艺事，赞助宫廷画家，并因此而增强宫中收藏，然均不专注于书画收藏。十六世纪末至十七世纪初，是明代最为衰弱的时期，许多重要作品，因此不明不白地从皇宫中消失，流入民间。1644年满清入关时，情况更是混乱不堪。

本译文的插图请参见英文原文。

清代早期的皇帝：顺治与康熙

继大明王朝起于东北边界的满清，在其大军入关帮助围剿北京的叛乱之前，已根据中国的体制，建立了一个新兴的军事强权。在接手北京城时，他们所面对的是一片混乱的景象：京城被掠劫一空、政权群龙无首，明思宗自缢于煤山，而叛将李自成的大军正欲进兵城下。不久，叛军被逐出京城并被剿平，满清占领北京，并于未来几年间陆续征服了中国的大部分国土。地处京城中心的皇城，一部分已在早先被洗劫焚毁，但宫中仍然保存的书画收藏，则为满清入主中国的合法性起了重要的作用[8]。

满清入主中国的第一个皇帝顺治(1644–1661在位)即位时，还只是个孩子。在他仍年幼时，朝廷政事由几位摄政代理。他在位的十几年间，满清所面临的是延伸清朝军事控制以及对所征服地区政局的稳定。在此局势下，即使朝廷的中国专家顾问了解书画收藏对满清统治中国重要的象征意义，清廷对他们所据有的艺术品，仍无暇顾及。书画图轴在那时，多是嘉奖有功将领与官员的礼物。顺治在位时，除了他自己的创作，史料里并无任何显示清廷收集书画活动的证据[9]。

皇太子玄烨(1654–1722)，因父亲罹患"天花"駕崩，而于1661年登极为康熙皇帝[10]，上述的情况才开始有了些微的改变。康熙即位时还不及七岁，由四位摄政掌权，直到1669年。康熙在位的早年，反清复明的抵抗势力仍强，"清朝" 清朝將"漢人"漢人降將有功者分封管理一部分南方及西南方省份。然不久之后，三位中国藩王先后舉兵反叛，其三藩勢力，幾及全國之半，形同割據。此番形势，到1680年代，才在明宗室保护者被杀，三藩之亂一一平定，和明朝时期的疆域纳入满清版图之后，渐渐稳定下来。由此可见，由于军事与政治等种种原因，康熙在位的前二十年，即使年轻的康熙皇帝本人对书法情有独钟，清廷仍旧无暇进行对书画艺术品的搜集。

然而，在他当政的中后期，康熙开始争取对中国汉人文化与知识分子的认同，并透过对艺术发展的提倡与支持，进行宫廷书画收藏的活动。画家与画匠们得以在启祥宫中的如意馆画室工作[11]， 祭祀所用及非正式的肖像画与宫廷生活的种种景象，则由画师们描绘纪录。为人所知的宫廷画家，如焦秉贞与其学生冷枚(约1670–1742后)，创作运用西洋透视和明暗技法的绘画。宫廷中以绘画知名的高官，如王原祁(1642–1715)与蒋廷锡(1669–1732)，则为康熙晚期领导山水画与花鸟画风格的个中翘楚。王原祁为名画家与收藏家王时敏(1592–1680)之孙，王时敏曾与董其昌学画，王原祁因此在绘画上，追随十七世纪时期由董其昌所大力提倡的正统派传统。他将此种为中国上层知识分子所推崇的画风带入宫中，使其成为清代宫廷画的重要风格。蒋廷锡在1699年中举后，先为宫廷画师，后才跻身仕途。王与蒋之作品，均直接收入清廷内府收藏。康熙帝常在蒋所作之画中题款，也于满人画家赫頣与高其佩(1660–1734)画上亲作题跋，并将二人作品纳入宫中收藏[12]。康熙在朝最重要的绘画工程，要数康熙帝为其多次南巡所绘制的长卷图画。康熙在位时，自1684年起，总共南巡六次。此大手笔的作风目的在于对南方臣民显示大清朝廷的政权与实力。南巡图此一系列长卷绘画的工程，是在第二次南巡归来后开始策划的。正统派宫廷画家王翚(1632–1717)，以其在宫中的职位，主持繪製此堪稱巨制的《南巡圖》系列[13]。 通过此工程，康熙帝以自己的形象为中心，直接地进入了中国的文化核心。

同样的，在文学工程方面，康熙帝組織编輯與出版《康熙字典》与汉语辞典《佩文韵府》，亦是占有中国文化精髓的一种手段。这些重要的作品，均由康熙詔修，由许多学者集结无数心血，历时多年才完成。即使康熙皇帝未能竭尽心力搜罗古代书画，他仍能轻易地将他的声名透过史籍而流传。1705年，康熙诏令王原祁及其他四位学者，参与编辑《佩文斋书画谱》的工作。此书画谱共计一百卷，于1708年完成，至今仍为研究中国书画的重要参考资料。这一系列的文学工程，对康熙来说，比起他对画家的赞助与宫廷书画的收藏，显得更迫切、更重要。在一幅为宫廷画家所绘的康熙帝闲居肖像中，康熙一副文士模样，坐拥群书之间，身旁却无任何图画或古董。画中的图书以西洋透视法描绘，显见康熙渊博的学问与对新知的探讨，及其对宫廷画家的影响(见图 1)。

私人收藏与宫廷品味的形成

顺治与康熙时期，民间收藏书画的风气相当兴盛。其中最知名的收藏家的艺术品味与收藏类别，很明显地影响了后来宫廷收藏的趋向。因此，这些大收藏家，也就值得在此一提。满清入关后的几十年间，宫廷中重要的收藏均由孙承泽(1593–1675)与梁清标(1620–1691)等大臣负责[14]。孙梁二人，在满清入主中国前，均在明朝宫中任职，李自成在北京称王时，两人亦继续留在宫中，后来则投附满清。孙承泽，明朝时累官至刑科都给事中，降清后仍任同职，1652年官至吏部左侍郎。两年后，因宫廷政争而遭解职。退休之后的孙承泽寄情艺术研究，于1660年作了《庚子消夏记》，为自己毕生所有的收藏与曾见识过的书画作品作注解析。虽然孙并未给每一画作特定的细目，他为艺术品所作的研究与鉴赏，为后世留下了重要的参考资料。梁清标虽未留与后人任何关于他个人收藏的目录，但从今天传世的、带有他钤印与亲笔题签的画作来看，梁不但曾拥有相当大型的收藏，还曾收有如今世人公认国宝级的宋元书画。在当时，梁清标是最受时人推崇的鉴藏家。许多他收藏过的早期画作，后来均被内府收藏。比起孙承泽，世人对梁清标生前所知甚为有限。梁在投效满清之前，曾事李自成。仕途历经顺治与康熙两朝，后擢为保和殿大学士。梁将自己所有的收藏留给子孙，但不幸的是其后代将之散失殆尽。许多曾为他收藏的名画，如《悟阳子养性图》（见图录第10号），后来均收归内府收藏。

其他与清廷有直接关系、年轻一辈的鉴藏家，如宋荦(1634–1713)[15]、耿昭忠(1640–1686)[16]与高士奇(1645–1703)[17]，以及满洲官员与收藏家索額圖(1703年歿)[18]，均在康熙年间建立起自己的私人收藏。宋荦之父宋权(1598–1652)在清兵入关时，任順天巡撫，他降清后仍被派任原职，1652年去世时，职位为國史院大學士與太子太保。倚仗父亲的馀荫，宋荦得以在宫中赢得顺治与康熙皇帝的重视。他后任江西与江苏巡抚，表现出色。其后发家致富，在1699、1703与1705年康熙南巡时，担任招待皇帝出入食宿的工作。宋荦在任巡抚期间，还成为远近知名的诗人与艺术赞助者，并在那时积极地建立起自己的书画收藏。不少带有他印款的名画，后来亦纳入清廷内府收藏。

耿昭忠家早在清入关前，即已为满清供职，入编正黄旗下。其父耿继茂(1671年卒)在清入主中国时，建国有功。耿昭忠因此关系娶了一位和硕公主，成为额驸。虽然他的哥哥耿精忠为清初的“三藩”之一,随吴三桂在南方叛清,后兵败身死，耿昭忠仍深受清廷倚重，受任太子少师，耿得以藉此发展他个人的重要收藏。据传为九世纪画家董源所作的《夏景山口待渡图》，即为耿旧藏之一。此图后来也被溥仪带到东北去。

高士奇出身寒微，但为康熙帝所赏识，虽从未通过京城高等会考，仍供奉内廷，任“南书房行走”一职，并成为康熙亲信。他积聚可观的财富，虽曾因植党营私与贿赂而被弹劾，却仍然与皇帝保持着极为亲近的私人关系。在1693年去职时，他完成了《江村消夏录》，将他过去三年间所见之书画目录作记。高士奇为将书画作品以细目与特征作详细记录的第一人，其内容包括尺寸、材料、题款、钤印、以及题跋。但高并未循孙承泽之法为各作品附加评注，但他将书法与绘画分类整理，并编列成表。有趣的是，高士奇将所谓可进奉的或可当作礼品赠送的、和最不重要的作品分成一类，将其它最珍贵、应永久收藏的画作分在另一类。身为康熙皇帝身边，专司书画收藏顾问工作的官员，高士奇仍当仁不让地将自己的个人利益放在职业忠诚之前。但即使如此，高的大部分收藏，后来还是一并进了内府的皇家收藏。

在宫中所有的满洲人中，索額圖是其中最重要的收藏家之一。他是皇帝的叔叔，皇子胤礽的叔公。这样的皇室背景，使他在宫中深具影响力，却也促成他后来因康熙立储与皇子争位的斗争而被罢免。他聚集财富，因此也得以累积了大批包括古青铜器、书法与绘画的私人收藏。不少他曾收过的知名作品，后来也被送进了皇宫。

另一位值得一提的鉴藏家是安岐(1683–约1744)，年纪最轻，一生活跃于收藏界，直到十八世纪。安家本为朝鲜人，从事盐业贩卖。在清入关前，即已入满清包衣一籍[19]。安岐年轻时，即有幸观赏梁清标与耿昭忠家藏的作品。1715年，安与王翚相识，见识了由董其昌鉴定的一幅为宋代早期名僧巨然所作名画。同年间，王翚为安岐作一肖像，画中王将其置身于庭园山水之间，身旁围绕着图卷画轴[20]。因安家以贩盐发家，安岐具有相当的财力大量收集古书画。他在自己的收藏著录《墨缘汇观》里写道，能见到并拥有这些书画，实是天命缘分使然。他沿用高士奇的方法，将所藏精品逐条著录，每条先标其尺寸、质地、题款、印鉴与题跋，后叙其内容、流传，并附加他个人相当中肯的品评。

雍正时期

1722年十二月康熙皇帝驾崩时，他的第四子胤禛(1678–1735)继位为雍正皇帝(1723–35在位)[21]。因为激烈的争夺储位斗争，使雍正即位后，始终猜疑其他兄弟。雍正用各种方式将他们罢黜免职，削去他们对八旗军控制的权力，并降为侍从。通过这些手段，雍正将大权牢牢在握。身为皇帝，雍正是个能干勤恳的领袖，他进行改革，力行整治朝纲，同時整顿康熙晚年逐渐形成的官僚与腐敗现象。他的政绩，得以为其子乾隆皇帝(1736–95在位)的王权，建立一套運行有效的統治體制。

历史为雍正对宫中的书画收藏一事，记载甚少。只略微提及他如父亲康熙一样，赞助宫廷画师，并扩充宫内的收藏。此记载甚为确切，而事实上，雍正在即位之前，曾命画师作他与其妻为农夫农妇耕织之图。他将此画与其他类似的作品装订成画册，不为外界所知。此画册实为雍正有意的政治宣传，旨在出示给未来的执政者，使其了解他对一般平民百姓的关怀[22]。雍正也诏令宫中创作长卷，一如他父亲为南巡图作画的意图，记载了他亲政时的种种事迹[23]。一些小尺寸的画册，每一幅描绘他身着不同的衣着打扮，显示不同的身份地位[24]。像他早先画有的耕织图，这些图像表现了他集所有身份于一身的形象。其中一件全身肖像画（见图2），描写雍正在书房里阅读。他手执一书，身边架上放满书册。虽然拥有相当的书法造诣，雍正并未像他父亲，在他的私人生活画像中，以饱学之士的形象面世（见图1）。从这些画中可知，宫廷绘画在雍正时期，已达到相当精致的水准。但雍正对艺术最大的贡献，在于他对陶瓷制作的赞助和倾心。其陶瓷作品臻于完美的水平，即使后世最精美的创作，亦难以媲美。雍正并将宫中最珍奇的古玩与陶瓷，绘制成图，记录于长卷之中，其选择，无疑反映了他的个人品味与对陶瓷艺术的偏爱[25]。

乾隆时期

雍正皇帝的第四子弘历(1711–1799)，于1735年即位，是为乾隆[26]。他在位的六十年间，疆土扩张，国富民安，宫中的收藏进入了真正的成长时期。乾隆在位的早年，以父亲建立的帝业为基础，进一步地实行中央集权，以其他亲王的生命与权位为代价，巩固他个人的皇权。在位中期，乾隆贪逸骄奢的倾向开始出现，致使了晚年时期朝廷贪污猖獗蔓延。因此，即使乾隆有着不凡的政绩，他王位的继承人并未承续任何他在1735年后所巩固的政治基础。

比起他的父祖，乾隆皇帝更清楚地意识到清宫收藏对清王朝统治中国的合法性意义。他自比唐太宗及宋徽宗两位鉴藏家皇帝，搜罗天下的作品，俨然为满清奉天承运、一统中国的政权拥有者。然而，作为一个皇帝，乾隆亦有着强烈的自觉，不让历代史家以此抨击他如宋徽宗一样，因耽于艺事而疏忽朝政、置国家于不顾。自皇子时代即已热衷收藏，作了皇帝后，乾隆更大规模地收集书画艺术品。十七世纪与十八世纪早期的私人收藏，均陆续为乾隆收购入宫，其中许多作品为皇宫失而复得之物。最重大的一次收购，来自于高士奇与安岐一千多件的图轴，由小舅子傅恒办助，于1746年全数购得。还有一部分知名的书画，由朝中大臣以赠送皇帝为名入贡进宫。朝中大臣与名诗人沈德潜(1673–1769)，即进呈了张择端的《清明上河图》这一旷世之作。该画在日后被溥仪携带出宫。

清宫中的书画收藏，在乾隆在位的短短九年里，达到了前所未有的盛况。为了有系统地为此收藏作记录，乾隆于1744年一月，下令编纂宫中佛教与道教书画品目录《秘殿珠林》。以汉武帝宫中的“秘殿”为名，此目录记载了271件作品，并于该年夏天编纂完成。1744年春，当《秘殿珠林》编修工作仍进行之时，乾隆又明令制定非宗教性书画的编纂工程，并将此清代内府所藏書畫的著錄，并命名为《石渠宝笈》。此名源自汉朝开国皇帝高祖刘邦，将在秦宫室里发现的图籍藏于石渠阁的这一史迹。《石渠宝笈》初编收入了1774件作品，历时一年半完成，于1745年秋成书并进呈乾隆。《宝笈》总工程由尚书張照(1691–1745)负责编修之管理工作。張照博學多識，与乾隆一样，崇尚书法艺术，尤其钟情宋代大师与董其昌（见图录第19号）等书家。張照之外，另四位参与编修《宝笈》者均为朝中大臣与学者。由于《宝笈》初编为一目录集，所有收录作品，均依照作品所保管的宫殿名称分类编制。每件作品被分级别，以上品或次品分两等级。所有上品，参照十七世纪如孙承泽、高士奇等著名私人藏家所用的详细目录分类方式，编次入书。

至1791年，清宫增收的书画品，半数以上来自于宫廷画家与乾隆自己的作品，需要另增补《续编》入《石渠寶笈》與《秘殿珠林》中。两件《续编》均于1793年完成编撰。编修的组织原则大致与初编相同，但作品已不再以等级划分，所有书画均一视同仁，翔实记载。1799年乾隆死后，其子嘉庆皇帝(1796–1820在位)有感于继续编目的需要，在1815年下诏三编《石渠寶笈》與《秘殿珠林》，并于次年完成。有鉴于乾隆皇帝的关注与支持，前后数十年间，这些目录的编修者得以更有效率地完成此一大规模的编纂工程。

乾隆在位的六十年中，积极地投入清宫的收藏工作。他不但与目录编修者共事，更亲自为各书画作品作研究，还为藏品作了无数的题跋[27]。他认为书法为艺术之精髓，竭尽心力搜取最知名的传世名迹。其中最令乾隆皇帝陶醉的是拥有代表王羲之(约303–约361)、王献之(344–387)父子书法传统的历代杰作。老天不负其苦心，乾隆终于获得了二王以及王羲之之侄王珣(350–401)的书法。为了纪念此举，乾隆称此三件作品为“三希”，并将自己的书斋命名为“三希堂”[28]。1749年，乾隆敕令编修《三希堂法帖》，上溯三世纪、下至十七世纪初，由135位历代大书家所写的340件名作的一部大型丛帖终于编刻完成。这样的文艺工程，显示了乾隆对中国文化精深的造诣，也因此对中国的精英分子保证了历代文物所蕴含的价值，其不仅受到竭力的保存，也得以传续后代子孙。乾隆借用耿昭忠拥有的一方鉴藏印，为自己镌刻了一方《宜子孙》印玺。虽意在传承自己的子孙，乾隆亦藉此传达了此举背后的深意。在此，他明白地自承为中国文化传统的守护者。

乾隆皇帝对宫中书画藏品的珍爱程度，可从他对十四世纪大画家黄公望(1269–1354)与倪瓒(1306–1374)作品的题款中一见端倪。在董其昌的书画理论倡导之下，明朝人将黄公望、吴镇(1280–1354)、倪瓒与王蒙(约1308–1385)奉为“元朝四大家”。乾隆不计一切，为充实内府收藏四处收罗此四大名家的作品。其中最有名的即是黄公望成名于明代、享誉十七世纪的杰作《富春山居图》。此卷本为沈周(1427–1509)所藏，董其昌在一睹真迹风采时，对它佩服得五体投地，在卷首跋文中连称“吾师乎，吾师乎！”。

1745年，人人向往的《富春山居图》被征入宫，黄公望为子明作此画的原由，由画家写在图卷之尾[29]。乾隆与大臣们认定此卷即是曾为沈周所有、董其昌所见、鼎鼎大名的黄公望之作，马上将此画收入《石渠寶笈》之中。没想到，第二年，朝中又呈上了另外一幅购得的《富春山居图》，从题款可知，此卷是画家为无用所绘，而非名为子明之人[30]。《无用卷》的出现，引起了该画的真伪问题之争议。乾隆与书画顾问、《石渠寶笈》编修者之一梁诗正(1697–1763)商议，鉴别该画，认定先前一本为真迹。然而，《子明卷》自此便成了乾隆毕生收藏中，最念念不忘的一个讨论公案。从1745年至1794年，乾隆陆续在

《子明卷》画上题跋，总计五十六次，长长短短、印鉴累累，凡空隙处，几乎为之充塞(见图3)[31]。他对《山居图》爱不释手，不仅常在宫中展阅，出外巡游时也随身携带，在灵感来时随时题款，并书写当时境况以誌留念。乾隆在画上的题跋大多为诗词，其它也有散文式的记录。其中一记录，讨论了《子明卷》与《无用卷》的关系。对乾隆而言，此图卷为他一生的伴侣。晚年的时候，乾隆在子明卷《山居图》的卷首作了最后的题跋留念："以後展玩，亦不復題識矣"。为了证明他贵为皇帝对此画的拥有权，乾隆在此卷上的题款，无疑对画面作了彻底的改变。《无用卷》虽然在1746年购得，但并未马上被收入《石渠寶笈》之中。直到《三编》完成时才划入"石渠宝笈次等"，收入内府。当时，《寶笈》主编胡敬(1769–1845)意欲质疑《子明卷》一本的真伪，但这在乾隆还在世时是不可能发生的[32]。

倪瓚的名作《狮子林图》(见图4)也是十七世纪时大名鼎鼎的作品。身为画家与学者，倪在明代末年享有相当高的声誉。他舒朗简约的构图章法与以干笔线条入画的风格，受到许多十七世纪画家的效法，被认为是文人画的理想画风。《狮子林图》是倪瓚为人熟知、少数的图卷式作品之一。在1744年被宫廷购得并收入《石渠寶笈》目录前，曾为孙承泽与高士奇收藏[33]。孙在他的收藏目录中，巨细无遗地将收得此画卷的始末作了详细地交待[34]。它在清兵攻入南京城时，一度被带到北方作战利品。当时，因画卷里带有南明朝的纪年，以及南明朝廷恶名昭彰的弄臣马士英(1591–1646)所作的题跋，所有的题款遂被人一并地从图卷上切除。1654年间，孙承泽将之重新装裱，记载收得该画的情形。乾隆在此画入宫时，将其再次裱褙，在画前加了一段前迎，并在画前附上自己的题诗。诗中言及不知狮子林一址是否仍在。

乾隆在位期间，六次在此画面上题款，并在画后上写了题跋。题跋中记了他与此画神交的种种情形。1757年乾隆第二次南巡时临幸苏州，发现狮子林仍在。虽然园林已不称狮子林，归黄氏家族所有，乾隆因此图得以确认原址的存在，感到喜出望外。他马上派人兼程赶回北京，把图卷带到苏州，让他将此发现题记在画卷中，并为他先前的题诗作改动。1762年第三次南巡时，他再次将图卷带到苏州的狮子林，还亲自为此卷临摹了一个副本。乾隆在1765年第四次南巡时，重复此举，并把自己的抄本与原作加以比较，在两图卷上加了题跋。乾隆对狮子林图卷与狮子林庭园欣赏有加，眷恋之余，将该庭园于北京畅春园及承德避暑山庄内依样仿建。1774年承德狮子林竣工时，乾隆又一次重临此画，并又一次地在倪瓚的原作上题款，纪念此举。1784年第六次南巡，他最后一次在画上作题跋。在题记中，乾隆纠正了世人以为狮子林曾为倪瓚别业的误解。他还指出，该园原为一佛教禅林，倪在原图卷的题辞中亦曾提及此一史实。如同他为黄公望《富春山居图》所作的序跋，乾隆不但将倪瓚的作品作了根本的改变，更在为其改观的过程中，进一步地突显他天子的形象。

乾隆也购得诗人画家徐贲(1335–1380)所画《狮子林十二景点图》的两种版本。一本为册页，另一本则为手卷[35]。乾隆认定册页为真品，手卷为摹本，并断定其为明代一佚名画家所绘。1468年乾隆购得杜琼(1396–1474)画狮子林图时，曾指示杜在画中注明该画是以徐贲之作为蓝本。拥有倪瓚的手卷和徐贲的册页，乾隆注意到，杜琼的狮子林图却更接近倪瓚的风格，而全无徐贲的格调。在1771与1772年，乾隆三次在杜琼的画上加了题跋，并在1772年的一个题款上，试图调和此风格上的歧异。由此可见，即使杜琼狮子林图的灵感来自于徐贲的十二景图，因所作之图为单景山水，仍未能脱离倪瓚狮子林图的原创观念[36]。

乾隆在他最后的题跋中，表达了他对《狮子林图》历史真伪价值的考量，以及他在讨论杜琼之作所持实事求是的求真态度，表示了他堪称为历史学家，以实证主义精神探究的人文素养。这种"考证"的文人作风，正是十八世纪知识分子研究学问的核心态度[37]。他对历史准确性的重视，反映在他许多亲笔御批的题跋里。举个例子来说，在他收购到一幅曾为董其昌所有、传为十世纪画家董源所作的大型山水时，便根据自己对该画题跋与相关书籍的研究，对其主题作了诠释[38]。在此之前，董其昌早已为此画作了一番调查，认定该作应为宋太祖(960–976在位)时的宫廷画家董源，在南唐覆灭后、宋兵进南京城时为太祖所画。鉴赏家张丑(1577–1643)曾有另一种说法，他认为该画的主题意指宋太祖的登极大典。乾隆并未采信这两种解释，而提出他个人的看法：该图描写的是古代祈雨的仪式。根据他对一些早期纪录的详细研究，乾隆指出董其昌与张丑的说法，均无根据，亦无法证实。他证明了宋太祖在此之前并未到过南唐国都南京，接受南唐君主的受降；董源也不可能在太祖即位时到宋朝的国都开封去，因为当时南唐还未向北宋政权投降。在否定了董与张的说法后，乾隆查遍古书记载，相信此画真正的主题，可从《左传》中证实为一个祈雨之仪式。题跋中可见的是，乾隆运用以事实作佐证的"考证"方法，表明他是一个根据原文资料、细心求证史实的考据专家。如此的学者风范与能力，贴切地反映了乾隆作为中国统治者所俱有的素质。

乾隆对书画艺术的鉴赏能力，包括了他对资料的研究与哲学思考的判断，给予他利用自己收藏的绘画，作为政治筹码的绝佳机会。1746年，他在宋代画家李迪的《牧笛图》上指出，该画真正的主题是关于苏武的故事[39]。苏武是汉朝的一个使节，因出使匈奴被扣，而羁留北方大漠长达十九年之久。在流放北海时，苏武在北方，娶妻生子、放牧劳作并繁衍生息，但始终忠于西汉朝廷。乾隆深信如此，下令朝臣将苏武忠贞的节行写在题跋中，并把画名改为《冰天汉节》，亲自书写四字于卷首。

1788年乾隆为该图写了另一题跋，这次，他提到了苏武与乾隆清军旗下的云南按察史杨重英。杨在1760年间出兵缅甸，但兵败被擒。乾隆认为杨的气节远高于苏，因杨虽从未结婚，却不着缅甸衣冠，也未失去身为一位大清武将的自尊。杨在被囚二十一年后，终于回到北京，受到皇帝英雄式的欢迎。在杨回国之前，乾隆曾几次谈及有关忠臣的一些历史事件。在《二臣传》中，乾隆曾抨击晚明降清、并对满清建国有功的大臣，谴责他们是前朝的叛徒。他写这段题跋的历史背景，即来源于这样的心情。同时，乾隆并大兴文字狱，镇压任何被认为不忠于清廷的文章[40]。藉此机会，乾隆再一次地重申他作为政权统治者的绝对权利。

乾隆时期为清朝聚集历代艺术文化遗产的最高峰时期。在此几十年间，全中国最珍贵的书画收藏汇集清廷内宫，提供了满清统治中国的绝对权威，确保了他统治全国的合法性。当乾隆命郎士宁(1688–1766)与丁观鹏(活跃于1726–1770)为他做肖像画，描绘他闲坐庭园中赏画博古，身边围绕无数的古董书画时，他意在昭告天下，他所拥有的这些，是所有中国的过去(见图5)。满清一统中国的大业，亦已成为乾隆皇帝统治下的文化大业。

最后的皇帝

嘉庆皇帝在位时，虽然在胡敬(1769–1845)的监督下，于1816年完成了编修皇家目录《秘殿珠林三编》与《石渠宝笈三编》的巨制，却也开始了清宫皇室书画收藏的衰落。许多作品成了皇室赐给皇亲国戚、宦官与大臣们的礼品，而从此离开了皇宫。成亲王永瑆(1752–1823)获赐了宫中最早的书法杰作之一，陆机(261-303)的《平复帖》，以及传为唐朝大师韩干所画的《照夜白》图卷[41]。后来的道光皇帝(1821-1850在位)与其后的几代皇帝，均延续这种常规。恭亲王奕訢(1833-1898)获赐了宋徽宗所画的《五色鹦鹉图》与陈容的《九龙图》[42]。嘉庆皇帝仿效父亲乾隆皇帝，在宫中所藏书画上钤入自己的鉴藏印玺。他之后所有十九世纪的清代皇帝，则未如此效法。嘉庆之后，只有宣统皇帝溥仪，在皇室收藏的图轴上加钤鉴藏玺。

结语

1911年清廷覆亡，书画收藏的千年传统或有变迁，但作为政治合法性的象征，它的作用仍继续存在。即使溥仪认定走私故宫藏品出紫禁城，可为他的将来提供有力的财源，但他仍然保存了最重要的书画作品，并在他称帝满洲国时，将这些书画带到东北。其他于1924年溥仪出宫时留在宫中的书画，则与其他所有的收藏，被当时的政府视为“国宝”[43]。当中日战争局势转剧之时，中华民国政府针对其非凡的重要性，为不使国宝落入日本人手中，随即将这批收藏中最精美的部分运到西南大后方去。二次大战结束后，这些收藏被转送到国民政府的首都南京，以此表明南京政权的合法地位。不久之后，国民党在内战国共斗争中逐渐失势，再决定将其中最重要的收藏，秘密地运到其撤守的台湾。这些收藏，如今是台北国立故宫博物院的镇馆之宝。其他从内宫带出而散失各地，及后来被溥仪带到东北的书画收藏，则在中华人民共和国成立后，由政府积极奔走搜寻、一一寻回，有的重回到北京故宫，有的被辽宁省博物馆收藏。身为国宝，这些失而复得的前清藏品，也同样成了新政府成立的合法依据。即便在今日，它们依旧是“宜子孙”的最佳佐证。

（简菱仪译）

注解:

1. 溥仪英国籍的私人教　庄士顿(Reginald F. Johnston)在他的作品《紫禁城的黄昏》描述了溥仪紫禁城里的生活。
2. 见溥仪,《从皇帝到公民：爱新觉罗　溥仪的自传》,由 W.J.F. Jenner 翻译并加总序与篇序(牛津：牛津大学,1987),第128—29页。
3. 有关溥仪从皇宫带出的书画之历史事件,参见杨仁恺,《国宝沉浮录：故宫散佚书画鉴伪考略》(上海：上海人民美术出版社,1991)；另参考 Jeannette Shambaugh Elliott and David Shambaugh,《中国皇室艺术宝藏漂泊之旅》(西雅图与伦敦：西雅图大学出版,2005)。
4. 以下描述根据雷德侯(Lothar Ledderose),〈一些有关中国宫廷收藏的观感〉,《东方陶瓷学会会刊(*Transactions of the Oriental Ceramic Society*)》,第43期(1978/79),第35—46页。有关九鼎之研究,参见张光直(K. C. Chang),《艺术,迷思与仪式：古中国赢取政治权威之途径》(剑桥,麻萨诸塞州：哈佛大学出版,1983),特别堑　5—97页.
5. 张彦远,《历代名画记》,由 William R. B. Acker 翻译,《唐代与唐代前关于中国绘画的论作》(莱顿：E. J. Brill,1954),第75—80页。
6. 有关故宫收藏之历史以及特定的书画收藏,参见杨仁恺,《国宝沉浮录》,第1—15页；Elliott and Shambaugh,《漂泊之旅》,第3—47页；以及张临生,〈国立故宫博物院：一个收藏的历史〉,收录于《中华瑰宝：台北国立故宫博物院的宝藏》,方闻与屈志仁合编(纽约：大都会博物馆,1996),第3—25页.
7. 见傅申,〈祥哥剌吉公主：书画收藏家〉，收录于《阴影下之花朵：中国与日本绘画历史中之女性》,Marsha Weidner 编(火奴鲁鲁：夏威夷大学出版,1990)，第55—80页;及 Marsha Weidner,〈几个关于蒙古宫廷绘画与艺术赞助的观点〉，收录于《艺术家与赞助者：一些关于中国绘画的社会经济现象》，李铸晋(Chu-tsing Li)编 (劳伦斯：堪萨斯大学艺术史系,1989),第37—59页。
8. 关于满清的崛起与北京的沦陷之讨论,有若干参考来源。尤其见 Frederick Wakeman, Jr.,《大业：十七世纪中国满清帝国秩序的重建》(伯克莱：加州大学,1985)。
9. 清世祖顺治皇帝的十九幅画作,被记载在《秘殿珠林初编》与《石渠宝笈初编》中。初于1745年完成,后重刊并合编为《秘殿珠林石渠宝笈合编》,十二册(上海:上海书局,1988),第一册,第9—10页,与第二册,第257—58页。画作图片,见《故宫书画图录》,第10册(台北：国立故宫博物　1992),第7—8页。
10. 关于康熙皇帝与其統治時期,见史景迁 (Jonathan D. Spence),《中国皇帝：康熙康熙自画像》(纽约：Knopf,1974)。《中国的三个皇帝，1662—1795》，康熙为此书画展图录焦点主题之一，Evelyn S. Rawski 与 Jessica Rawson合编(伦敦：皇家学院,2005)；见本书中 Evelyn S. Rawski,〈“盛世”：康雍乾时期之中国〉,图录第22—40页,与 Regina Krahl,〈康熙皇帝：战士,学者,科学家〉,图录第208—39页。
11. 见房兆楹,〈玄烨〉。《清代名人传略》,恒慕义(Arthur W. Hummel)编(华盛顿特区：U. S. Government Printing Office,1943),第327—31页。清代宫廷绘画,见聂崇正,〈清代宫廷画,收录于《中国的三个皇帝,1662—1795》,(见注10),第76—115页。
12. 康熙皇帝所题款之画作,见《秘殿珠林石渠宝笈合编》中之《石渠宝笈》(1745),第1册,第406、451—2、672、675页,与第2册,第786、813—15、1164页。
13. 见Chin-sung Chang〈山水清晖：王　(1632—1717)与中国清代早期全景山水画之制作〉(博士论文,耶鲁大学,2004)与何慕文(Maxwell K. Hearn),〈文献与肖像：康熙乾隆南巡图〉收录于《乾隆皇帝时期的中国绘画》，周汝式与 Claudia Brown 合编,*Phoebus*,第6,第1期(Tempe:亚利桑那州立大学,1988),第91—131页。
14. 有关孙承泽资料，参见 Dean R. Wickes,〈孙承泽〉。《清代名人传略》(见注11),第669—70页;谢巍,《中国画学著作考录》(上海书画出版社,1998),第434—35页;与 Hin-cheung Lovell,《中国绘画目录与相关文献之注释书目》(安娜堡：密西根大学,1973),第34—35页。有关梁清标资料，参见李雪曼 (Sherman E. Lee)与何惠鉴(Wai-kam Ho),〈梁清标收藏的本质与重要性〉,《中央研究院国际汉学会议论文集》(台北:中央研究院历史语言研究所艺术史组,1981),第102—57页。
15. 关于宋荦与其父宋权,见〈宋荦〉及〈宋权〉,《清代名人传略》(见注11),第688—90页。
16. 见罗覃(Thomas Lawton),〈耿昭忠注释〉,《艺术的诠释:中国绘画与诗词论文集》特别艺术刊号译文,屈志仁编 (香港:翻译中心,香港中文大学,1976),第144—51页。
17. 见房兆楹,〈高士奇〉,《清代名人传略》(见注11),第413—15页;谢巍,《中国画学》，第478—80页;及 Lovell,《书目注释》,第38—41页。
18. 见房兆楹,〈索额图〉,《清代名人传略》(见注11),第663—66页。
19. 见房兆楹,〈安岐〉,《清代名人传略》(见注11),第11—13页;及罗覃(Thomas Lawton),〈安岐的墨缘汇观〉,《庆祝蒋复聪先生七十岁论文集》(台北:故宫博物院,1969年),第13—35页。
20. 此画现今为美国克里夫美术馆所藏。见《八代之中国绘画：美国堪萨斯市纳尔逊—艾京斯艺术博艾京斯艺术博物馆与克里夫兰美术馆之收藏》(克里夫兰：克里夫兰美术馆,1980),第351—52页。
21. 关于雍正皇帝,见房兆楹,〈胤祯〉,《清代名人传略》(见注11),第915—20页；及 Regina Krahl,〈艺术收藏家及赞助者〉,《中国的三个皇帝》(见注10),第240—45页。雍正在位期间政绩简介,参见史景迁(Jonathan D. Spence)在《因书叛国》中精辟的介绍,(纽约:维京企鹅,2001)。
22. 见聂崇正编,《清代宫廷绘画》(上海：上海科学技术出版社, 1999),第11期,第74—90页。
23. 见聂崇正,《清代宫廷绘画》第14号,第101—3页,及第15号,第104—5页；Rawski and Rawson,《中国的三个皇帝》(见注10),第126—27页。
24. 见聂崇正,《清代宫廷绘画》第16期,第106—11页,及第18期,第118—23页；Rawski and Rawson,《中国的三个皇帝》(见注10),第248—49页；巫鸿,〈皇帝的化妆 — 雍正与乾隆的“服装像”〉,*Orientations*,第26册,第7期(七月/八月号,1995),第25—41页。
25. 此二画卷目前均在伦敦,一为 Percival David 中国艺术基金会之收藏,另一为维多利亚与艾伯特博物馆之藏品。见 Rawski and Rawson,《中国的三个皇帝》(见注10),第252—55页。

26. 不少文献记录了乾隆皇帝与他的统治时期。见房兆楹,〈弘历〉,《清代名人传略》(见注11), 第369—73页; Harold L. Kahn,《皇帝眼中的君主专制: 乾隆政权的形象与现实》(剑桥,麻萨诸塞州: 哈佛大学出版,1971); 周汝式与 Claudia Brown,《优雅之笔: 乾隆皇帝时的中国绘画,1735—1795》(凤凰城:凤凰城美术馆,1985年);《乾隆皇帝的文化大业》(台北: 国立故宫博物院,2002);张弘星,《乾隆皇帝: 紫禁城的国宝》(爱丁堡:苏格兰国立美术馆,2002); Patricia Berger,《帝国性空: 中国清代的佛教艺术与政权》(火奴鲁鲁:夏威夷大学出版,2003); Chuimei Ho 与 Bennet Bronson,《壮丽的紫禁城: 乾隆皇帝的辉煌帝业》(伦敦: Merrell 与 Chicago:菲尔德美术馆,2004); 见 Gerald Holzwarth,〈艺术赞助者乾隆皇帝与北京故宫收藏的形成〉,与 Jessica Rawson,〈The Qianlong Emperor: Virtue and the Possession of Antiquity〉,收录于《中国的三个皇帝》(见注10),分别为第41—53页与第270—75页。
27. 有关乾隆皇帝身为艺术鉴赏家的讨论,参见古原宏伸(Kohara Hironobu),〈乾隆皇帝鉴赏中国绘画的能力〉,《乾隆皇帝时期的中国绘画》(见注13),第56—73页。
28. 关于此名之选择与其多重含义,参见Holzwarth,〈艺术赞助者乾隆皇帝〉,第44—45页。
29. 关于讨论《子明卷》的详细资料,见《故宫书画图录》,第17册(1998),第281—88页。
30. 关于讨论《无用卷》的详细资料,见《故宫书画图录》, 第17册(1998),第289—98页。
31. 见《子明卷》在《乾隆皇帝的文化大业》中之讨论, 第80—81页。
32. 见《秘殿珠林石渠宝笈合编》中之《石渠宝笈三编》, 第9册,第518—22页; 与《故宫书画图录》, 第17册,第296页。
33. 见《秘殿珠林石渠宝笈合编》中之《石渠宝笈》, 第1册,第593页; 与张弘星,《乾隆皇帝》, 第94—95页。
34. 孙承泽,《庚子消夏记》(1660;重版,台北:汉华文化事业股份有限公司, 1971 [民国60年]),2.9a—10a,第95—97页。
35. 徐贲的册页图集被记录在《石渠宝笈续编》。见《故宫书画图录》,第22册(2003),第148—53页; 图卷则直到该宫廷目录编写《石渠宝笈三编》时才予收入,见《秘殿珠林石渠宝笈合编》中之《石渠宝笈三编》, 第12册, 第4413—14页。
36. 关于杜琼的画作与相关资料,见《故宫书画图录》, 第6册(1991),第137-38页。
37. 关于乾隆在位年间其个人在考证学上之成就,参见 Benjamin A. Elman,《从哲学到文献学: 中国帝制晚期的知识与社会现象》(剑桥,麻萨诸塞州: 东亚研究学会,哈佛大学出版,1984); 与 R. Kent Guy,《皇帝的四库: 乾隆晚期的学者与政府》(剑桥,麻萨诸塞州: 哈佛大学出版,1987)。
38. 《龙宿郊民图》收载入在《石渠宝笈续编》。见《故宫书画图录》,第1册(1989),第77—80页,其真正主题仍待考证; 相关讨论资料,参见启功,〈董源的"龙宿郊民图"〉,睹朗趸》杂志, 第5期(1978),第50—51页。
39. 见《故宫书画图录》, 第16册(1997),第157—60页; 以及《乾隆皇帝的文化大业》, 第77页。
40. 参见 Pamela Kyle Crossley,《半透明的镜子: 清皇权思想体系的历史与本质》(伯克莱与洛杉矶:加州大学出版,1999),第290—96页; 与富路德(L. Carrington Goodrich),《乾隆的文字狱》(巴尔地摩,马里兰州: Waverly Press,1935)。
41. 见杨仁恺,《国宝沉浮录》, 第56页。陆机的书法《平复帖》现藏北京故宫,韩干《照夜白》先由 Percival David 爵士所藏,后为纽约大都会博物馆收藏。
42. 此两幅画作如今均为波士顿美术馆藏品。
43. 有关故宫收藏的早期历史与关于"国宝"的观念,见李铸晋(Chu-tsing Li),〈故宫收藏的近代史〉,《美国中国艺术协会资料档案》,第12期(1958),第61—75页; 及 Elliott and Shambaugh,《漂泊史》,第3章。

Talented Sons of Heaven
A Brief History of the Chinese Imperial Painting and Calligraphy Collection

Willow Weilan Hai Chang

Everywhere under Heaven
Is no land that is not the king's.
To the borders of all those lands
None but is the king's subject.
(trans. Arthur Waley, emended)[1]

In several thousand years of centralized, authoritarian rule in China, it had been established that everything in the land—which includes the land itself, products, people, and all forms of wealth, be it material or spiritual—was at the disposal of the imperial establishment. Works of art, as products of human civilization and as witnesses to history, have always been regarded as the bearers of cultural heritage and therefore have been treasured and collected by the rulers.

According to historical documents, artistic works of painting and calligraphy became objects of interest and collection for the Chinese imperial families between the Han and Six Dynasties period. Beginning in the Qin and Han dynasties, the arts of painting and calligraphy were set to develop into long lasting traditions that would reach their first height during the Six Dynasties.[2] Many emperors were also painters or calligraphers. There were no fewer than a dozen such artist-emperors from Yuandi of the Han (r. 48–33 BCE) to Yuandi of the Liang (r. 552–55) dynasty.[3] They were, moreover, actively involved in the theoretical discussions of painting and calligraphy. Wudi of the Liang dynasty, for example, wrote *Guan Zhong You shufa shier yi* (Twelve observations on the calligraphy of Zhong You),[4] and in an exchange of nine letters with the famous Daoist thinker and calligrapher Tao Hongjing (456–536) ,[5] he took delight in evaluating the works of two of the most popular calligraphers of the time, Zhong You (151–230) and Wang Xizhi (ca. 303–ca. 361).[6] In the Han dynasty, the invention of paper had technologically facilitated the creation and dissemination of written and painted works, and paper books were beginning to become widespread.[7] The development of mounting techniques during the Six Dynasties period reflected one of the needs of society with regard to collecting painting and calligraphy, and it also stimulated creative production. Technical exchange from one field to another led to the maturity of art collecting as well as the techniques of mounting and finishing. Among the earliest named mounting experts in recorded history was Fan Ye (398–445) of the Liu Song dynasty.[8] Appreciation of and passion for art, from the upper class to the masses, had caused painting and calligraphy to become valuable symbols of culture. In an anecdote about Wang Xizhi aiding a peddler by inscribing her fans, the addition of a mere five characters increased their value fivefold, and demand ran higher than supply. This story illustrates how well aware the general public was of good calligraphy and that painting and calligraphy had a tremendous influence in shaping society and its cultural values.[9]

A society with considerable knowledge and recognition of the importance of artistic creation was ready for collecting painting and calligraphy. With the advantage of their sovereign authority, members of the Chinese imperial families inevitably became the main force in collecting, gathering ever larger quantities of painting and calligraphy into the imperial storehouses. If it can be said that early bronze and jade objects were collected as emblems of the state, possession of which signified power and status, then paintings and calligraphy indicated possession of the best cultural and artistic achievements that Chinese civilization had thus far been able to produce. As examples of the visual embodiment of the spirit, they had been relentlessly sought after by rulers of successive dynasties, who have themselves become the subject of paintings (see fig. 1); in addition, some emperors demonstrated particular interests and initiative and were able to obtain art treasures through unusual means at whatever costs, resulting in massive collections. The rise of imperial collectors in the fourth century during the Six Dynasties period is well documented, and this tradition lasted until the early years of the twentieth century, which saw the end of the Qing dynasty. Throughout more than fifteen hundred years of history, the collecting, appreciation,

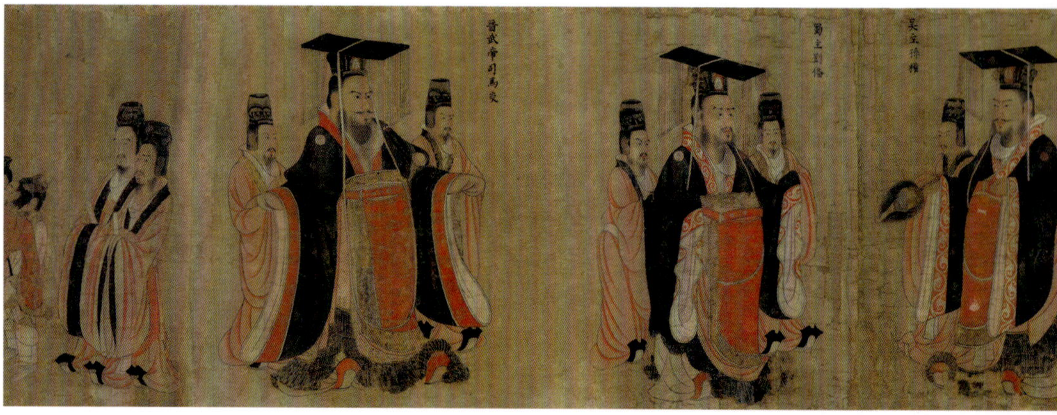
晉武帝司馬炎
蜀主劉備
吳主孫權

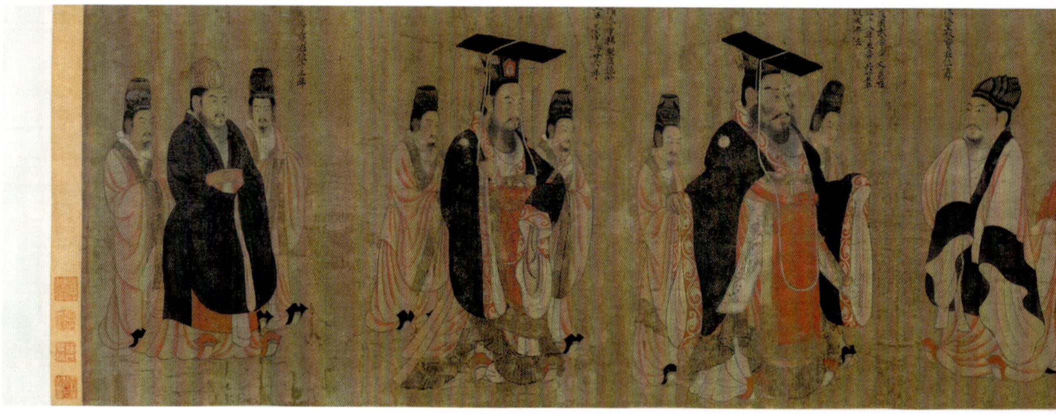

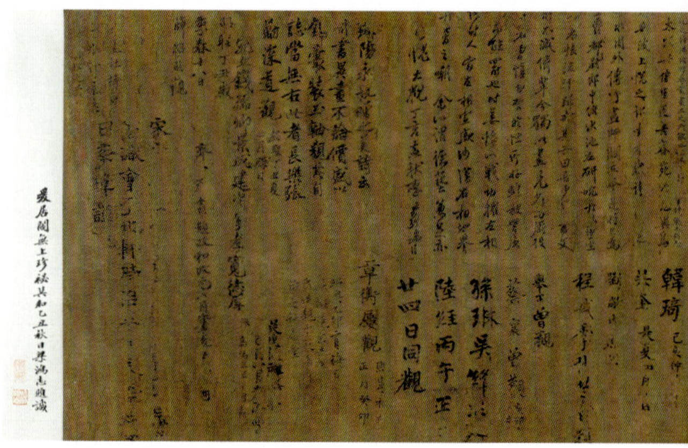

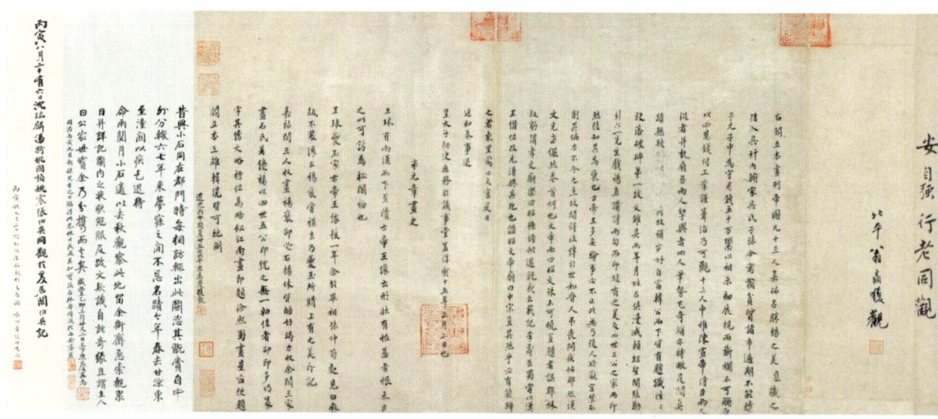

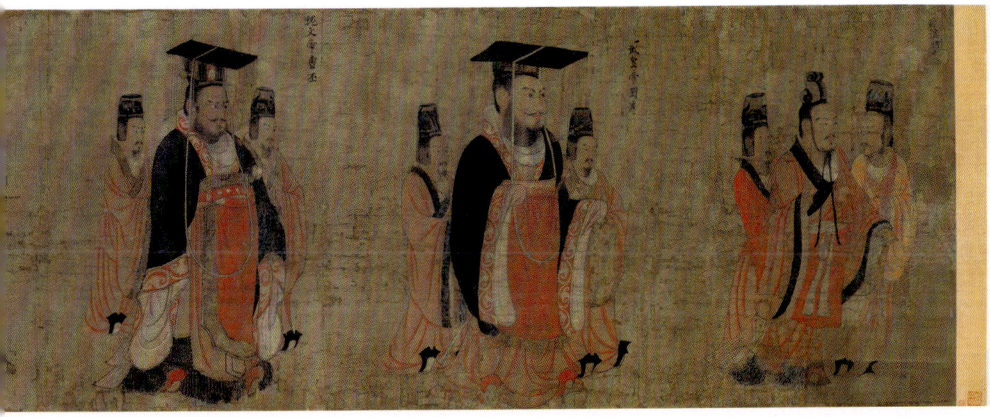

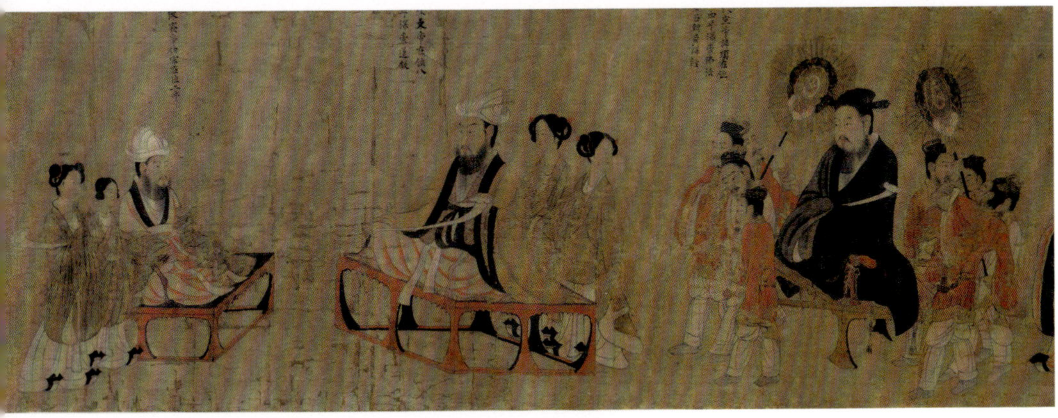

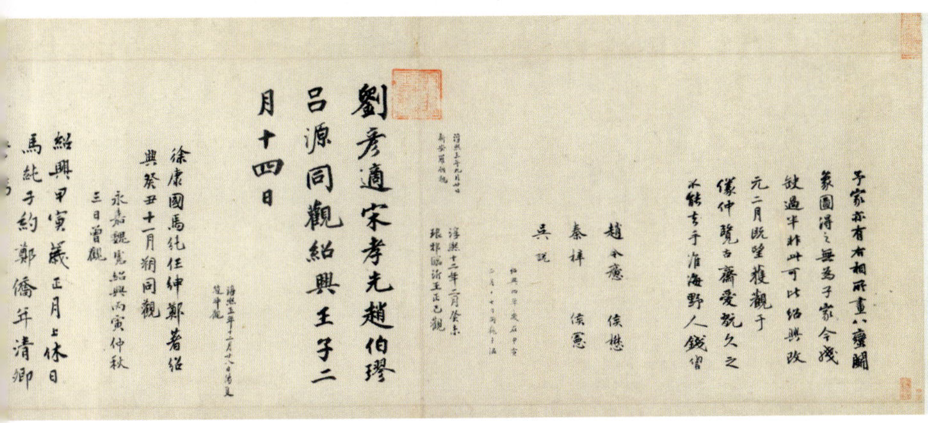

Fig. 1. Attributed to Yan Liben (ca. 600–673), *The Thirteen Emperors.* Handscroll. Ink and color on silk. Museum of Fine Arts, Boston. Denman Waldo Ross Collection (MFA 31.643). Photograph © 2008 Museum of Fine Arts, Boston
唐，传阎立本，历代帝王图，手卷局部，绢本设色，
美国波士顿美术馆

conservation, and cataloguing of painting and calligraphy by the imperial family never stopped. Although it waxed and waned at different times, the collection was handed down from generation to generation, leaving clear records of its development and acquisitions and becoming a typical form of cultural transmission in China.

I. The Principal Emperors and Members of the Imperial Family Involved in the Painting and Calligraphy Collections of Successive Dynasties

Wudi, or Emperor Wu (r. 141–87 BCE), of the Han dynasty was probably the originator of China's imperial collection. According to Tang dynasty literature, "Emperor Wu of the Han created a treasure building to store illustrations and books. Emperor Ming of the Eastern Han (28–75) loved the art of painting; he set up painting studios and established the Hongdu Academy to promote the fine arts, whereupon artistic talents from all over gathered."[10] In approximately two thousand years since that time, there were no fewer than a dozen emperors who had made great contributions to the collecting of painting and calligraphy. It has been estimated that from the Jin to the early Ming dynasty there were 177 historical figures who would qualify as connoisseurs, among whom fourteen or fifteen individuals were indeed emperors, making up close to ten percent of the total. Combining this early history with what we know of the later emperors, the following is an outline of the major contributors (including usurpers who did not occupy the throne for a lengthy period) to the Chinese imperial collection of painting and calligraphy from the usurper Huan Xuan and the Liang emperor Wudi of the Six Dynasties to the Qianlong emperor of the Qing dynasty.[11]

The Six Dynasties—Huan Xuan; Liu Yu (Emperor Wu of Liu Song); Liu Yu (Emperor Ming of Liu Song); Xiao Daocheng (Emperor Gao of Southern Qi); Xiao Yan (Emperor Wu of Liang); Xiao Yi (Emperor Yuan of Liang)

Huan Xuan (369–405) of the Eastern Jin dynasty was a native of Qiao (present-day Huaiyuan, Anhui). He was talented, strong, and bold in nature.[12] Starting as a military official in charge of Jingzhou and Jiangzhou, he rose to power and took control of the region in the middle and upper reaches of the Yangzi River. In 402, Huan Xuan captured the Eastern Jin dynasty capital Jiankang (present-day Nanjing) and usurped the throne; he thereafter helped himself to the entire collection of the Eastern Jin imperial court. He was an inexorable art lover and, as a calligrapher, liked to compare himself to Wang Xizhi. Such claims, however, have never been generally acknowledged,[13] although some of his calligraphic works had been collected by the imperial court of the Southern Qi dynasty, which was established by the Xiao family during the Southern Dynasties period.[14] Huan Xuan had small boats built so as to bring his favorite paintings and calligraphic works with him wherever he traveled.[15] Not only was he addicted to the art but he was avaricious:[16] "His desire led him to hunt for extant masterpieces of painting and model calligraphy and to take them by force."[17] He had allegedly stolen a cabinet full of paintings left with him for safe keeping by the then famous painter Gu Kaizhi, who had sealed the cabinet with paper. But upon his return, the owner found the seal tampered with and the cabinet empty. Gu Kaizhi knew who must have taken the works of art, but was in fear of Huan's power. He had no choice but to play down the incident, saying "paintings, like humans, are soul incarnates; they transcend as they immortalize."[18] In so doing, Huan Xuan was able to amass the best paintings and calligraphy of his time.

Liu Yu (363–422), a native of Pengcheng (present-day Xuzhou, Jiangsu) and a military man who rose through the ranks, usurped the Eastern Jin throne to establish the Liu Song dynasty and became known as Wudi. Without lifting a finger, he thus acquired the Eastern Jin court collection, including all the masterpieces seized by Huan Xuan. Liu Yu also liked paintings, so he kept enriching the imperial collection. A significant increase in acquisitions occurred in 467 (3rd year of Taishi) under Liu Yu (Mingdi), who was a voracious reader and loved literature. After succeeding to the throne, Mingdi started recruiting scholars and talents and devoted attention to the art collection: on one front he instructed his ministers to do an inventory of the existing pieces in the court collection; on another he sent expeditions to remote areas to recover court paintings and calligraphic works dispersed during the chaotic period of war in which Qianfeidi, the previous emperor, had been deposed. In addition, he allocated funds for the retrieval of works of art previously in the court collection. Men were sent to the remote regions of Wu, Jing, and Xiang (present-day Hunan) to search for lost paintings and calligraphic works, donations and contributions from ministers and dukes were accepted, and within a few months "masterpieces miraculously gathered." Almost all important works from the Six Dynasties up to that time, including those by such masters as Wang Xizhi, his son

Wang Xianzhi, Zhong You, Zhang Zhi, and others, were assembled into a huge collection, boasting some 707 scrolls of calligraphy by the Wangs and 697 characters originally written on paper by Zhong You.[19]

A Shandong native and a warlord who had served as commander of the imperial bodyguards at the Liu Song court, Xiao Daochen (427–482) murdered the emperor Shundi (Liu Zhun; b. 467) in 479, establishing the Southern Qi dynasty under the rule of the Xiao family and becoming the emperor known posthumously as Gaodi. Xiao Daochen liked literature and was a quite sophisticated connoisseur of the arts. All the treasures of the Liu Song dynasty court became his collection. He rated the works of art on the basis of their quality and excellence rather than their age. Starting from the painter Lu Tanwei (act. 465–72) and moving on to Fan Weixian (or Huaixian), he left evaluations of forty-two artists, ranking each one of them; twenty-seven slipcased works of art and 348 scrolls were reserved for his own enjoyment in his leisure time.[20] He thought that the twelve slipcases of calligraphy in the court collection was far from enough, so he ordered Wang Sengqian (426–485), a great-great grandson of Wang Xizhi, to search for more calligraphic works. This resulted in the addition of ten scrolls by such calligraphers as Zhang Zhi of the Eastern Han dynasty (25–220) to the imperial collection.[21] Gaodi (Xiao Daochen) also painted, and according to Tang dynasty records, his paintings included *Horse in the Low-lying Lands* (*Wowa ma tu*) and *Screen of Filial Piety* (*Xiaozi pingfeng tu*).[22]

Xiao Yan (464–549), a member of the Southern Qi royal family, seized power in 502 (the 2nd year of Zhongxing) when he was governor of Yongzhou, taking over the throne of the Qi emperor Xiao Baorong. He thereupon established the Liang dynasty and assumed the title of emperor, becoming Wudi of Liang (see fig. 2). According to historical records, he was a man "of innately unusual qualities and incisive talents, capable of composing all kinds of poetry and prose on the spur of the moment, and his casual improvisations all turned out to be works of literature. Also, he was as polite, frugal, sober, and respectful as he was multi-talented and knowledgeable, a truly rare combination."[23] He had a high level of connoisseurship in calligraphy. In addition to his exchange of correspondence with Tao Hongjing on the calligraphy of Zhong You and Wang Xizhi, he also left extensive comments on works by thirty-four calligraphers from the end of the Han to the Liang dynasty using concise yet witty language, a style typical of the Six Dynasties.[24] Xiao Yan took good care of the masterpieces in the

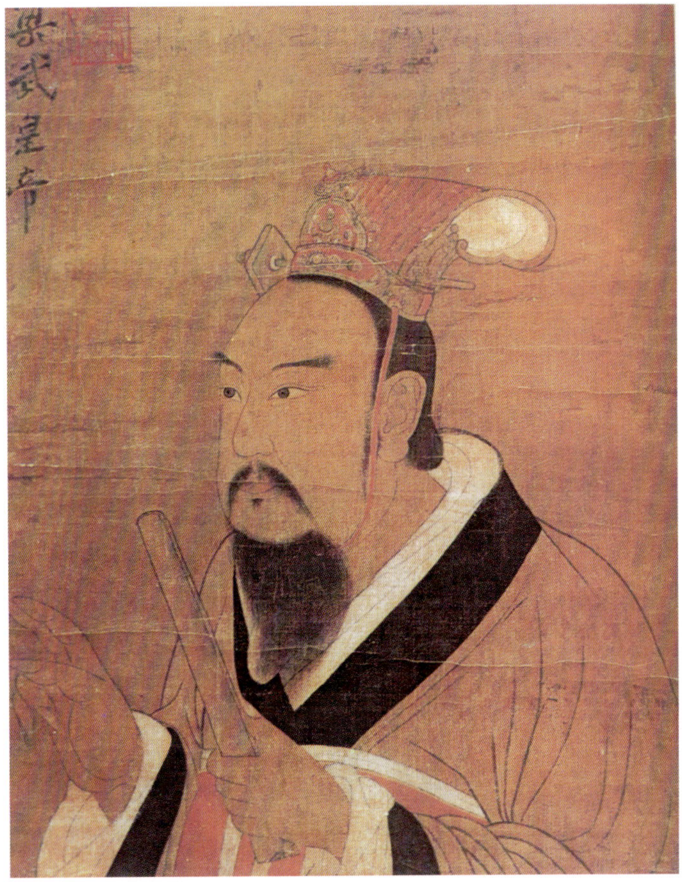

Fig. 2. Anonymous, *Portrait of Liang Wudi* [r. 502–49]. Hanging scroll. Color on silk. National Palace Museum, Taipei, Taiwan
佚名，梁武帝半身像，立轴，绢本设色，台北国立故宫博物院

court collection of the Southern Qi royal Xiao family and made great efforts to locate all dispersed works of art. He ordered the remounting and labeling of the paintings and calligraphic works, using for the best of them coral scroll weights, brocaded silk, and jade pins with gilt inscriptions.[25] Tao Hongjing, a famous calligrapher, Daoist, and connoisseur of the time, had the favor of being rewarded by Wudi with the opportunity to appreciate the imperial calligraphy collection. Tao thought there were no more than two dozen such pieces. When the number of pieces he was allowed to view reached two hundred seventy, he realized how many more there must have been and exclaimed, "The imperial collection is deep as an ocean, impossible for one bottle to absorb."[26] According to written accounts, the court collection was inventoried during Wudi's reign, and there was a book titled *Liang taiqing mu* (Catalogue of the Liang collection), which was used as a reference in the Tang dynasty when Pei Xiaoyuan compiled his *Zhenguangong sihuashi*

(History of paintings in imperial and private collections). The names of artists and titles of the works of art cited were all based on the *Liang taiqing mu*.[27]

Xiao Yi (Liang dynasty emperor Yuandi; 508–554), son of Xiao Yan, was a superior talent who also practiced painting. Six of his paintings were included in the *Zhenguangong sihuashi*.[28] Xiao Yi's fascination with art reached a stage of madness. After succeeding to the throne, he launched incessant quests for works of all the well-known artists, resulting in a huge collection with a size far beyond that of any in the previous dynasties. Initial damage to this huge court collection was inflicted in 548 (the 2nd year of Taiqing) during the Hou Jing Rebellion, when hundreds of works were unfortunately burnt. Later, all the paintings and calligraphic works in the court collection were transported to the city of Jiangling, which was sacked in 554 (the 3rd year of Chengsheng) by General Yu Jin of the Western Wei dynasty. Before the fall of the city, Xiao Yi had piled up all his important paintings, model calligraphy, and books, amounting to some 140,000 items (some say 240,000), and ordered the courtier Gao Shanbao to set fire to the pile. Then, when the emperor tried to jump into the blazing pile and immolate himself along with the treasures, he was held back by the palace guards. Furious, he hacked at the palace pillars with his sword and, heaving a great sigh, said, "Such is Xiao Shicheng's (his style name) fate, so let the elegant arts also end tonight."[29] When Yu Jin and his men arrived, they were able to salvage from the smoldering ashes some four thousand scrolls, which were then transported to Chang'an. This incident was documented as the single worst catastrophe ever in the history of Chinese art! The huge loss was irreparable. Also lost was the *Liang taiqing mu* and, along with it, a record of the precise number of works, as well as their specifics and artistic significance. People at the time commented that this was an unprecedented shame.[30] These 140,000 works of model calligraphy, famous paintings, and ancient books and records constituted the most comprehensive collection that any Chinese imperial court had been able to amass up to that time, and it vanished in a single fire.

Sui, Tang, and the Five Dynasties— Yang Jian (Emperor Wen of Sui); Li Shimin (Emperor Taizong of Tang); Li Houzhu (Southern Tang Dynasty)

Yang Jian (541–604), who had been given the title Duke of Sui by the Northern Zhou dynasty, took over the throne in 581 becoming Wendi of the Sui dynasty (589–618). He sacked the city of Jianye (Nanjing) in 589 (the 9th year of Kaihuang) and captured Chen Shubao (Emperor Houzhu of the Chen dynasty; 553–604), reunifying China and ending more than two hundred years of separation between the south and the north. Soon afterwards, Yang Jian ordered his military advisors Pei Ju and Gao Ying to search for works of art previously in the collection of the Wei and Jin courts and thus obtained some eight hundred scrolls. Two buildings were then erected in the East Capital (Dongjing, another name for Luoyang) behind the Guanwen Dian hall: Miaokaitai on the east for storing model calligraphy and Baojitai on the west for famous paintings from antiquity. These were the first of such buildings specially built and designated for the collection of paintings and calligraphy by the imperial court.[31] In 616 (the 12th year of Daye), Yang Guang (Sui dynasty emperor Yangdi; 569–618) went on an inspection tour to Jiangdu (Yangzhou) and brought the model calligraphy and famous paintings from the East Capital with him on the Grand Canal. Along the way, however, the transport boats tipped over and most of the works fell into the water. Chinese art suffered another catastrophe! Yang Guang himself was murdered in Jiangdu by the commander of the bodyguards, Yuwen Huaji (d. 619), who then plundered the rest of the works of art that had survived to reach Yangzhou and took them to Liaocheng. There, they were obtained by Dou Jiande, leader of the peasant rebels. Whatever was left in the East Capital fell into the hands of warlord Wang Shichong. By that time, the original art collection of the Sui dynasty imperial court had been completely dispersed.[32]

Li Yuan (566–635), a garrison commander stationed at Taiyuan, proclaimed himself king of Tang in 617, even though the Sui court had conferred on him the title Duke of Tang because of his military strength. In the next year, he ascended the throne in Chang'an (Xi'an), establishing the Tang dynasty and becoming Emperor Gaozu. In 622 (the 5th year of Wude), he captured the territory of Zheng, eradicated Wang Shichong, Dou Jiande, and other rivals, and brought about the grand reunification of the entire country. Thus, the court treasures from both capitals (Luoyang and Chang'an) and whatever was left of the masterpieces in Yangzhou all became his assets. When the collections were being transported up the Yellow River en route to Chang'an, however, the ships were overturned by the strong currents at the Sanmenxia Gorge. Only one or two pieces out of every ten were saved from the disaster; the rest of them were all lost![33]

Love of painting and calligraphy was very widespread among members of the Tang imperial family. Many of them turned out to be artists, for example, the Duke of Han (Li Yuanchang), who liked to paint horses; the Duke of Jiangdu, who was good at painting birds and cicadas; and the Duke of Siteng, who was good at painting bees and cicadas.[34] Of particular importance to the arts was Li Shimin (the Tang emperor Taizong; 599–649), second son of Emperor Gaozu (see fig. 3). He was a man of Herculean courage and great vision, a heroic warrior on horseback, but at the same time an admirer of literati arts. While he was still the Duke of Qin, he had already started collecting works of art; after he ascended the throne in 626, he was even more enthusiastic about collecting. He was so particularly fond of Wang Xizhi's calligraphic works that he vowed to seek them out from all sources, regardless of cost. In 632, the sixth year of his reign (the Zhenguan era), he ordered an inventory and conservation project to sort out all the calligraphy pieces in the imperial collection. In 636 (the 10th year of Zhenguan), he issued a decree to seek and purchase all existing calligraphic works by Wang Xizhi using gold and silk for payments. In 638 (the 12th year of Zhenguan era), the father of Wang Fangqing contributed more than forty works by Wang Xizhi, his great-great grandfather. With this donation, plus all other acquisitions from around the country, the number of Wang calligraphy originals amounted to more than 290 works in standard script and running script mounted into some seventy scrolls and over 2,000 works in cursive script mounted into eighty scrolls for Taizong's easy viewing and copying.[35] Taizong had long been fixated on Wang Xizhi's original *Lanting xu*, or "Preface to Orchid Pavilion." He obtained the work by sending his advisor Xiao Yi to the Yongxin temple in Kuaiji to befriend the monk Biancai (see fig. 4); he then duplicated the text by having it carved onto a piece of jade and ordered rubbings to be made from the slab as gifts to dukes, princes, and ministers close to him.[36] Moreover, Taizong personally wrote the preface to a sutra for the monk Huairen (a Tang calligrapher) by collecting calligraphic characters from Wang Xizhi's works. Carved as a stele, this preface is now a national treasure housed in the Xi'an Beilin Museum.[37] Despite being the emperor, he also deigned to personally write Wang Xizhi's biography.[38] He so loved Wang Xizhi's calligraphy that he was as if mad with intoxication. On his deathbed, Taizong's only wish was to be buried with the original "Preface to Orchid Pavilion," and he asked his son, the future Emperor Gaozong, to be filial and not disobey him.[39] Allegedly, Wang Xizhi's masterpiece *Yue Yi lun* (On Yue Yi), which is considered "number one in standard script," was also buried in his mausoleum, Zhaoling. It is now preserved only on stone.[40] Thus, one can see

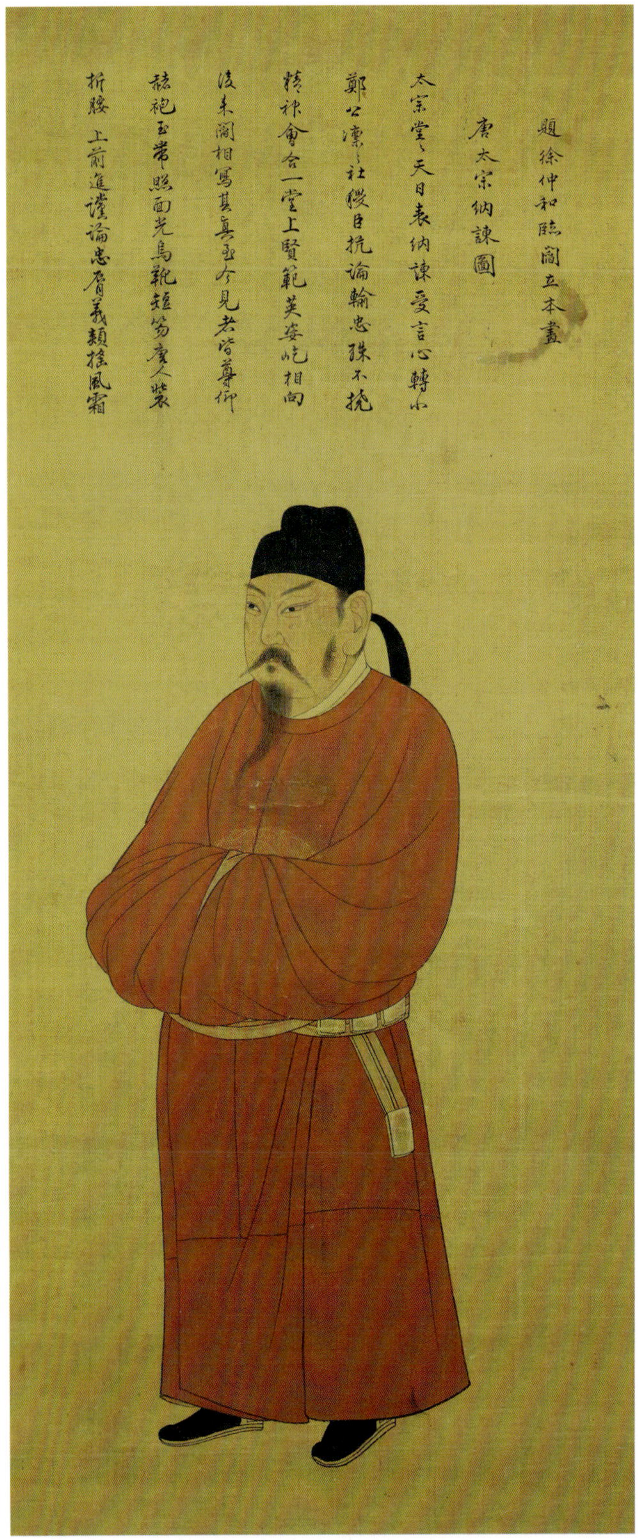

Fig. 3. Anonymous, *Standing Portrait of Tang Taizong* [r. 627–49]. Hanging scroll. Color on silk. National Palace Museum, Taipei, Taiwan
佚名，唐太宗立像，立轴，绢本设色，台北国立故宫博物院

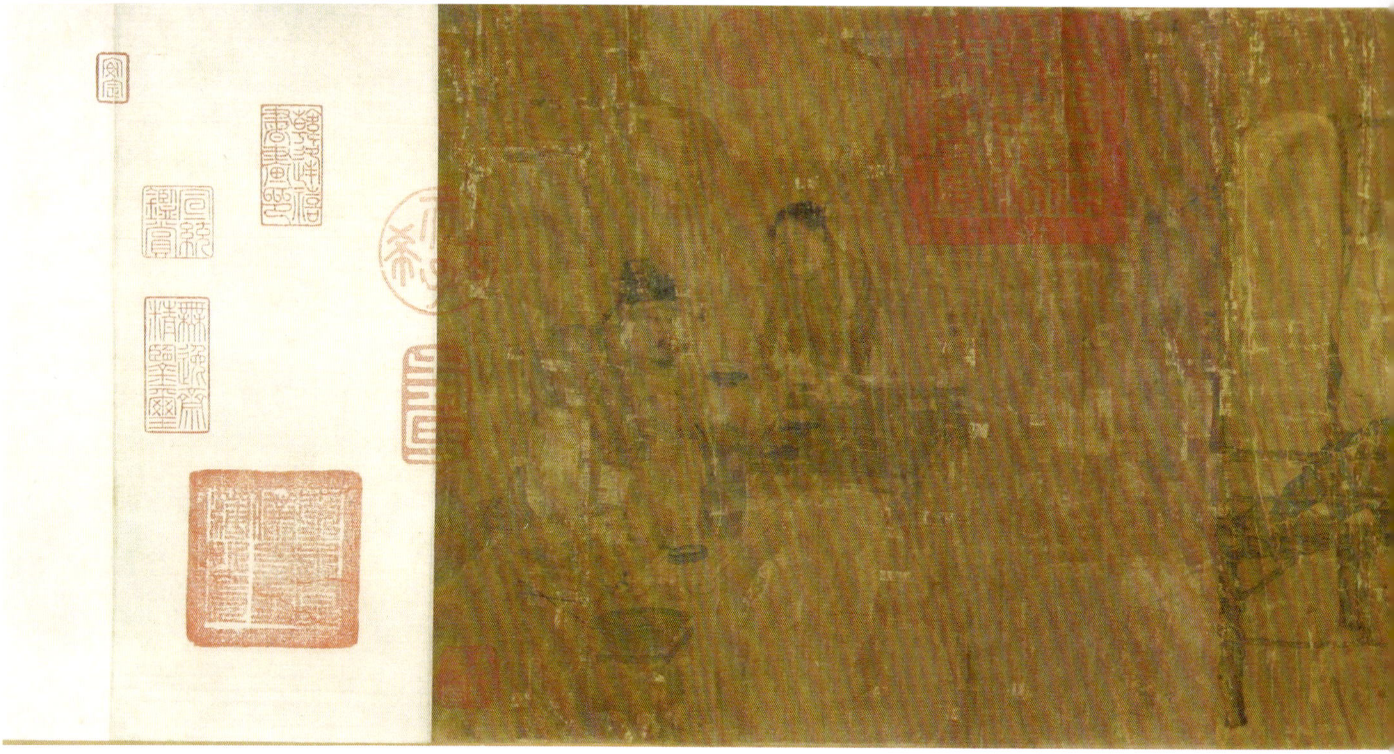

the depth of Taizong's fascination with Wang Xizhi's calligraphy. Veneration for Wang's calligraphy during the Tang and successive dynasties had a lot to do with this emperor's high esteem.

Taizong was an accomplished calligrapher himself, who knew how to learn by copying works by old masters. His running cursive script was modeled after that of the two Wangs (father and son); it was elegant and smooth in style, with excellent use of *feibai*, or "flying white" (uncovered areas left in the passage of a stroke, indicating swift movement), and dynamic brushstrokes.[41] Taizong enjoyed discussing calligraphy with Yu Shinan (558–638), a master calligrapher of the day, and frequently showed his own calligraphic works to his ministers. He also had an unconventional and incisive way of discussing calligraphy, using his profound military experience as metaphors for brush technique; he realized that the most important quality to strive for in the art of calligraphy was structural strength.[42]

Not only did Taizong continue the quest for good works of painting and calligraphy from the civilian population throughout the Zhenguan era, he also exercised imperial prerogatives to place restrictions on the art collectors among the populace. Civilian collections were probably limited to only eulogies and letters of concern for the sick, leaving all other forms of calligraphy reserved for the imperial establishment. As a result, masterpieces long held among the populace were all rounded up into the court collection.[43] The Tang commentator Bian Sheng wrote that "during the Zhenguan (627–49) and Kaiyuan (713–741) periods, there was unprecedented prosperity; the emperors were all divine and multi-talented, and scholars were refined and well-versed in the arts. They all sought to purchase ultimate treasures and made huge acquisitions. For this reason, the court has a large and comprehensive collection of pictures and books."[44] Earlier in the Tang dynasty, during the Wude era (618–26), there were only some three hundred scrolls of painting and calligraphy in the court collection, including the few works remaining from the Sui dynasty. With Taizong's efforts, the court collection now boasted some 1,510 scrolls of authentic works by Zhong You, Wang Xizhi, and his son Wang Xianzhi,[45] along with the twenty or so extant masterpieces from the Six Dynasties that are documented in the *Zhenguangong sihuashi* and not a small number that are undocumented.[46] During the reign of Li Longji (the Tang emperor Xuanzong; 685–762), the imperial Hanlin Academy was established, talented and learned scholars in the literary arts were summoned, and they were granted the title of *daizhao* (imperial attendant). Meanwhile, the court greatly expanded its collection with the newly acquired private family collections of Xue Ji, Li

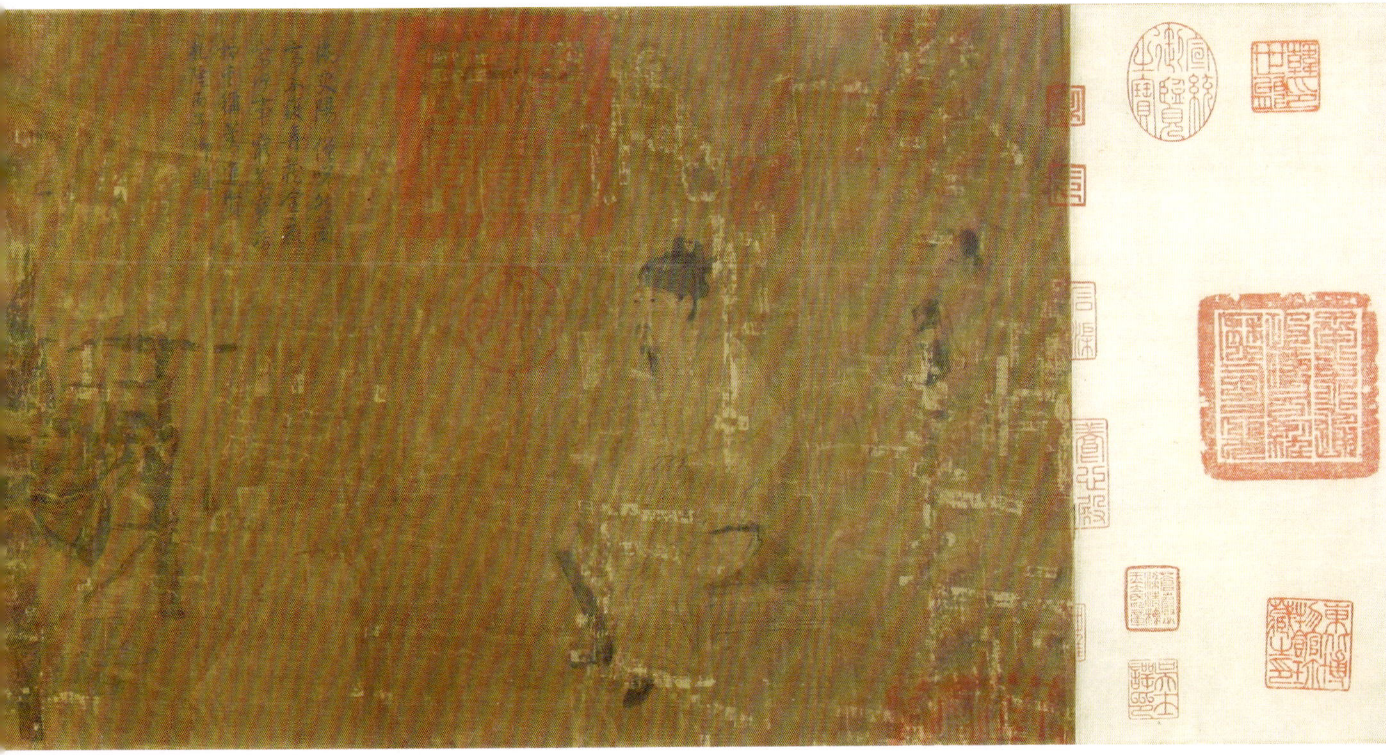

Fig. 4. Attributed to Yan Liben (ca. 600–673), *Xiao Yi Acquires the Orchid Pavilion Manuscript*, Southern Song (1127–1279). Handscroll. Color on silk. Liaoning Provincial Museum
南宋，传唐阎立本，萧翼赚兰亭图，手卷，绢本设色，辽宁省博物馆

Fan, and Wang Fangqing, and in the Kaiyuan era, there were even instances of rewards bestowed for donations made to the imperial storehouse. With all these measures and sources, China's imperial art collection reached a second peak.

During the Five Dynasties period, both Li Jing (the Southern Tang emperor Zhongzhu) and his sixth son, Li Yu (the emperor Houzhu; 937–978), were famous poets of their generation, especially the younger emperor Li. Assuming the sobriquet Hermit of Mount Zhongshan, he was good at both calligraphy and painting. In calligraphy, he used a tremulous brushstroke, which was known as *jincuo dao* (gold filigree stroke) His paintings are marked by a calligraphic quality, and the subjects of landscape, figures, birds, and bamboo all show individuality. An imperial art academy was also established in Jinling, attracting great artists from all over the country to compete with those at the court of the Later Shu dynasty in Chengdu, making both cities centers of artistic activity. The florescence of painting and calligraphy stimulated inventions in the making of ink, paper, and tools, such as the *chengxintang* paper and *litinggui* ink made in the time of Li Yu.[47] "Extremely talented and knowledgeable, Li Houzhu enjoyed reading, owned a large collection, and was an excellent connoisseur."[48] Works of painting and calligraphy that he had viewed and studied would have his collection seals and poetic inscriptions. In terms of quantity, however, his collection was no match for the Tang imperial collection.

The Two Song Dynasties—Zhao Guangyi (Emperor Taizong); Zhao Ji (Emperor Huizong); Zhao Gou (Emperor Gaozong)

It was not by chance that the Song dynasty saw the emergence of a famous artist-emperor, one who was an excellent painter, calligrapher, and connoisseur—Huizong (1082–1135). After Song dynasty founder Zhao Kuangyin (known posthumously as Taizu) was proclaimed emperor in the Chenqiao Revolt of 959, the famous paintings and model calligraphy held by the neighboring kingdoms of Southern Tang, Later Shu, and Wuyue were brought as booty into the Song court in Kaifeng as each state was annexed, thus reassembling several centuries of treasures dispersed from the late Tang court.[49] When Zhao Guangyi (939–997), the future Song emperor Taizong, was governor of Jinling

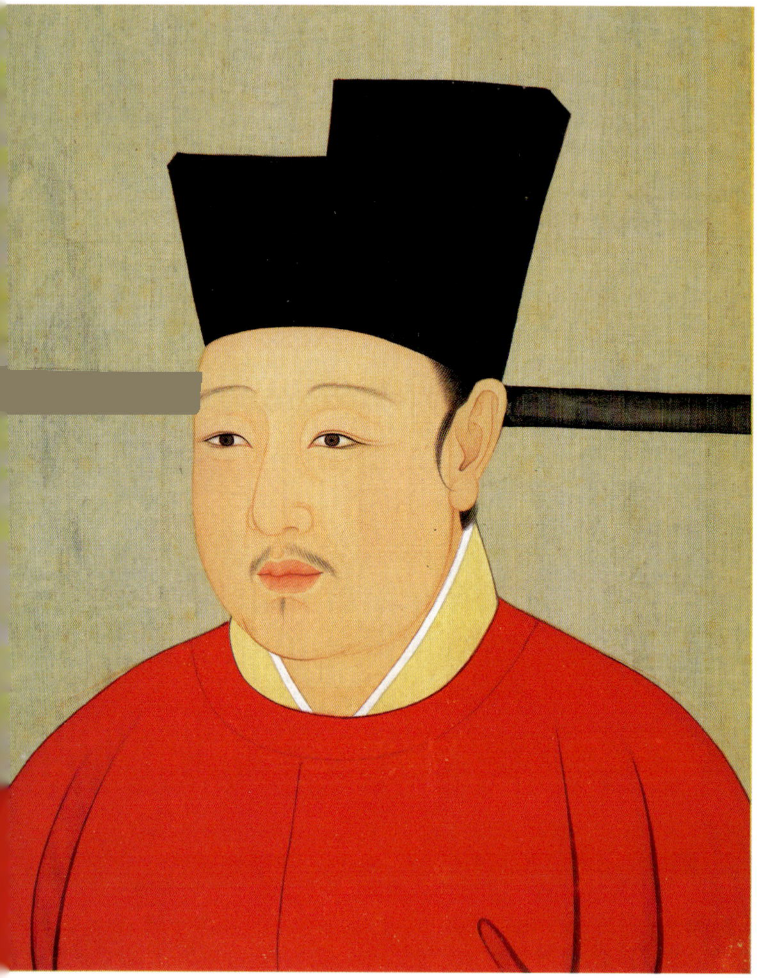

Fig. 5. Anonymous, *Portrait of Song Huizong* [r. 1100–25]. Album. Color on silk. National Palace Museum, Taipei, Taiwan
佚名，宋徽宗半身像，册页，绢本设色，台北国立故宫博物院

(Nanjing), he had to use his knowledge and connoisseurship to resolve a dispute over the ownership of some paintings and ended up purchasing the paintings himself; they were sixteen scrolls of Luohan portraits by the Southern Tang dynasty artist Wang Qihan (an attending court artist at the Southern Tang imperial academy; act. 961–75). Sixteen days later, Zhao Guangyi ascended the throne as the emperor and thereupon renamed the paintings "Harbinger Luohans," which was full of auspicious meaning.[50] During his reign, he increased the number of candidates for imperial examinations, ordered the compilation of the encyclopedia *Taiping yulan* (Imperially reviewed encyclopedia of the Taiping era), and promoted literacy and creative expression. At the beginning of his reign, out of his love for painting and calligraphy, he ordered local collection campaigns all over the nation in order to locate important works of art and sent the imperial attendants Huang Jucai and Gao Wenjin to search for paintings among the civilian population as well as to record and rate the acquisitions. In 988 (the 1st year of Duangong), a storage building was erected inside the Chongwenyuan (Center for Literary Studies) for the safe keeping of the artifacts, both ancient and contemporary. Assistant Minister of Official Personnel Affairs Li Zhi, who was also manager of the Imperial Library, was given the task of screening pictures and books for imperial review; he selected for his majesty some ten thousand volumes of originals from the three imperial studios.[51]

Succeeding emperors of the Song dynasty all had a part in boosting the art collection of the court. Zhao Zhen (Emperor Renzong, r. 1023–63) was adept in painting; he painted, for example, the *Bodhisattva of the Dragon Tree*. By the Zhenghe era (1111–17), Zhao Ji, the emperor Huizong (see fig. 5), had in his collection over six thousand antiquities, which he stored separately in the Chongzheng Dian hall and Xuanhe Dian hall. As his collection expanded, more rooms were built, including Baohe Dian hall, Jigu Ge court, Bogu Ge court, and Shanggu Ge court, all for the storage of antique jade, seals, ritual bronze vessels of all kinds, paintings, and model calligraphy. An outstanding artist himself, Huizong acknowledged that painting and calligraphy were his only passions. So his ministers selected the best in the court collection, including authentic works from Cao Buxing of the Three Kingdoms to Huang Jucai of the Song period, for imperial viewing during leisure moments; they were compiled into the *Xuanhe ruilan* (Xuanhe's wise review). The emperor also spent lots of time at the Xuanhe Dian hall, painting and inscribing poems.[52] During his thirty-five years on the throne, he "neglected administration, employed crafty sycophants, and mismanaged state affairs, leading to his own capture and the downfall of the nation. The only merit he had was in the practice of calligraphy and painting landscapes, figures, flowers and birds, and ink bamboo, all of which were skillful works of the utmost beauty, rendered in exquisite detail. He understood well the nature of his subjects and was excellent at distinguishing them. Masterful in calligraphy, he started by working in the style of Huang Tingjian but later achieved his own style, known as 'slender gold'" (see fig. 6).[53]

During his rule, Huizong further developed the Hanlin Painting Academy, which had been established since the beginning of the Song dynasty; he implemented a painting school and promoted art education. Every ten days or so he would bring out two cases of painting scrolls from the court

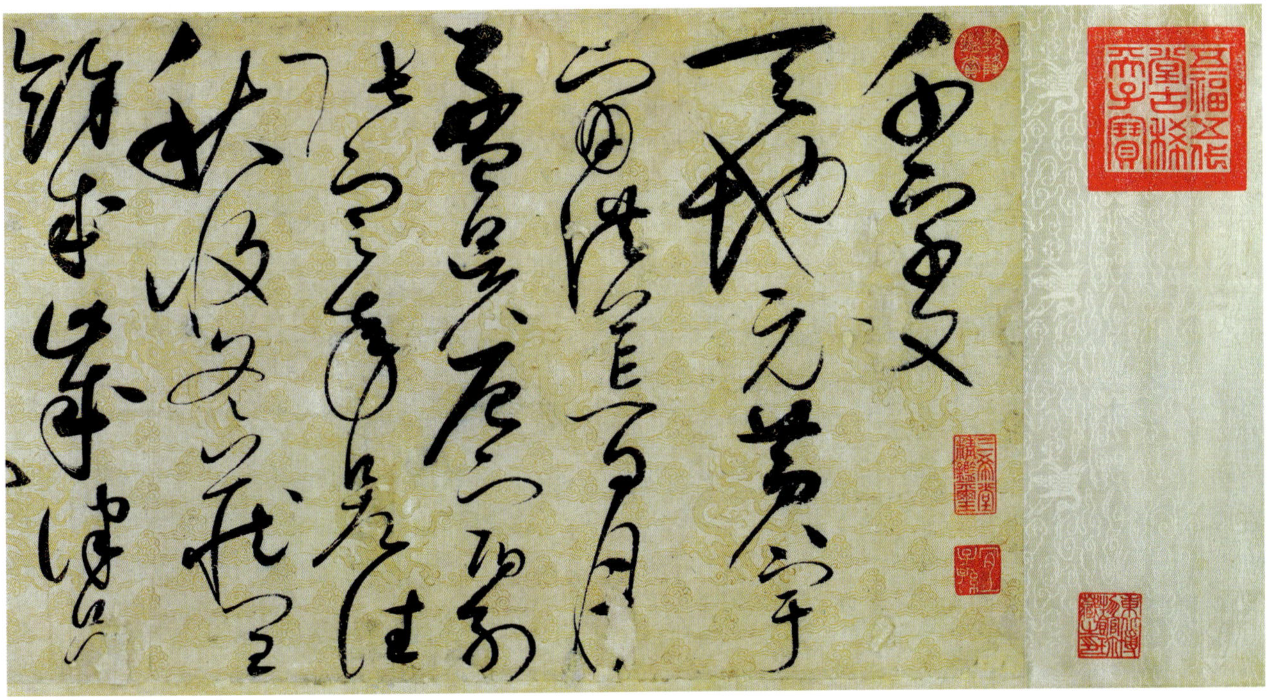

Fig. 6. Zhao Ji (Emperor Huizong; 1082–1135), Front section of *Thousand-Character Essay*. Handscroll. Ink on painted-gold cloud and dragon paper. Liaoning Provincial Museum
北宋，宋徽宗赵佶，千字文（书卷之首），手卷，描金云龙笺纸本水墨，辽宁省博物馆

collection for the students to view and copy, a routine activity known as "a study session." Examinations in which "paintings are matched to poems" were also held, not only promoting an abundance of rich literary flavor in paintings but also greatly enriching the artists' self-cultivation. The emperor himself also commented on the paintings' weak and strong points, sharing his own experiences with observation and realism in painting.[54] A large number of painting masters gathered at his court and produced the "Xuanhe style," blending the skills of realistic painting with a poetic appearance. His "Xuanhe Academy," therefore, became the pinnacle of Chinese court academies, hailed in the annals of China's dynastic history. The works produced by these court artists added substantially to the court collection; at the same time, Huizong himself, in his supreme capacity as emperor, resorted to all possible means to search for important works of painting and model calligraphy all over the nation, resulting in a hundred-fold increase in the number of items in the court collection. During the Xuanhe era, the emperor ordered the compilation of the *Xuanhe shupu* (Xuanhe calligraphy catalogue) and the *Xuanhe huapu* (Xuanhe painting catalogue), monumental records that documented items in the imperial collection at that time, including 1,248 scrolls of model calligraphy from the period of the Wei-Jin dynasties (220–317) and 6,396 paintings of famous artists, beginning with Cao Buxing of Wu in the Three Kingdoms period and running through the Jin dynasty up to Huang Jucai of the Northern Song—a total amount of 7,644 scrolls. This amount did not include works by Zhao Ji himself or works of the artists at the academy. Had these works been included in the catalogue, the number would be over ten thousand. This was the third peak for China's imperial art collection.

The Jin people from the north, who were Jurchens, rose to power and soon forced the ruling Zhao family of the Song dynasty to flee south across the Yangzi River, where it established a remnant court as the Southern Song dynasty in remote Lin'an (Hangzhou). When order was temporarily restored, the Southern Song court started to collect famous paintings and model calligraphy dispersed from the previous capital, Bianliang (present-day Kaifeng), during the chaos. They also traded with the Jin occupiers in an effort to retrieve some of the works, but restoring the previous Xuanhe collection to its original level seemed an impossible task.[55] Zhao Gou (Emperor Gaozong, r. 1127–62) himself claimed that "since the establishment of this court, appraisal and identification of genuine works of art have been carried out, and all important

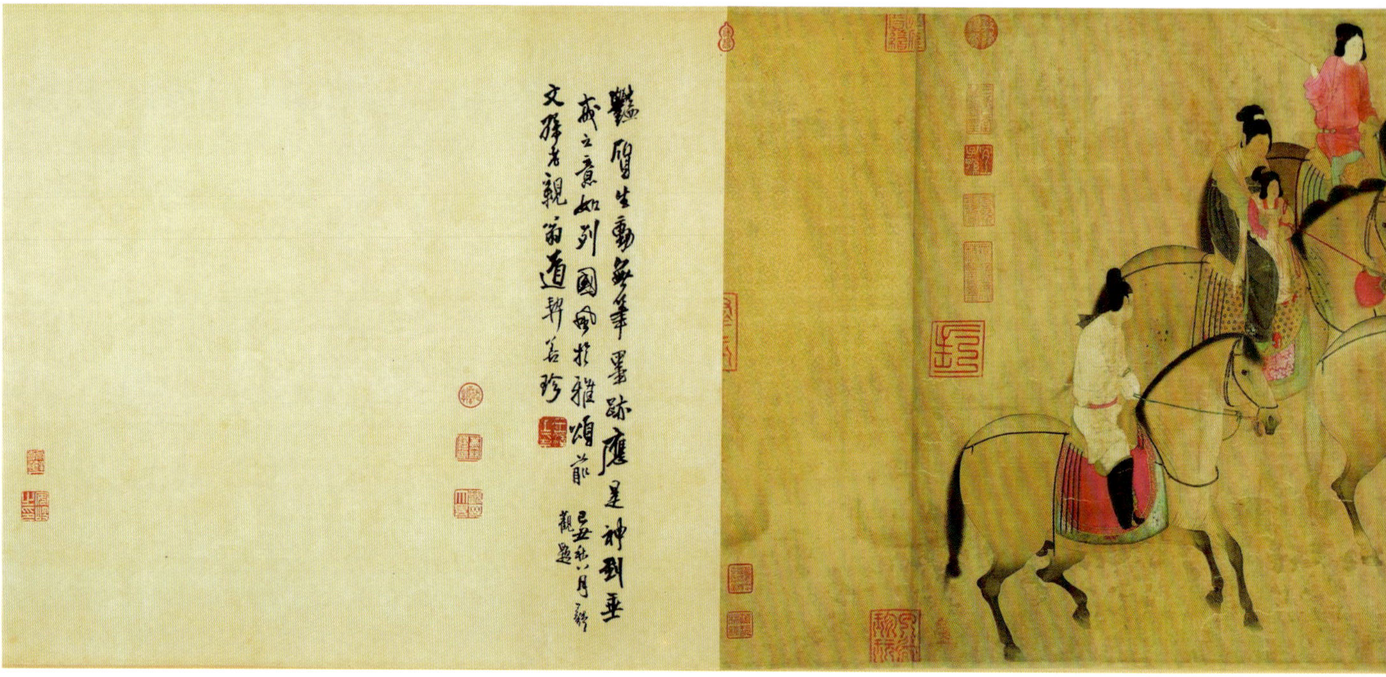

remains of model calligraphy have been returned to the court. My predecessor had made visits of acquisition, rewards of gold, silk, or high ranks have been given, and envoys have been dispatched for negotiation; a lot has been done."[56] However, according to Yang Wangxiu, the head librarian of the Imperial Library during the Qingyuan era of the Southern Song dynasty who wrote *Zhongxing guange chucang tuhua ji* (Record of the paintings stored in the Song dynasty Zhongxing Guange hall), the Southern Song court only had some 1,098 important scrolls dating back to the Wei-Jin, representing about only one eighth or one ninth of the total Northern Song imperial collection of famous paintings.[57]

Jin and Yuan Dynasties—Wanyan Jing (Emperor Zhangzong of Jin); Tugh Temür (Emperor Wenzong of Yuan); Princess Sengge Ragi

Rising to power from the banks of the Songhua River, the Jurchens established the Jin dynasty and, upon defeating the Northern Song dynasty, occupied the northern territories of China to remain a formidable threat to the passive Southern Song dynasty in Hangzhou. The Jurchens, however, were not that impressed with the famous paintings and model calligraphy that they had looted from the Northern Song capital at Kaifeng. Some were traded back through the Southern Song negotiators and some were kept for the Jin court, where they remained until the time of Wanyan Jing (1168–1208), the Jin dynasty emperor Zhangzong. Wanyan Jing's mother was the daughter of Zhao Ji, the Song emperor Huizong. Therefore, Wanyan Jing was influenced by Han Chinese culture, which was deeply instilled in him since childhood. He was also proficient in Chinese literature, calligraphy, and painting. During his reign (1190–1208), he ordered officials to seek out for purchase the paintings and calligraphic works dispersed from the Xuanhe court collection, and those who were not willing to part with the items were required to lend them to the court for duplication; the owners were paid half the offered price as a fee when the work of art was returned. In 1192 (the 1st year of Mingchang), he ordered the compilation of the *Pindi fashu minghua ji* (Record of model calligraphy and famous paintings), a project of some 550 volumes compiled by both Wang Tingyun and Zhang Rufang. Famous masterworks that had been viewed by the emperor often carried his inscriptions, rendered in a style of calligraphy similar to that of Huizong's "slender gold."[58] His inscriptions are found on such extant works as *Lady Guoguo on a Spring Outing* (*Guoguo furen youchun tu*; fig. 7) and *Ladies Pounding Silk* (*Daolian tu*).[59]

Rising out of the steppes, the Mongols established the Yuan dynasty after eliminating the Jin and conquering the Southern Song dynasty. The Yuan court collection was largely indebted to the foundation laid by Kublai Khan (1215–1294), and much of that collection had belonged to the Southern Song court. In 1276,

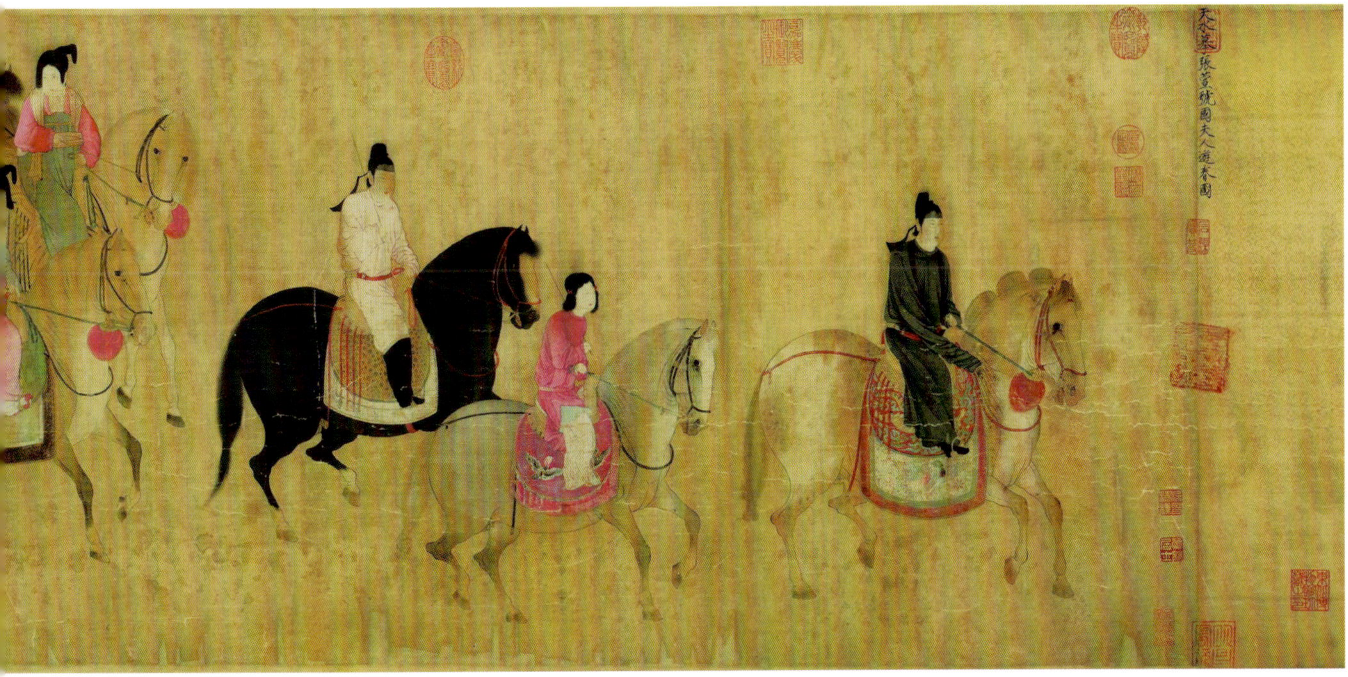

Fig. 7. Attributed to Zhao Ji (Emperor Huizong; 1082–1135), Copy after Zhang Xuan's (713–755) *The Spring Party of Lady Guoguo*, Northern Song dynasty (960–1126). Handscroll. Color on silk. Liaoning Provincial Museum
北宋，传宋徽宗，摹张萱虢国夫人游春图，手卷，绢本设色，辽宁省博物馆

the Yuan general Bayan (1236–1295) led his troops into Lin'an and quickly sealed the court collections and confiscated the books (*tushu*) of the official archives and ritual temples.[60] Although the acquisition of paintings and calligraphic works from the Southern Song court collection was not total, it was not an insignificant quantity. By 1277, according to an estimate by Jiao Qing'an, a court mounter, as many as 1,009 scrolls needed to be re-mounted.[61] With the addition of the Jin court collection, which was acquired and stored in the Wanyi warehouse in the Yuan capital Dadu (present-day Beijing), the paintings gathered from both south and north China and cared for by the Imperial Library, and what was purchased from all sources, the magnificent Yuan court collection was formed.[62] It boasted some 2,008 works of calligraphy and 1,556 scrolls of painting.[63]

Since the early years of the Yuan dynasty, when Kublai Khan (Emperor Shizu) had advocated the learning of the Chinese language, the practice of calligraphy became the most basic cultural requirement. Consequently, the Yuan emperors were all influenced by Han culture, showing respect for the wise; they also gradually developed a strong interest in the art of painting and calligraphy. In 1272 Kublai Khan set up the Imperial Library to administer books and ritual objects. Among his successors, Emperor Renzong (Ayurparibhadra, r. 1311–20) loved painting, treating such southern artists as Zhao Mengfu and Wang Zhenpeng with courtesy. In 1318 he organized a party for viewing Wang Xizhi's *Timely Clearing after Snowfall Calligraphy Model-book* (*Kuaixue shiqing tie*) and asked Zhao Mengfu and others to add colophons. Emperor Renzong took no pleasure in amusements or pearls and jewels but was "conversant with antiquity and esteemed culture," a characteristic greatly admired by his ministers.[64]

Admiration for Han culture during the Yuan dynasty led to the emergence of a rare female connoisseur, the sister of Emperor Renzong, Princess Sengge Ragi (ca. 1283–1331). After her husband died in 1310, she never remarried, apparently turning her attention to collecting. She collected jades, but of particular importance is her collection of paintings and calligraphy. In 1311 Renzong conferred on her the title of "Imperial Sister." The two seals, "Huangzi tushu" (Imperial Sister's pictures and books) and "Huangzi zhenwan" (Imperial Sister's curios), that appear on the works of art she had owned were most likely placed after the year 1311.[65] In 1323, the imperial sister convened a rare and historic gathering of some 20 to 30 literati talents in Dadu at the

Tianqing Temple, to the south of the city, for the viewing of her collection. There were extremely rare pieces and all the participants celebrated the event with poems and inscriptions. According to Yuan Jue (1266–1327), who was one of the participants, there were forty works of model calligraphy, religious paintings, and paintings of figures and beasts as well as flowers and birds and ink bamboo on display. Among them were works by such famous artists as Huizong, Zhou Fang, Juran, Yan Wengui, and others from the Tang to Song dynasties as well as the contemporary (Yuan) artist Wang Zhenpeng.[66]

Collecting and appreciating painting and calligraphy became a most common practice in the imperial family during the reign of Tugh Temür, the Yuan emperor Wenzong (r. 1328–32). The greatest proponent of art among the Yuan emperors, and the most refined, Wenzong could himself also wield a brush to paint, and his calligraphy is frequently seen in collections of Yuan colophons. The accomplishment most indicative of his dedication to art was Kuizhang Ge studio, which was established in 1329 (the 2nd year of Tianli). It was located to the west of the Taiyechi pool in the imperial garden, in the approximate vicinity of the White Pagoda (Baita) in the Beihai district of present-day Beijing. Although the studio had only three rooms, the collected items had to be of classic beauty and taste or they would not be admitted. Decorated like study rooms, the studio housed the best paintings and calligraphic works of the Yuan imperial collection and were staffed by the most knowledgeable art scholars of the time (see fig. 8). Emperor Wenzong made frequent visits there to view painting and calligraphy and to discuss them with the scholars. And often, when the creative mood struck, he would even pick up the brush to write in the studio and bestow the calligraphic works on his officials as gifts. The Kuizhang Ge studio also instituted academic posts and gave degrees in art. A grand scholar degree at the studio was for a civil official of the second rank, a very high position in an era where all officials were distinguished by a total of only nine ranks, with the ninth being the lowest rank.

Renowned Yuan dynasty master painter Ke Jiusi started at the studio as an advisor; he was promoted to doctor of appraisal the following year on the twenty-fifth day of the first month and was responsible for the inspection and storage of paintings and calligraphy. The Kuizhang Ge studio lasted eleven years until 1340. Initially built as a place for intimate talks and lengthy discussions between Wenzong and his advisors, it remained active as a center of collecting and art appreciation for the Yuan imperial court, even though the untimely death of Wenzong at the early age of twenty-nine resulted in the decline of its activities. According to Fu Shen in his *Yuandai huangshi shuhua shoucang shilue* (A brief history of the Yuan dynasty imperial fine art collection), there were at least eighty to ninety very important pieces in its collection, a figure based on works with the collection seal of the Tianli era and that of the Kuizhang Ge studio. It is also possible that this figure might be just a fraction of the entire collection. In the period from 1340 to 1341, the emergence of the master Mongol calligrapher Kangli Naonao restored interest in the arts of painting and calligraphy for the Yuan court, and the Kuizhang Ge studio was revived but renamed Xuanwen Ge.

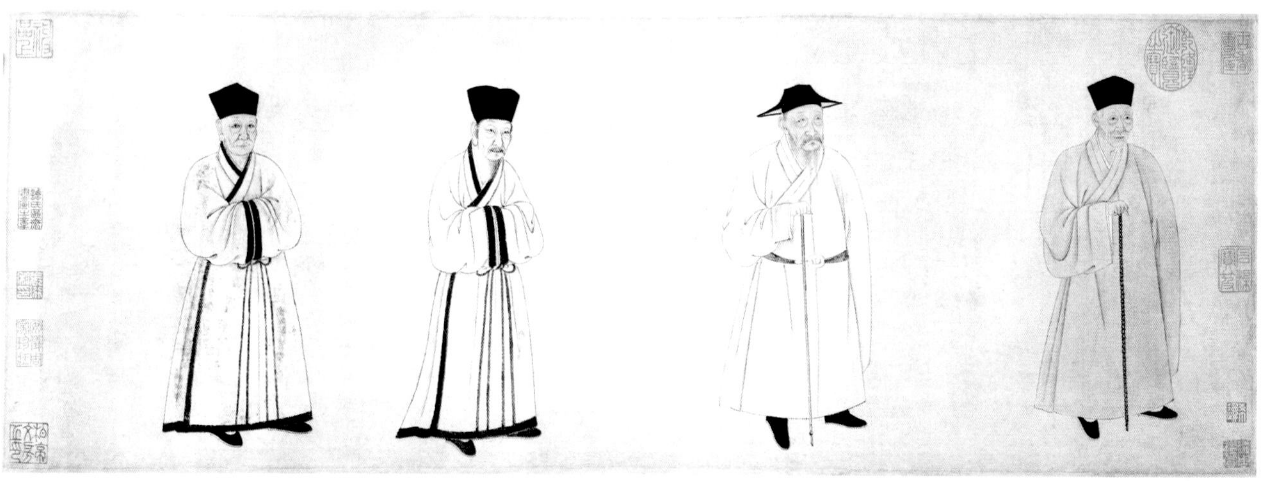

Fig. 8. Anonymous, *Four Scholars of the Yuan dynasty*, Yuan dynasty, ca. 1323–33. Handscroll. Ink and color on paper. Cincinnati Art Museum (1948.82)
元，佚名，元代四学士像，手卷，纸本水墨设色，美国辛辛纳提艺术博物馆

Together with the Duanben Tang hall, which had been built in 1349 to teach the princes to read and write, it became the place for appreciating calligraphy and painting within the palace until the downfall of the Yuan dynasty.[67]

Ming Dynasty—Zhu Zhanji (Emperor Xuanzong of Ming)

In the peasant uprisings of the late Yuan dynasty, Zhu Yuanzhang (1328–1398), was a novice monk who made a living by begging and miraculously became a monarch in the middle of the chaos of war. In 1368, he set up a capital at Jinling (Nanjing), established the great Ming dynasty, and named his reign period Hongwu. Within the Hongwu court there was an Inspection Department which oversaw cultural relics; because the eunuchs were in charge, every model calligraphy and famous painting that had been captured or handed over as a donation was gathered together and returned to the Inspection Department for safekeeping. The calligraphic works and paintings thus handed down were affixed with the half seal of the Inspection Department in the lower right corner, evidence of having passed through the collection of the early Ming court.[68] Although there is no clear record of an imperial painting academy in the Ming dynasty (except for the Xuande period), the "Renzhi Dian palace, Wuying Dian palace, and the Wenhua Dian palace all carried out the functions of a painting academy, ...taking what is a palace in name and conducting a painting academy in actuality."[69] Around the emperor, there was also no lack of people who loved calligraphy and painting. According to the Qing dynasty *Minghua lu* (A record of celebrated paintings) by Xu Qin, foremost among those who are enumerated as capable of painting in the three hundred years of the Ming dynasty are four emperors and fourteen princes. These four emperors are Zhu Zhanji (Emperor Xuanzong, r. 1426–35), Zhu Jianshen (Emperor Xianzong, r. 1465–87), Zhu Youcheng (Emperor Xiaozong, r. 1488–1505); and Zhu Houzhao (Emperor Wuzong, r. 1506–21).[70]

Xuanzong (1398–1435) is particularly outstanding. He was the grandson that Emperor Chengzu, Zhu Di (1360–1424), had dreamed of, and he was much doted on. Chengzu personally sent his own esteemed minister, the learned monk Yao Guangxiao (d. 1418), to counsel his beloved grandson. Xuanzong was intelligent and industrious and lived up to his grandfather's high expectations. Under the policies enacted when his father succeeded to the throne as Renzong (r. 1424–25), Xuanzong continued to cut the taxes that had burdened the farmers, treated his scholars with respect, put down disorder, and dispersed the military. The benevolent policies of both father and son brought about what is referred to in history as the "Ren Xuan Governance." Historical records document Xuanzong's artistic versatility and his extraordinary attainments in painting: "Xuanzong took care in writing *ci* poems. He was outstandingly good at painting; his landscapes, figures, flowers and birds, and grasses and insects are equally beautiful. His talent is a heaven-endowed skill and not under the control of men. On his paintings, he would usually write the date and the name of the person who is to receive the painting; he would affix the seals 'Guangyun zhibao,' 'Wuyingdian bao,' and 'Yongxi Shiren.'"[71] Not only was Xuanzong the best painter among the Ming emperors, but the Xuande painting academy established during his reign embraced all artists, giving the practice of painting and calligraphy a boost. However, with the exception of what were received as donations or confiscated by bureaucrats, it seems that the imperial collection did not seek out the vestiges of famous painting and calligraphy that had been handed down among the populace, nor were there any other notable achievements in appreciation research. After the Jiajing era (that of Emperor Shizong, Zhu Houming; r. 1522–64), the court went so far as to have offered treasures from their storehouses for sale in exchange for funds when they did not even have enough to pay the army.[72]

Qing Dynasty—the Kangxi Emperor (Xuanye); the Qianlong Emperor (Hongli)

Although ruled by the Manchus, the Qing dynasty (1644–1911) gave rise to two emperors who were extremely interested in Chinese culture. After their consolidation of control over the whole of China, the Qing court became committed to the collection of all Chinese treasures including bronze vessels, stone objects, paintings and calligraphy, *kesi* embroidery, and albums of rubbings. These items were stored at the Forbidden City in Beijing and the vacation palaces in Fengtian (Shenyang), Rehe or Jehol (Chengde), and other imperial resorts, making this last dynasty the richest imperial collector with the largest and most comprehensive collection China had ever seen.

This great enterprise was established by two emperors, Kangxi and Qianlong. Both were extremely drawn to Han culture and understood the importance of sinicization for the consolidation of their rule. The most obvious sinicization criterion was the ability to write Chinese characters and to practice calligraphy and painting. The Kangxi emperor, Xuanye (r. 1662–1722), was immersed in Han culture since childhood

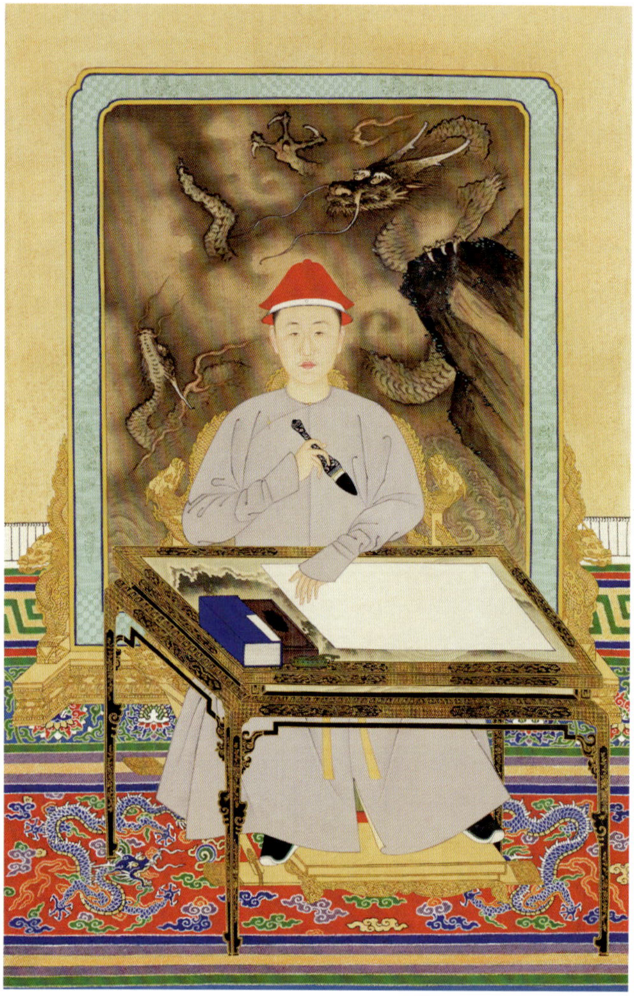

Fig. 9. Anonymous court artists, *Portrait of the Kangxi Emperor in Informal Dress Holding a Brush*, Qing dynasty, Kangxi period (1662–1722). Hanging scroll. Color on silk. Palace Museum, Beijing
清，佚名（宫廷畫家），康熙皇帝便服写字像，立轴，绢本设色，北京故宫博物院

and had a strong interest in painting and calligraphy. Aesthetically he was greatly influenced by Dong Qichang (1555–1636) of the late Ming dynasty, who once theorized that "calligraphy and painting are of great importance; the former conveys ideas, the latter conveys images, and there is nothing greater than the application of both."[73] Not only did Kangxi himself indefatigably follow Dong's calligraphy and painting in all respects, but as a result there were no ministers in his court who did not hasten to emulate him. The general mood was changed at once, and works by Dong and members of his Huating School were therefore collected in large quantities by the court. Gao Shiqi (1645–1703), a court official close to Kangxi whose private collection boasted paintings and calligraphy from many previous dynasties, even had a special catalogue made for works by Dong, revealing one aspect of the prevailing customs of the time.[75] During the Kangxi emperor's sixty-one-year reign, the Qing imperial court had accumulated a considerable number of important paintings and model calligraphy, mostly contributed by ministers and officials. One listing in Gao Shiqi's *Shu hua lu* (Catalogue of painting and calligraphy) specified "works for contribution"; many of these were fakes however. Apparently, there was at that time a lack of qualified court connoisseurs and appraisers for authentication.[76]

The swallowing up of practically all existing important works of painting and model calligraphy by the Qing imperial court was accomplished during the sixty-year reign of Hongli (the Qianlong emperor, r. 1736–95). Not only did Hongli himself practice calligraphy, painting, and poetic composition as daily lessons (see fig. 9),[77] but his enthusiasm for calligraphy and poetry led him to the habit of having his ministers, at all kinds of banquets and gatherings, join him in the game of improvising poems, some of which were permanently carved onto the stone clasps used to tie up slipcases. His enthusiasm even encouraged some of his close court officials to become calligraphers, for example, Zhang Zhao and Liang Shizheng as well as his eleventh son, Yongxin (Prince Cheng), who eventually became an influential Qing calligrapher.[78] By the time of Qianlong's administration, the Qing dynasty had already gone through a period of nearly a hundred years of peace. Since the late Ming and early Qing dynasties, the important paintings and model calligraphy dispersed in the chaos of war had been sought out by collectors among the populace and gradually came to be concentrated in the hands of a few very wealthy families. This was a factor in the formation of Hongli's imperial collection. Hongli had an obsession for painting and calligraphy as well as a strong desire to own the works, and in his position as the supreme ruler of the nation, he had all the power to do so. All he had to do was issue an order, naming a specific person from whom he expected a donation or setting a purchase price at his own discretion, to gather all of China's important paintings and model calligraphy within the palace walls of a single imperial family. All possible measures were taken by Hongli to bring into his court one after another some of the most important Qing dynasty private collections, such as those of Song Quan and his son Song Luo of Shangqiu, Henan; the one-time minister of Zhending Liang Qingbiao; the Shangdong collector Zhang Xianshan; the Suzhou antique dealer Gui Xizhi; the Weiyang merchant Jiang Mengming; Kangxi's confidant Gao Shiqi; and others. Works of art stored in the Guxiang Shuwu (Ancient Fragrance Library), which belonged to the famous collector An Qi (Yizhou), were all celebrated classics of the Jin, Tang, and Song dynasties and earlier. After mediation by Shen Deqian, a venerable member of the scholar gentry from the Jiangnan region, this substantial collection was acquired in its entirety for the court, adding the most important and finishing touch to the Qing imperial collection of painting and calligraphy. During his reign, the Qianlong emperor made visits to the provinces of the Jiangnan region in search of books for the compilation of the *Siku quanshu* (Comprehensive library of the Four Treasuries), which he had commissioned. He took the opportunity to not only collect a large number of books but also round up more private art collections and bring the new acquisitions back to the Qing court. For instance, some Song and Yuan dynasty paintings and calligraphic works in the collection of the rare-book collector Ji Cangcui and his father, Ji Yinshi, of Taixing, Jiangsu Province, were simply taken away from them by the emperor.[79] At this point, Emperor Hongli had successfully acquired all the famous collections under heaven, with the exception of a few pieces left outside the court. Later additions were sporadic if any. The Qing court thus filled in its art collection with an unprecedented number of important works of painting and model calligraphy, which were stored separately at a dozen locations including the Yushufang (Imperial Library) and the Yangxin Dian (Hall of Mental Cultivation). There were about two thousand important Sui, Tang, Song, and Yuan dynasty works of art and another two thousand Ming dynasty works. Including the large number of Qing dynasty works and those by emperors, the total came to more than ten thousand works. China's imperial collection of paintings and calligraphy had reached another peak, which was also its last.

A general survey reveals the following sources for the paintings and calligraphy in China's imperial art collections: court collections inherited from a previous dynasty by the victor of a conflict; tribute received from officials; requisitions by purchase or annexations from private collectors and the general public; and works created by members of the imperial family and court painters. Throughout the course of the last millennium or two, there had been at least four reigns in which the imperial art collection reached a peak—that of the Liang dynasty emperor Yuandi during the Six Dynasties period, the Tang emperor Taizong, the Song emperor Huizong, and the Qing dynasty Qianlong emperor. These works of painting and calligraphy have gone through incredibly rough circumstances; beyond their scattering and reassembling during the military conflagrations accompanying the frequent rise and collapse of dynasties, they have suffered a great deal of calamities, both

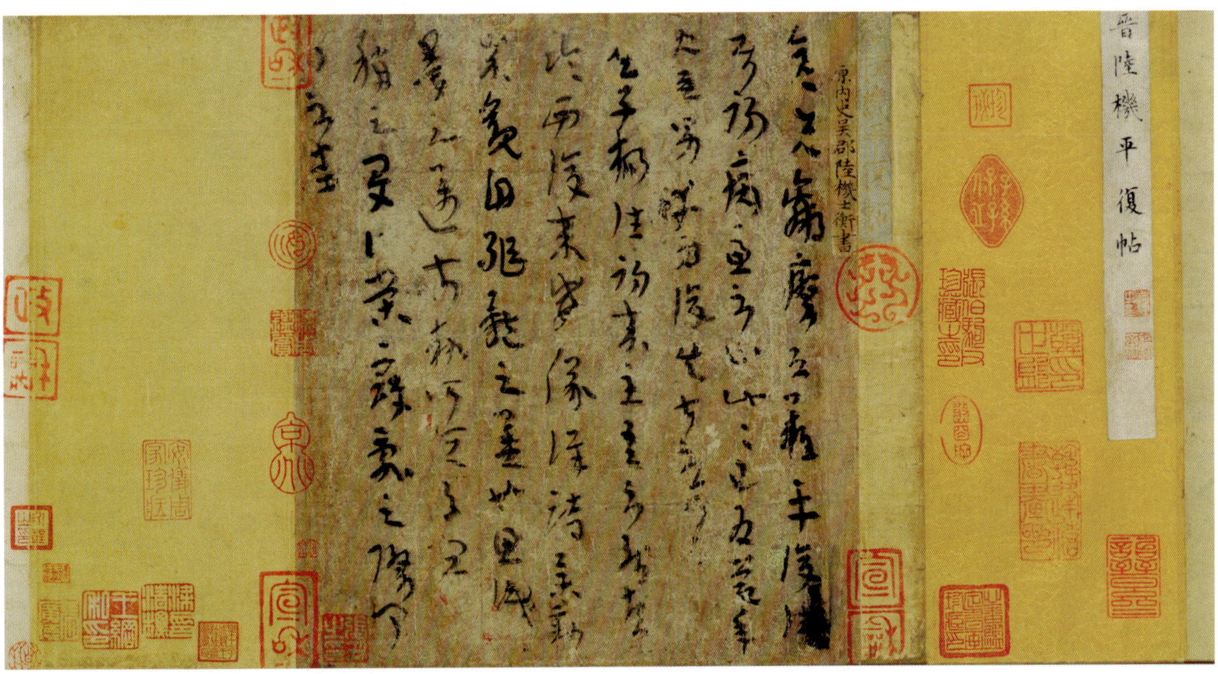

Fig. 10. Lu Ji (261–303), *Pingfu Calligraphy Model-book (Pingfu tie)*. Jin dynasty (265–317). Handscroll. Ink on paper. Palace Museum, Beijing
晋，陆机，平复帖，手卷，纸本水墨，北京故宫博物院

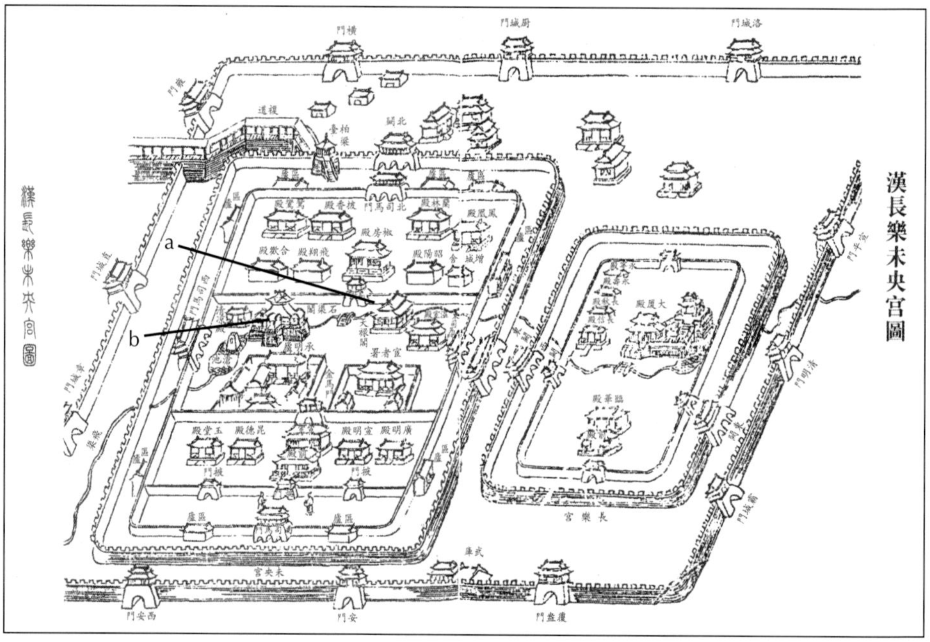

Fig. 11. Diagram of the location of Tianlu (a) and Shiqu (b) Pavilions within the Han palace. After Bi Yuan (1730–1797), *Guanzhong Shengji Tuzhi* (Xi'an: Sanqin chubanshe, 2004), p. 117
天禄(a)、石渠(b)阁在汉宫的位置图，参考清代毕沅撰《关中胜迹图志》（西安，三秦出版社，2004），第117页。

intentional and unpredictable. According to Mr. Yang Renkai, there have been at least seven great tragedies in the history of China's art collection, beginning with the Six Dynasties and Song periods, during which numerous works of art have been dispersed or lost to fire, water damage, and war.[80] The dispersal of the imperial collections was also due to the frequent bestowal of gifts, for example, as dowries, birthday presents, and rewards to distinguished imperial relatives and favored officials. All of these were common occurrences. In the last-mentioned type of dispersal, for example, the Qing emperors frequently and randomly picked works that did not carry the two royal seals "Shiqu baoji" and "Baoji chongbian" for gifts to princes and ministers.[81] Towards the end of the Qing dynasty, this became a routine practice. One of the earliest scrolls in the former Qing court collection and now in the Palace Museum, Beijing, is what remains of the original model calligraphy known as *Pingfu tie* (fig. 10) by the Western Jin dynasty master Lu Ji (261–303), which was given away as a gift before the time of the last emperor, Puyi (r. 1909–11). Fortunately, this work was acquired by the art collector and famous late Qing-early Republican period poet and collector Zhang Boju (1898–1982) for a huge sum of money, and it was able to remain in China.[82]

The imperial art collection suffered its saddest fate during the late Qing period, as China's last imperial dynasty moved towards its demise. First, the Allied Forces of the Eight Western Powers ransacked and burned the Yuanming Yuan imperial gardens. Then the collection was further depleted by the last emperor, Puyi, in the form of rewards to his brother Pu Jie. In a period of some 140 days from September 1922 to January 1923 (the 13th day 7th month to the 12th day 12th month, 14th year of Xuantong), Pu Jie was awarded 1,313 items, including paintings, calligraphy, and rare books. Among them, 216 items were volumes and sets of rare books of the Song dynasty, and 1,097 items were paintings and calligraphic works in scroll and other formats. In the very first month, these awards were mainly books. Starting from November 16, 1922, however, the gifts became mainly paintings and calligraphic works. The items were being transported out of the Forbidden City at a rate of twenty to thirty pieces per day everyday.[83] Thus, what was once kept under the same roof as part of China's imperial collection drifted from place to place and scattered to the ends of the earth to be acquired one after another by private collectors and museums all over the world.

II. The Management, Connoisseurship, and Cataloguing of China's Imperial Art Collection

1. Storage Departments and Personnel

Throughout the dynasties, China's imperial painting and calligraphy collection had always been stored within the inner palace. Records of this practice from the Han to the Six Dynasties period can be found in the *Suishu jingji zhi* (Sui Annals – Chronicles of classics and books): "During the Han dynasty, classics and books were stored at the Tianlu Ge

[Heavenly Emolument] pavilion. During the Guangwu Restoration, the Shishi [Shiqu, or Stone Channel; fig. 11] and Lan Tai [Orchid] pavilions were packed with books. New collections had to be housed in the Dongguan Ge and Renshou Ge pavilions. When the Wei supplanted the Han, books were stored at three buildings located in or outside the Mishu (Department of Secretaries). Illustrations were also stored there. By the Eastern Jin, pictures and books were stored at the Mi Ge (Secure or Secret Pavilion), Wenhua Dian hall, and Hualin Yuan compound (which housed Buddhist texts and reference books)."[84] After that, the Sui dynasty emperor Yangdi built the Miaokai Tai (Excellent Model) and Baoji Tai (Treasured Paintings) pavilions behind the Guanwen Dian hall in the East Capital (Luoyang) to store paintings and calligraphy.[85] In the Tang dynasty, buildings that housed the imperial collection were called *tianfu* (celestial house), *yufu* (imperial house), or *neiku* (court storage),[86] whereas actual management was performed by the Jixianyuan (House of the Virtuous), the Hanlin Academy, and Hongwenguan (Office for the Promotion of Letters).[87]

In 988 (the 1st year of Duangong) during the Song dynasty, Emperor Taizong established at the center of the Chongwen Yuan (Compound of Literary Studies) a Mi Ge pavilion, where a selected collection of some ten thousand books were stored for imperial use.[88] The Mi Ge was an impressive edifice known at the time as the Wooden Tower of Heaven.[89] Several thousand pieces of treasured calligraphy and ink originals were housed in the Chunhuazhong Ge pavilion. Additional storage locations inside the palace included the three pavilions Tianzhang Ge, Longtu Ge, and Baowen Ge as well as the library of the inner garden. They rivaled the Tianlu Ge and Shiqu pavilions, which were the painting and calligraphy storage facilities of the Han dynasty palace, and the Miaokai and Baoji towers of the Sui dynasty.[90] The Southern Song imperial painting and calligraphy collection was stored in the Mi Ge pavilion within the palace; it was administered by the Mishu, or Department of Secretaries, and the official position of Superintendent of Secretaries was established to manage the department. The Zhongxingguan Ge pavilion is regarded as one of its storage places.[91]

The imperial painting and calligraphy collection was managed throughout the Yuan dynasty by the Department of Secretaries, which was established in 1272 (the 9th year of Zhiyuan) and had four officials of the third rank with a staff of six workers. There was a position of "senior painting and calligraphy appraiser" earlier in the staffing. No works of art were allowed to be taken out of the department without the permission of the emperor or the supervisor.[92] During the reign of the Yuan emperor Wenzong (1328–1332), the Kuizhang Ge pavilion was established to store antiques, paintings, and calligraphy, and an academy was also set up for the management and connoisseurship of the works of art. Critiques were led by five preeminent scholars who were civil officials of the second rank and had a pay rate of one hundred and one strings of cash and three coins and thirty-three cents plus ten bushels and five pecks of rice. On the staff were "doctors in book appraisal" who specialized in the identification and appraisal of paintings and calligraphy, were civil officials of the fifth rank, and had an honorarium of forty-one strings of cash plus four bushels and five pecks of rice. Each official serving at the Kuizhang Ge pavilion carried with him a special insignia inscribed on one side with three gold characters, *kui*, *zhang*, and *ge*, in seal script and on the other side with the name of the same institution in both Mongolian and Uighur scripts. Carrying such an insignia gave one "unlimited access";[93] it was a symbol of wealth, power, and prestige. By the time of Emperor Shundi (Huizong, r. 1333–68), the Kuizhang Ge pavilion was converted to Xuanwen Ge at the insistence of the great calligrapher Kangli Naonao (1295–1345), but staffing and funding for the institution was much down graded. Positions offered were instructors of literature and doctors of appraisal, which were merely fifth- or sixth-rank officials. This situation lasted till the collapse of the Yuan dynasty.[94]

During the Hongwu reign (1368–98) of the Ming dynasty, the painting and calligraphy collection was kept at the Jichasi (Bureau of Auditing and Investigation) and managed by court eunuchs. Later, during the Xuande reign (1425–35), the places where the Xuande emperor and his painting academy spent much of their time creating paintings and calligraphy and conducting activities of appraisal and connoisseurship were the Wuying Dian (Military Heroism Hall) and Wenhua Dian (Cultural Splendor Hall). However, more research is needed to unveil the details of the imperial art collection during the Ming dynasty.

In the early years of the Qing dynasty, the Neiwufu (Management Authority of Internal Affairs) was reinstalled; it oversaw seven departments, three bureaus, and some fifty institutions, all catering to the needs of the imperial household and the court staff.[95] According to the *Shiqu baoji chubian* (First compilation of the Treasured boxes of the Stone Channel), paintings and calligraphic works were stored at fourteen separate locations out of concern for possible hazards such as palace fire and to ensure that the treasures wouldn't be ruined all at once or vanish from one location.[96] The Yushufang, or Imperial Library, had the largest concentration of artwork in its storage, constituting thirteen out of the total number of volumes in the *Shiqu baoji* catalogue. The next largest concentration was the Qianqing Gong (Palace of Heavenly Purity) collection and the equally large collection at the Yangxin Dian hall, each of which constituted nine volumes. Next in size was the collection at the Chonghua Gong (Palace of Double Glory), amounting to eight volumes. The collections at the Sanxi Tang (Studio of Three Rare Treasures), the Xueshi Tang (Hall for Learning from the Odes), and the Huachan Shi (Zen of Painting Studio) constituted one volume each, as did those at the Changchun Shuwu (Everlasting Spring Study), the Suian Shi (Ease and Peace Studio), and the Youyu Zhai studio. Elsewhere, the collections of the Cuiyun Guan hall and the Shufang Zhai, the Jingyi Xuan, and the Sanyou Zhai studios together constituted one volume.[97] At the time of the second compilation of the *Shiqu baoji,* more works of art were collected and stored at such places as the Xi Yuan, the Yuanming Yuan, and the Changchun Yuan gardens, and the Three Mountains.[98]

Those involved with the painting and calligraphy collection included the Ruyiguan (Ruyi Design Studio) and the Xiabiaozuo (Joinery and Mounting Workshop), both under the management of the Zaobanchu (Department of Imperial Workshops), which had been established inside the Yangxin Dian hall early in the Kangxi reign. Also involved was the Yushuchu (Imperial Press), which was responsible for the tracing, carving, rubbing, and printing of imperial manuscripts and masterpieces of calligraphy and had under its management the Kezizuo (Character-carving Workshop), the Biaozuo (Mounting Workshop), the Mokezuo (Inkstick-carving workshop), and the Mozuo (Ink-making Workshop). All the painting and calligraphy storage facilities were under the Neiwufu, and each location had a manager of varying bureaucratic status who was compensated according to his rank. For example, at the Imperial Library, which had most of the artwork, there was one head keeper who was an eighth-rank eunuch-in-waiting with a monthly pay of four silver ingots and four *hu* of rice, plus a compensation of seven coins and thirty-three cents. The rest of the twelve eunuch staff members were each paid a monthly salary of two silver ingots and one and a half *hu* of rice plus a compensation of six coins and sixty-six cents. Their job was to collect and store books, paintings, and calligraphy as well as to perform other duties related to the safe keeping of the works, such as house cleaning and guard duty.[99] Most of them were, however, petty officials of the eighth rank or no rank at all. Such a system persisted until the Jiaqing reign, well into the final decline of the Qing dynasty, when the *Guochao gongshi* (History of the imperial courts) was compiled.[100]

2. Management of the Imperial Painting and Calligraphy Collection

1) Conservation of Painting and Calligraphy

The safe keeping of paintings and calligraphy requires storage free of excessive humidity yet with adequate ventilation. For this purpose, boxes and containers made of wood, bamboo, and rattan have been used. This is a time-honored practice. The Tang dynasty writer Zhang Yanyuan (b. ca. 815) mentions, for example, that the paintings and calligraphy in his family collection were stored in suitcases of plaited bamboo.[101] For extra protection, the treasured items can be bagged in silk sleeves.[102] Another important measure for the conservation of artwork in ancient times was the annual airing of books and scrolls during hot, sultry summer days, a practice that had begun as early as the Southern Dynasties (420–589). Tang dynasty records indicate that Empress Wu Zetian (r. 690–704) had her courtiers air out the paintings and calligraphic works at the Yisui Dian hall.[103] It was also an annual routine for the Mi Ge pavilion of the Song court to air out its collection of books and scrolls during *futian* (hot summer period).[104] Another measure was to place among the books and scrolls aromatic herbs such as common jasmine orange (*Murraya paniculata*), sweet-flag (*Acorus calamus*), and angelica root (*Angelicae dahuricae*), all of which are insect repellent.[105] Records also show that the court of the Jin dynasty emperor Zhangzong (r. 1190–1208) began to use sandalwood scroll rollers for the paintings and calligraphy in the court collection, because it was found that "sandalwood is moisture proof, and the use of sandalwood rollers has great benefits; when the box is opened there is a pleasant aroma instead of a moldy smell, and insects have been repelled."[106]

2) Mounting of Paintings and Calligraphy and the Imperial Formats

Ever since the Eastern and Western Jin dynasties (281–420), the mounting of paintings and calligraphy has been a specialized profession. According to written records, the use of teal-green silk twill and hawksbill turtle-shell knobs were distinctive mounting features of the Liang dynasty (502–589; ruled by the Xiao family) imperial collection.[107] Different mounting materials were used depending on the class ranking of the individual paintings and calligraphic works. Those mounted with hawksbill turtle-shell knobs, woven ribbons, and jade pins with gilt characters, as well as some additionally mounted with red sandalwood (Pterocarpus santalinus) rollers, were first-class calligraphic works. Some second-class calligraphic works were also mounted with red sandalwood rollers, and those of still lower classes were finished with lacquered knobs.[108]

There was an established system for the mounting of works in the imperial collection during the Tang dynasty. The official in charge of mounting and finishing in the mid-Zhenguan era (627–649) was Chu Suiliang (596–ca. 658). Works mounted during the Zhenguan and Kaiyuan reigns all uniformly had white sandalwood (Symplocos paniculata) rollers finished with red sandalwood knobs, and purple silk gauze mounting fabric and woven ribbons were distinctive features of the official mounting format.[109] Mounting techniques saw greater refinement during the reign of Empress Wu Zetian. Interestingly, some officials in charge of hiring skilled craftsmen to restore masterpieces for the court in this period replaced the originals with copies, sending back the fakes and keeping the originals for themselves. This might have been the earliest known record of such a deplorable practice.[110]

The following mounting features were observed in the court of the Southern Tang emperor Li Houzhu (r. 960–975): "The mounting fabrics include dark brocades woven with designs of large or small reverting phoenixes, cranes among clouds, and flycatchers. Woven ribbons are used for tie strings and yellow sutra papers for title labels on most scrolls. The names of the mounting finisher and supervisor are often written on the back of the scroll, along with indications of the work's class ranking. Also *chengxintang* paper is available for the use of famous people in their calligraphy and paintings."[111]

Works of painting and calligraphy that had been in the imperial collection of the Song dynasty Xuanhe (1119–25) court can be identified by their uniform mounting formats: they use either *kesi* silk tapestry or silk brocades with archaic motifs for the wrapping section of the scroll. The *kesi* fabric or brocade come in various colors; the *geshui* divider panels (left and right margins) are fine yellow silk tabby; and for the colophon space at the end section, Korean spun-silk paper is used.[112] According to the Southern Song emperor Gaozong's (r. 1127–62) recollection, the treasured pieces in the Northern Song court collection were mounted using white coral knobs and had the three seals "Daguan," "Zhenghe," and "Xuanhe"; one of these seals was carved in the Qin dynasty small seal script. He further recalls that the back of the scrolls had descriptive titles and class rankings, all hand inscribed by the emperor, and that works of lower ranking were stored in the *waimi*, or "outer confidential house."[113] Elsewhere it is observed that "for the title labels on the mounting, Emperors Huizong (r. 1101–25) of the Song and Zhangzong of the Jin dynasty both preferred cobalt-blue paper and titles written in gold pigment for a spectacular contrast. Their second choice was Jinshu Temple sutra paper."[114]

Dynastic changes have certainly left their marks on presentation formats; in some cases the new acquisitions were entirely remounted. That was the case for the Southern Song imperial collection during the Shaoxing reign (1131–62), when the court developed its own standard mounting formats and conventions for the placement of seals. Regardless of their original mounting formats, newly acquired works from various previous dynasties were all remounted for the sake of uniformity before they were admitted into the court collection. This undoubtedly inflicted great damage on the works of art.[115] The Song dynasty painting and calligraphy connoisseur Zhou Mi had detailed accounts of these practices in his *Qidong yeyu* (Unofficial anecdotes from Eastern Qi), in which he devotes an entire chapter to "Mounting formats of the Shaoxing Imperial Court." His documentation preserves information on the mounting style of the Southern Song dynasty court—the various mounting materials used for different works according to their class ranking, the determination of dimensions, and the conventions of seal placement. He tells us, for instance, about the mounting of "original masterpieces beyond rating, such as ink originals from both Han dynasties, the Three Kingdoms, the two Jin dynasties, the Six Dynasties, the Sui and Tang dynasties, and works by emperors and ministers. (These, together with works that have imperial inscriptions and are marked with the character *miao* [excellent]), are mounted in *kesi* or brocades with architectural motifs or green brocades with reed-mat patterns. The frontispiece section is finished using self-patterned white twill with pheasants among ginger-shaped cloud motifs. Korean silk paper is used for the colophon space at the end...Seals placed in the heading section include 'neifu tushu' [pictures and calligraphy of the court] and 'neidian shuji' [inner palace literary property]. Inscriptions can also be left in this section. The seal 'yufu tuji' [imperial house pictures and books] is used on seams, and the seal 'Shaoxing' is to be found at the very end. After all that, the scroll is handed over to Mi Youren [1074–1151] to be identified, who then personally inscribes his evaluations in the colophon space towards the end of the scroll."[116]

Modeled after the Northern Song dynasty court, the Jin dynasty court also set up a system of its own for the mounting of its art collection. The title labels were removed, the wrapping sections were replaced, and the frontispieces, colophons, and seals were remounted into Jin formats. The following seals are found on the margin areas and colophon spaces: "Mingchang baowan," "yufu baohui," "neidian zhenwan," "Mingchang," "Mifu," "Qunyuzhongmi," and "Mingchang yujian."[117] The Yuan dynasty court did not have a distinctive mounting format of its own for its collection.

There are detailed records for the mounting of the Ming painting and calligraphy collection. In his *Huishi beikao* (Reference for painting related topics), Wang Yuxian of the Qing dynasty documents the following: "[Mounting] formats after the Xuanzong emperor of Ming became very sophisticated in form and elegant in taste. Not only did the imperial court use jade clips with gilt characters on works that were much more elaborately mounted than any of the preceding dynasties, scholars families in general also had carefully designed and crafted mounting formats." Wang goes on to describe how works on paper and silk were treated with different techniques. Proportionally, large pieces and small scrolls all have their respective and specified size ratios for tops, bottoms, and sides. Works done on a full sheet of rice paper, for example, were mounted with a three-inch top divider and a two-inch bottom divider.[118]

The Neiwufu of the Qing court had under its administration the Zaobanchu, or Department of Imperial Workshops, which employed a staff of 594 people during the Kangxi reign. This department was greatly expanded during the Qianlong period. Its joinery and framing workshops were among those responsible for the mounting of painting and calligraphy in the imperial collection.[119] After his close examination of the actual works in the Qing imperial collection, Yang Renkai summarized his observations on the various aspects of mounting as follows: "Vertical scrolls are bagged in silk sleeves. Handscrolls are wrapped in custom-made silk wrapping cloths of light yellow or light green patterned twill with white satin lining. On the outside of each wrapping cloth is identification information, such as the title of the wrapped work of art, name of the artist, year, class ranking, and so forth. Besides that, each work has a white jade clip with relief carving on the front and its title incised on the back and inlaid with gold. The identifying characters on the scroll are identical to those on the outside of the wrapping cloth. Each scroll is kept in a wooden box made of *nanmu* (*Phoebe nanmu*), or South China teak, and each box is custom made according to the size of the scroll. Large standing cabinets made of red sandalwood were used for the storage of the works at each location. Some of these cabinets were so tall that they almost reached the ceiling."[120] A study of the Qing dynasty archives can reveal some sporadic but interesting records. For example, the Qianlong emperor preferred the color blue. He often used gold characters on blue paper in his calligraphy (a fashion continued since the reign of Huizong in the Song dynasty), and frequently ordered a one-inch blue silk border when having works of art mounted. He preferred silk textiles from the Suzhou Imperial Weaving Workshop.[121] The above information gives us a general idea of the characteristic features of the painting and calligraphy mountings of the Qing imperial court.

3. IMPERIAL AUTHENTICATION AND CONNOISSEURSHIP

The most obvious records of an emperor's viewing of a work of art are the inscriptions and seals that he would leave on it.

1) The Emperors' Viewing Seals

By the time of the Sui dynasty, no imperial collection seal had yet been found on any work of art. In the Tang dynasty however, "Emperor Taizong (r. 626–49) wrote two small characters, *zhen* and *guan*, and made them into two small seals." This might be the forerunner of what was to become a routine practice of emperors leaving their seals on paintings and calligraphic works. Later, Emperor Xuanzong (r. 712–56) wrote "*kai* and *yuan*, two small characters that were made into one seal."[122] In both instances, the characters were only the reign name and the sizes of seals were small, showing considerable modesty. According to records by Mi Fu (1051–1107), seals during the Zhenguan and Kaiyuan reigns were small, used over the seam lines, and about one inch in size.[123] Since that time, emperors of successive dynasties all had their own collection seals for placement on paintings and calligraphy after viewings. Seal legends can include reign titles and the names of storage locations. The character *bao*, or "treasure," was first used by Emperor Li Houzhu of the Southern Tang dynasty in his seal "Jianye wenfang zhibao" (Treasure of the Jianye Studio). Based on currently available sources, it appears that use of the character *bao* became more frequent in seals after the reign of the Yuan dynasty emperor Wenzong. By the time of the Qing dynasty, expressions often seen in seals were *yulan* (for imperial viewing), *jianshang* (identification and appreciation), and *jiancangxi* (imperial identification and collection seal). In particular, the Qianlong emperor owned an impressive array of these seals, some of them in large sizes, such as "taishang huangdi zhibao" and "bazheng

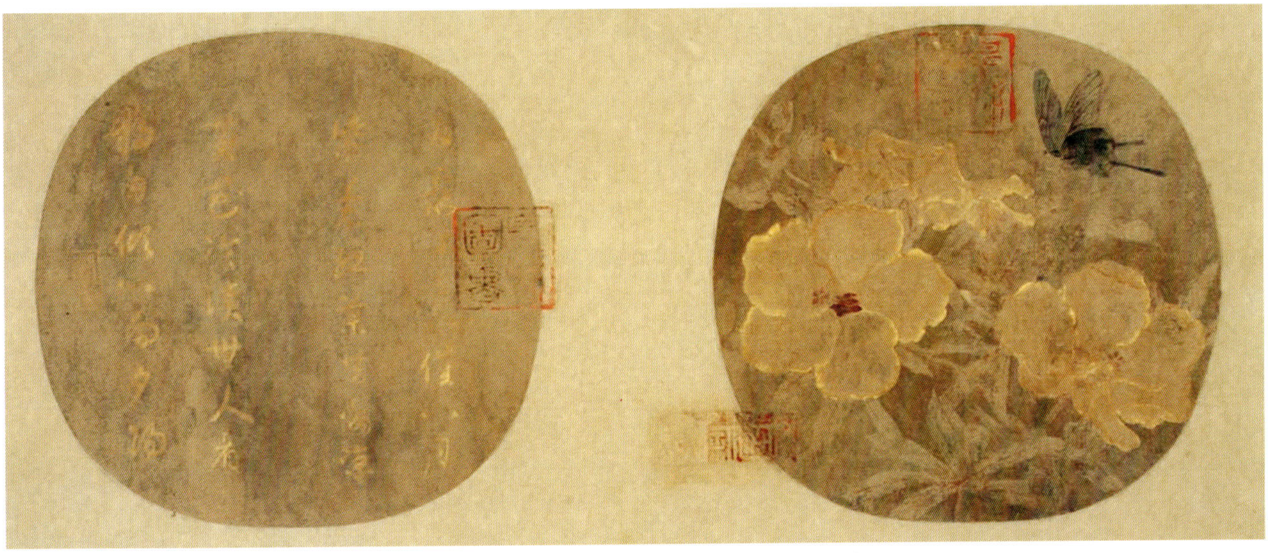

Fig. 12. Zhao Gou (Emperor Gaozong; r. 1127–63), Inscription of poem on *Flower and Butterflies* by an anonymous court artist. Fan. Color on silk. Shandong Provincial Museum
南宋，佚名（宮廷畫家），葵花蛱蝶图，宋高宗题诗，纨扇，绢本设色，山东省博物馆

maonian zhibao," which were made after his abdication. The frequently used identification and collection seals of his five-seal and eight-seal sets were enormous, especially compared to the seals first used by the Tang dynasty emperor Taizong. Indeed, when it comes to the modesty of the initial practice, either in terms of seal quantity or seal size, the two cannot even be mentioned in the same breath. Ruan Yuan, the Qing scholar who had taken part in the compilation of the *Shiqu baoji*, wrote in his *Shiqu suibi* (Notes on the Stone Channel) an entire section, titled "Lun qianbao," on the imperial seals used by the Qing monarchs. He describes in especially great detail the use of seals by the Qianlong emperor, providing a good reference source.[124] See Appendix A in this catalogue for the viewing and connoisseurship seals frequently used by the Qing emperors.

2) Poems and Inscriptions by the Emperors

The imperial practice of adding inscriptions and comments on works of art probably began in the Jin dynasty (265–420). In his *Zhenguan gongsi huashi* (Zhenguan history of paintings in imperial and private collections), Pei Xiaoyuan (act. 627–49) of the Tang dynasty records that inscriptions by the Jin dynasty emperor Mingdi (r. 323–25) and the Liang dynasty emperor Yuandi (r. 552–55) were found on three scrolls (including one titled *Two Capitals* [*Liang jing tu*]) by Yang Xiu of the Wei dynasty (220–65; ruled by the Cao family).[125] According to written records, Li Shimin, the Tang dynasty emperor Taizong, inscribed colophons on the end sections of paintings,[126] and Li Houzhu of the Southern Tang dynasty was probably the first to inscribe poetry on paintings.[127] Imperial inscriptions on paintings reached a climax during the reign of Emperor Huizong in the Song dynasty. Among the paintings recorded in Southern Song sources, there were thirty-one scrolls that had Huizong's inscriptions, most of which were in the form of poems.[128] This has been corroborated by such archeological discoveries as the Song dynasty silk fan decorated with sunflowers and butterflies unearthed in 1972 from the tomb of Zhu Tan (early Ming dynasty) at Zou County, Shandong Province. Gaozong's inscription of a poem was found on the reverse side of the fan (see fig. 12).[129] Emperors and empresses of the Southern Song took delight in this practice and left their inscriptions on works of art that they had viewed. Emperor Ningzong (1195–1224) left inscriptions on Ma Yuan's paintings and his empress, Yang Meizi, also left her inscriptions on many works of art.[130] The Yuan imperial family members were ethnic Mongols who rose from the steppes and could not read Han Chinese characters. Although some, such as Emperor Renzong (r. 1311–20), made some effort to practice calligraphy, they were, however, not ready to inscribe on paintings and calligraphy after viewing them. For that, they would turn to preeminent scholars instead; this practice lasted until the time of the Yuan emperor Yingzong (r. 1321–23).

Therefore, the end sections of paintings and calligraphy that had been in the collection of the Yuan dynasty court often had inscriptions and poems left by scholars, such as Ke Jiusi (1290–1343) and Yu Ji (1272–1348), who served at the Kuizhang Ge pavilion, where the Yuan imperial collection was stored.[131]

Although they were ethnically Manchu, the Qing imperial household's great emphasis on the study of Han culture was unprecedented. Not only were the Jingshan Official School and Xian'an Gong Official School set up within the palace for the children of the Upper Three Banner Army, but official Mongolian schools were also set up for the children of the Mongolian soldiers serving in the Eight Banner Army. It was mandatory for all royal princes to attend the imperial classrooms and to study assiduously.[132] Greatly impressed by the strictness of the imperial household rules imposed on the students as well as by their diligence, a Qing individual named Zhao Yi (1727–1814) exclaimed in praise that even career academicians would find it hard to contend with them. These imperial princes studied from dawn to dusk, day after day. Such unparalleled efforts enabled the Manchus, after their conquest of China, to successfully absorb the essence of Chinese culture and learn the secrets of maintaining both civil administration and military domination, thus securing their role as effective rulers of the Han Chinese population in spite of being an ethnic minority themselves.[133] Most Qing dynasty emperors could write well in Chinese. Of the hundreds of buildings in the palace and the assortment of architectural forms in the gardens, not a single one was left without a fancy name or a poetic reference. And the buildings were more often than not decorated with calligraphic signage originating from the imperial hand. Evidence of the rulers' cultural involvement is overwhelming when one flips through the pages of the *Guochao gongshi* (History of the imperial courts).[134] Other members of the imperial household could also write and paint; they enjoyed viewing works of art and were good at improvising poems and writing colophons. Among them, the Qianlong emperor was notorious for leaving a long trail overflowing with ink works and imperial poetry wherever he traveled. His inscriptions and poems can be found on almost every piece of calligraphy or painting that he had viewed. Sometimes one finds repeated inscriptions from different occasions on a single work. It was a phenomenal feat for one individual, the Son of Heaven ruling over so many (regardless of his level of sophistication and excellence, which is something else yet to be discussed), to have left us with more than forty-eight thousand poems in his lifetime, to have been so obsessed with Chinese art and literature, and to have been so diligently involved in creativity. His prolificacy resulted in the innumerable inscriptions seen on large numbers of extant works, especially on masterpieces which he viewed over and over again and inscribed repeatedly. Once, for example, he had mistaken one landscape scroll by the Yuan dynasty master Huang Gongwang (1269–1354) in the court collection for another and regarded it as the famed *Dwelling in the Fuchun Mountains* (*Fuchunshan ju tu*) mentioned in Dong Qichang's *Huachanshi biji* (Notes from the Zen Painter Studio). He liked it so much that he left a total of fifty-five inscriptions on the work, which he carried with him wherever he traveled—on his inspection tours to the South, on his fall hunting trips to the North, on his excursions to the East, and on his expeditions to the West.[135]

3) Appraisers and Connoisseurs Appointed by the Imperial Court

Appointed appraisers and connoisseurs responsible for the artwork in the imperial court collection often left acknowledgements, inscriptions, and seals on the works they inspected. At an early stage, it was customary for the responsible handler to leave a handwritten signature, known as *yashu* (signing in or acknowledgement), on a work. Probably begun in the Six Dynasties period at the Liu-Song court, this practice continued into the Sui dynasty.[136] In addition to the signature of the handler and conservator, inscriptions with year, month, day, and other information (such as "mounted under imperial order on the [number] day of the [number] month of the [named] year during the reign of Daye [605–617]") as well as other forms of inscription also began to appear.[137] During the Zhenguan reign of the Tang dynasty, the appraisers' official titles, if any, were added along with their handwritten signatures. Two small, round linked seals with the characters *zhen* and *guan* that make up the reign name were also added. These practices persisted into the mid-Kaiyuan period, when a colophon section was added at the end.[138] In some cases, signatures of the previous handlers were cut off and replaced with the signatures and official titles of the new handlers. A small seal with the two characters *kai* and *yuan* was sometimes affixed. Other seals of the period occasionally found on works of art include "Jixian," "Mi Ge," "Hanlin," and "Hongwen," all names of the storage facility or building that housed them, which were probably affixed by the managers of these facilities for identification.[139] The addition of department superintendents' seals and storage location seals to certify works of art was a practice that began in the Tang dynasty and lasted well into the Qing dynasty, when there were more than a dozen storage locations. Thus, in addition to appraisers' seals and those of the emperor, the Qing added the name seals of buildings that housed the collection, such as the Qianqing Gong (Palace of Heavenly Purity) and the Yangxin Dian (Hall of Mental Cultivation).

In the court management system, the *neiku* (court storage) or the *neifu* (inner house) inside the palace was usually the conservatory for paintings and calligraphy and antiquities. Works affixed with the seal "neifu" had most likely been in the collection of the imperial conservatory. The earliest examples of *neifu* seals are those used in the Tang dynasty, like the one found on the *Spring Excursion* (*Youchun tu*; fig. 13) by Zhan Ziqian of the Sui dynasty.[140] This management system and its practices continued into the Qing dynasty, when a work of art was handed into the *neifu* for identification and storage after being acquired by the court.[141] An inspection of the paintings and calligraphy of the former imperial collection in the Liaoning Provincial Museum revealed that some also have a title strip with a "neifu zhencang" (*neifu* collection) mark, indicating that the work was inspected and confirmed by the *neifu*; such a mark is usually accompanied by Qianlong's small, square seal impression reading "Qianlong chenhan" in red characters (see cat. no. 9).

4. Loan Procedures for Works of Art in the Imperial Collection

No significant amount of information has been found on the topic of loan procedures except for the little pamphlet published by the Qing Royal Estates Management Committee titled *Gugong yiyi shuji shuhua mulu si zhong* (Four catalogues of dispersed calligraphy and paintings from the imperial palace). It contains two interesting lists. One is dated to the third month of the *gengshen* year (1920) during the reign of Xuantong and is titled "Rough Log of Books, Calligraphy and Paintings, and Curious Objects Borrowed by Official Members of the Court." The log only lists the date, month, and year an item was borrowed and whether it had been returned or if it was still on loan. Many of the items in the log were works by Emperor Huizong of the Song dynasty, Dong Yuan, and other artists of the same caliber. No names of the handlers were entered. The "List of paintings and calligraphic works on loan" has a notation reading "Record of the Study," which might refer to the Imperial Study. This, too, is a record of works of art on loan to individuals; returns are marked off with a seal reading "shouhui" (returned).[142] This pamphlet may be evidence that the Qing court did allow works of art in its imperial collection to leave the palace on loan, but it does not provide further details on how the loan process worked or was handled. Nor does it give any indication of whether or not such practices or systems had been observed or existed during previous dynasties. More material evidence is needed for further study on this topic.

5. Cataloguing the Paintings and Calligraphy of the Imperial Collection

Writing about the imperial collection of painting and calligraphy was not only a personal hobby of the emperor, but it reflected his high regard for the works of art and his awareness of their importance. The earliest emperor to be seriously involved in this manner might be Xiao Daocheng, the Southern Qi dynasty emperor Gaodi (r. 479–82) in the Six Dynasties period. He wrote some three hundred volumes of art critiques, evaluating various artists and assigning them to different ranks. Unfortunately his writings have not survived. Guo Ruoxu of the Song dynasty recorded that he had once read a book titled *Minghuaji* (Collection of famous paintings), written by Gaodi. However, it cannot be confirmed whether or not he was talking about the same author.[143] Later on, the Liang dynasty emperor Wudi (r. 502–49) ordered his subordinates to compile a catalogue of paintings and calligraphy titled *Liang Taiqing mu* (Art catalogue of Liang Taiqing), which became a must-have reference book for connoisseurs of the Sui and Tang dynasties. Pei Xiaoyuan of the Tang dynasty relied heavily on this text when he wrote his *Zhenguan gong si huashi* (Zhenguan history of paintings in imperial and private collections).[144]

Shortly after he was enthroned, Emperor Huizong told his ministers, "What little leisure time I have in my busy schedule, I take no delight in anything except for painting." Therefore, the imperial collection swelled while his ministers tried to please the monarch by compiling the *Xuanhe Ruilan* (Xuanhe's wise review)—a work of some one thousand five hundred volumes divided into one hundred sleeved stacks—for the convenience of the emperor in viewing the collection whenever he wished.[145]

Later, Emperor Huizong ordered the compilation of the *Xuanhe shupu* (Xuanhe calligraphy catalogue) and the *Xuanhe huapu* (Xuanhe painting catalogue). The emperor's preface is dated to the second year of the Xuanhe reign (1120), but names of the compilers were not recorded. Sponsored by the imperial court and systematically arranged, these two monumental books were the first of their kind. They are major resources in the study, research, and connoisseurship of Chinese painting and calligraphy and

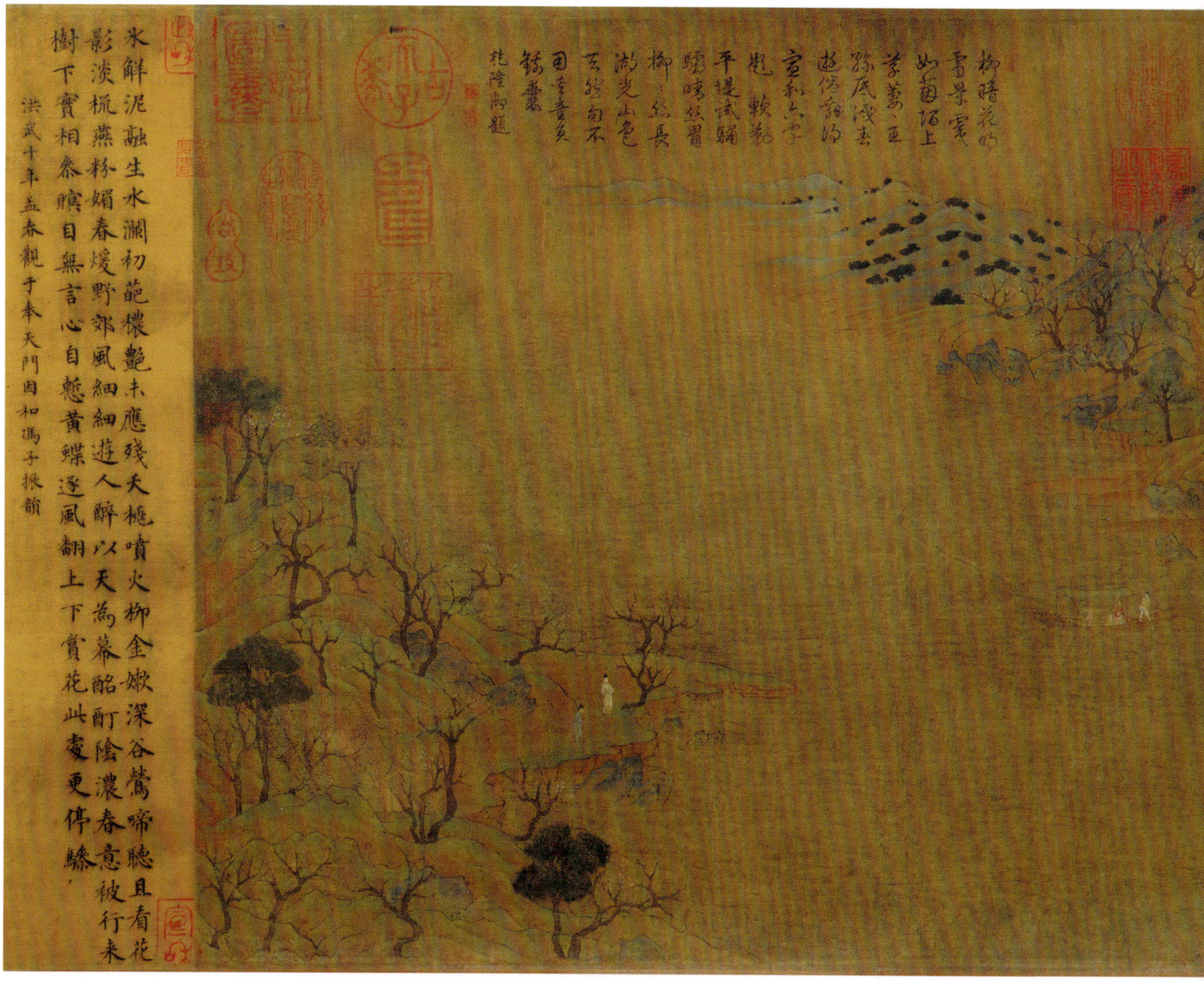

Chinese art history. With regard to early works of Chinese art, especially ones that have since been lost or destroyed, they serve as an archive of what once existed in history and would otherwise never be heard of again. The book provides a concise record of each artist's biographical data, the titles of his or her works, and the number of his or her works in the collection.

The *Xuanhe shupu,* which comes in twelve volumes, documents the calligraphic works in the collection of Huizong's court during the Xuanhe reign. This collection boasted a total of 1,198 works by more than one hundred and ninety calligraphers covering a period from the Han up to the early Song dynasty. The catalogue is divided into the following eight categories: calligraphy by emperors of various dynasties, seal script, clerical script, standard script, running script, cursive script, *bafen* script, and imperial decrees. Explanatory texts precede each of the eight categories and a brief biography of each calligrapher is provided. The works are rated and their styles and lineages explained. The *Xuanhe huapu* consists of twenty volumes and is divided into ten categories according to subject matter, as follows: religious subjects, figures, architecture, foreigners, dragons and fish, landscapes, animals and beasts, flowers and birds, ink bamboo, and fruits and vegetables. It records a total of 6,396 paintings in the court collection by 231 artists beginning from the Six Dynasties period. Introductions and critical essays precede each category, followed by biographies of the artists and then a list of the titles of their works and a total count.

The Qing dynasty saw the ultimate amassing of paintings and calligraphy from all periods in a court collection. Unprecedented attention was also paid to the writing of books and compiling of reference materials on the subject of painting

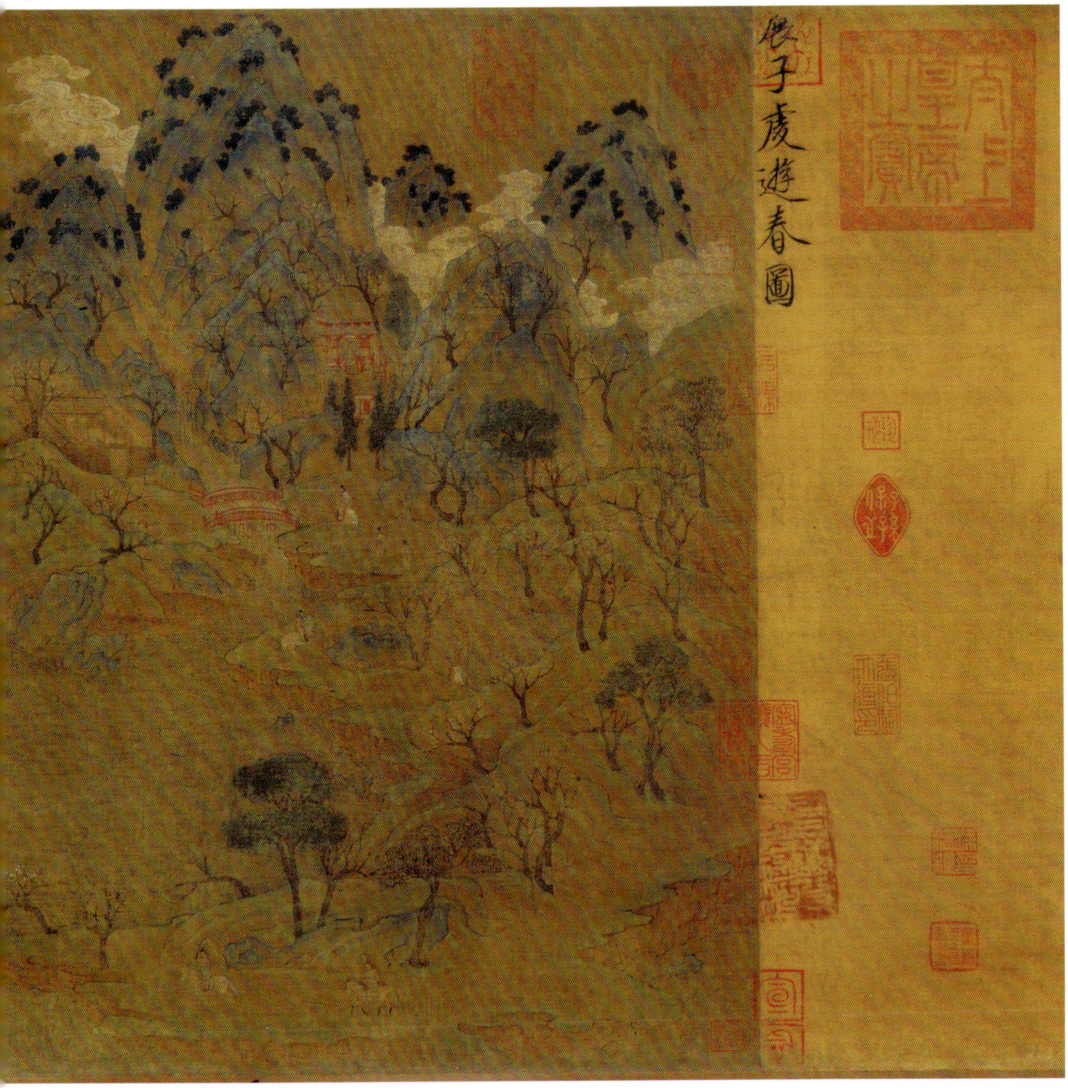

Fig. 13. Zhan Ziqian (act. late 6th century), *Spring Excursion*. Handscroll. Ink and color on silk. Palace Museum, Beijing
隋，展子虔，游春图，手卷，绢本设色，北京故宫博物院

and calligraphy. The first project was the compilation of the *Peiwenzhai shuhua pu* (Calligraphy and painting compendium of the Peiwen Studio), ordered by decree of the Kangxi emperor. It was started in the forty-fourth year of his reign (1705) with eight scholars in charge, including Sun Yueban (Assistant Minister of Rites and Chancellor of the Imperial Academy) as the head compiler, Song Junye (Deputy Auditor of the Censorate), and Wang Yuanqi (Attending Academician at the Hanlin Academy; 1642–1715). The project lasted two years. Kangxi wrote a preface for the compendium in which he emphasized the importance of paintings and calligraphy.[146] The contents are divided into such sections as discussions on calligraphy and painting; works of calligraphy and painting by emperors of successive dynasties; biographies of artists; works by anonymous artists of all dynasties; emperors of successive dynasties and their colophons on masterpieces of painting and calligraphy; critiques on calligraphy; and the collection and connoisseurship of painting and calligraphy in previous dynasties. Consisting of a total of a hundred volumes and drawing reference materials from 1,844 classic books, this compendium has the following features:

1. Inclusive of both calligraphy and painting, it changes the inadequate traditional format in histories of painting or of calligraphy in which one is presented separately from the other; the assembled descriptions of the paintings and calligraphy from all previous dynasties are imposing.
2. Rich in reference material, this compendium is all one would need to understand the general situation of collecting, research, and writings on the painting and calligraphy of previous dynasties.

3. A complete record of the imperial and private collections, it provides the reader with a comprehensive understanding of the situation in art collections, connoisseurship, research, and writings current at that time.

4. Transmitted together with the works of famous artists for their share of immortality, works of anonymous artists were saved from being lost. However, this was done mainly for the comprehensive arrangement of the literature and lacks a concern for connoisseurship. Therefore, the spurious and the genuine are intermixed.

There were a total of three projects of identification and categorization of the paintings and calligraphy in the Qing imperial collection launched during the Qianlong reign. The first project was begun in the second month of the ninth year of Qianlong (1744) and lasted a total of one year and eight months. Zhang Zhao (1691–1745), Liang Shizheng (1697–1763), and Dong Bangda (1699–1769) were appointed editors-in-chief. In the final compilations, all the works are divided into nine categories according to their mounting formats and their storage locations inside the palace—the Qianqing Gong palace, the Yangxin Dian hall, Chonghua Gong hall, and the Imperial Library among others. Each category is further separated into groups ranked either first class or second class. The nine categories are as follows:

- calligraphy albums
- painting albums
- albums combining calligraphy and painting
- calligraphy handscrolls
- painting handscrolls
- scrolls combining calligraphy and painting
- hanging calligraphy scrolls
- hanging painting scrolls
- hanging scrolls combining calligraphy and painting

First-class works appear in the front of a volume and second-class works in the rear. Characters from the *Qian zi wen* (Thousand-character essay) are used in the serial numbers. Physical properties of the items are noted, such as material used, size, format, collectors' seals, colophons, inscriptions by the Qianlong emperor, and imperial seals. For works deemed second class, only the titles and the artists' own inscriptions are listed but no information is included on dimensions and seals. More detailed documentation is given for a work in this class viewed by the Qianlong emperor. But the imperial inscriptions on such works are not included.

Works of art that were authenticated and rated first class would be affixed with a set of eight imperial seals: "Qianlong yulan zhibao," "Shiqu baoji," "Qianlong jianshang," "Sanxitang jingjian xi," "yizisun," and a few others that signify the buildings where the works were housed. The project identified and appraised a total of 2,286 items, which included 460 works of model calligraphy of all dynasties, 1,261 important paintings of all dynasties, 389 works of calligraphy and painting by various officials and artists serving the court at the time, and 176 pieces of model calligraphy by the Kangxi and Yongzheng emperors. The secular works were assembled into the forty-four volumes constituting the *Shiqu baoji* (Treasured boxes of the Stone Channel; fig. 14), while the smaller number of religious works were compiled into the *Midian zhulin* (Pearl forest of the Secret Hall).

The second project was launched in the spring of 1791 (the 56th year of Qianlong), when Wang Jie, Dong Gao (1740–1818), and Ruan Yuan (1764–1849) took the responsibility of sorting out and appraising the second batch of paintings and calligraphy. It lasted two years and was completed in the winter of 1793 (the 58th year of Qianlong). Based on the organizational format of the *Shiqu baoji*, the appraisal process went from one palace to another; each new item was identified and documented with better details. This time the works were not given a rating, nor were any comments recorded, but the current conditions of each painting or calligraphic work were carefully documented. The use of serial numbers with characters taken from the *Thousand-Character Essay* was dropped with the result that the titles are easier to identify. New imperial collection seals such as "Shiqu chongbian" and "Shiqu jijian," as well as the "Zhulin xinbian" seal for religious works, were added to the 1,845 new items of painting and calligraphy appraised. Most of these were the Qianlong emperor's own paintings and calligraphy, amounting to 1,160 items. Works by officials and court artists totaled 600, religious paintings of all dynasties totaled 300, and works co-created by Qianlong and others totaled another 157 items, constituting a grand total of 3,062 newly acquired works of art. All the works of this appraisal project were compiled into the forty-volume supplement *Midian zhulin Shiqu baoji xubian* (Second compilation of the "Midian zhulin" and "Shiqu baoji").

The third project, which resulted in the *Midian zhulin Shiqu baoji sanbian* (Third compilation of the "Midian zhulin" and "Shiqu baoji"), was launched in spring of 1815 (the 20th year of Jiaqing) and concluded in that winter, a period of ten months. Yinghe (1771–1840) and Hu Jing (1769–1845) were

Fig. 14. *Shiqu baoji* imperial catalogue and the Qing imperial seals
石渠宝笈及清宫鉴藏印

put in charge. In reality, Hu Jing was responsible for much of the editorial work. Later he wrote the *Xi Qing zhaji* (Notes from the Western Clarity retreat), giving a detailed account of the appraisal process he managed while at the court. Noteworthy aspects of this project were the addition of a large number of paintings and calligraphy by the Qianlong and the Jiaqing emperors, amounting to 2,493 great gems by father and son, and the relatively large number of (newly acquired) painting and calligraphy from all dynasties, amounting to 916 items; these volumes have tables of contents, making it easier to locate the entries for research. As a result of this project, an unspecified number of volumes of the *Midian zhulin Shiqu baoji sanbian* was produced. These works have new imperial seals that came into existence after the last compilation, including "Jiaqing yulan" (viewed by the Jiaqing emperor), and seals that the Qianlong emperor began using after his abdication, such as "taishang huangdi" (emperor emeritus), "guxi tianzi zhibao" (treasure of the emperor at age seventy), and "bazheng maonian zhibao" (treasure commemorating the advanced age of eighty). The formatting of the new compilation was based on the second compilation. At that time, only a part of this handwritten compilation was separately incorporated into the *Siku quanshu* (Comprehensive library of the Four Treasuries). No printed copies have been circulated, except for what Luo Zhenyu (1866–1940) was able to hand copy from the content pages and submit for wood-block cutting. There is no complete edition (fig. 14).

The 1911 Revolution led by Sun Yat-sen overthrew the Qing dynasty. After his abdication, the Xuantong emperor, Puyi lived inside the Forbidden City for eleven more years. During that period, he had ordered Zai Ying, Chen Baochen, and others to do an inventory of the works of art in the court collection. Puyi also affixed his seal "Xuantong yulan" (viewed by the Xuantong emperor) to some of the works that he viewed. A lithographed edition of *Dianhuamu* (List of paintings in the inventory) was printed and copies were distributed among persons related to him. A small number of these works were stored in the old Qing capital Shengjing, also known as Shenyang, and the imperial villas of Jehol (now called Chengde). Although Jin Liang's *Shengjing shuhua lu* (Catalogue of calligraphy and paintings in the capital Shengjing) documents these works, it was still hard to avoid leaving out some.[147]

Conclusion

China is an ancient and still thriving civilization. Its culture owes a great deal of its long continuity to the abundance of cultural artifacts, whether in the form of utensils or of calligraphy and painting, that have survived and been passed on. Regardless of whether the imperial collection was originally intended to serve as a single person's personal hobby or was motivated by great foresight and the realization of the importance of an art collection, China's imperial households have in actuality successfully preserved much of what Chinese culture has been able to produce. By collecting paintings and calligraphy, keeping good records, conducting research, and passing on the works of art, they have enabled several thousand years of the Chinese civilization to have demonstrable existence in the form of texts, images, and artifacts. Moreover, having the effect of "enhancing ethics and aiding in enlightening the public,"[148] painting and calligraphy serve as important tools in preserving China's cultural heritage and are regarded as occupying a place of great importance within the imperial collection.

There is a popular Chinese saying, "Mount your horses to gain control of a nation, get off your horses to run a country," which in the terminology of governance would be "conquer with force, but rule by virtue of culture." As an obvious sign of being educated and cultivated, the possession of works of painting and calligraphy helps the rulers to maintain spiritual accord and ideological communication with the social elite and to gain recognition by other members of society, making it easier to rule. To that end, emperors and rulers of successive dynasties have made great efforts as well as remarkable contributions.

First of all, an overview of China's history finds that such a large number of emperors who have become collectors of calligraphy and painting is a phenomenon unique to Chinese culture and very unlikely to be found in the histories of other nations. Secondly, whether from the standpoint of building special storage facilities or establishing an administrative system, or efforts at aesthetic appreciation and cataloguing, the Chinese imperial households showed an increasingly strong awareness of the importance of collecting painting and calligraphy. Such interest reached extreme proportions during the Qing dynasty, when there were more than a dozen storage locations for paintings and calligraphy inside the palace as well as a complete set of management teams. Several compilation projects of books on art were ordered under imperial decree. Moreover, the great importance attached by the Qing rulers to the collection and transmission of paintings and calligraphy is also indicated by the number of collection seals, the contents of the seals as well as the size of the seals. One seal from a set of eight collection seals belonging to the Qianlong emperor reads "yizisun" (Suitable for sons and grandsons).[149] This phrase is a concept known in antiquity. During the pre-Qin era, when bronze vessels were very important, they were considered treasures to be inherited by the family or by the throne. Propitious phrases such as "zisun yong bao yong" (for use by sons and grandsons forever) often appear in bronze inscriptions. When the Qianlong emperor placed the "yizisun" seal on many famous pieces of painting and calligraphy he had viewed,[150] his intentions were readily understood. Whether in their content, events represented, or artistic expression, all these works of art have their unique aspects which serve to admonish, inspire, provide relaxation, or teach artistic skills. Therefore, calligraphy and painting were cherished by the emperors, who regarded them as tools in the transmission and promotion of China's cultural lifeblood and to guarantee the continuity of the throne. The Kangxi emperor wanted them to be "perpetual,"[151] and the Qianlong emperor remarked, "They should be hereditary and passed down to my offsprings."[152]

There is no doubt that with such efforts, calligraphy and painting scrolls, as the most characteristic of all Chinese art forms and bearers of the wisdom and sensibilities of the Chinese people, have acted like a magnet and adhesive to unify and reflect a people's spiritual world, and have created a cultural landscape unique to China. Chinese paintings and calligraphy in collections around the world speak best for Chinese art and culture. Their distinctive features enable Chinese art to stand out in the arena of the world's arts, while their rich content has not only preserved ancient Chinese civilization but also serve to enrich the entire history of human civilization. From this standpoint, how can we underestimate the contributions made by the emperors of successive dynasties through the collecting of painting and calligraphy?

Translated by David Huiwei Shen

Notes

1. Arthur Waley, trans., *The Book of Songs* (New York: Grove Press, 1960), p. 320.
2. According to Zhang Yanyuan (b. ca. 815), "The wonder of pictorial arts came into vogue during the Qin and Han"; see Zhang Yanyuan, *Lidai minghua ji* [Record of famous painters of successive dynasties], *juan* 1, reprinted in *Guhua pinlu* [Classification of ancient painters], Siku yishu congshu [Art books from the Comprehensive library of the Four Treasuries] (Shanghai: Shanghai guji chubanshe, 1991), p. 812/280. The Kangxi emperor wrote in his "Preface" to the *Peiwenzhai shuhua pu* that "The pictorial arts started during Qin and Han, and flourished in the Six dynasties." See *Peiwenzhai shuhua pu* [Calligraphy and painting compendium of the Peiwen Studio] (Beijing: Zhongguo shudian, 1984), vol. 1, preface.
3. Zhang Yanyuan, *Fashu yaolu* [Essentials of calligraphy], reprinted in *Guhua pinlu* [Classification of ancient painters], Siku yishu congshu [Art books from the Comprehensive library of the Four Treasuries] (Shanghai: Shanghai guji chubanshe, 1991), pp. 812/108, 165.
4. Ibid., p. 812/121.
5. Tao Hongjing was a native of Moling, what is now Nanjing and was a Daoist philosopher and herbalist who lived in reclusion in the Maoshan Mountains in the period from the Southern Qi to the Liang dynasty. He declined repeated invitations from the Liang emperor Wudi to serve him at his court. Because the emperor sought him out for consultation on all matters, the people called him the "Prime Minister in the Mountains." See *Cihai* [Sea of words], concise ed. (1979; reprint, Shanghai: Shanghai cishu chubanshe, 1986), p. 438.
6. Zhang Yanyuan, *Fashu yaolu*, pp. 812/121–25.
7. If there were works of painting or calligraphy to speak of during the period from the Qin to the Han dynasty, they would probably have been done on silk. While archeological evidence has confirmed that supposition, it has been separately recorded in Yu He's (fl. ca. 470) *Lun shu biao* [Memorial on calligraphy] that by the late Eastern Han period, when a great percentage of calligraphy was still being produced on silk, artists such as Zhang Zhi, Zhang Chang, and Mao Hong wrote on either silk or paper. Cited in Zhang Yanyuan's *Fashu yaolu*, pp. 812/118–120.
8. A special section in the *Lidai minghua ji* gives a detailed account of the techniques of mounting since the Jin dynasty. Some of the best mounting experts were listed such as Fan Ye, Xu Yuan, and Yu He during emperor Mingdi's time. Zhang Yanyuan, *Lidai minghua ji*, p. 812/302.
9. See Yu He, *Lun shu biao*, cited in Zhang Yanyuan, *Fashu yaolu*, p. 812/120.
10. Zhang Yanyuan, *Lidai minghua ji*, *juan* 1, p. 812/208.
11. Zhang Yingwen (16th century) mentions the following individuals as connoisseur emperors: Huan Xuan, Wudi of Liang, Yuandi of Liang, Houzhu of Chen, Yangdi of Sui, Taizong of Tang, Xuanzong of Tang, Li Houzhu, Taizong of Song, Huizong of Song, Gaozong of Song, Zhangzong of Jin, Wenzong of Yuan, and King Qian Chu of the Wuyue kingdom. See Zhang Yingwen, *Qing mi cang* [Pure and arcane collecting], *juan* 2, reprinted in *Meishu congshu* [Fine art series], ed. Huang Binhong and Deng Shi (1947; reprint, Nanjing: Jiangsu guji chubanshe, 1997), vol. 1, p. 491.
12. It is recorded that "His mother saw a meteor shooting into a basin, and she drank that water, guaranteeing that when he grew up, he would be handsome, graceful in manners, versatile in the arts, and excellent in literature. Fearful of his talents and pomposity, others kept him at bay and the court did not trust him." "Huan Xuan zhuan," *Jinshu* [Book of Jin], Ershisishi, *juan* 99 [The twenty-four chronicles] (Beijing: Zhonghua shuju, 1995), p. 2585.
13. Zhang Yanyuan, *Fashu yaolu*, p. 812/113.
14. Ibid., p. 812/165.
15. See "Huan Xuan zhuan," *Jinshu* [Book of Jin], Ershisishi, *juan* 99 [The twenty-four chronicles] (Beijing: Zhonghua shuju, 1995), p. 2592.
16. "Greedy, fond of exotic things, and addicted to treasures, he could not keep his hands off of jewelry. He was always trying to take into his own possession good pieces of calligraphy and painting or gardens and residences belonging to others." Ibid., p. 2594.
17. Zhang Yanyuan, *Lidai minghua ji*, *juan* 1, p. 812/280.
18. *u Jin yangqiu* [Sequel to the chronicles of Jin], cited in Pan Tianshou, *Lidai huajia pingzhuan* [Biographies and commentaries on painters of successive dynasties] (reprint, Hong Kong: Zhonghua shu ju, 1986), p. 7.
19. See Yu He, *Lun shu biao*, cited in Zhang Yanyuan, *Fashu yaolu*, p. 812/118.
20. Zhang Yanyuan, *Lidai minghua ji*, p. 812/280.
21. Zhang Yanyuan, *Fashu yaolu*, p. 812/165.

22. Pei Xiaoyuan, *Zhenguan gong si huashi* [History of paintings in imperial and private collections], in *Meishu congshu* (see note 11), vol. 1, p. 808.

23. *Liangshu* [Book of Liang], *juan* 1, Ershisishi [The twenty four chronicles] (Beijing: Zhonghua shuju, 1995), p. 1.

24. See Jiang Chenying, *Zhanyuan tiba* [Inscriptions noted at Zhanyuan garden], cited in *Zhongguo shuhua quanshu* [Complete series of Chinese calligraphy and painting], ed. Lu Fusheng (Shanghai: Shanghai shuhua chubanshe, 1994), vol. 7, p. 967.

25. Zhang Yanyuan, *Fashu yaolu*, p. 812/119.

26. Ibid., p. 812/122.

27. Pei Xiaoyuan, *Zhenguan gong si huashi*, in *Meishu congshu* (see note 11), vol. 1, p. 804.

28. Ibid., p. 808. He Yanzhi's *Lanting ji* [Record of the Orchid Pavilion preface] of the Tang dynasty tells us that the *Envoys from Vassal Kingdoms* (*Zhigong tu*) painted by the Liang dynasty emperor Yuandi was inherited by his great grandson Xiao Yi, who, while serving as chief inspector at the Tang court, used it to successfully entice the monk Biancai of Yongxin Temple in Kuaiji into trading Wang Xizhi's *Preface to Orchid Pavilion* (*Lanting xu*) to the Tang emperor Taizong. Cited in Zhang Yanyuan, *Fashu yaolu*, p. 812/157.

29. In one souce, Zhang Yanyuan, ibid., p. 812/166, documents the total as 140,000 scrolls and in another, *Lidai minghua ji*, *juan* 1, p. 812/281, as 240,000 scrolls.

30. Commenting on this event, Yan Zhitui (531–568) writes in his *Guan wo sheng fu* [Looking at my life], "Millions of people taken as prisoners, a thousand wagon-loads of books reduced to flying ashes—nothing like this has ever taken place in recorded history. For all those under heaven it is the end of civilization!" Cited in Zhang Yanyuan, *Lidai minghua ji*, *juan* 1, p. 812/281.

31. Ibid., *juan* 1, p. 812/281.

32. See Yang Renkai, *Guobao chenfu lu* [The loss and recovery of national treasures] (Shenyang: Liaohai chubanshe, 1999), p. 3

33. "Jingji zhi" [Treatise on bibliography], *juan* 32, in the *Suishu* [Book of Sui], Ershisishi [The twenty four chronicles] (Beijing: Zhonghua shuju, 1995), p. 908.

34. Zhu Jingxuan, *Tangchao minghua lu* [Masterpieces of the Tang dynasty], cited in *Meishu congshu* (see note 11), vol. 2, p. 1010.

35. Zhang Yanyuan, *Fashu yaolu*, pp. 812/172–176.

36. Chen Jiru, *Ni gu lu* [Fondness for antiquities], *juan* 3, cited in *Meishu congshu* (see note 11), vol. 1, p. 633.

37. *Xi'an beilin bowuguan* [Introduction to the Xi'an Forest of Stelae] (Xi'an: Shaanxi renmin chubanshe, 2000), p. 39.

38. *Peiwenzhai shuhua pu*, vol. 1, p. 2.

39. The Lanting gathering is a celebrated literary event in Chinese culture. In 353 (the 9th year of Yonghe), during the Eastern Jin dynasty, Wang Xizhi and more than forty companions took part in an elegant gathering at Lanting (the Orchid Pavilion). The participants drank wine and composed poems, and when the mood hit him, Wang Xizhi, picked up the brush and wrote out, as if assisted by some supernatural power, an incredible essay, leaving us the famous work *Lanting xu* (Preface to [the collection of poems at] the Orchid Pavilion) in running script. This work was inherited by his seventh generation grandson Zhiyong, who became a monk at the Yongxin Temple in Kuaiji and, upon his death, left it to his disciple Biancai. Emperor Taizong of the Tang dynasty had summoned Biancai to the court several times, making all kinds of offers to obtain the work without avail. Finally, Chief Inspector Xiao Yi, a great grandson of the Liang emperor Yuandi, disguised himself as a student and showed Biancai many other works of calligraphy by Wang, inducing him to produce the original. He was thus able to acquire the *Lanting xu* for Emperor Taizong. See Zhang Yanyuan, *Fashu yaolu*, pp. 812/156–58.

40. Shen Kuo, *Yuankan Mengxi bitan* [Dream Pool essays, Yuan printing] (Beijing: Wenwu chubanshe, 1975), *juan* 17, p. 17.

41. See Zhang Yanyuan, *Fashu yaolu*, *juan* 4, p. 812/173. According to Shen Roujian, ed., *Zhongguo meishu cidian* [Dictionary of Chinese art] (Taipei: Xiongshi meishu chubanshe, 1989), p. 322, "his other extant works include *Wenquan ming* and *Jinci ming*."

42. Zhang Yanyuan, *Fashu yaolu*, pp. 812/172–73.

43. Shen Kuo (1031–1095) writes in his *Mengxi bitan* that ink originals from the Six Dynasties and Song periods in the collection of the civilian population were all eulogy papers for the dead, which were exempt from the ban on collecting masterpieces of calligraphy imposed during the Zhenguan reign. Shen Kuo, *Yuankan Mengxi bitan*, p. 17.

44. See the section on connoisseurship and collecting in Zhang Yanyuan, *Lidai minghua ji*, p. 812/297.

45. *Tangchao xushu lu* [Tang dynasty writings on calligraphy], cited in *juan* 4 of Zhang Yanyuan, *Fashu yaolu*, p. 812/172.

46. Pei Xiaoyuan, *Zhenguan gong si huashi*, in *Guhua pinlu* (see note 3), pp. 812/17–29.

47. Shen Roujian, *Zhongguo meishu cidian*, p. 109.

48. Guo Ruoxu, *Tuhua jianwen zhi* [Experiences in painting], in *Guhua pinlu* (see note 3), p. 812/569.
49. According to Guo Ruoxu (11th century), "[when] Taizu conquered the lower reaches of the Yangzi, the paintings acquired were all sent to the academy. There were over fifty scrolls at first, but by the mid-Jingde and Xianping eras, there remained only the three scrolls of *Attending Buffalo in the Rain at a Village* (*Yu cun muniu tu*) by an anonymous artist, the three scrolls of *Wild Geese in the Winter* (*Hanlu yeyan*) by Xu Xi, and the two scrolls of *Five Kings Drinking Yogurt* (*Wu wang yin lao tu*) by Zhou Wenju. The scrolls were ordered remounted." Ibid., p. 812/562.
50. Ibid., p. 536.
51. Ibid., p. 510.
52. The Song emperor Huizong's hanging scroll *Tossing Sticks into a Wine Jar* (*Touhu tu*), signed as painted by the imperial hand at the Xuanhe Palace, is documented in Wu Xiu, *Qingxiaguan lunhua jueju* [Qingxiaguan collection of quatrains on painting], cited in *Meishu congshu* (see note 11), vol. 2, p. 1056.
53. According to Tao Zongyi, *Shushi huiyao* [Concise history of calligraphy], *juan* 6, Siku quanshu zhenben shiji [Precious editions from the Comprehensive library of the Four Treasuries, tenth collection], ed. Wang Yunwu (Taipei: Wenshizhe chubanshe, 1974), p. 3, "Huizong's running cursive script is expressive and powerful. He learned by studying the style of Xue Ji (649–713) and later developed an incredibly original style of his own, which he called 'slender gold'."
54. See Song Huizong, *Xuanhe lunhua zaping* [Xuanhe art critiques], *juan* 1, in *Meishu congshu* (see note 11), vol. 3, p. 1778.
55. Zhou Mi, *Qidong yeyu* [Unofficial anecdotes from Eastern Qi], *juan* 6, Congshu jicheng chubian [Collection of serialized books, first compilation], no. 2779–82. (Beijing: Zhonghua shuju, 1985), vol 1, p. 63.
56. Song Gaozong, *Siling hanmo zhi* [Siling discussions on ink calligraphy], reprinted in *Guhua pinlu* (see note 3), p. 812/432.
57. See Yang Wangxiu, *Zhongxing guange chucang tuhua ji* [Record of the paintings stored in the Zhongxing Guange hall], cited in *Meishu congshu* (see note 11), vol. 3, p. 2388. According to what is recorded in the *Zhongxing guange lu* [Zhongxing Guange hall catalogue], there were 215 scrolls of calligraphy and 1,260 scrolls of paintings; see Yang Renkai, *Guobao chenfu lu*, p. 6.
58. Shen Roujian, *Zhongguo meishu cidian*, p. 147.
59. Yang Renkai, *Guobao chenfu lu*, p. 7.
60. Fu Shen, *Yuandai huangshi shuhua shoucang shilue* [Brief history of the Yuan dynasty imperial collection] (Taipei: Guoli gugong bowuyuan, 1981), p. 4.
61. Ibid.
62. According to what is recorded for 1342 in *Yuan mishu jianzhi* [Treatise on the Directorate of the Yuan Imperial Library], cited in ibid., p. 87.
63. Ibid., pp. 92–93.
64. From a "commissioned inscription" by the Mongol scholar Hudoudar, an attending-secretary of the Hanlin Academy and compiler at the Office of National History, left on the *Timely Clearing after Snowfall Calligraphy Model-book* (*Kuaixue shiqing tie*), cited in Fu Shen, *Yuandai huangshi shuhua shoucang shilue*, p. 4.
65. The collection of the National Palace Museum, Taipei, has a a waist-length portrait of the Liang emperor Wudi (*Liang Wudi banshenxiang*) with a seal reading "Huangzi zhen wan" (For the Imperial Sister); see ibid., p. 20, plate 16. A relief seal reading "Huangzi tushu" (Artwork belonging to the Imperial Sister) is also seen on Zhao Chang's *Butterfly* (*Jia die tu*), Song Gaozong's *Nymph of the Luo River in Cursive Script* (*Caoshu Luoshen fu*), and Wang Zhenpeng's *Boya playing a Qin* (*Boya guqin tu*); see Yang Renkai, *Guobao chenfu lu*, pp. 15–16.
66. Yuan Jue, *Qing Rong ji* [Collection of writings by Qing Rong], *juan* 45, reprinted in *Sibu congkan chubian suoben* [Concise edition of the first compilation of the Four sections of literature] (Shanghai: Shangwu yinshuguan, 1928), and cited in Fu Shen, *Yuandai huangshi shuhua shoucang shilue*, pp. 16–18.
67. Fu Shen, *Yuandai huangshi shuhua shoucang shilue*, pp. 35–42
68. Yang Renkai, *Guobao chenfu lu*, p. 8.
69. Yang Boda, *Qingdai huayuan* [The Qing court academy] (Beijing: Zijincheng chubanshe, 1993), pp. 23–24.
70. Xu Qin, *Ming hua lu* [Ming dynasty paintings], reprinted in *Meishu congshu* (see note 11), vol. 2, p. 1723.
71. Xu Qin, *Ming hua lu*, reprinted in *Zhongguo shuhua quanshu* (see note 24), vol. 10, pp. 1 and 5.
72. Yang Renkai, *Guobao chenfu lu*, p. 8.
73. Dong Qichang, *Gudong shisan shuo* [Thirteen topics on antiques], reprinted in *Meishu congshu* (see note 11), vol. 2, p. 1194.

74. The late Ming dynasty Huating School established in the Jiangnan region by Gu Zhengyi and others is often considered one branch of the Songjiang School headed by Dong Qichang; see Shen Roujian, *Zhongguo meishu cidian*, p. 79.
75. A note in Gao Shiqi's *Jiangcun xiaoxia lu* [Record of Gao Shiqi's summer pastime] specifically declares that "Sir Dong Wenmin's paintings rate as number one in contemporary times, and lots of his originals are around, enough for a separate volume"; see *Gengzi xiaoxia ji* [Gengzi summer pasttime], Siku yishu congshu [Art books from the Comprehensive library of the Four Treasuries] (Shanghai: Shanghai guji chubanshe, 1991), pp. 812/470.
76. Gao Shiqi, *Jiangcun shuhua mu* [Catalogue of Gao Shiqi's calligraphy and painting], reprinted in *Zhongguo shuhua quanshu* (see note 24), vol. 7, p. 1068.
77. Wan Yi, Wang Shuqing, and Liu Lu, *Qingdai gongting shi* [History of the Qing dynasty court] (Tianjin: Tianjin baihua wenyi chubanshe, 2004), p. 280, quotes Zhao Yi (1727–1814) as saying that the poems Qianlong wrote in his youth were gathered by the poet-in-waiting Gu Chengtian into the *Leshantang quanji.*
78. Ibid., p. 293.
79. Yang Renkai, *Guobao chenfu lu*, pp. 27–28.
80. Ibid., pp. 2–6.
81. Ruan Yuan, *Shiqu suibi* [Notes on the Stone Channel], *juan* 1, reprinted in *Biji xiaoshuo daguan* [Compendium of notes and novels] (Yangzhou: Jiangsu Guangling guji keying chubanshe, 1984), p. 369.
82. Yang Renkai, *Guobao chenfu lu*, p. 109.
83. According to the incomplete count by the Qing Royal Estates Management Committee in *Gugong yiyi shuji shuhua mulu si zhong* [Four catalogues of dispersed calligraphy and paintings from the imperial palace] (Beijing: Gugong bowuyuan, 1926).
84. "Jingji zhi," pp. 905–7.
85. Zhang Yanyuan, *Lidai minghua ji*, p. 812/281.
86. Zhang Yanyuan, *Fashu yaolu*, pp. 812/166, 172.
87. Ibid., p. 812/154.
88. Guo Ruoxu, *Tuhua jianwen zhi*, p. 812/510.
89. According to the Song writer Shen Kuo, "The most magnificant building inside there is the Mi Ge, tall and over-shadowing. Tradition has it that it is called the Wooden Tower of Heaven. " Shen Kuo, *Yuankan Mengxi bitan, juan* 24, p. 13.
90. Guo Ruoxu, *Tuhua jianwen zhi*, p. 812/510.
91. Zhou Mi, *Yunyan guoyan lu* [Private collections viewed], Congshu jicheng chubian, no. 1553 (see note 55), p. 58. See also Yang Wangxiu, *Zhongxing guange chucang tuhua ji*, reprinted in *Meishu congshu* (see note 11) , vol. 3, p. 2388.
92. Fu Shen, *Yuandai huangshi shuhua shoucang shilue*, pp. 78–79.
93. Yang Yu, *Shanju xinhua* [New stories from mountain dwellings], p. 11, cited in Fu Shen, *Yuandai huangshi shuhua shoucang shilue*, pp. 41–42.
94. Ibid., p. 66.
95. Wan Yi, Wang Shuqing, and Liu Lu, *Qingdai gongting shi*, pp. 73–74.
96. Shen Kuo, in his *Yuankan Mengxi bitan, juan* 1, p. 15, cites past examples of separated storage to reduce the odds of fire and water damage.
97. *Shiqu baoji* [Treasured boxes of the Stone Channel], first compilation (Shanghai: Shanghai guji chubanshe, 1981), vol. 1, contents page.
98. Wan Yi, Wang Shuqing, and Liu Lu, *Qingdai gongting shi*, pp. 295–96.
99. E'ertai, Zhang Tingyu, et al., *Guochao gongshi* [History of the imperial courts] (Beijing: Beijing guji chubanshe, 1987), vol. 2, pp. 456–58.
100. Qing Gui and Dong Gao, *Guochao gong shi zheng xubian* [Official version of the history of the Qing imperial court], in Zhongguo shixue congshu [Collected works of Chinese historiography] (Taipei: Mingu wushinian dongfang xuehui, 1961), vol. 5.
101. Zhang Yanyuan, *Fashu yaolu*, p. 812/104.
102. According to Xu Hao in his *Guji ji* [Record of ancient traces], "Princess Anle was so fond of Wang Xizhi's work *Yue Yi lun* that she acquired from the court of Zhongzong that she had the work placed in a woven bag and stored inside a plaited bamboo suitcase"; see Zhang Yanyuan, *Fashu yaolu*, p. 812/154.
103. See Wu Pingyi, *Xushi fashu ji* [Collected calligraphy by Xu], in Zhang Yanyuan, *Fashu yaolu*, p. 812/151.
104. Guo Ruoxu, *Tuhua jianwen zhi*, pp. 812/510, 561. According to the Chinese traditional calender, *futian* (hot season) lasted approximately from mid July to late August; see *Cihai*, p. 217.
105. Shen Kuo, *Yuankan Mengxi bitan, juan* 3, p. 11.
106. The remark by Wang Sishan is recorded in *Liuru Jushi huapu* [Collection of paintings by Liuru Jushi], reprinted in *Meishu congshu* (see note 11), vol. 2, p. 1228.

107. According to Wu Pingyi in his *Xu shi fa shuji*, "Those mounted in teal green and turtle-shell knobs are old mounts from Liang dynasty, with identification information on the wrapping section"; cited in Zhang Yanyuan, *Fashu yaolu*, p. 812/151.
108. According to the Liang dynasty calligrapher-in-waiting Yu He in his *Lun shu biao* [Memorial on calligraphy], cited in Zhang Yanyuan, *Fashu yaolu*, pp. 812/118, 119, 165.
109. Zhang Yanyuan, *Lidai minghua ji*, p. 812/303.
110. Ibid., p. 812/281.
111. Guo Ruoxu, *Tuhua jianwen zhi*, p. 812/569.
112. Yang Renkai, *Guobao chenfu lu*, p.6.
113. Song Gaozong, *Siling hanmo zhi*, p. 812/432.
114. Zhou Jiazhou, *Zhuanghuang zhi* [On the art of mounting], reprinted in *Meishu congshu* (see note 11), vol. 1, p. 79.
115. Zhou Mi, *Qidong yeyu, juan* 6, pp. 63.
116. Ibid., *juan* 6, pp. 63–72.
117. Yang Renkai, *Guobao chenfu lu*, pp. 7–8.
118. Wang Yuxian, *Huishi beikao* [Reference for painting], cited in *Gengzi xiaoxia ji* (see note 75), pp. 826/116–17.
119. Wan Yi, Wang Shuqing, and Liu Lu, *Qingdai gongting shi*, p. 296.
120. Yang Renkai, *Guobao chenfu lu*, p. 41. For a record of the cultural artifacts, paintings, and calligraphy stored in the Jianfu Gong palace behind the Yangxin Dian hall, see also Puyi, *Wode qianbansheng* [The first half of my life] (Beijing: Dongfang chubanshe, 2007), p. 126.
121. Xing Yongfu and Shi Liwu, ed., *Qinggong Rehe dang'an* [Qing imperial archives at Jehol], National Archives Series (Beijing: Zhongguo dangan chubanshe, 2003), pp. 481–86.
122. Zhang Yanyuan, *Lidai minghua ji*, p. 812/301.
123. Mi Fu, *Shu shi* [History of calligraphy], reprinted in *Meishu congshu* (see note 11), vol. 1, p. 658.
124. Ruan Yuan, *Shiqu suibi, juan* 1, p. 396.
125. Pei Xiaoyuan, *Zhenguan gong si huashi*, in *Meishu congshu* (see note 11), pp. 808, 812.
126. Zhang Yanyuan, *Fashu yaolu*, p. 812/152. According to Mi Fu, Taizong had inscribed three characters onto Xie An's *tie* (model-book); see Mi Fu, *Shu shi*, p. 806.
127. Guo Ruoxu, *Tuhua jianwen zhi*, p. 812/569.
128. Yang Wangxiu, *Zhongxing guange chucang tuhua ji*, p. 2388.
129. *Wenwu*, no. 5 (1972): plate 3.1.
130. Lee Hui-shu, *Exquisite Moments: West Lake and Southern Song Art* (New York: China Institute Gallery, 2001), pp. 86–93.
131. Fu Shen, *Yuandai huangshi shuhua shoucang shilue*, chaps. 1, 2. See also the Yuan dynasty chapter in Yang Renkai, *Guobao chenfu lu*, p. 8.
132. Wan Yi, Wang Shuqing, and Liu Lu, *Qingdai gongting shi*, p. 80.
133. Zhao Yi, *Yanpu zaji* [Anecdotes to air under the eaves], *juan* 1, Qingdai shiliao biji congkan [Notes on Qing history series] (1982; Beijing: Zhonghua shuju, 1997), p. 8.
134. "On Palaces," in E'ertai, Zhang Tingyu, et al., *Guochao gongshi, juan* 11–15, pp. 177–349.
135. Wan Yi, Wang Shuqing, and Liu Lu, *Qingdai gongting shi*, p. 294.
136. Zhang Yanyuan, *Lidai minghua ji*, pp. 812/299–300.
137. Ibid., p. 812/300.
138. Ibid., p. 812/301.
139. See the "Xu zigu bawei yashu" [Account of postscripts and *yashu* security signatures since antiquity] in Zhang Yanyuan, *Lidai minghua ji*, p. 812/301.
140. Zhan Ziqian's *Spring Excursion* is documented as having two *neifu* seals in Ruan Yuan, *Shiqu suibi*, p. 368.
141. Ibid., p. 369.
142. *Gugong yiyi shuji shuhua mulu si zhong* [Four catalogues of dispersed calligraphy and paintings from the imperial palace] (Beijing: Gugong bowuyuan, 1926), front illustrations.
143. Guo Ruoxu, *Tuhua jianwen zhi*, p. 812/509.
144. Pei Xiaoyuan. *Zhenguan gong si huashi*, in *Guhua pinlu* (see note 3), pp. 812/17–29.
145. Deng Chun, *Hua ji* [Painting sequel], reprinted in *Huashi* [The history of painting], Siku yishu congshu (see note 3), p. 813/505.
146. *Peiwenzhai shuhua pu*, vol. 1, p. 2.
147. Yang Renkai, *Guobao chenfu lu*, p. 30.
148. Zhang Yanyuan, *Lidai minghua ji, juan* 1, p. 812/279.
149. See David Sensabaugh's essay in this publicaton, p. 24.
150. See the section "On Seals" in Ruan Yuan, *Shiqu suibi*, p. 396.
151. In the Kangxi emperor's original preface to *Peiwenzhai shuhua pu*, vol. 1, p. 2.
152. From the Qianlong emperor's imperial decree published in *Shiqu baoji*, Siku yishu congshu [Art books from the Comprehensive library of the Four Treasuries] (Shanghai: Shanghai guji chubanshe, 1991), vol. 1, p. 824/1.

儒雅天子

中国皇家书画收藏史论

海蔚蓝

序言

“普天之下，莫非王土；率土之滨，莫非王臣”（注1），中国几千年的集权专制统治，决定了这块土地上的一切都握于王权之掌心，土地、物产、人、和人所创造的财富：物质的和精神的。艺术品作为人类文明的产物和历史的见证，历来为统治者视为文化传承的载体而珍藏。

从有关文献记载看，书画艺术品为中国皇家关注并收藏，约在汉代至六朝时期。自秦汉以来（注2），书画渐兴，汇成长流，生波逐浪，在六朝时期形成了中国书画创作的第一个高峰，许多帝王亦为书画家，自汉元帝（在位公元前48－33）到梁元帝（在位552－555）不下十多位。（注3），他们并积极加入品评书画的理论行列，例如梁武帝有论钟繇书法十二意（注4），并曾和著名的道教思想家、书法家陶隐居（注5）往返信函九封，津津乐道当时最推崇的钟繇和王羲之的书法之短长（注6）。客观上，汉代以来纸张的发明，为书画的创作和普及创造了便利，纸书开始流行（注7）。同时书画装裱技术在六朝时的发展，映证了社会上对收藏书画的需求，也促动了创作、书画收藏与装裱技术多向刺激而发展完善的必然现象，目前所见于记载的，最早留名于青史的书画装裱专家，便是刘宋时的范晔（398－445）等人（注8）。对书画的欣赏和热情，自上而下，使之成为有文化有价值的象征，王羲之（约303－约361）为卖扇妇人题扇，仅书五字，其扇价便翻了五倍，并且供不应求，这个故事从侧面反映了民众对书法艺术的认识，和书画对形成一个社会的文化基础所起的巨大作用（注9）。

在有了相当的书画创作和对书画重要性的认同的社会基础上，遂成就了书画收藏的气候，而凭着中国皇权的专利，皇室成员自然而然地成为收藏书画的主力，将书画越来越多地纳入皇家的府库之中，如果说早期的金石器物，是作为权力和地位的国家重器的象征来被收藏的话,书画则成为中国文化和艺术最高成就的象征，作为精神的形象表率，为历代王朝所孜孜追求，加之历代某些皇帝个人的特别爱好和倡导，不惜从各种渠道搜集珍藏,汇聚一堂,若自有明确记载的帝王收藏家的四世纪的六朝算起，到二十世纪初的清末，在一千五百多年的历史中,皇家的书画收藏和鉴赏，管理和著录,虽然高低跌宕，但代代相传，有其发展延续的清晰脉络，成为中国文化传承的典型形式之一。

I. 历代收藏书画的主要帝王和皇室成员

中国皇室书画收藏的始作俑者，可能是汉武帝（在位，公元前141－87年），唐代人曾说：“汉武创置秘阁，以聚图书，汉明[东汉明帝,28－75]雅好丹青，别开画室，又创立鸿都门学以集奇艺，天下之艺云集”（注10），其后的两千多年的历史中，对收藏书画有贡献的帝王不下十几位，前人曾有评论，将汉末至清初的历史中够资格称为书画鉴赏家的，列为177人，其中帝王者十四五人，约占总数的十分之一，始自六朝的桓玄，梁武帝到吴越王钱椒等（注11），兹结合历史上另一些对中国书画收藏有贡献的帝室（包括短时篡位者），择要简述如下。

六朝 — 桓玄、宋武帝刘裕、宋明帝刘彧、齐高帝萧道成、梁武帝萧衍、梁元帝萧绎

东晋时的桓玄（369－405），谯国人（今安徽怀远），才华横溢，雄强不羁，（注12）。曾任荆江二州刺史，称霸于长江中上游，于公元402年攻入东晋首都建康(今南京)，篡帝位，于是东晋内府所藏书画，尽归他掠为己有。他对书画痴爱不已，首先他自己就是一个书法家，曾自比为王羲之，别人未给与认同（注13），但南朝的萧齐王朝曾收集他的书法作品入内库秘阁（注14）。桓玄曾制作小船，将喜欢的书画随身携带赏玩（注15）。他爱书画且贪心（注16），“欲使天下法书名画尽归己有”（注17）。据说当时著名的画家顾恺之曾将自己的一橱柜的画寄存于桓玄处，以纸封为记，桓破而得之，复封上，顾归而见空柜，知道为桓所取，但摄于其权势，只得解嘲道：“画通灵化而去，亦犹人之登仙了”（注18）。在他手上，一时聚敛了当时最好的书画。

军伍出身的彭城（今江苏徐州）人刘裕（363－422）篡位东晋建立刘宋王朝，是为武帝。他垂手而得东晋内府的珍藏，包括桓玄所攫走书画名作在内。刘裕也雅好绘画，故不断地充实库藏。特别到了明帝刘彧泰始三年（467），明帝好读书，爱文义，即位后，引进才学之士，并留意书画：一面命臣下清理旧日内库藏品，一面诏令寻求前废帝战乱时散失的书画，还出资将内库书画赎回。随后遣使到三吴、荆、湘等偏远地区去搜集散佚的书画，连同群臣所

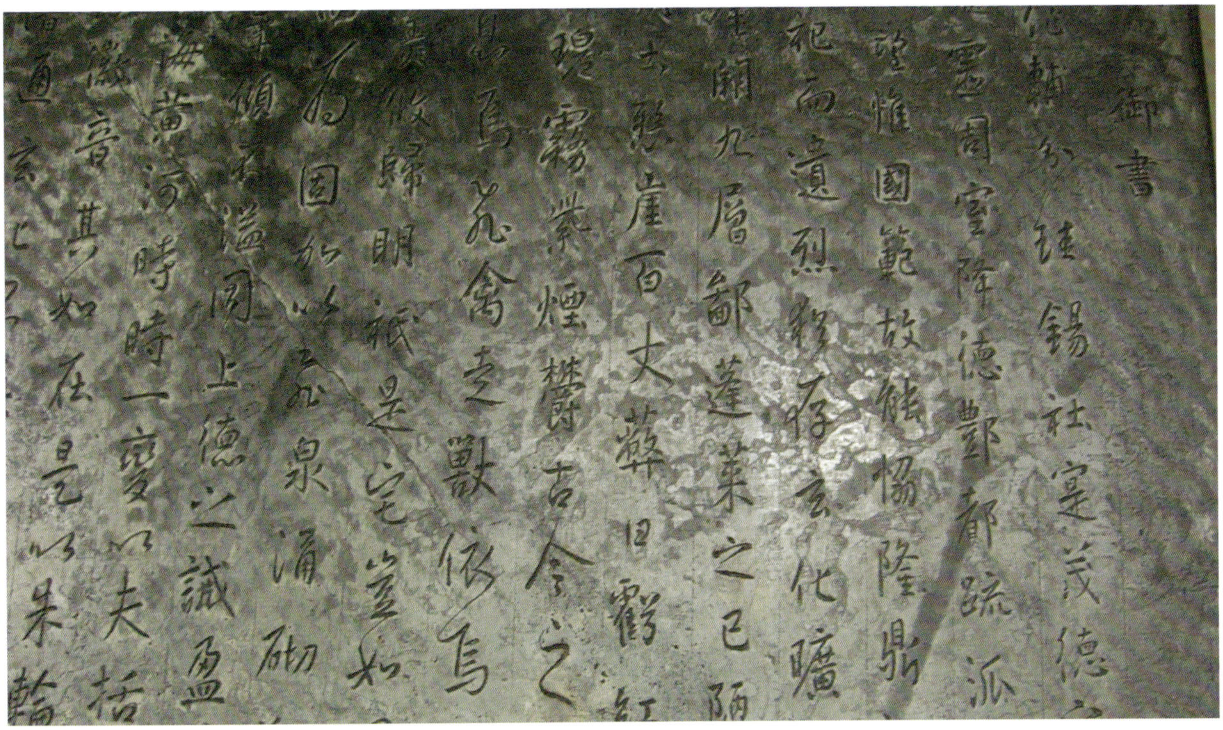

图一. 唐，太宗李世民，温泉铭（局部），石碑藏于山西省太原晋祠，海蔚蓝拍摄
Detail of Tang Taizong's (599–649) *Wenquan ming* stele in the Jinci temple, Taiyuan, Shanxi Province. Photo by Willow Weilan Hai Chang

献，不数月之间，“奇迹云萃”，几乎将六朝时书法名家如王羲之父子、钟繇、张芝 的作品收集周全，如王书藏有707卷，钟繇纸书697字等（注19）。

同样是军事霸主，曾为刘宋王朝的禁军将领的萧道成（427－482，祖籍山东），于公元479年弑刘宋顺帝刘准（生于467年），建立萧齐王朝，是为高帝。萧道成性好文学，尤擅鉴赏，凡内库中刘宋时宝藏，悉为所有。并根据作品优劣，评定甲乙，不以年代远近而论高低。自画家陆探微（活跃于465－472）至范惟（怀）贤四十二人评为四十二等，二十七帙，三百四十八卷，供其暇时披览欣赏（注20）。并觉得内府收藏的书法作品太少仅有十二帙而已，又命王僧虔（426－485，王羲之的四世孙）四处访求，得到张芝等十多位书家之作十卷，奏入秘阁（注21）。他自己亦善丹青，其画被唐人记载者有“渥洼马图”和“孝子屏风图”（注22）。

与萧道成同族的萧衍（464－549），于中兴二年（502），当他任雍州刺史时，乘乱夺权，得萧齐皇帝萧宝融禅位，称国号曰梁，是为梁武帝，史书记载此人“生有奇异之气……天性睿敏，下笔成章，千赋百诗，直疏便就……恭俭庄敬，艺能博学，罕或有焉”(注23)。他对书法的品评鉴赏品味很高，除了之前所述，有评钟繇之书法和与陶弘景书函往来论钟繇王羲之书法外，还有论汉末至梁三十四人的书评，用语清妙俊发，为典型的六朝清言（注24）。他对萧齐内府所藏的名书画，极为珍惜，并搜访天下散佚的书画，命臣下重新装裱题检，将最好的书画作品用珊瑚轴，锦绣织带，金题玉躞（注25）。当时著名的道士、书法家和鉴赏家陶弘景有幸被梁武帝赐书卷赏玩，初以为不过二三十件而已，直至阅览了二百七十件，不由惊叹“天府如海，非一瓶可汲”。(注26)。据记载，梁武帝时曾整理宫中的书画收藏，并编有《梁太清目》一书，此书在隋唐时代一定是鉴藏家们所必备的参考书，唐代裴孝源编撰《贞观公私画史》一书时，还曾依据《梁太清目》来注明画家或画名（注27）。

萧衍之子梁元帝萧绎（508－554），才艺过人，兼善绘事，《贞观公私画史》载有其六卷画（注28）。萧绎对书画的热爱简直到了疯狂的地步，继位之后，锐意访求名迹，致内府所藏书画，远远超过前代。可惜先是太清二年（548）遭侯景之乱，内府珍藏被焚数百函。随后将内库所有书画，载往江陵，不幸在承圣三年（554）江陵为西魏于谨攻陷。失守前梁元帝萧绎将所有法书名画和典籍十四万卷（或为二十四万卷），派遣后阁舍人高善宝前往火焚，萧氏欲投火中，与珍藏同归于尽，为宫宾所阻，他气得用利剑斫折殿柱，长叹息道："萧世诚（绎字）遂至于此，儒雅之道今夜穷乎！"（注29）事后，于谨诸人于煨烬中拾得书画四千余轴，运往长安。这是我国书画名作见于文献记载的最大一次浩劫！毁灭的再也不能复苏了。《梁太清目》一书失传，无从查封具体件数，以及其所藏书画的艺术价值，时人评为有史以来所未有的耻辱（注30）。十四万卷（或二十四万卷）法书名画典籍，这个中国皇室书画收藏的第一个高峰之所聚，也就如此毁于一炬。

隋唐五代 — 隋文帝杨坚、唐太宗李世民、南唐李后主

北周隋国公杨坚（541－604）于581年受北周禅为隋文帝，于开皇九年（589）陷建业（南京）虏陈后主叔宝（553－604），结束了两个多世纪南北分裂的局面，中国重归统一。杨坚遂命元帅记室参军裴矩、高颖搜集魏晋内府中书画，得八百余卷，在东京（洛阳）观文殿后面修建二台；东为妙楷台，藏自古法书；西为宝迹台，藏自古名画，是皇家为书画收藏而特意修造的专门建筑（注31）。隋炀帝杨广（569－618）于大业十二年（616）幸江都（扬州），东都法书名画随之由运河载往，中途船只覆灭，大半落水，我国法书名画又一次遭受厄运！杨广在江都为禁军将领宇文化及（卒于619）所弑，运扬州的劫余书画，则由宇文掠去聊城，为农民起义首领窦建德所得；至于东都留下的藏品，落入割据势力王世充之手，隋王朝珍藏历代名迹遂遭离散（注32）。

公元617年，太原留守唐国公李渊（566－635），拥兵称唐王，受隋禅，翌年即帝位于长安（西安），国号曰唐，是为唐高祖。武德五年（622年），攻克郑地，先后灭王世充、窦建德等，天下又归一统，于是两都（洛阳与长安）内库珍迹以及扬州所余精品，均归其所有。在由船只护送回长安的路上，沿黄河逆流而上，道经三门峡之砥柱，水流湍急，竟遭覆灭之灾，所存不过十分之一二而已！（注33）。

唐代皇室对书画的爱好是很普遍的，皇室子弟中颇有善于丹青者，如汉王元昌善画马，江都王善画雀蝉，嗣滕王善画蜂蝉（注34），而唐高祖之次子唐太宗李世民（599－649）尤有大气魄和造诣，他既是马上英雄，也心仪儒雅之道，为秦王之时，便已留心搜藏，登极之后，更是热心收藏，尤其珍爱王羲之的书法，不惜一切四处征求。贞观六年敕命整理御府书法，贞观十年命以金帛购求天下王书，贞观十二年，王方庆之父献上高祖王羲之的真迹四十余卷，太宗并购求得到人间王氏书，凡真行二百九十余纸，装为七十余卷，草书二千纸，装为八十卷，以便太宗经常披览，并随时临摹（注35）。唐太宗曾耿耿于怀，非要得到王羲之的兰亭序不可，后由监察御史萧翼从会稽永欣寺的辩才和尚处赚得兰亭序，并刻之于玉石（注36），随即敕命拓书人拓之，赠送皇太子诸王和近臣。他还亲自为怀仁（唐代书法家）集王羲之字的圣教序作序，此一国宝级石碑现藏于西安碑林博物馆(注37)。他酷爱王羲之，如醉如痴，身为皇上，还曾"亲叙王羲之传"（注38）。太宗临崩，只求兰亭序一物与之随葬，要求其子高宗诚孝勿违（注39）。据说王羲之唯一留存于石上之作的"乐毅论"，被誉为"正书"第一者，也随葬了昭陵（注40），可见唐太宗沉迷王羲之书法之深，唐代及后世之尊王之风，可谓得力于他的推崇。他自己也是一个相当出色的书法家，善临古帖，行草师法二王，清远高致，善飞白书，笔力遒劲（注41）（见图一）。太宗喜欢与当时著名的书法家虞世南论书，也常将自己的书法作品出示群臣，并有别致精辟的论书之道，因其善于用兵，尝以用兵之勇来比喻书法的用笔，悟到最关键者是求书法的骨力（注42）。

唐太宗即位之后，不仅于贞观年间进一步访求搜集在民间的书画佳作，并以皇家的特权，对民间收藏者有相当的限制，大约除吊丧问疾的书简仍可为民间所藏以外，其他都只有皇家才能收藏，因此，久藏民间的剧迹佳作，一时荟萃于内府（注43）。唐代人便盛赞道："贞观开元之代，自古盛时，天子神圣而多才，士人精博而好艺，购求至宝，归之如云，故内府图书谓之大备"（注44）。从唐初武德年间内库仅有的三百多卷书画连同隋代所留下的数量有限的书画，经太宗李世民的搜集，此时光是钟繇、王羲之父子真迹，即有1510卷之富（注45），还有《贞观公私画史》所记之六朝名作，尚存二十余件，未记者不在少数（注46）。后来在玄宗李隆基（685－762）时，不仅开始设立翰林院，广延文章才学之士，冠之以"待诏"的头衔，并且又新收薛稷、李范、王方庆诸家私藏书画，开元年间，甚而有悬爵赏赐入库的例子，皇室收藏得以通过这种种渠道得到充实，从而形成了中国皇室书画收藏的第二个高峰。

五代时南唐中主李璟及其第六子后主李煜（937－978）都为一代名词人，尤其是李后主，自号钟山隐翁，亦善书画，书作颤笔，号为"金错刀"，画以书法入之，而山水、人物、禽鸟、墨竹皆别具一格。设立皇家画院，吸引了天下名手汇集金陵，与后蜀之成都媲美，成为当时艺术之两大都会。书画之兴，亦促进了纸墨工具的发明，李后主时创制了"澄心堂"纸和"李庭圭墨"（注47）。"李后主才高识博，雅尚图书，蓄聚既丰，尤精赏鉴"，所有内府的书画凡经他所鉴赏的多钤鉴藏印并押字题诗（注48）。但其收藏的数量和质量都无法与唐朝比较。

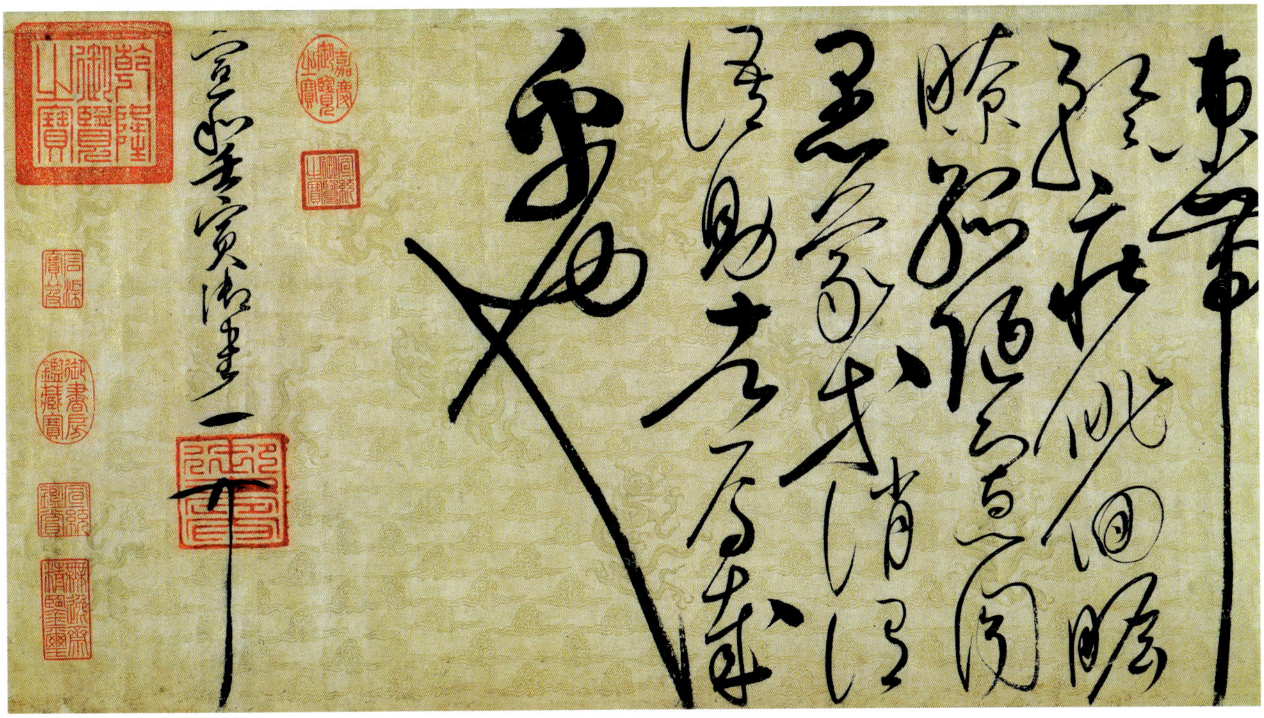

图二. 宋徽宗赵佶，千字文（书卷之尾），手卷，描金云龙笺，纸本水墨，辽宁省博物馆

Zhao Ji (Emperor Huizong; 1082–1135), End section of *Thousand-Character Essay*. Handscroll. Ink on paper. Liaoning Provincial Museum

两宋 — 太宗赵光义、徽宗赵佶、高宗赵构

声名显著的书画家、书画鉴赏家皇帝—宋徽宗（1082－1135）的出现，并非偶然。自宋代开国皇帝宋太祖赵匡胤于959年陈桥兵变称帝，前后吞并各国如南唐、后蜀、吴越诸国所有之法书名画，均作为战利品运往开封内库，从唐末散佚了数十百年的珍品，又重新聚集起来（注49）。太祖之子宋太宗赵光义（939－997）当初尹京督金陵（今南京）的时候，便在解决争讼时，因懂鉴赏，而得以重金购到南唐画家王齐翰（961－975间为南唐皇家画院翰林待诏）的十六轴罗汉图，十六日后，他登极为皇帝，故将这些画命名为富有吉祥含意的“应运罗汉”（注50）。他在位期间不仅通过增加科举进士名额，敕修《太平御览》，促进了文风的昌炽，并且因为对书画的爱好，即位之初，便下诏国内郡县搜访名迹，又命待诏黄居采、高文进搜求民间图画，铨定等级目录。端拱元年（988）建置秘阁于崇文院的中堂，用来庋藏古今名迹，并派吏部侍郎李至兼秘书监，点检供御图书，选三馆正本万卷实之秘监以进御（注51）。

其后，宋代的几位皇帝在文物书画上皆有贡献，如仁宗赵祯（在位1023－1063）善画，曾画“龙树菩萨”。到了徽宗赵佶的政和年间（1111－1117），他收藏的古物已达到六千多件，分别收藏在崇政殿、宣和殿。以后由于古物增多，又建保和殿、稽古阁、博古阁、尚古阁，专门储藏古玉、印玺、各种鼎彝礼器、法书和图画。他自己也是一个成就突出的艺术家，自道书画是唯一爱好，臣下尽选内府精品一千五百件，自曹不兴到黄居采，编为《宣和睿览》，供其随时赏玩，也常在宣和殿作画题诗（注52）。其在位35年，“怠于政治，任用奸邪，国事大坏，终于身虏国亡。惟好书、画、山水、人物、花鸟、墨竹，无不精工极妍，刻划入细，而又善体物情，精于鉴别。工书，初学黄庭坚，后自成一体，号‘瘦金书’”（见图二）（注53）。

在其执政期间，徽宗又进一步发展了自宋代立国以来便设置的“翰林图画院”，设立画学，推行艺术教育，每旬出示御府所藏图轴两匣，给画院学艺等人观摩学习，称为“习学”，并试行“诗题甄试画士”，不仅使绘画富有浓郁的文学气息，而且使画家的修养更为丰富沉厚，他自己也品评绘画之短长，传授观察写实和绘画的体会（注54），一时间丹青好手云集，形成了将写实画艺和诗意相融合的“宣和体”，宣和画院亦成为中国皇家画院的巅峰，标榜史册。宫廷画家的佳作充实了内府的收藏，此外，宋徽宗亦利用自己至高无上的权力，通过各种途径，采用各种手段广搜天下名贵绘画、法书，御府收藏因之百倍富于前朝。

宣和年间，他所敕命编辑的《宣和书谱》和《宣和画谱》，记录了宣和内府秘阁所藏书画，自魏晋迄于北宋初期法书1248轴，三国吴曹不兴画、晋到北宋名画如黄居寀之画共6396轴，总计7644轴。这还不包括赵佶本人的作品和画院作品在内，再加上画院作品未入《画谱》者，当不在万轴（卷）之下！形成中国皇室书画收藏的第三个高峰。

北方女真族的金人崛起，很快便逼迫赵宋王朝南渡长江，成立了偏隅临安（杭州）的南宋王朝，当局势逐渐稳定，南宋王朝即着手在民间搜集从汴梁（今开封）流散出来的法书名画，并通过与金人的往来，从榷场中交换一部分作品，但欲恢复宣和旧观已非易事（注55）。虽然宋高宗赵构（在位1127－1162）自己说道"本朝自建隆以后，评定僭伪，其间法书名迹，皆归秘府。先帝时又加采访，赏以官职金帛，至遣使寻访，颇尽探讨"（注56）。据南宋庆元年间秘书省的秘书监杨王休所撰的《中兴馆阁储藏图画记》，当时南宋内府所藏的名画，自魏晋以来者不过1098轴（册），大约只占北宋皇家收藏总数的八九分之一而已（注57）。

金元 — 金章宗完颜璟、元文宗图帖睦尔、皇姊大长公主祥哥剌吉

松花江上崛起的女真族，建立金国，灭了北宋，占据着中国的北部，与偏安杭州的南宋对峙。对从北宋都城开封掠来的法书名画，不甚重视，一部分通过榷场为南宋换了回去，一部分藏入金内府，直到金章宗完颜璟（1168－1208）时，才有改观。完颜璟的母亲是宋徽宗赵佶的女儿，因而他自小便深受汉文化的影响，精通汉学，工书善画，尤喜书法，在位期间（1190－1208），曾令官员购求宣和内府遗散的书画，藏书家不愿出售者，劝其交给官府录写后交还，并给半价。明昌元年（1192），并曾令王庭筠、张汝方合纂《品第法书名画记》五百五十卷。经他亲自鉴赏过的名作，常有其题签，书法仿效宋徽宗赵佶的瘦金体（注58），例如传世的《虢国夫人游春图》《捣练图》等作就是完颜璟手笔题签（注59）。

图三. 元代皇姊祥哥剌吉（约1283-1331）书画收藏印："皇姊图书"（朱文方印）和"皇姊珍玩"（白文方印）
Appreciation seals of the Princess Sengge Ragi of the Yuan dynasty, "Huangzi tushu" (square/relief), and "Huangzi zhenwan" (square/intaglio)

来自草原的蒙古族人建立了元代，灭亡了金代和南宋，其内府藏品的基础是由元世祖忽必烈（1215－1294）奠定的，藏品的主要来源是南宋内府的旧藏。1276年，元将伯颜（1236－1295）入临安（今杭州）之后，即封府库，收史馆礼寺图书，及百官符印（注60）。从南宋内府收藏得到的书画虽非全部，但数量不菲，到1277年，据内府裱褙匠焦庆安的计算，光是需要重裱的画轴便计有1009轴（注61）。加上元大都万亿库内收藏从金代内府得到的库藏，南北所得图画均运至秘书监收藏，和四方购纳所得，合成元代内府收藏的大观（注62），计有书法二千零八单，名画一千五百五十六轴（注63）。

元代初年，自世祖忽必烈始便倡导学习汉文，习字书法成为汉化的最基本的要求，因此元代皇帝多习染汉族文化，礼贤下士，也渐渐对书画艺术产生浓厚的兴趣。忽必烈在1272年设立秘书监掌管图书礼器，其后的仁宗皇帝（爱育黎拔力八达，在位1311－1320）爱好书画，礼遇南人画家赵孟頫、王振鹏，1318年召群贤观赏过王羲之的"快雪时晴"帖，并命赵孟頫等人题跋。仁宗皇帝不喜游乐，不爱珠宝，而独独"博古尚文"，为臣下所倾倒（注64）。

对汉文化的敬仰，还使元代皇室中产生了一位中国历史上少见的女书画收藏家，仁宗之姊祥哥剌吉（约1283－1331），她的丈夫在1310年去世，此后她未再嫁，似乎专注于收藏，她收藏有玉器，但尤著于书画收藏。1311年仁宗封其为"皇姊"，其收藏过的书画作品上出现的"皇姊图书"和"皇姊珍玩"方印应该是在1311年始用（注65）（见图三）。1323年，皇姊召集了历史上少见的女性主人的雅集，二三十位文人雅士聚集于大都（今北京）城南的天庆寺，观赏皇姊收藏，其中不乏书画剧迹，与会文人并尊皇姊之命赋诗题跋。据与会并尊命题诗的袁桷（1266－1327）记载，其藏品有四十件之众，包括法书，宗教画，人物走兽，花鸟墨竹等，其中不乏如宋徽宗和唐宋名家如周昉、巨然，燕文贵和当代（元代）画家王振鹏的作品。（注66）。

到元文宗图帖睦尔（在位1328－1332）时，皇家的书画收藏鉴赏风气最甚，文宗是元代最风雅最倡艺术的皇帝，他自己也能挥毫书画，其御书墨迹常见于元代文集的各家题跋中，他倾心书画的最具标志性的作为，是于天历二年（1329）所创立的奎章阁，此阁设于皇宫园林的太液池之西，约在今北京北海的白塔附近，虽然只有三间屋，却非古雅之物不得入储，这布置得如书房一般的地方，藏有元代皇家收藏中最好的书画作品，并选择最有书画知识的学士入直，文宗皇帝则常常御驾观赏书画，并与诸学士清论

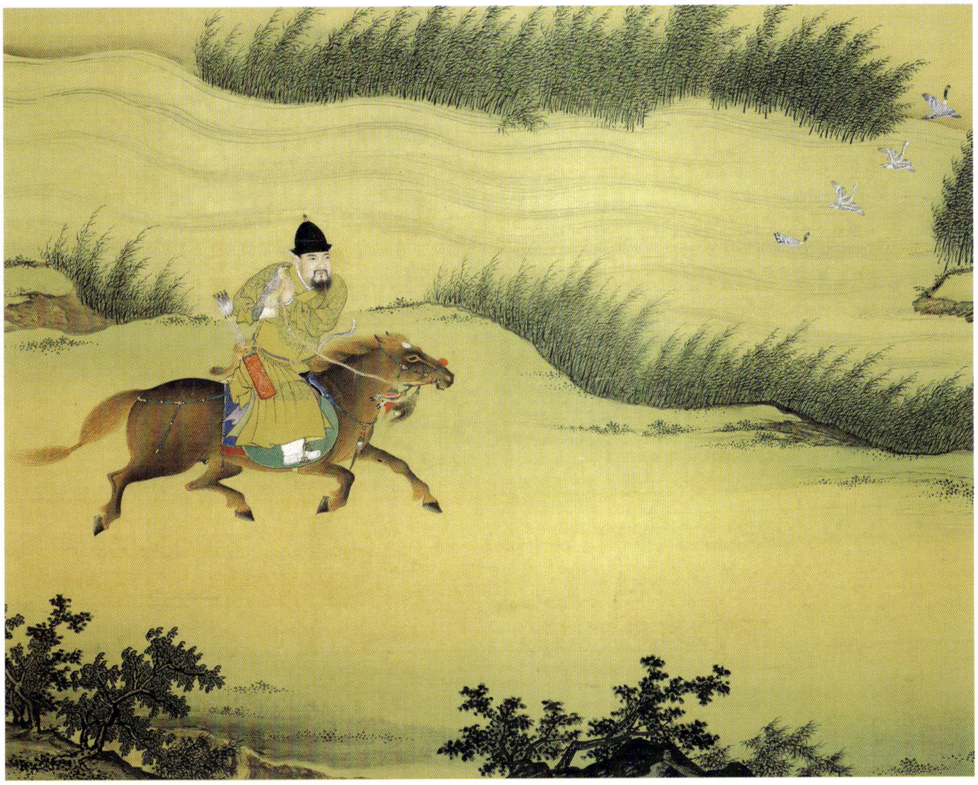

图四. 佚名，明宣宗（1398-1435）马上像，立轴，绢本设色，台北国立故宫博物院
Anonymous, *Portrait of Ming Xuanzong on a Horse*. Hanging scroll. Color on silk. National Palace Museum, Taipei, Taiwan

书画，甚而兴致所至，常在奎章阁挥笔书写，赐书臣下。奎章阁设立的学士院，置建书画博士，大学士官阶为正二品，在以九品为官序的年代，可谓身居要职。元代著名画家柯九思初为参书，翌年正月二十五日拜鉴书博士，负责书画鉴藏。奎章阁自1329年创立至1340年，长达11年之久，虽在1332年文宗英年（29岁）驾崩后，便走下坡，虽然其设立的初衷是以文宗广贤纳谏，与辅佐之臣可得以促膝长谈之地，但却成为元代皇室书画收藏和皇室书画鉴赏的核心之处，其所藏珍品剧迹，据傅申先生《元代皇室书画收藏史略》主要按照后代存世者有天历和奎章之印的书画作品来统计，也有将近八九十件，可能仅是一小部分而已。1340至1341年间，大书家康里夔夔重振元代皇室对书画的重视，将奎章阁更名为“宣文阁”而保留，并与1349年成立的教皇子们读书的端本堂一起，成为宫内书画鉴赏的场地直至元代灭亡（注67）。

明代 — 明宣宗朱瞻基

元末的农民战争中，朱元璋（1328—1398），一个靠乞讨为生的小和尚，奇迹般地在战乱中成为了国君，于1368年定都金陵（南京），建立了大明王朝，年号洪武。洪武时期内廷有稽察司监管文物，由太监掌管，凡是俘获或献缴的法书名画，统归稽察司保存，传世书画在右下角钤有稽察司半印者，都是明初内廷收藏过的佐证（注68）。明代虽然没有明确记载皇家设立画院的资料，但“仁智殿、武英殿、文华殿都履行着画院的职责”，“以直殿的名义，行画院之实”（注69）。帝王中也不乏喜爱书画之人，据清代徐沁《明画录》所载明朝三百年中能绘事者，首先列举了四位皇帝和十四位王子。这四位皇帝是：宣宗朱瞻基（在位1426－1435），宪宗朱见深（在位1465－1487），孝宗朱佑樘（在位1488－1505）和武宗朱厚照（在位1506－1521）（注70）。

宣宗朱瞻基（1398－1435）尤为杰出，他是明成祖朱棣（1360－1424）好梦中得来的孙子而备受宠爱，成祖亲派自己尊敬的大臣，博学的僧人姚广孝（卒于1418）来辅导这位心爱的孙子。宣宗聪明勤奋，不负祖父的厚望，执政后继承父皇仁宗（在位1424－1425）的政策，继续减税重农，礼贤下士，平乱撤兵，父子俩的仁政创造了历史上所称的“仁宣之治”。史书记载其多才多艺，丹青造诣非常：“宣庙留神词翰，尤工绘事，山水人物花鸟草虫并佳，天纵异能随意所至皆非人力能及，上御书年月及赐臣下衔名，用广运之宝或武英殿宝及雍熙世人图章”（注71）（见图四）。宣宗不仅是明代皇帝中最好绘事者，并且在位期间设立宣德画院，延揽各方艺士，书画风气为之一振。但皇家的书画收藏，除了献纳或臣僚没籍者外，似乎并没有力求民间流传的名迹，也未有其他显著的鉴赏研究之功。嘉靖（明世宗朱厚熜在位1522－1564）以后，还因为军饷不足，甚而还曾把内库珍品出卖给豪强以换取资金（注72）。

清代 — 康熙皇帝玄烨、乾隆皇帝弘历

中国封建社会的最后一朝清代（1644－1911），虽为满人统治，却出现了两位对中国文化极有兴趣的皇帝，在定鼎天下之后，清室便致力于各种珍宝包括金石、书画、缂丝拓本等的搜集庋藏，分藏于北京紫禁城皇宫，及奉天（沈阳）行宫、热河（承德）行宫等处，使中国这一最后的封建王朝成为古代文物书画的集大成者，成就了中国皇家书画收藏的最后一个高峰。

这个大业是由康熙、乾隆两个皇帝奠定的。这两个皇帝极其爱好汉文化，并深知汉化对巩固统治的重要性，而汉化的标准，最明显的形式之一就是会写字，能书绘画。康熙皇帝玄烨（在位1662－1722）从小对汉文化习染深，对书画兴趣浓，在书画的审美取向上极受明末董其昌（1555－1636）的影响，董其昌有论“至书与画，尤当贵重，书以传意，画以传形，用莫大焉”（注73）。康熙皇帝不但其本人笃好不倦，书画上处处步伍董氏，致使朝廷内大臣亦莫不趋之若鹜，风气为之一变，从而宫廷中庋藏董氏和华亭派作品最盛（注74）。康熙皇帝玄烨的侍臣高士奇（1645－1703）私家所藏历代书画，还特别将董氏作品列为专目，可见时代风尚之一斑（注75）。在康熙皇帝六十一年的统治时期，清代皇室已积累了一批法书名画，主要来源为臣工的贡献，高士奇《书画目》中，就列有“可进御”一项，其进献的多为赝品，宫廷中显然缺乏鉴藏的人员来分辨真伪（注76）。

将天下的法书名画几乎囊括无遗，集中于清内府的大业，是在乾隆皇帝弘历（在位1736－1795）统治的六十年里实现的。弘历本人不仅以作书作画作诗为常课（注77），他对书法的热忱和不断在各种宴会中与群臣联句吟诗，并书写成帙勒石，甚而影响了宫廷近臣成为书家如张照，梁诗正等，他的第十一子成亲王永瑆也成为清代有影响的书家（注78）。当他执政之时，清代已有了近百年的和平时期，从明末清初以来，因为战乱而散佚的法书名画，通过民间收藏家的搜求，已渐渐归入几家巨富之手，正为弘历的庋藏创造了条件。弘历嗜好书画，占有欲极强，作为一国之主，他可利用无上的权力，一道谕旨，或指名献纳，或酌情价购等方法，来将天下的法书名画集于一个皇家宫墙之内。清代的一些著名收藏家，如河南商丘宋权、宋荦父子、曾为显宦的真定相国梁清标、还有山东张先山、苏州古玩商归希之、维扬商人江孟明、近臣高士奇等人的藏品，均先后为弘历以各种方式罗致到皇宫之中。而由另一个著名收藏家安岐（仪周）之“古香书屋”收藏的晋唐两宋以下名迹，经江南名士沈德潜的从中斡旋，最后全部进入宫中，为清内府书画收藏的充实添上了最后也是最重要的一笔。乾隆年间，当乾隆皇帝敕纂《四库全书》时，到江南诸省访求图书，借此机会不仅搜集了图书版本，也将私人收藏的书画罗致于清宫，如江苏泰兴善本鉴藏家季沧苇和乃父季因是收藏的宋元书画便被皇上据为己有（注79）。至此，弘历皇帝已搜集尽天下名家收藏，以后只是零散的增添而已，清内府遂有着前所未有的法书名画的集大成，分藏于御书房，养心殿等十几处，其中隋唐宋元的法书名画近两千件，明代作品亦存两千件左右，加上御笔和清代作品，总数可在万件以上，形成了中国皇室书画收藏的又一个高峰，也是最后的高峰。

纵观中国皇家书画收藏的来源，或由战胜者承袭前代的库藏，或接纳官员的进贡，或从民间和私人手上征购吞并，或有皇室成员和宫廷画家作品的入藏，在一两千年中，至少形成了六朝梁元帝，唐代太宗，宋代徽宗和清代乾隆皇帝时皇家书画收藏的四次高峰。这些书画作品的命运不胜坎坷，且不说朝代嬗递之际，兵燹散聚，还有许多人为和不测之灾，据杨仁恺先生的初步统计，中国书画收藏散佚的大悲剧自六朝到宋，或毁于火，或落于水，或失于兵燹，不下7次。(注80)。此外，皇家的书画收藏也常作为各种礼品赏赐而散佚，如作为陪嫁品，寿礼，和赏赐贵戚和臣下的礼品，均屡见不鲜，即以最后一类举例来说，清代皇室收藏的书画中，若是没有加钤“石渠宝笈”、“宝笈重编”二玺的作品，皇上便常拿来赏赐给诸王，及其官员（注81）。清代末年，赏赐之风更兴，如现藏于北京故宫博物院，曾为清宫收藏的中国书画卷轴中最早的法书名迹西晋陆机（261－303）的《平复帖》，便早在末帝溥仪之前就被赏赐出宫，后为清末民初的著名词人和书画收藏家张伯驹（1898－1982）巨金购得，而得以留在中国（注82）。

中国历代皇室书画收藏的命运，最可悲的莫过于清末，随着中国封建社会最后一朝的走向灭亡，先是遭西方八国联军的掠烧圆明园，之后，又被末代皇帝溥仪，以赏赐其弟溥杰为名，从宣统十四年（1922年）七月十三日起到十二月十二日的一百四十多天中，共赏赐溥杰书画和善本书籍1313件卷，其中以宋版本为主的善本书216套册，各类书画卷册1097件，在最初的一两个月里，以赠送善本书为主，自9月28日始，便以书画为主，每天以二三十幅的数量和速度被运出皇宫，（注83），以后又由于其他的政治原因，曾经汇集于一室的中国皇家书画收藏遂颠沛流离，散落天涯，为世界各地博物馆及私人陆续收藏。

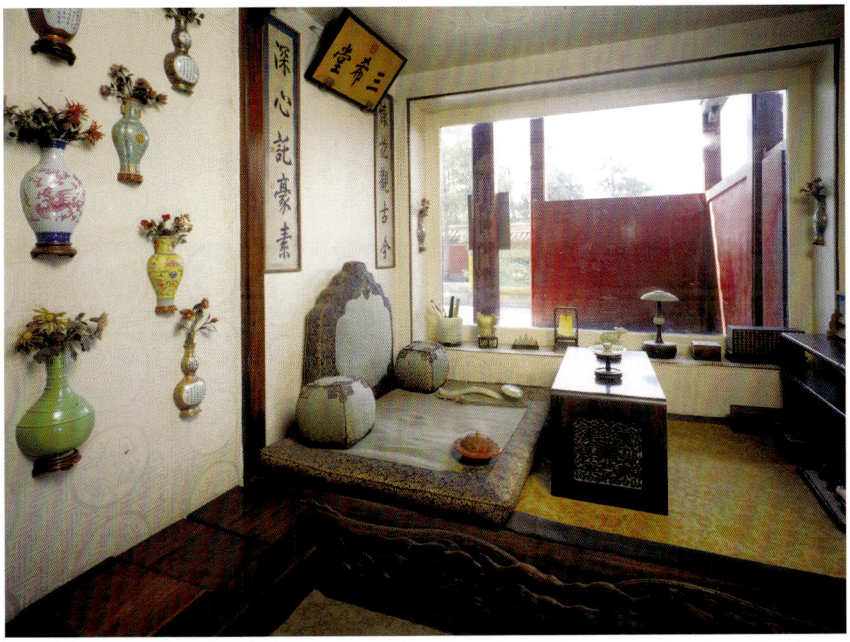

图五. 紫禁城，三希堂，
北京故宫博物院
The Sanxi Tang (Hall of Three Rarities) in the Forbidden City, Beijing. Photo provided by the Palace Museum, Beijing

II. 皇家书画藏品的保管、鉴赏和著录

1. 保管部门和人员

历代皇室的书画收藏都被藏于内宫，从汉代至六朝，据《隋书。经籍志》记载，“汉代，经籍藏于‘天禄阁’，光武中兴，书籍贮满石室（渠）、兰台，又于东观阁和仁寿阁集新书。魏代汉，书籍藏秘书中外三阁，其中有‘图赞’等。东晋，图书藏于秘阁、文华殿，华林园（藏释典）”（注84）。隋唐时代，隋炀帝在东京洛阳观文殿后建妙楷、宝迹二台以储书画（注85）。唐代对皇家书画收藏之所称为天府、御府、内库等（注86），具体管理的部门如有集贤院，翰林院和弘文馆等（注87）。

宋代，宋太宗端拱元年（988）以崇文院之中堂置秘阁，选点万余卷藏之，以供御览（注88）。秘阁的建筑宏伟，时人喻之为“木天”（注89）。还有书法墨宝数千件藏于淳化中阁，除此之外，宫内还有天章、龙图、宝文三阁，后苑有图书库，皆为藏所，可与汉宫中专门储藏书画的天禄、石渠，以及隋代的妙楷和宝迹台阁相侔（注90）。南宋皇宫书画收藏则藏于内府之秘阁，属秘书省管辖并设官职为秘书监者总管，中兴馆阁当是其收藏地之一（注91）。

元代内府书画，自元始至元末，都归秘书监掌管，秘书监于至元九年（1272）设立，官三品，官四员，吏属六人。早期并设有“辨验书画直长一员”，在管理制度上，书画作品非奉圣旨及上位，不得出监（注92）。至文宗时（在位1328－1332）成立奎章阁，置放古董书画，并设学士院及一套班子，来管理、鉴赏和谈论，以大学士五名为首，官阶为二品，俸禄为一百一贯三钱三分三厘，米一十石五斗，其中的鉴书博士专司鉴赏书画，官五品，俸禄为四十一贯，米四石五斗，所有奎章阁的官员都佩带特制牙牌，“金书奎章阁三字，一面篆字，一面蒙古字，畏吾儿字”，佩此可以“出入无禁”（注93），可谓高官厚禄，显赫一时。到顺帝惠宗时（1333－1368），奎章阁有赖大书家康里巎巎（1295－1345）之坚持，而转世为宣文阁，但所设编制和待遇都大大差矣，仅设授经郎和鉴书博士，都仅为五六品官而已，直至元亡（注94）。

明代洪武年间（1368－1398）书画藏品归内廷的稽察司保存，由太监掌管，其后宣德年间（1425－1435）武英殿、文华殿等地为宣德皇帝和画院创作书画的场地，或也鉴赏书画，但皇家书画收藏的具体状况仍有待于更多资料的披露。

清代初年重设内务府，下设七司三院和将近五十个不同机构，以掌管宫内事物（注95）。据《石渠宝笈》初编记载，所储书画地点共有十四处。其储放诸地的原因可能是出于安全的考虑，以防一旦水火无情，不致全部毁于一地（注96）。其中储存量最大的是御书房，所藏者占《石渠宝笈》中的十三卷，其余依次为乾清宫，养心殿各九卷，重华宫占八卷，三希堂（见图五），学诗堂，画禅室各一卷，长春书屋，随安室，攸芋斋共占一卷，翠云馆，漱芳斋，静怡轩，三友斋共占一卷（注97）。至《石渠宝笈》重编时，又见书画收藏有储放在西苑，圆明园，长春园和三山等处者。（注98）。

与书画收藏有关的如康熙初年设于养心殿内的造办处所辖的如意馆，匣裱作；御书处，负责临摹，拓刻皇帝诗文手迹法帖，下设刻字作，裱作，墨刻作，墨作。储藏书画之各处属内务府管理，又各设头目，其机构和待遇如：

收藏书画最多的御书房，设首领一名，为八品侍监，每月银四两，米四斛，公费银七钱三分三厘。太监十二名，每月银二两，米一斛半，公费银六钱六分六厘。专司收储书籍，古今字画，洒扫，坐更等事（注99），但都为区区八品小官或无官品者。上述之制，到清末的嘉庆年间续编国朝宫史时，几乎没变。（注100）

2. 书画的保管方法

1）书画的保管

书画的储存需要防湿并透气，因此多存放在竹木或藤制品的箱匣中，此习由来已久，唐代张彦远（约生于815年）讲道，他家的书画藏品便是存放在篋笥中的（注101）。对珍贵之品，还可加锦囊丝袋（注102）。另外，每年夏伏天曝书也是古代书画保管的重要一着。此习自南朝（420－589）已开始，唐代的文献中也有记载，武则天时（在位690－704）由宫人出书画在亿岁殿曝之（注103）；宋代秘阁每年夏伏天曝书也是常规（注104）。还有在所藏书（画）中置放香草如七里香，菖蒲，白芷之类来防虫蠹的方法（注105）。据记载，金章宗（在位1190－1208）内府所藏书画也开始用檀香木做轴，因为“檀香辟湿气，画必用檀轴有益，开匣有香而无糊气又辟蠹也”（注106）。

2）书画的装裱和皇家式样

书画装裱技术自两晋以来已成为专门技艺，据记载六朝时萧梁皇家（502－589）收藏的装裱特色是青绫裱，玳眉轴（注107），并按照书画的优劣，配有不同的装裱材料，如装有玳眉轴，织成带和金题玉躞的，及一部分装有紫檀轴者，都是第一流的书法作品；一部分装有紫檀轴的书法作品次之，再以下的书法作品，便仅以漆轴头为之（注108）。唐代内库所藏名迹在装裱上有一定的制度。唐代贞观（627－649）中褚遂良（596－约658）掌监裱褙，贞观开元中的装裱并一律用白檀身紫檀首，紫罗裱织成带，以为官画之裱（注109）。唐代武则天时，装裱技术一定更为精进，甚至有官员遂招巧工修内库书画，将真迹换成临摹者送回内库，自己则将真品留下，或许是这类恶行的最早纪录。（注110）。

南唐李后主（在位960－975）宫内所收书画，“有织成大回鸾、小回鸾、云鹤、练鹊、墨锦裱饰，提头多用织成绚带，签贴多用黄经纸，背后多书监装褙人姓名及所较品第，又有澄心堂纸以供名人书画”（注111）。

宋代皇家装裱凡经宣和（1119－1125）御府收藏过的书画，装祯形制包首用各色缂丝或古锦，鹅黄细绢为前后隔水，拖尾赙纸用高丽茧纸（注112）。据南宋高宗（在位1127－1162）所追记北宋皇家珍藏的书画作品，藏在内府的珍品必定是用白玉珊瑚为轴，钤大观、政和、宣和印章，其中一印并以秦代印玺篆书风格，后有内府标题品次，皆皇帝御题，其次者则储于外秘（注113）。此外，“书画装裱所用的贴笺，宋徽宗（在位1101－1125）、金章宗(在位1190－1208)多用瓷蓝纸，泥金字，殊臻壮伟之观。金粟笺次之”（注114）。

在朝代更换之际，对新收藏入库者，也有整体上重新装裱的例子，如南宋内库书画的装裱形制和钤印，便立有一定的制度，不管入库的历代作品原装如何，为了整齐划一，一入绍兴（1131－1162）内库，便全部改装，这无疑是对文物的破坏（注115）。宋代的书画鉴定家周密（1232－1298）著有《齐东野语》记载很详细，专列一章介绍“绍兴御府书画式”，保留了南宋皇家书画装裱的样式，其按照书画的品次高下而用不同的装裱材料，尺寸定式和印记等。例如，对超出等级之外的高古法书名画，如“出等真迹法书，两汉、三国、二晋、六朝、隋、唐君臣墨迹。（并系御题签，各书妙字）用缂丝作楼台锦裱，青绿覃文锦里，大姜牙云鸾白绫引首，高丽纸谭……引首前后用内府图书、内殿书记印，或有题跋，与缝上用御府图籍印，最后用绍兴印，并降付米友仁（1074－1151）亲书审定，题于谭卷后”（注116）。

金代内库书画收藏的一个特色，即仿照北宋内府装帧之例，也设有一套制度，除去题签以外，包首、引首、谭尾、钤印都要换成自己的形制。前后隔水、谭纸钤“明昌宝玩”、“御府宝绘”、“内殿珍玩”、“明昌”、“秘府”、“群玉中秘”、“明昌御鉴”等印玺。（注117）。元内库书画装裱则无明显特色。

明代内廷书画的装裱，据清代王毓贤《绘事备考》记载颇详：“明宣宗（1426－1435）以后格愈精式愈雅，不独御府装潢金题玉躞，度逾前代，即士大夫家镡（应为贝旁）裱寻常卷轴亦皆有体有裁，斟酌尽善”，对纸质和绢质者，皆有不同的处理方式，格式上对大轴小轴的上下左右的尺寸比例等也都有定制，例如大整幅上引首三寸，下引首二寸等等（注118）。

清宫内务府设有造办处，康熙年间（1662－1722）约有五百九十四人，乾隆时（1736－1795）更为扩大，其中的匣作、裱作当是皇家书画装裱的承做者之一（注119）。据杨仁恺在实际考察清代皇室收藏的书画作品的装裱后，总结道：“立轴有锦套，手卷也有为它专制的淡黄或淡青花绫包袱，白软缎作里，上面钤印墨色所包书画的品名，作者姓名，年代，以及评定等级，每件专用。除此而外，每件作品都定制有白玉签（即撇子），正面浮雕图案，里刻品名，并填赤金，文字与包袱皮里一致。每件书画都有楠木匣盛装，其长短大小是根据书画本身的体积定作的。

各处储藏书画原先用的是大立柜，多为紫檀木制成，有的高达屋顶”（注120）。若检查一些清代档案，零星地也有些记载，如乾隆皇帝比较喜欢蓝色，书法常用蓝笺金字（承袭了自宋徽宗肇始的品味），也常喜欢吩咐装裱时用一寸蓝绫边，丝织品也多来自苏州织造府（注121），据此可对清宫皇家的书画装裱特色略有了解。

3. 皇家鉴定与押印

历代皇帝鉴赏书画后的记录，最明显的是书画上的题诗，题跋和钤印。

1）御览钤印

皇帝书画收藏的钤印约到隋代时（589－618）还没有，但自唐“太宗皇帝（在位626－649）自书贞观二小字作连珠小印”，或为帝王于书画上钤印之始，其后玄宗（在位712－756）自书“开元二小字成一印”（朱文长方印）（注122），无论是印文（仅有年号），还是尺寸（仅为小印），还是非常谦恭的。据米芾（1051－1107）记载，贞观开元皆小印，便于印缝，都不过一寸左右而已（注123）。自此以后，历代帝王均有书画印鉴，于观赏书画后用，印文有以帝号入印文者，有以收藏地入印文者，收藏印文中用“宝”字者，从目前的资料来看，似始自南唐李后主（在位960－975，有“建业文房之宝”），自元代文宗（在位1328－1332）以后常见用“宝”字入印。至清代皇帝的鉴藏印多有“御览”，“鉴赏”的字样，也出现“鉴藏玺”的字样，此外，清代乾隆皇帝，洋洋大观地以数量众多而较大尺寸的五玺八玺，作为鉴藏印，尤其是他在逊位后制作的大玺，如“太上皇帝之宝”、“八征耄念之宝”等，与唐代太宗首开皇帝钤印于书画、首倡此风时的谦和，确实不可同日而语了。清代曾参加编撰《石渠宝笈》的阮元（1764－1849），在其《石渠随笔》一书中单独列有“论钤宝”一节，对清代皇室用印，尤其是乾隆皇帝的用印有详细地说明，可作参考（注124）。清代皇家常用的鉴藏印，也可参考此图录附录A。

2）御题诗跋

帝王在画上题记者或始于晋朝，唐人裴孝源（活跃于贞观年间627－649）的《贞观公私画史》中录有曹魏（220－265）时的杨修所画的“两京图”等三卷图轴，其上有晋明帝（在位323－325）的题记，六朝时的梁元帝（在位552－555）也有题跋印记（注125）。从目前资料来看，最早见于记载，在画上题诗者恐怕是南唐李后主（注126）。在画上跋尾的，则有唐太宗李世民（注127）。皇帝御题诗跋之风，到宋代徽宗尤为炽烈，在南宋人记载的书画中，经徽宗御题的31轴书画中，大多均为其题诗（注128）。此记载亦与考古发现所见相呼应，如1972年在山东省邹县明初朱檀墓中出土的宋人葵花蛱蝶图纨扇之背，便有其题诗（注129）。南宋的帝王皇后，显然也乐于此事，多于观赏书画后题诗跋者，如宁宗（在位1195－1224）有御题马远诗画册，宁宗皇后杨妹子也于许多书画上有题诗跋，（注130）。元代皇室是起于荒漠的蒙古族，不解汉文，虽然仁宗文宗等几位皇帝也都练习汉字书法，但在书画鉴赏之余的题跋，一般均命大学士来题，此习约延至元英宗。因此经元代皇室收藏的书画拖尾，常常有当时收藏书画之所“奎章阁”学士们如柯九思（1290－1343）、虞集（1272－1348）等人的题咏和跋文。（注131）。

清代皇室虽为满族，但对研习汉文的重视，前所未见。不仅宫内设景山官学和咸安宫官学，教上三旗子弟；设蒙古官学，教蒙古八旗子弟，所有的皇子们都要到上书房刻苦学习（注132）；清人赵翼（1727－1814）曾对清朝皇子读书的家法严峻和皇子读书的勤勉感慨万千，叹道即使一般靠读书吃饭的人也不能与之相比，皇子们从黎明到黄昏，日日不断，这种史无前例的状况，使清人在得天下后，又深得中国文化之理，得文武之道的奥秘，从而保证了清人能以异族而长久占据统治汉人的地位（注133）。清朝几代皇帝，都能写字，宫中数千百的楼阁亭台，无一未有清名雅号，长赋小诗，且常为皇帝的御制御笔，翻开《国朝宫史》，比比皆是（注134）。即使是皇室成员，于创作和观赏书画，赋诗题跋，皆常可亲为。乾隆皇帝尤是独占头鳌，所到之处，诗痕墨迹不断，他所鉴赏过的书画作品上，几乎都题有诗跋，有的还反复多次，他的水平如何是另一回事，作为万人之上的天子，一生留下了四万八千多首诗，对中国诗文书画有如此兴趣和如此勤勉的，史所罕见，经其御题诗文的书画则数不胜数。对一些喜爱的名书画，他还反复观赏题跋，如他误以为大内所藏的元人黄公望的山水长卷，为董其昌《画禅室笔记》中提到的“富春山居图 ”，竟然前后题跋五十五次，并不论南巡，秋弥，东幸，西行，到处都带着，以便随时观赏（注135）。

3）皇帝敕命内府的鉴赏

皇家的书画收藏亦经专人鉴赏并常有押署，题跋和钤印为记。早期多为经手人签名，称之为押署。押署始自六朝刘宋内府，此习沿至隋代（注136），由鉴藏人押署，并开始增添年月日和增加跋文，如有“大业某年某月某日奉敕装”的字样（注137）。唐代贞观年间，鉴定人除签名押署外，还增加其官爵名称，上钤贞观连珠小玺。开元中亦如此，并增加跋尾（注138）。间有割去前人签署，代以后人的押署官爵，也有钤开元二字小印的，并间或有钤用

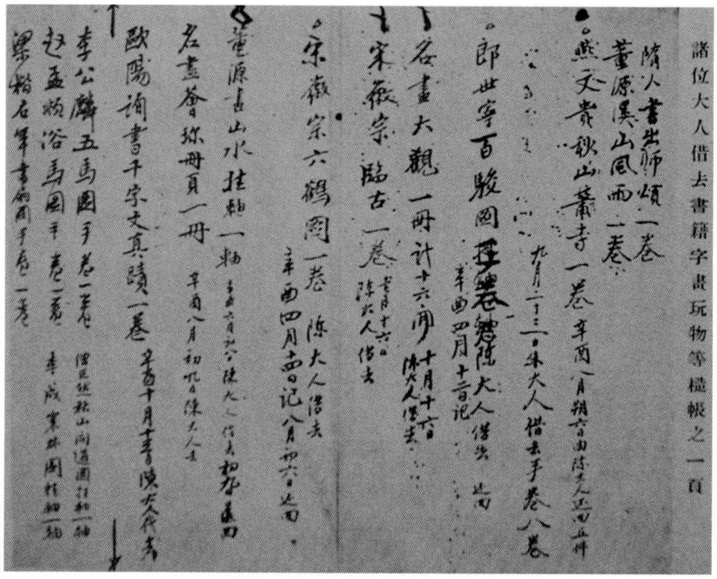

图六. 清宫诸位大人借书画单，载《故宫已佚书籍书画目录四种》（国立北平故宫博物院，1926年）
Inventory list of the paintings and calligraphy borrowed from the Qing palace. From the *Gugong yiyi shuji shuhua mulu si zhong* (Beijing: The Palace Museum, 1926)

集贤、秘阁、翰林、弘文诸印的，当属各部门掌管加钤的印信，以资识别（注139）。唐代以来，这种按照各部门的主管或保藏地点再加印记为凭的做法，直至清代宫廷中亦采之，清代皇家书画藏于十几处，除了鉴赏者和皇帝的印记外，都再加上各收藏处的印记，如乾清宫，养心殿等。在宫廷的管理体系中，内府通常是保管书画古董的机构，有些钤有“内府”印的画作显然经过这一部门的观赏和记录。最早的“内府”印约见于唐代，在隋代展子虔（活跃于6世纪）的“游春图”上（注140）可见。这一管理系统和习惯持续到清代，书画进宫后，先交付内府储藏并审鉴（注141）。从观赏到的清宫收藏的书画来看，在书画的题签上，也常能见到“内府珍藏”的字样，并常与“乾隆宸翰”的朱文小方印同时出现(参见图录第9号)。

4. 皇家书画收藏的外借制度

关于这一点的资料还了解不多，但在民国十五年由清室善后委员会刊行，标明为故宫博物院的《故宫已佚书籍书画目录四种》的一本小册子中，有两份很有意思的目录，一份为宣统庚申年三月的“诸位大人借去书籍字画玩物等糙账”，仅列某大人某年某月借去，或还回，或未还，其中不少是宋徽宗，董源之类名家的作品，也未写明经手人。另一份清单名为“外借字画浮记簿”，注明“书房记”，或是御书房所记，也是为私人借还书画的记录（见图六），并且似乎在已还的账上再加盖“收回”的印记（注142）。这份资料或许可以证明清室皇家书画收藏中的外借制度，但具体如何运作，或前代各朝是否都有类似的制度及如何运作，暂时都还没有见到更多的资料来论述，留待日后更多的发现。

5. 皇家书画收藏的著录

皇家书画收藏的著录，不仅是皇帝个人的爱好，也直接体现了对书画的重视，最早者或可追溯到六朝时的齐高帝萧道成（在位479－482），他曾编书三百多卷，品评画家等次等，但未有传世，宋代郭若虚（活跃于11世纪）记载所读过的书中有高帝所撰《名画集》一书，不知是否为同一者（注143）。其后，有六朝梁武帝（在位502－549）敕令下属整理的书画目录《梁太清目》，此书大约是隋唐书画鉴藏家必备的参考书，唐代裴孝源作《贞观公私画史》的时候，还多所凭据（注144）。

宋徽宗即位不久，便告知臣下，“万几余暇，别无他好，惟好画耳”，因此，秘府收藏日剧，臣下精选上自三国曹不兴，下至宋代黄居采的作品，共一千五百件分为一百帙十四门，名为《宣和睿览》以供皇上随时观赏（注145）。

此后宋徽宗又敕修《宣和书谱》和《宣和画谱》两书，无编者姓名，御制序言纪年为宣和二年（1120年），这是皇家主办的第一部系统的著录，是研究中国书画历史和鉴藏的重要著作，籍此对中国早期的书画作品，尤其是已经在历史过程中散佚和毁灭的书画家的作品，起了钩古钓沉的作用。该著录对藏品作者简历、品名、数量均有简要纪录。

《宣和书谱》，二十卷，记宋徽宗宣和内府所藏法书墨迹，包括上自汉下迄宋初的190多位著名书法家的作品1198件，分历代诸帝王书，以及篆、隶、正、行、草、八分、制诰等八门，每门前有叙论，并于法书目录前系书家小传，品第风格源流，叙论详明。《宣和画谱》，二十卷，分道释、人物、宫室、番族、龙鱼、山水、畜兽、花鸟、

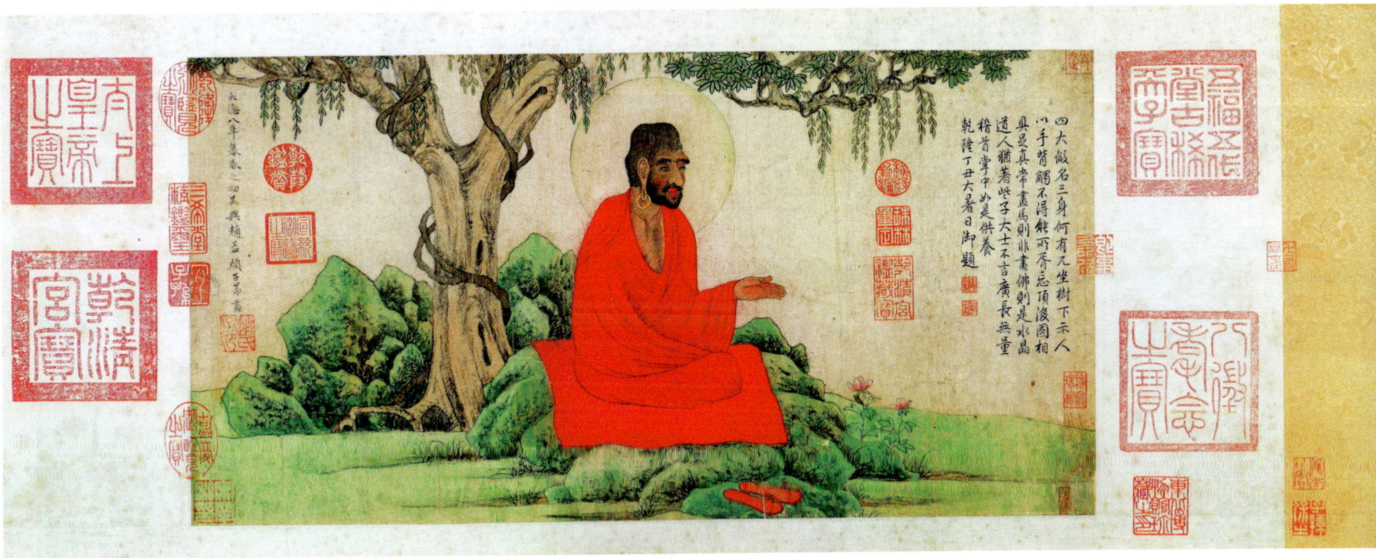

图七. 元，赵孟頫（1254－1322），红衣西域僧，手卷，纸本设色，辽宁省博物馆（清宫钤盖鉴藏印之例）
Zhao Mengfu (1254–1322), *A Foreign Monk in Red Robes*. Handscroll. Ink and color on paper. Liaoning Provincial Museum.

墨竹、蔬果等十个门类，记录宫廷所藏六朝以来历代画家231位画家的作品，共6396件。每门先作叙论，次为画家评传，后列作品名目及件数。

清代是中国封建时代皇家书画集大成的时期，对书画的著录也是史无前例的重视，先是康熙皇帝敕纂《佩文斋书画谱》。清代康熙四十四年(1705年)，礼部侍郎仍管国子监祭酒事孙岳颁领衔，与都察院左副御史宋骏业，翰林院侍读学士王原祁（1642－1715）等八人奉旨纂辑，历时两年多完成。康熙皇帝为书画谱写了序，极言书画之重要（注146）。其内容分论书论画、历代帝王书画、书画家传、历代无名氏书画、历代帝王与名书画跋、书辩证、历代书画鉴藏等，共100卷。该书特点是：1）书画同谱，以改古代集录书画者如书断画断书史画史等各自成篇的不足，汇辑历代书画著录（作），洋洋大观；2）内容资料丰富，一部书画谱在手，即可了解历代书画收藏、研究、著录的概况；3）宫廷内府与私人收藏俱录，使人对当时社会收藏、鉴赏、研究和著录情况有一个较全面地了解；4）无名氏书画，不使其遗佚，与有名氏并传不朽。但这主要是以文献整理为主，缺少对书画的鉴藏辨识，故真赝相错。所录者共一千八百四十四种。

清宫对皇家书画收藏的鉴别整理始于乾隆，前后共有三次。第一次是在乾隆九年二月到十年十月十日，共历时一年八个月时间，由大学士张照（1691－1745）、梁诗正（1697－1763）和董邦达（1699－1769）等人主编，根据宫中藏书画地点的乾清宫、养心殿、重华宫、御书房等处，和书画装裱的形式：书册、画册、书画合册、书卷、画卷、书画合卷、书轴、画轴、书画合轴，分为九类，每类又分上等和次等，上等在前，次等附后，用千字文编号，记载材质、尺寸、款识、收藏印记、题跋及弘历题字、内府印玺等；次等者则仅录作品名称，本人款识，不记尺寸、印章，如经乾隆过目的，仍然详录，只是他本人题跋文字从略。凡是经过鉴定的书画，上等作品所钤印玺有五：如“乾隆御览之宝”、“石渠宝笈”，“乾隆鉴赏”、“三希堂精鉴玺”、“宜子孙”并加钤储藏宫殿的印记 （见图七）。共鉴定了历代法书460件，历代名画1261件，本朝臣工书画389件，玄烨、胤禛书法176件，总计2286件。编成《石渠宝笈》共四十四卷。有关宗教题材的释道类书画则收入《秘殿珠林》初编（图六）。

第二次是在乾隆五十六年春，由王杰、董诰（1740－1818）、阮元（1764－1849）等人负责，开始第二批书画的鉴定整理，至乾隆五十八年冬完成，历时两年多，在《石渠宝笈》的基础上，仍按储藏宫殿逐项鉴定，但纪录更为翔实，不分上等次等的等级或臣工意见，所有书画现状都一一记入，取消千字文编号，眉目清楚。内府玺印加钤“石渠重编”、“石渠继鉴”，宗教作品则加钤“珠林新编”等印。鉴定书画1845件，主要是弘历书画1160件，臣工画600件。此外有关宗教书画的鉴定整理，计历代的300件，弘历和臣工的157件，总共整理了3062件。鉴定纪录编为《秘殿珠林。石渠宝笈续编》四十卷。

第三次是嘉庆年间的《秘殿珠林石渠宝笈三编》。于嘉庆二十年，自春至冬，前后历时十个月，由英和（1771－1840）、胡敬（1769－1845）等人负责，实际由胡敬主持实际工作，后他写有《西清札记》，对当时入宫鉴定整理的情形记载颇详。这次整理的特点是以乾隆皇帝弘历和嘉庆皇帝颙琰父子的书画为多，计2493件，历代书画较多，为916件，记录目次，以供查考，还是有便。此次整理编出《秘殿珠林。石渠宝笈三编》若干卷，又加钤“嘉庆御览”等玺印。乾隆逊位后，又在书画上添钤“太上皇帝”、“古稀天子之宝”、“八征耄耋之宝”等大玺。形式同于重编，当时仅有部分抄本分别编入《四库全书》，无印本流传，只有罗振玉就抄本录出目次付梓，未有全本。

1911年，孙中山领导的辛亥革命，推翻清朝，中国封建社会的最后一位皇帝宣统溥仪逊位后，仍留居故宫十一年，在此期间曾命载瀛、陈宝琛等人查点过一次清内府所藏的历代书画，并在观赏过的书画上加钤“宣统御览之宝”，并石印《点画目》一书，分送有关人员。少数藏于盛京沈阳和热河行宫，有金梁纂《盛京书画录》记载，但还难免有遗漏的（注147）。

结语

中华文化作为一个仍然存在的古老文明，其之所以能够绵延生存的原因，与其具有丰富的文化遗产密切相关，无论是器物或书画，历千年而传承不止。中国皇室的书画收藏，且不论其初衷是否出于个人嗜好，或高瞻远瞩地意识到书画收藏的重要性，客观上由于皇室对文化产物，包括书画作品所进行收藏、记载、研究和传承，而使中国数千年的文明成为从文字图像和实物都有据可循的史实，并且发挥着书画“成人伦、助教化”的作用（注148），使书画在皇室收藏中占据重要的地位。中国人常说“马上得天下，马下治天下”，在“文治武功”的统治术中，书画常成为一个显而易见的有文化修养的、和与社会精英及社会认知得到精神沟通的标记，而有助于国家的统治，为此，历代帝王的努力和贡献不菲。

首先，纵观中国历史，有如此之多的帝王成为书画收藏家，便是一个极为特别的中国文化现象，是世界上其它国家的历史中所罕见的。其次，无论是特意建造储藏之所还是建立一个管理体系，还是在鉴赏和著录上的努力来看，中国皇家对书画收藏重要性的认识越来越强烈，尤其在清代达到极致，皇宫中不仅有十几处专门收藏书画之所，和一套完整的管理班子，并且多次由皇家敕命修撰书画著录。另外，从书画收藏印鉴的数量，印文的用语，印章的尺寸等方面，也都体现对书画收藏和传承重要性的高度重视。乾隆皇帝书画鉴赏所用的八玺之一，便有一颗印玺之文曰“宜子孙”（注149）。“宜子孙”的观念自古有之，先秦时期以铜器为重器，作为传家传国的宝物，每在铸造的铭文中有“子孙永宝用”的吉语。乾隆皇帝将“宜子孙”印作为其御用宝玺的八玺之一，钤于他观赏过的著名书画上（注150），其苦心一目了然。这些书画无论是内容，记事，或艺术表现都有其独到之处，或可警世，或可励志，或可养心，或可传艺，而值得为皇帝们所宝爱，使书画作为传承中华文化血脉的载体，以保世祚之长久。故康熙皇帝欲使之“以永传也”（注151），乾隆皇帝则道“所当敬为什袭，贻我后人”（注152）。

无疑，在这样的努力之下，绘于卷轴之上的书画作为中国艺术最具特色的形式，承载着中华民族的心智和情怀，犹如磁铁和粘合剂，凝聚并体现了一个民族的精神世界，塑造了独一无二的中华文化面貌。各地收藏的中国书画作品，便是中国艺术和文化的最好代言人，其强烈的个性，使中国艺术得以屹立于世界艺术之林，而其丰富的内涵不仅保存了中国这一古老的文明，并且也丰富了整个人类的文明史。如是观之，历代帝王书画收藏的贡献孰可轻乎？

注解：

1. 《诗经。小雅。北山》载《十三经注疏》（北京，中华书局，1983年），第195页。
2. [唐]张彦远《历代名画记》，“图画之妙，爰自秦汉”（上海古籍出版社1991年），第812/280页；康熙皇帝在其为《佩文斋书画谱》的序言中亦有此说：“图画之事，始自秦汉，盛于六朝”，《佩文斋书画谱》第一册，御制佩文斋书画谱序（北京市中国书店，1984年）。
3. [唐]张彦远《法书要录》，载四库艺术丛书《古画品录》（上海古籍出版社，1991年），第812/108、165页。
4. 同上书，第812/121页。
5. 即陶弘景，456－536，秣陵，今南京人，南朝齐梁时道教思想家，医学家。隐居江苏茅山，梁武帝力邀不出，帝凡事皆问之，人称“山中宰相”。《辞海》（上海辞书出版社1979版缩印本，1986年重印），第438页。
6. [唐]张彦远《法书要录》，载四库艺术丛书《古画品录》（上海古籍出版社1991年），第812/121至125页。
7. 春秋战国到两汉，如果有书画作品的话，大约还是以帛书帛画为多见的。一方面考古发现可以作证，另据唐代张彦远《法书要录》“虞禾论书表”记载，直至东汉晚期的书家，帛书仍然占有很大的比例，如张芝，张昶，毛宏等或书法于缣素或有纸书。载四库艺术丛书《古画品录》（上海古籍出版社，1991年），第812/118至120页。
8. [唐]张彦远《历代名画记》中专列一节，讲述装裱技术自晋代以来已有，并列自刘宋以来著名的几位装裱师，如刘宋的范晔，徐爰，明帝时的虞禾等，均载四库艺术丛书《古画品录》（上海古籍出版社，1991年），第812/302页。
9. [唐]张彦远《法书要录》“虞禾论书表”，载四库艺术丛书《古画品录》（上海古籍出版社，1991年），第812/120页。
10. [唐]张彦远《历代名画记》卷一，载四库艺术丛书《古画品录》（上海古籍出版社1991年），第812/280页。

11. [清]张应文《清秘藏》卷下，提到的帝王鉴赏家为：桓玄，梁武帝，梁元帝，陈后主，隋炀帝，唐太宗，唐玄宗，李后主，宋太宗，宋徽宗，宋高宗，金章宗，元文宗，吴越王钱椒等，载于黄宾虹、邓实《美术丛书》第一卷（江苏古籍出版社，1997年），第491页。
12. 《二十四史。晋书》卷99，“其母因见月下流星入盆中，饮水保之，及长，形貌缳秀，风神疏朗，博综艺术，善属文，常负其才地，以雄豪自处，众咸惮之，朝廷疑而不用”（北京中华书局，1995年），第2585页。
13. [唐]张彦远《法书要录》，载四库艺术丛书《古画品录》（上海古籍出版社，1991年），第812/113页。
14. 同上书，第812/165页。
15. 《二十四史。晋书。桓玄传》卷99（北京中华书局，1995年），第2592页。
16. 同上书，“性贪鄙，好奇异，尤爱宝物，珠玉不离于手。人士有法书好画及佳园宅者，悉欲归己”（北京中华书局，1995年），第2594页。
17. [唐]张彦远《历代名画记》卷一，载四库艺术丛书《古画品录》（上海古籍出版社，1991年），第812/280页。
18. 《历代画家评传》潘天寿“顾恺之”，引《续晋阳秋》（香港中华书局，1986重版），第7页。
19. [唐]张彦远《法书要录》引《虞禾论书表》，载四库艺术丛书《古画品录》（上海古籍出版社，1991年），第812/118页。
20. [唐]张彦远《历代名画记》卷一，载四库艺术丛书《古画品录》（上海古籍出版社，1991年），第812/280页。
21. [唐]张彦远《法书要录》，载四库艺术丛书《古画品录》（上海古籍出版社，1991年），第812/165页。
22. [唐]裴孝源《贞观公私画史》载黄宾虹、邓实《美术丛书》第一卷（江苏古籍出版社，1997年），第808页。
23. 《二十四史。梁书》卷一（北京中华书局，1995年），第1页。
24. [明]姜宸英《湛园题跋》，载卢辅圣主编《中国书画全书》第七册（上海书画出版社，1994年），第967页。
25. [唐]张彦远《法书要录》，载四库艺术丛书《古画品录》（上海古籍出版社1991年），第812/119页。
26. 同上书，第812/122页。
27. [唐]裴孝源《贞观公私画史》，载黄宾虹、邓实《美术丛刊》第一卷（江苏古籍出版社，1997年），第804页。
28. 同上书，第808页；[唐]张彦远《法书要录》引唐何延之兰亭记，梁元帝绘制的“职贡图”传到他的曾孙唐代的监察御史萧翼之手，并由其以此为诱饵，为唐太宗从会稽永欣寺的辨才和尚处赚得了王羲之的兰亭序。载《古画品录》（上海古籍出版社，1991年），第812/157页。
29. [唐]张彦远《法书要录》第812/166页，记载为十四万卷；又见于《历代名画记》卷一，记载为二十四万卷，载四库艺术丛书《古画品录》（上海古籍出版社，1991年），第812/281页。
30. [唐]张彦远《历代名画记》卷一，记载颜之推（531－568）《观我生赋》对此次历史事件所作评论道：“人民百万而囚虏，书史千两（辆）而烟扬，史籍以来，未之有也。普天之下，斯文尽丧！”载四库艺术丛书《古画品录》（上海古籍出版社，1991年），第812/281页。
31. 同上书，第812/281页。
32. 杨仁恺《国宝沉浮录》（辽海出版社，1999年），第3页。
33. 《隋书》卷三十二，《经籍志》，载《二十四史》（北京中华书局，1995年），第908页。
34. [唐]朱景玄《唐朝名画录》载黄宾虹、邓实《美术丛刊》第二卷（江苏古籍出版社，1997年），第1010页。
35. [唐]张彦远《法书要录》，载四库艺术丛书《古画品录》（上海古籍出版社1991年），第812/172至176页。
36. [明]陈继儒《妮古录》卷三，载黄宾虹、邓实《美术丛书》第一卷（江苏古籍出版社，1997年），第633页。
37. 《西安碑林博物馆》（陕西人民出版社，2000年），第39页。
38. [清]康熙皇帝序载《佩文斋书画谱》第一册（北京市中国书店，1984年），第2页。
39. 兰亭雅集是中国文化的著名典故，东晋时，王羲之等四十余人于永和九年在兰亭修禊雅集，饮酒赋诗，兴致所至，王羲之挥笔撰文书写，似有神助，留下了行草名迹“兰亭序”，传到七世孙智永，智永出家会稽永欣寺，百年之后遗付弟子辩才。唐太宗几次诏辩才入宫，供养善诱，无从得之，最后由监察御史，梁元帝的曾孙萧翼，乔装打扮书生模样，以王的其他名迹书法，诱得辩才出示之而为太宗赚得了兰亭序。见张彦远《法书要录》，载四库艺术丛书《古画品录》（上海古籍出版社，1991年），第812/156至158页。
40. [宋]沈括《元刊梦溪笔谈》卷十七（北京文物出版社，1975年），第17页。
41. [唐]张彦远《法书要录》卷四，载四库艺术丛书《古画品录》（上海古籍出版社，1999年），第812/173页；另参见沈柔坚主编《中国美术词典》，并记载他仍有传世之作，为行书刻本“温泉铭”和“晋祠铭”（台湾雄狮美术出版社，1989年），第322页。
42. [唐]张彦远《法书要录》，载四库艺术丛书《古画品录》（上海古籍出版社，1991年），第812/172至173页。
43. 沈括《梦溪笔谈》卷十七，讲到民间所藏六朝晋宋书法作品都多为吊丧问疾的信笺，因贞观年间有严法禁止民间收藏佳作，只有这类信笺例外（北京文物出版社，1975年），第17页。
44. [唐]张彦远《历代名画记》卷二，论鉴藏收藏购求阅玩一节，载四库艺术丛书《古画品录》（上海古籍出版社，1991年），第812/297页。
45. [唐]张彦远《法书要录》卷四引《唐朝叙书录》，载四库艺术丛书《古画品录》（上海古籍出版社，1999年），第812/172页。
46. [唐]裴孝源《贞观公私画史》，载四库艺术丛书《古画品录》（上海古籍出版社，1991年），第812/17至29页。
47. 沈柔坚主编《中国美术辞典》（台北雄狮美术出版社，1989年），第109页。
48. [宋]郭若虚《图画见闻志》，载四库艺术丛书《古画品录》（上海古籍出版社，1991年），第812/569页。
49. [宋]郭若虚《图画见闻志》记载：“太祖平江表，所得图书赐学士院。初有五十余轴，及景德、咸平中，只有《雨村牧牛图》三轴（无名氏）《寒芦野雁》三轴（徐熙笔）《五王饮酪图》二轴（周文矩笔），悉令重装褙焉”。载四库艺术丛书《古画品录》（上海古籍出版社，1991年），第812/562页。
50. 同上书，第812/536页。
51. 同上书，第812/510页。
52. [清]吴修《青霞馆论画绝句》记载宋徽宗“投壶图”立轴上署宣和殿御制。载黄宾虹、邓实《美术丛书》第2卷（江苏古籍出版社，1997年），第1056页。

53. [元]陶宗仪《书史会要》卷六，“徽宗讳佶，哲宗弟，万几之余，翰墨不倦，行草正书，笔势劲逸，初学薛稷，变其法度，自号‘瘦金书’，意度天成，非可以陈迹求也”。王云五主编，载《四库全书珍本十集》（台北文史哲出版社，1974年），第3页。
54. 宋徽宗著《宣和论画杂评》一卷，载黄宾虹、邓实《美术丛书》第3集（江苏古籍出版社，1997年），第1778页。
55. [宋]周密《齐东野语》卷六，载《丛书集成初编》（北京中华书局，1985年）第1册，第63页。
56. 宋高宗御撰《思陵翰墨志》，载四库艺术丛书《古画品录》（上海古籍出版社，1991年），第812/432页。
57. [宋]杨王休《中兴馆阁储藏图画记》，载黄宾虹、邓实《美术丛书》第3卷（江苏古籍出版社，1997年），第2388页。另可参考杨仁恺《国宝沉浮录》，据《中兴馆阁录》记载，计有法书二百一十五轴，名画1260轴（册）（辽海出版社，1999年），第6页。
58. 沈柔坚主编《中国美术辞典》（台湾，雄狮美术出版社，1989年），第147页。
59. 杨仁恺《国宝沉浮录》（辽海出版社，1999年），第7页。
60. 傅申《元代皇室书画收藏史略》（台北国立故宫博物院，1981年），第4页。
61. 同上书，第4页。
62. 同上书，引元代秘书监志1342年纪录（台北国立故宫博物院，1981年），第87页。
63. 同上书，第92至93页。
64. 同上书，引翰林待制承直郎，兼国史院编修官，臣护都沓儿在“快雪时晴帖”的“奉敕恭跋”中的赞语（台北国立故宫博物院，1981年），第9页。
65. 同上书，《梁武帝半身像》有“皇姊珍玩”印，藏台北故宫博物院（台北国立故宫博物院，1981年），第20页，图版16。杨仁恺《国宝沉浮录》，赵昌《蛱蝶图》，宋高宗《草书洛神赋》和王振鹏《伯牙鼓琴图》钤有“皇姊图书”朱文大印（辽海出版社，1999年），第15至16页。
66. 傅申《元代皇室书画收藏史略》，引自袁桷《清容集》卷四十五，[载《四部丛刊初编缩本》，商务印书馆1928]（台北国立故宫博物院，1981年），第16至18页。
67. 同上书，第35至42页。
68. 杨仁恺《国宝沉浮录》（辽海出版社，1999年），第8页。
69. 杨伯达《清代院画》（紫禁城出版社，1993年），第23至24页。
70. [清]徐沁《明画录》载黄宾虹、邓实《美术丛书》第2卷（江苏古籍出版社，1997年），第1723页。
71. [清]徐沁《明画录》，载卢辅圣主编《中国书画全书》第十册（上海书画出版社，1996年），第1、5页。
72. 杨仁恺《国宝沉浮录》（辽海出版社，1999年），第8页。
73. [明]董其昌《骨董十三说》，载黄宾虹、邓实《美术丛书》第二集（江苏古籍出版社，1997年），第1194页。
74. 沈柔坚主编《中国美术辞典》，华亭派，明晚期江南画派，由顾正谊等创，常称为“松江画派”之一支，董其昌为其代表画家（台北雄狮美术出版社，1989年），第79页。
75. [清]高士奇《江村销夏录》凡例中特意申明“董文敏公书画为近代第一，所见真迹甚多，另为一卷”，载四库艺术丛书《庚子销夏记》（上海古籍出版社，1991年），第812/470页。
76. [清]高士奇《江村书画目》，载卢辅圣主编《中国书画全书》第七册，（上海书画出版社，1994年），第1068页。
77. 万依、王树卿、刘潞《清代宫廷史》引赵翼之语，乾隆青少年时代的诗文则由词臣顾成天收集整理为《乐善堂全集》（天津百花文艺出版社，2004年），第280页。
78. 同上书（天津百花文艺出版社，2004年），第293页。
79. 杨仁恺《国宝沉浮录》（辽海出版社，1999年），第27至28页。
80. 同上书，第2至6页。
81. [清]阮元《石渠随笔》卷一，载于《笔记小说大观》（扬州，江苏广陵古籍刻印出版社，1984年），第369页。
82. 杨仁恺《国宝沉浮录》（辽海出版社，1999年），第109页。
83. 据《故宫散佚书籍书画目录》的不完全统计，清室善后委员会（故宫博物院，民国十五年，1926年）。
84. 《二十四史。隋书。经籍志》（北京中华书局，1995年），第905至907页。
85. [唐]张彦远《历代名画记》卷一，载四库艺术丛书《古画品录》（上海古籍出版社，1991年），第812/281页。
86. [唐]张彦远《法书要录》卷四，载四库艺术丛书《古画品录》（上海古籍出版社，1991年），第812/166页，812/172页。
87. [唐]张彦远《法书要录》卷三，载四库艺术丛书《古画品录》（上海古籍出版社，1999年），第812/154页。
88. [宋]郭若虚《图画见闻志》，载四库艺术丛书《古画品录》（上海古籍出版社，1991年），第812/510页。
89. [宋]沈括《元刊梦溪笔谈》：“内诸司舍屋唯秘阁最宏壮，阁下穹隆高敞，相传谓之木天”，卷二十四（北京文物出版社，1975年），第13页。
90. [宋]郭若虚《图画见闻志》，载四库艺术丛书《古画品录》（上海古籍出版社，1991年），第812/510页。
91. [宋]周密《云烟过眼录》，载《丛书集成初编》（中华书局，1985年），第58页。另参见[宋]杨王休《中兴馆阁储藏图画记》，载黄宾虹、邓实《中国美术丛书》第三卷（江苏古籍出版社，1997年），第2388页。
92. 傅申《元代皇室书画收藏史略》（台北国立故宫博物院，1981年），第78至79页。
93. 傅申《元代皇室书画收藏史略》，引杨瑀《山居新话》第11页，（台北国立故宫博物院，1981年），第41至42页。
94. 同上书，第66页。
95. 万依、王树卿、刘潞《清代宫廷史》（天津百花文艺出版社，2004年），第73至74页。
96. [宋]沈括《元刊梦溪笔谈》卷一，引用历史上藏书分散以防水火之例（北京文物出版社，1975年），第15页。
97. 《石渠宝笈》初编第一册目录（上海古籍出版社，1981年）。
98. 万依、王树卿、刘潞《清代宫廷史》（天津百花文艺出版社，2004年），第295至296页。
99. [清]鄂尔泰、张廷玉《国朝宫史》下册，（北京古籍出版社，1987年），第456至458页。
100. [清]庆桂、董诰等《中国史学丛书。国朝宫史正续编》（台北，民国五十年东方学会印，1961年），第5册。
101. [唐]张彦远《法书要录》序，载四库艺术丛书《古画品录》（上海古籍出版社，1991年），第812/104页。
102. [唐]张彦远《法书要录》唐徐浩古迹记，“唐代安乐公主得到中宗内府藏品，因爱王羲之的‘乐毅论’，以织成袋，盛置竹箱”载四库艺术丛书《古画品录》（上海古籍出版社，1991年），第812/154页。

103. [唐]张彦远《法书要录。武平一之〈徐氏法书记〉》，载四库艺术丛书《古画品录》（上海古籍出版社，1991年），第812/151页。
104. [宋]郭若虚《图画见闻志》载四库艺术丛书《古画品录》（上海古籍出版社，1991年），第812/510，812/561页。伏天是中国农历的算法，相当于阳历的七月中旬到八月下旬，《辞海》缩印本（上海辞书出版社，1986年），第217页。
105. 参见[宋]沈括《元刊梦溪笔谈》卷三（北京文物出版社，1975年），第11页。
106. [元]王思善之语载《六如居士画谱》，载黄宾虹、邓实《美术丛书》第2卷（江苏古籍出版社，1997年），第1228页。
107. [唐]张彦远《法书要录》武平一"徐氏法书记""青绫褾玳眉轴者，云是梁朝旧迹，褾首各题篇目行字等数，章草书多于其侧帖以真字楷书"，载四库艺术丛书《古画品录》（上海古籍出版社，1991年），第812/151页。
108. [唐]张彦远《法书要录》引"梁中书侍郎虞禾论书表"，载四库艺术丛书《古画品录》（上海古籍出版社，1991年），第812/118至119,165页。
109. [唐]张彦远《历代名画记》，载四库艺术丛书《古画品录》（上海古籍出版社，1991年），第812/303页。
110. 同上书，第812/281页。
111. [宋]郭若虚《图画见闻志》，载四库艺术丛书《古画品录》（上海古籍出版社，1991年），第812/569页。
112. 杨仁恺《国宝沉浮录》（辽海出版社，1999年），第6页。
113. 宋高宗《思陵翰墨志》，载四库艺术丛书《古画品录》（上海古籍出版社，1991年），第812/432页。
114. [明]周嘉胄《装潢志》，载黄宾虹、邓实《中国美术丛刊》第一卷（江苏古籍出版社，1997年），第79页。
115. [宋]周密〈齐东野语〉卷六，载《丛书集成初编》（北京中华书局，1985年），第63页。
116. [宋]周密《齐东野语》卷六，载《丛书集成初编》（北京中华书局，1985年），第63至72页。
117. 杨仁恺《国宝沉浮录》（辽海出版社，1999年），第7至8页。
118. [清]王毓贤《绘事备考》，载四库艺术丛书《庚子销夏记》（上海古籍出版社，1991年），第826/116至117页。
119. 万依、王树卿、刘潞《清代宫廷史》（天津百花文艺出版社，2004年），第296页。
120. 杨仁恺《国宝沉浮录》（辽海出版社，1999年），第41页。另见溥仪《我的前半生》，对养心殿后的建福宫内藏文物书画的记载（北京，东方出版社，2007年），第126页。
121. 邢永福、师力武主编《清宫热河档案》（国家档案编纂委员会档案丛刊，中国档案出版社，2003年），第481至486页。
122. [唐]张彦远《历代名画记》，载四库艺术丛书《古画品录》（上海古籍出版社，1991年），第812/301页。
123. [宋]米芾《书史》载黄宾虹、邓实《美术丛书》第一卷（江苏古籍出版社，1997年），第658页。
124. [清]阮元《石渠随笔》，载《笔记小说》（江苏扬州广陵古籍刻印社，1984年），第396页。
125. [唐]裴孝源《贞观公私画史》，载四库艺术丛书《古画品录》（上海古籍出版社，1991年），第808、812页。
126. [宋]郭若虚《图画见闻志》，载四库艺术丛书《古画品录》（上海古籍出版社，1991年），第812/569页。
127. [唐]张彦远《法书要录》，载四库艺术丛书《古画品录》（上海古籍出版社，1991年），第812/152页。据米芾所记，太宗亦曾在谢安帖上御跋三字，《书史》载黄、邓《美术丛刊》第一卷（江苏古籍出版社，1997年），第806页。
128. [宋]杨王休《中兴馆阁储藏图画记》，载黄宾虹、邓实《美术丛书》第三卷（江苏古籍出版社，1987年），第2388页。
129. 《文物》1972年5期，图版参：1。
130. 李慧淑《 Exquisite Moment: West Lake and Southern Song Art 》（纽约华美协进社中国美术馆，2001年），第86至93页。
131. 参见傅申《元代皇室书画收藏史略》（台北国立故宫博物院1981年），第一，二章；杨仁凯《国宝沉浮录》（辽海出版社，1999年），第14至16页。
132. 万依、王树卿、刘璐《清代宫廷史》（天津百花文艺出版社，2004年），第80页。
133. [清]赵翼《檐曝杂记》卷一，载《清代史料笔记》（北京中华书局，1997年），第8页。
134. [清]鄂尔泰、张廷玉《国朝宫史》，卷十一至十五，宫殿（北京古籍出版社，1987年），第177至349页。
135. 万依、王树卿、刘璐《清代宫廷史》（百花文艺出版社，2004年），第294页。
136. [唐]张彦远《历代名画记》，载四库艺术丛书《古画品录》（上海古籍出版社，1991年），第812/299至300页。
137. 同上书，第812/300页。
138. 同上书，第812/301页。
139. [唐]张彦远《历代名画记。叙自古跋尾押署》，载四库艺术丛书《古画品录》（上海古籍出版社，1991年），第812/301页。
140. [清]阮元《石渠随笔》记载隋代展子虔游春图，便有内府印二颗，载《笔记小说大观》（江苏扬州广陵古籍刻印社，1984年），第368页。
141. 同上书，第369页。
142. 《故宫已佚书籍书画目录四种》（北京故宫博物院，民国十五年版，1926年）。
143. [宋]郭若虚《图画见闻志》，载四库艺术丛书《古画品录》（上海古籍出版社，1991年），第812/509页。
144. [唐]裴孝源《贞观公私画史》，载四库艺术丛书《古画品录》（上海古籍出版社，1991年），第812/17至29。
145. [宋]邓椿《画继》，载四库艺术丛书《画史》（上海古籍出版社，1991年），第813/505页。
146. 康熙皇帝序《佩文斋书画谱》第一册（北京市中国书店，1984年），第2页。
147. 杨仁恺《国宝沉浮录》（辽海出版社，1999年），第30页。
148. [唐]张彦远《历代名画记》卷一，载四库艺术丛书《古画品录》（上海古籍出版社，1999年），第812/279页。
149. 参见江文苇在本图录中的文章，第24页。
150. [清]阮元《石渠随笔》"论钤宝"，载《笔记小说大观》（江苏扬州广陵古籍刻印社，1984年），第396页。
151. 康熙皇帝御制佩文斋书画谱序《佩文斋书画谱》，第一册（北京市中国书店，1984年），第2页。
152. 乾隆皇帝上喻《石渠宝笈》卷一，载四库艺术丛书（上海古籍出版社，1991年），第824/1页。

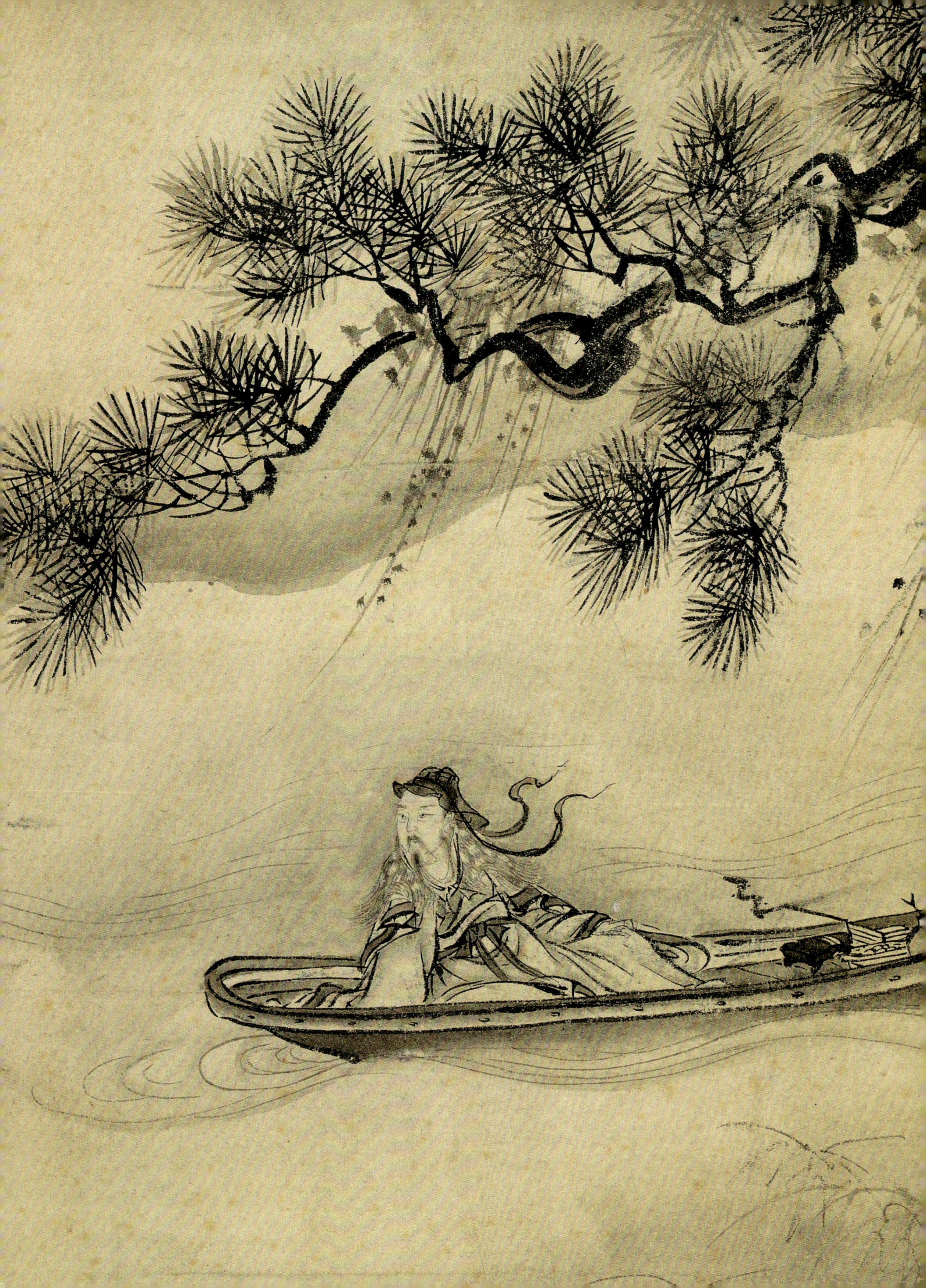

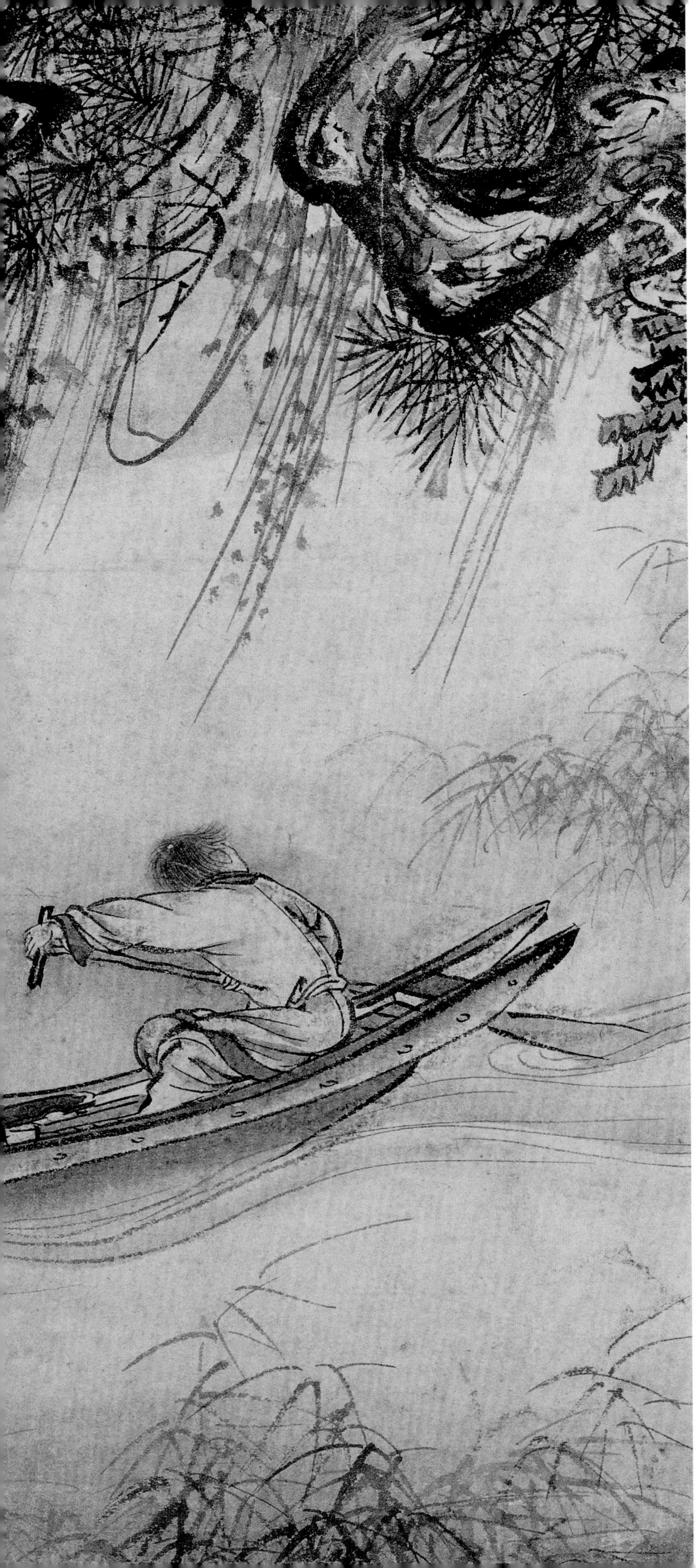

Catalogue I
Works Recorded in the Imperial Catalogues

图录第一部分
皇家著录中的书画作品

Contributors 作者

WWHC Willow Weilan Hai Chang 海蔚蓝
HWL Huang Weili 黄伟利
DAS David Ake Sensabaugh 江文苇

Translators 译者

DHWS David Huiwei Shen 沈慧伟
MSW Mansheng Wang 王满晟
LYC Ling-Yi Chien 简菱仪

Measurements, unless specified otherwise, are for the actual work of art and does not include mounting. The inscriptions of colophon writers listed in the heading of each entry are either appended to or located on the actual art work. Seals are listed as either "relief" (leaving an impression of red characters) or "intaglio" (leaving an impression of white characters). Additional information about mounting is included only if it is of significant interest. Much of the seal information has been provided by the Liaoning Provincial Museum with additional research by Professor Zhou Xiaolu, David Ake Sensabaugh, and Willow Weilan Hai Chang.

书画尺寸皆以画芯为准，不包括装裱。跋文作者包括该作品上各处所出现者。印鉴亦注明朱文或白文。除特殊装裱者有介绍外，其他从略。印鉴主要参照辽宁省博物馆的资料并由周晓陆教授、江文苇和海蔚蓝核实。

Overleaf: Detail of leaf 7 from cat. no. 4

1
明　王绂　湖山书屋图
手卷，纸本水墨
Wang Fu (1362–1416)
Studios among Lakes and Mountains, 1410

Handscroll; ink on paper
29 x 828.2 cm

ARTIST'S SEALS: Binghu qiuyue (rectangular/intaglio), Mengduan (square/intaglio)

IMPERIAL SEALS: Qianlong, r. 1736–95] Qianlong yulan zhibao (large square/relief), Qianglong yushang zhibao (square/relief), Shiqu baoji (rectangular/relief), Yangxindian jiancangbao (rectangular/relief), Qianlong jianshang (round/intaglio), Sanxitang jingjianxi (rectangular/relief), Yizisun (square/intaglio), Guxi tianzi (round/relief), Wufu wudaitang guxi tianzi (large square/relief), Bazheng maonian zhibao (large square/relief); [Jiaqing, r. 1796–1820] Jiaqing yulan zhibao (oval/relief); [Xuantong (Puyi), r. 1909–11] Xuantong jianshang (square/relief), Wuyizhai jingjianxi (rectangular/relief), Xuantong yulan zhibao (square/relief)

OTHER SEALS: [Wen Zhengming, 1470–1559] Wen Zhengming yin (rectangular/intaglio), Heng (half square of Hengshan seal/relief); [Wen Peng, 1498–1573] Wen Peng yin (square /relief and intaglio); [Xiang Yuanbian, 1525–1590] Xiang Zijing jia zhencang (rectangular/relief), Tianlaige (rectangular/relief), Mo-Lin (linked square seals/relief), Jingyin'an zhu (square/relief), Xiang Molinfu miji zhiyin (rectangular/relief), Pingsheng qishang (square/intaglio), Xiang Yuanbian yin (square/relief), Zi (half seal/intaglio), Zhipu (half seal of Liuyi zhipu, intaglio), Ruoshui xuan (rectangular/relief), Tuimi (double-gourd/relief), Xiang Molin jianshangzhang (rectangular/ intaglio), Molin (rectangular seam seal/relief); [An Qi, 1683–ca. 1744] Chaoxian ren (rectangular/intaglio), An Qi zhiyin (square/intaglio), An Yizhoujia zhencang (rectangular/relief), Anshi Yizhou shuhua zhizhang (rectangular/intaglio), Yizhou zhencang (rectangular/relief), Siyuan tang (square/intaglio), Lucun (square/relief); [unidentified] Youxi hanmo (square seam seal/relief)

COLOPHON WRITERS (SEALS): Qianlong emperor (Shiqu jijian [square/relief], Jixia yiqing [square/intaglio], Qianlong chenhan [square/relief]); Wen Zhengming (Wen Zhengming yin [square/ intaglio], Hengshan [square/relief]); Yu Yunwen, 1512–1579 (Zhong Wei [rectangular/intaglio], Chengsheng linfan [square/relief])

WRAPPER: Ginger-yellow brocade, inscribed "Wang Fu Hushan shuwu zhenji. Shangdeng cangyi. Qianlong jiunian chunyue chen Zhang Zhao deng fengchi bianci"

画家印鉴：冰壶秋月（白文长方印）、孟端（白文方印）

皇家印鉴：[清乾隆皇帝弘历，在位1736–1795]乾隆御览之宝（朱文大方印）、乾隆御赏之宝（朱文方印）、石渠宝笈（朱文长方印）、养心殿鉴藏宝（朱文长方印）、乾隆鉴赏（白文圆印）、三希堂精鉴玺（朱文长方印）、宜子孙（白文方印）、古希天子（朱文圆印）、五福五代堂古稀天子宝（朱文大方印）、八征耄念之宝（朱文大方印）。[清嘉庆皇帝颙琰，在位1796–1820]嘉庆御览之宝（朱文椭圆印）。[清宣统皇帝溥仪，在位1909–1911]宣统鉴赏（朱文方印）、无逸斋精鉴玺（朱文长方印）、宣统御览之宝（朱文方印）。

其他印鉴：[文征明，1470–1559]文征明印（白文长方印）、衡（朱文印，衡山朱文印半边）。[文彭，1498–1573]文彭印（朱白文方印）。[项元汴，1525–1590]项子京家珍藏（朱文长方印）、天籁阁（朱文长方印）、墨林（朱文连珠印）、净因庵主（朱文方印）、项墨林父秘笈之印(朱文长方印)、平生奇赏（白文方印）、项元汴印（朱文方印）、子（白文半印）、之圃（六艺之圃，白文半印）、若水轩（朱文长方印）、退密（朱文葫芦印）、项墨林鉴赏章（白文长方印）、墨林（朱文长方骑缝印）。[安岐，1683–约1744]朝鲜人（白文长方印）、安岐之印（白文方印）、安仪周家珍藏（朱文长方印）、安氏仪周书画之章（白文长方印）、仪周珍藏（朱文长方印）、思原堂（白文方印）、麓村（朱文方印）。另有骑缝印：游戏翰墨（朱文方印）。

题跋者（钤印）：清乾隆皇帝弘历（石渠继鉴[朱文方印]、几暇怡情[白文方印]、乾隆宸翰[朱文方印]）。文征明，1470–1559（文征明印[白文方印]、衡山[朱文方印]）。俞允文，1512–1579（中尉[白文长方印]、乘胜林樊[朱文方印]）。

画袱：姜黄色织花锦。内面书写：王绂湖山书屋真迹。上等藏一。乾隆九年春月臣张照等奉敕编次。

Wang Fu's *Studios among Lakes and Mountains* was among the many handscrolls surreptitiously taken out of the Forbidden City by Puyi and his brother Pujie (1907–1994) before November of 1924. It had been in the palace collection since not long before 1744 when it was included in *Shiqu baoji* (Treasured boxes of the Stone Channel), the catalogue of the imperial collection of calligraphy and painting commissioned by the Qianlong emperor at the beginning of the year.[1] Before entry into the palace, it had belonged to An Qi, the son of a Korean bondservant who had amassed a fortune during the Kangxi reign (1662–1722) through the salt monopoly.[2] The family wealth had allowed An Qi to become one of the foremost connoisseurs and collectors of the early eighteenth century. *Studios among Lakes and Mountains* was given a short notice in an addendum to the sixth fascicle of An Qi's catalogue of his own collection, *Moyuan huiguan* (Notes on works in ink that I had the good fortune to see), prefaced in 1742, although presumably the painting had already left the collection by that time.[3] During the Yongzheng reign (1723–35), the An family had experienced political difficulties resulting in the forced sale of some of An Qi's paintings. It was not until 1746, probably after An Qi's death and after the completion of the imperial catalogue, that many works from the collection were acquired by the palace. With its sixteenth-century colophons by Wen Zhengming and Yu Yunwen, *Studios among Lakes and Mountains* was designated as a first-class work by the editors of the imperial catalogue.

Studios among Lakes and Mountains was painted in 1410 for Lin Zhong, the director of the Ministry of Personnel early in the Yongle reign (1403–24). It was completed in mid-autumn of that year. In his inscription at the end of the scroll (detail d), Wang Fu recorded that Lin had supplied him with both the paper and the subject matter for the painting. In fulfilling Lin's request he felt that his painting was a modest effort for such fine paper but Lin knew him and would understand. Lin came from Huating in Songjiang, south of present-day Shanghai, and Wang painted for him a scene of lakes and hills typical of the water country in the delta region south of the Yangzi River. The scholarly dwellings nestled in the landscape among fishing villages and farming communities seem separated from the outside world even while being surrounded by it. They are quiet domains accented by tall pine trees with straight branches. What Wang has achieved in his scroll is to combine the landscape of reclusive residences developed during the last decades of the Yuan dynasty—the thatched hut pictures (*caotang tu*) which embodied the dilemma of whether to serve or retire in formal juxtapositions of open and closed compositions—with the tradition of long panoramic landscapes inherited from the Song and practiced in the Yuan period by such painters as Huang Gongwang (1269–1354). Wang Fu's *Studios among Lakes and Mountains* bears many resemblances to Huang's *Dwelling in the Fuchun Mountains* (*Fuchun shanju tu*) completed in 1350. In both paintings, areas of foreground and distance alternate in rhythmic progression, and in both pictures, dry brushstrokes are woven together to capture the earthy surfaces of land while at the same time maintaining formal independence as strokes. Wang Fu appears to go one step beyond Huang Gongwang in the formalization of his brushwork.

More is known about Wang Fu than about most early Ming painters.[4] He was born in 1362 in Wuxi, Jiangsu, the home of the late Yuan painter Ni Zan (1306–1374). At the age of fifteen he became a student in the government-run county school, but perhaps because of some minor infraction he was not able to continue his studies. He returned home and at about that time married and had two children. In 1378, after living at home for two years, he responded to a government call for unemployed licentiates to travel to the capital at Nanjing to fill positions in the bureaucracy. His time in the capital was short, however, and it is not clear whether he was ever given an appointment. In 1380, for reasons that remain unclear, he was banished to Datong in the northern part of Shanxi Province where he served as a frontier guard under extreme hardship. It is most likely that he was caught up in the purge of government officials surrounding the fall of the prime minister Hu Weiyong, who was accused of treason and executed in 1380. Recent studies of Wang Fu's life suggest that he was in Datong for twelve years before he was able to return to Wuxi. It is possible that a son adopted in Shanxi may have served out the remainder of his sentence.[5] Wang Fu lived in Wuxi at Mount Jiulong for the next decade writing poetry and painting and adopted Jiulong Mountain Man (Jiulong Shanren) as his byname. He painted landscapes in the manner of his fellow townsman Ni Zan and emulated other late Yuan-early Ming masters, such as Wang Meng (ca. 1308–1385), as well. In painting bamboo he followed Wu Zhen (1280–1354). After the death of Zhu Yuanzhang (1328–1398), the first Ming emperor, and the coup staged by his fourth son Zhu Di (1360–1424), who became the third emperor of the Ming dynasty in 1402, Wang Fu was recommended for office in the Wenyuan Ge pavilion in the capital because of his renown as a calligrapher. He was in Nanjing for the next decade and at one point accompanied an imperial son-in-law on a tour to Sichuan. From around 1409 to

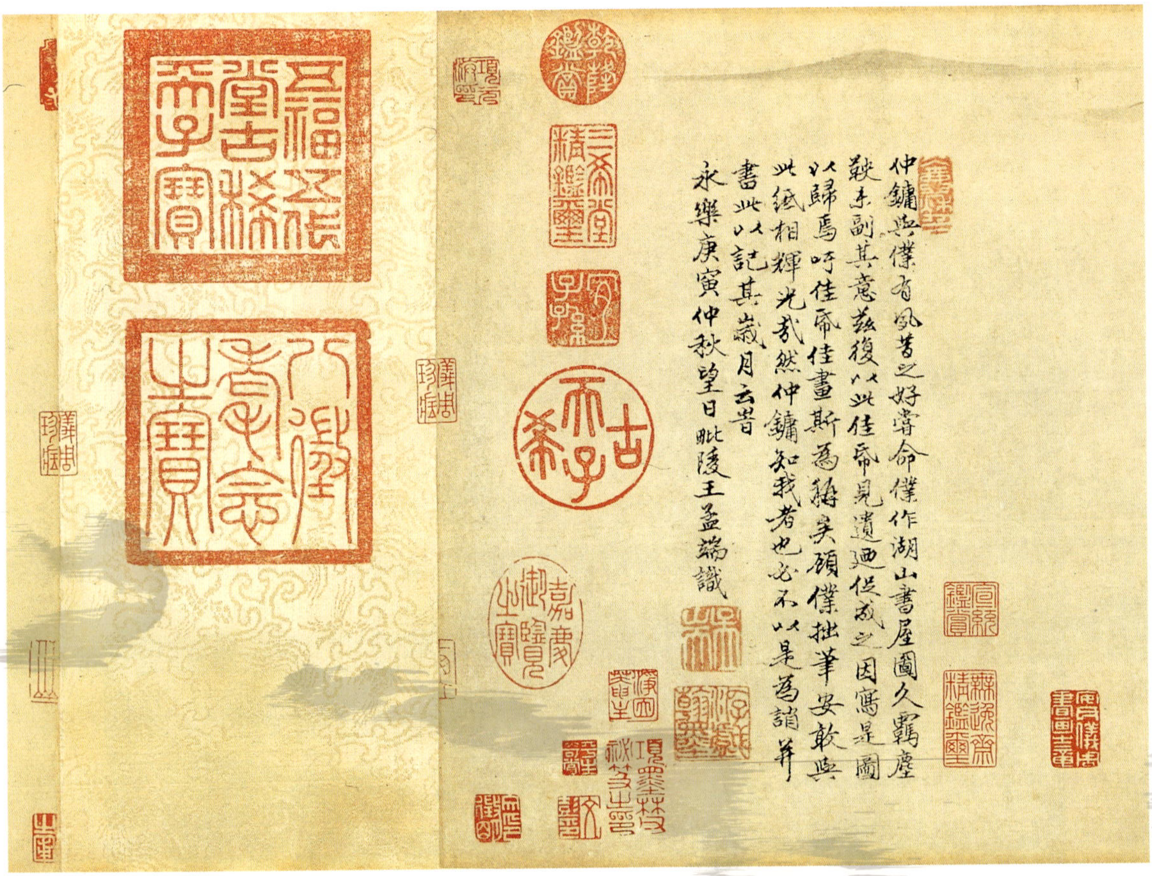
仲鏞與僕有夙昔之好嘗命僕作湖山書屋圖久羈塵
鞅未副其意茲復以此佳紙見遺迺促成之因寫是圖
以歸焉吁佳紙佳畫斯爲稱矣顧僕拙筆安敢與
此紙相輝光哉然仲鏞知我者也必不以是爲誚并
書此以記其歲月云爾
永樂庚寅仲秋望日毗陵王孟端識

1 (detail c 局部)

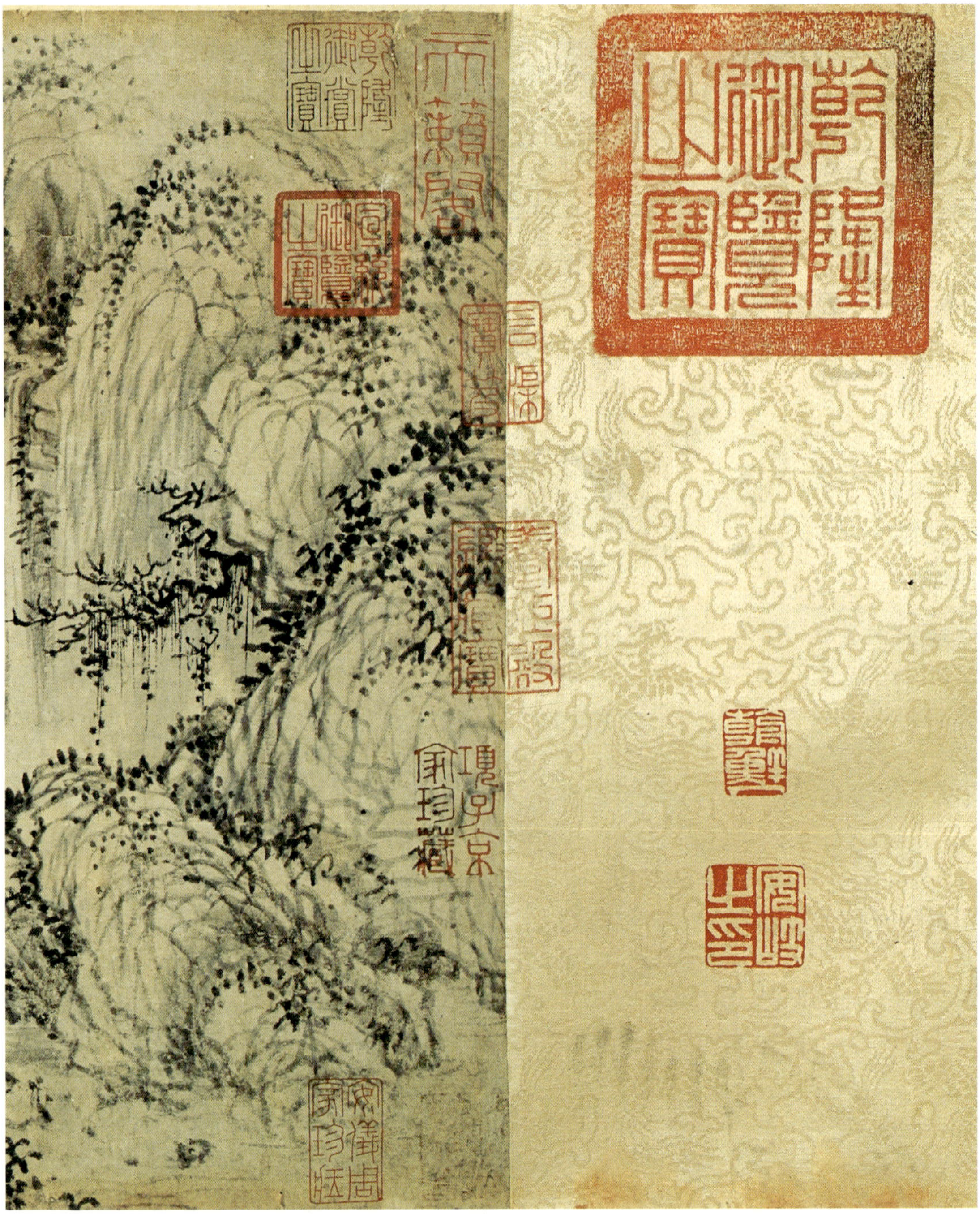

1 (detail d 局部)

1410 he was in the retinue of the Yongle emperor, Zhu Di, during an inspection tour to the north, where the emperor was preparing Beijing to serve as the northern capital. *Studios among Lakes and Mountains*, painted in the autumn of 1410, would presumably have been executed after his return from the north. In 1412 Wang Fu was raised to the rank of drafter (Zhongshu sheren) in the Central Drafting Office, a low rank but still one indicative of the esteem in which he was now held, and in the following year again accompanied the court on a trip to Beijing. He remained in Beijing until his death in 1416.

In a 1516 colophon attached to the painting, the great Ming scholar-painter Wen Zhengming praises Wang Fu's principled character for not allowing himself to be ensnared by his art, but at the same time he places Wang only in the top grade of the "capable" (*neng*) class of painters, after the "inspired" and the "excellent." He further cites critical opinion that Wang Fu combined the professional with the scholarly in equal measure. This ambivalent estimation of Wang Fu persisted into the Qing period. After writing in his *Daguanlu* (A record of magnificent works that I have seen) of 1712 that *Studios among Lakes and Mountains* was a true passage of landscape, Wu Sheng continues that Wang Fu had a uniformity of texturing and washes and a stability of composition that resembled the habits of a professional painter.[6] He attributes this to a lack of continuity in the transmission of painting from the masters of the late Yuan, particularly from Ni Zan and Wang Meng, to the painters of the early Ming. For Wu Sheng, the tradition of painting had nearly died out with Ni Zan's and Wang Meng's deaths in 1374 and 1385 respectively, leaving painters like Wang Fu bereft of teachers. Both Wen Zhengming and Wu Sheng were impressed by the length of the handscroll, however, and, as Wu remarked, such long scroll compositions by Wang were rare. Wang Fu's sustained achievements of composition and brushwork in *Studios among Lakes and Mountains* belies the statements by Wen Zhengming and Wu Sheng. He is recognized now as one of the important links in the formation of the Wu School of painting of which Shen Zhou (1427–1509) was the greatest early exponent.[7]

DAS

Notes

1. *Shiqu baoji* [Treasured boxes of the Stone Channel] (1745), reprinted in *Midian zhulin Shiqu baoji hebian* [Pearl forest of the Secret Hall and Treasured boxes of the Stone Channel, combined edition], 12 vols. (Shanghai: Shanghai shudian, 1988), vol. 2, p. 595.
2. For biographical information on An Qi, see Fang Chao-ying, "An Ch'i," in *Eminent Chinese of the Ch'ing Period*, ed. Arthur W. Hummel (Washington: U. S. Government Printing Office, 1943), pp. 11–13, and Thomas Lawton, "The Mo-yuan hui-kuan by An Ch'i," in *Qingzhu Jiang Fucong xiansheng qishisui lunwenji* [Symposium in honor of Dr. Chiang Fu-tsung on his seventieth birthday] (Taipei: Guoli gugong bowuyuan, 1969), pp. 13–35.
3. An Qi, *Moyuan huiguan* (preface dated 1742), reprinted in *Zhongguo shuhua quanshu* [Complete writings on Chinese calligraphy and painting], vol. 10 (Shanghai: Shanghai shuhua chubanshe, 1996), p. 415.
4. For biographical information, see Yu Jianhua, *Wang Fu* (Shanghai renmin meishu chubanshe, 1961); Lee Hwa-chou, "Wang Fu," in *Dictionary of Ming Biography*, ed. L. Carrington Goodrich (New York: Columbia University Press, 1976), pp. 1374–75; Song Houmei, "Mingchu huajia Wang Fu de yinju yu Zhuchalu zhuangzhi niandai kao" [An investigation into the chronology for the early Ming painter Wang Fu's retirement and his Bamboo Tea Stove], *Gugong xueshu jikan* [Palace Museum research quarterly] 2, no. 3 (1985): 13–27; and Kathlyn Liscomb, "Wang Fu's Contribution to a New Painting Style in the Ming Dynasty," *Artibus Asiae* 48, no. 1/2 (1987): 39–78.
5. Song Houmei, "Mingchu huajia Wang Fu."
6. Wu Sheng, *Daguanlu* (preface 1712), *juan* 19, p. 13a–13b, reprinted in *Yishu shangjian xuanzhen* [Selected writings on art appreciation] (Taipei: Hanhua, 1970), pp. 2325–6.
7. See Hou-mei Sung Ishida [Song Houmei], "Early Ming Painters in Nanking and the Formation of the Wu School," *Ars Orientalis* 17 (1989): 73–115; and Liscomb, "Wang Fu's Contribution."

王绂的《湖山书屋图》为溥仪与其弟溥杰(1907–1994)在1924年十一月前，暗中从紫禁城运出的众多图卷之一，此图於1744年前即已入清内府。乾隆皇帝为记载清宫所藏历代书画藏品，于该年下令编纂《石渠宝笈》。被收入《石渠宝笈》目录之前，原为安岐旧藏。安岐父为朝鲜包衣，在康熙期间(1662–1722)因垄断天津盐业而成巨富。庞大家业与财富，得以使安岐成为十八世纪早期最重要的鉴藏家。安岐为自己的收藏写了一部作序于1742年的目录集《墨缘汇观》，《湖山书屋图》记载在该著录的第六卷附录中。此图可能在此目录完成时已离安府，雍正在位期间(1723 –35)，安家因政治因素，被迫出售安岐一部分的旧藏。安岐所曾拥有的大批书画精品，要到1746年安岐谢世、《宝笈》完成后，才陆续地被宫廷收购。《湖山书屋图》带有十六世纪文征明与俞允文之题跋，《宝笈》编者将其收录于上等之列。后为溥仪与其弟溥杰（1907–1994）

在1922年十一月前，暗中从紫禁城运出的众多图卷之一。

此图为王绂在1410年永乐年间(1403–24)为林钟（字仲镛）所画，林于永乐早期(1403–24)担任吏部郎中。此画于是年秋天完成。王绂在卷尾题字中写道，林为此画提供题目与画纸，王意欲遂林所愿，却觉如此珍贵的画纸来作画太过看重他，但王相信林了解他这番心意。林为松江华亭人，即今上海市南区，王绂因此画了长江三角洲南岸、太湖一带水乡泽国的景色。画中文人居处隐于山水之间，渔家农村则错落其中；峰谷间松林茂密，更添宁静闲适的江南气息。整个湖山清野，绝尘避世。王不但成功地将元代晚期草堂图中表现退隐与入世、开放与自闭空间构图的双重矛盾情结，融入画面中，更传承了始自北宋、实践于元朝黄公望(1269–1354)式的全景山水长卷，意象清新，浑然天成。王绂此《湖山书屋图》与黄公望1350年完成的《富春山居图》确有着许多的相似之处。两图均将山水景致以近距远距相互交替的形式处理，在图面上创造一种交错有致的韵律感；山石表面均以干笔皴擦，景色交织一气；用笔则顿挫转折，点皴勾线，极有法度。然在依循传统之外，王绂的笔法，却比黄公望更讲究形式的表达。比起其它明代早期画家，王绂生平较为完整详尽。1362年生于无锡，为元末画家倪瓒(1306–1374)的同乡。十五岁时为弟子员，然因故未能继续学业。王绂回到家乡，不久娶妻并生有二子。1378年，朝廷征召赋闲在家的知识分子，王绂即被举荐进京。王逗留南京的时间相当短暂，是否谋得官职亦未知。1380年，丞相胡惟庸被控为逆党而遭处死，朝廷因此事兴大狱，牵连甚广。王绂亦因不明原因而坐累，被发放到山西大同充当戍卒。近世研究得知，王被罚以苦役十二年后，才得回乡。据说在山西时，王过继了一个祀子，后由他为王服完剩余的刑期。王绂回乡后十年间，隐居九龙山(即惠山)，赋诗作画，自号九龙山人。王绂之山水，取法倪瓒，兼及王蒙(约1308–1385)等元末明初大家，画竹则师法吴镇(1280–1354)。明朝开国皇帝朱元璋(1328–1398)薨后，第四子朱棣（1360–1424)主导政变，于1402年登基为明朝第三位皇帝。同年间，王绂因善书而被举荐进京，供事文渊阁。供职南京十年间，王曾一度随皇驸马出行四川。1409至1410年期间，担任永乐皇帝朱棣之随从，前往北京巡视，从事迁都的筹备工作。《湖山书屋图》作于1410年秋，应是北京之行结束后的作品。1412年，王绂授中书舍人一职，职位虽低，却受到相当的重视。翌年，王再度随明成祖北巡，驻留北京，直到1416年过世。

1516年时，此图卷附加了明代大画家文征明的题款，文中称美王绂高尚自持的性格：“人品特高，能不为艺事所役”。但却只将王之绘画成就评为“能品上”，即能品级别里的上品之作，非在其上的“妙品”与“神品”之列。文征明说明此因王绂兼容文人与职业画风之故。这种对王绂绘画矛盾的评价与看法，持续到清代。直至1712年吴升在《大观录》中指出《湖山书屋图》为一真山水杰作。吴升认为王绂皴擦渲染，笔调圆熟，构图形式统一，诚为职业画家之风。但他进一步分析，其真正原因在于元代后期，大师如倪瓒与王蒙等人的风格传统，并未直接延续到明代早期。在倪与王分别于1374与1385年谢世后，中国绘画传统面临了几乎灭绝的境况，留给王绂这些明代画家无师可事、无法可循的艺术真空状况。然而，文征明与吴升两人均对此长卷的尺寸予以赞赏。吴升指出，王绂鲜有如此形制的长卷创作。事实证明，王绂的《湖山书屋图》无论在章法、笔意上的成就，均超过文征明与吴升的评价。如今，王绂被公认是影响以沈周(1427–1509)为早期代表人物的吴门画派最重要的画家之一。

江文苇（LYC译）

注解：

1. 《石渠宝笈》(1745)，重刊于合刊本《秘殿珠林石渠宝笈合编》，12册(上海: 上海书店，1988)，第2册，第595页。
2. 有关安岐生平事迹，参见房兆楹<安岐>《清代杰出的中国人》，恒 慕义（Arthur W. Hummel）编（华盛顿特区：国会图书馆，1943），第11–13页；罗覃（Thomas Lawton）<安岐的墨缘汇观>，收录于《庆祝蒋复聪先生七十岁论文集》(台北:故宫博物院, 1969)，第 13–35页。
3. 安岐，《墨缘汇观》（1742年作序），重刊于《中国书画全书》（上海：上海书画出版社，1996），第10册，第415页。
4. 有王绂岐生平事迹，参见俞劍华，《王绂》(上海：人民美术出版社,1961)；李华宙<王绂（Wang Fu）>，收于《明代名人传》，L. Carrington Goodrich 编(纽约:哥伦比亚大学出版，1976), 第1374–75页;宋后楣，<明初画家王绂的隐居与竹茶炉创制年代考>《故宫学术季刊》，第2册，第3期(1985)，第13–27页；Kathlyn Liscomb，<王绂对明代新绘画风格的贡献>, *Artibus Asiae*，第48册，第1/2期(1987)，第 39–78页。
5. 宋后楣，《明初画家王绂》。
6. 吴升，《大观录》(序言作于1712年)，第19卷，第13a–13b页, 重刊于《艺术赏鉴选珍》(台北:汉华文教事业股份公司，1970)，第2325–6页。
7. 见宋后楣（Hou-mei Sung Ishida），<明代早期在南京的绘画与吴派的形成>，*Ars Orientalis*，第17期（1989），第73–115页；Kathlyn Liscomb，<王绂对明代新绘画风格的贡献>，*Artibus Asiae*, 第48册，第1/2期(1987)，第39–78页。

2
明 戴进 达摩至慧能六代祖师图
手卷，绢本水墨设色
Dai Jin (1388–1462)
The Six Patriarchs of Chan Buddhism: Bodhidharma to Huineng
Handscroll; ink and color on silk
33.8 x 220 cm

ARTIST'S SEALS: Qiantang daishi (square/intaglio), Wenjin (square/relief)
IMPERIAL SEALS: [Qianlong, r. 1736–95] Wufu wudaitang guxi tianzi bao (large square/relief), Bazheng maonian zhibao (large square/relief), Midian zhulin (square/relief), Qianqinggong jiancangbao (rectangular/relief), Qianlong jianshang (round/intaglio), Qianlong yulan zhibao (oval/relief), Sanxitang jingjianxi (rectangular/relief), Yizisun (square/intaglio), Midian xinbian (round/relief), Zhulin chongding (square/intaglio), Zizhen (square/intaglio), Taishang huangdi zhibao (large square/relief), Qianqinggong bao (square/relief); [Jiaqing, r. 1796–1820] Jiaqing yulan zhibao (oval/relief); [Xuantong (Puyi), r. 1909–11] Xuantong yulan zhibao (oval/relief)
COLOPHON WRITERS (SEALS): Zhu Yunming, 1461–1527 (Zhu Yunming yin [square/relief], Xizhe [square/relief]); Tang Yin, 1470–1524 (Wu qu [round/relief], Nanjing jieyuan [square/relief], Liuru jushi [square/relief]); Cao Xun, dates unknown (Cao Xun [round/relief], E xue [square/intaglio]); Cao Rong, 1613–1685 (Cao [round/relief], Cao Rong [square/relief], Jiangongshi [square/relief])

画家印鉴：钱塘戴氏（白文方印）、文进（朱文方印）
皇家印鉴：[清乾隆皇帝弘历,在位1736–1795]五福五代堂古稀天子宝（朱文大方印）、八征耄念之宝（朱文大方印）、秘殿珠林（朱文方印）、乾清宫鉴藏宝（朱文长方印）、乾隆鉴赏（白文圆印）、乾隆御览之宝（朱文椭圆印）、三希堂精鉴玺（朱文长方印）、宜子孙（白文方印）、秘殿新编（朱文圆印）、珠林重定（白文方印）、子贞（白文方印）、太上皇帝之宝（朱文大方印）、乾清宫宝（朱文方印）。[清嘉庆皇帝颙琰,在位1796–1820]嘉庆御览之宝（朱文椭圆印）。[清宣统皇帝溥仪,在位1909–1911]宣统御览之宝（朱文椭圆印）
题跋者(钤印)：祝允明，1460–1527（祝允明[朱文方印]、晞哲[朱文方印]）。唐寅，1470–1524（吴趋[朱文圆印]、南京解元[朱文方印]、六如居士[朱文方印]）。曹勋，生卒年不详（曹勋[朱文圆印]、峨雪[白文方印]。曹溶，1613–1685（曹[朱文圆印]、曹溶[朱文方印]、鉴躬氏[朱文方印]）。

In the sixteenth century the critic Wang Shizhen (1525–1590) wrote the following: "Dai Jin of Qiantang painted incessantly during his whole life, yet he could never buy a full meal. This was his minor misfortune. After his death he was famous in Wu, but when a hundred years had passed he was no longer considered equal to Shen Zhou. This was his greater misfortune. But in the eyes of real connoisseurs he will be considered the foremost of all Ming painters."[1] Wang, a member of the generation born after Shen Zhou's death in 1509, inscribed this on a now-lost painting by Dai Jin. By the eighteenth century, Dai Jin's reputation had truly been eclipsed by that of Shen Zhou. In the first part of the imperial catalogue of calligraphy and painting *Shiqu baoji*, completed in 1745, only four works by Dai were included—two fully catalogued and two simply listed—while sixty-six paintings by Shen Zhou were included. *The Six Patriarchs of Chan Buddhism* was not catalogued until the second part of the imperial catalogue was completed in 1793, at the end of the Qianlong reign. It represented works acquired by the palace in the intervening forty-seven years. The scroll was one of four more works by Dai to be added to the palace collection; meanwhile another forty-seven paintings by Shen Zhou had been acquired. The scroll's value was undoubtedly enhanced by the presence of colophons by Zhu Yunming (1461–1527) and Tang Yin (1470–1524), two famous representatives of Suzhou literati culture. Because of its Chan Buddhist subject matter the painting was included in the part of the catalogue reserved for Buddhist and Daoist paintings and texts titled *Midian zhulin* (Pearl forest of the Secret Hall).[2] Eight official Qianlong seals were affixed to the painting surface and four more to the mounting. One seal of the Jiaqing emperor was added to the painting surface and a single seal of Puyi (the Xuantong emperor) was added at the end of the scroll. The quality of the painting may well have been recognized when it was examined in the palace in the early 1920s, and it subsequently became one of the scrolls given to Pujie (1907–1994), Puyi's younger brother, to smuggle out of the palace.

The Six Patriarchs of Chan Buddhism represents the history of Chan Buddhism in China up to Huineng (638–713) and the division of the sect into a Southern and a Northern school. At the beginning of this painting, Dai Jin depicted Bodhidharma, the first Chan patriarch in China, meditating against a wall. The monk standing in attendance is presumably Huike, the second patriarch, who was to cut off his arm as an indication of his desire to study with Bodhidharma. The cave in which Bodhidharma sits is described in detail down to the bamboo water pipes along the ceiling. In the following scene, Huike, the stump of his left arm hidden under his monastic robes, is seated on a rock dais under the branches of an overhanging pine tree. He is in conversation with a scholar-official whose hat ties hang down behind him. The third patriarch, Sengcan, likewise sits on a rock dais. He holds a chowrie and is engaged in discussion with a monk. Daoxin, the fourth patriarch, is shown standing; he leans against a particularly spiky tree and points at the character *fo*, or "Buddha," written on the surface of a flat-topped rock. He is accompanied by a monk and a servant. The fifth patriarch, Hongren, sits formally on a high chair made of unfinished wood, backed by rocks. Like the second patriarch he is engaged in conversation with a scholar-official. The final scene of the sixth patriarch, Huineng, shows him seated on an armchair-like rock dais with carved arms. He is engaged in conversation with a layman. The scroll closes with two servants preparing a stove in front of a view of distant mountains. In composing the scroll, Dai has used trees to separate each scene and to articulate movement through the scroll. As in the opening scene, he has consistently described details. The brushwork defining the contours of the rocks and the tree trunks is agitated, as if each line was a linked sequence of dots.

Dai Jin was one of the most versatile and prolific of Ming painters.[3] He was born in 1388 into a Hangzhou family of professional craftsmen. By some accounts his father was a painter, and early in the Yongle reign (1403–24) he accompanied his father to the capital in Nanjing to seek his fortune as a painter. An anecdote reveals that he was already a skilled draftsman at the time: it is told that upon arriving in Nanjing, a porter stole his luggage and he immediately drew such a faithful likeness of the porter that the man was identified and the luggage recovered. Despite his skill he did not find employment in Nanjing and returned to Hangzhou. Later, during the Xuande reign (1426–35) he made another trip to the capital, this time to Beijing, with the recommendation of a eunuch named Fu. He is said to have submitted paintings to the court, and some accounts state that they were viewed by the emperor with his painting advisor Xie Huan (act. 1368–1437) in attendance. Xie is said to have pointed out hidden political messages that caused Dai Jin to be dismissed from the court and the eunuch Fu to be executed. The main sources for Dai Jin's biography were written over a hundred years after the events that they relate and are frustratingly inexact. Some have Dai fleeing the capital at night and being pursued back to Hangzhou and ultimately to Yunnan, where he received the patronage of the family of Mu Ying (1345–1392), the dukes of Qianguo. There is no question that Dai Jin enjoyed their patronage, but it is more likely that this occurred in Nanjing at their ducal residence rather than in distant Yunnan.[4] A new artistic direction related to the interests of the Nanjing aristocracy can be seen in his incorporation of elements of Northern Song monumental landscape painting into his own landscapes. It also seems clear that after the death of the Xuande emperor in 1435, Dai Jin did obtain a position as a painter at court, although he may not have stayed for long. Dai's final years were spent in his native Hangzhou.

Very few of Dai Jin's paintings are dated, and the dating of this scroll poses problems. It is generally assumed on stylistic grounds that it was painted early in his career during one of his periods in Hangzhou, perhaps after his trip to Nanjing or after his first trip to Beijing. An early dating, however, is complicated by the evidence of the inscriptions by Zhu Yunming and Tang Yin. Both refer to the owner of the scroll at the time that they wrote as being the dedicatee of the painting. This would suggest that the painting would have to be a late work, since Zhu Yunming was born only the year before Dai Jin was to die and Tang Yin was not born until eight years later.

DAS

Notes

1. Wang Shizhen from *Yanzhou shanren gao* [Manuscripts of the recluse of Yanzhou] quoted in *Peiwenzhai shuhuapu* [Calligraphy and painting compendium of the Peiwen Studio] (1708), *juan* 86, p. 66a, as reprinted in *Yingyin Wenyuange Siku quanshu* [Photographic reprint of the Wenyuange copy of the Imperial Library] (Taipei: Taiwan Shangwu yinshuguan, 1983), vol. 822, p. 676. Translation from Osvald Sirén, *Chinese Painting: Leading Masters and Principles*, vol. 4 (New York: The Ronald Press, 1958), p. 133.
2. *Midian zhulin xubian* in *Midian zhulin Shiqu baoji hebian hebian* [Pearl forest of the Secret Hall and Treasured boxes of the Stone Channel, combined edition], 12 vols. (Shanghai: Shanghai shudian, 1988), vol. 3, pp. 140–42.
3. For studies of Dai Jin's life and attempts to date his works, see in particular Hou-mei Sung Ishida [Song Houmei], "From the Min-Che Tradition to the Che School (Part 2), Predecessors of the Che School: Hsieh Huan and Tai Chin," *Gugong xueshu jikan* [Palace Museum research quarterly] 7, no. 1 (1989): 1–15; Mary Ann Rogers, "Visions of Grandeur: The Life and Art of Dai Jin," in Richard M. Barnhart, *Painters of the Great Ming: The Imperial Court and the Zhe School* (Dallas: Dallas Museum of Art, 1993), pp. 127–94; and Shan Guoqiang, "Dai Jin zuopin shixu kao" [An investigation into the chronological sequence of Dai Jin's works], *Gugong bowuyuan yuankan* [Palace Museum Bulletin], no. 4 (1993): 11–36.
4. See Shi Shouqian [Shih Shou-chien], "Zhepai huafeng yu guizu pinwei" [The style of the Zhe school and aristocratic taste], in *Fengge yu shibian: Zhongguo huihuashi lun* [Style and social change: Essays on the history of Chinese painting] (Taipei: Yunchen wenhua, 1996), pp. 181–228.

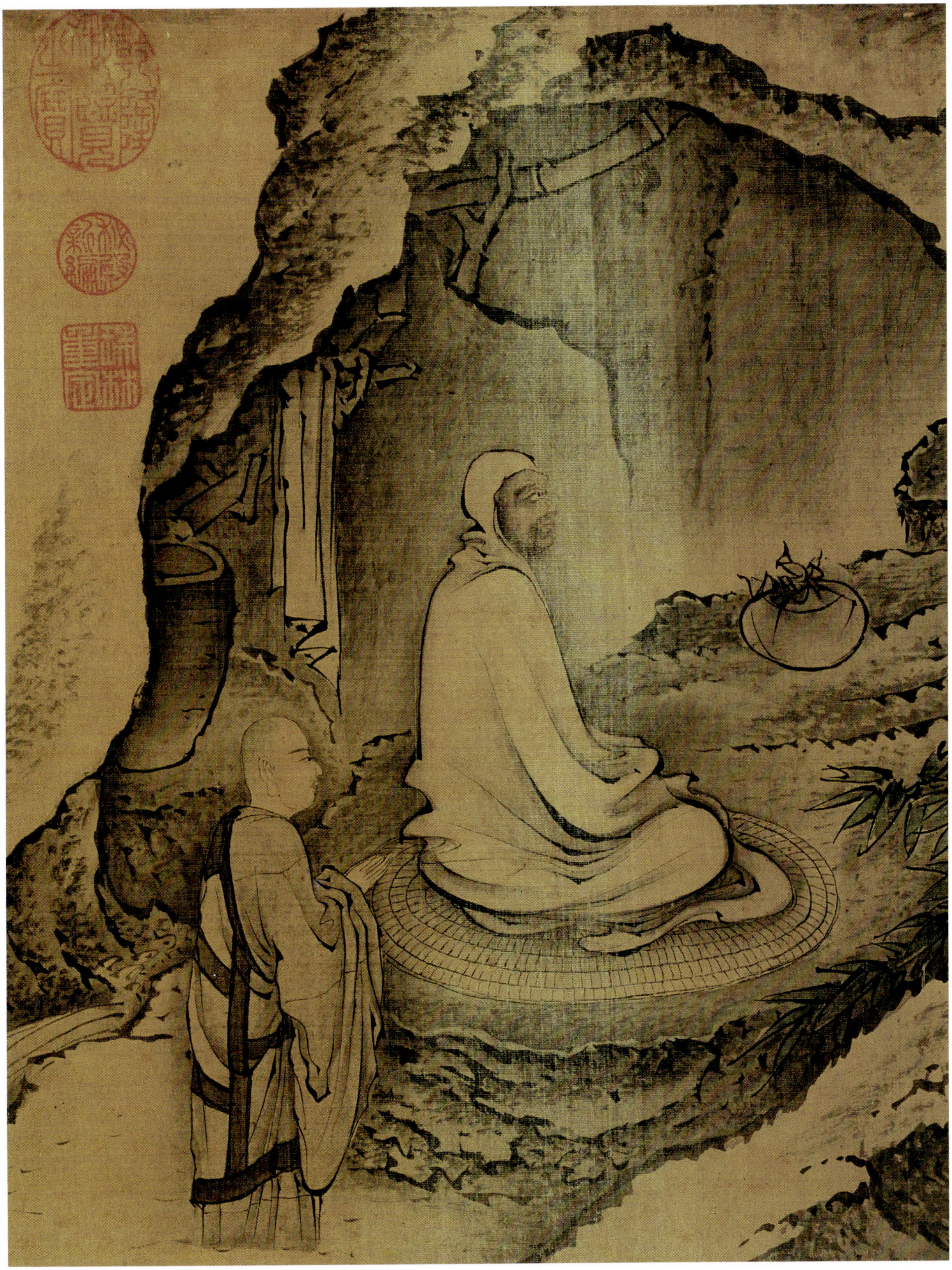

2 (detail 局部)

2

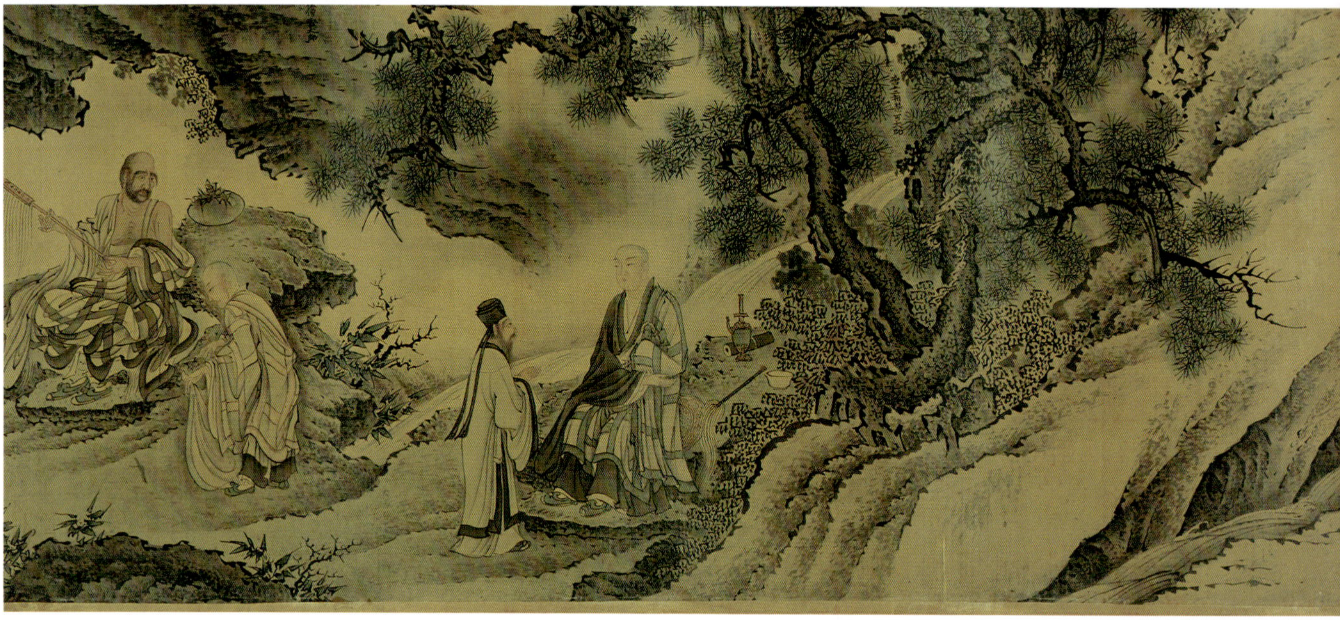

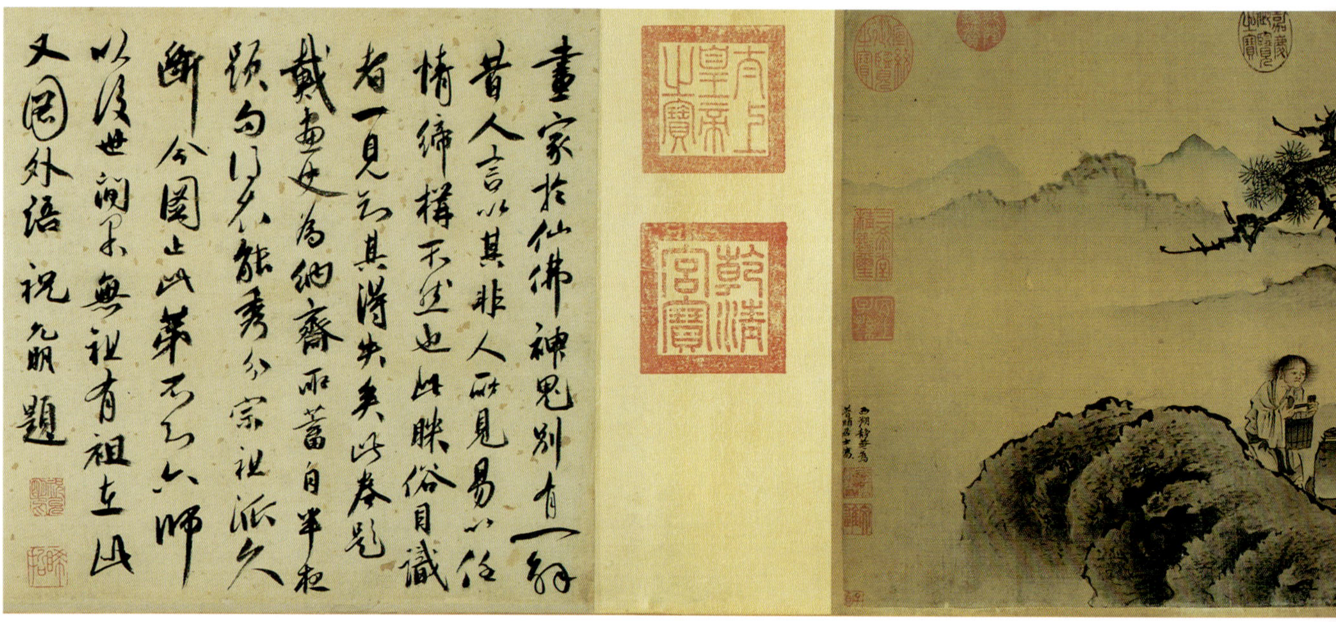

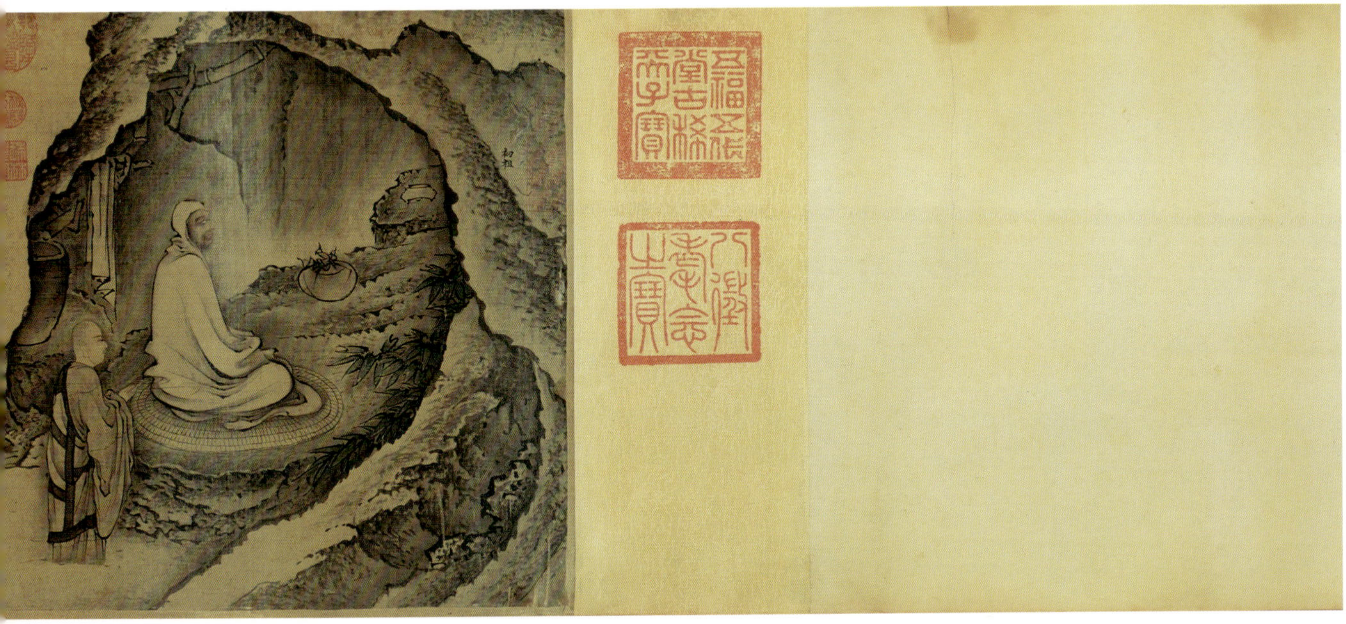

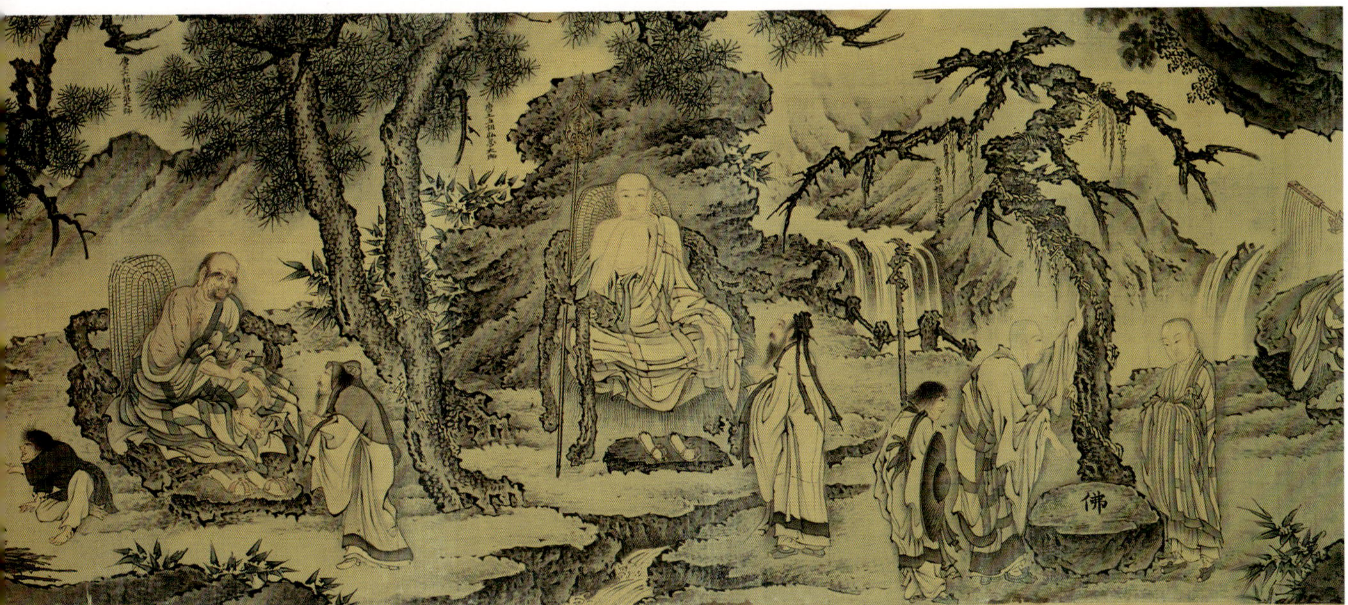

2

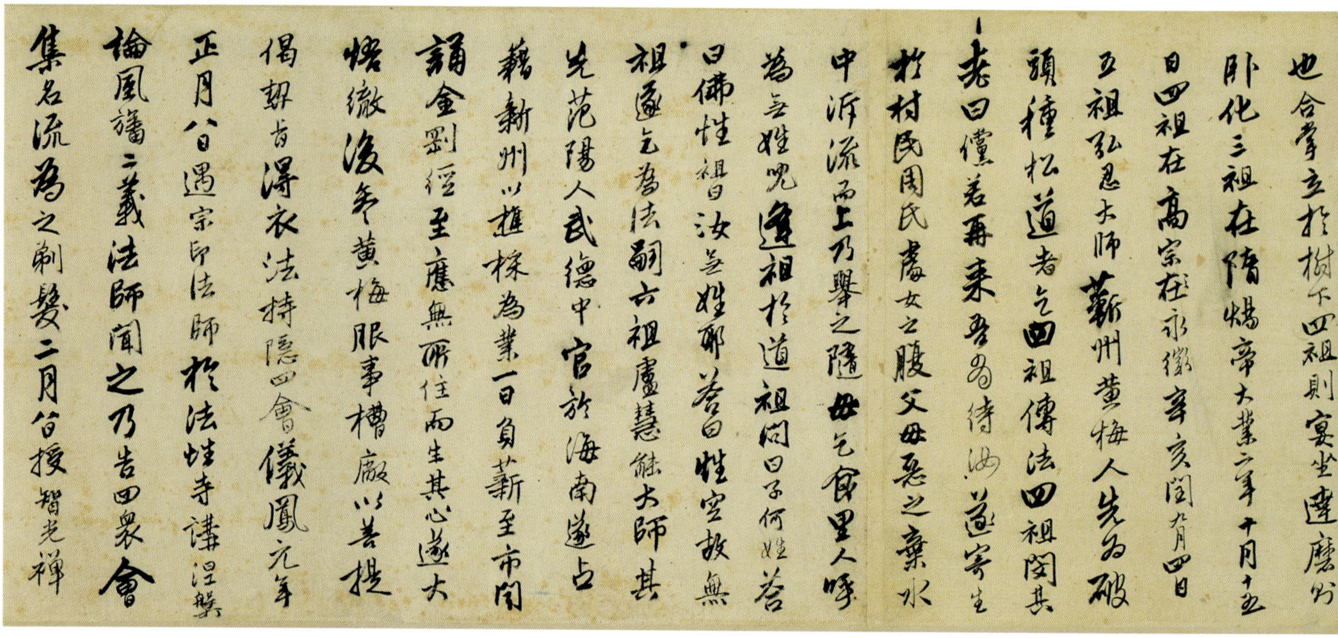

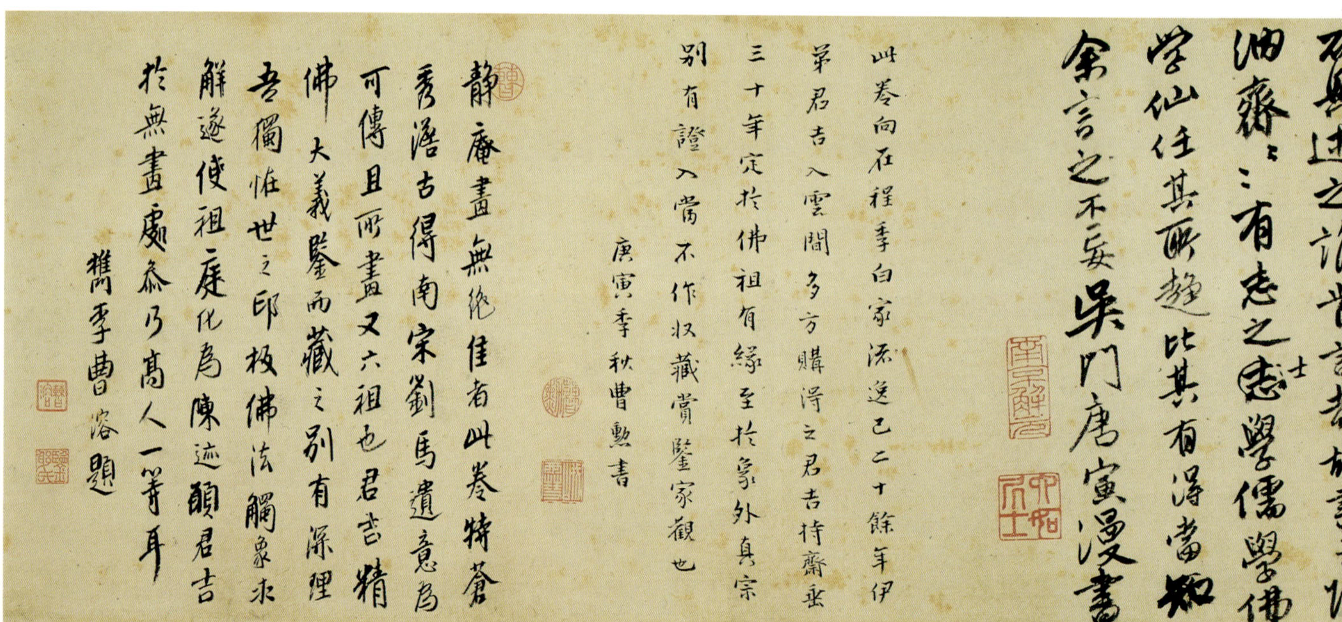

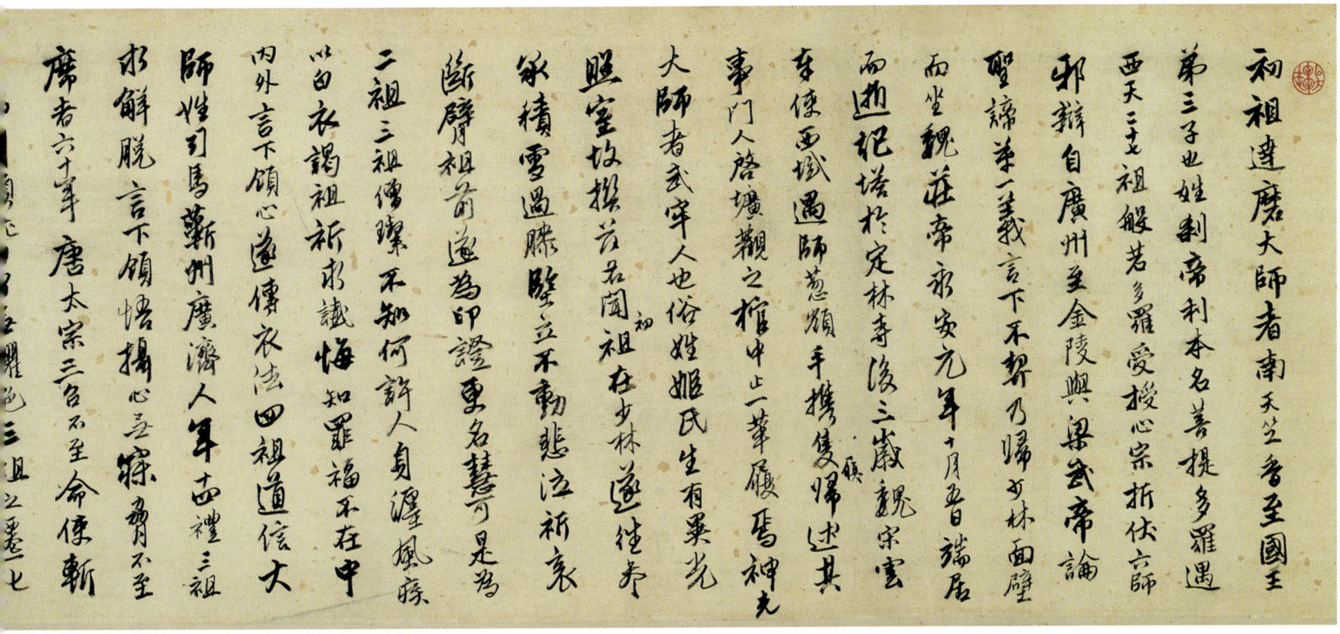

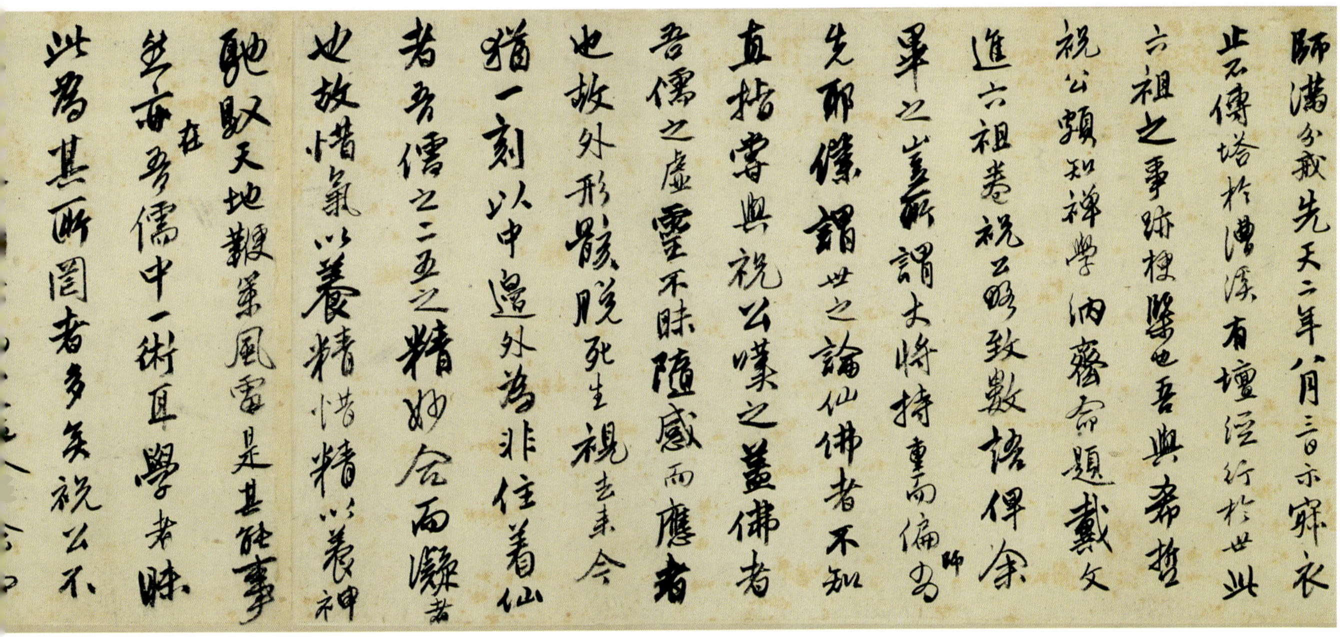

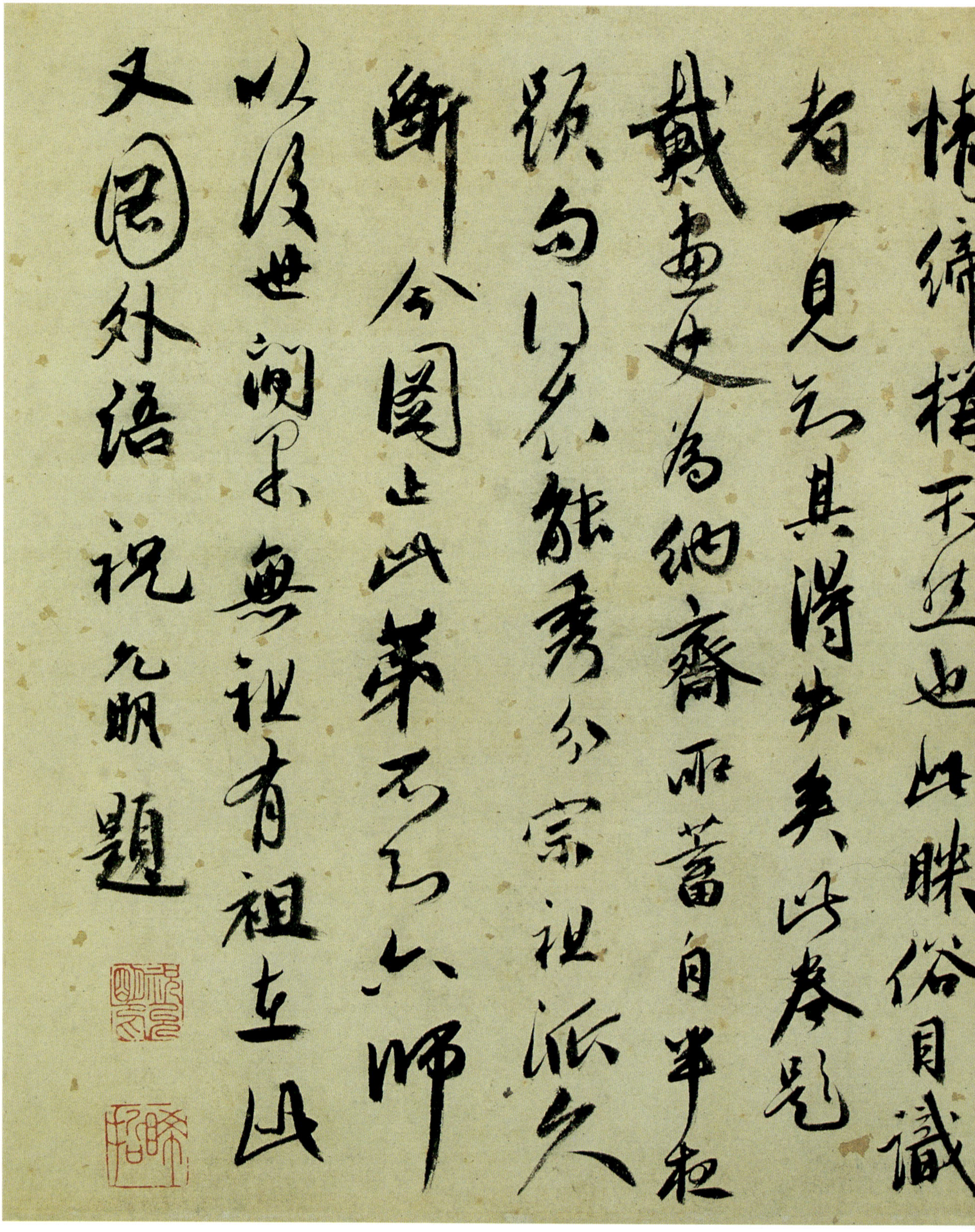

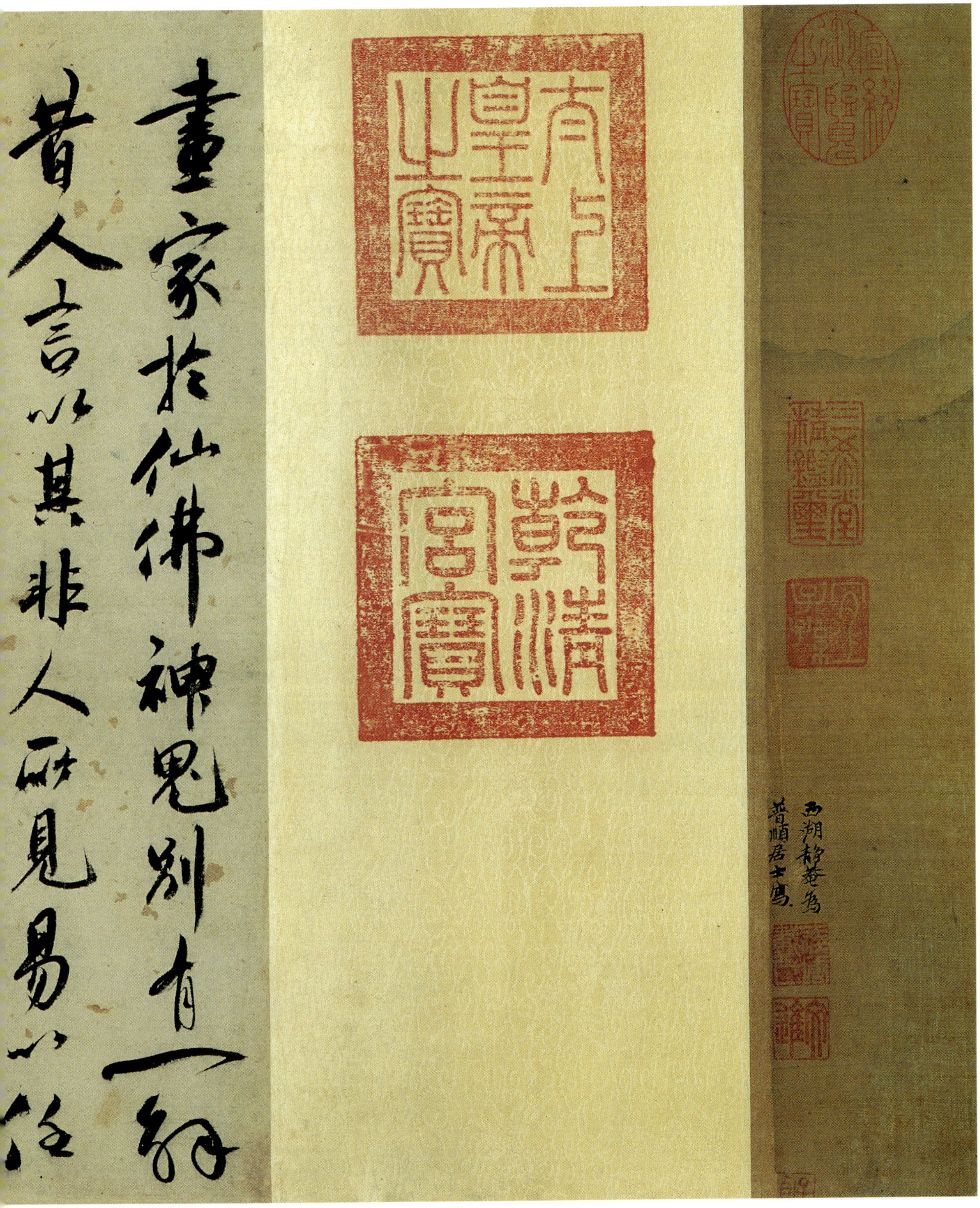

2 (section 局部)

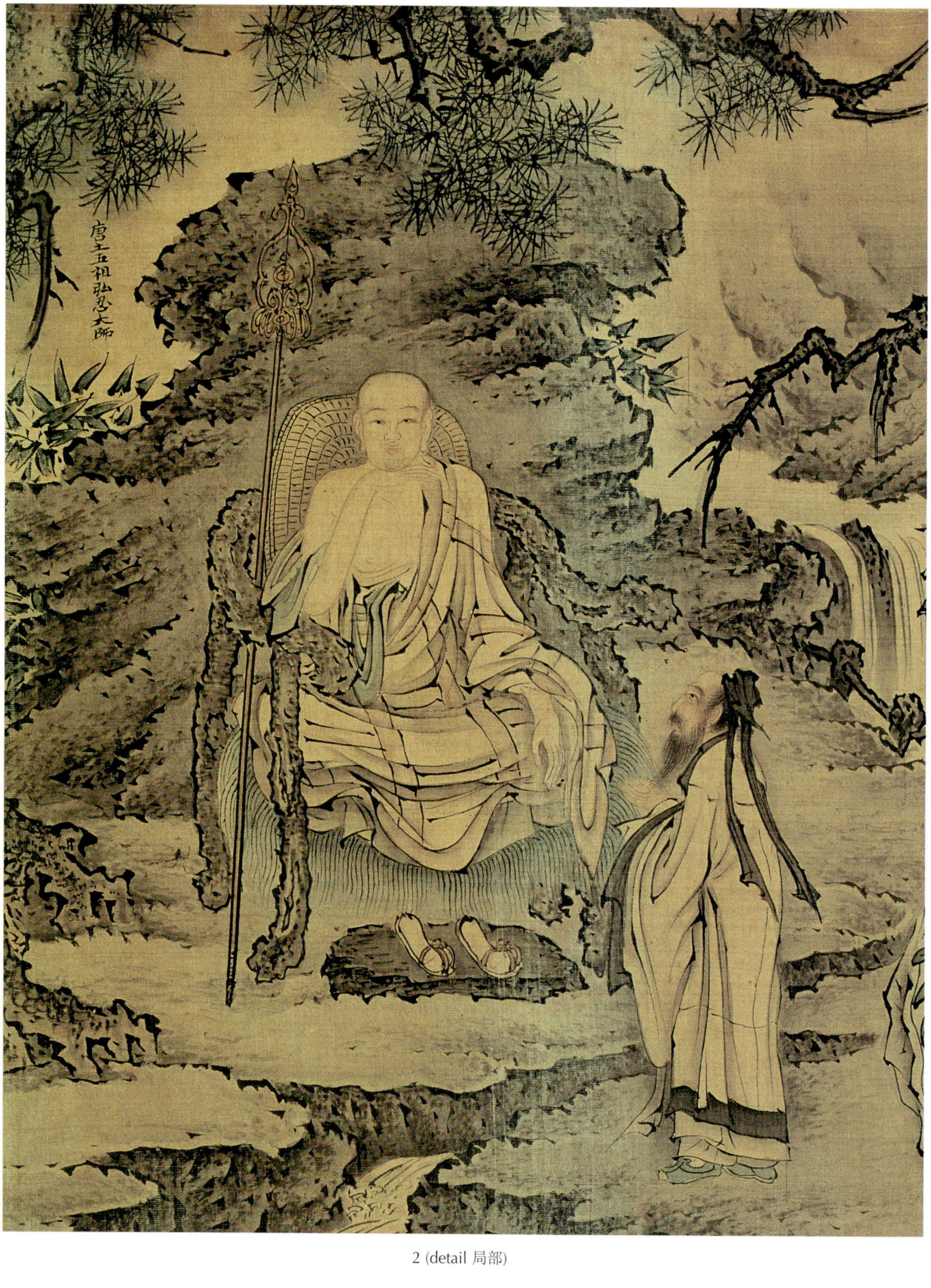

2 (detail 局部)

十六世纪艺术评论家王士贞(1525–1590)，生于沈周（卒于1509）之后的时代。他曾如此评述一幅戴进如今已逸失的作品：“钱塘戴文进，生前作画不能买一饱，是小厄。后百年，吴中声价，渐不敌相城翁[沈周]，是大厄。然令具眼观之，尚是我明最高手”。戴进的画名，早在十八世纪前就已被沈周所取代。清皇室於1745年完成的收藏目录《石渠宝笈》，在第一部分宫廷书画中只收有四幅戴进的作品,其中两幅带详细编目，另两幅只记画作条目。然而沈周部分则收录了六十六幅之多。此幅《达摩至慧能六代祖师图》，直到1793年乾隆晚期、《石渠宝笈》第二部分完成时才追加入档，此画可视为清皇室前前后后四十七年间所收书画的代表作。在此期间，戴进的四件作品被收入内府，沈周之作则有四十七件之多。此图卷之价值，无疑因祝允明(1461–1527)与唐寅(1470–1524)两位苏州文人画派大家的题跋而大增。此画并由于佛教禅宗的主题，被收录于《石渠宝笈》的《秘殿珠林》道释图画与书籍部里。乾隆御印八玺直接钤在画面上，另外四方打在裱褙部分。画上另有嘉庆鉴藏玺，溥仪（宣统皇帝）的鉴赏印则钤在画卷之末。此画之品位特色当已于1920年代在宫中审定，为溥仪赏其弟溥杰的图卷作品之一，后被挟带出宫。

此图描写中国佛教禅宗传承至六祖慧能(638–713)及其分裂成南北宗之历史故事。在卷首，戴进描绘禅宗初祖达摩面壁参禅。侍立一旁的僧人为欲虔心出家学佛而自断一臂的二祖慧可。达摩祖师坐禅之石窟细节交待详细，连窟顶竹管水渠亦一目了然。在接续的画面中，慧可端坐在枝干盘结的古松下，左臂的残肢在袈裟下隐约可见。石台上的慧可正与一绂带垂肩、文官模样的人交谈。第三图中，三祖僧璨亦盘坐石台之上，手持拂尘，与一僧人絮絮交谈。图中四祖道信一手倚着一棵虬结的古松，另一手则指着平台上写着的“佛”字。两身旁随侍一僧一侍。五祖弘忍危坐一粗木高椅，背靠山石，和二祖一样，与另一文人倾谈。最后一画面中，六祖慧能坐在圈椅模样的石座上，和一方外人士交谈。图卷结尾画两侍者着意炉火，背后远山一片。戴进利用树木布局，将每一场景清楚的分隔，并用此将图画里的故事依序连接。如图首初祖一图，全图所有细部均据实描绘。山石树干之轮廓，以颤动激劲的折笔交待，笔笔线条如同以点串联而成。

戴进是明代最多才多艺、最多产的画家。他生于1388年杭州的一个工匠之家。另有一说其父系职业画家，进承家学，于永乐末年(1403–24)随父应诏入京，欲以画业兴家。有一则轶事提及戴进当时已是一个手艺娴熟的画匠。据说，戴进初到南京，即遭一挑夫窃走随身行李，戴马上凭记忆，画了该挑夫的肖像，惟妙惟肖的肖像，很快便协助了将人赃俱获，找回了行囊。但是尽管身怀绝技，戴进却并未在南京觅得任何工作，只好返回家乡杭州。宣德年间(1426–35)，戴由一姓傅的宦官推荐，再次赴京。据说他将画作呈送入宫，让皇帝与他的书画顾问谢环(活动于1368–1437)过目。谢因指摘画中所带的政治意味，致戴进受遣返，傅宦官亦因此而被处死。戴进的生平事迹由后人于戴死后一百多年写就，许多事件语焉不详并错误百出。一些记载更提及戴连夜逃离京城，潜回杭州，最后远走云南，终于在那儿受到黔国公沐英(1345–1392)一家的资助。戴进受到沐英礼遇是事实，但此事应在京城南京的沐英家发生，并非远在云南。原因在于戴进将北宋的全景山水画融入其个人作品而形成的山水画风，在南京得到了贵族阶级的赏识，而成为一种时尚的新艺术品味。另可确定的是，戴进在宣德皇帝于1435年去世后，于画院中曾经谋得一职。然戴并未久留，其晚年是在老家杭州度过的。

戴进画作少有纪年，因此为此图卷推断创作之年代增加了困难。如以艺术风格取法的方式来看，此图应是戴杭州时期早年之作，在南京之行、或者第一次造访北京之后。但以此断代，却与祝允明与唐寅的题跋相矛盾。两画家均提及为当时画卷的收藏者撰写题跋一事。但祝允明生于戴进死前一年，唐寅要于八年后才出生，此事实指出该画应属戴进晚年之作。

江文苇（LYC译）

注解：

1.王世贞,《弇州山人稿》，引述自《佩文斋书画谱》(1708)，第86卷，第66a页，见于《影印文渊阁四库全书》重刊本（台北：台湾商务印书馆，1983），第822册，第676页。译文见于喜龍仁（Osvald Sirén）《中國繪畫：大師與原理》中之引文（纽约：The Ronald Press, 1958)，第4册，第133页。

2.《秘殿珠林续编》收录于《秘殿珠林石渠寶笈合编》，12册(上海:上海书店，1988)，第3册，第140–42页。

3.有关戴进生平事迹与作品纪年,特别参见宋后楣（Hou-mei Sung Ishida），<元末闽浙画风与明初浙派之形成（二），浙派前辈：谢环与戴进〉，《故宫学术季刊》,第7册，第1期（1989），第1–15页; Mary Ann Rogers，<宏观：戴进的生平与艺术）收于班宗华（Richard M. Barnhart),《大明画家：宫廷画与浙派画》(达拉斯:达拉斯美术馆，1993),第127–194页; 单国强，<戴进作品时序考>，《故宫博物院院刊》，第4期 (1993)，第11–36页。

4.石守谦，<浙派画风与贵族品味>,《风格与世变：中国绘画史论》(台北:允晨文化，1996)，第181–228页。

3
明 朱瞻基 万年松图
手卷，纸本水墨
Zhu Zhanji (Emperor Xuanzong, 1398–1435)
Ten-Thousand-Year-Old Pine Tree, 1431

Handscroll; ink on paper
33 x 453 cm

ARTIST'S SEALS: Huangdi zunqin zhibao (large square/relief), Wuyingdian bao (square/relief)

IMPERIAL SEALS: [Qianlong, r. 1736–95] Yushufang jiancangbao (oval/relief), Qianlong yulan zhibao (square/relief), Shiqu baoji (rectangular/relief); [Jiaqing, r. 1796–1820] Jiaqing yulan zhibao (oval/relief); [Xuantong (Puyi), r. 1909–11] Xuantong yulan zhibao (oval/relief)

OTHER SEALS: [Wang Duo, 1592–1652] Wang Duo zhiyin (square/intaglio); [Museum of the Northeast] Dongbei bowuguan zhencang zhiyin (square/relief)

画家印鉴：皇帝尊亲之宝（朱文大方印），武英殿宝（朱文方印）

皇家印鉴：[清乾隆皇帝弘历，在位1736－1795]御书房鉴藏宝（朱文椭圆印）、乾隆御览之宝（朱文方印）、石渠宝笈（朱文长方印）。[清嘉庆皇帝顒琰，在位1796－1820]嘉庆御览之宝（朱文椭圆印）。[清宣统皇帝溥仪，在位1909－1911]宣统御览之宝（朱文椭圆印）。

其他印鉴：[王铎，1592－1652]王铎之印（白文方印）。[东北博物馆]东北博物馆珍藏之印（朱文方印）。

Zhu Zhanji (sobriquet, Changchun Zhenren) was the great-grandson of Zhu Yuanzhang (Emperor Taizu of the Ming dynasty) and the eldest son of Zhu Gaochi (Emperor Renzong). His inaugural reign was named Xuande, and he was given the temple name Xuanzong. Known among Ming emperors for his abilities in painting and calligraphy, he secured himself a permanent position in the history of Chinese art. He studied painting and calligraphy painstakingly, excelling in figures, flora and fruits, and birds and insects. Boldly executed, his calligraphy was full-bodied and mature. It was recorded that he often saw himself as an artistic rival to Emperor Huizong of the Song dynasty.[1] During his reign (1426–35), the Xuande Academy was established to support talented artists, and his taste was to have a profound influence on court paintings as well as artistic circles of his day.

The evergreen stands for staunchness and longevity in Chinese culture. Titled "Ten-Thousand-Year-Old Pine Tree," this work was made by the emperor as a birthday gift to his mother.[2] Painted on paper in a horizontal format, the composition presents a section of the old pine in a close up, cut-off view. The sturdy trunk and the gnarled, twisted branches are executed in heavy and unhurried brushstrokes; light and dense texture strokes of the scale-like bark impart a sense of movement and rich three-dimensionality while swift and meticulous lines give the needles a densely clustered, flourishing appearance. Climbing vines, expertly rendered with fluid lines, random dots, and texture strokes, add interest to the aged pine, which is full of life and rustic meaning.

This long handscroll's frontispiece was inscribed by the artist himself: "On this first day of the fourth month in the sixth year of the Xuande period [May 12, 1431], your eldest son, the emperor, painted this Ten-Thousand-Year-Old Pine for the pleasure of the Renshou Gong palace." Placed over the inscription is a large seal that reads "Huangdi zunqing zhibao" (Treasure for the emperor's respected elders); this royal seal was used especially on paintings or calligraphy made for the artist's elders. Using artwork as a gift is an extremely ennobling and tasteful practice.[3] On both the right and left margins bordering the painted area and on seam lines within the painting are four impressions of the same "Wuyingdian bao" (Treasure from the Wuying Dian hall) seal, a square seal with red legend frequently used on paintings and calligraphic works by Emperor Xuanzong.

Xuanzong was a prolific artist whose extant works include *The Marquis of Wuhou at Rest* (*Wuhou gaowo tu*), dated the third year of the Xuande period (1428); *Pine Shade near Lotus Pond* (*Songyin lianpu tu*); and the *Calligraphy of Three Emperors* (*San di shu*), a scroll combining the works of emperors Taizu, Renzong, and Xuanzong. All the above works were formerly in the court collection, but in 1922 (the 14th year of Xuantong) they were awarded to Pujie as gifts.[4] *Xuanzong's Melon and Rat* (*Gua shu tu*), completed in 1427 (the 2nd year of Xuande), and the calligraphic work *Song on Snow* (*Xue yi ge*), written in 1433, are in the collection of the Palace Museum, Beijing. The whereabouts of his *Five Cats* (*Wu mao tu*), dated to the equivalent of 1429, is unknown.[5] In the contents pages of his *Shiqu suibi* (Notes on the Stone Channel), Ruan Yuan of the Qing dynasty had listed a life drawing of two gibbons by Xuanzong.[6] Hu Jing, who was one of the compilers of the third edition of the imperial catalogue *Shiqu baoji* (Treasured boxes of the Stone Channel), documented Xuanzong's flower-and-insect paintings in his *Xi Qing zhaji* (Notes from the Western Clarity retreat).[7] From these limited sources, one can see that there were at least about a dozen surviving works by the Ming emperor Xuanzong towards the end of the Qing dynasty in the early twentieth century.

Originally in the Ming dynasty court collection during the Xuande period, this work was acquired by the famous late Ming-early Qing artist and collector Wang Duo, who had served at the Ming court as minister of rites. It was then re-acquired by the imperial court, probably during the Kangxi or Qianlong period. According to the *Shiqu baoji*, which ranks it as an A-minus, the work was stored at the imperial study.[8]

On January 5, 1923 (the 19th day of the 11th month in the 14th year of the Xuantong period), this scroll was removed from the Forbidden City when the last emperor, Puyi, awarded it to his brother.[9] It was transported first to Tianjin and then to the "imperial palace" in Changchun. After World War II, it was carried by Puyi and his fleeing entourage to the city of Linjiang, Jilin Province, where it was recovered by the People's Liberation Army. The work was then submitted to the People's Bank of the Northeast, which in turn handed it over to the Northeastern Committee for the Management of Cultural Relics. It was later acquired by the Museum of the Northeast, which is currently the Liaoning Provincial Museum.[10]

WWHC (trans. DHWS)

Notes

1. Yang Renkai, ed., *Liaoningsheng bowuguan cang shuhua zhulu: Huihua juan* [Writings on paintings and calligraphic works in the collection of the Liaoning Provincial Museum: Volume on art] (Shenyang: Liaoning meishu chubanse, 1999), p. 280.
2. *Ming shilu* [Veritable record of the Ming] (hand-copied manuscript; [Nanjing]: Jiangsu Library of Sinology, n. d.), *juan* 78, p. 2.
3. During the Qianlong emperor's celebration of his mother's seventieth birthday, he presented her with ninety-nine gifts every day. Topping each daily list of gifts were his imperial calligraphy works in the form of couplets and overhead boards. See E'ertai, Zhang Tingyu, et al., *Guochao gongshi* [History of the imperial courts] (Beijing: Beijing guji chubanshe, 1987), vol. 2, pp. 410–26.
4. *Gugong yiyi shuji shuhua mulu si zhong* [Four catalogues of dispersed calligraphy and paintings from the imperial palace] (Beijing: Gugong bowuyuan, 1926), pp. 6, 8, 10, and 14.
5. Shen Roujian, ed., *Zhongguo meishu cidian* [Dictionary of Chinese art] (Taipei: Xiongshi tushu, 1989), p. 167.
6. Ruan Yuan, *Shiqu suibi* [Notes on the Stone Channel], *juan* 5, reprinted in *Biji xiaoshuo daguan* [Compendium of notes and novels] (Yangzhou: Jiangsu Guangling guji keyinshe, 1984), p. 383, which also documents a calligraphy scroll collaboratively created by the Xuanzong emperor and his father, Emperor Renzong.
7. See the contents page of Hu Jing, *Xi Qing zhaji* [Notes from the Western Clarity retreat] (Beijing: Laixunge, 1934).
8. *Shiqu baoji* [Treasured boxes of the Stone Channel] (Taipei: Guoli gugong bowuyuan, 1971), vol. 2, p. 1052.
9. Registered under the serial number *Jing* 261 in *Gugong yiyi shuji shuhua mulu si zhong*, p.16.
10. Yang Renkai, *Liaoningsheng bowuguan cang zhulu huihua juan*, p. 281.

朱瞻基自号长春真人，为明太祖朱元璋的曾孙，明仁宗朱高炽长子，建元宣德，庙号宣宗。他对中国书画潜心研摹，工画人物，花果，翎毛，草虫，其书法于圆熟之外，以遒劲出之，文献记载往往与宋徽宗争胜（注1）。他在位时（1426－1435）成立宣德画院以资艺术人才，其品味所倡对宫廷绘画和当时的画坛影响很大，他是明代皇帝中能以书画闻名者，并在中国书画艺术史上占有一席之地。

常青的松树在中国文化中代表着坚贞和长寿，此"万年松图卷"当是宣宗皇帝为其母贺寿之作（注2），画面在横向的纸幅中，以截面的构图来表现老松，枝干用笔沈稳厚重，虬曲遒劲壮实；浓淡有致的皴法表现鳞皮，生动而富有立体感；利落缜密的线条，表现松针的茂密峥嵘蓬勃；流畅的线条和皴点，使攀缘的野藤给古松增添了生趣，生气勃勃而古朴隽永。

长卷的引首作者自题："宣德六年四月初一日，长子宣德皇帝敬写万年松图，奉仁寿宫清玩"，下钤"皇帝尊亲之宝"朱文方印。这一玺是专为长辈所作的书画而用，以书画作为礼品是极体面和有品味的（注3）。画心和前后隔水钤有"武英殿宝"朱文方印四处，这是宣宗皇帝书画作品中常用的印玺。

明宣宗善于丹青，其传世作品还有"武侯高卧图"卷（宣德三年作），"松荫莲浦图"一卷；与太祖仁宗皇帝合作"三帝书"一卷，均为内府收藏，而在宣统14年（1922年）均赏赐给溥杰（注4）。另宣德二年作（1427）"瓜鼠图"卷，八年作（1433）"雪意歌"书法，均藏北京故宫博物院，另有四年（1429）作"五猫图"不知流落何处（注5）。清代阮元《石渠随笔》的目录中记载有宣宗皇帝写生小品，双猿大轴（注6），参加编撰《石渠宝笈》三编的胡敬，则在所著《西清劄记》的目录中，记载了宣宗的花卉草虫图等（注7）。仅从这些有限的记载，可以略知，在清末到二十世纪初期，明宣宗的画作至少还有十幅左右为人所知。

本卷装裱为锦本包首，引首为洒金笺，隔水皆为绫本，画心为纸本。此件作品原藏明代宣德内府，在明末清初曾入著名书画家、收藏家和官至明朝礼部尚书的王铎之手。约在康熙乾隆年间收回宫中，据《石渠宝笈》记载，此画列为"次等致一"（注8），藏于御书房。末帝溥仪于宣统十四年十一月十九日，以赏其弟溥杰为名而流落宫外(注9)。曾被运往天津，后又被运往长春伪宫，第二次世界大战胜利后，溥仪携逃至吉林省临江市，被人民解放军截获，交东北人民银行转交东北文物管理委员会，后归东北博物馆，即今辽宁省博物馆所藏（注10）。

海蔚蓝

注解：

1. 杨仁恺主编《辽宁省博物馆藏书画著录》绘画卷（辽宁美术出版社,1999），第280页。
2. 《明实录》卷七十八，第二页，宣德六年四月"辛丑，皇太后圣节，上率亲王上寿"，江苏国学图书馆传钞本。
3. [清]鄂尔泰、张廷玉等编撰，《国朝宫史》下册，乾隆皇帝为母后做七十大寿时，每天恭进九十九件礼物，礼品单上首先敬献的常常是他御笔的书法对联和匾额，可作参考（北京古籍出版社，1987），第410－426页。
4. 《故宫已佚书籍书画目录四种》（故宫博物院，民国十五年版，1926），第6、8、10、14页。
5. 沈柔坚主编《中国美术辞典》（台北雄师美术出版社，1989），第167页。
6. [清]阮元《石渠随笔》卷五，载《笔记小说大观》，也记载有宣宗与其父仁宗合作的书法卷（江苏广陵古籍刻印出版社，1984），第383页。
7. [清]胡敬《西清劄记》目录，亦记录了宣宗的松荫莲浦图（民国二十三年，来薰阁版，1934）。
8. [清]《石渠宝笈》初编下册（台湾，国立故宫博物院，民国六十年，1971），第1052页。
9. 《故宫已佚书籍书画目录四种》此一卷宫中登记号为静字二百六十一号（故宫博物院，民国十五年版，1926），第十六页。
10. 杨仁恺主编《辽宁省博物馆藏书画著录》绘画卷，（辽宁美术出版社，1999），第281页。

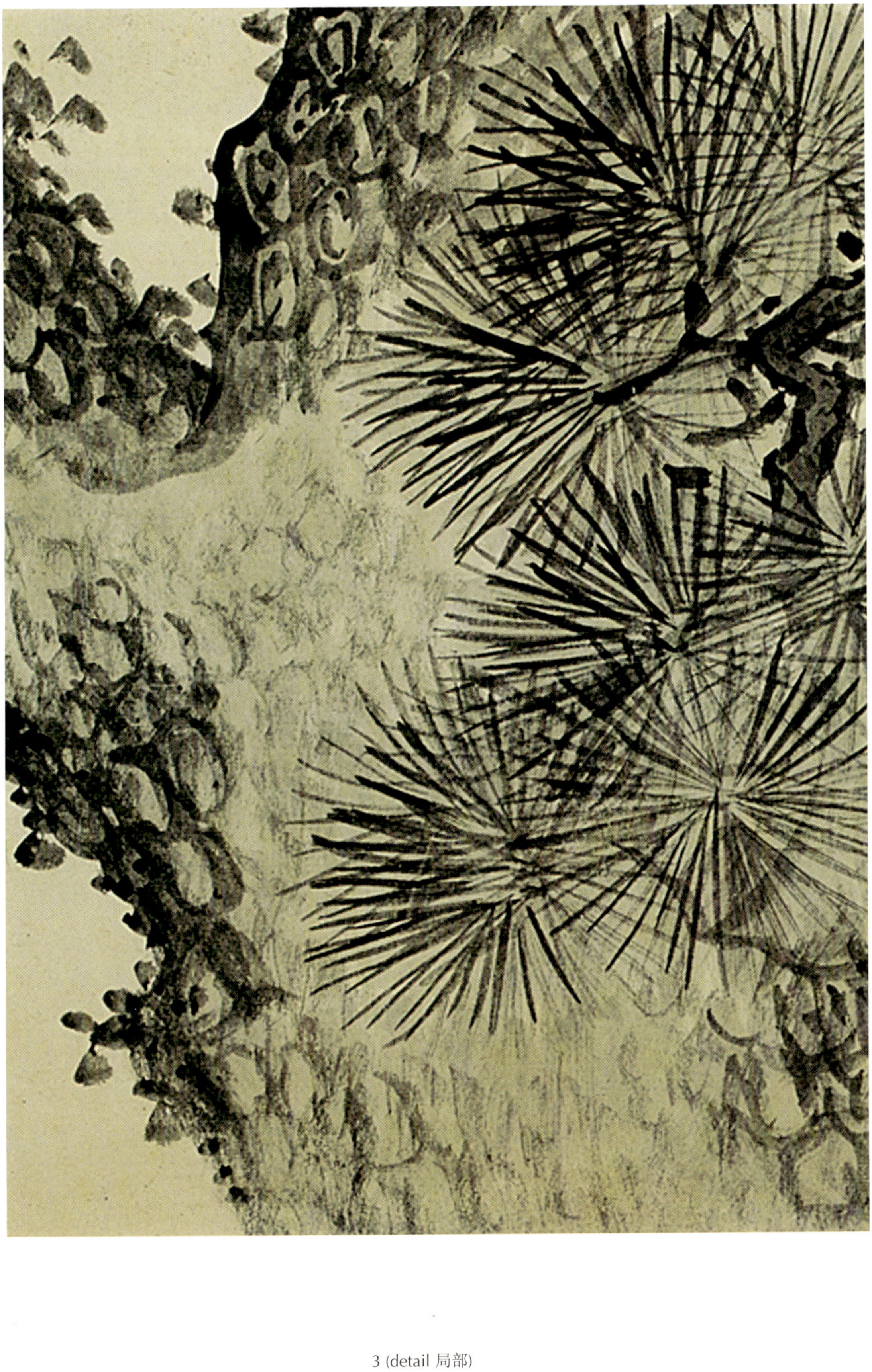

3 (detail 局部)

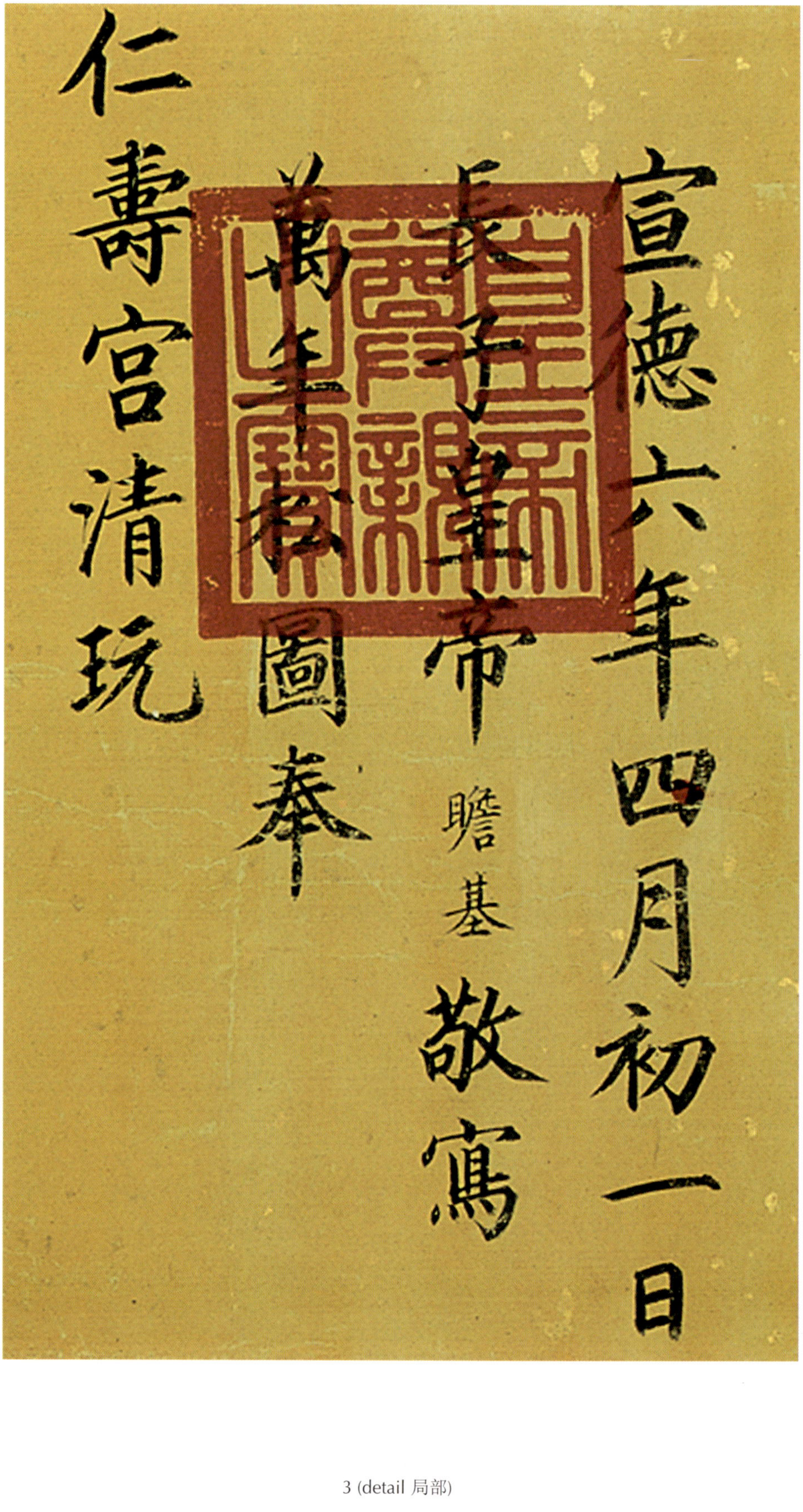

3 (detail 局部)

4
明　马轼　李在　夏芷　归去来辞图
手卷, 纸本水墨及淡设色
Ma Shi, Li Zai, and Xia Zhi (act. ca. 1426–35)
Coming Home, after the Poem by Tao Qian

Handscroll; ink and light color on paper
27.7 x 656 cm

ARTISTS' SEALS: Lianchuan Ma Shi (square/relief); Li Zai tushu (square/relief); Xia Zhi (square/relief), Tingfang (square/relief)

IMPERIAL SEALS: [Qianlong, r. 1736–95] Shiqu baoji (rectangular/relief), Shiqu dingjian (round/relief), Baoji chongbian (square/intaglio), Qianlong yulan zhibao (oval/relief), Leshoutang jiancangbao (rectangular/intaglio), Ningshougong xuru shiqu baoji (square/relief), Qianlong jianshang (round/intaglio), Sanxitang jingjianxi (rectangular/relief), Yizisun (square/intaglio); [Jiaqing, r. 1796–1820] Jiaqing yulan zhibao (oval/relief); [Xuantong (Puyi), r. 1909–11] Wuyizhai jingjianxi (rectangular/relief), Xuantong jianshang (square/relief)

JADE CLIP INSCRIPTION: Qianlong yushang. Ma Shi, Li Zai, Xia Zhi hezuo Guiqulaici tu

画家印鉴：练川马轼（朱文方印），李在图书（朱文方印），夏芷（朱文方印）、庭芳（朱文方印）。

皇家印鉴：[清乾隆皇帝弘历，在位1736－1795]石渠宝笈（朱文长方印）、石渠定鉴（朱文圆印）、宝笈重编（白文方印）、乾隆御览之宝(朱文椭圆印)、乐寿堂鉴藏宝（白文长方印）、宁寿宫续入石渠宝笈（朱文方印）、乾隆鉴赏（白文圆印）、三希堂精鉴玺（朱文长方印）、宜子孙（白文方印）。[清嘉庆皇帝颙琰，在位1796－1820]嘉庆御览之宝（朱文椭圆印）。[清宣统皇帝溥仪，在位1909－1911]无逸斋精鉴玺（朱文长方印）、宣统鉴赏（朱文方印）。

玉别子镌：乾隆御赏。马轼、李在、夏芷合作归去来辞图

Ma Shi, Li Zai, and Xia Zhi were all court painters during the Xuande reign (1426–35), serving as artists-in-waiting (*daizhao*) at the imperial art academy. One way or another, they all had contact with Dai Jin, the leading artist of the Zhe School. A native of Jiading (present-day Shanghai), Ma Shi (courtesy name, Jingzhai; act. late 14th–mid 15th century) shared with Dai Jin a great reputation in the capital as an artist. Also good at divining by astrology, he was promoted to doctor of time-keeping at the Imperial Board of Astronomy. Li Zai (courtesy name, Yizheng; d. 1431), a native of Putian, Fujian, was enrolled in the imperial art academy during the Xuande reign and, like Dai Jin, served at the Renzhi Dian hall as an artist-in-waiting. Xia Zhi (courtesy name, Tingfang; act. 1426–35), a native of Qiantang, Zhejiang, studied with Dai Jin. When the latter was purged from the court by the forces of jealousy, Xia hid himself in a monastery and continued to paint. Few of his works have survived. According to comments by their contemporaries, the leading landscape artist of the time was Shang Xi (act. 1426–35), and the three artists discussed here, although well-known, were considered secondary in fame.[1]

This scroll mounts together separate works by the three above-mentioned artists. The landscape compositions here are chiefly modeled on the paintings of the Southern Song academy: there is a tendency to emphasize one corner of the composition, there are clearly conceived edges and angles, and the axe-cut texture strokes of Ma Yuan (act. ca. 1190–1230) and Xia Gui (act. ca. 1200–ca. 1230) can be seen in many places where the brushwork is bold and unconstrained. The finer, smoother areas draw from the brushwork of the Northern Song artist Guo Xi (ca. 1000–ca. 1090). These are common features shared by landscape paintings of the early Ming period. Thus, this scroll has significant research value for the study of early Ming dynasty painting.

The nine paintings extant on this scroll all depict Tao Yuanming's poem "Coming Home." According to the *Shiqu baoji*, the following scenes were all done by Ma Shi: (1) *Moving Smoothly Forward in a Boat* (*Zhou yaoyao yi qing yang*), signed "Ma Shi"; (2) *Asking Other Travelers the Way* (*Wen zhengfu yiqian lu*), affixed with the seal "Lianchuan Ma Shi"; (3) *Children Waiting at the Door* (*Zhizi houmen*), affixed with the seal "Lianchuan Ma Shi"; (6) *Farmers Telling Me Spring is Here* (*Nongren gaoyu yi chun ji*), signed "Jingzhan"; and (8) *Going Outdoors Alone to Enjoy Nature* (*Huai liangchen yi guwang*), signed "Ma Shi."[2] The following three paintings were done by Li Zai: (4) *Clouds Float Idly out of the Canyon* (*Yun wuxin yi chuxiu*), affixed with the seal "Li Zai tushu"; (5) *Feeling the Lonely Pine with My Hand, I Linger* (*Fu gusong yi panhuan*), inscribed "Putian Li Zai painted this lingering scene at a lonely pine in the fall of the *jiachen* year [1424]" and impressed with one seal, "Li Zai tushu"; and (9) *Facing the Clear Stream, I Start a Poem* (*Lin qingliu er fushi*), impressed with the seal "Li Zai tushu." There is only one painting by Xia Zhi, the seventh, *Or Asking for a Wagon* (*Huo mingjinche*).[3]

"Coming Home" is a masterpiece of Chinese literature by the celebrated Eastern Jin dynasty poet Tao Yuanming (also known as Tao Qian, 365–427; see Appendix B). It portrays an aloof scholar who rejects officialdom to return to the field and enjoy the pleasures of hoeing the earth, cultivating chrysanthemums, drinking wine until intoxicated, talking of

4

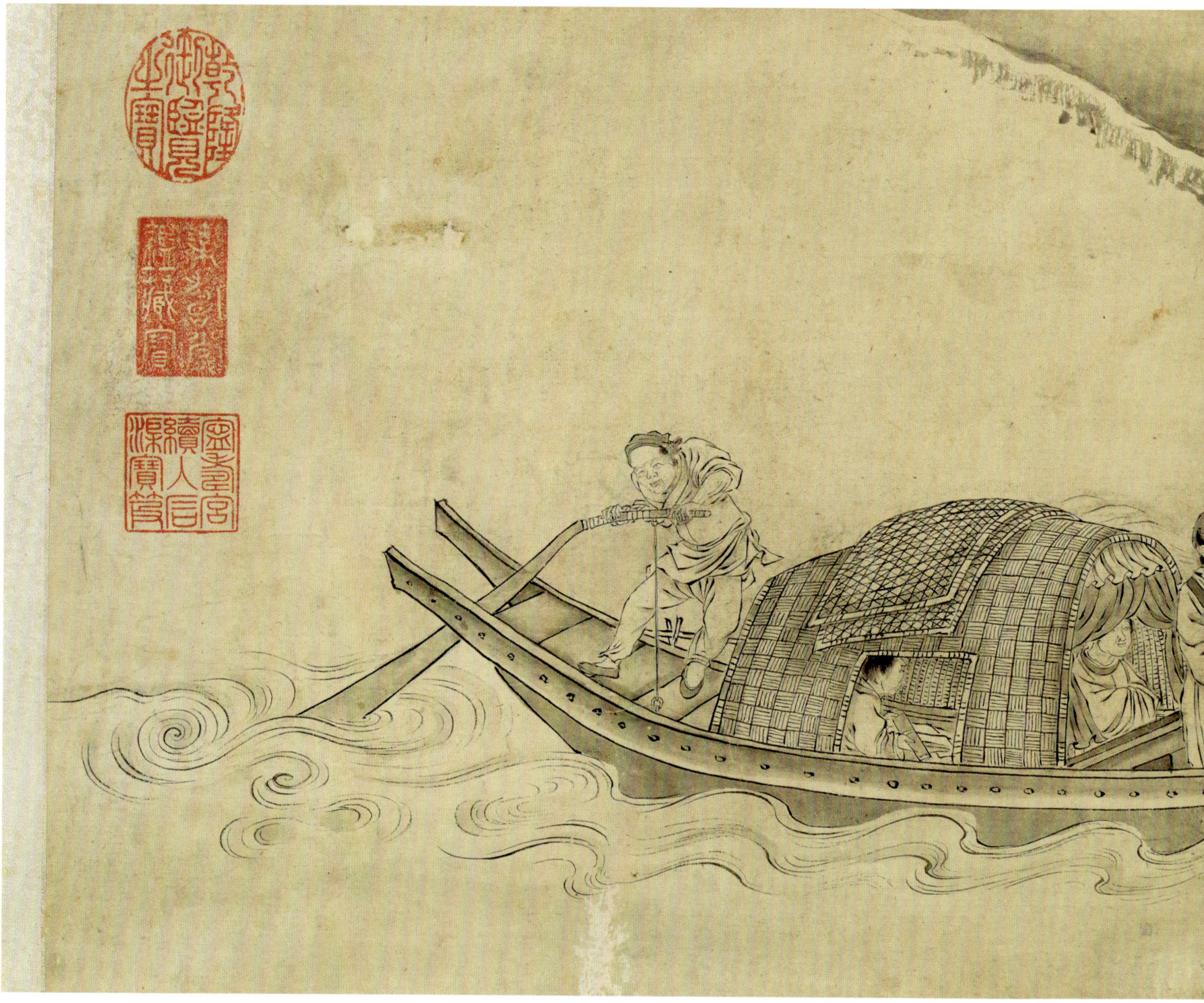

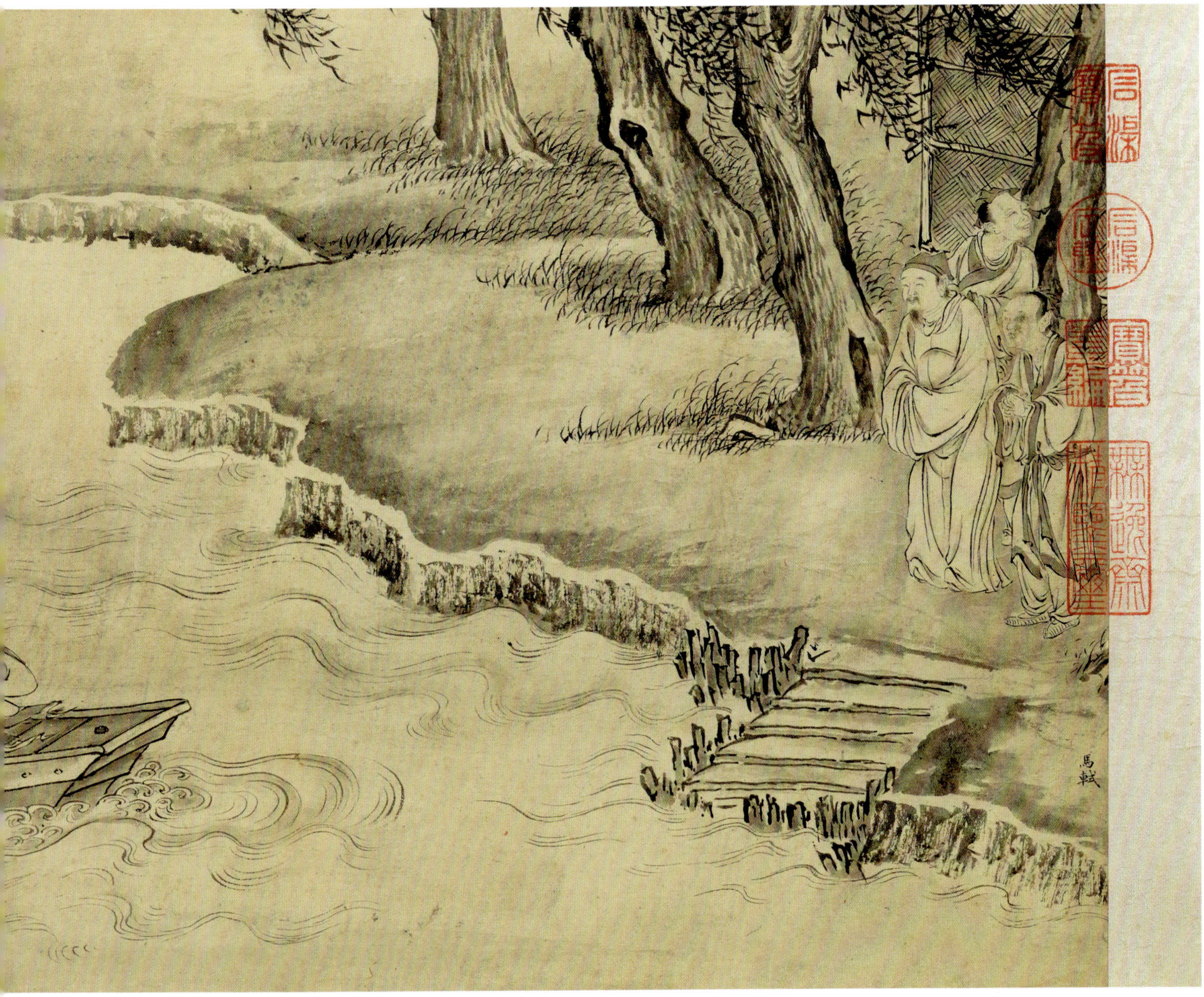

(1) *Moving Smoothly Forward in a Boat* 舟遥遥以轻飏

4

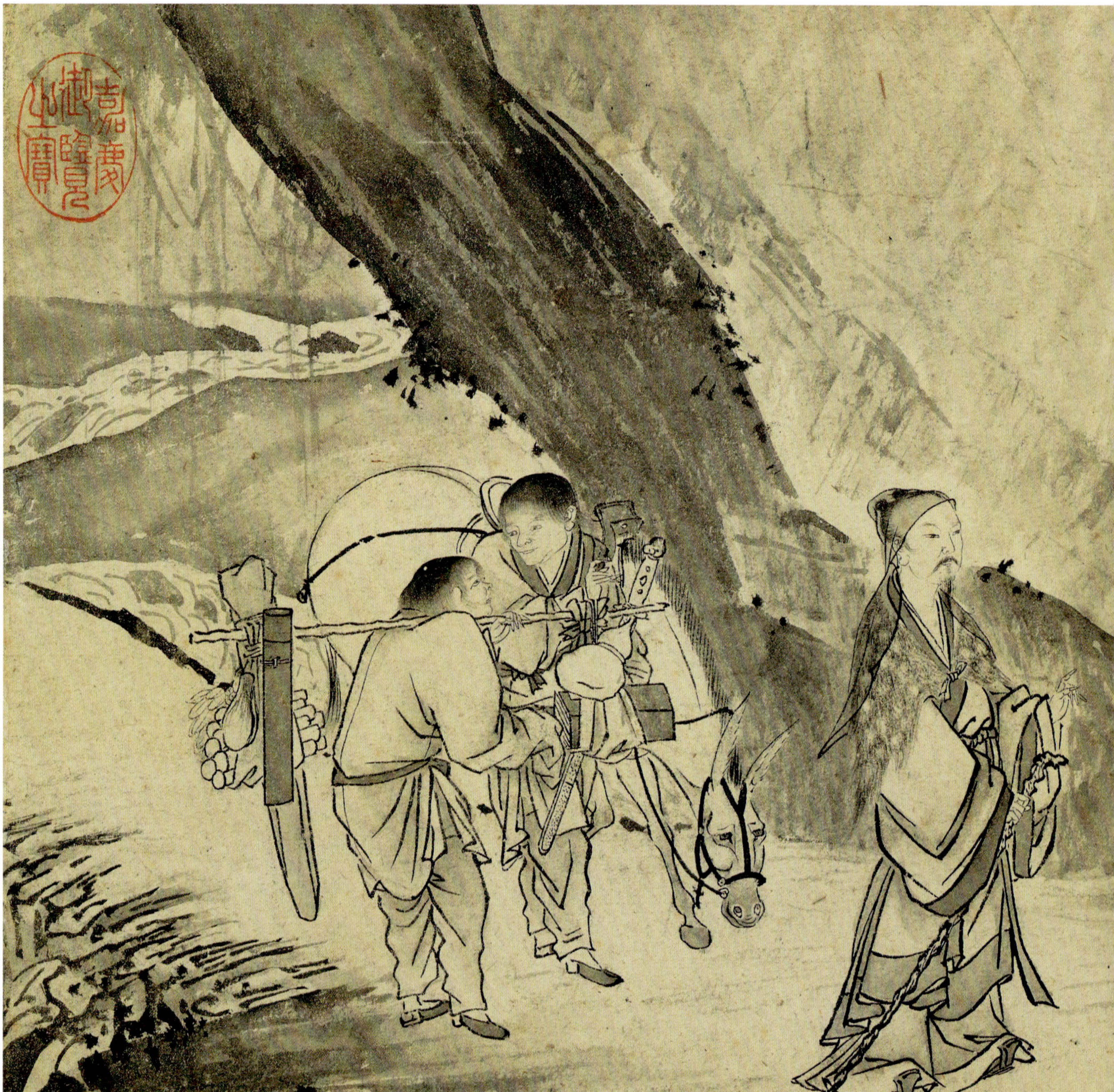

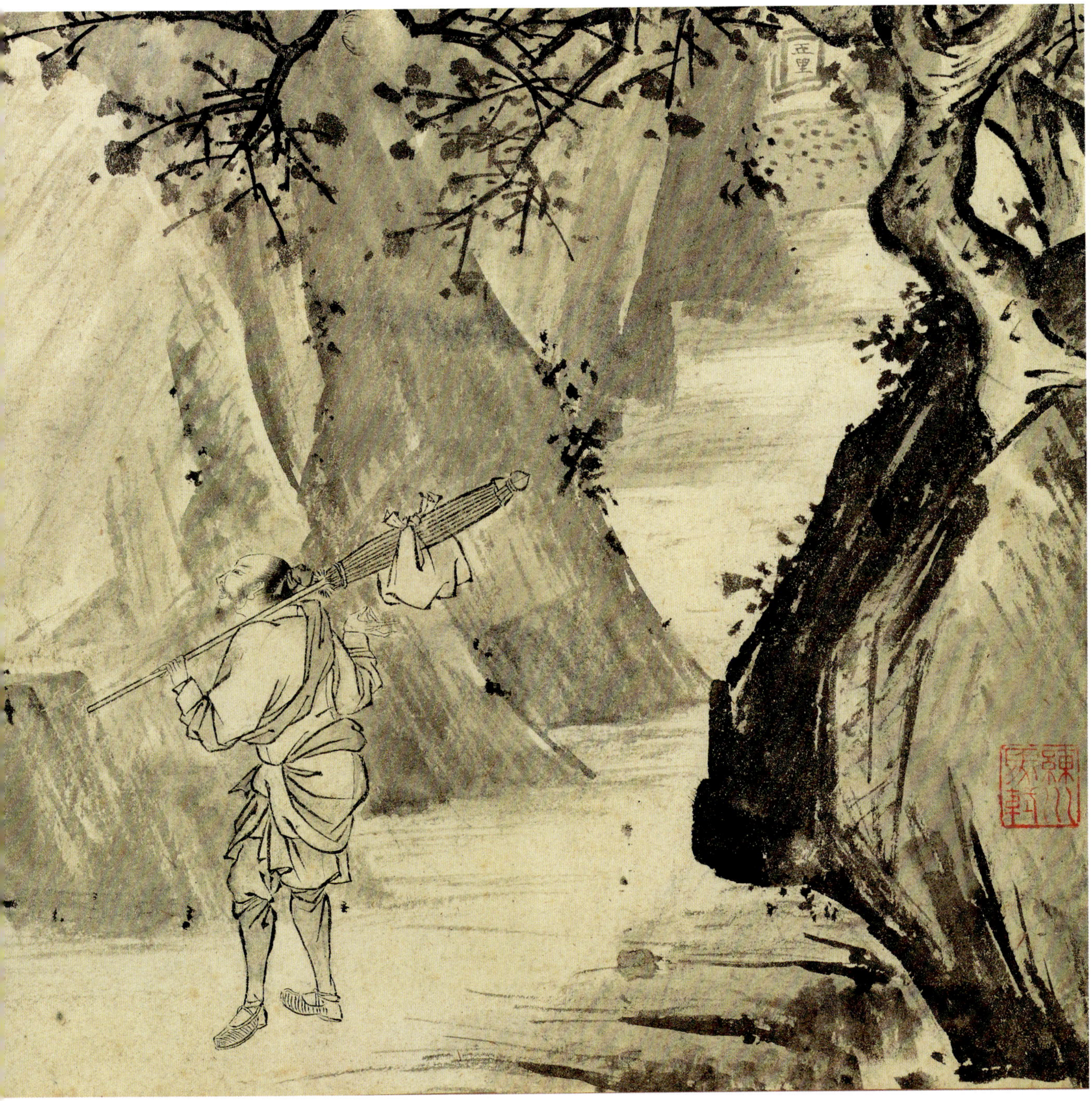

(2) *Asking Other Travelers the Way* 问征夫以前路

4

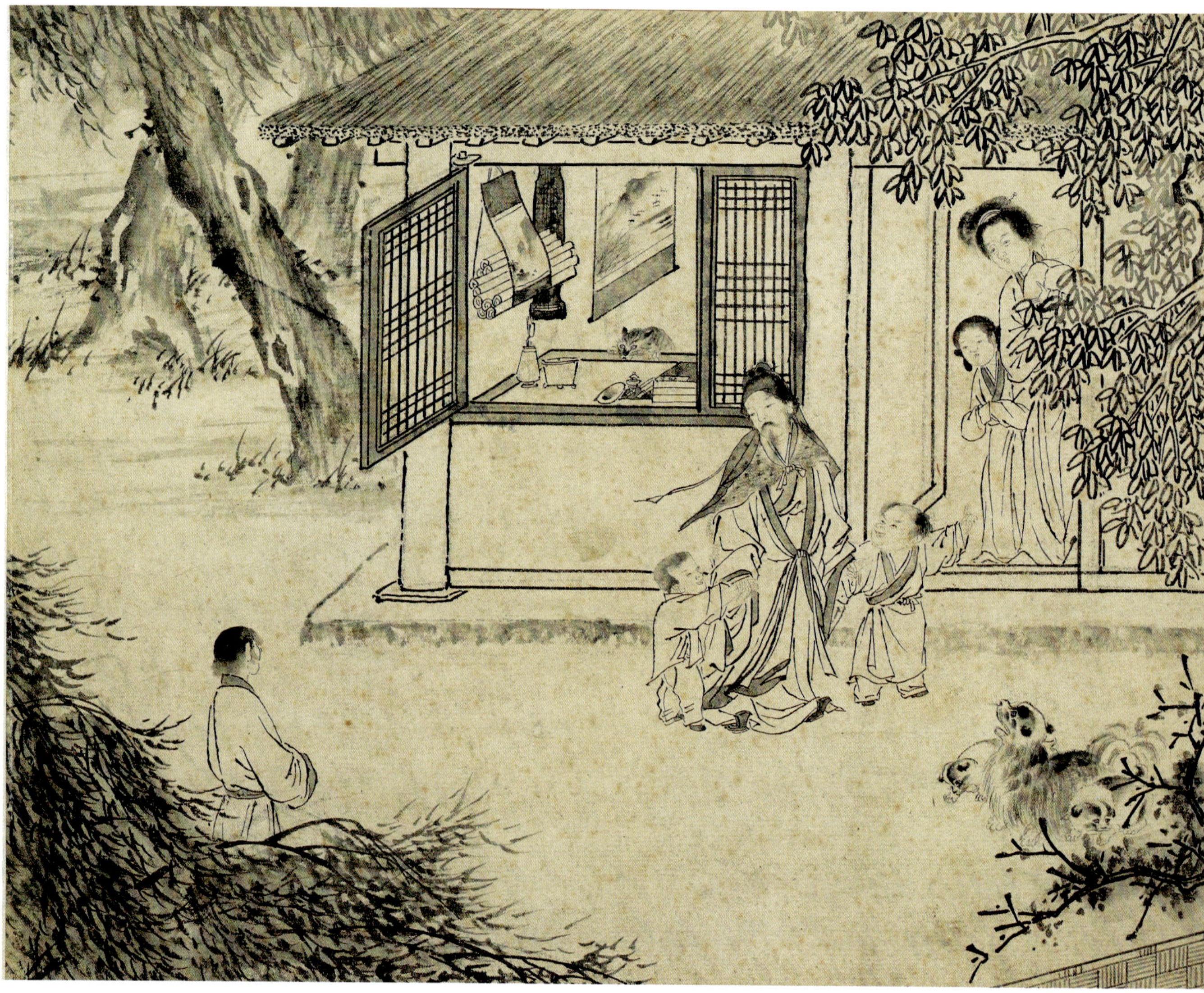

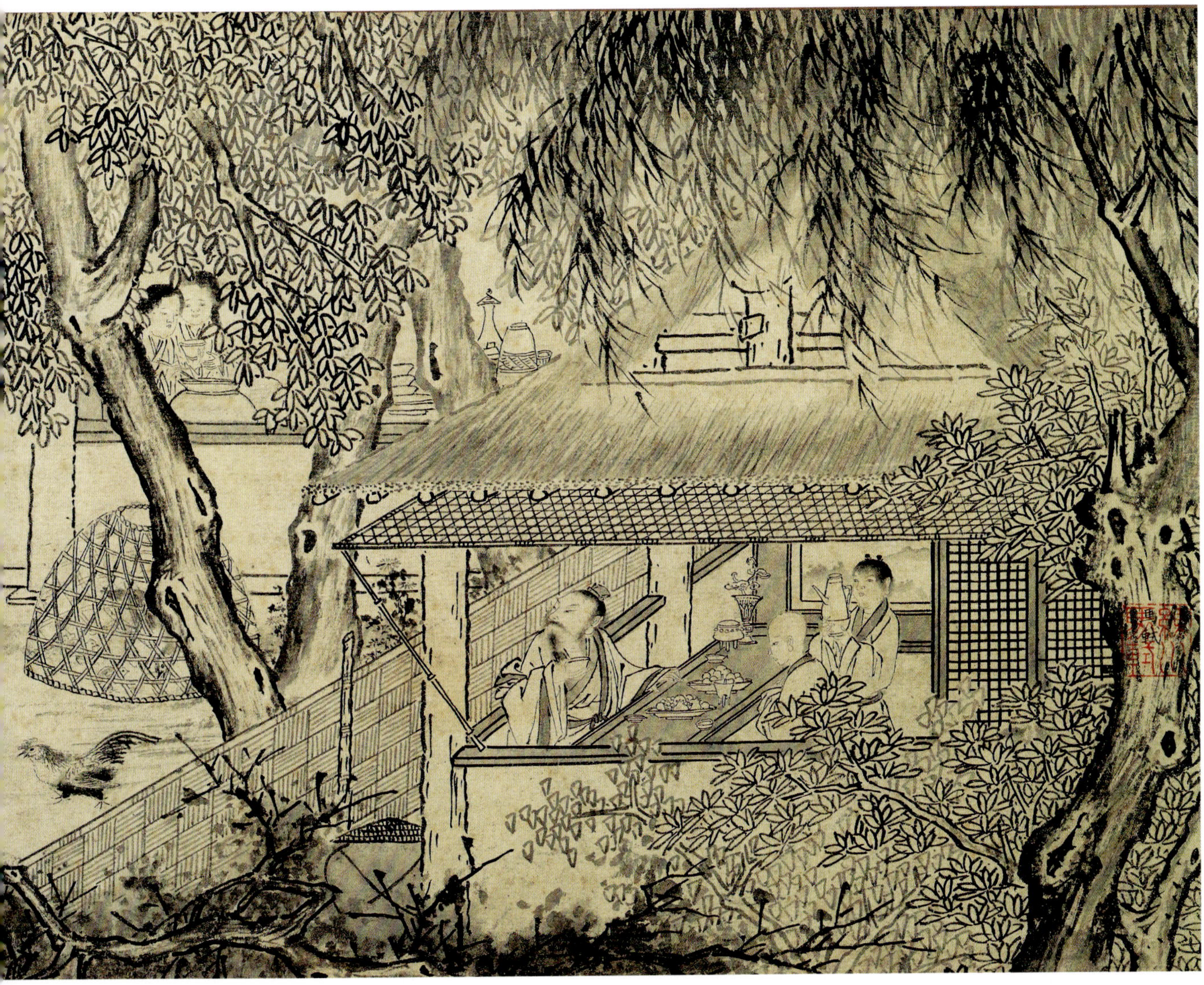

(3) *Children Waiting at the Door* 稚子候门

4

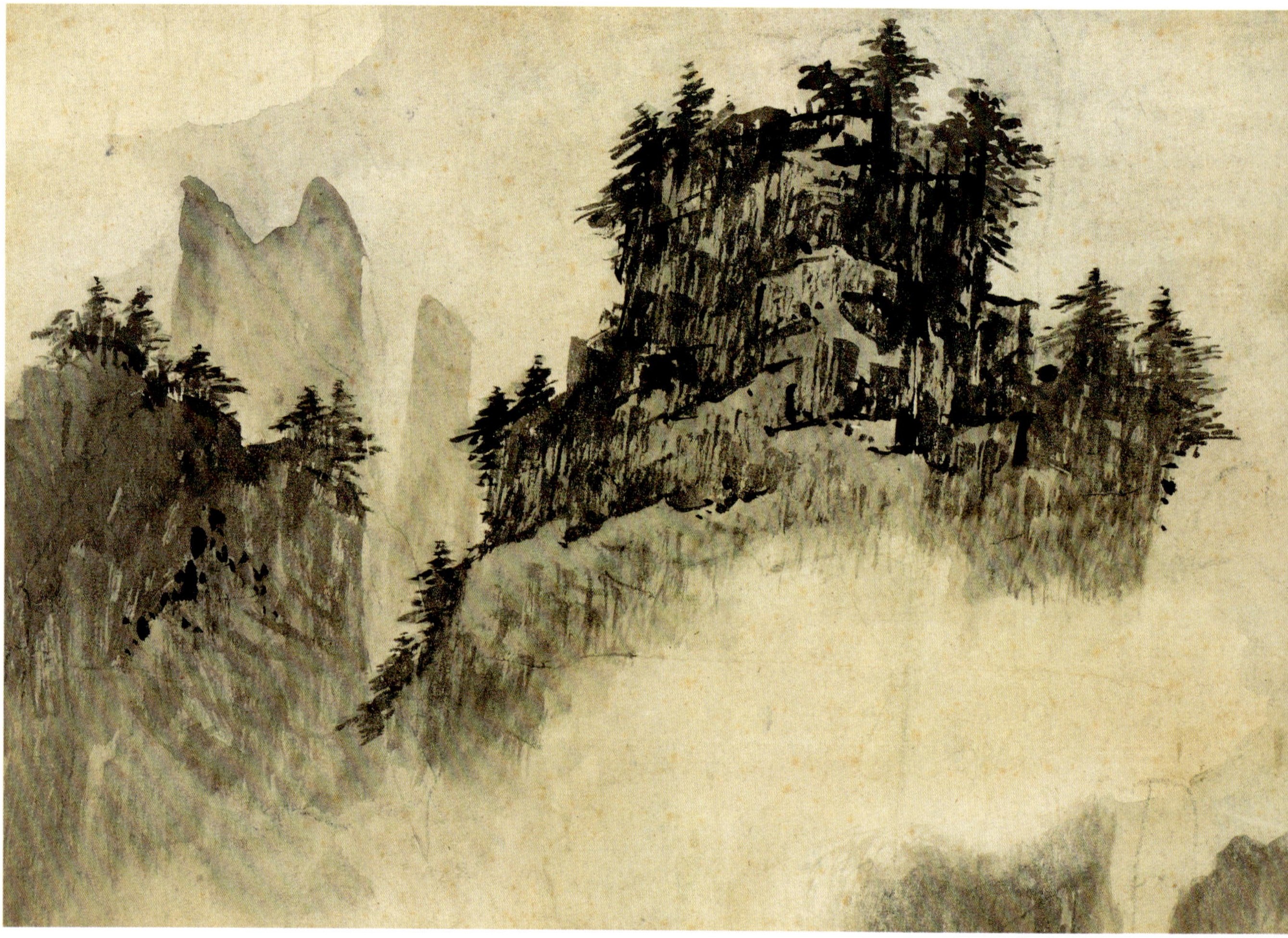

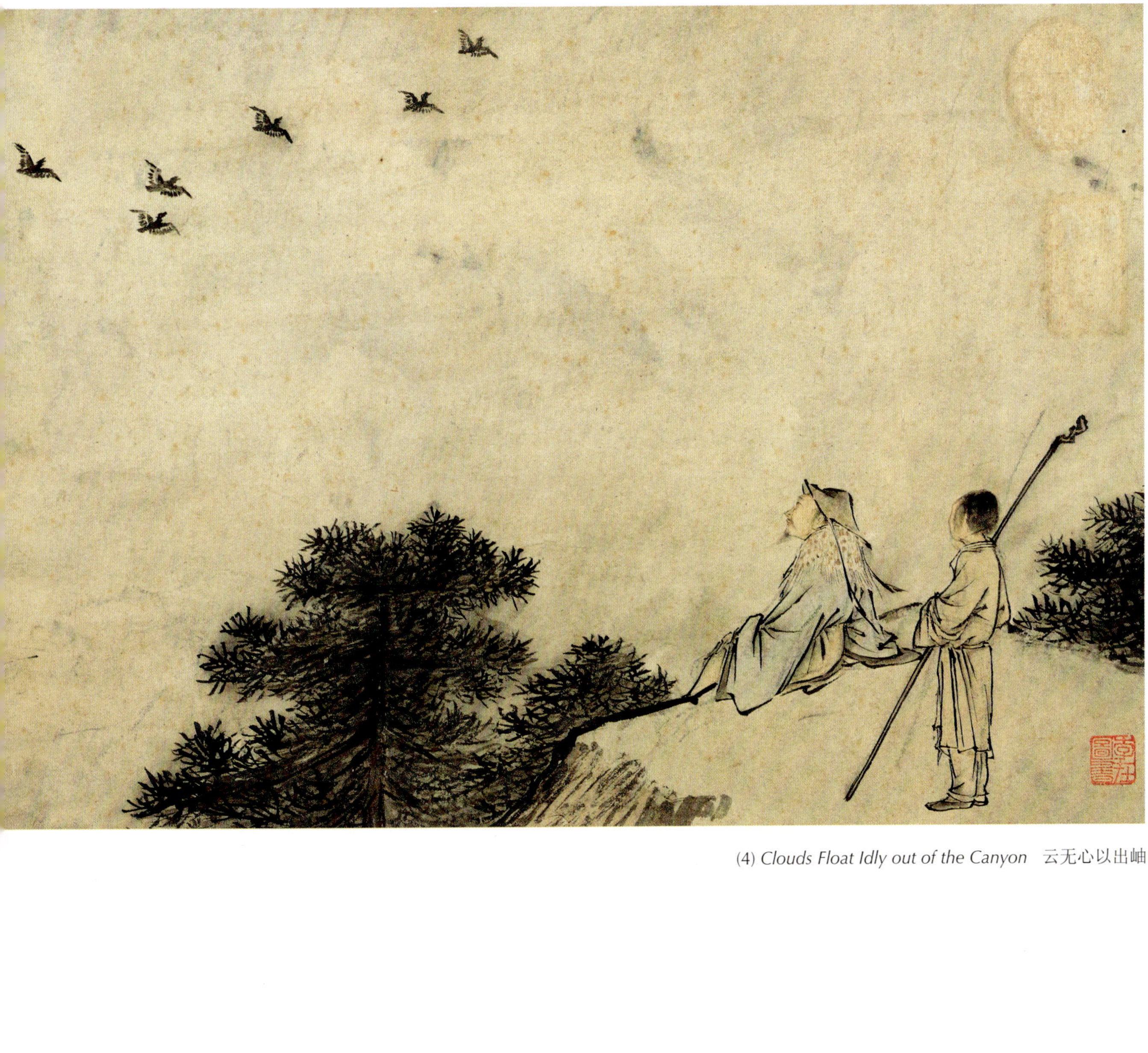

(4) *Clouds Float Idly out of the Canyon* 云无心以出岫

4

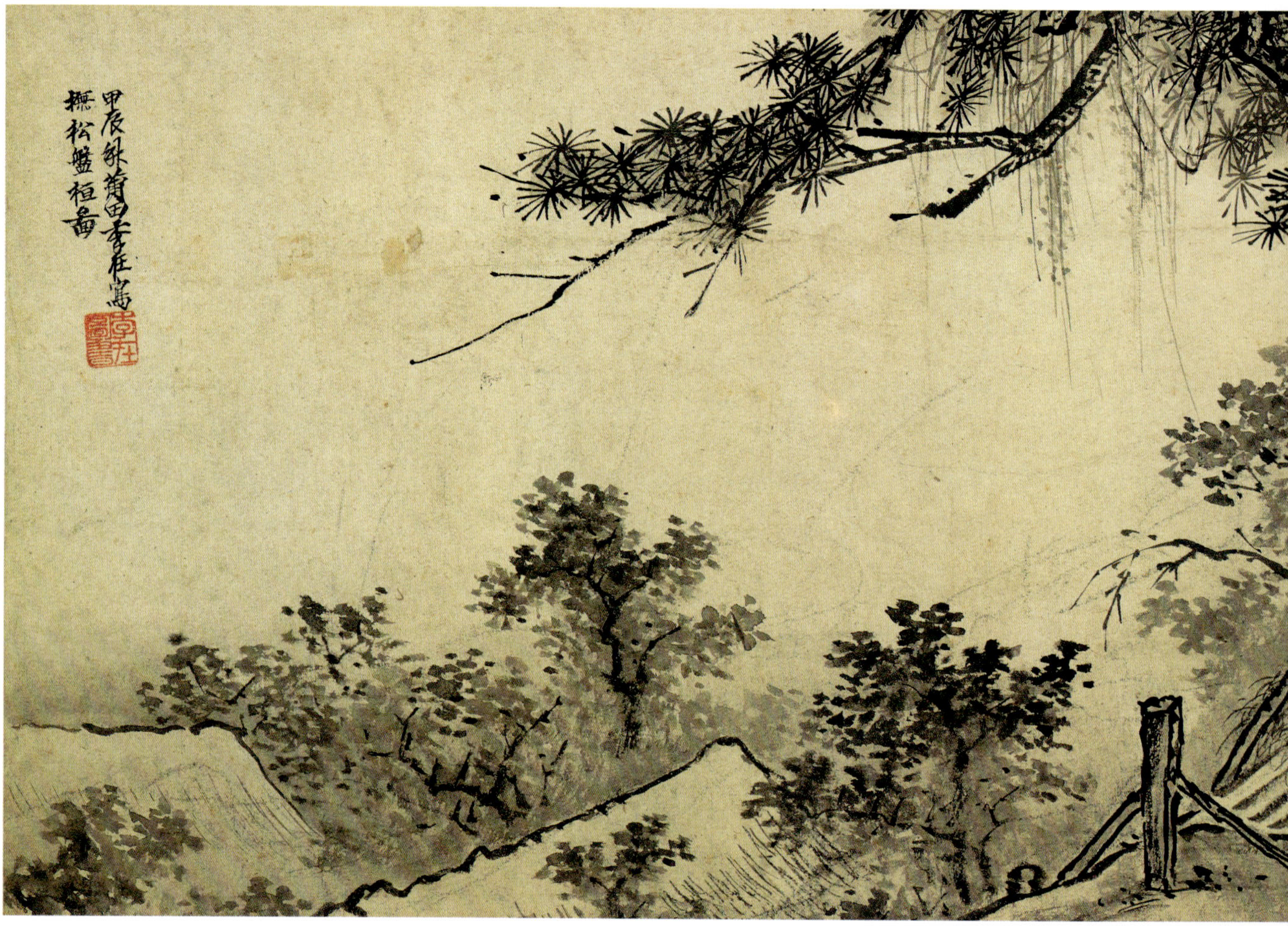

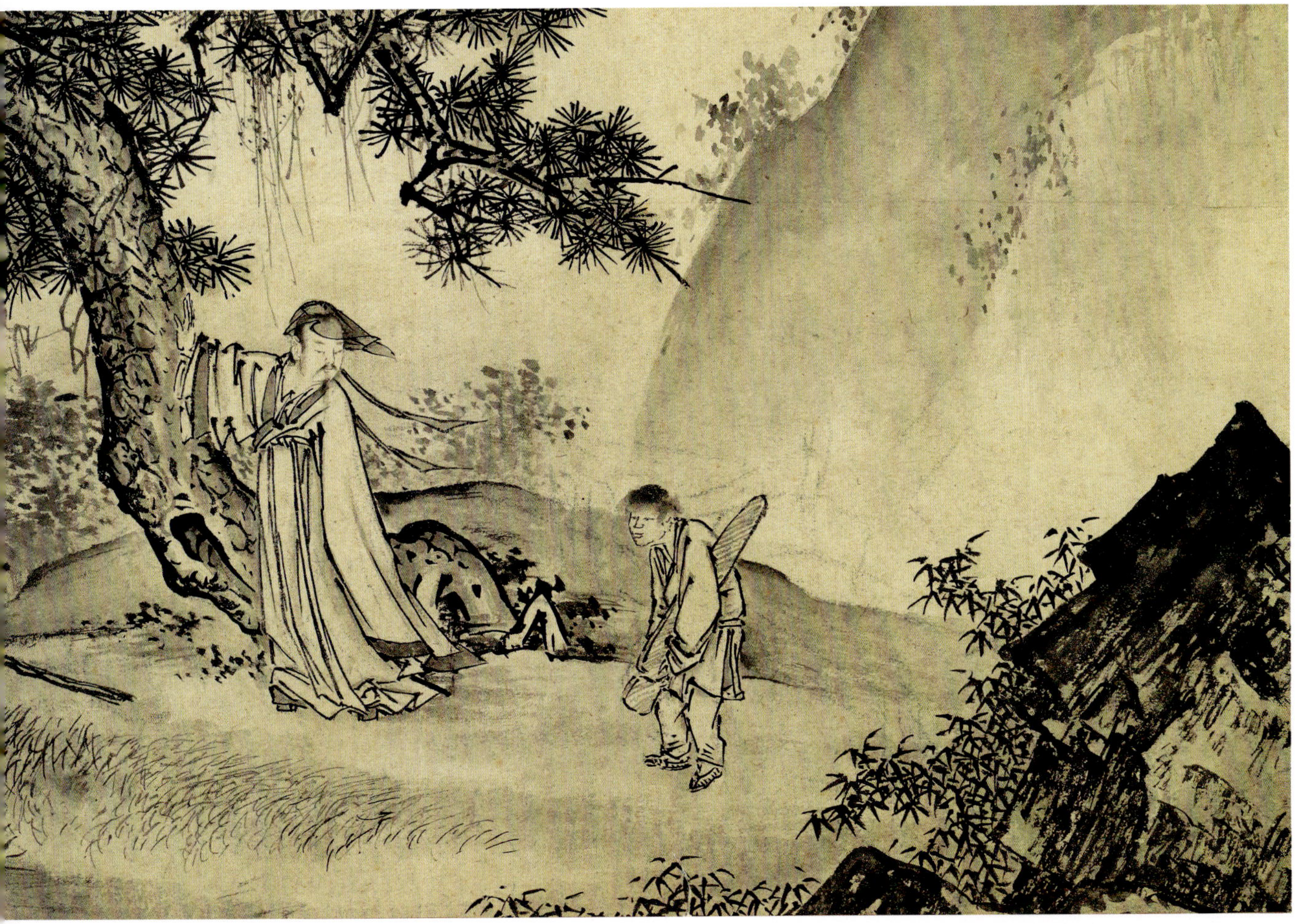

(5) *Feeling the Lonely Pine with My Hand, I Linger* 抚孤松以盘桓

4

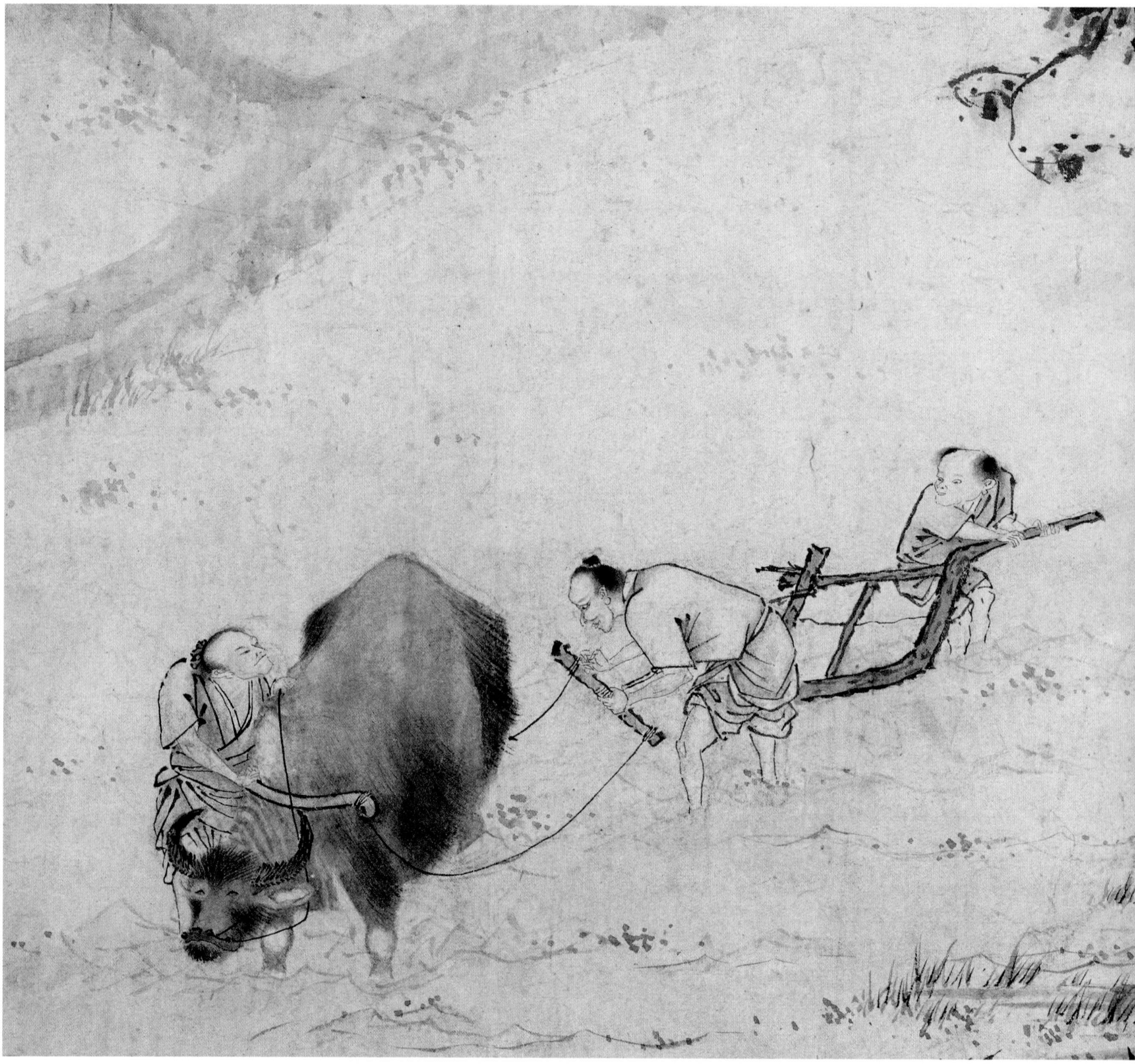

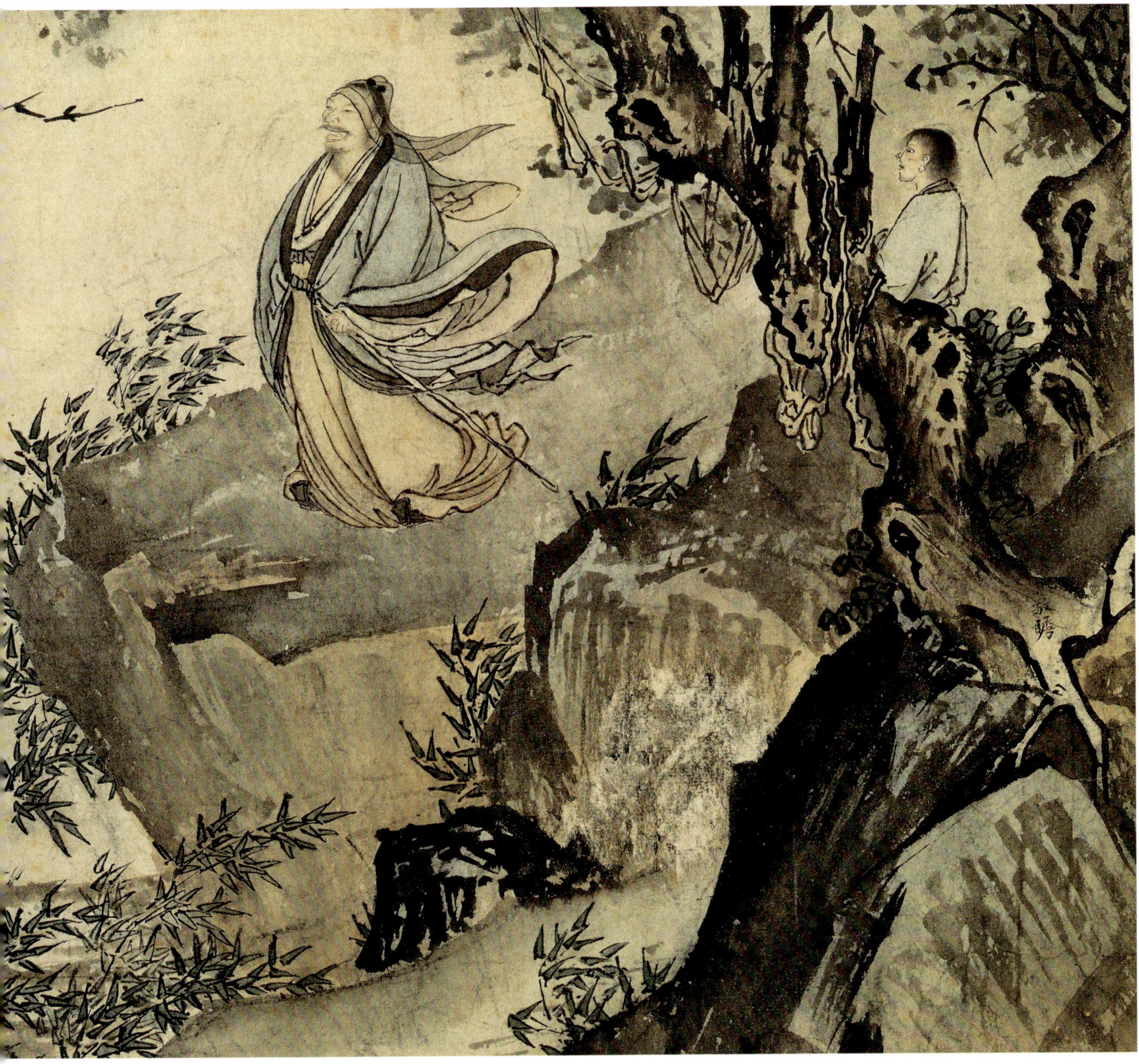

(6) *Farmers Telling Me Spring is Here* 农人告余以春及

4

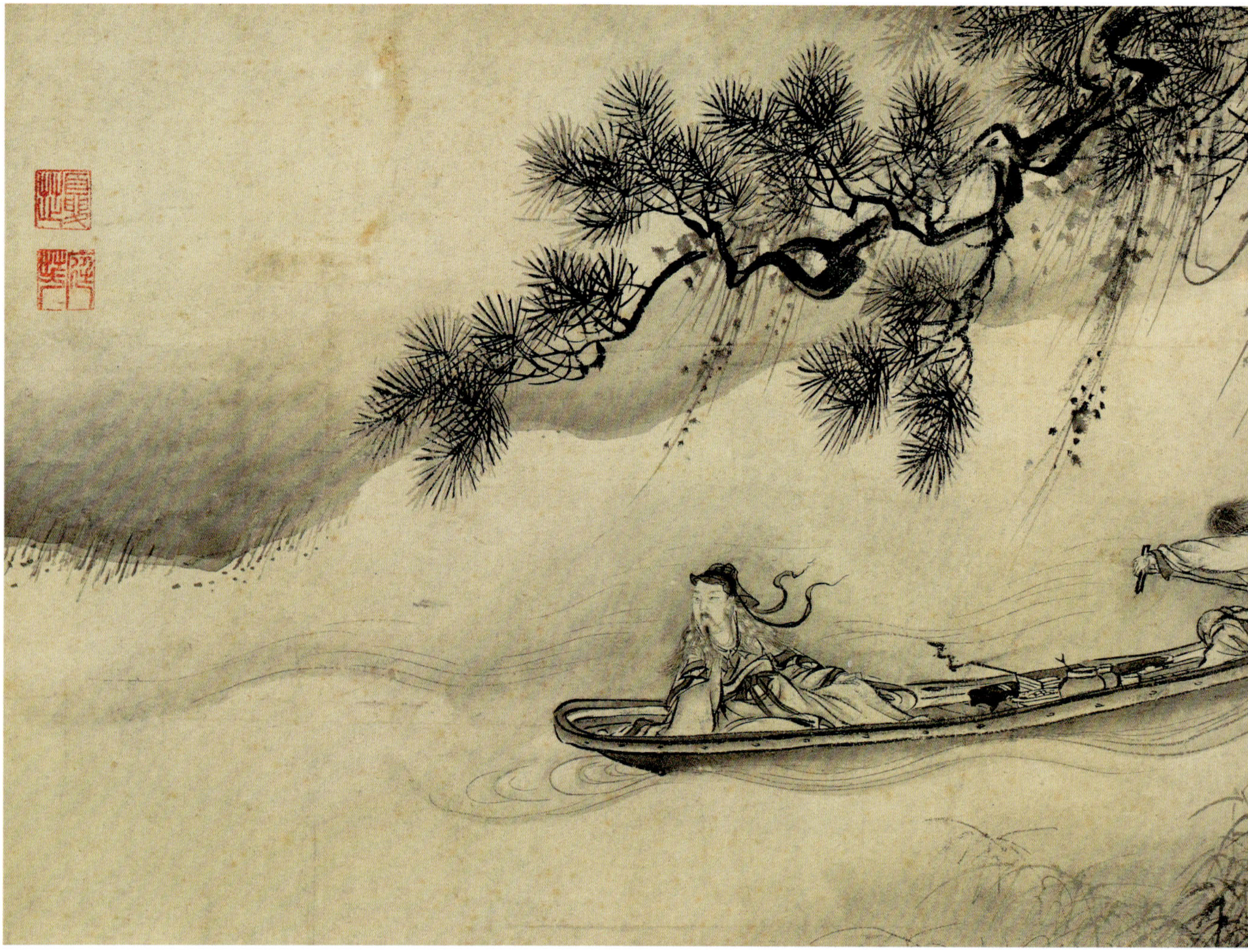

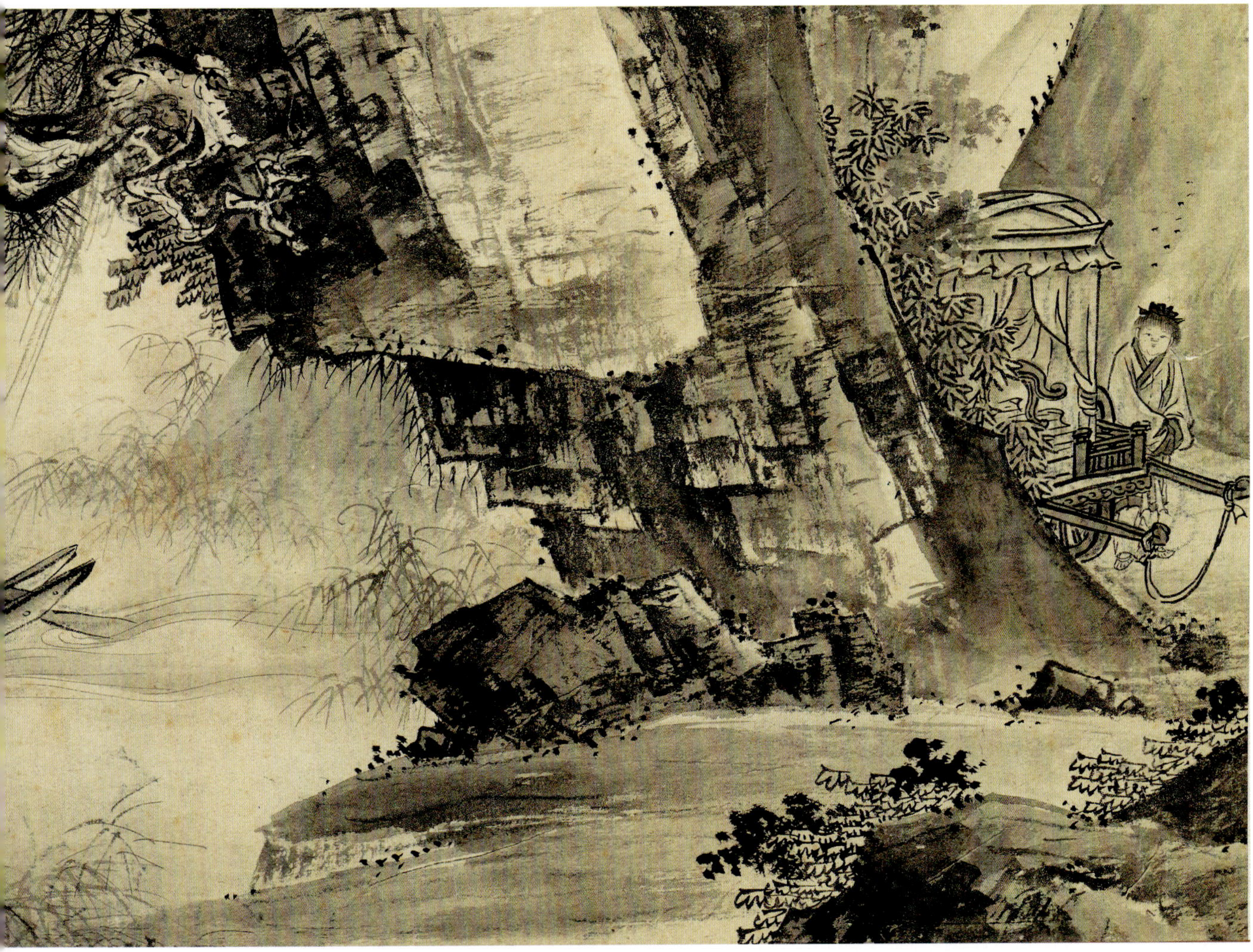

(7) *Or Asking for a Wagon* 或命巾车

4

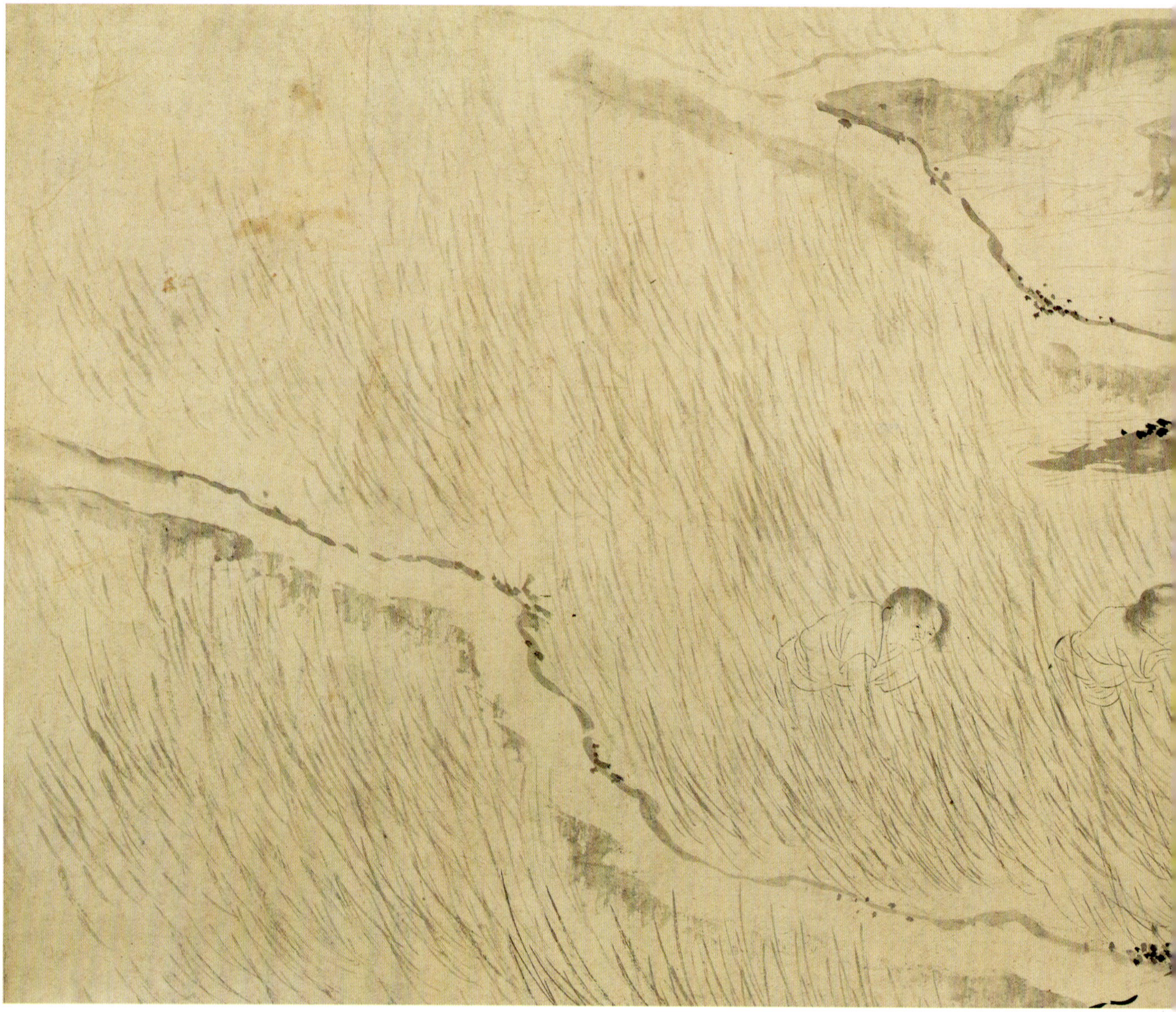

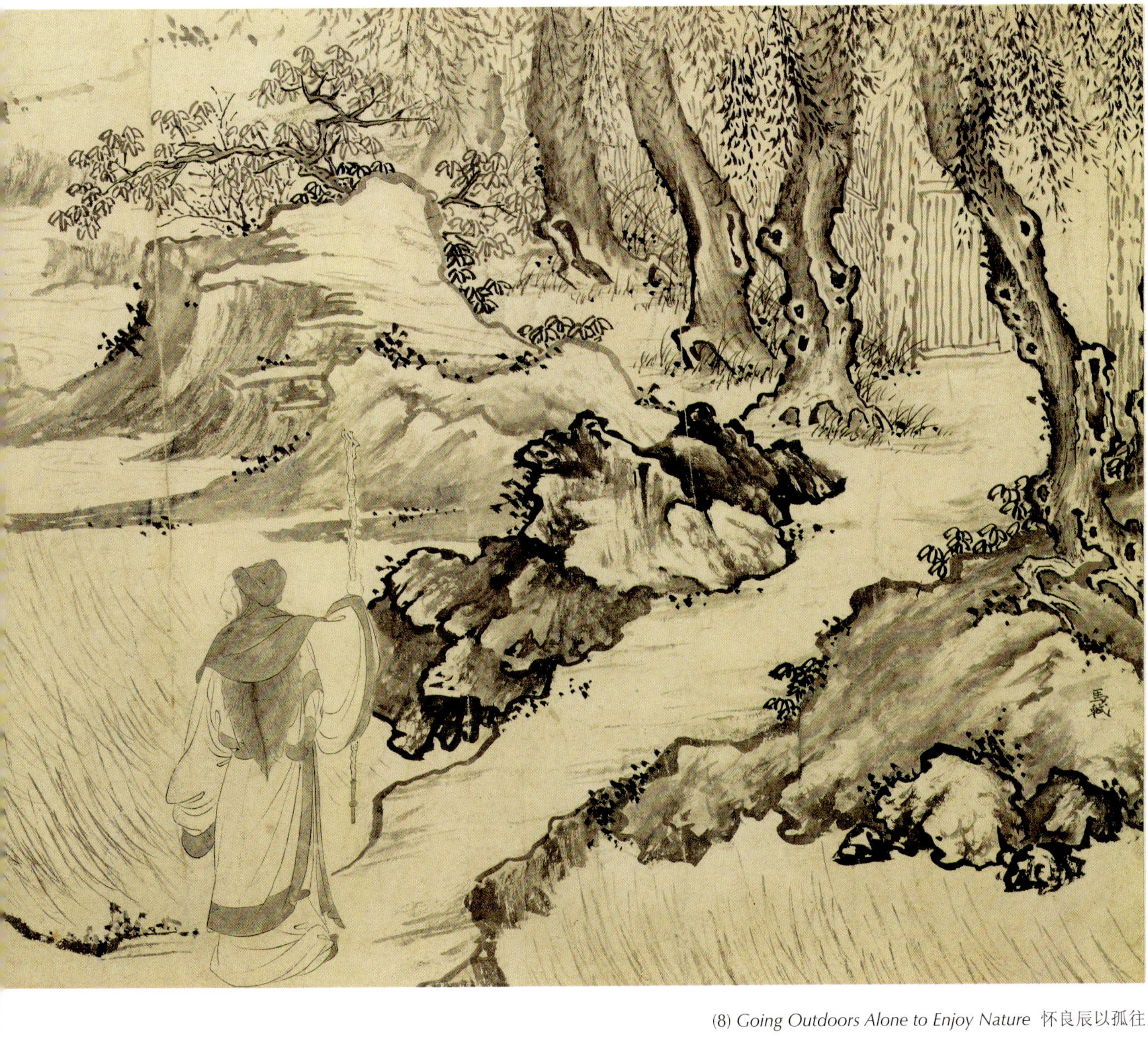

(8) *Going Outdoors Alone to Enjoy Nature* 怀良辰以孤往

4

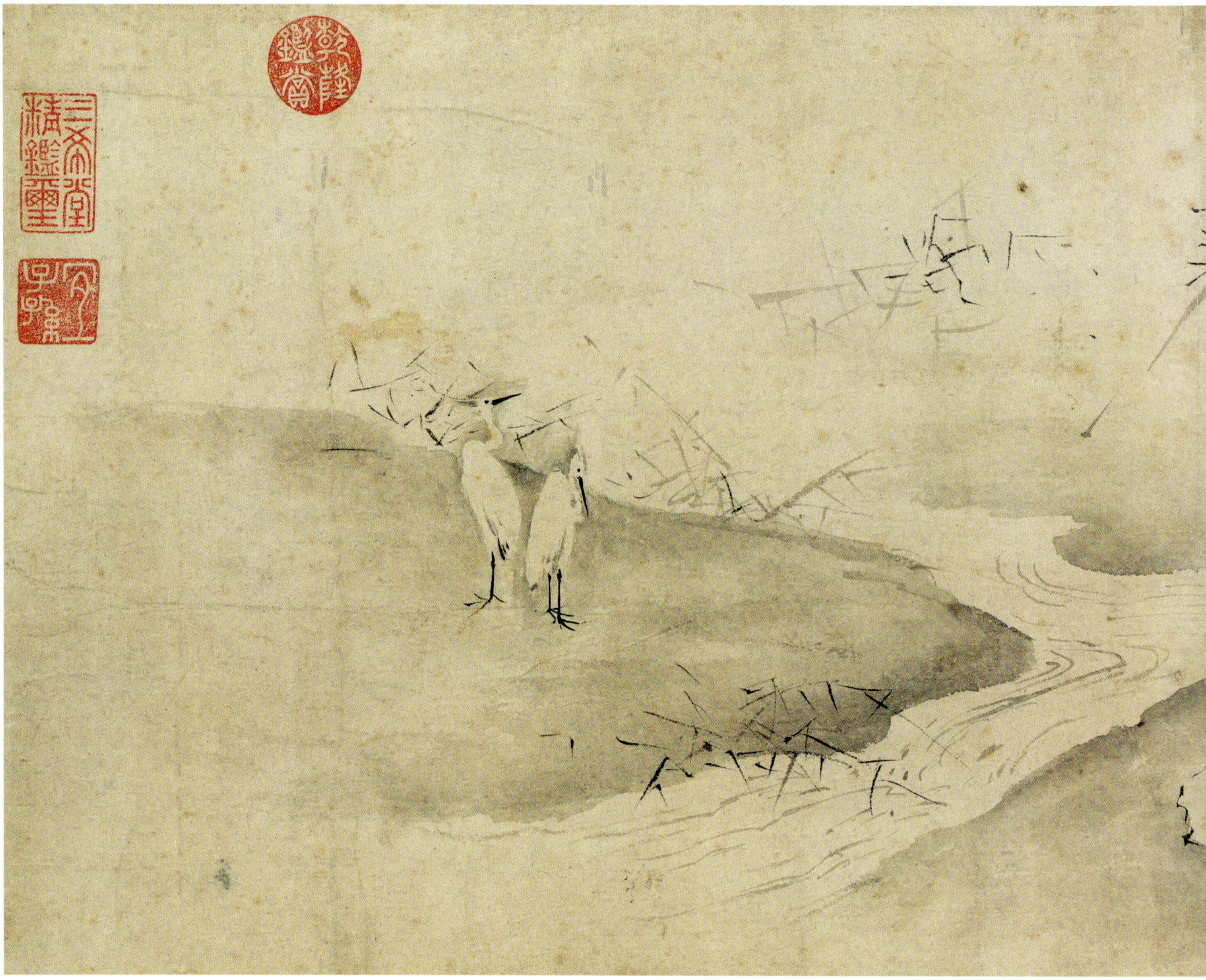

5
明　沈周　千人石夜游图
手卷, 纸本水墨设色
Shen Zhou (1427–1509)
Night Excursion to the Thousand-Man Rock, ca. 1493

Handscroll; ink and color on paper
30.2 x 446 cm

ARTIST'S SEALS: Qinan (square/relief), Shitian (square/intaglio)
IMPERIAL SEALS: [Qianlong, r. 1736–95] Shiqu baoji (rectangular/relief), Chonghuagong jiancangbao (rectangular/relief), Shiqu dingjian (round/relief), Baoji chongbian (square/intaglio), Qianlong yulan zhibao (oval/relief), Qianlong jianshang (round/intaglio), Sanxitang jingjianxi (rectangular/relief), Yizisun (square/intaglio); [Jiaqing, r. 1796–1820] Jiaqing yulan zhibao (oval/relief); [Xuantong (Puyi), r. 1909–11] Xuantong yulan zhibao (square/relief)
COLOPHON WRITERS (SEALS): Xu Lin, 1462–1538, as *daibi* for Shen Zhou (Qinan [square/relief], Shitian [square/intaglio], Baishiweng [square/intaglio]); Yang Xunji, 1456–1544

画家印鉴：启南（朱文方印）、石田（白文方印）
皇家印鉴：[清乾隆皇帝弘历，在位1736－1795]石渠宝笈（朱文长方印）、重华宫鉴藏宝（朱文长方印）、石渠定鉴（朱文圆印）、宝笈重编（白文方印）、乾隆御览之宝（朱文椭圆印）、乾隆鉴赏（白文圆印）、三希堂精鉴玺（朱文长方印）、宜子孙（白文方印）。[清嘉庆皇帝颙琰，在位 1796–1820] 嘉庆御览之宝（朱文椭圆印）。[清宣统皇帝溥仪，在位1909–1911]宣统御览之宝（朱文方印）。
题跋者(钤印)：沈周,1427－1509，徐霖代笔，霖字子仁，1462－1538(启南[朱文方印]、石田[白文方印]、白石翁[白文方印])。杨循吉，1456－1544。

Tiger Hill, with its many scenic spots such as Thousand-Man Rock, was already a destination for visitors to Suzhou in Shen Zhou's time. Residents of the city made the short trip by boat, particularly during festivals, and often left poetic and prose records of their visits. Shen Zhou was one of the first to create pictorial as well as poetic records of his visits to Tiger Hill.[1] His poem recording a particular night excursion to Thousand-Man Rock was quite well known to his contemporaries and was included in the 1506 gazetteer of Suzhou, *Gusuzhi*.[2] The transcription of his poem, along with poems written in response to it by his young friend and fellow poet the bibliophile Yang Xunji (1456–1544), comprise the main body of this scroll. In fact, Shen Zhou's note at the end of the scroll records that Yang Xunji was so irrationally fond of the original poem that, after Yang had responded to it, Shen wrote another poem. Yang again answered, and Shen in turn responded to the last of Yang's poems. Shen Zhou had composed the first poem some years before he came to write them out on a rainy day in the summer of 1493. He did it on a day after getting up from an illness, and once he had begun to write, he did not have the strength in his arm to finish. Fortunately Xu Lin (sobriquet, Ziren), another young friend and noted calligrapher, was there to complete the task for him. In the note recording the circumstances surrounding Yang Xunji's response to the poems, Shen Zhou concludes by saying that Thousand-Man Rock was one of the scenic spots in the Wu region that everyone felt compelled to visit and to compose poetry about and that these compositions were then turned into scrolls which everyone wanted to collect. Shen Zhou often wrote out his own poems, and this scroll was one such case. His painting, which precedes the poems in this scroll, becomes a pictorial preface to the poetic exchange. The painting bears only a seal belonging to Shen Zhou; presumably it was executed about the same time that the poems were transcribed.

Shen Zhou's depiction of his night excursion to Thousand-Man Rock presents the flat, terrace-like formation up close as if seen from a low vantage point. He has cropped the composition so that the expanse of the rock is the focus; the banks and trees as well as the surrounding hillside are cut off at top and bottom much in the same way which the Xuande emperor had painted the pine tree in his *Ten-Thousand-Year-Old Pine Tree* of 1431 (cat. no. 3.). This type of composition had been developed by Wang Fu (1362–1416) in depicting passages of bamboo, but Shen Zhou was the first to fully explore the potentials of such compositions in landscape painting. A lone figure walking with a staff, the artist, appears at the opening of the scroll followed by the expanse of the rock, which ends against the enclosing hillside with steps leading upward. By framing the Thousand-Man Rock with trees at the beginning and the hillside at the end of the scroll Shen Zhou has played off the flat surface against the busier areas at the beginning and end. It is a seemingly simple composition that belies the careful arrangement of forms. The flatness of the expanse creates a calm mood despite the natural tilt of the rock surface. Shen Zhou washes the surface with a pale green color that asserts the flatness of the form while suggesting a scene bathed in moonlight. The long, drawn-out brushstrokes used to create the land have a bluntness that, combined with the rich, round dotting employed for foliage, further enhances the serene quality of the evening visit. The brushwork also imparts a

5

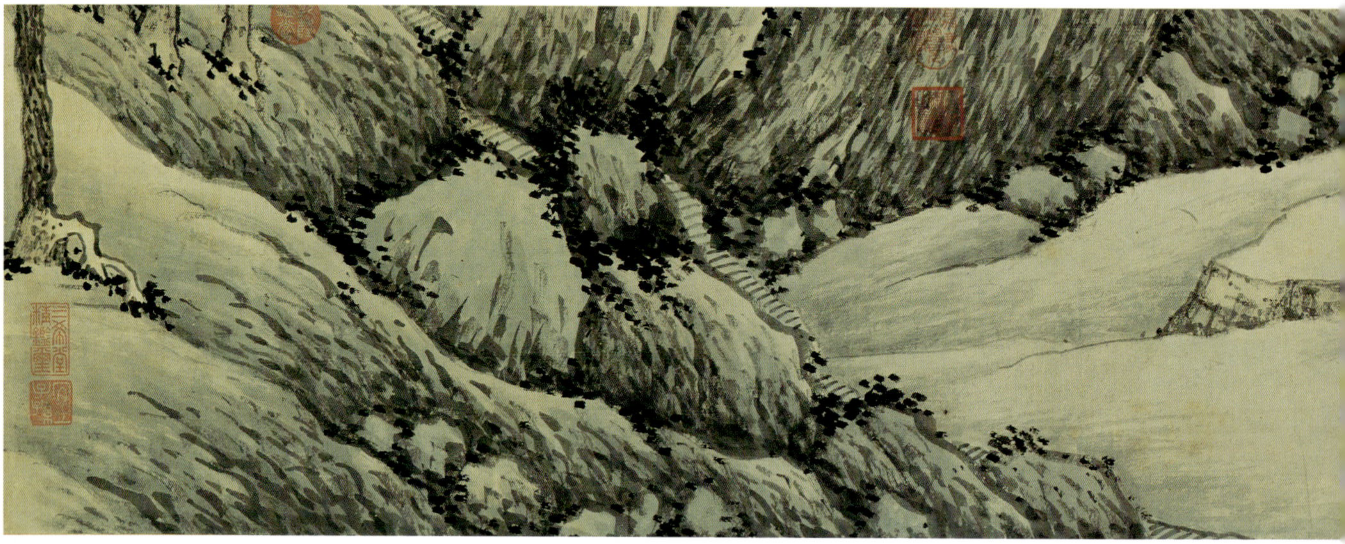

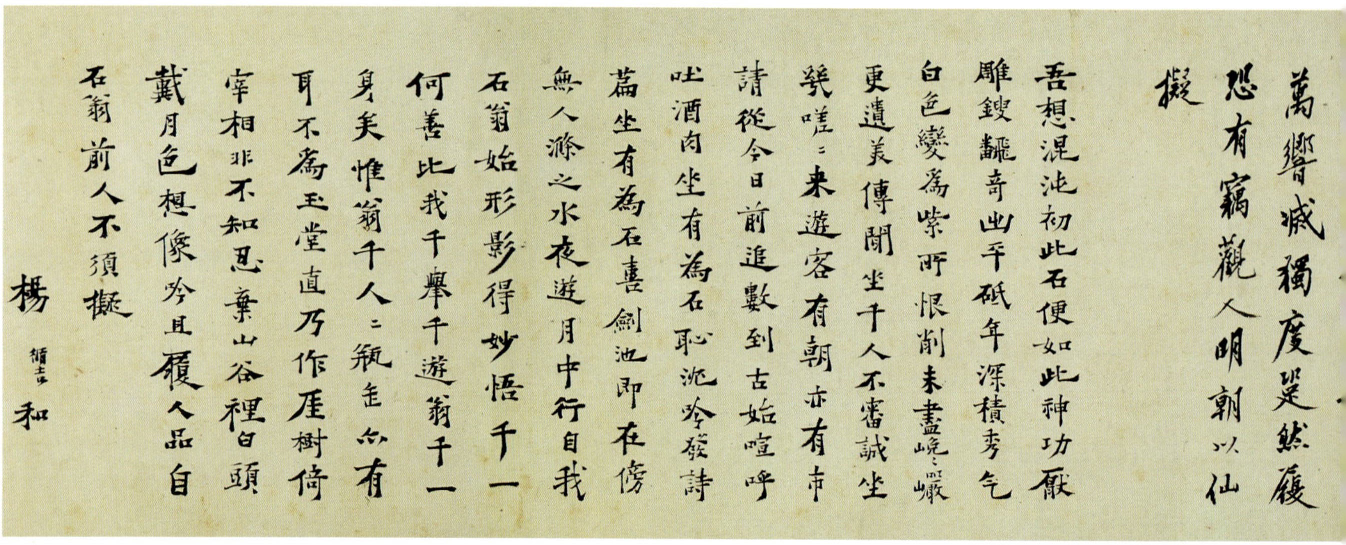
萬響滅獨度跫然履
恐有竊觀人明朝以仙
擬
吾想混沌初此石便如此神功厭
雕鏤巃奇出乎砥年深積秀气
白色變爲紫所恨削未盡嶢〻巖
更遺美傳聞坐千人不審誠坐
幾嗟〻来遊客有朝亦有市
請從今日前進數到古始喧呼
吐酒肉坐有爲石恥泚吟發詩
蓋坐有爲石書劍池即在傍
無人滌之水夜遊月中行自我
石翁始形影得妙悟千一
何善比我千舉千遊翁千一
身美惟翁千人〻稱生亦有
耳不爲玉堂直乃作崖樹倚
宰相非不知思棄山谷裡白頭
戴月色想像吟且履人品自
石翁前人不須擬
楊循吉和

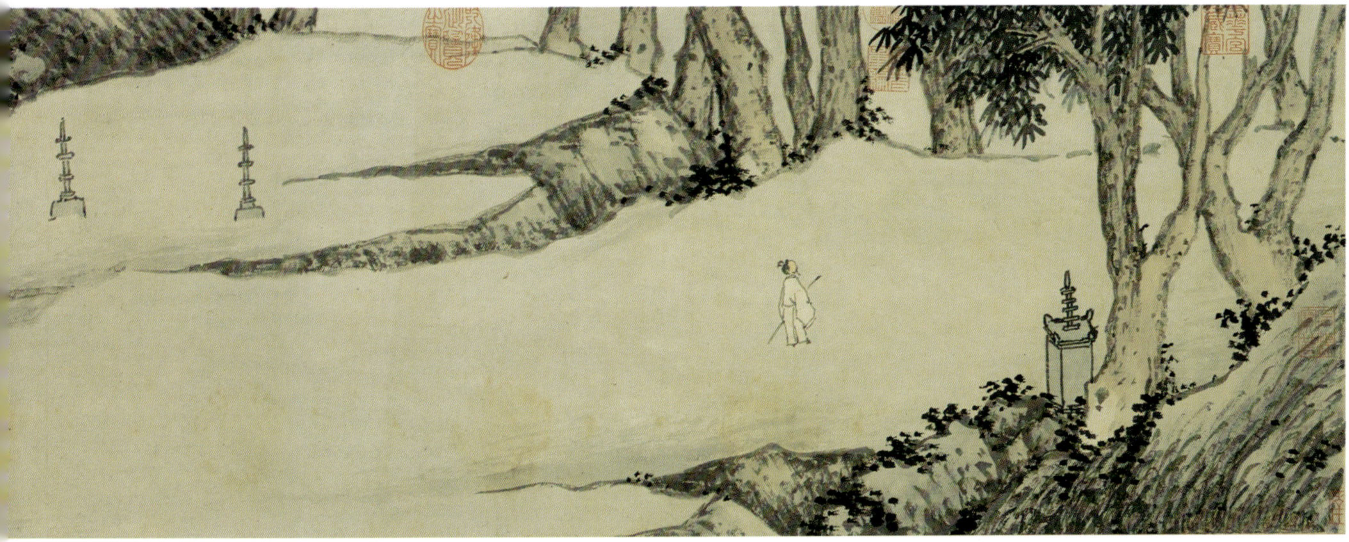

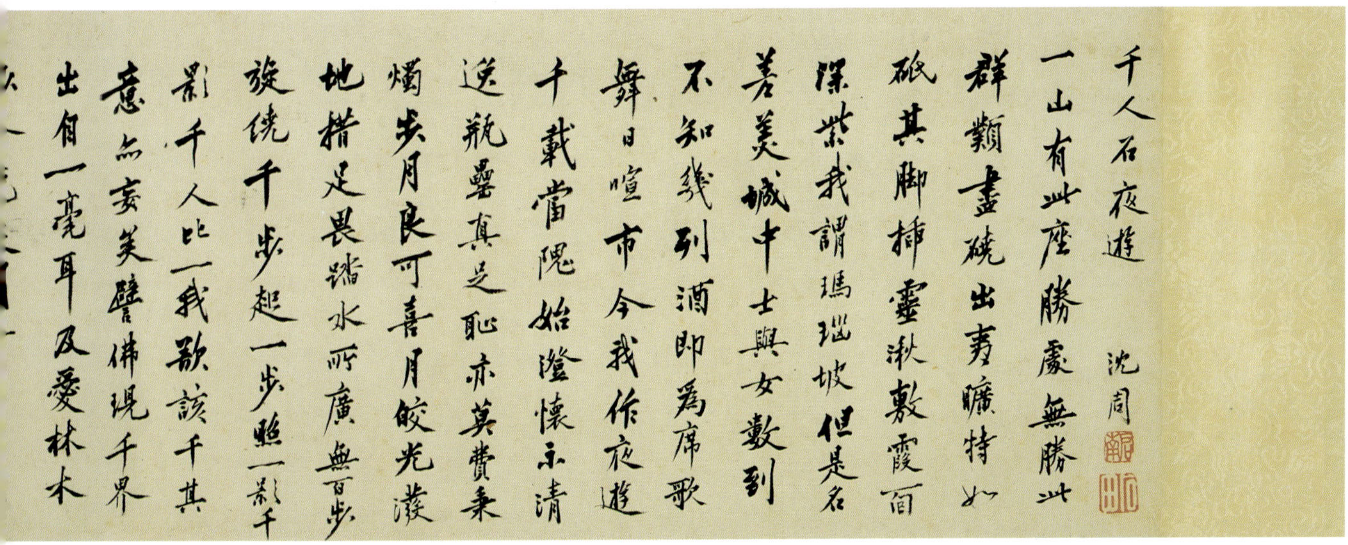
千人石夜遊 沈周
一山有此座勝處無勝此
群類盡硗出夷曠特如
砥其脚插靈湫數霞百
深紫我謂瑪瑙坡但是名
差美城中士與女數到
不知幾列酒即爲席歌
舞日喧市今我作夜遊
千載當隗始澄懷示清
送瓶罍真足恥亦莫費秉
燭步月良可喜月皎光潑
地措足畏踏水所廣無百步
旋繞千步起一步照一影千
影千人比一我歡該千其
意亦妄矣譬佛現千界
出自一毫耳及愛林木

5

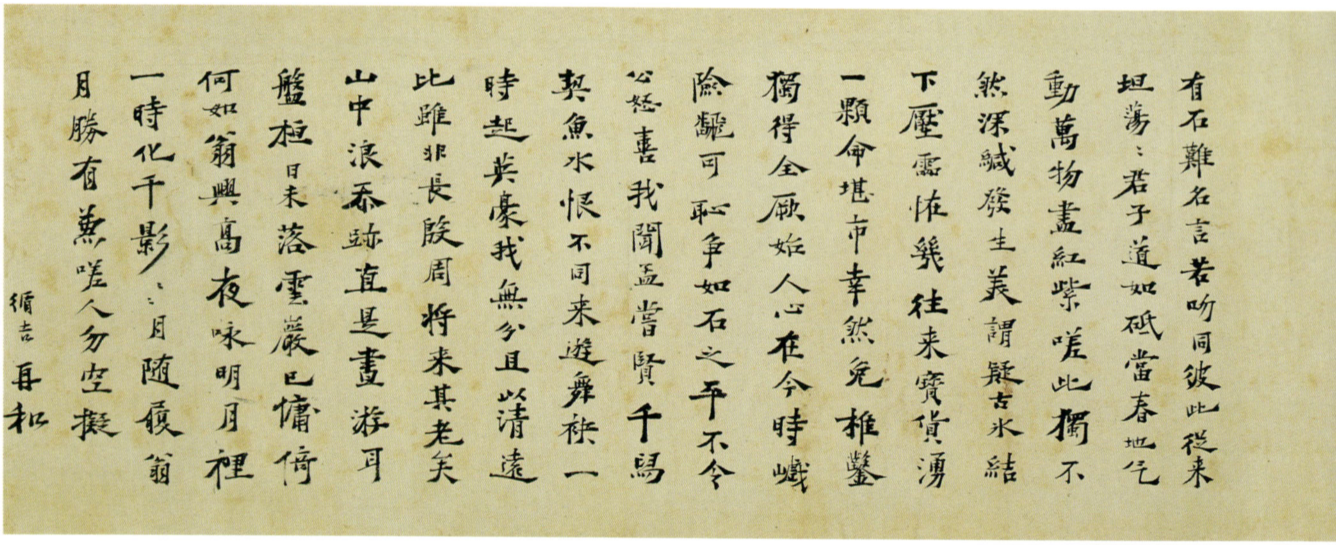

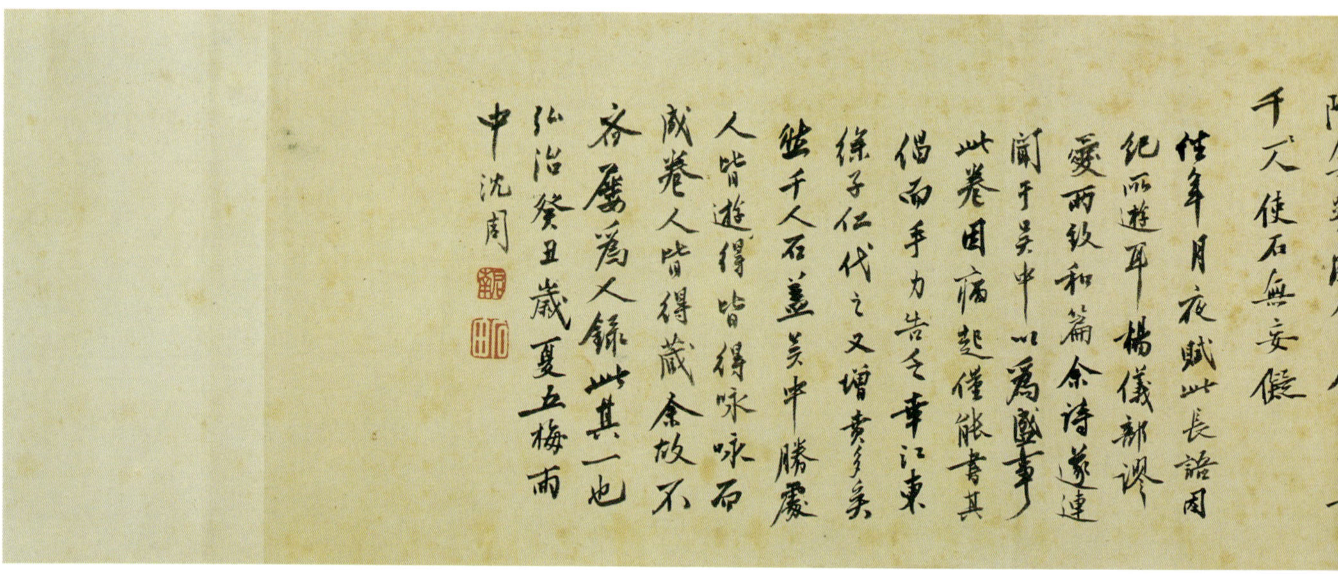

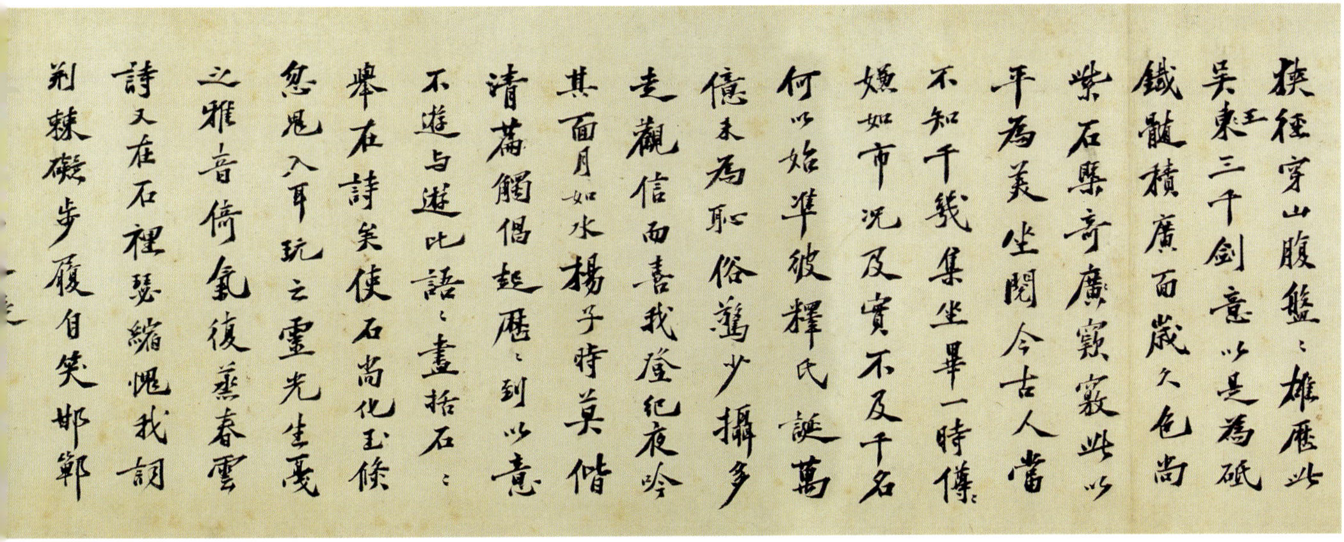
狹徑穿山腹盤盤雄歷此
吳東王三千劍意以是為砥
鐵髓積廣百歲久色尚
紫石槩奇廣竅窾此以
平為美坐閱今古人當
不知千載集坐畢一時傳
媿如市況及實不及千名
何以始準彼釋氏誕萬
億未為恥俗鶩少攝多
支觀信而喜我登紀夜吟
其面月如水楊子特莫偕
清蒲觸倡起歷歷到以意
不遊与遊比語語盡括石石
舉在詩矣使石尚化玉條
忽見入耳玩之靈光生憂
之雅音倚氣復蒸春雲
詩又在石裡瑟縮愧我詞
剏棘礙步履自笑邯鄲

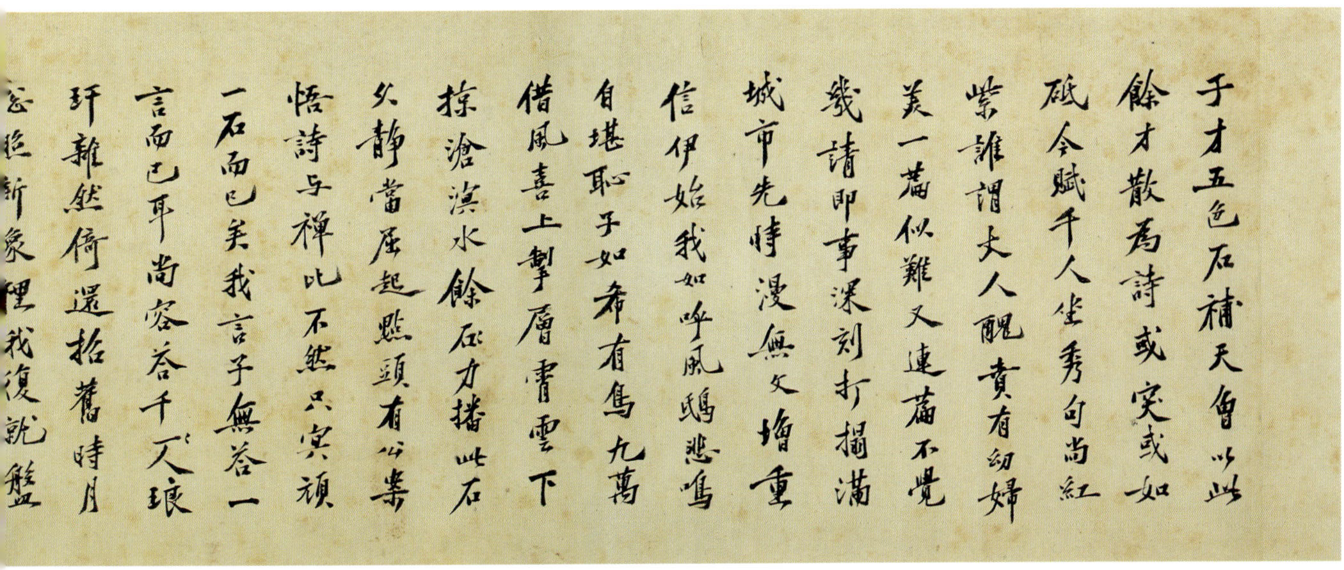
子才五色石補天曾以此
餘才散為詩或突或如
砥今賦千人坐秀句尚紅
紫誰謂丈人醜貴有幼婦
美一蒲似難又蓮蒲不覺
幾請即事渫刻打揭滿
城市先特漫無文增重
信伊始我如呼風鳴悲鳴
自堪恥子如希有鳥九萬
借風喜上掣層霄雲下
捺滄溟水餘石力播此石
久靜當屋起點頭有此案
悟詩与禪比不然只宾頑
一石而已矣我言子無答一
言而已耳尚容吞千人琅
玕雜然倚還拾舊時月

sense of warmth, amply conveying the mood of the artist's solitary visit to this scenic spot.

Shen Zhou was born in 1427 into a landowning family in Xiangcheng, a small town just to the north of Suzhou.[3] His ancestors had moved the family to that location in the fourteenth century, and since the beginning of the Ming dynasty the family had held the position of tax gatherers for the immediate area. Neither his grandfather nor father had served in government, preferring to remain home as recluse-scholars. The family had direct links to the world of the late Yuan scholar-painters—his great grandfather had been a collector and connoisseur as well as a friend of the painter Wang Meng (ca. 1308–1385), and his grandfather, who was also a collector, was compared in the *Ming History* (*Ming shi*) to the late Yuan man of culture Gu Dehui (1306–1369). Gu was remembered for the elegant gatherings (*yaji*) held at his estate in nearby Kunshan. Shen thus grew up in an atmosphere that preserved the ideal of the man of culture (*wenren*) as it had unfolded in the fourteenth century. When it came time for his education, he was tutored by his father's teacher's son, Chen Kuan, the grandson of the late Yuan painter Chen Ruyan (ca. 1331–1371). This gave the young Shen Zhou a further link to the world of the fourteenth-century men of culture. As a painter he was taught by his father and uncle and studied the works of the fourteenth-century masters, particularly the works of the painters who came to be known as the Four Masters of the Yuan: Huang Gongwang (1269–1354), Wu Zhen (1280–1354), Ni Zan (1306–1374), and Wang Meng. At one point he owned Huang's famous scroll *Dwelling in the Fuchun Mountains* (*Fuchun shanju tu*) and later, after he had sold the scroll, made a copy of it from memory. The late Ming critic Li Rihua (1565–1635) summed up his development as a painter in the following way: "Shitian [Shen Zhou] first learned to paint from his father and his uncle; then he studied various old masters and knew them all perfectly. In his middle age he chose Huang Gongwang as his master, but in his later years he was completely carried away with Mei Daoren [Wu Zhen]. His heart was drunk as if intoxicated with Wu Zhen's art; he blended so closely with it that some of his works could not be distinguished from Wu Zhen's if they were mixed up." In his depiction of the Thousand-Man Rock, Shen Zhou indeed employed the thick line drawing and juicy ink dots of Wu Zhen.

Like his grandfather, his father, and his uncle, Shen Zhou did not seek a career in government, although he undoubtedly could have received an appointment through recommendation. When he was pressed by friends who wanted to recommend him for office, he cited his filial duty to his mother as the main reason for not leaving home. His mother lived to be ninety-eight, dying just two years before Shen Zhou himself. Although Shen had a national reputation during his lifetime as both a poet and a painter, as a commoner without official rank he could be called upon to perform menial tasks by local government officials. One often repeated story, which may be apocryphal, tells of a new prefect in Suzhou being given Shen Zhou's name and asking the artist to paint the walls of his official residence. Shen Zhou did so, saying that it was his duty to comply. Only later did the official find out that the artist was known personally to high officials in the capital. When he returned to Suzhou and paid a visit to Shen Zhou, he was received with courtesy. Such stories are used by traditional biographers to reveal Shen Zhou's character. What may lie behind such stories is the reality that Shen must have garnered an income from his calligraphy and painting. It is worth remembering that on the summer day in 1493 when his arm was tired, Xu Lin wrote in his stead.

By the late sixteenth to early seventeenth century, Shen Zhou's reputation as a painter exceeded that of his contemporaries. He came to be considered the founder of a tradition of scholar painting in the Wu region, called the Wu School (*Wumen huapai*), and later, along with his pupil Wen Zhengming (1470–1559), Tang Yin (1470–1524), and Qiu Ying (ca. 1495–1552), he was grouped as one of the Four Great Masters of the Ming dynasty. The Qianlong emperor did much to cement Shen's reputation as one of the preeminent painters of the Ming period by assembling almost all of his best works in the palace collection. This scroll joined forty-seven paintings catalogued in the second part of the imperial catalogue, *Shiqu baoji xubian* (Treasured boxes of the Stone Channel, continued), finished toward the end of the Qianlong reign in 1793. They were added to the sixty-six paintings already in the collection when the first part of the catalogue was completed in 1745. Qianlong impressed eight seals on the surface of the painting; the Jiaqing emperor and Puyi left one seal each.

DAS

Notes

1. For Shen Zhou and depictions of Tiger Hill, see Yoshida Haruki, "Guanyu Huqiushan tu zhi wojian" [My view concerning pictures of Tiger Hill], in *Wumen huapai yanjiu* [Research on Wu School painting] (Beijing: Zijincheng chubanshe, 1993), pp. 65–75.
2. *Gusu zhi* [Gazetteer of Suzhou Prefecture] (1506), ed. Wang Ao et al., *juan* 8, p. 2b, reprinted in Zhongguo shixue congshu [Collected works of Chinese historiography] (Taipei: Taiwan Xuesheng shuju, 1965), p. 131.
3. For general biographical information, see Zheng Bingshan, *Shen Shitian* [Shen Shitian (Zhou)] (Shanghai: Shanghai renmin meishu chubanshe, 1958); Richard Edwards, *The Field of Stones: A Study of the Art of Shen Chou (1427–1509)* (Washington: Smithsonian Institution, 1962); and Richard Edwards, "Shen Chou," in *Dictionary of Ming Biography*, ed. L. Carrington Goodrich (New York: Columbia University Press, 1976), pp. 1173–77.
4. *Ming shi*, *juan* 298 (Beijing: Zhonghua shuju, 1974), vol. 13, p. 7630.
5. Li Rihua from *Liuyanzhai biji* quoted in *Peiwenzhai shuhuapu* [Calligraphy and painting compendium of the Peiwen Studio] (1708), *juan* 56, p. 29b, as reprinted in Yingyin *Wenyuange Siku quanshu* [Photographic Reprint of the Wenyuange Copy of the Imperial Library] (Taipei: Taiwan Shangwu yinshuguan, 1983), vol. 821, p. 400. Translation by Oswald Sirén, *Chinese Painting: Leading masters and Principles*, vol. 4 (New York: The Ronald Press, 1958), p. 152.
6. *Shiqu baoji xubian* [Treasured boxes of the Stone Channel, continued] in *Midian zhulin Shiqu baoji hebian* [Pearl forest of the Secret Hall and Treasured boxes of the Stone Channel, combined edition], 12 vols, (Shanghai: Shanghai shudian, 1988), vol. 5, pp. 1606–07.

早在沈周的时代，苏州虎丘千人石已是天下知名的游览胜地。当地人多乘船到此游憩，每逢节庆假日，更是如此。骚人墨客，经常过访，并作诗记游，沈周则是为虎丘之行作画并题诗的第一人。该诗作记载他某次夜访千人石之事，为当时人所熟知，于1506年入载《姑苏志》中。此记游诗，连带其友、诗人与書誌編纂家杨循吉(1456－1544)与之唱和的作品，构成此图卷的主体。沈周在卷末题款，述及此事的原委。杨循吉对沈之原诗异样喜爱，在杨以诗回赠其作之后，沈作了另一诗相和。杨则再次以诗数首答复，沈就又一次回应杨之作。沈周第一首诗虽早已作成，但诗本身要到1493年夏天才由沈周书写纪录。据说，沈周欲于病中起身书写此诗，但才提笔，却无力完成。所幸，沈的好友名书家徐霖(1462－1538)在场，代笔将诗写就。在记录关于杨循吉作诗与之唱和的事件中，沈周于结语里说，千人石为吴郡人人均欲参访作诗的景点，将这些作品收入画卷中，则人人将競相收藏。作为画家，沈周通常为画赋诗，此画亦不例外。然图卷画在诗之先，反而变成了诗作交换主题的画序。此图只钤一沈周印，图画本身可能是在诗作写成时同时完成的。

为描绘他夜游千人石一事，沈周以一视线稍低的平远法，将平坦如露台的主景拉前。他并将构图缩近，以此凸显千人石山岩的旷阔。堤岸树木与周围山坡，均截去了上下两部分，与宣德皇帝在他1431年的《万年松图》中(见图录第3号)对松树的处理手法相似。此种构图法由王绂(1362－1416) 始创，运用于描绘竹林。但在山水画的布局中将此法充分发挥，沈周则为第一人。图中画家自己一人倚杖独行，出现在卷首，眼前一片廣袤的石岩。石岩之尽，山坡与登高石级相接。全画由千人石与古树交待于前，山坡接续于尾，画卷景色两端起伏，中间平广。沈周的构图看似简约，章法形势布置却极巧妙而富动感。平缓广阔的路面，即便石面凹凸倾斜，仍显得静谧祥和。沈周以淡綠设色石面，突显石块的平整，并表现了夜色中月光铺地的质感。地面以略带粗硬、细长堆叠的披麻皴为表，圆形苔点皴点于上，交待石上花草枝叶，更增夜游静寂之象。笔法线条圆润饱满，平添画家静夜独游胜景的孤寂感。

沈周于1427年生于苏州城北相城的一个地主之家。祖先于十四世纪时迁到相城，明朝时以收取租税为业。沈之祖父与父亲均未做官，一生在家退隐耕读。沈家与元代文人画坛有着直接的脐带联系,其曾祖父为一鉴藏家，既记载和元代大画家王蒙（约1308－1385）有交往。祖父亦为收藏家，在《明史》曾有记载，与元代文人顾德辉(1306－1369) 相提并论，顾以在崑山自家住宅组织“雅集”而为世人所知。生长于十四世纪充满文人思潮的环境里，沈周由父亲业师的儿子陈宽启蒙，陈为元代末期画家陈汝言(约1331－1371) 之孙。这层关系将少年沈周与十四世纪文人传统更直接地串联起来。沈周从父亲和伯父习画，并潜心研究十四世纪诸家作品，尤其是黄公望(1269－1354)、吴镇(1280－1354)、倪瓒(1306－1374)与王蒙元四大家的杰作。沈并一度藏有黄公望的稀世名作《富春山居图》，沈在出售此图卷后，凭记忆了一个副本。晚明评论家李日华(1565－1635)对沈画艺的发展作了以下的总结："石田[沈周]绘事，初得法于父叔，于诸家无不漫烂。中年以子久(黄公望)为宗，晚乃醉心梅道人(吴镇)，酣肆融洽，杂梅老真迹中有不复能辨者"。从描绘此千人石的画卷里，的确可看出沈周运用吴镇浓墨粗笔之线条，以及湿墨皴点草木山水的风格特色。

沈周虽然可轻易获举荐入仕，但却与祖父、父亲与伯父一样，不求闻达，也从未求取功名。每当友人相劝提议举荐，沈均以奉养老母、无法离家为由而推拒。沈周之母得享高寿，九十八岁去世后两年，沈才谢世。一生诗名、画名享天下，以一无官职的平民身份为人所知，沈周随时可能为当地官员传唤，从事卑微的工作。一则轶闻曾传说苏州一新到任的地方官，听说沈周画名，嘱沈为其官邸之楹庑作画。沈周依从，并称此为他本应服从之事。事后，该官员知悉沈在京师为众高官所敬重，回到苏州后，兼程到沈家拜访，沈周仍以礼殷勤相待。后世传记史家以此类故事，彰显沈周的性格为人。但由此可知，沈周肯定从他的书画创作中赚取收入。值得再提的是，1493年夏，沈周手臂无法提笔时，作品是由徐霖代笔完成的。

在十六世纪末与十七世纪初，沈周的画已超越了当代所有的画家。他被公认为吴郡地区传统文人画"吴门画派"的创始人。他与后来的文徵明(1470－1559)、唐寅(1470－1524)、仇英(约1495－1552)被画坛称为"明四家"。为巩固沈周身为明朝最卓越的画家之一，乾隆皇帝搜罗了几乎所有沈周最出色的作品，纳入宫中收藏。此画与其他四十六件沈周的画作收录入清内府于1793年末乾隆晚年编辑完成的《石渠宝笈续编》中。在此之前，六十六件沈周的作品已收编在1745《石渠宝笈》里。此画带乾隆的鉴藏八玺，钤于画芯，另有嘉庆、溥仪各一鉴藏玺。

江文苇（LYC译）

注解：

1. 有关沈周及对虎丘的描述，详见于吉田晴纪(Yoshida Haruki)，〈关于虎丘山图之我见〉，《吴门画派研究》(北京:紫禁城出版社, 1993)，第65－75页。
2. 《姑苏志》(1506)，王鏊与其他人合编，第8卷，第2b页。重刊于《中国史学丛书》中(台北:台湾学生书局, 1965)，第131页。
3. 有关沈周生平事迹，参见郑秉珊，《沈石田》(上海:人民美术出版社, 1958)；Richard Edwards，《石田：沈周艺术之研究》(华盛顿:史密斯博物馆, 1962)；Richard Edwards,〈沈周〉, 收于《明代名人傳》，L. Carrington Goodrich 编(纽约:哥伦比亚大学出版, 1976)，第1173－77页。
4. 《明史》，298卷（重刊本）（北京：中華書局, 1974)，第13册，第7630页。
5. 李日華，《六研齋筆記》引自《佩文齋書畫譜》(1708)，第56卷，第29b页，重刊于《影印文淵閣四庫全書》（台北：台湾商務印書館，1983)，第821册，第400页。译文见于喜龍仁（Osvald Sirén）《中國繪畫：大師與原理》中之引文（纽约：The Ronald Press, 1958)，第4册，第152页。
6. 《石渠宝笈续编》，《秘殿珠林石渠宝笈合编》，12册(上海:上海书店, 1988)，第5册，第1606－07页。

6
明　　祝允明　小楷东坡记游
手卷, 纸本水墨
Zhu Yunming (1461–1527)
***Calligraphy on the Travel Notes by Su Dongpo,* 1513**
Handscroll; ink on paper
37 x 1065 cm

ARTIST'S SEALS: Zhu Yunming yin (square/intaglio), Zhizhi sheng (rectangular/intaglio)

IMPERIAL SEALS: [Qianlong, r. 1736–95] Qianlong yulan zhibao (oval/relief), Shiqu dingjian (round/relief), Baoji chongbian (square/intaglio), Yangxindian jiancangbao (rectangular/relief), Qianlong jianshang (round/ intaglio), Sanxitang jingjianxi (rectangular/relief), Yizisun (square/intaglio), Shiqu baoji (square/relief); [Jiaqing, r. 1796–1820] Jiaqing yulan zhibao (oval/relief); [Xuantong (Puyi), r. 1909–11] Xuantong yulan zhibao (oval/relief)

OTHER SEALS: [Xiang Yuanbian, 1524–1590] Xiang Yuanbian yin (square/relief), Zijing fu yin (square/relief), Jingyin'an zhu (square/relief), Zijing (double-gourd/relief), Xiang Molin jianshangzhang (rectangular/relief), Zhenshang (oval/relief); [Wang Shizhen, 1526–1590] Langya Wang Jingmei shi jiacang tushu (rectangular/relief); [He Liangjun, 1506–1573] Yuanlang jianding (rectangular/relief), Qingsenge shuhuaji (rectangular/relief); [Bian Yongyu, 1645–1712] Bianshi lingzhi (rectangular/relief), Lingzhi (square/relief), Shigutang shuhua yin (rectangular/relief); [Luo Kun, dates unknown] Dongyue Luo Ran (square/intaglio), Banshanyuan (square/intaglio); [Zhang Bi, 1527–1613] Zhongwu Lushi Songhuatang yin (rectangular/relief); [additional seals] Wendinggong yi (square/relief), Yushan ren (rectangular/relief), Lengjia jushi (square/relief), Longxi buyi (rectangular/relief), Kuaiji (rectangular/relief), Kang chen (rectangular/relief), Shen Yinfan (square/intaglio), Bimo zhiwai (square/intaglio), Weixian (rectangular/intaglio), Zhuyuan (square/relief)

COLOPHON WRITERS (SEALS): Wang Chong, 1494–1533 (Wang Chong siyin [square/intaglio]); Wen Peng, 1498–1573 (Wen Peng zhiyin [square/relief], Wen Shoucheng shi [square/relief]); Wang Shizhen, 1526–1590 (Yuanmei [square/intaglio]); Zhang Fengyi, 1550–1636 (Zhangsheng Boqi [square/intaglio], Fengyi [square/intaglio]); Cao Rong 1613–1685 (Cao Rong zhiyin [square/intaglio], Jiegong [square/intaglio]); Luo Kun, dates unknown (Luo dalang [square/intaglio], Jiangdongsheng [square/intaglio]); Zhang Bi, 1527–1613 (Chenbi [square/relief], Dengzishi [square/intaglio], Dengzi [square/relief])

JADE CLIP INSCRIPTION: Qianlong yushang. Zhu Yunming kaishu Dongpo youji

书家印鉴：祝允明印（白文方印）、枝指生（白文长方印）

皇家印鉴：[清乾隆皇帝弘历，在位1736－1795] 乾隆御览之宝（朱文椭圆印）、石渠定鉴（朱文圆印）、宝笈重编（白文方印）、养心殿鉴藏宝（朱文长方印）、乾隆鉴赏（白文圆印）、三希堂精鉴玺（朱文长方印）、宜子孙（白文方印）、石渠宝笈（朱文方印）。[清嘉庆皇帝颙琰，在位1796－1820] 嘉庆御览之宝（朱文椭圆印）。[清宣统皇帝溥仪，在位1909－1911] 宣统御览之宝（朱文椭圆印）。

其他印鉴：[项元汴，1524－1590] 项元汴印（朱文方印）、子京父印（朱文方印）、净因庵主（朱文方印）、子京（朱文葫芦印）、项墨林鉴赏章（白文长方印）、真赏（朱文长椭圆印）。[王世贞，1526－1590] 琅琊王敬美氏家藏图书（朱文长方印）。[何良俊，1506－1573] 元朗鉴定（朱文长方印）、清森阁书画记（朱文长方印）。[卞永誉，1645－1712]卞氏令之（朱文长方印）、令之（朱文方印）、式古堂书画印（朱文长方印）。[罗坤，生卒年不祥] 东越罗髯（白文方印）、半山园（白文方印）。[张陛，1527－1613] 中吴陆氏松华堂印（朱文长方印）。并有:文定公裔(朱文方印)，玉山人(朱文长方印)，棱伽居士(朱文方印)，陇西布衣(朱文长方印)，会稽(朱文长方印)，康臣(朱文方印)，沈胤范(白文方印)，笔墨之外(白文方印)，惟宪(白文长方印)，竹院(朱文方印)。

题跋者(钤印)：王宠,1494－1533 (王宠私印[白文方印])。文彭，1498－1573 (文彭之印[朱文方印]、文寿承氏[朱文方印])。王世贞, 1526－1590 (元美[白文方印])。张凤翼，1550－1636 (张生伯起[白文方印]、凤翼[白文方印])。曹溶，1613－1685 (曹溶之印[白文方印]、洁躬[白文方印])。罗坤, 生卒年不详(罗大郎[白文方印]、江东生[白文方印])。张陛，1527－1613 (臣陛[朱文方印]、登子氏[白文方印]、登子[朱文方印])。

玉别子镌：乾隆御赏。祝允明楷书东坡游记

Zhu Yunming (courtesy name, Xizhe) adopted the sobriquets Zhisheng and Zhizhisheng (meaning "polydactyl") because he was born with an extra digit. A *juren* (successful candidate at the provincial exams) during the Hongzhi reign, he was appointed county magistrate of Xingning and later promoted to city controller of Yingtianfu (Nanjing). He was good at poetry and calligraphy and became known, along with Wen Zhengming, Xu Zhenqing, and Tang Yin, as one of the "four talents of the Wu region." His calligraphy imitated that of the Jin and Tang dynasty masters and was also influenced by styles of the Song and Yuan periods, making him extremely versatile. Wang Shizhen (1526–1590), the leading literary figure of the Ming dynasty, had this to say about him: "Below Dalin, but superior to all those around Beihai." By these comments, Wang Shizhen had placed him below Wang Xianzhi, son of the Six Dynasties calligrapher Wang Xizhi, but above Li Yong and other Tang dynasty calligraphers. Still, Zhu was recognized by his contemporaries as the "leading calligrapher of the Ming dynasty."[1]

This scroll copies the seven-part travel notes of the Song dynasty literary giant Su Shi (1037–1101): (1) Inviting a friend to stroll under the moon on the twelfth day of the tenth month in the sixth year of Yuanfeng [1083]; (2) Buying a field in Huangzhou, catching an illness, and enquiring after an eccentric person; (3) Traveling with my youngest son through the remains of Buddhist temples in Baishui on the twelfth day of the tenth month in the first year of Shaosheng [1094]; (4) My first tour of Lushan; (5) On the day of *shangyuan* [15th day into the new year] in the *jimao* year [1099]; (6) Living in Xuzhou; and (7) [My old friend] Li Chun (courtesy name, Xisheng). Su's travel notes are short, yet their sentiments are always movingly sincere and uninhibited. For instance, this excerpt from the first passage records how one night in the sixth year of Yuanfeng (1083), the bright and beautiful light of the moon enters his room as if eagerly beckoning him. He goes to Chengtian Temple seeking his good friend Zhang Huaimin, who has not yet gone to sleep. The two then stroll in the moonlight-bathed courtyard. The most subtle lines are the following:

> There is moonlight every night.
> There is bamboo everywhere.
> But there is nobody like the two of us,
> Just idling away, doing nothing else.

Just like a dream world! What a transcendental scholar! A mix of poetry and prose, Su's travel notes are full of witty philosophical sayings about life and are passionately recited generation after generation. In the second passage, he describes his encounter with a deaf but extraordinarily sensitive person who inspires him to write these lines: "Who says youth never returns. Look, the running stream can make a turn to flow west." And in the fourth passage, he reflects on his first tour of the Lushan Mountains with lines of poetry:

> Not to see the true nature of the Lushan Mountains—
> The very reason is that you are located within them.

With that, he confidently remarked "All poems about the Lushan Mountains are now finished."[2]

The calligraphy of this scroll was executed in 1513. Its commemorative inscription reads, "Written after a moonlit walk while staying at the Eastern Zen Temple [Dongchan si] on the twelfth day of the eighth month in the *guiyou* year."[3] To have a solitary walk in the moonlight while staying at a Chan temple is already a unique form of tranquility. A work created in an environment and state of mind that is far from worldly concerns can be said to have connected with the spirit of heaven and earth and the three realms of human existence. No wonder there is a transcendental quality in this calligraphy. The style of the scroll's small standard (*xiaokai*) script comes from the *Jizhi biao*, a classic work by the Six Dynasties calligrapher Zhong You. In terms of brushwork, the strokes are based on the techniques for seal and clerical scripts; they are supple in appearance and strong in substance. Executed with a centered brush, the strokes have a smooth and charming finish. The brushwork is calm and unhurriedly confident; it has a primitive simplicity, free from impurities. This work in small standard script is rare considering that Zhu is known for his cursive script. Structurally, the characters show interesting variations and are tastefully arranged; their subtleties deserve recognition. Ruan Yuan, in his first compilation of the *Shiqu baoji*, comments, "Entirely after Zhong You, [this is] executed with great care, order, and solid technique; it is drastically different from the 'mad grass' scripts and imitations out there."[4]

Zhong You was the most famous calligrapher of the Three Kingdoms period. Records show that he learned from Cai Wenji; Zhong You then passed the style on to Madam Wei, who in turn passed it on to Wang Xizhi. In early times, many beginners chose to start with Zhong's style in learning calligraphy.[5] Extant works by Zhong You have always been extremely rare. In the Southern Dynasties period, the Liang dynasty rulers, surnamed Xiao, sent agents in search of painting and calligraphy masterpieces. Their court collection, which included 707 original works of calligraphy by Wang Xizhi and his son, had acquired only fragments of Zhong You's calligraphy on paper, totaling some 697 characters. Emperor Wudi of the Liang dynasty loved Zhong's calligraphy and wrote an essay titled "Twelve Observations on the Calligraphy of Zhong You." In addition, there was an exchange of nine letters with Tao Yinju (Tao Hongjing) in which they take delight in evaluating the works of Zhong You and Wang Xizhi.

The naturalness and ingenuity in Zhong You's calligraphy has long been celebrated. Yu Jianwu of the Liang dynasty during the Southern Dynasties period once commented, "Zhong's calligraphy is first in naturalness, second in skill. It rivals the Xuchang steles in excellence, demonstrates the ultimate literary ambience of the Yexia strips."[6] His contemporary Wang Shizhen made the following remark when he saw this work: "Delighted to see this scroll; I feel ambitious now. Sitting on my desk, it seems to serve the same purpose for me as several jars of wine would have for Master Ruan."[7]

The first person to leave an inscription after viewing the scroll was Wang Chong (1494–1533), a mid-Ming dynasty calligrapher who shares the same reputation for calligraphy as Wen Zhengming and Zhu Yunming himself. They are known as the Three Master Calligraphers of the Wu School. Wang Chong viewed this scroll in the eighth month of the *xinsi* year (1521). Later viewers who also left inscriptions include Wen Peng (1498–1573), Wang Shizhen, Zhang Fengyi (1550–1636), Cao Rong (1613–1685), Luo Kun, and Zhang Bi. Cao Rong's inscription, left in mid winter of the *gengxu* year (1670), expresses his worries that many of the calligraphic works in the court collection had been dispersed into the civilian population during the past two decades. Zhang Bi's colophon was written in 1671, when the work was evidently still among the populace. The multiple collection seals also confirm that the work had been circulating all over the country and had been in the possession of such private collectors as Zhejiang's Xiang Yuanbian and Shandong's Wang Jingmei. Acquired by the imperial court during the reign of Qianlong, this became the emperor's favorite work; he had all of his eight imperial seals affixed on it.[8] The Jiaqing and Xuantong emperors also affixed their imperial seals onto it. On January 10, 1923 (the 24th day of the 11th month, the 14th year of Xuantong), Puyi awarded it to his brother Pujie as a gift.[9] The scroll was transported to Tianjin and the "imperial palace" in Changchun. It left the palace after the Japanese surrendered in 1945. The Liaoning Province Antiques and Cultural Relics Shop acquired it in 1973, and it later went into the collection of the Liaoning Provincial Museum.[10]

The white jade clip attached to the scroll's ribbon tie is incised with characters that read "Qianlong's imperial appreciation; Zhu Yunming's standard script *Calligraphy on the Travel Notes by Dongpo*."

WWHC (trans. DHWS)

Notes

1. According to Zhang Bi as cited in *Shiqu baoji xubian* [Treasured boxes of the Stone Channel, continued] (Taipei: Guoli gugong bowuyuan, 1971), p. 1036.
2. *Shiqu baoji xubian*, pp. 1034–35.
3. Ibid., p. 1036.
4. Ruan Yuan. *Shiqu suibi* [Notes on the Stone Channel], *juan* 5, reprinted in *Biji xiaoshuo daguan* [Compendium of notes and novels] (Yangzhou: Jiangsu Guangling guji keyinshe, 1984), p. 384.
5. Zhang Yanyuan, *Fashu yaolu* [The art of calligraphy], *juan* 1, reprinted in *Guhua pinlu* [Classified record of ancient paintings], Siku yishu congshu [Art books from the Comprehensive library of the Four Treasuries] (reprint, Shanghai: Shanghai guji chubanshe, 1991), pp. 812/110–111. Later generations also consider Zhong Yuan and Wang Xizhi to be the originators of the art of calligraphy. Song emperor Huizong, "in his daily practice of calligraphy, would only take Zhong and Wang as models. Afterwards he experienced a transformation and developed a style of his own." *Siling hanmo zhi* [Records of the calligraphy from Siling imperial mausoleum], reprinted in *Guhua pinlu*, p. 812/427.
6. Zhang Yanyuan, *Fashu yaolu, juan* 3, p. 812/130.
7. *Shiqu baoji xubian*, p. 1036. Master Ruan, or Ruan Ji (210–263), was one of the Seven Sages of the Bamboo Grove in the Six Dynasties period; he loved drinking. See *Cihai* [Sea of words] (Shanghai: Shanghai cishu chubanshe, 1979), p. 408.
8. *Shiqu baoji xubian*, p. 1036.
9. Registered under the serial number *Yong* 9 in *Gugong yiyi shuji shuhua mulu si zhong* [Four catalogues of dispersed calligraphy and paintings from the imperial palace] (Beijing: Gugong bowuyuan , 1926), p. 18.
10. Yang Renkai, ed., *Liaoningsheng bowuguan cang shuhua zhulu: Shufa juan* [Writings on paintings and calligraphic works in the collection of the Liaoning Provincial Museum: Volume on calligraphy] (Shenyang: Liaoning meishu chubanse, 1999), p. 246.

祝允明，字希哲，因生枝指，号枝生，枝指生。弘治间中举人，授兴宁县令迁应天府通判。善诗书，与文征明、徐祯卿、唐寅并称“吴中四才子”。书学晋唐，下逮宋元，无所不能，王世贞评为“大令之下，北海诸君之上”，即不及六朝书家王羲之之子王献之，而高于唐代书家李邕等人，但仍为时人推为“明朝第一”（注1）。

此卷抄录宋代文豪苏轼的七段记游：1。元丰六年（1083）十月十二日邀友月下漫步；2。黄州买田得疾寻访异人；3。绍圣元年（1094）十月十二日，与幼子过游白水佛迹寺；4。初入庐山游；5。已卯上元；6。在徐州时；7。（吾故人）黎醇，字希声。苏氏之记游，篇幅短小，却总是涌动着率真不羁之情。如摘抄的第一段记载元丰六年，十月十二日夜，明媚的月光照进了他的房间，仿佛殷勤相邀，他便到承天寺去找不眠的好友张怀民，两人遂在月光如水的庭院里漫步。最妙的便在：“何夜无月，何处无竹，但少闲人如吾两人耳”。何等高士，犹如梦境！苏的记游且文且诗，常出语精辟，抒发人生哲理，为后人不绝传颂，如第二段记与黄州聋哑异人相见，作诗道：“谁道人生无再少，君看流水尚能西”。如第四段，初入庐山游，作绝句云：“不识庐山真面目，只缘身在此山中”，并自信道：“庐山诗尽于此矣”（注2）。

此卷书法作于1513年，落款记载：“癸酉八月十二日，步月宿东禅寺书此”（注3）。月下独步，安宿禅寺，已是一个独特宁静,清尘远虑的创作心境和环境，可谓接天地人三界灵气，书法怎能不超远逸外乎？此卷小楷风格出自六朝书法家钟繇之“季直表”，笔意自篆隶来，用笔柔中带刚，清圆秀媚，神闲气定，古朴而逸脱，在以草书名世的祝氏作品中不多见。字的结构安排，富于变化，而错落有致，耐人寻味。阮元在《石渠宝笈》初编中评道：“全学钟繇，谨饬有法度，迥异外间狂草伪笔”（注4）。钟繇是三国时最著名的书法家，据载，钟受传于蔡文姬，钟传之于卫夫人，卫夫人传之于王羲之，当年许多人学书法，都先学钟体（注5）。钟繇书法传世极少，南朝萧梁遣使搜购名书画，内府所藏王羲之父子书法有七百零七卷，却只得到钟繇纸书六百九十七字。梁武帝很喜爱钟的书法，曾专门写了“观钟繇书法十二意”，并和陶弘景有九封信函往返论钟繇和王羲之的书法短长。钟繇书法的天然神妙之趣，早就为人赞颂，南朝萧梁时的庾肩吾便论道：钟天然第一，功夫次之，妙尽许昌之碑，穷极邺下之牍（注6）。当明代文坛领袖王世贞（1526－1590）获见祝允明这卷出自钟繇风格的书法时，喜不自禁，谓之“今见此卷，不觉雄心勃勃，置之几案间，可当阮公数斗美酒”（注7）。

此卷第一个观赏题跋者为王宠（1494－1533），明代中叶的著名书法家，书与文征明，祝允明同名，时人所谓吴门三家者，其观于辛巳年八月（1521）。后观并题跋者有文彭（1498－1573）、王世贞、张凤翼（1550－1636）、曹溶（1613－1685）、罗坤、张陞。曹溶的跋作于庚戌仲冬（1670），并感叹二十年来内府书法真迹流落人间之事。似乎暗示此卷或曾藏于明代皇家内府中。张陞的跋作于辛亥四月（1671），显然当时仍然流落民间。诸多的鉴藏印也可见此卷显然曾经辗转东西南北，为多位私人藏家收藏，如浙江的项元汴，山东的王世贞等。约在乾隆年间入宫，是为乾隆心爱者，钤有八玺全（注8），并有嘉庆和宣统皇帝的御览之玺印。宣统十四年十一月二十四日，由末帝溥仪以赏赐为名赠送给其弟溥杰，（注9），前后运往天津和长春伪宫，1945年日本投降后由伪宫散出，1973年为辽宁省文物店购得，后为辽宁省博物馆珍藏（注10）。

此卷为花织锦包首，玉池为淡青色云凤花绫，前后隔水皆为淡黄色云凤纹花绫，画心和拖尾则为纸本，并有玉别子和乾隆御刻:乾隆御赏。祝允明楷书东坡游记。

海蔚蓝

注解：

1. [清]张陞语，载《石渠宝笈》续编(台湾国立故宫博物院, 1971)，第1036页。
2. [清]《石渠宝笈》续编(台湾国立故宫博物院, 1971)，第1034－1035页。
3. [清]《石渠宝笈》续编(台湾国立故宫博物院, 1971)，第1036页。
4. [清]阮元《石渠随笔》，载《笔记小说大观》(江苏广陵古籍出版社, 1984)，第384页。
5. [唐]张彦远《法书要录》卷一，载四库艺术丛书《古画品录》(上海古籍出版社, 1991)，第812/110－111页；后世亦以钟王为书法之本原，宋徽宗“尝曰学书当以钟王为法，然后出入变化，自成一家”，见《思陵翰墨志》，载四库艺术丛书《古画品录》(上海古籍出版社, 1991)，第812/427页。
6. [唐]张彦远《法书要录》卷三，载四库艺术丛书《古画品录》（上海古籍出版社, 1991），第812/130页。
7. [清]《石渠宝笈》续编，王世贞跋（台湾国立故宫博物院, 1971），第1036页。阮公即阮籍（210－263），六朝竹林七贤之一，嗜酒。参见《辞海》（上海辞书出版社1979），第408页。
8. [清]《石渠宝笈》续编（台湾国立故宫博物院, 1971），第1036页。
9. 《故宫已佚书籍书画目录四种》，此一卷宫中登记号为永字九号（故宫博物院，民国十五年版, 1926），第十八页。
10. 杨仁恺主编《辽宁省博物馆藏书画著录。书法卷》（辽宁美术出版社, 1999），第246页。

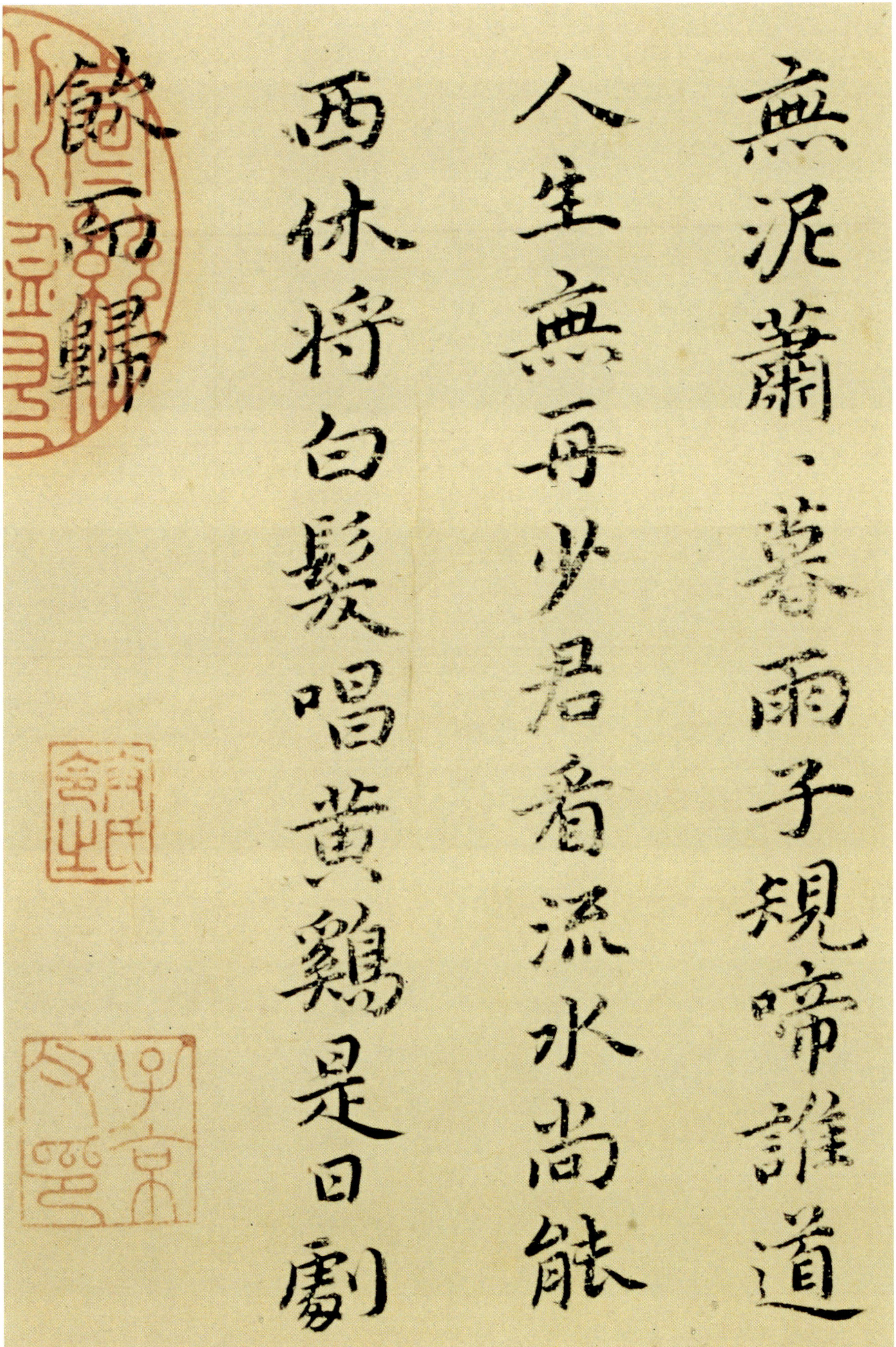

6 (detail 局部)

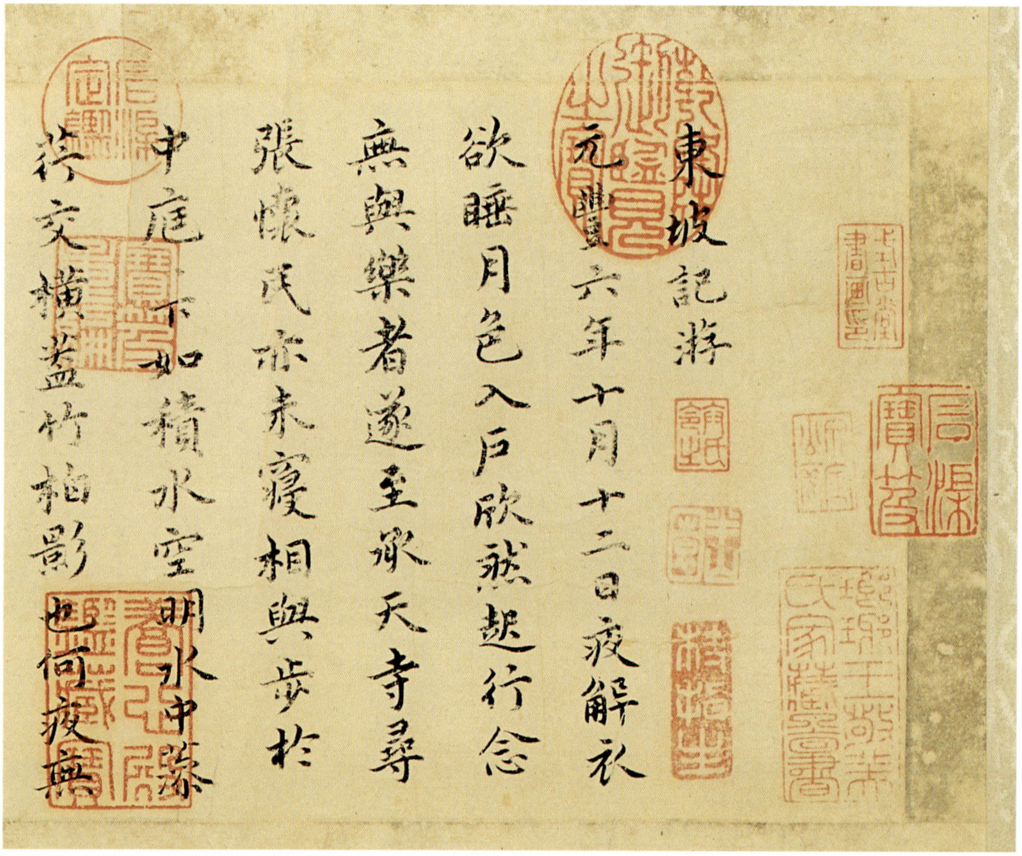
東坡記游
元豐六年十月十二日夜解衣
欲睡月色入戶欣然起行念
無與樂者遂至承天寺尋
張懷民懷民亦未寢相與步於
中庭庭下如積水空明水中藻
荇交橫蓋竹柏影也何夜無

6 (detail 局部)

7
明　　文征明 浒溪草堂图
手卷, 纸本水墨设色
Wen Zhengming (1470–1559)
The Huxi Thatched Hut, 1535/36

Handscroll; ink and color on paper
26.6 x 142.5 cm

ARTIST'S SEAL: Zhengming (square/intaglio)

IMPERIAL SEALS: [Qianlong, r. 1736–95] Qianlong yulan zhibao (square/relief), Shiqu baoji (rectangular/relief), Qianlong yushang zhibao (rectangular/relief), Yushufang jiancangbao (oval/relief), Sanxitang jingjianxi (rectangular/relief), Yizisun (square/intaglio), Qianlong jianshang (round/intaglio); [Jiaqing, r. 1796–1820] Jiaqing yulan zhibao (oval/relief); [Xuantong (Puyi), r. 1909–11] Xuantong yulan zhibao (square/relief)

OTHER SEALS: [Wen Dian (1633–1704)] Zhuwu Wen Dian (square/intaglio), Zhuwu (rectangular/relief); [Museum of the Northeast] Dongbei bowuguan zhencang zhiyin (square/relief)

COLOPHON WRITERS (SEALS): Wen Zhengming (Wen Zhengming yin [square/intaglio], Wuyan shi yin [square/intaglio]; Lu Can, 1494–1551 (Jun-Ming [linked seal; double square /relief], Shifan shanren [square/intaglio], Luyuan [rectangular/relief]); Gu Lan, *juren* in 1498 (Rongfu [square/intaglio], Wuliu jingtang [square/intaglio]); Wang Guxiang, 1501–1568 (Youshi [rectangular/relief], Guxiang [square/relief], Luzhi [square/relief]); Zhang Yu, dates unknown (Benhong [square/relief], Ganjieli ren [square/relief]); Tang Zhen, dates unknown (Tangshi zizhong [square/intaglio], Shuangwu caotang [square/intaglio]); Yuan Zhi, 1502–1547 (Yuanshi yongzhi [square/intaglio], Bingshu jinshi [square/relief]); Gu Wen, *juren* in 1528 (Xingzhifu [square/relief], Zhoushan zhuren [square/intaglio]; Wang Zhideng, 1535–1612 (Jiechaotang yin [square/relief], Wang Zhideng yin [square/intaglio]); Wang Shimin, 1592–1680 (Wang Shimin yin [square/intaglio], Xilu laoren [square/intaglio]); Wen Nan, 1596–1667 (Duanwen [square/relief], Wenquyuan [square/intaglio], Wuzhu [rectangular/relief]); Jin Junming, 1602–1675 (Jin Junming yin [square/intaglio], Bumei minghuai [square/relief], Lu-Chai [linked seal; double rectangle/relief]); Wen Dian (Wen Dian [square/intaglio], Dian [square/relief], Zhuwu shanren [square/intaglio])

画家印鉴：征明（白文方印）

皇家印鉴：[清乾隆皇帝弘历, 在位1736－1795] 乾隆御览之宝（朱文方印）、石渠宝笈（朱文长方印）、乾隆御赏之宝（朱文扁方印）、御书房鉴藏宝（朱文椭圆印）、三希堂精鉴玺（朱文长方印）、宜子孙（白文方印）、乾隆鉴赏（白文圆印）。[清嘉庆皇帝颙琰,在位1796－1820]嘉庆御览之宝（朱文椭圆印）。[清宣统皇帝溥仪,在位1909－1911]宣统御览之宝（朱文方印）。

其他印鉴：[文点,1633－1704] 竺坞文点（白文方印）、竺坞（朱文长方印）。[东北博物馆]东北博物馆珍藏之印（朱文方印）。

题跋者(钤印)：文征明,1470－1559（文征明印[白文方印]、悟言室印[白文方印]）。陆粲，1494－1551（浚、明[朱文连珠方印]、石风山人[白文方印]、录原[朱文长方印]）。顾兰,. 1498年举人（荣父[白文方印]、五柳京堂[白文方印]）。王穀祥，1501－1568（酉室[朱文长方印]、穀祥[朱文方印]、禄之[朱文方印]）。张裕，生卒年不详（本弘[朱文方印]、甘节里人[朱文方印])。汤珍，生卒年不详（汤氏子重[白文方印]、双梧草堂[白文方印]）。袁袠，1502－1547（袁氏永之[朱文方印]、丙戌进士[朱文方印]）。顾闻，1528年举人（行之父[白文方印]、周山主人（[白文方印]）。王穉登，1535－1612（解嘲堂印[朱文方印]、王穉登印[白文方印]）。王时敏，1592－1680（王时敏印[白文方印]、西庐老人[白文方印]）。文枏,1596－1667（端文[朱文方印]、文曲辕[白文方印]、无住[朱文长方印]）。金俊明，1602－1675（金俊明印[白文方印]、不寐明褱[朱文方印]、鹿、柴[朱文连珠长方印]）。文点，1633－1704（文点[白文方印]、点[朱文方印]、竺坞山人[白文方印]）。

In the twelfth month of the *yiwei* year in the Jiaqing reign (corresponding to a period from December 24, 1535 to January 22, 1536), Wen Zhengming painted a picture titled *The Huxi Thatched Hut* at the request of a Mr. Shen Tianmin. The painting commemorated Shen's place of retreat and his choice of byname (*hao*). Wen Zhengming prefaced his poetic colophon after the painting as follows: "Master Shen Tianmin's family lived for generations at Hushu [Hu Villa], and although he now lives in the city, he has not forgotten the mulberries and catalpas of old and so has taken the byname Huxi [Hu Stream]. He wants to seek out the famous men of the age to sing of this event. I have painted a picture and composed this poem for the various gentlemen to answer."[1] Wen Zhengming follows with a discussion of the character used for *hu* and how it changed over time and then writes his poem. The painting, then, is in response to a specific request and may have been a return favor for Shen Tianmin, or Shen may have recompensed Wen Zhengming in some way for the painting.[2] Shen was clearly successful in getting members of the elite to contribute to his scroll. Wen's pupil Wang Guxiang (1501–1568) wrote the frontispiece and contributed a poem, and Lu Can (1494–1551; *jinshi* 1526) composed a record of the thatched hut in the autumn of 1537. Other poems were written by Gu Lan (*juren* 1498), Zhang Yu, Tang Zhen, Yuan Zhi (1502–1547), and Gu Wen (*juren* 1528).

Wen Zhengming's painting opens with a scene of the thatched hut set among trees by the bank of a lake. The master of the thatched hut is entertaining a guest while tea is being prepared by two servants in an adjacent room. There are other buildings including a library seen through the trees. Along the lake shore, a gentlemen and his servant have arrived by boat and are advancing toward the hut. The scene then extends out to a view across the lake and a few buildings on the opposite shore. A few moored boats and a bank bring the view back to the foreground; the composition closes with an inlet surrounded by a few houses. The scene is that of the water country in the area around the city of Suzhou where Wen Zhengming and Shen Tianmin both lived. Wen has used fine brushwork and a blue-and-green color palette that harks back to early traditions of colored landscape painting. His meticulous brushwork gives the painting a sense of refined elegance, while the blue and green mineral colors provide classical associations for Shen Tianmin to savor.

For his depiction of Shen Tianmin's Huxi Thatched Hut, Wen Zhengming draws on a type of painting that was developed during the mid-fourteenth century, when many had sought refuge from the troubled political climate of the late Yuan dynasty by retreating from public life. These men had celebrated their places of reclusion with cumulative scrolls that included the name of the retreat written out in an epigraphic script type, a depiction of the retreat, a prose record, and poems composed at the retreat, poems often written on the single occasion of an elegant gathering (*yaji*). The paintings, which may be called "thatched hut pictures" (*caotang tu*), posed the question of whether to retreat or to advance into public life in formal terms by juxtaposing the closed world of the retreat with an opening to the outside world.[3] Here, Wen Zhengming follows this type of composition, although he does not open up the space at the end of the scroll in quite the same way. Perhaps for Shen Tianmin the question of whether to advance or retreat was not so pressing. In any event, the type of painting had become a staple of scholar painting in the Wu region by Wen's time and was often combined with the function of celebrating the choice of a byname, as in this scroll.[4]

Wen Zhengming early on complained in a letter to his patron Wang Ao (1450–1524) that the completion of obligations such as this painting for Shen Tianmin was the kind of chore that kept him from his preparations for the examinations.[5] Wen, who was born into a distinguished Suzhou family in 1470, studied diligently for the examinations that would lead to a career in government and took them ten times between 1485 and 1522, each time failing to pass. In 1523 at the age of fifty-three he finally achieved office through recommendation by the provincial governor and was appointed to a position in the Hanlin Academy in Beijing. He spent the next several years in the capital during a time of political controversy at the beginning of the Jiajing reign (1522–66). Wen Zhengming found the life in the capital not to his liking and asked to return home; he was finally granted permission to do so in 1527. From then until his death in 1559 he became the dominant figure in the world of Suzhou painting. Beginning in 1489 Wen had studied painting with Shen Zhou and continued to study with him until Shen's death in 1509. Wen's career as a painter is not mentioned by his second son, Wen Jia (1501–1583), in the biography of his father that he wrote after his father's death. It was Wen Zhengming's official career and his scholarship, not his painting, that defined him in the eyes of his contemporaries. Within fifty years of his death, however, he and his teacher, Shen Zhou, were seen as the greatest masters of painting in Suzhou and as the founders of a Wu school of painting (*Wumen huapai*).

The Huxi Thatched Hut was preserved on and off by the descendants of Shen Tianmin during the sixteenth and seventeenth centuries. At one point it was lost to the family and then reacquired. The great painter and connoisseur Wang Shimin (1592–1680) saw the painting and added a colophon to it as did several of Wen Zhengming's descendants: Wen Nan in 1657 and Wen Dian in 1676. All lamented the passing of the elegant way of life depicted in the scroll and marveled at its preservation. By 1744 the painting had entered the palace collection and was included as a first-class work in the imperial catalogue *Shiqu baoji*.[6] Although he did not inscribe the painting, the Qianlong emperor left his seals on the painting surface and on the mounting. Both the Jiaqing emperor and Puyi left their seals on the mounting preceding the painting, and Puyi passed it to his brother Pujie (1907–1994) to take out of the Forbidden City before November of 1924. The painting went with Puyi to Changchun when he became ruler of Manchukuo under the Japanese.

DAS

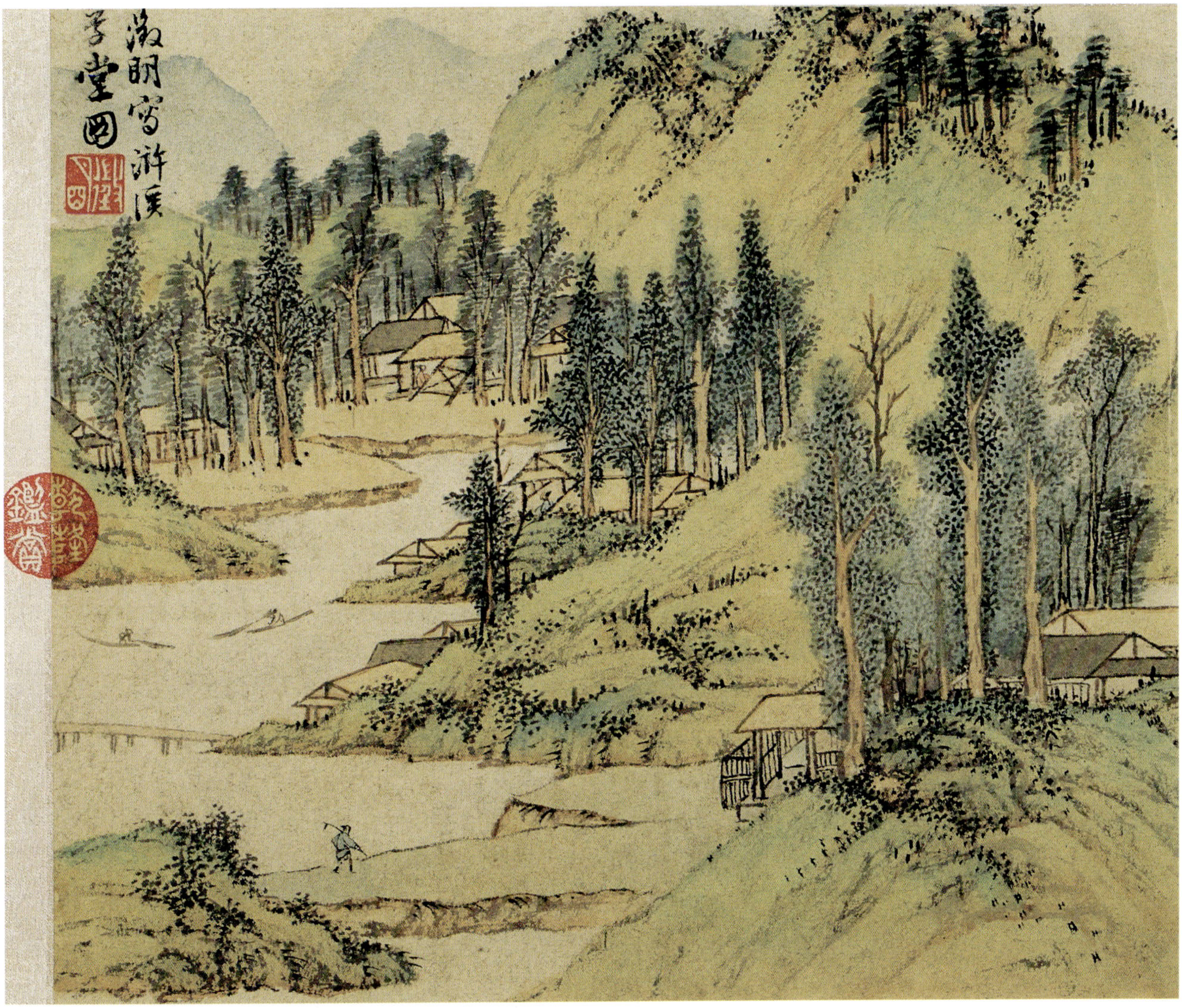

7 (detail 局部)

Notes

1. Wen's colophon is recorded in *Shiqu baoji*, reprinted in *Midian zhulin Shiqubaoji hebian* [Pearl forest of the Secret Hall and Treasured boxes of the Stone Channel, combined edition], 12 vols (Shanghai: Shanghai shudian, 1988), vol. 2, pp. 1031–33.
2. Wen Zhengming's social paintings are the subject of Craig Clunas, *Elegant Debts: The Social Art of Wen Zhengming*, 1470–1559 (Honolulu: University of Hawaii Press, 2004).
3. For a discussion of this type of painting, see David Ake Sensabaugh, "Guests at Jade Mountain: Aspects of Patronage in Fourteenth-Century K'un-shan," in *Artists and Patrons: Some Social and Economic Aspects of Chinese Painting*, ed. Chu-tsing Li (Lawrence, KS: Kress Foundation Department of Art History, 1989), pp. 93–100, and David Ake Sensabaugh, "A Few Rocks Can Stir the Emotions: Chinese Gardens and Scholars," *Orientations* 31, no. 1 (Jan. 2000): 32–39.
4. See Liu Jiuan, "Wumen huajia zhi biehaotu jianding julie" [Distinguishing examples of byname pictures by painters of the Wu School], in *Wumen huapai yanjiu* [Research on Wu School painting] (Beijing: Zijincheng chubanshe, 1993), pp. 35–46.
5. Wen's letter to Wang Ao is discussed in Clunas, *Elegant Debts*, pp. 44–45, and in Anne de Coursey Clapp, *Wen Cheng-ming: The Ming Artist and Antiquity* (Ascona: Artibus Asiae Publishers, 1975), pp. 2–3. For biographical information on Wen Zhengming in addition to Clunas and Clapp, see Richard Edwards, *The Art of Wen Cheng-ming* (1470–1559) (Ann Arbor: University of Michigan, 1976); Jiang Zhaoshen, *Wen Zhengming yu Suzhou huatan* [Wen Zhengming and painting in Suzhou] (Taipei: Guoli gugong bowuyuan, 1977); and Liu Gangji, *Wen Zhengming* (Changchun: Jilin meishu chubanshe, 1996).
6. *Shiqu baoji* (see note 1).

嘉庆年间，乙未臘月（相当于西历1535年至1536年的冬天），因沈天民相求，文征明作了《浒溪草堂图》。此画是纪念沈以自己别号取名的别业而作，文征明为诗作序，并将其题于画卷之后："沈君天民，世家浒墅，今虽城居，而不忘桑梓之旧。因自号浒溪，将求一时名贤咏歌其事。余既为作图，复赋此诗，以为诸君倡"。在题跋后，文征明说明了草堂以"浒"为名之原由，以及草堂几番易名之始末。画作本身因沈天民特意相求而作，应为画家回报之举，或则由沈与画家协议决定报酬之作。此画完成后，沈得其他艺坛精英题跋助阵，文之弟子王谷祥(1501－1568)为之写卷头语并作一诗，陈粲(1494－1551;1526年进士)于1537年为草堂作纪。其他诗作由顾兰(1498年举人)、张裕、汤珍、袁袠(1502－1547)与顾闻(1528年举人)题写。

在卷右方开卷处，文征明将草堂设在湖边高树浓荫之下。草堂内，一高士案前与客对坐，隔壁厢房里，两个小厮正忙着备茶待客。书房与其他房舍，设在不远处树林边。湖汀上，一文人与仆从，刚下船缓步迈向草堂方向。景色一路向西，湖水开阔。几间房舍并立于对岸群树之间。几艇帆樯，陪衬湖滨景致，将视线带到前景。卷尾处一水湾及房舍，则将全图带入尾声。图中景象为文征明与沈天民在苏州城附近居住过的水乡。文以细笔描绘，青綠设色，如同高古的青綠山水。笔法轻灵细劲，将画境衬托得清幽雅致。石青石綠，秀润相衬，一派古意盎然，为沈天民所宝爱。

此卷的风格形式，为一十四世纪中期所发展的画风。元代晚期，许多人从动荡不安的政治局势中隐退。这些人为纪念他们隐居之所，收罗以自己隐居处为题的图卷。其形式包括了格言式之卷首，居处为画题之图，一篇相关的记录文章，与在自家居处所创作的诗词。诗中通常是某次"雅集"聚会的纪事。此类可称之为"草堂图"的作品，反映了当时文人内心对退处江湖抑或心存魏阙所持的矛盾心态。然而章显于图画中的，常是将隐居所封闭的世界与周围开放空阔的山水世界同时并置。此画中，虽然卷尾处未尽采用开放空间的惯例，文征明仍大致沿用了"草堂图"的基本构图。或许，对沈天民，入仕或隐居的抉择，不是非常迫切的个人问题。但在吴郡地区，这类绘画，与誌记别号于画中的风气，成了文征明所处时代文人画的一个独特的艺术现象。

文征明早先曾在信中向他的赞助人王鏊(1450－1524)抱怨，这种为他人作画的杂务与负担，让他无暇准备会试。文1470年生于苏州一显赫世家，自幼即勤勉向学，冀望仕途。但在1485年与1522年间，十次参加生员岁考，却次次名落孙山。1523年五十四岁那年，终于被举荐进京，在翰林院担任待诏的职位。文在北京供职的几年间，正逢嘉靖初年(1522－66)政治纠纷频仍的时期。文征明心中悒悒不乐，遂上书请求辞官回家，几番尝试，到1527年才获批准南归。从此至1559年去世为止，文征明成为苏州画坛最为举足轻重的人物。文征明自1489年起即师事沈周习画，直到沈1509年逝世为止。但文之二子文嘉(1501－1583)，在文死后为父所撰的传记中，却对文之画名只字未提。原因在于当时，文征明是以他的功名与学问知名于世。然而，文去世后五十年间，文与其师沈周，被后人公认为是苏州画坛之名家以及"吴门画派"之宗师。

《浒溪草堂图》在十六及十七世纪间，断断续续地为沈天民的后人保存下来。其间曾一度流失，后又被寻回。知名画家与鉴赏家王时敏(1592－1680)曾得观此图，并为之作跋。文之后人文柟与文点也分别于1657与1676年作了题跋。三人均为文感叹画中情致难再，并惊叹图画保存之完好。1744年前，此画已被收入清宫，并在皇室目录《石渠宝笈》中被奉为上等。乾隆虽未曾题款，但在画中及裱褙处均钤有印玺。嘉庆与溥仪也在前隔水裱褙处加盖了御印。溥仪后将此画转给溥杰(1907－1994)，并于1924年十一月稍早带出了紫禁城。溥仪在日本扶植下成立满洲国傀儡政权时，此画亦一并被携至长春。

江文苇（LYC译）

注解：

1. 文之题跋记录于《石渠宝笈》，重刊于《秘殿珠林石渠宝笈合编》，12册(上海:上海书店,1988),第2册,第1031－33页。
2. 关于文征明应酬画作的讨论，见Craig Clunas,《雅债：文证明的应酬社交性艺术，1470－1559年》(火奴鲁鲁:夏威夷大学出版,2004)。
3. 关于此类绘画，请见江文苇（David Ake Sensabaugh）,〈玉山之客：十四世纪昆山人的艺术赞助〉,收于《艺术家与赞助者：一些关于中国绘画的社会经济现象》，李铸晋（Chu-tsing Li）编，（劳伦斯：堪萨斯大学艺术史系，1989年），第93－100页；江文苇（David Ake Sensabaugh），〈石中见真情：中国庭院与文人〉, *Orientations*, 第31册,第1期(2000年1月号)，第32－39页。
4. 见劉九庵，〈吳門畫家之別號圖鑒別擧列〉，《吳門畫派研究》（北京：紫禁城出版社，1993），第35－46頁。
5. 有关文给王鏊之信的讨论，见Clunas,《雅债》，第44－45页；Anne de Coursey Clapp,《文证明：明代画家与古风》(Ascona: Artibus Asiae Publishers, 1975)，第2－3页。有关文征明生平事迹，参见Clunas 与 Clapp, 并参见 Richard Edwards,《文征明的艺术》(安娜堡:密西根大学, 1976);江兆申，《文征明與蘇州畫壇》（台北：國立故宮博物院，1977）；劉綱紀，《文徵明》（長春：吉林美術出版社，1996）。
6. 《石渠宝笈》(见注1)。

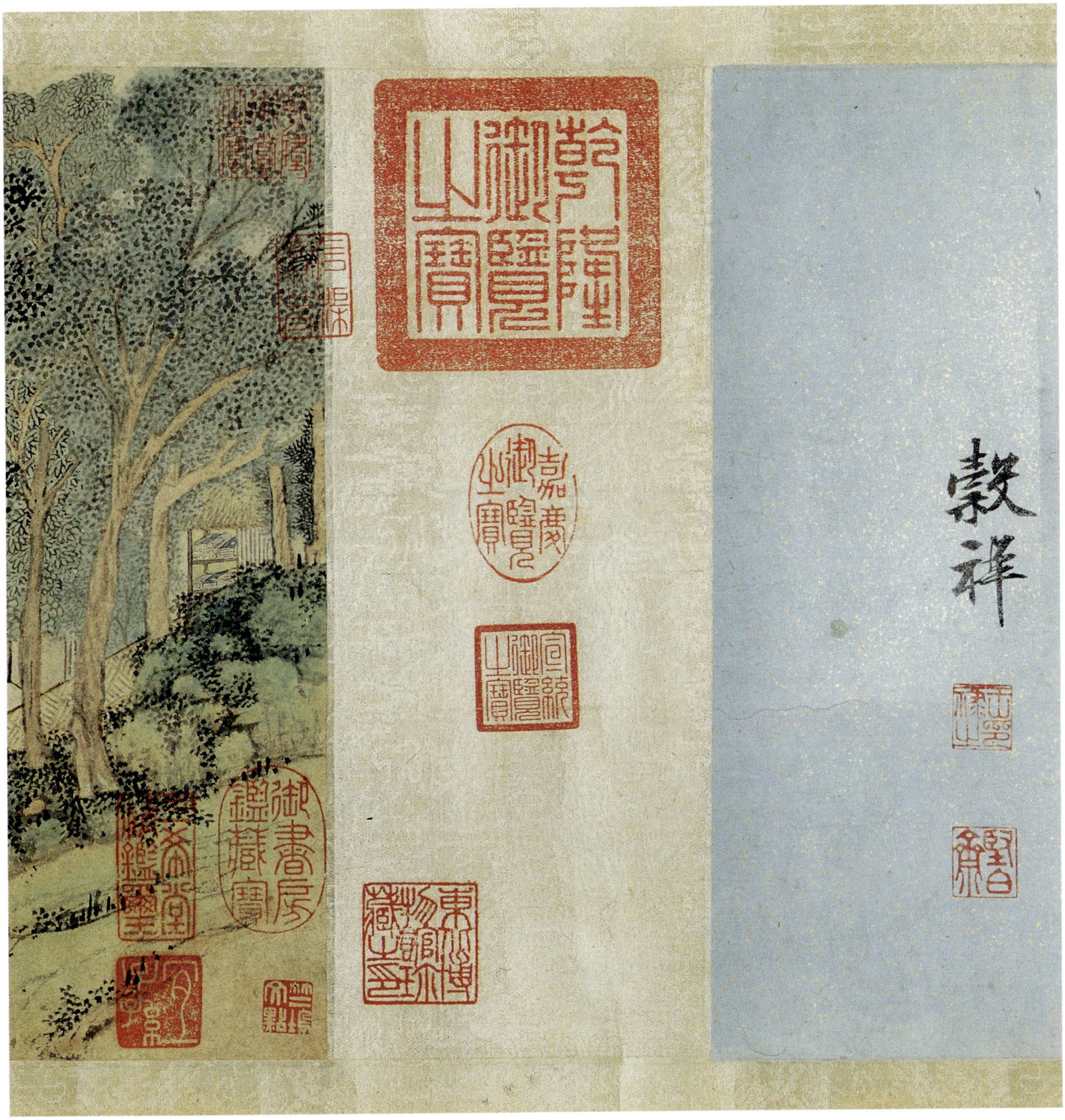

7 (detail 局部)

7

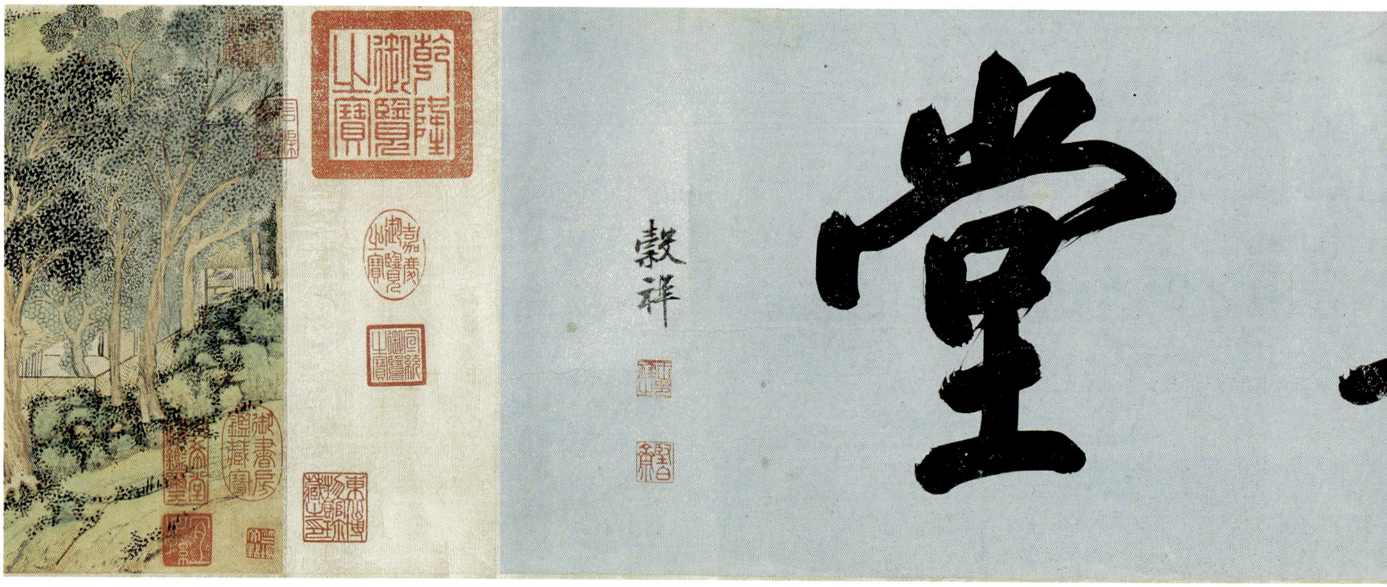

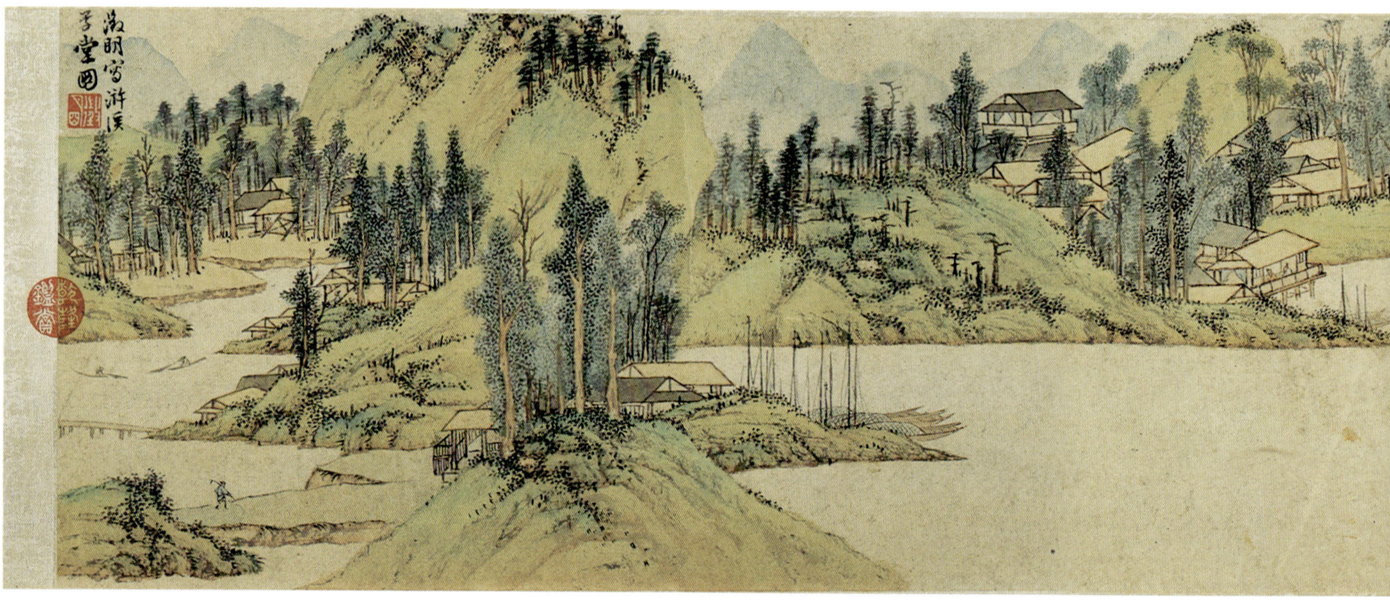

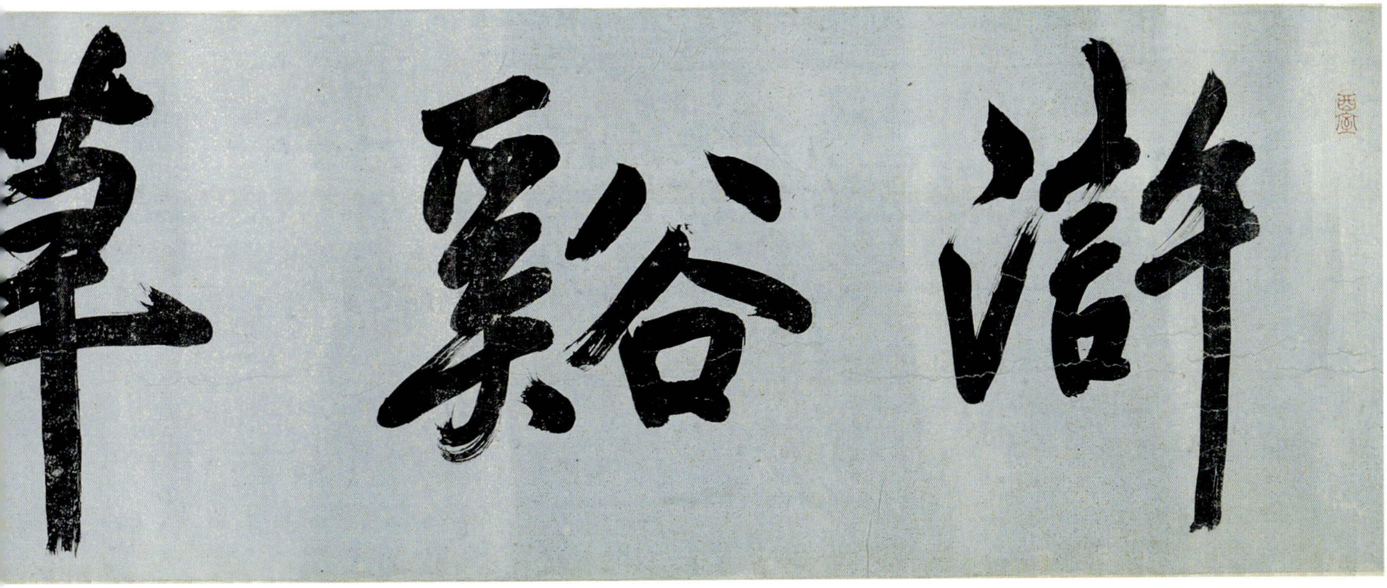

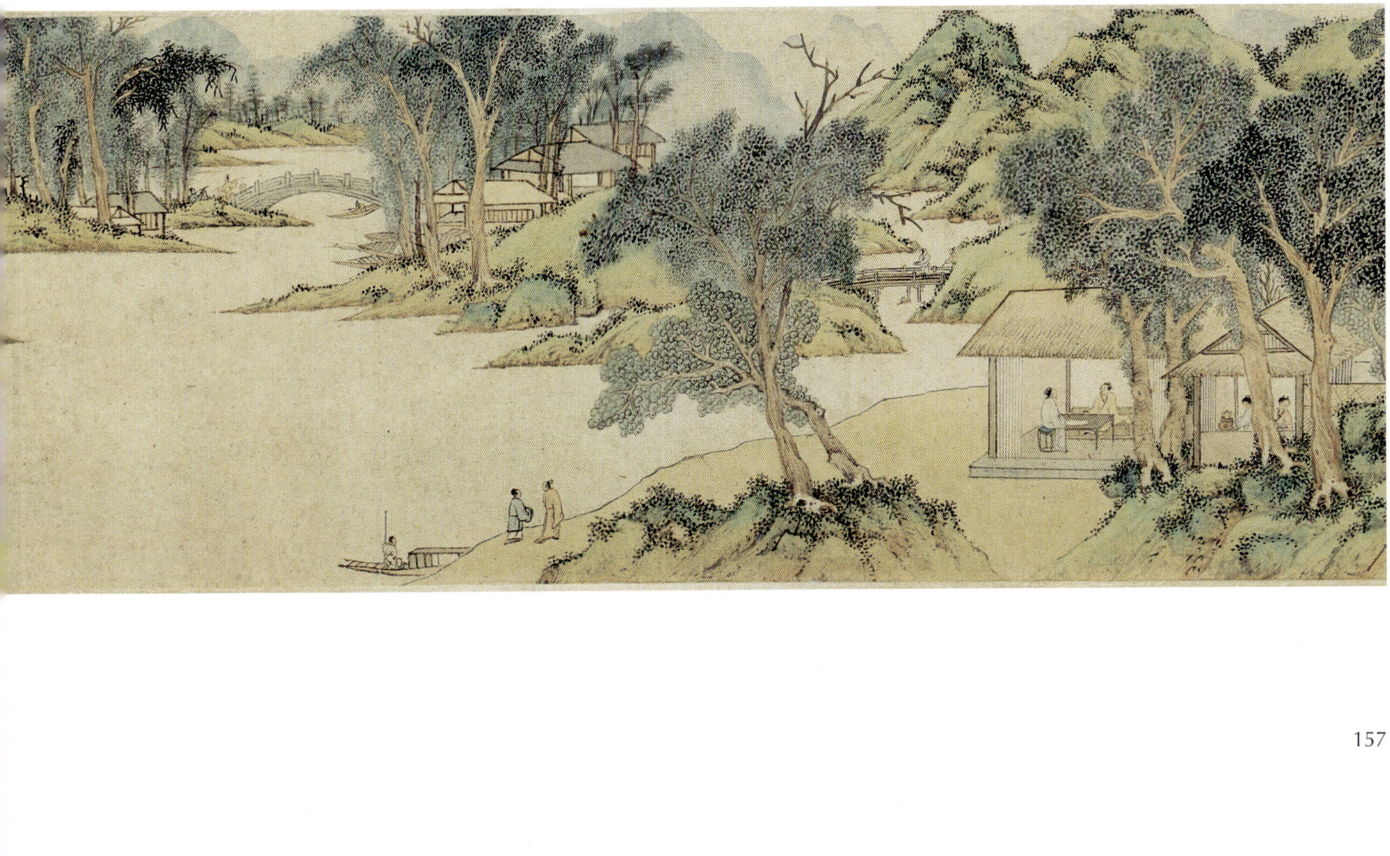

7

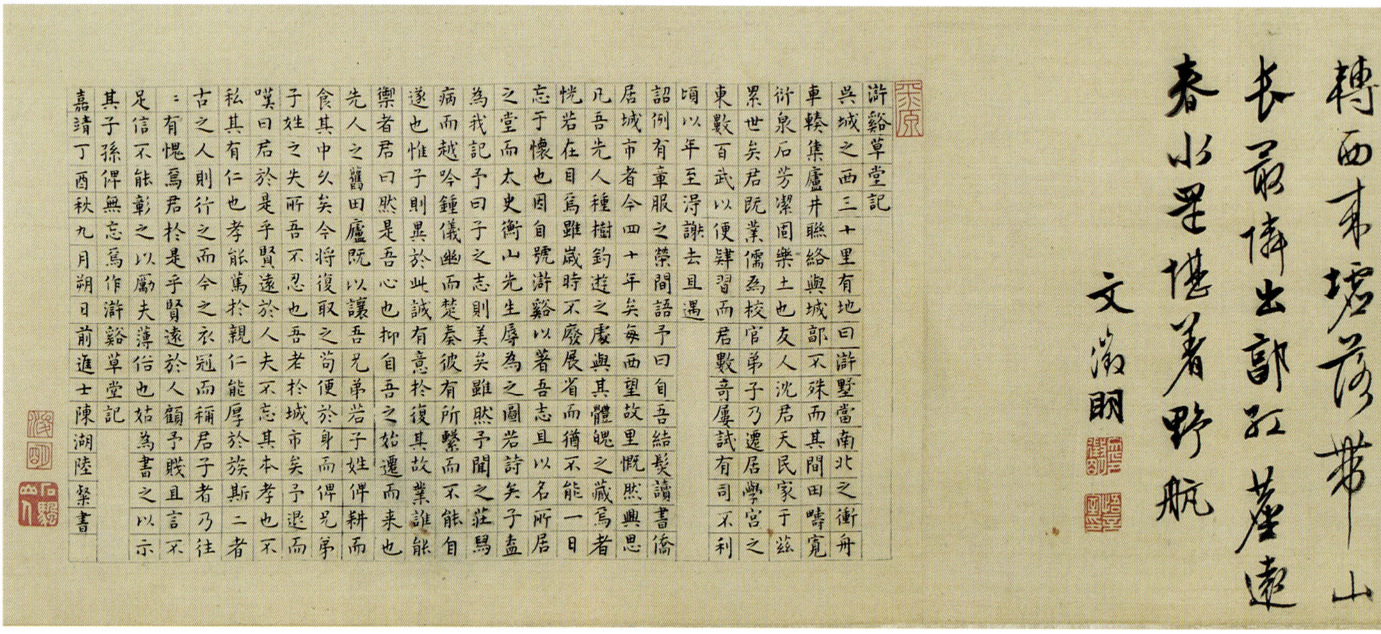

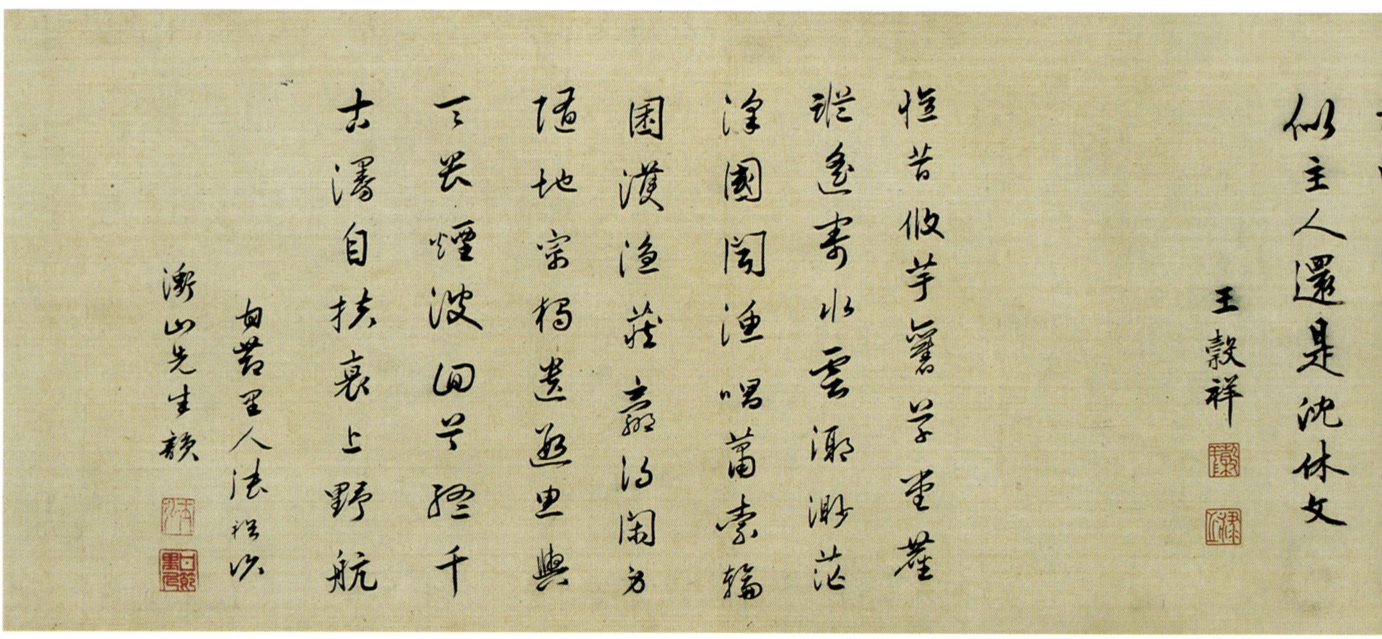

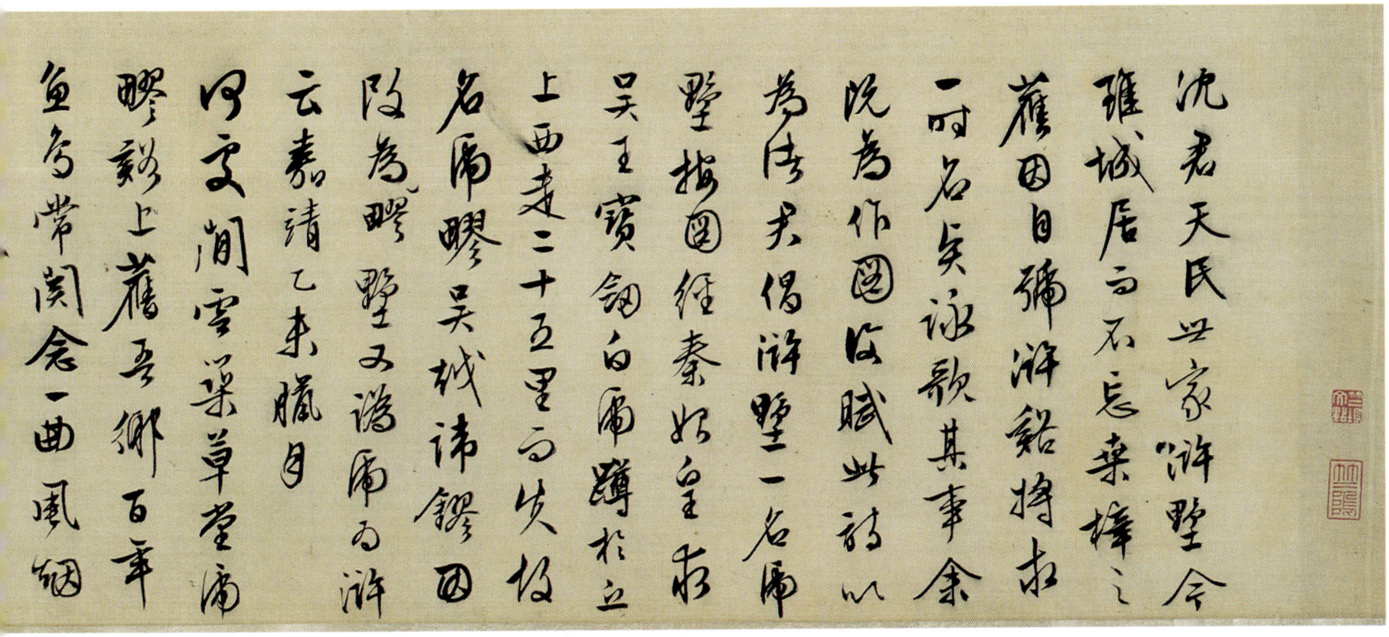

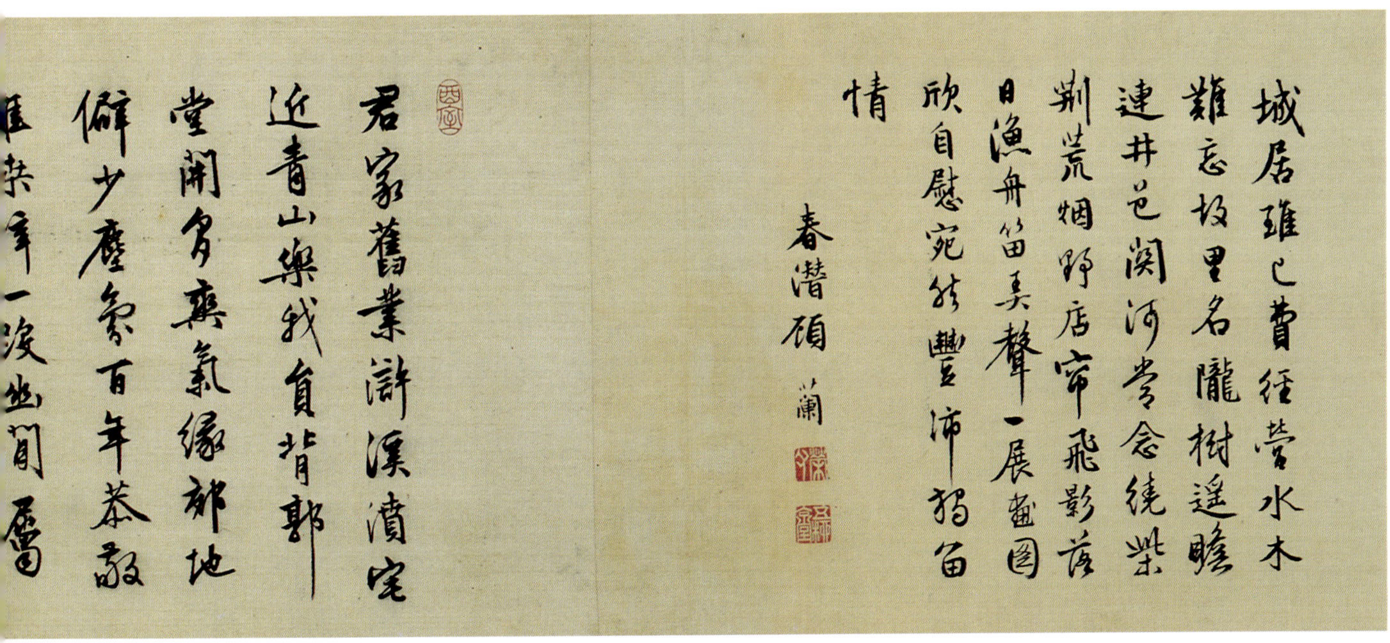

7

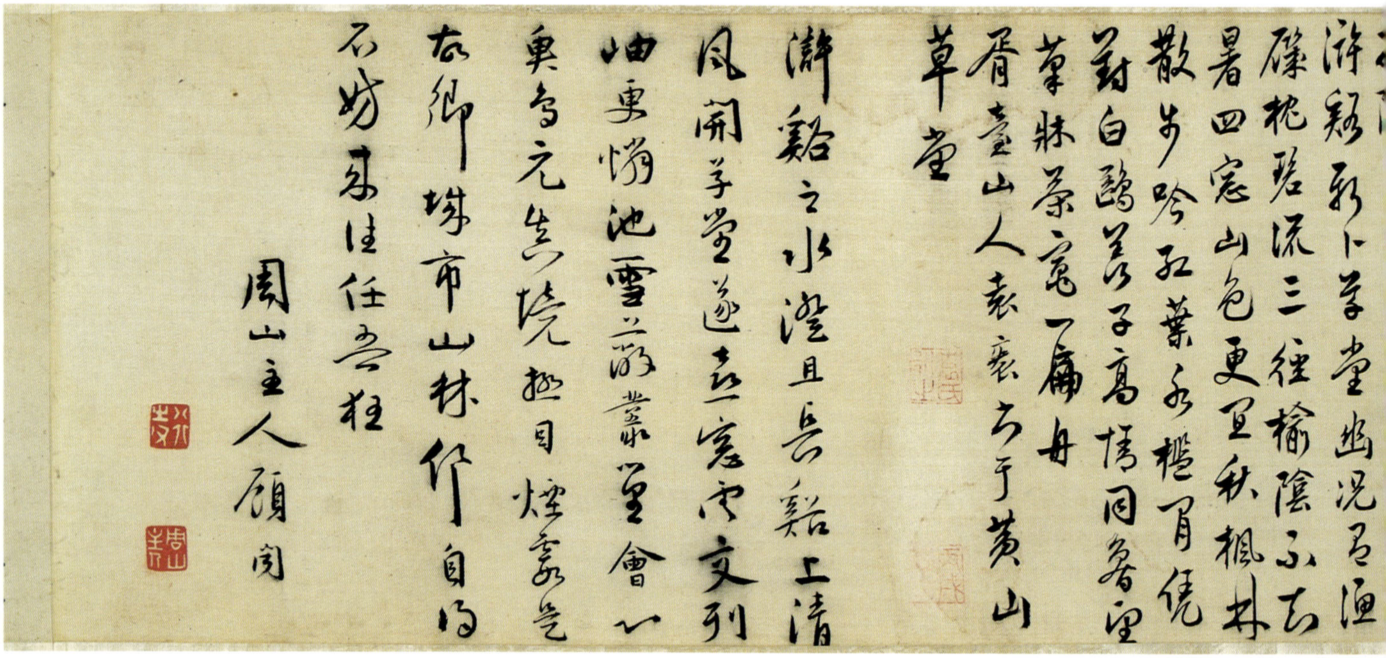

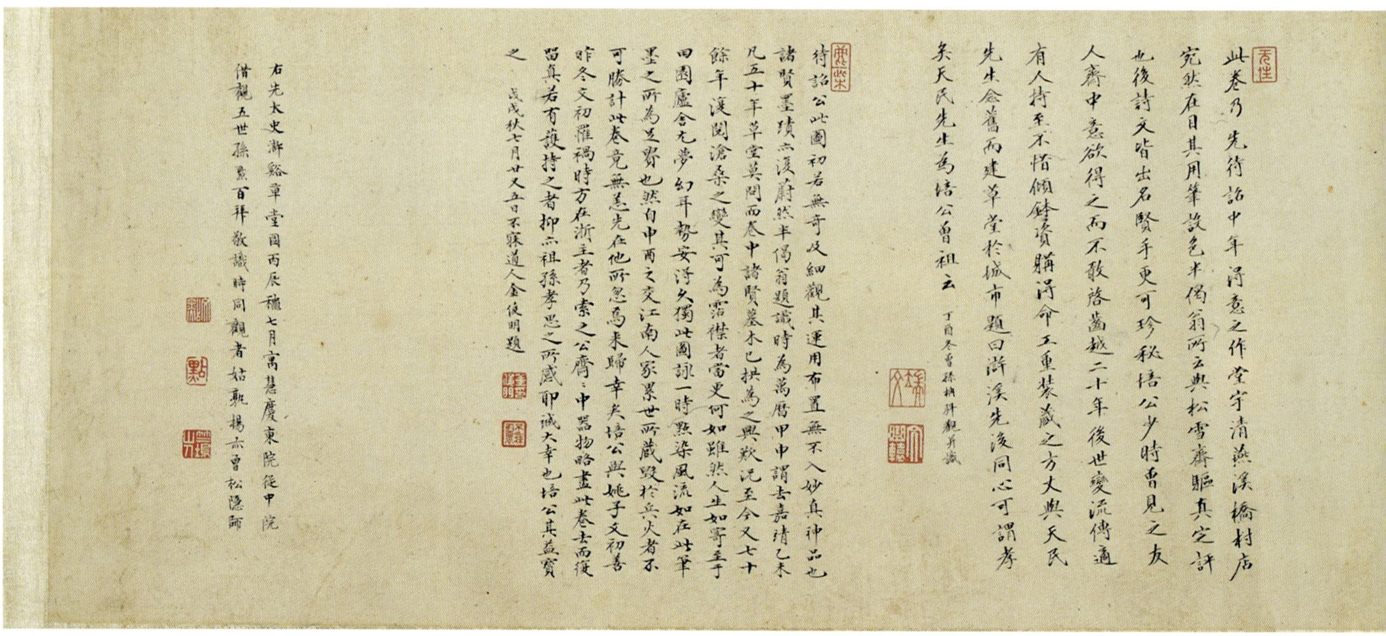

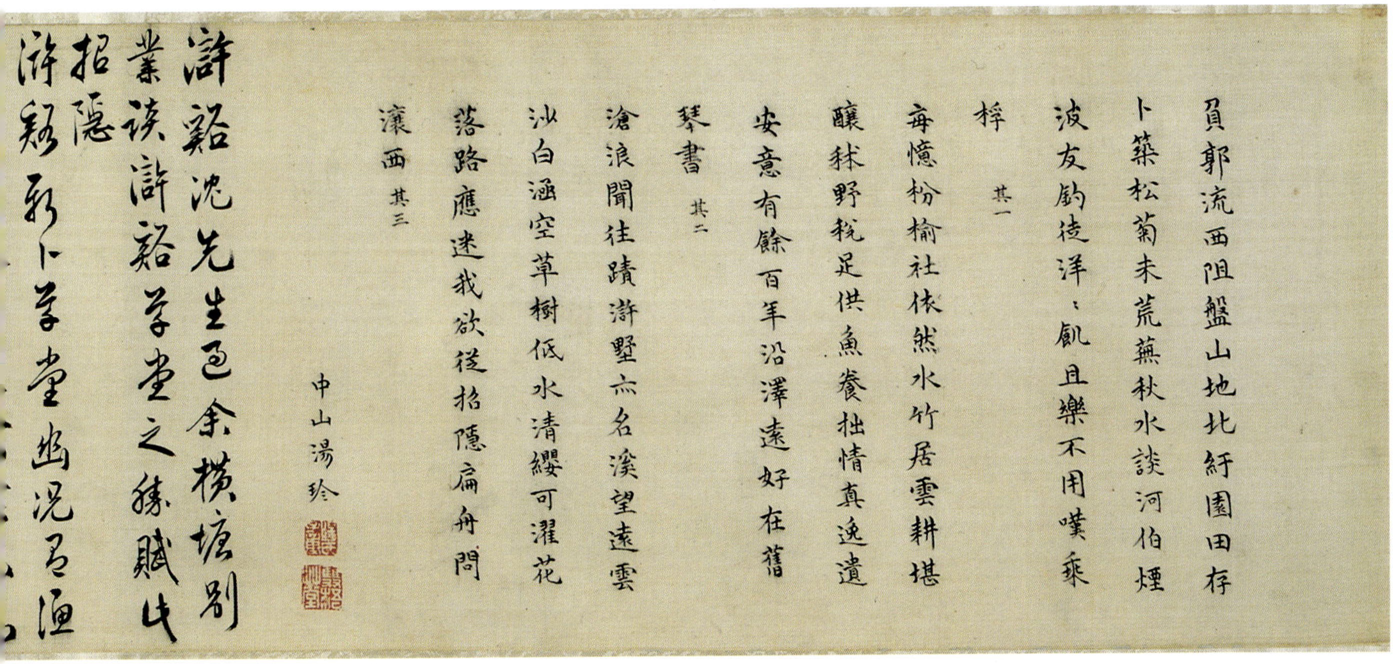
負郭流西阻盤山地北紆園田存
卜築松菊未荒蕪秋水談河伯煙
波友釣徒洋洋飢且樂不用嘆乘
桴 其一
每憶枌榆社依然水竹居雲耕堪
釀秫野税足供魚飬拙情真逸遺
安意有餘百年沿澤遠好在舊
琴書 其二
滄浪聞往蹟滸墅亦名溪望遠雲
氿白涵空草樹低水清纓可濯花
落路應迷我欲從招隱扁舟問
瀼西 其三
中山湯珍
滸谿沈先生邑余橫塘別
業談滸谿草堂之勝賦此
招隱

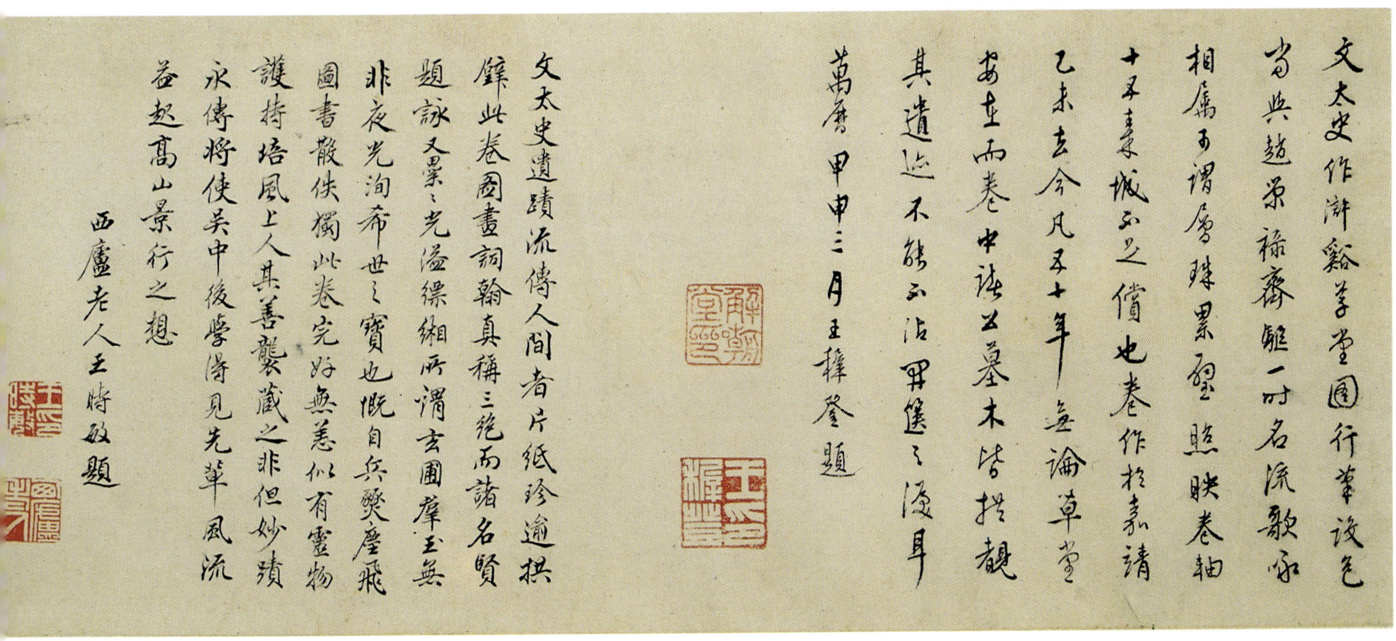
文太史作滸谿草堂圖行草詩色
尚典趙榮祿齋軀一时名流歌詠
相屬可謂貫珠累璧照映卷軸
十年袁城公之僧也卷作於嘉靖
乙未去今凡五十年無論草堂
安在而卷中諸公墓木皆拱覩
其遺迹不能不治
萬曆甲申三月王穉登題
文太史遺蹟流傳人間者片紙珍逾拱
璧此卷圖畫詞翰真稱三絕而諸名賢
題詠又纍纍光溢縹緗所謂玄圃瘴玉無
非夜光洵希世之寶也既自兵燹塵飛
圖書散佚獨此卷完好無恙似有靈物
護持培風上人其善襲藏之非但妙蹟
永傳將使吳中後學得見先輩風流
益起高山景行之想
西廬老人王時敏題

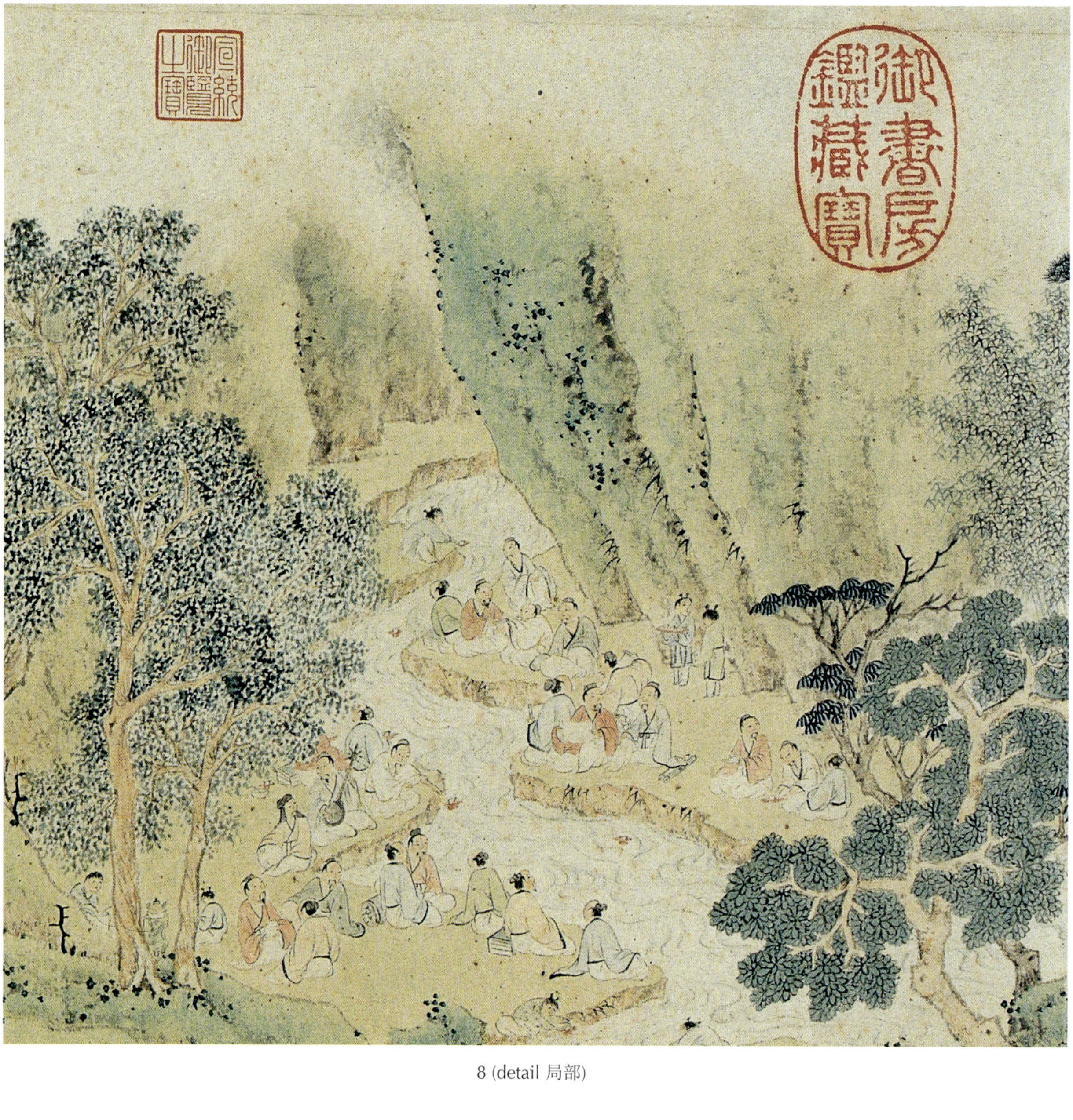

8 (detail 局部)

8
明　　祝允明 书兰亭序文征明补图
合卷, 纸本水墨设色
Zhu Yunming (1461–1527) and Wen Zhengming (1470–1559)
Calligraphy and Painting of the Orchid Pavilion

Handscroll; ink and color on paper

Painting: 20.9 x 77.5 cm; calligraphy: 23.3 x 48.4 cm

ARTISTS SEALS: [Zhu Yunmin] Zhishan (square/intaglio), Zhu Yunming yin (square/intaglio), Xizhe (square/relief); [Wen Zhengming] Wen Zhongzi (square/intaglio), Wuyanshi yin (square/intaglio)

IMPERIAL SEALS: [Qianlong, r. 1736–95] Qianlong yulan zhibao (oval/relief), Shiqu dingjian (round/relief), Baoji chongbian (square/intaglio), Yushufang jiancangbao (oval/relief), Qianlong jianshang (round/intaglio), Shiqu baoji (oval/relief), Sanxitang jingjianxi (rectangular/relief), Yizisun (square/intaglio); [Jiaqing, r. 1796–1820] Jiaqing yulan zhibao (oval/relief); [Xuantong (Puyi), r. 1909–11] Xuantong yulan zhibao (square/relief), Xuantong jianshang (square/relief), Wuyizhai jingjianxi (rectangular/relief)

OTHER SEALS: [Hua Yun, 1488–1560] Conglong (square/intaglio); [Fang Zhenguan, 1679–1747] Fang Zhenguan shending (square/relief); [Wang Shu, 1668–1743] Gongshou (square/relief), Wang Shu yin (square/intaglio); [Museum of Northeast] Dongbei bowuguan zhencang zhiyin (square/relief)

COLOPHON WRITERS (SEALS): Wen Zhengming (Zhengming [square/intaglio]); Wang Shu (Shu [square/relief], Liangchang shanxia ren [rectangular/intaglio], Wang Lang [square/relief], Xuzhou [square/relief], Ruolinfu yin [square/relief])

画家印鉴：[祝允明]枝山（白文方印）、祝允明印(白文方印)、晞哲（朱文方印）；[文征明]，文仲子（白文方印）、悟言室印（白文方印）

皇家印鉴：[清乾隆皇帝弘历，在位1736－1795]乾隆御览之宝（朱文椭圆印）、石渠定鉴（朱文圆印）、宝笈重编（白文方印）、御书房鉴藏宝（朱文椭圆印）、乾隆鉴赏（白文圆印）、石渠宝笈（朱文长方印）、三希堂精鉴玺（朱文长方印）、宜子孙（白文方印）。[清嘉庆皇帝颙琰，在位1796－1820]嘉庆御览之宝（朱文椭圆印）。[清宣统皇帝溥仪，在位1909－1911]宣统御览之宝（朱文方印），宣统鉴赏（朱文方印），无逸斋精鉴玺（朱文长方印）。

其他印鉴：[华云，1488－1560]从龙（白文方印）。[方贞观，1679－1747]方贞观审定（朱文方印）。[王澍，1668－1743]恭寿（朱文方印），王澍印（白文方印）。[东北博物馆]东北博物馆珍藏之印（朱文方印）

题跋者（钤印）：文征明（征明[白文长方印]）。王澍（澍[朱文方印]、良常山下人[白文长方印]、王郎[朱文方印]、虚舟[朱文方印]、若林父印[朱文方印]）。

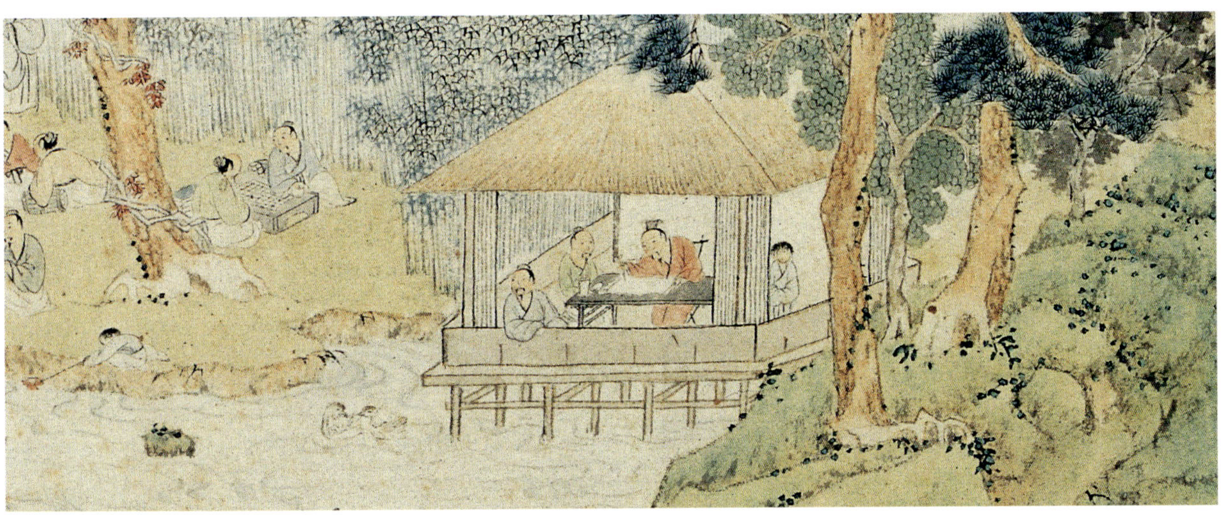

8 (detail 局部)

8

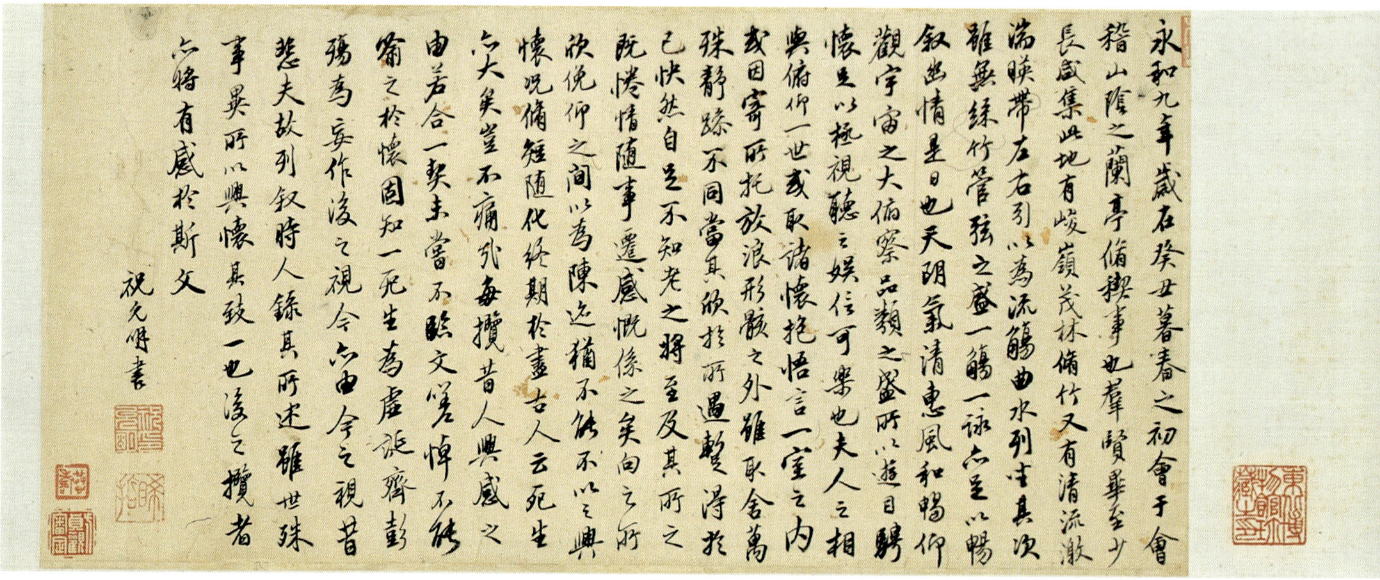

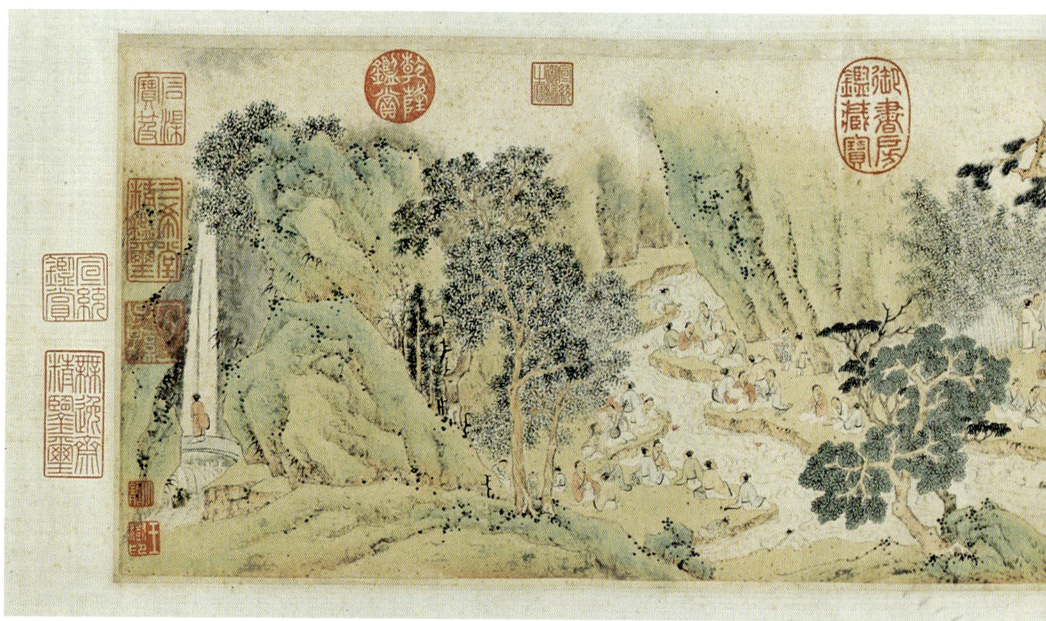

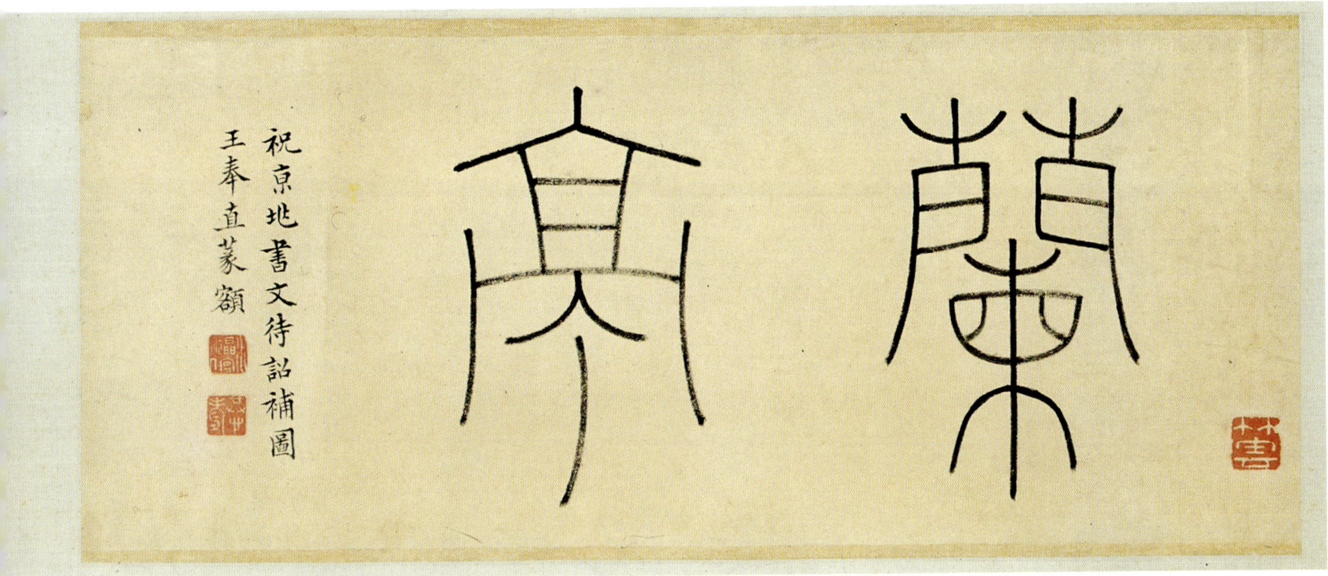
蘭亭
祝京兆書文待詔補圖
王奉直篆額

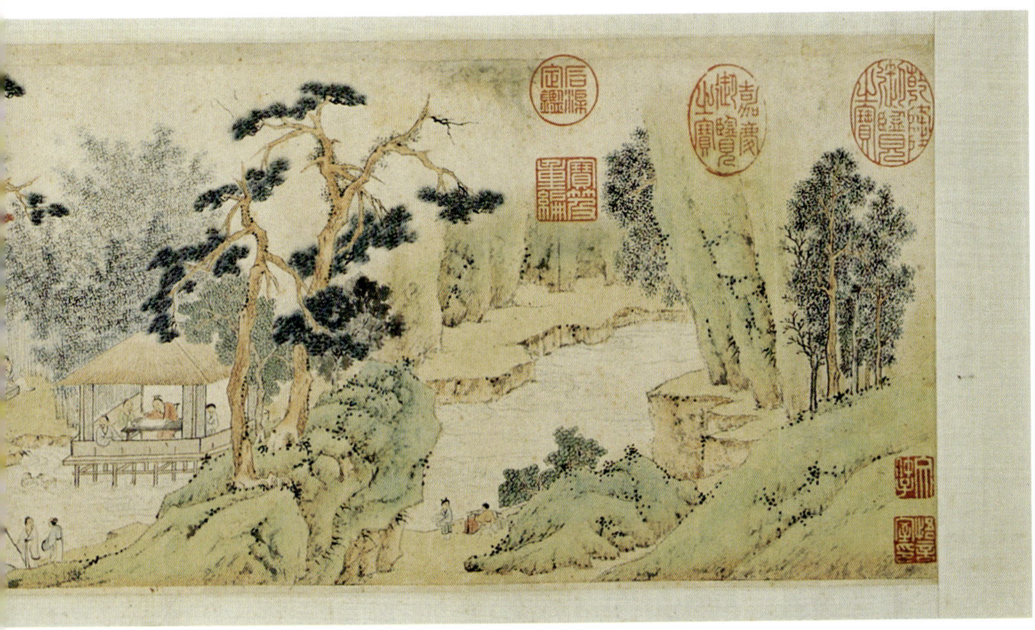

8

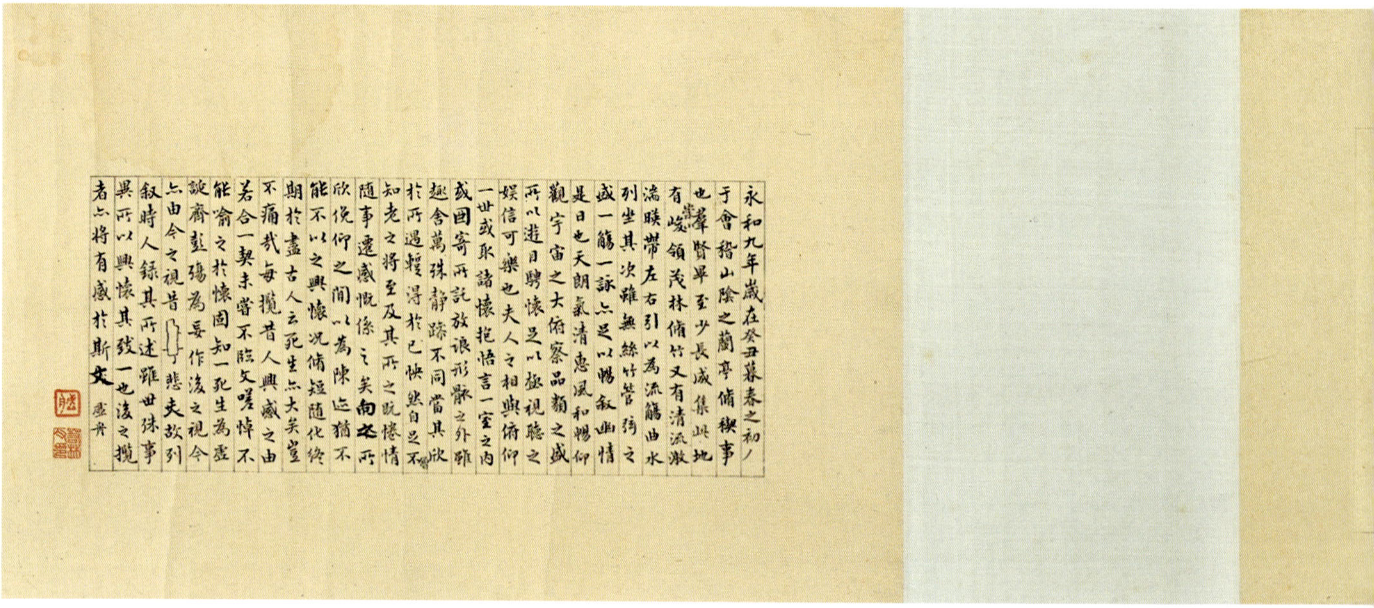

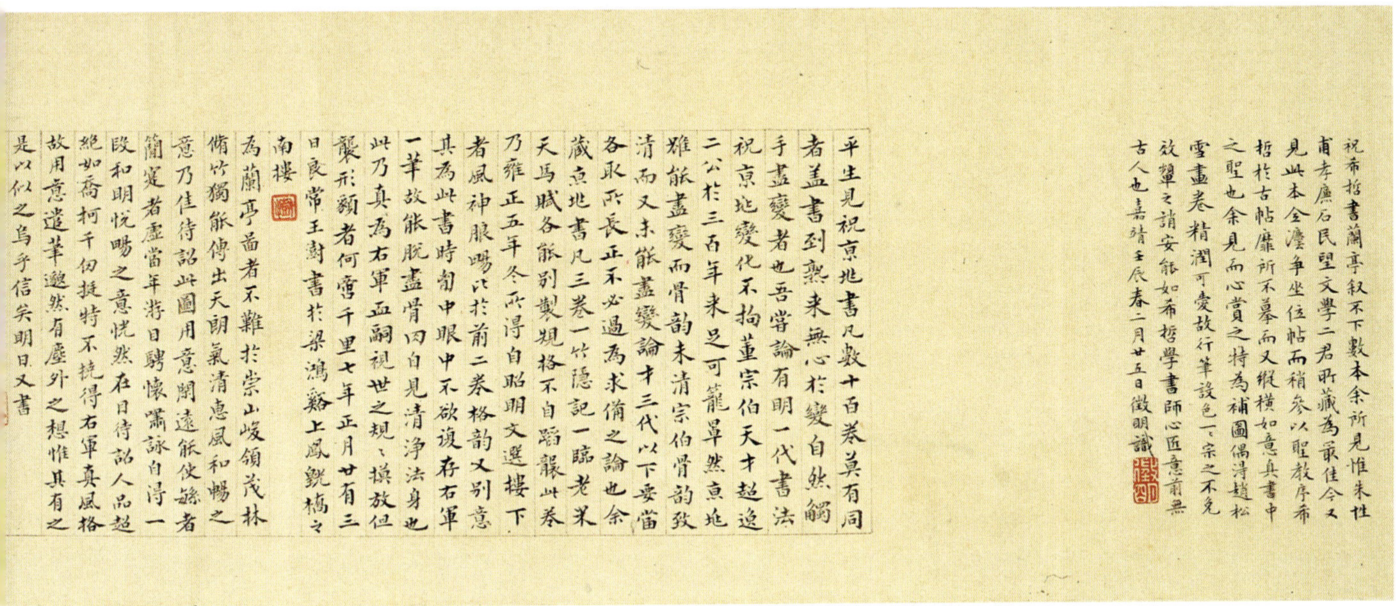
祝希哲書蘭亭叙不下數本余所見惟朱性
甫李應石民望文學二君所藏為最佳今又
見此本全瀍争坐位帖而稍參以聖教序希
哲於古帖靡所不摹而又縱橫如意其書中
之聖也余見而心賞之特為補圖偶得趙松
雪畫卷精潤可愛故行筆設色一一宗之不免
效顰之誚安能如希哲學書師心匠意前無
古人也嘉靖壬辰春二月廿五日徵明識
平生見祝京兆書凡數十百卷莫有同
者蓋書到熟來無心於變自然翩
手盡變者也吾嘗論有明一代書法
祝京兆變化不拘董宗伯天才超逸
二公於三百年來足可籠罩然京兆
雖能盡變而骨韵未清宗伯骨韵致
清而又未能盡變論才三代以下要當
各取所長正不必過為求備之論也余
藏京兆書凡三卷一竹隱記一臨老米
天馬賦各能別製規格不自蹈襲此卷
乃雍正五年冬所得自昭明文選樓下
者風神朗暢只於前二卷格韵又別意
其為此書時胸中眼中不欲復存右軍
一筆故能脫盡骨肉自見清淨法身也
此乃真為右軍丞嗣視世之規規摹放但
襲形貌者何啻千里七年正月廿有三
日良常王澍書於梁鴻谿上鳳皇橋之
南樓
為蘭亭畫者不難於崇山峻領茂林
脩竹獨能傳出天朗氣清惠風和暢之
意乃佳待詔此圖用意閑遠能使觀者
簡覽者盡當年游目騁懷嘯詠自得一
段和明悅暢之意恍然在目待詔人品超
絕如喬柯千仞挺特不撓得右軍真風格
故用意遣筆邈然有塵外之想惟其有之
是以似之烏乎信矣明日又書

This is an exquisite combination scroll mounted with the artwork of two prominent mid-Ming dynasty artists: the calligrapher Zhu Yunming and painter Wen Zhengming. Both works refer to a collection of poems improvised at a gathering of literati and talents at Lanting (Orchid Pavilion) and the documentation of the event by the apotheosized master calligrapher Wang Xizhi (ca. 303–ca. 361) in an epoch-making masterpiece—the *Preface to the Orchid Pavilion* (*Lanting xu*).

Although he held a number of official government posts, including at one time the position of controller at the Yingtianfu regional government, Zhu Yunming devoted himself mostly to calligraphy. He developed a natural and intuitive approach using flexible brush techniques that allowed him to establish a new style of calligraphy for the Ming dynasty and earned him the reputation of "Number One among Contemporary Calligraphers" of his time.

A leading artist at the time, Wen Zhengming was so inspired by this particular "copy of antiquity" by Zhu that he created a painting titled *Gathering at the Orchid Pavilion* to match the calligraphy. At the end of the scroll, he also inscribed a colophon in small-standard script stating that this was one of the best of Zhu's many copies of the Orchid Pavilion that he had seen and expressed his admiration for Zhu Yunming as a "Sage in Calligraphy." The reclusive setting and peaceful atmosphere described in the *Preface* is effectively captured in this painting.

Impressed by this combination scroll and its mood, renowned Qing dynasty calligrapher Wang Shu (1668–1743) wrote the title "Orchid Pavilion" in seal script as a frontispiece for the scroll, showcasing the superb level of his calligraphy. After a long colophon, Wang Shu made a copy of the complete text of the *Orchid Pavilion Preface*. Judging from the imperial collection seals on the scroll, we know that it was acquired by the Qing imperial court during Qianlong's reign. Wang Shu died in 1743 (the 8th year of Qianlong), making him the last possible private collector of this scroll before it went into the imperial court.

HWL (trans. DHWS)

这是明中期最著声望的书法家祝允明（1461－1527年）和画家文征明（1470－1559年）各自创作的一个精品合卷，作品的内容源于书圣王羲之（约303－约361年）的"兰亭雅集"及其旷世名作《兰亭序》。

祝允明虽然任有应天府通判等官职，但一生的精力主要用在了书法方面，他发挥天性，得心应手，以灵活多变的笔法，开创了明代书法艺术的新格调，被称为"当朝第一书家"。画坛领袖文征明深为祝允明这件"临古"书作而感动，激赏中创作了《兰亭雅集图》卷，卷后以他精美的小楷题写了跋文，文中述及，他见过多本祝允明临写的《兰亭序》，唯独见到此本分外喜爱，感叹祝允明真是"书中之圣也"。《兰亭雅集图》中的景致幽深而清雅，贴切而又生动地表现了《兰亭序》原文的意境。

清代著名的书法家王澍（1668－1743年），受到前面书、画中气氛的感染，于卷前引首处以篆书题写了"兰亭"二字，体现他书法的高超造诣，并在卷后题写长篇跋语外，又恭谨地临写了一遍《兰亭序》全文。王澍卒于乾隆八年（1743年），从卷中钤盖的御藏印判断，此卷在乾隆年间已经进入清宫内府，那么王澍就是此卷的最后一位私人收藏者了。

黄伟利

9
明　唐寅　临李公麟饮中八仙图
手卷, 纸本水墨
Tang Yin (1470–1524)
In Imitation of the "Eight Drunken Immortals" by Li Gonglin, 1517

Handscroll; ink on paper
31.9 x 631.7 cm

ARTIST'S SEALS: Tang Bohu (square/relief), Tang Yin siyin (square/intaglio); Nanjing jieyuan (rectangular/relief), Wu qu (round/relief)

IMPERIAL SEALS: [Qianlong, r. 1736–95] Qianlong yulan zhibao (oval/relief), Qianlong jianshang (round/intaglio), Shiqu baoji (square/relief), Yangxindian jiancangbao (rectangular/relief), Qianlong yulan zhibao (square/relief), Guxi tianzi (round/relief), Wufu wudaitang guxi tianzi bao (large square/relief), Bazheng maonian zhibao (large square/relief), Sanxitang jingjianxi (rectangular/relief), Yizisun (round/intaglio), Yongbi zaixin (square seam seal/intaglio), Yuyi yuwu (square seam seal/relief); [Jiaqing, r. 1796–1820] Jiaqing yulan zhibao (oval/relief); [Xuantong (Puyi), r. 1909–11] Xuantong yulan zhibao (square/relief), Xuantong jianshang (rectangular/relief), Wuyizhai jingjianxi (rectangular/relief)

OTHER SEALS: [Museum of the Northeast] Dongbei bowuguan zhencang zhiyin (square/relief)

COLOPHON WRITERS (SEALS): Tang Yin (Tang Bohu [square/relief], Liuru jushi [square/relief]); Zhu Yunming, 1461–1527 (Zhu Yunming yin [square/intaglio], Xiaoyao tingzi [rectangular/intaglio], Xizhe [square/relief]); Li Yinchang, dates unknown (Lishi Yinchang [square/intaglio])

JADE CLIP INSCRIPTION: Qianlong Yuqian. Tang Yin lin Li Boshi yinxian tu (filled with gold)

画家印鉴：唐白虎（朱文方印）、唐寅私印（白文方印）、南京解元（朱文长方印）、吴趋(朱文圆印)。

皇室印鉴：[清乾隆皇帝弘历，在位1736－1795]乾隆御览之宝（朱文椭圆印）、乾隆鉴赏（白文圆印）、石渠宝笈（朱文方印）、养心殿鉴藏宝（朱文长方印）、乾隆御览之宝（大朱文方印）、古希天子(朱文圆印)、五福五代堂古稀天子宝(大朱文方印)、八征耄念之宝（大朱文方印）、三希堂精鉴玺（朱文长方印）、宜子孙（白文圆印）、用笔在心（白文方骑缝印）、寓意于物（朱文方骑缝印）。[清嘉庆皇帝顒琰，在位1796－1820]嘉庆御览之宝（朱文椭圆印）。[清宣统皇帝溥仪，在位1909－1911]宣统御览之宝（朱文方印）、宣统鉴赏（朱文长方印）、无逸斋精鉴玺（朱文长方印）。

其他印鉴：[东北博物馆]东北博物馆珍藏之印（朱文方印）

题跋者（钤印）：唐寅，1470－1524（唐白虎[朱文方印]、六如居士[朱文方印]）。祝允明，1461－1527（祝允明印[白文方印]、逍遥亭子[白文长方印]、晞哲[朱文方印]）。李胤昌，生卒年不详（李氏胤昌[白文方印]）。

玉别子镌：乾隆御签。唐寅临李伯时饮仙图（填金）

Tang Yin (courtesy name, Baihu; sobriquet, Liuru Jushi) was a native of Wuxian County (present-day Suzhou, Jiangsu). An expert in painting landscapes, trees, and rocks as well as figures, he was one of the Four Masters of the Wu School.

Executed in a purely monochrome-outline, or *baimiao*, technique, this scroll depicts a gathering of thirty-five people in the midst of a mountain forest, capturing completely the expressions of stroking the *qin* zither, playing the flute, raising their wine cups, chanting poetry, enjoying calligraphy and painting, lying about, or returning home drunk. It is a copy of *Drunken Immortals* by the Northern Song painter Li Gonglin (sobriquet, Longmian; ca. 1041–1106). At the end of this long scroll, Tang Yin, describes the circumstances of his painting: During the Zhende reign in the "long summer" of the *dingchou* year (1517), while vacationing at Shihu (present-day Suzhou, Jiangsu), he was delighted to see the scroll of drunken immortals by Li Longmian, shown to him by one of the guests. As a result, he stayed on for the next several months copying it. He writes, "I'm not quite able to emulate the charm, but viewer, please don't laugh at this." However, in Zhu Yunming's colophon are comments of great appreciation for the genuine-looking copy: "Tang Jushi can capture the mood and spirit of the original; his brushwork is just like the cursive script technique of the Jin dynasty masters, without a drop of worldly intentions. The *baimiao* technique is more difficult than painting with color; the former requires knowledge of an archaic clumsiness. Besides, few can handle such a long scroll."[1] Tang Yin was about forty-five when he painted this scroll. His brush technique has liveliness and archaic clumsiness, producing strokes that resemble silver wire and iron hooks. The texture strokes are tastefully applied, mixing dry and wet brush and light and dark washes to achieve rich textures that evoke feelings of a distant fairyland. Zhu Yunming's calligraphy on this scroll is fully mature and refined, done when he was about sixty years of age.

Written by the great Tang dynasty poet Du Fu (712–770), the "Eight Drunken Immortals" is a poem that celebrates the carefree and untrammeled nature of eight individuals of the Tang period who were variously poets, high ranking officials, or members of the imperial family and who all loved drinking and enjoyed freedom of expression. The eight drunken immortals are identified as He Zhizhang (d. 744), Li Jin, Li Shizhi (d. 747), Su Jin, Jiao Sui, Cui Zongzhi, Li Bai (701–762), and Zhang Xu. They have been much admired and emulated by generations of Chinese literati who consider themselves independent and above the rest. This poem by Du Fu has also been widely quoted and recited and has frequently served as a subject for calligraphers and painters.[2] A copy of the entire text for the poem "Eight Drunken Immortals" was added by Li Yinchang for the end section of this scroll (see Appendix B).

Affixed to the painting are the name seals of the artist, mood seals (*xian zhang*), and seals of connoisseurs such as the Ming dynasty calligrapher Zhu Yunming, who wrote a colophon in standard script on the painting, and Li Yinchang, who wrote a long seven-character *shi* poem. Although information about its succession of owners at the end of the Ming dynasty is unknown, the scroll was most probably remounted after it went into the collection of the Qing court. The scroll has a brocade wrapping section with a label inscribed "Tang Yin's copy of Li Boshi's Drunken Immortals" in Qianlong's imperial handwriting as well as the notice *neifu zhencang* (Treasured collection of the court) and the seal "Qianlong chenhan" (Qianlong's imperial writing), rating it as number one among the top-rated works of art to be stored at the Yangxin Dian (Hall of Mental Cultivation).[3]

Affixed to the painting are the eight frequently used seals of the Qianlong emperor as well as the collection viewing seals of the Jiaqing and Xuantong emperors. Its eventual route into the collection of the Liaoning Provincial Museum is the same as that of Zhu Zhanji's *Ten-Thousand-Year-Old Pine Tree* (cat. no. 3).

WWHC (trans. DHWS)

Notes

1. *Shiqu baoji* [Treasured boxes of the Stone Channel] (Taipei: Guoli gugong bowuyuan, 1971), p. 633.
2. Among the gifts awarded to Pujie by Puyi on the 22 day of the 11th month in the 14th year of the Xuantong reign, was Cheng Liang's *Eight Drunken Immortals*, registered under the serial number Yong 281 in *Gugong yiyi shuji shuhua mulu si zhong* [Four catalogues of dispersed calligraphy and paintings from the imperial palace] (Beijing: Gugong bowuyuan, 1926), p. 17.
3. *Shiqu baoji*, p. 632.

唐寅字伯虎，号六如居士，吴县（今江苏苏州）人。善画山水、树石、人物，为吴门四家之一。

此卷纯为白描，山林之间，共有35位人物，抚琴，吹笛，把酒，吟诗，书画，闲卧，醉归，神态毕具，为临北宋李公麟《饮仙图》，画后唐寅记载了绘画经过：正德丁丑年长夏（1517），在石湖（今江苏苏州）避暑时，有客人出示李龙眠饮仙图卷，自己非常喜欢，因而留下几个月临摹，"不能效颦耳，观者勿哂"。而在祝允明的跋语中，对唐寅几可乱真的临摹之作赞赏不绝"唐居士能画其神情意态毕具，其用笔如晋人草书之法，无一点尘俗气，白描更难于设色，彼用心于古拙，此长卷亦非人之所及也"（注1）。唐寅作此卷时约四五十岁，用笔古拙生动，银线铁钩，皴檫之干湿浓淡有致，渺若仙境。祝允明的书法用笔淳厚，意气密丽，约为其六十左右所书。

"饮中八仙诗"为唐代大诗人杜甫（712—770）所作，指唐代的八位酒仙贺之章（744卒）、汝阳王李琎（唐玄宗时人）、李适之（卒于747）、苏晋（唐玄宗时人）、焦遂（生卒年不详）、崔宗之（生卒年不详）、李白（701—762）和张旭（生卒年不详），此八人或为诗人，或为高官，或为皇室成员，但皆天然率真，我行我素，借酒而畅达情性，历来为标榜特立独行的中国文人所爱，杜甫此诗为人所传诵，书画家亦不乏这一题材的作品（注2）。此卷拖尾有明末清初人李胤昌书法抄录杜甫的"饮中八仙歌"。

钤印有画家名章，闲章和观赏者如明代书法家祝允明在画心的楷书题跋，李胤昌有七言长诗题跋。虽然明末的递藏情况不明，但入清宫后，或曾重新装裱，本卷锦包首，包首外有"唐寅临李伯时饮仙图"，"内府珍藏"字样和"乾隆宸翰"朱文方印，定为上等第一，贮于养心殿内（注3）。引首为经背纸，隔水皆为绫本，画心和拖尾为纸本。画上钤有乾隆八玺，并有嘉庆和宣统皇帝的鉴藏玺。其后为辽宁省博物馆收藏的途径与图录第3号"万年松图卷"相同。

海蔚蓝

注解：

1. ［清］《石渠宝笈》初编（台湾国立故宫博物院，1971），第633页。
2. 《故宫已佚书籍书画目录四种》记载，末帝溥仪于宣统十四年十一月二十二日赏赐溥杰的书画中，有程梁"饮中八仙图"一卷，宫中登记号为永字二百八十一号（故宫博物院，民国十五年版，1926），第十七页。
3. ［清］《石渠宝笈》初编（台湾国立故宫博物院，1971），第632页。

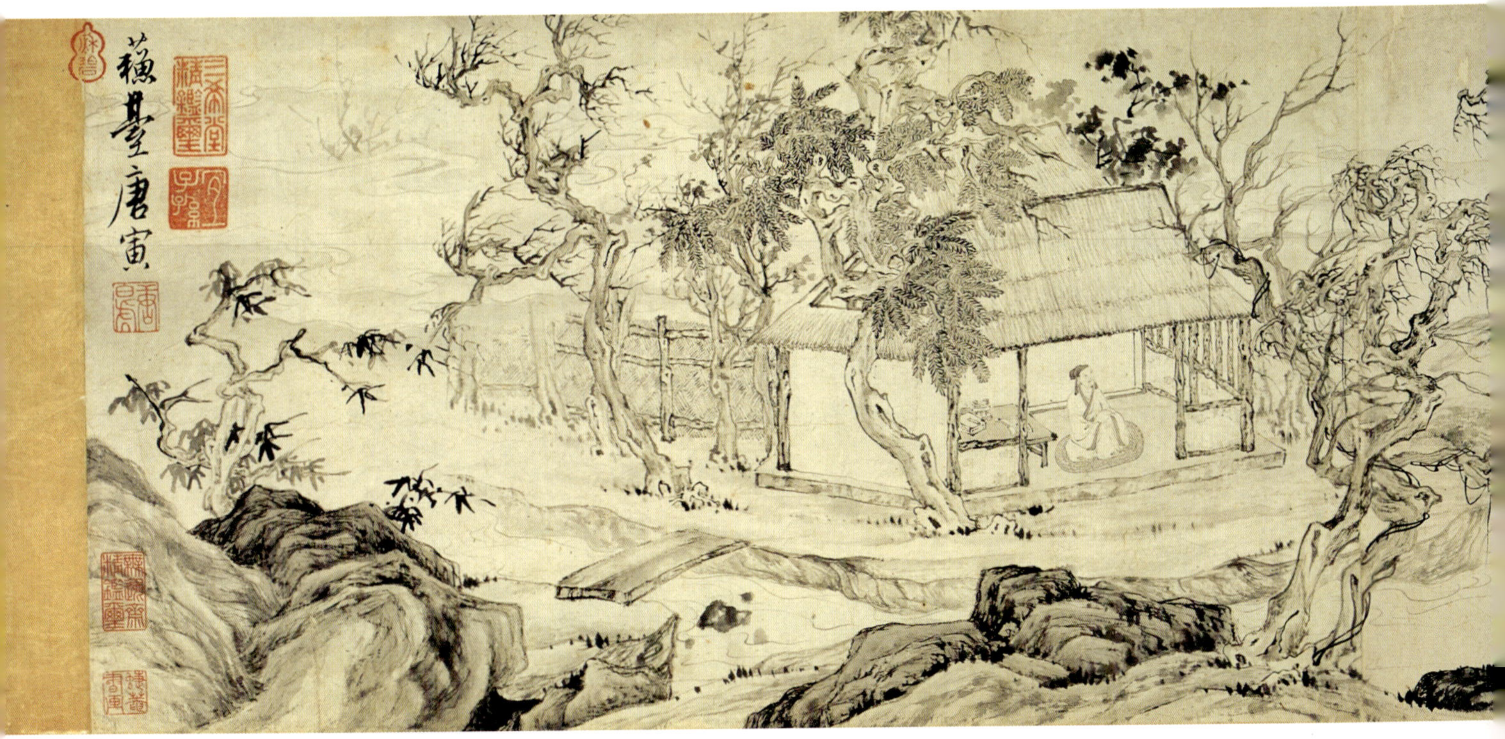

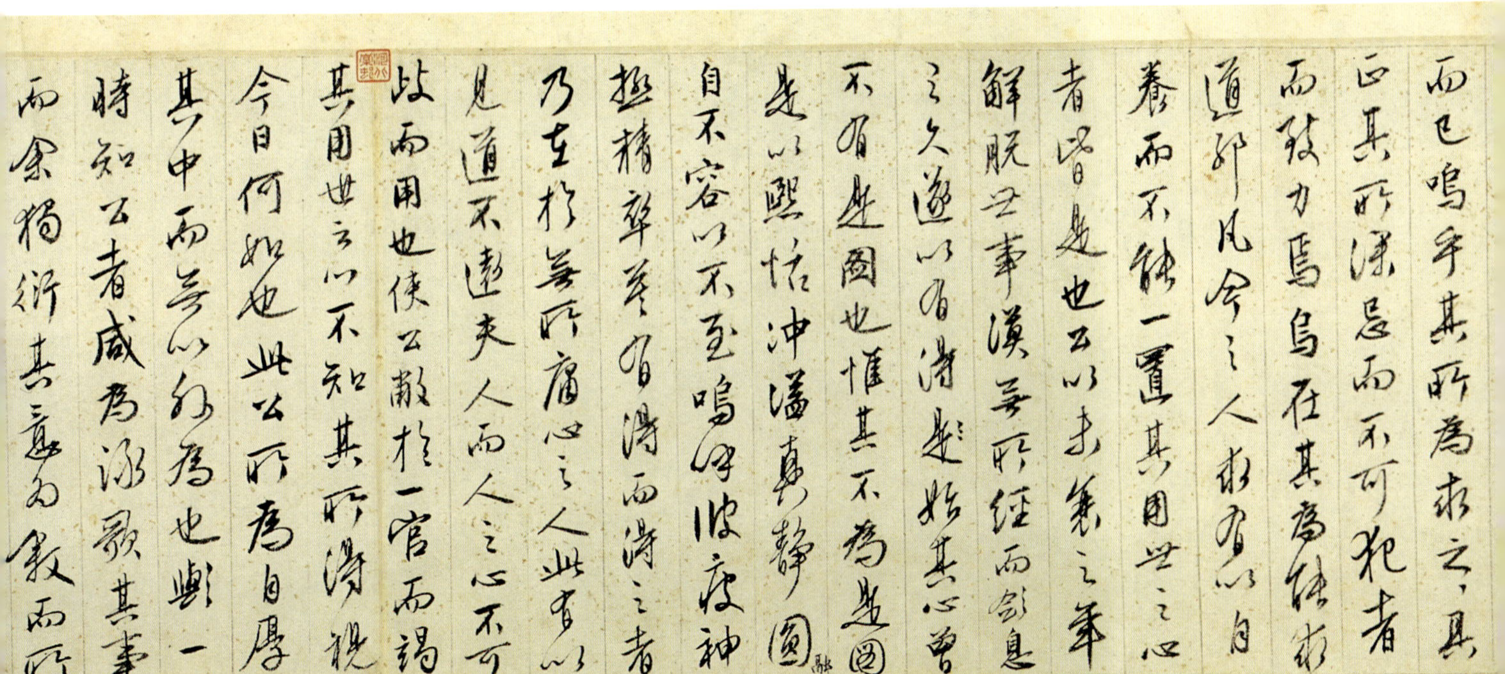

而已嗚呼其所為求之其
正其所謀是而不可犯者
而致力焉烏在其為絲求
道耶凡今之人求官以自
養而不能一置其用世之心
者皆是也公以未艾之年
解脫世事漠無所經而創息
之久遂以有濟是始其心曾
不有是圖也惟其不為是圖
是以熙怡沖澹真靜是圖
自不容以不至嗚呼彼度神
極精華有濟而濟之者
乃在於無所庸心之人此有以
見道不遠夫人而人之心不可
岐而用也使公敝於一官而竭
其用世之心以不知其所濟視
今日何如也此公所為自厚
其中而無以外為也斷一
時知公者咸為詠歌其事
而余獨衍其意趣而敘而所

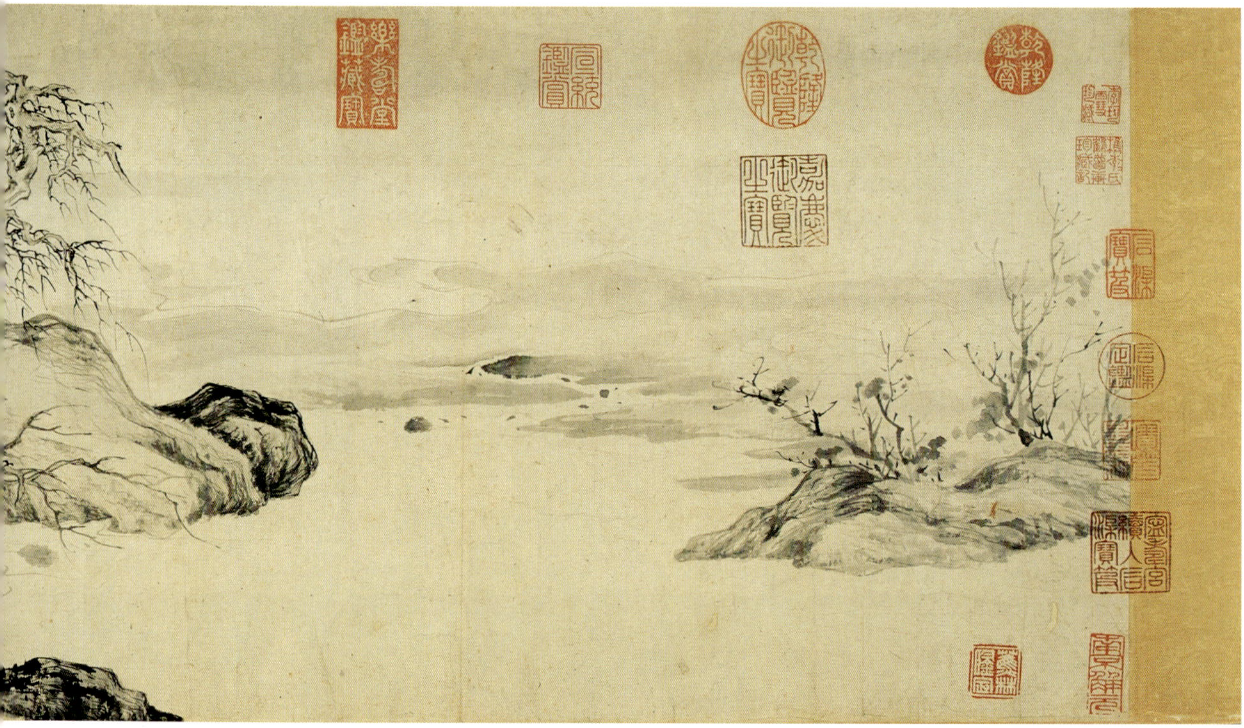

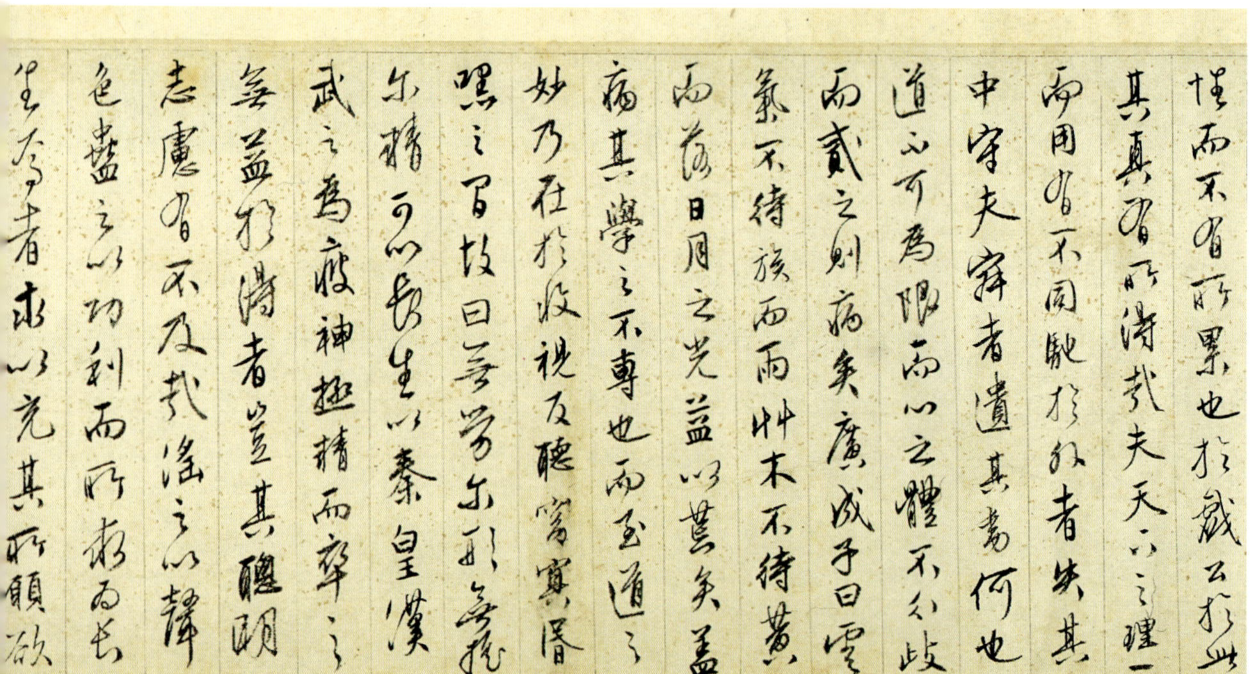

惟而不省所累也於戲出於此
其真習所得哉夫天下之理一
而用智不同馳於外者失其
中守夫雜者遺其旁何也
道不可為限而心之體不分歧
而貳之則病矣廣成子曰雲
氣不待族而雨草木不待黃
而落日月之光益以荒矣蓋
病其學之不專也而至道之
妙乃在於收視反聽寂寞昏
默之間故曰無勞爾形無搖
爾精可以長生以秦皇漢
武之為欲神趣精而卒之
無益於得者豈其聰明
志慮智不及哉深之以肆
色蠱之以功利而所欲而長
生不可者求以充其所願欲

10
明　唐寅　悟阳子养性图
手卷, 纸本水墨
Tang Yin (1470–1524)
Master Wuyang in Self-Cultivation, ca. 1514

Handscroll; ink on paper
29.5 x 103.5 cm

ARTIST'S SEALS: Tang Bohu (square/relief), Nanjing jieyuan (rectangular/relief)

IMPERIAL SEALS: [Qianlong, r. 1736–95] Shiqu baoji (rectangular/relief), Shiqu dingjian (round/relief), Baoji chongbian (square/intaglio), Ningshougong xuru shiqu baoji (square/relief), Qianlong jianshang (round/intaglio), Qianlong yulan zhibao (oval/relief), Leshoutang jiancangbao (rectangular/intaglio), Sanxitang jingjianxi (rectangular/relief), Yizisun (square/intaglio); [Jiaqing, r. 1796–1820] Jiaqing yulan zhibao (square/relief); [Xuantong (Puyi), r. 1909–11] Xuantong jianshang (square/relief), Wuyizhai jingjianxi (rectangular/relief)

OTHER SEALS: [Li Zhaoheng, ca. 1592–ca. 1662] Li Kexue zhencang (square/relief), Zuililishi hemengxuan zhencangji (square/relief); [Liang Qingbiao, 1620–1691] Jiaolin jianding (square/intaglio), Qiubi (double-gourd/relief), Yexi yuyin (rectangular/relief), Cangyan (square/relief), Cangyanzi (round/relief), Jiaolin jushi (square/intaglio), Hebei Tangcun (square/relief); [Zhu Zhengchu, dates unknown] Zhu Zhengchu (square/intaglio), Songzhai (square/intaglio), Diean shuhua (square/relief)

COLOPHON WRITERS (SEALS): Wen Zhengming, 1470–1559 (Wen Zhengming yin [square/intaglio]), Hengshan [square/relief]); Lu Shidao, b. 1517 (Luzichuan [square/relief], Jiajing wushu jinshi [square/relief])

画家印鉴：唐白虎（朱文方印）、南京解元（朱文长方印）

皇家印鉴：[清乾隆皇帝弘历,在位1736－1795]：石渠宝笈（朱文方印）、石渠定鉴（朱文圆印）、宝笈重编（白文方印）、宁寿宫续入石渠宝笈（朱文方印）、乾隆鉴赏（白文圆印）、乾隆御览之宝（朱文椭圆印）、乐寿堂鉴藏宝（白文长方印）、三希堂精鉴玺（朱文长方印）、宜子孙（白文方印）。[清嘉庆皇帝颙琰，在位1796－1820]：嘉庆御览之宝（朱文方印）。[清宣统皇帝溥仪，在位1909－1911]：宣统鉴赏（朱文方印）、无逸斋精鉴玺（朱文长方印）。

其他印鉴：[李肇亨, 约1592－约1662]李珂雪珍藏（朱文方印）、槜李李氏鹤梦轩珍藏记（朱文方印）；[梁清标，1620－1691]蕉林鉴定（白文方印）、秋碧（朱文葫芦印）、冶溪渔隐（朱文长方印）、苍岩（朱文方印）、苍岩子（朱文圆印）、蕉林居士（白文方印）、河北棠村（朱文方印）。[朱正初，生卒年不详]朱正初（白文方印）、松斋（白文方印）、蝶庵书画（朱文方印）。

题跋者（钤印）：文征明,1470－1559（文征明印[白文方印]、衡山[朱文方印]）。陆师道，生于1517（陆子传[朱文方印]、嘉靖戊戌进士[朱文方印]）。

Tang Yin was born in the same year as Wen Zhengming (see cat. nos. 7, 8), and the two became friends despite the differences in their social background.[1] Tang came from a family engaged in business in Suzhou. His father, a restaurateur, was determined that his son receive an education that would allow him to climb the ladder of success through the examination system to a career in government. Tang Yin, although undisciplined, was a brilliant student and easily passed the first examination on the local level. He quickly came to the attention of the city's elite, and through Wen Lin (1445–1504), Wen Zhengming's father, he was introduced to prominent figures of the older generation, such as Shen Zhou (see cat. no. 5) and Wu Kuan (1435–1504), and became a close friend of the slightly older calligrapher Zhu Yunming (1461–1527; see cat. nos. 6 and 8). By 1486 he was already painting and probably married. His future seemed very bright. His world changed abruptly, however, between 1493 and 1494 when his father, his wife, his younger sister, and his mother all died in succession leaving him in charge of his younger brother. In depression, he slipped back into his undisciplined way of life, drinking heavily and carousing with friends. This libertine lifestyle deflected him from his studies and his goal of success in the examinations. His friend Zhu Yunming counseled him to either keep up his studies or give up his goal and burn his books. Tang Yin reapplied himself, and in 1498 he went to Nanjing to take the provincial level examination. He passed in first place and henceforth used a seal reading "Graduate with highest honors in Nanjing" (*Nanjing jieyuan*).

Flush with his success on the provincial level he went to Beijing to take the metropolitan examination, the third and final exam that would open the doors to high office. His reputation preceded him, and he was expected to place very high. Unfortunately he was caught in an examination scandal, accused of having learned of the questions before the examination, and jailed along with his traveling companion, a wealthy young man from Suzhou who confessed under torture to having attempted to learn the questions in advance. Tang's hopes of a career were ruined, and he returned to Suzhou in disgrace. Only friends like Zhu Yunming and Wen Zhengming stood by him. Ultimately, however, his lifestyle drew him apart from Wen Zhengming; the two were temperamental opposites.

Tang was forced to make a living, and he did so by selling his writings and his paintings. Having initially learned painting through Shen Zhou and the older generation of scholar painters in Suzhou, he now turned for instruction to Zhou Chen (d. ca. 1536), the leading professional painter in the city. From Zhou he learned the brush schemata and compositional modes that would make him a viable commercial painter. In particular he studied the Song dynasty painters Li Tang (ca. 1070s–ca. 1150s) and Liu Songnian (act. ca. 1175–after 1207). He appears to have done quite well, soon moving to a residence at Peach Blossom Bank in the section of the city where both Zhu Yunming and Wen Zhengming lived. Later, however, his way of life intruded on his business career and he fell into debt. In 1514 along with Wen Zhengming and others he was invited by Zhu Chenhao (d. 1521), the Prince of Ning, to serve on his staff in Nanchang, Jiangxi. Tang Yin accepted and moved to Nanchang, little suspecting that the prince was plotting rebellion. When the prince's intentions became clear, Tang Yin feigned madness in order to be dismissed. He returned to Suzhou where he resumed his career as a painter, painting until his death in 1524.

Tang Yin's many surviving works reveal the great range of a very versatile painter. Among his landscapes, some are polished, conservative works in the style of Li Tang that he had learned from Zhou Chen. For the most part these works are executed in ink and color on silk and appear to reflect his patrons' taste. Tang Yin is nevertheless able to infuse most of them with an energetic brushwork that defines him as a painter. Other works are executed in ink monochrome or ink and light color on paper, often in the more intimate format of the handscroll. A few of these works relate specifically to the world of his old friends and intellectual peers, but the majority of them, again, appear to have been commissions.

Tang's image of Master Wuyang (Wuyangzi) in his studio is such a work. It is a commemorative painting done for a man whose surname, Gu, is known, but who is otherwise unrecorded. It is a handscroll executed in ink only and is mounted together with a preface to Master Wuyang's poetry composed and written out by Wen Zhengming in the ninth lunar month of 1514. Tang Yin signed the painting but did not dedicate it. It is in Wen Zhengming's preface that Master Wuyang's surname is mentioned, and it is the dated preface that gives an approximate date for Tang's painting. Presumably both the painting and the preface were commissioned by Gu when he retired to Suzhou after a long career in government and assumed the byname Master Wuyang.

Tang Yin's painting opens with a view across water to a spit of land and distant hills. The opening section is executed in soft washes of pale ink. The focus quickly comes to the foreground where a pair of dynamically twisting trees with spiky branches devoid of foliage divides the composition. The trees serve as a pivot for the movement of the composition, one reaching into the opening section while the other reaches over the hut where Master Wuyang sits in contemplation. The hut and the figure are large, close to the picture plane, and are executed in thin lines of light ink in the *baimiao*, or plain drawing, technique associated with the late Northern Song scholar-painter Li Gonglin (ca. 1041–1106). This imparts a scholarly air to the painting, and undoubtedly flattered Master Wuyang, who becomes the true focus of the composition. The painting closes with a further passage of landscape: the studio is approached by a small bridge that reinforces the solitude of the thatched hut where Master Wuyang sits in self-cultivation. The dynamic movement of the tree branches suggests a wind blowing through the scene, yet Master Wuyang appears undisturbed.

The juxtaposition of the open view of the outside world and the closed world of the thatched hut follows a type of composition—the "thatched hut picture" (*caotang tu*)—that had its origins in the mid-fourteenth century, when many men of culture sought refuge in retirement and wished to celebrate their place of retreat. Tang Yin executed many paintings of this type, and his contribution to the genre was to enlarge the figure so that it is in effect a portrait. Wen Zhengming's *The Huxi Thatched Hut* (cat. no. 7) is a painting of this genre and, with its anonymous figures, contrasts markedly with Tang Yin's painting.[2]

Before its entry into the palace collection in the eighteenth century, the scroll was seen by Lu Shidao, who left a colophon, and owned by Li Zhaoheng (ca. 1592–ca. 1662), the son of the official and art critic Li Rihua (1565–1635). Later it was owned by Liang Qingbiao (1620–1691), the most important collector and connoisseur of the early Qing period. It was not catalogued for the palace collection until the second part (*xubian*) of the *Shiqu baoji*, which was completed in 1793.[3] There are eight seals of the Qianlong emperor, one of the Jiaqing emperor, and two of Puyi, the Xuantong emperor. Puyi and his younger brother Pujie were responsible for secretly taking this and other scrolls out of the Forbidden City before Puyi was expelled in November 1924. When Puyi became ruler of Manchukuo in 1932, the scrolls accompanied him to Changchun. With the collapse of Manchukuo in 1945, the scrolls were dispersed, and only after the founding of the People's Republic of China in 1949 were as many of the scrolls as could be located collected to form the foundation of the collection of the Liaoning Provincial Museum.

DAS

Notes

1. For Tang Yin's life and art, see in particular T. C. Lai, *T'ang Yin: Poet/Painter, 1470–1524* (Hong Kong: Kelly and Walsh, 1971); Jiang Zhaoshen, *Guanyu Tang Yin de yanjiu* [Research concerning Tang Yin] (Taipei: Guoli gugong bowuyuan, 1976); Chu-tsing Li, "T'ang Yin," in L. Carrington Goodrich, ed., *Dictionary of Ming Biography* (New York: Columbia University Press, 1976), pp. 1256–59; and Anne de Coursey Clapp, *The Painting of T'ang Yin* (Chicago: The University of Chicago Press, 1991).
2. Anne Clapp in chapters 3 and 4 of *The Painting of T'ang Yin* discusses Tang Yin's commemorative paintings in detail. See also Liu Jiuan, "Wumen huajia zhi biehaotu jianding julie" [Distinguishing examples of byname pictures by painters of the Wu School] in *Wumen huapai yanjiu* [Research on Wu School painting] (Beijing: Zijincheng chubanshe, 1993), pp. 35–46; and David Ake Sensabaugh, "Guests at Jade Mountain: Aspects of Patronage in Fourteenth-Century K'un-shan," in *Artists and Patrons: Some Social and Economic Aspects of Chinese Painting*, ed. Chu-tsing Li (Lawrence, KS: Kress Foundation Department of Art History, 1989), pp. 93–100.
3. *Shiqu baoji xubian* [Treasured boxes of the Stone Channel, continued] (1793), reprinted in *Midian zhulin Shiqu baoji hebian* [Pearl Forest of the Secret Hall and Treasured boxes of the Stone Channel, combined edition], 12 vols. (Shanghai: Shanghai shudian, 1988), vol. 6, pp. 2867–68.

唐寅与文征明同年（见目录图7与8），两人虽家世背景不同，但仍结为好友。唐出身苏州世商家庭，父亲開設酒店食肆，但执意其子刻苦学习并求仕进。唐寅生性放任，天资聪颖，年轻时即已轻易考取生员。不久后结識吳地大儒、文征明之父文林(1445－1504)。因此，被引介给沈周（见图录第5号）、吴宽（1435－1504)等文坛耆宿，并与年纪稍长的书法家祝允明（1461－1527年; 见图录第6与8号)成为至交。1486年时，唐寅已成婚并开始作画，未来显得无限美好，但不久即遭逢重大的家庭變故。1493与1494一年之间，唐寅的父親、妻子、妹妹与母親相繼去世，留下唐寅照顾幸存的弟弟。痛心之余，唐寅开始过着放荡不羁的生活，终日与狐朋狗党纵情饮酒。生活放纵的唐寅，似乎已把功名一事置之度外。后来由于祝允明的勸慰，告诫他如不发愤用功，不如焚书弃学。唐寅这才重新振作，在1498年赴南京赶考，参加乡试，得了第一名解元。唐寅「南京解元」的印章，如此得名。

意兴风发的唐寅，旋赴北京赶考，参加第三次、而且是最后一次登龙门的会试。盛名在外，人人看好唐寅拔得头筹。不幸，因考试洩题疑案受到牵连诬告，唐寅被控考前已预知试题。一同赴考的一苏州富家子弟，因不堪刑求，声称已事先得获试卷考题。唐寅因此被革士籍，一生仕途从此破灭。失意潦倒地返回苏州，其间，只有祝允明和文征明予以帮助。然而，因气质相左，唐寅与文征明最后还是分道扬镳。

为了生计，唐寅开始鬻画为生。之前师事沈周与其他苏州文人画派老将的唐寅，转向苏州当时最有名的职业画家周臣 (约卒于1536年) 请益。唐寅从周臣处学到了笔法线条与构图形势，使他能娴熟地以卖画为专业。但唐在周臣指导下，最重要的是学会并融會運用了李唐 (约1070年代－约1150年代) 与劉松年諸大家的山水风格。唐卖文鬻画似乎相当成功，旋将住处搬到苏州城北祝允明和文征明居住的桃花坞。不久，唐的生计不堪奢侈过度而债台高筑。1514年宁王朱宸濠 (卒于1521) 邀请唐与文征明一行人至江西南昌为其门客。唐寅即刻举家迁居南昌，不疑宁王造反之事。但在知悉宁王異謀之举后，唐寅佯狂装疯，蒙骗宁王，最后才获遣散。回到苏州之后，唐寅重操旧业，直到1524年去世。

唐寅存世之作，显示了他身为画家画艺领域之宽广与多样。以山水画来说，一部分的作品采用学自周臣工细、保守的李唐画风。大部分作品为绢本水墨设色，反映了买画顾客的喜好与品味。然而，这些画中仍可窥见唐堪称大家的苍劲活泼的笔法。还有其他纸本作品，有的以单色白描写就，有的以水墨淡彩敷色，装裱成供私人玩赏的图卷。其中有些属特定的，与有关至交友好、文坛同侪交游而画的作品。然大部分唐寅画作，仍为受人委託、买卖之作，

《悟阳子养性图》即是此类作品。此画此画是唐寅应一身世不祥的顾姓人士所邀而作。图画清一色单色白描，以悟阳子所做一诗为序，由文征明于1514年阴历九月题诗，一起装裱成图卷。画款署“唐寅”，但未加题献。悟阳子之姓则从文征明的诗序中得知，而其纪年的序文，亦为断定此画提供了大致的年代。想必图画本身与序文两者均由此顾姓先生所索求，在他为官多年后，退休定居于苏州，并取悟阳子为别号。

画卷之首，唐寅以松笔淡墨画一小山岩，岩后山陵连绵，杳无边际。焦点很快地接续到前景中两棵盘缠错结的枯树，枝枝如钉，将全图一分为二，为视觉构图的中轴点，一边联系着开卷部分，另一边则藉以将视线延伸到草堂里静坐的悟阳子。茅房与主角均特意在比例上放大，且接近前景，用北宋文人画家李公麟(约1041－1106)白描技法，以淡墨作游丝描。笔法高古，流露出文人画之无穷的典雅古韵，并加强了对悟阳子的刻画，使其自然地成为全画的真正主题。画尾以山石小径结束全景，茅庵附近并设一石桥，为悟阳子修性之所增加了一份孤寂感。图中树枝摇曳，显示山风正阵阵吹袭着茅屋，屋中悟阳子寂然静坐，丝毫不为所动。

图中自然世界的空旷与茅庵窄小的个人世界，交相并置，延续了“草堂画”的构图形式。此起源于十四世纪中期的文化特征，以描绘文人期待归隐山林，并誌记退隐居处的时代风格。唐寅画过许多这类的作品，在此类型的画中，唐寅常刻意加大了画中人物的比例，使其主角人物带有肖像画的特质。文征明《浒溪草堂图》（见图录第7号）只描绘不知名的高士于其中，与唐寅的此类风格比较，两者有着强烈的对比。

是卷入清内府前，曾为陆师道过目题跋，并先后经高官之子李肇亨(约1592－约1662)、评论家李日华 (1565－1635) 与清代早期最重要的鉴藏家梁清标 (1620－1691) 收藏，《石渠宝笈》原先未收录其中，直到1793年《石渠宝笈续编》完成时才见著录。卷中有乾隆钤八方御印、嘉庆一方、宣统帝溥仪两方鉴藏印。溥仪在1924年被逐出紫禁城前，早已与弟弟溥杰将此画与其他图卷偷运出宫。1932年溥仪就位满洲国皇帝时，此画被他一起带到长春。1945年满洲国覆亡，诸多图卷一尽散失，不知所终。直到1949年中国人民共和国成立后，此图与其他作品才在中国政府极力搜寻下，重新面世，成为辽宁省博物馆的建馆收藏之一。

江文苇（LYC译）

注解：

1. 有关唐寅的生平与艺术，详见T. C. Lai，《诗人画家唐寅，1470－1524》(香港：Kelly and Walsh, 1971)；江兆申，《关于唐寅的研究》(台北：国立故宫博物院，1976)；李铸晋（Chu-tsing Li），〈唐寅〉，收于《明代人物传记辞典》，L. Carrington Goodrich 编(纽约：哥伦比亚大学出版，1976)，第1256－59页；Anne de Coursey Clapp，《唐寅之画》(芝加哥：芝加哥大学出版，1991)。
2. Anne De Coursey Clapp，《唐寅之画》(芝加哥：芝加哥大学出版，1991)，第3－4章，详细讨论了唐寅的纪念性画作。另见劉九庵，<吴门畫家之別號图鉴别举列>，《吳門畫派研究》（北京：紫禁城出版社，1993），第35－46页；江文苇（David Ake Sensabaugh)，〈玉山之客：十四世纪昆山人的艺术赞助〉，收于《艺术家与赞助者：一些关于中国绘画的社会经济现象》，李铸晋（Chu-tsing Li）编（劳伦斯：堪萨斯大学艺术史系，1989年)，第93－100页。
3. 《石渠宝笈续编》(1793)，重刊于《秘殿珠林石渠宝笈合编》，12册(上海：上海书店，1988)，第6册，第2867－68页。

11
明 仇英 清明上河图
手卷, 绢本水墨设色
Qiu Ying (ca. 1405–1552)
Qingming Festival on the River
Handscroll; ink and color on silk
30.5 x 987.5 cm

ARTIST'S SEALS: Qiu Ying Shifu (square/intaglio), Shizhou (double-gourd/relief)

IMPERIAL SEALS: [Qianlong, r. 1736–95] Shiqu baoji (rectangular/relief), Qianlong yulan zhibao (oval/relief), Qianlong jianshang (round/intaglio), Shiqu dingjian (round/relief), Baoji chongbian (square/intaglio), Sanxitang jingjianxi (rectangular/relief), Qianqinggong jiancangbao (rectangular/relief), Yizisun (square/intaglio); [Jiaqing, r. 1796–1820] Jiaqing yulan zhibao (square/relief); [Xuantong (Puyi), r. 1909–11] Xuantong yulan zhibao (oval/relief)

OTHER SEALS: [Xiang Yuanbian, 1525–1590] Zuili Xiangshi shijia baowan (rectangular/relief); [Museum of the Northeast] Dongbei bowuguan zhencang zhiyin (square/relief)

画家印鉴: 仇英实父（白文方印），十洲（朱文葫芦印）

皇家印鉴: [清乾隆皇帝弘历，在位1736－1795]石渠宝笈（朱文长方印）、乾隆御览之宝（朱文椭圆印）、乾隆鉴赏（白文圆印）、石渠定鉴（朱文圆印）、宝笈重编（白文方印）、三希堂精鉴玺（朱文长方印）、乾清宫鉴藏宝(朱文长方印)、宜子孙（白文方印）。[清嘉庆皇帝颙琰，在位1796－1820]嘉庆御览之宝（朱文方印）。[清宣统皇帝溥仪，在位1909－1911]宣统御览之宝（朱文椭圆印）。

其他印鉴: [项元汴，1525－1590] 檇李项氏士家宝玩（朱文长方印）。[东北博物馆] 东北博物馆珍藏之印（朱文方印）。

Song dynasty artist Zhang Zeduan's long scroll *Qingming Festival on the River* depicts in vivid detail scenes of festivity in the then capital Bianliang (present-day Kaifeng, Henan Province) on the day of the Qingming Festival. His painting became a classic model for urban genre scenes in later Chinese paintings. Some four hundred years later, Qiu Ying, an outstanding Ming dynasty artist, did the same thing by assembling various scenes of the entire city of Suzhou into a panoramic whole, later also referred to by many as his "Qingming Festival on the River."

A famous city in the Jiangnan region, Suzhou of the sixteenth century was enjoying great economic prosperity through its network of canals and roads for easy transportation and commerce and the flourishing of its sericulture and silk weaving industry. The literati who gathered there actively mingled among the upper classes. Their calligraphy works and paintings, having a higher level of literacy and elegance, were much favored and eagerly collected by rich merchants and officials. Qiu Ying, who lived during the mid-sixteenth century, was one of the best painters among them, especially renowned for his paintings of people and his brilliant blue-and-green landscapes. This *Qingming Festival on the River* scroll reflects Qiu Ying's multiple talents and his overall mastery of realistic rendering skills.

Starting from the suburbs of the city, the scenes of spring in the Jiangnan region are unveiled section by section. First, a stretch of misty willows is seen amidst rice paddies, occasionally dotted with village dwellings and herdboys putting buffalo to pasture. Enjoying a spring ramble are also gallants from rich families riding horses and women being carried in sedan chairs. Upstream along the canal, the river gradually widens and more boats are seen, some anchored and some with sails set. There are also more farm houses, temples, and other buildings on the banks. A crowd gathers in front of a stage to watch a play while others pass by heading towards the city itself. Among the travelers are farmers, merchants, artisans, scholars, herbalists, and government officials.

The painting reaches its first climax right at the top of an arched bridge where a throng of people create a bustling scene. Once over the bridge, sections of the city's encircling wall are seen at intervals, leading the viewer into the busy downtown area. Here a second climax in the painting occurs, marked by row upon row of buildings spread along a web-like framework of intersecting streets. There are markets, courthouses, luxurious residences, ordinary homes, bars, and shops. The sense of prosperity of this metropolis is clearly felt in the vivid and detailed rendering of the huge variety of businesses it has to offer: rice stores, oil stuffs, woodworking workshops, jewelry shops, travel goods stores, drugstores, artwork mounting studios, and fortune tellers, all set among an overwhelming number of commercial signs on boards and banners.

Lavishly dressed performing girls in brothels and full-house entertainment clubs indicate a booming entertainment industry. In the finishing sections of the scroll, parts of the city wall are seen again, hidden among other elements, separating the inner city from the surrounding areas where scenes of bustling city life gradually give way to natural settings that cause one to feel peaceful and refreshed. Then fancy dwellings appear along the horizon across stretches of water, indicating a celestial domain, a place of hope and longing for those folks who are still caught in this dusty world.

After Qiu Ying made his *Qingming Festival on the River*, several copies similar to this one came into wide circulation, which had a strong impact and established a popular format for this type of painting. The imperial seals on the scroll indicate that this work was added to the collection of the Qing imperial court during the reign of Qianlong (1736–95). Coincidentally, this scroll was brought to Manchuria by the last emperor, Puyi, along with the original Song dynasty *Qingming Festival on the River* by Zhang Zeduan. Both works were acquired by the Liaoning Provincial Museum (known as Museum of the Northeast at the time) in the early 1950s. Later, Zhang Zeduan's *Qingming Festival on the River* was moved to the Palace Museum, Beijing, while this scroll by Qiu Ying remained at the Liaoning Provincial Museum.

HWL (trans. DHWS)

宋代画师张择端的《清明上河图》卷，生动地描绘了当时的首都汴梁（今河南省开封市）城乡的清明节日盛况，成为中国画中反映城市风俗的一个经典样式。约在四百多年后，明代的杰出画家仇英，采用相似的形式将苏州全景式地画了下来，后人也将其命名为《清明上河图》。

16世纪的苏州，是经济富裕的江南名城，这里河网密布，水陆交通开阔，尤以桑蚕养殖和手工丝织业的发达而带动了商业的繁荣。聚集于此的文人们活跃在上流社会，他们创作的绘画书法作品，具有高雅的文学趣味，并受到富商或官宦们的喜爱和收藏。生活在16世纪中期的仇英，便是其中最为著名的画家之一，尤以人物画和青绿山水画而著称。

此《清明上河图》卷，反映了仇英多方面的绘画才能和驾驭大局的写实功力。画卷从都市的郊野开始，江南的春月，一派烟峦绿柳，田野中偶见村舍放牛的牧童，也有富家公子骑着骏马、女子坐着轿子在踏青。沿河上行，河面渐宽，或行或止的船只，和位于两岸边的田舍、庙宇等房屋逐渐多了起来，围在戏台旁看戏的人群，匆忙从各方奔向城里的人们，其中有农民、商人、工匠、书生、郎中、官吏各色人等。人群在一座拱形的石桥上形成了繁闹的场面，将画卷推向了第一个高潮。过了拱桥，隐约出现的城墙将观者引入了繁华的市区，将画卷推向了又一个高潮，鳞次栉比的建筑，连绵交叉的街市，衙门、豪宅、民居、酒肆、店铺，一派都市的繁荣，汇集了市井各行各业的百态，当时的米行、油坊、木器行、金银首饰店、车马店、药铺、装裱店、算命的卦摊等一应俱全，牌幌如云。在"青楼"、"歌榭"中弹唱的盛装女子以及熙熙攘攘的人群，表现了当时娱乐业的繁荣。画卷最终，又是隐约的城墙，将城分为内外区，都市繁华渐渐淡化在城外令人心旷神怡的自然景象中。在水天之际出现的琼楼玉宇，是尘世中的人们所向往的天宫仙界。

在仇英的这卷作品以后，民间又出现了多种类似的仿制本，逐渐成为世传《清明上河图》的流行式样，影响广泛。卷中的御藏印表明，此卷在乾隆年间（1736－1795年）进入清宫内府收藏。巧合的是，它与宋代张择端原作的《清明上河图》，曾一同被末代皇帝溥仪带到了东北，并于上世纪50年代初，一同入藏辽宁省博物馆（时称东北博物馆）。随后，张泽端作的《清明上河图》调藏到北京故宫博物院，这卷仇英作《清明上河图》，仍藏在辽宁省博物馆。

黄伟利

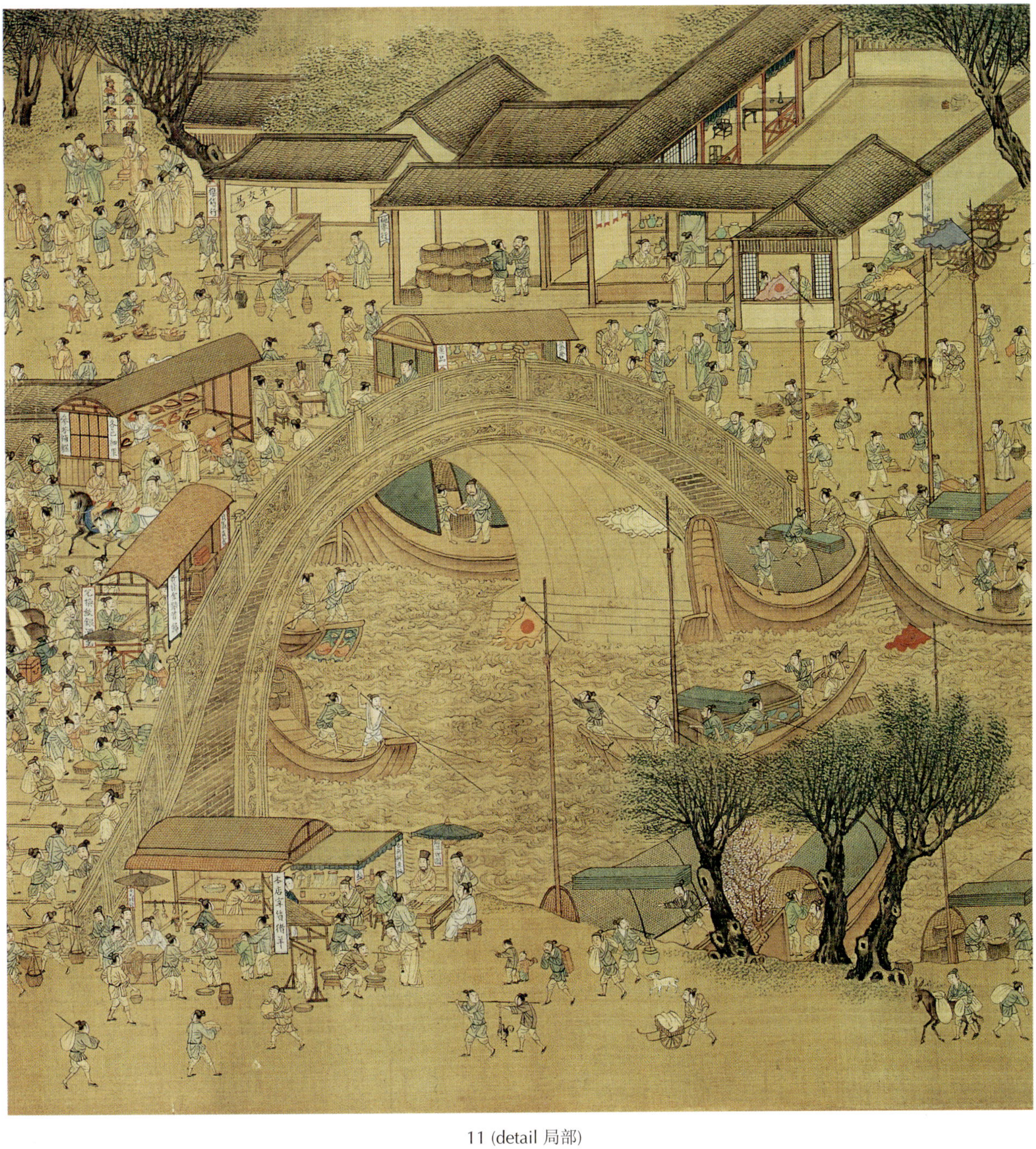

11 (detail 局部)

11

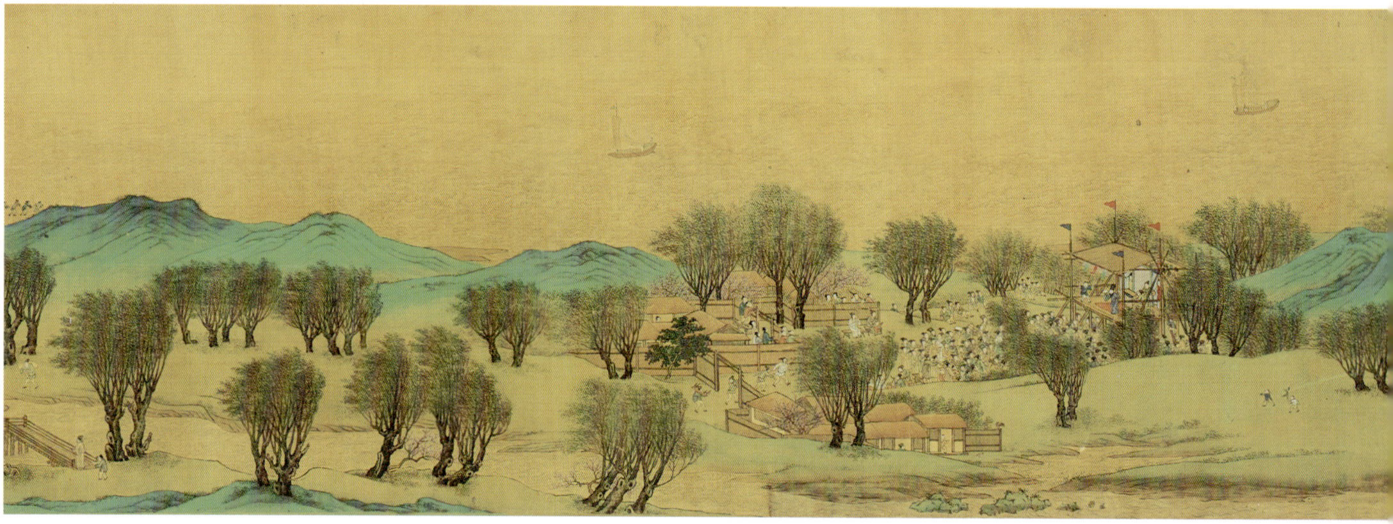

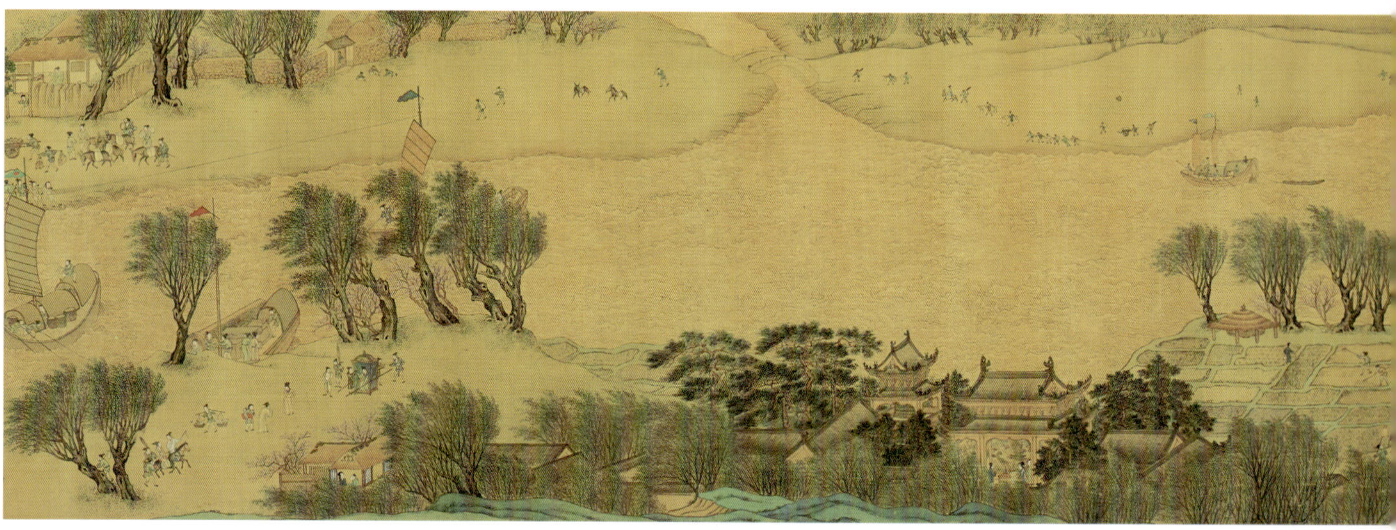

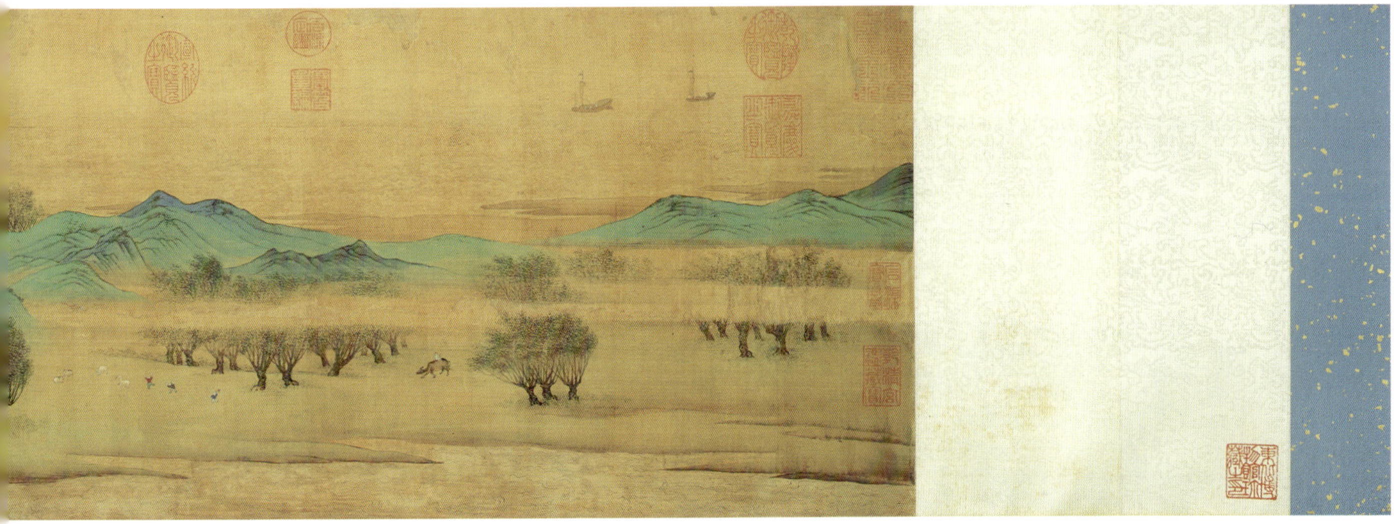

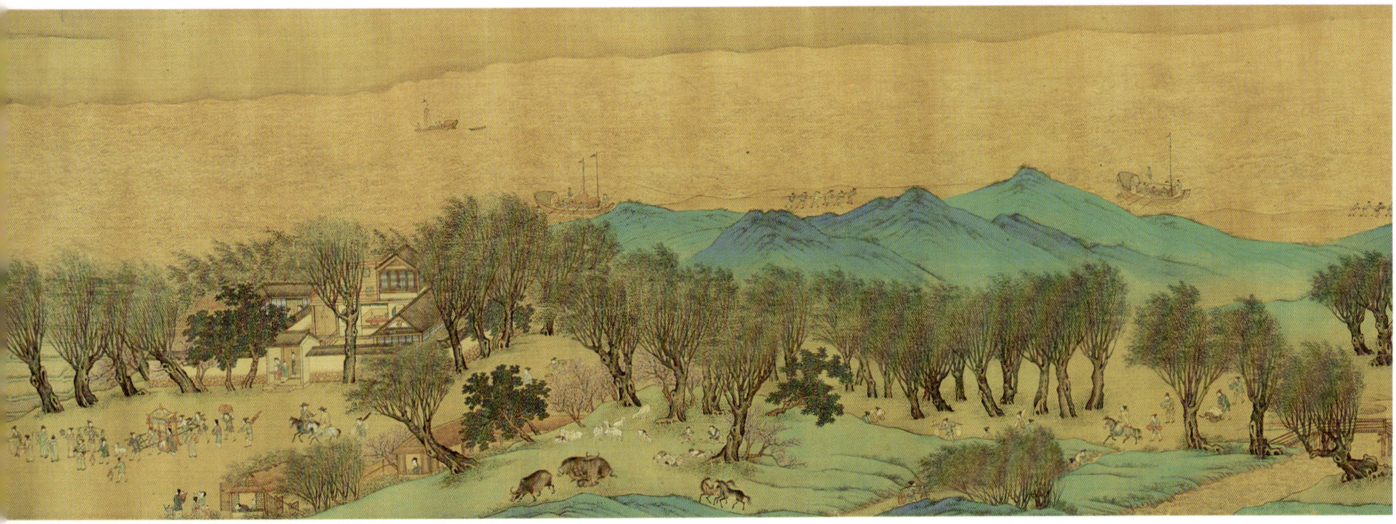

11

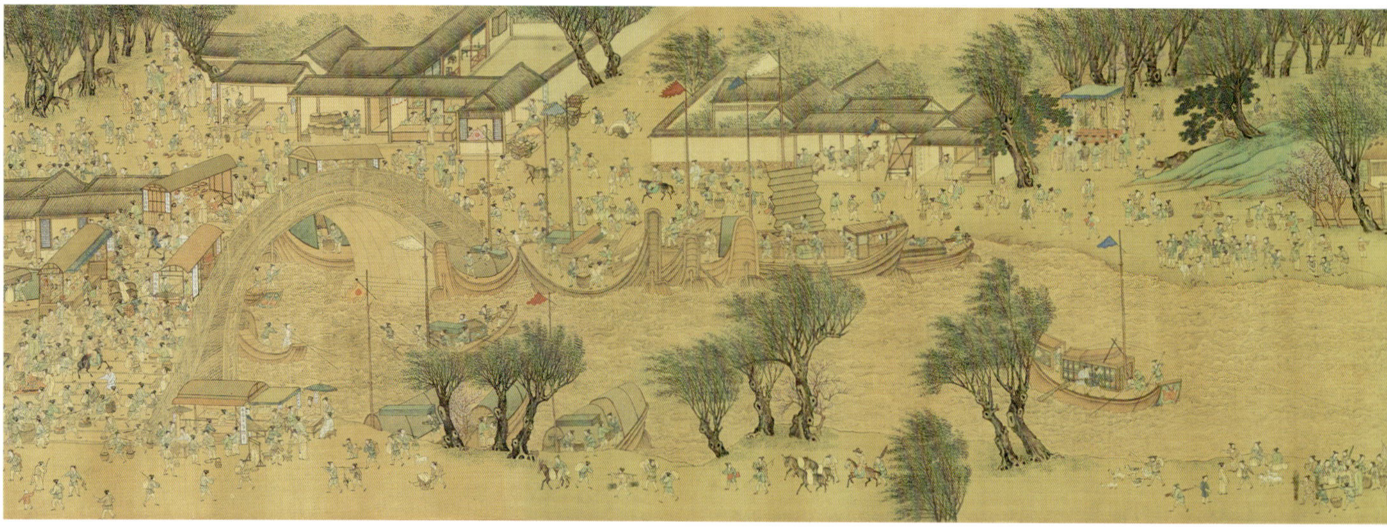

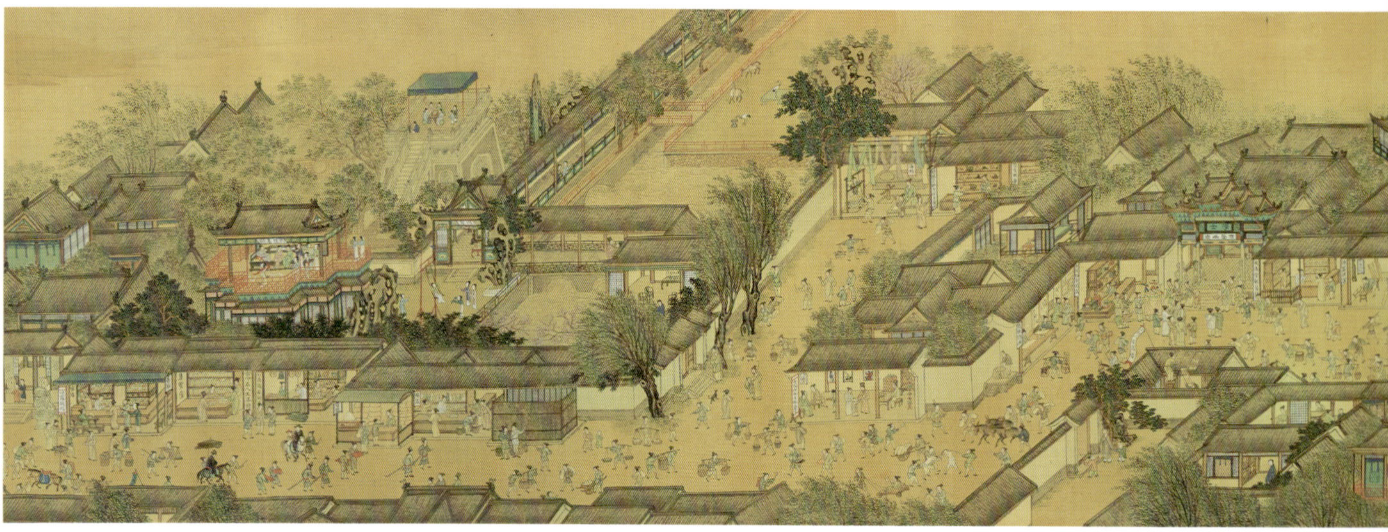

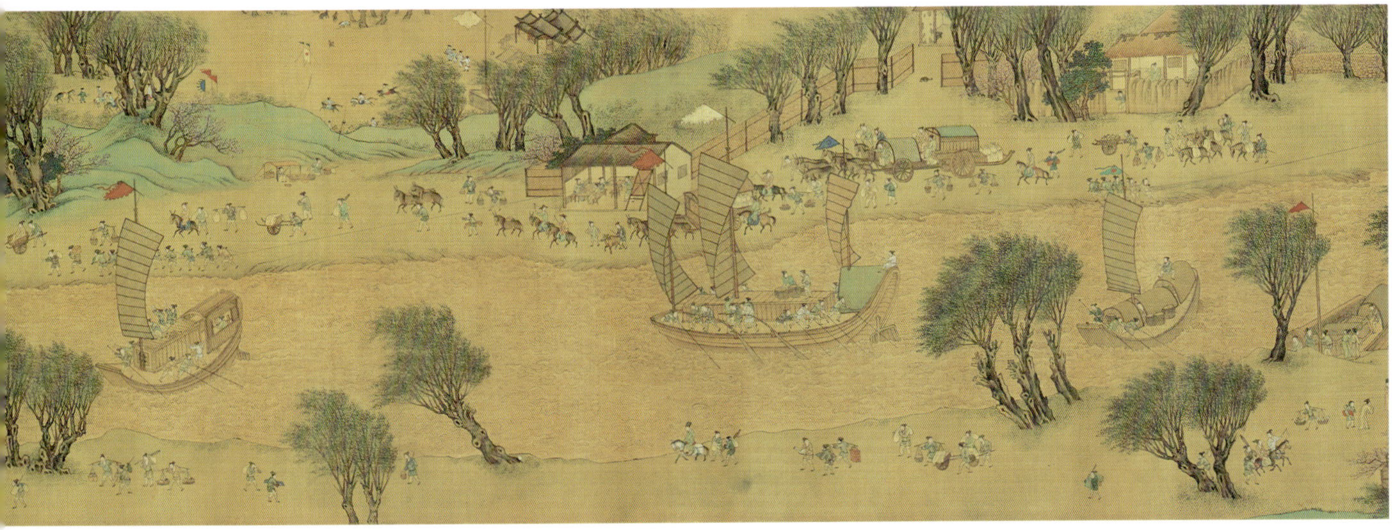

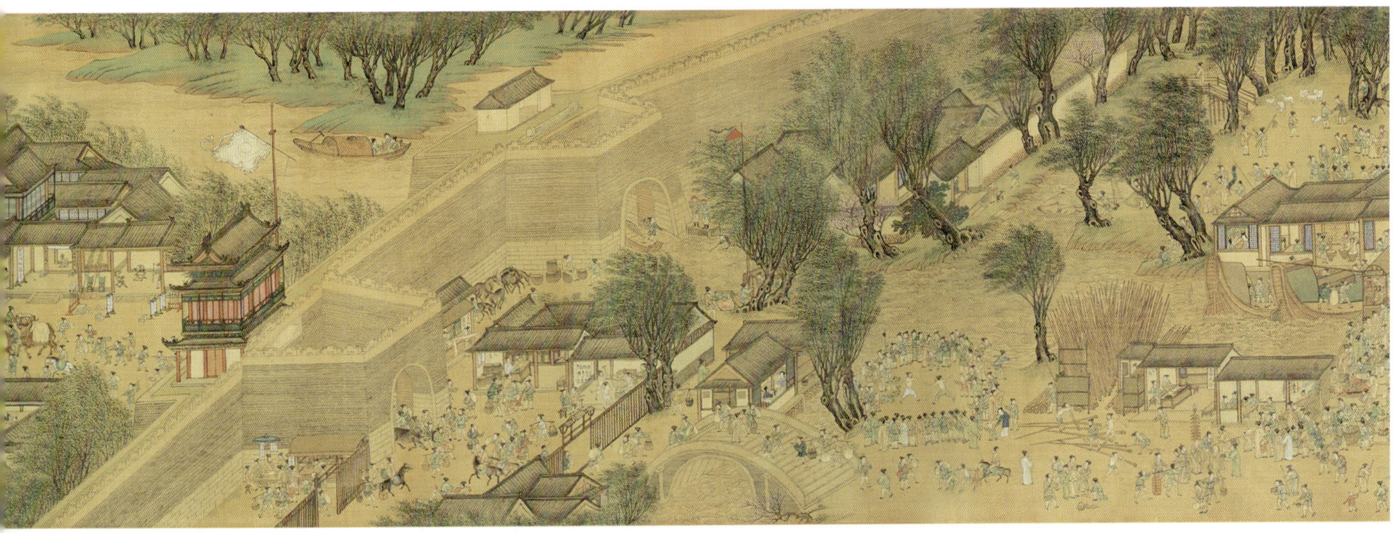

11

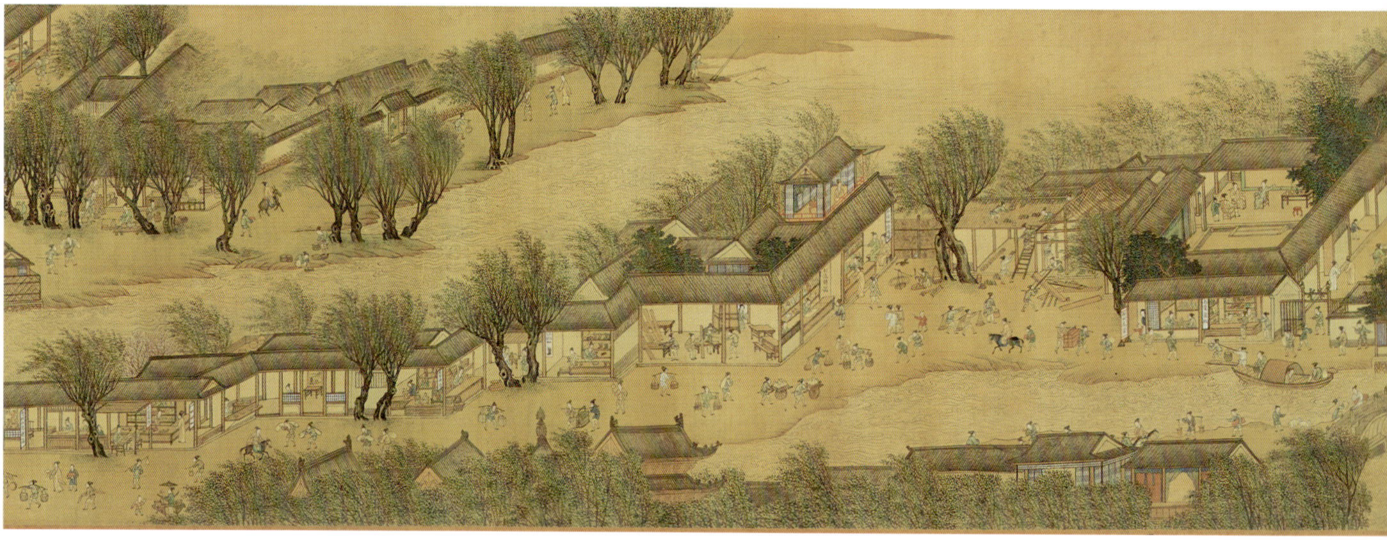

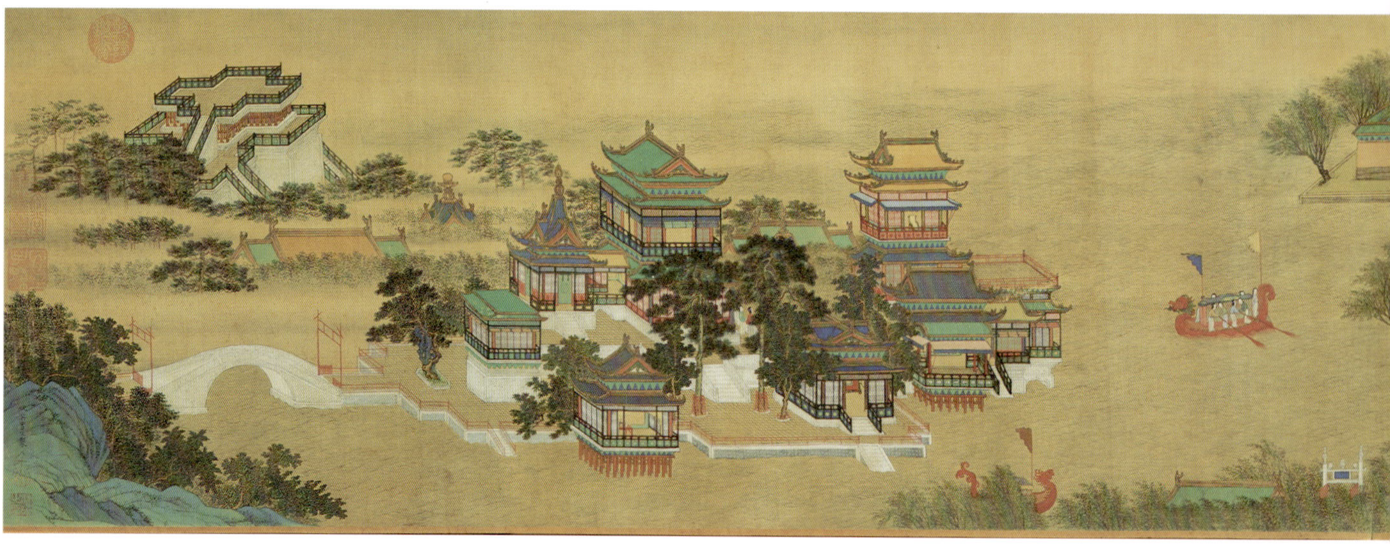

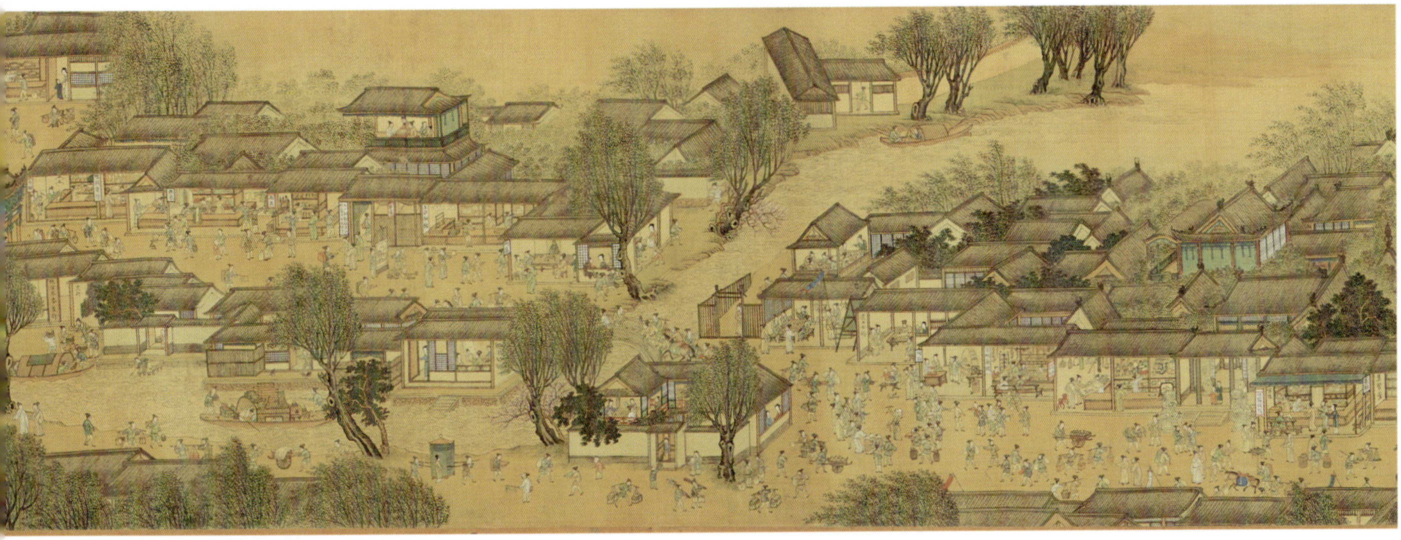

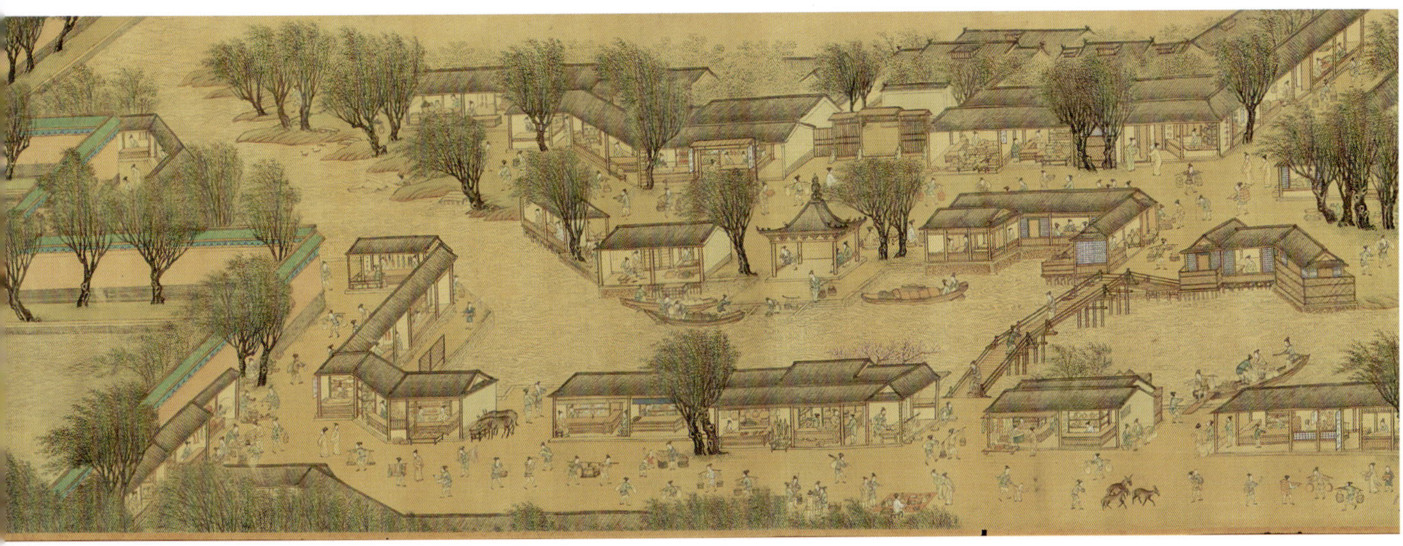

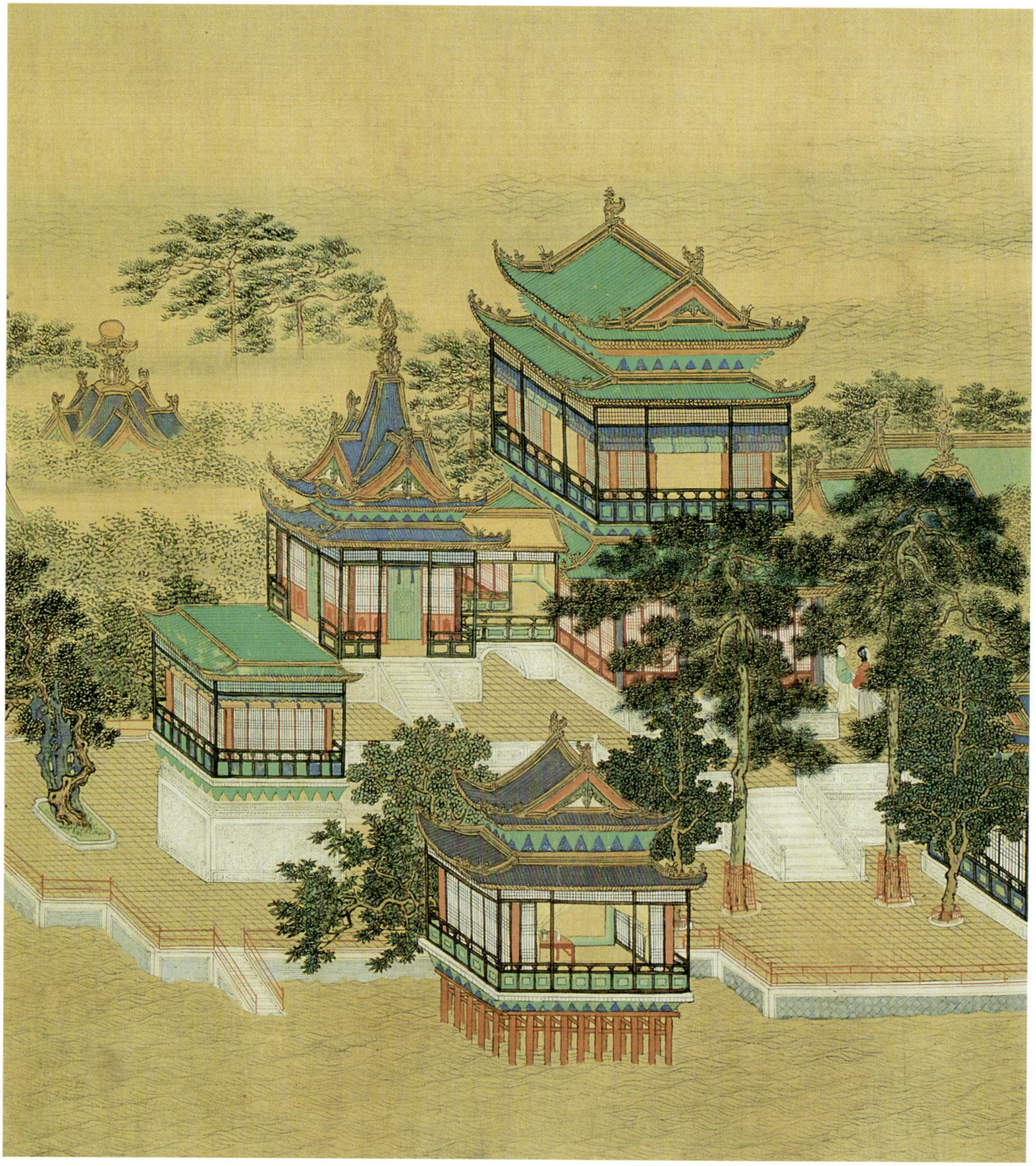

11 (detail 局部)

12
明　　文征明 桃源问津图
手卷，纸本水墨设色
Wen Zhengming (1470–1559)
***Peach Blossom Spring*, 1554**
Handscroll; ink and color on paper
32 x 578.3 cm

ARTIST'S SEAL: Zheng-Ming (linked seal; double square/relief)

IMPERIAL SEALS: [Qianlong, r. 1736–95] Shiqu baoji (rectangular/relief), Qianlong yulan zhibao (oval/relief), Shiqu dingjian (round/relief), Baoji chongbian (square/intaglio), Yangxindian jiancangbao (rectangular/relief), Qianlong jianshang (round/intaglio), Sanxitang jingjianxi (rectangular/relief), Yizisun (square/intaglio); [Jiaqing, r. 1796–1820] Jiaqing yulan zhibao (oval/relief); [Xuantong (Puyi), r. 1909–11] Xuantong jianshang (square/relief), Wuyizhai jingjianxi (rectangular/relief)

OTHER SEALS: [Wang Zuhuai, Ming dynasty] Wang Zuhuai yin (square/intaglio); [Gao Shiqi, 1645–1703] Gaoshi jiangcun caotang zhencang tushu zhiyin (rectangular/intaglio), Banxuan songyue (square/intaglio), Yangeng caotang danren Gaoshi Shiqi jianding shuhua zhiyin (square/relief), Zhuchuang (rectangular/relief), Jingjixuan tushu yin (square/intaglio), Huayuan caotang (rectangular/intaglio), Jujian (rectangular/relief), Qinglianzi (rectangular/intaglio), Lianpu qingshang (square/relief); [Gao Dai, *jinshi* in 1550] Kuang an (square/relief), Chen Dai siyin (rectangular/intaglio; repeated once); [Gao Han] Gao Wenkegong zengsun Han zhencang (square/intaglio); [Museum of the Northeast] Dongbei bowuguan zhencang zhiyin (square/relief); [undecipherable]

COLOPHON WRITERS (SEALS): Gao Shiqi (Shiqi [square/relief], Gao Danren [square/intaglio], Shi-Qi [linked seal; double square/relief]), Gao Shiqi tushu ji (rectangular/relief); Zhang Zhao, 1691–1745 (Zhang Zhao zhiyin [square/intaglio], Jingnan [square/relief]

JADE CLIP INSCRIPTION: Qianlong yushang. Wen Zhengming taoyuan wenjin tu

画家印鉴："征""明"朱文连珠方印

皇室印鉴：[清乾隆皇帝弘历，在位1736－1795]石渠宝笈（朱文长方印）、乾隆御览之宝（朱文椭圆印）、石渠定鉴（朱文圆印）、宝笈重编（白文方印）、养心殿鉴藏宝（朱文长方印）、乾隆鉴赏（白文圆印）、三希堂精鉴玺（朱文长方印）、宜子孙（白文方印）。[清嘉庆皇帝颙琰，在位1736－1795]嘉庆御览之宝（朱文椭圆印）。[清宣统皇帝溥仪，在位1909－1911]宣统御览之宝（朱文椭圆印）、宣统鉴赏（朱文方印）、无逸斋精鉴玺（朱文长方印）。

其他印鉴：[王祖槐，明代人]王祖槐印（白文方印）。[高士奇，1645－1703] 高氏江村草堂珍藏书画之印（白文长方印）、半轩松月（白文方印）、巖耕草堂澹人高氏士奇鉴定书画之印（朱文方印）、竹窗（朱文长方印）、静寄轩图书印(白文方印)、华原草堂(白文长方印)、菊涧(朱文长方印)、青莲子(白文长方印)、莲浦清赏(朱文方印)。[高岱,1550年进士]旷庵（朱文方印）、臣岱私印（白文长方印）。[高涵，生卒年不详]高文恪公曾孙涵珍藏（白文方印）。[东北博物馆]东北博物馆珍藏之印（朱文方印）。另有一印不可辨识。

题跋者（钤印）：高士奇（士奇[朱文方印]，高澹人[白文方印]、士、奇[朱文连珠方印]、高士奇图书记[朱文长方印]）。张照，1691－1745（张照之印[白文方印]、泾南[朱文方印]）。

玉别子镌：乾隆御赏。文征明桃源问津图

Wen Zhengming was one of the Four Masters of the Wu School during the Ming dynasty. His original given name was Bi and his courtesy name, Zhengzhong. He adopted Hengshan Jushi as a sobriquet and was given the private posthumous title of Master Zhenxian. He was a native of Changzhou (present-day Suzhou, Jiangsu). A court painter and scholar-in-waiting at the Hanlin Academy, he took Zhao Mengfu as his personal model. Wen Zhengming was accomplished in poetry, calligraphy, and painting. His calligraphy is based on the style of the Jin and Tang dynasty masters: his small standard script is reminiscent of Wang Xizhi's (ca. 303–ca. 361) *Eulogy to Yue Yi*, and in his running-cursive script, he achieved the brushwork of the monk Zhiyong (7th century). Also, his large characters resemble those of Huang Tingjian (1045–1105), and his seal script is modeled on that of Zhong You (151–230). In landscape he took Shen Zhou as his master and became more expressive. He had a self-assured brush and frequently achieved excellence through detailed rendering. Talented, compassionate, and brilliant, he maintained an air of detachment from worldly pursuits, a virtue highly regarded by the literati. He had an unyielding character towards the wealthy and powerful.[1]

The subject for this painting comes from the story "Peach Blossom Spring," a prose work by the Six Dynasties literatus and recluse Tao Yuanming, who lived in a period of raging wars and frequent changes of dynasties (see Appendix B). He describes an ideal pastoral landscape isolated from the outside world. Peach trees are in bloom everywhere; there is neither warfare nor politics. He had created a harmonious and tranquil Chinese-style utopia. Ever since this story, the fairyland of Peach Blossom Spring has become a longed-for paradise and the subject of many works of painting and calligraphy. At the end section of this scroll is an inscription left by the great Qing dynasty collector Gao Shiqi (1645–1703), who mentions having once seen long scrolls with illustrations of "Peach Blossom Spring" by the Song dynasty artists Zhao Qianli (Zhao Boju, act. 1127–62) and Zhao Xiyuan (1308–1385) in the collection of famous collector Liang Qingbiao (1620–1691). Among Wen Zhengming's contemporaries, there were others who also used this title for their paintings, such as the *Peach Blossom Spring*, by an anonymous artist, in the collection of The Art Institute of Chicago.[2]

The scenes in Wen Zhengming's painting unfold in basically the same sequence as described in Tao Yuanming's story of a fisherman's journey upstream: It depicts a gurgling stream lined with blossoming peach trees deep within the mountains. The fisherman passes through a cliffside cave and suddenly sees a brilliant vista of neatly ordered fields, neighborhoods with thatched dwellings and farmers happily tilling the earth. Here, the people seem to be carefree and content in the beautiful landscape. But when they hear that a traveler has arrived, they all come over to greet him. The fisherman is told that they originally took refuge here deep in the mountains to escape the upheavals of the Qin dynasty. Since then, they have been without knowledge of what has taken place in the outside world, enjoying the natural bonds of human relationships and an unaffected happiness.

The varied, imposing, and grand scenery is enhanced with a refined and careful application of colors. Great attention is paid to details through superb brushwork and ink quality. The rocks are textured with hemp-fiber strokes using dry brush and peppered with dark ink dots to represent moss. Tree trunks are outlined with hooked strokes and filled in with color washes while the leaves are rendered in both outline and dotting techniques, resulting in rich variety and liveliness. The inscription at the end of the painting reads, "In the *jiayin* year of the Jiajing reign, the sixteenth day of the second month [March 19, 1554], by Zhengming at age eighty-five." A pair of linked seals under the artist's signature reads "Zheng" and "Ming." According to Gao Shiqi, who had seen paintings of the same subject by Song dynasty artists, this painting by Wen is a close copy of the Peach Blossom Spring paintings by the two Zhaos of the Song dynasty with a few alterations. Although vigorous in terms of brushwork and well organized in composition, this carefully executed work by Wen does show a certain degree of rigidity perhaps because he was confined by a pre-existing model from which he was painstakingly seeking all the minute details to include.

A close inspection of the seals on the scroll reveals the succession of collectors who owned the painting. It was in the collection of Wang Zuhuai during the Ming dynasty. By the end of Ming period and early Qing dynasty, it was lost into the civilian population. It was then purchased on the street in Chang'an by the famous Qing dynasty collector Gao Shiqi, who not only left several seals on the scroll and but also added his own calligraphy in the form of the entire text of the essay "Peach Blossom Spring" and three subsequent inscriptions. This scroll was viewed by Zhang Zhao (1691–1745) in the fifth month of the *guisi* year (1713) in the Kangxi reign. It was in the collection of the Gao family for four generations until the time of Gao Han, whose one seal reads, "Gao Wenke's [Gao Shiqi] great grandson Han's treasured collection." After its acquisition by the Qing court around the time of the Qianlong emperor, the full array of

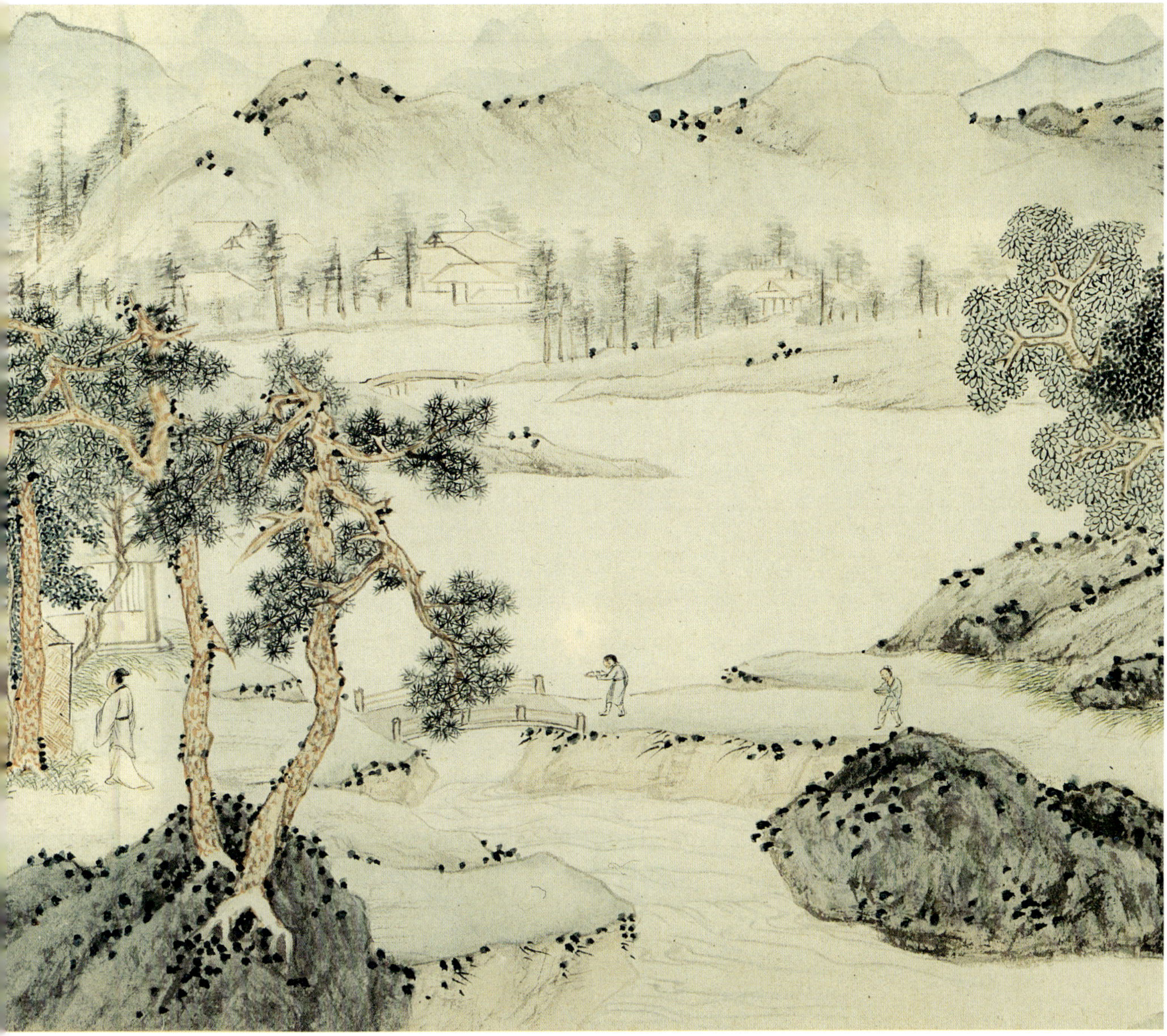

12 (section 局部)

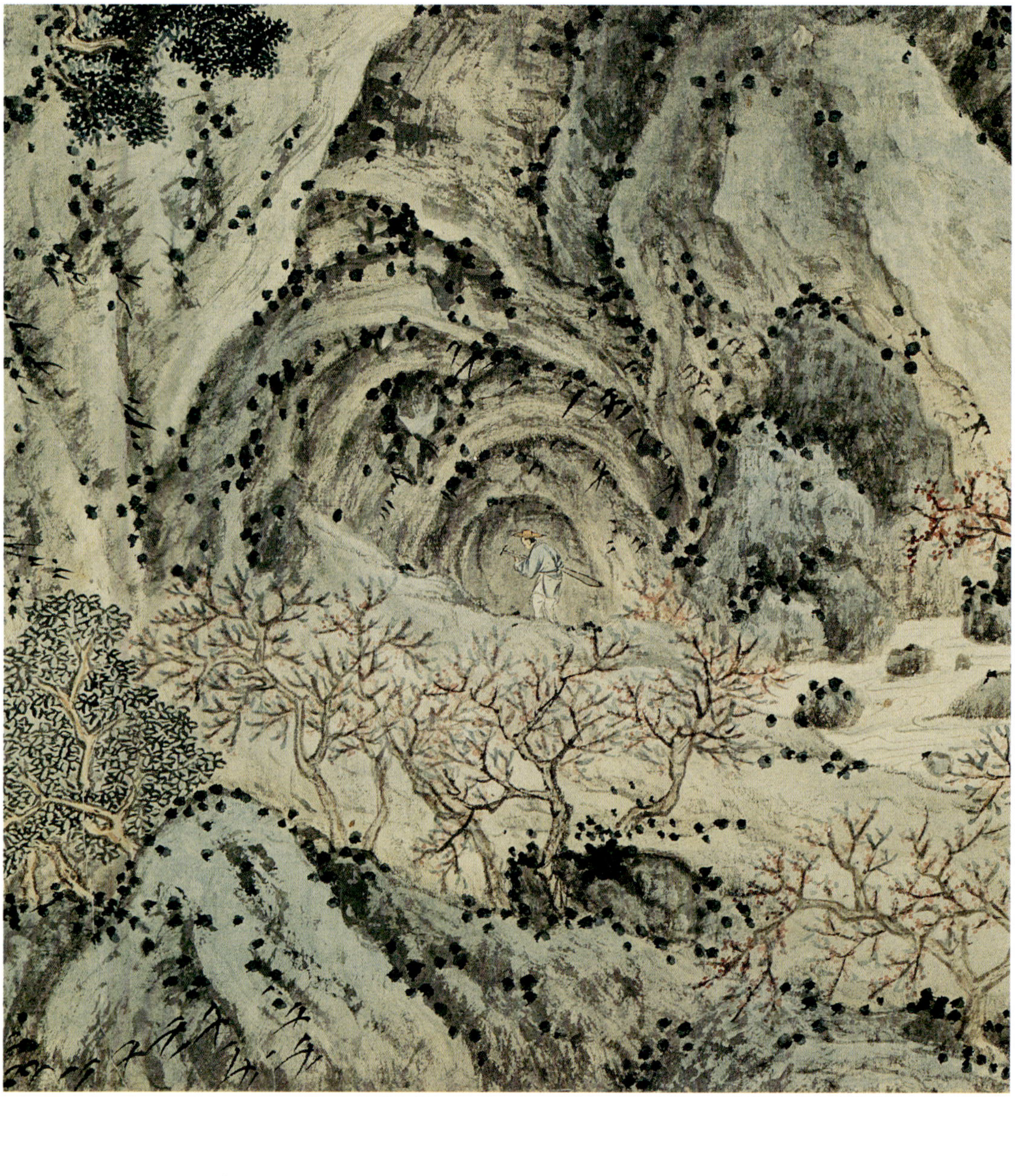

12 (detail 局部)

Qianlong's eight collection seals were added and then those of Jiaqing and Xuantong. The scroll left the Forbidden City after it was awarded to Pujie by the last emperor, Puyi, and was carried to Linjiang, Jilin Province, when Puyi fled there. It was recovered by the People's Liberation Army and then submitted to the People's Bank of the Northeast, which in turn handed it over to the Northeastern Committee for the Management of Cultural Relics. The scroll was later acquired by the Museum of the Northeast, which is currently the Liaoning Provincial Museum.[3]

WWHC (trans. DHWS)

Notes

1. Yu Jianhua, ed., *Zhongguo meishujia renming cidian* [Dictionary of Chinese artists] (Shanghai: Shanghai renmin meishu chubanshe, 1985), p. 39.
2. Jonathan Chaves, *The Chinese Painter as Poet* (New York: China Institute Gallery, 2000), pp. 60–61.
3. Luo Chunzheng in Yang Renkai, ed., *Liaoningsheng bowuguan cang shuhua zhulu: Huihua juan* [Writings on paintings and calligraphic works in the collection of the Liaoning Provincial Museum: Volume on art] (Shenyang: Liaoning meishu chubanse, 1999), p. 328–30.

文征明，明代吴门四家之一。名璧，字征仲，号衡山居士，私谥贞献先生，长洲（今江苏苏州人）。曾为宫廷画师翰林待诏，以元代赵孟頫为榜样，诗文书画均有造诣，书法法晋唐，小楷得乐毅（公元前3世纪）之韵，行草得智永（公元6世纪）笔法，大书仿黄庭坚（1045－1105），隶书仿钟繇而独步一世。山水师沈周而多添神采，得意之笔，往往以工致胜。才情旷达，气韵清高，深得文人之本，不为富贵权势者所折（注1）。

桃花源的画题，源于六朝时的文人隐士陶渊明（365－427）的散文《桃花源记》，当时朝代嬗递，战乱不已，陶渊明描述了一个理想的与世隔绝的山水田园，桃花盛开之处，没有战争，没有政治，创造了一个和谐宁静的，中国式的古典乌托邦世界。自此，桃源仙境历来成为人们向往的乐园，成为许多书画作品的题材，此画拖尾有清代大收藏家高士奇（1645－1703）的题跋，其中讲到宋代赵千里（赵伯驹，活跃于1127－1162）、赵希远（1308－1385），俱有桃源问津图长卷，曾为著名收藏家梁清标（1620－1691）收藏，高亦曾亲眼见过。即使在文征明的时代，也有以此题为画者，如有一位无名者的桃源图卷，现为美国芝加哥艺术学院所收藏(注2)。

此画的构图，循序按照陶渊明《桃花源记》的大意，描绘了群山怀抱中，溪流潺潺，桃花夹岸，穿越山崖岩洞，豁然开朗，田园井然，茅舍相邻，农人乐耕，人们悠然自得徜徉于山水之间，闻有客至，则纷纷前来问候，原来是自秦代避乱，逃居山中的人们，全然不知外面世界的变化，而共享天伦自然之乐。此图景物繁多，气势宏伟，设色典雅工整。笔墨工细，山作披麻皴，用枯笔干墨，浓墨点苔。树干钩染兼施，叶以夹点并用，极富生机，画末落款“嘉靖甲寅[三十三年]1554年）二月既望，征明时年八十有五”，下钤“征”、“明”二朱文连珠方印。此画据看过宋代赵氏画卷的高士奇说，文氏此卷是宗法宋代二赵的桃源问津图，而略变其法，虽然笔法苍劲，构图严谨，是文氏的精心制作，但也许既有前人的范本所限，又追求面面俱到，刻意求工，而有失板滞。

本卷的装裱包首为几何纹锦，隔水皆为黄色云凤纹绫，引首、画心、拖尾皆为纸本。从鉴藏印上看，明代曾为王祖槐收藏，明末清初流落民间，为清代著名书画收藏家高士奇在长安街头购得，画上钤有多方高氏鉴藏印，并有高氏抄录桃花源记原文和三次题记及题诗，康熙癸巳年五月（1713）并曾为张照（1691－1745）所观。此画在高家传藏了四代，至其曾孙高涵，钤有“高文恪公（高士奇）曾孙涵珍藏”白文方印，约在乾隆时入清宫。其后有乾隆的鉴藏八玺，嘉庆、宣统鉴藏玺，为末帝溥仪赏溥杰出宫后，由溥仪携逃至吉林省临江市，为解放军截获后，辗转由东北人民银行转交东北文物管理委员会，其后归东北博物馆即今辽宁省博物馆（注3）。

海蔚蓝

注解：

1. 俞剑华《中国美术家人名词典》（上海人民美术出版社，1985），第39页。
2. 齐皎翰《中国诗人画家》（纽约：华美协进社中国美术馆，2000），第60－61页。
3. 杨仁恺主编《辽宁省博物馆藏书画著录》绘画卷，罗春政撰写（辽宁美术出版社，1999），第328－330页。

13
明　　董其昌 临褚遂良庾信枯树赋
手卷，纸本墨书
Dong Qichang (1555–1636)
***In Imitation of "Ode of the Withered Tree" by Chu Suiliang,* 1626**
Handscroll; ink on paper
22.1 x 284.7 cm

IMPERIAL SEALS: [Qianlong, r. 1736–95] Qianlong yulan zhibao (oval/relief), Sanxitang jingjianxi (rectangular/relief), Yizisun (square/intaglio), Qianlong jianshang (round/intaglio), Shiqu baoji (rectangular/relief), Yushufang jiancangbao (oval/relief); [Jiaqing, r. 1796–1820] Jiaqing yulan zhibao (oval/relief); [Xuantong (Puyi), r. 1909–11] Xuantong yulan zhibao (oval/relief)

OTHER SEAL: [Museum of the Northeast] Dongbei bowuguan zhencang zhiyin (square/relief)

JADE CLIP INSCRIPTION: Qianlong yushang. Dong Qichang lin kushufu

皇家印鉴：[清乾隆皇帝弘历，在位1736－1795]乾隆御览之宝（朱文椭圆印）、三希堂精鉴玺（朱文长方印）、宜子孙（白文方印）、乾隆鉴赏(白文圆印)、石渠宝笈(朱文长方印)，御书房鉴藏宝(朱文椭圆印)。[清嘉庆皇帝颙琰，在位1796－1820]嘉庆御览之宝（朱文椭圆印）。[清宣统皇帝溥仪，在位1909－1911]宣统御览之宝（朱文椭圆印）。

其他印鉴：[东北博物馆]东北博物馆珍藏之印（朱文方印）

玉别子镌：乾隆御赏。董其昌临枯树赋

Dong Qichang (sobriquet, Xiangguang) was a native of Huating (present-day Songjiang, Shanghai). He attained the *jinshi* (successful candidate at the metropolitan exams) degree in 1589 (the 17th year of Wanli) under Emperor Shenzong and was later promoted to minister of rites. A gifted gentleman, he was a painter, a calligrapher, a connoisseur, and a great collector. He started his calligraphy training by studying the works of such Tang dynasty masters as Yan Zhenqing (709–785) and Yu Shinan (558–638) and later came to favor the works of Wei and Jin masters. He then turned to the works of Zhong You (151–230) and Wang Xizhi (ca. 303–ca. 361) and incorporated the brush techniques of such calligraphers as Li Yong (678–747), Xu Hao (703–782), and the Five Dynasties calligrapher Yang Ningshi (873–954). Claiming to have achieved "refinement in free expression," he tended to arrange his calligraphy in evenly spaced and free-flowing lines, a distinctive feature of his own. Together with Xing Tong (1551–1612), Mi Wanzhong (1570–1628), and Zhang Ruitu (d. 1644), he was considered one of the Four Masters of the Late Ming, a group which strongly influenced calligraphy during the late Ming and early Qing dynasties.[1]

"Ode of the Withered Tree" (*Kushu fu*) was a famous poem by the Northern Zhou dynasty poet Yu Xin (513–581), whose father, Yu Jianwu, was a famous Liang dynasty poet during the Southern Dynasties period (see Appendix B). Yu Xin made frequent visits to the Liang court with his father and the father-and-son poets Xu Chi and Xu Ling, and he accompanied Prince Xiao Gang (Emperor Jianwen, r. 550–51) in writing some extremely sentimental poems in what came to be known as the "Xu Yu style."

This sad and powerful poem borrows a verse by the mighty general Huan Xuan (369–404), who was moved by a withering tree at the end of its life cycle to realize that there was a lack of permanence in history, in time and space, and in human life. Chu Suiliang's version of the "Ode of the Withered Tree," according to his inscription at the end of his calligraphy, was written "on the eighth day of the tenth month in the fourth year of the Zhenguan reign [630], for the Duke of Yan." That work has a total of 467 characters arranged in thirty-nine lines. Marked by a continuous flow of *qi* energy, Chu's brushwork is reposed, dignified, and elegant, yet the strokes are vivid with random variations and refined movement. Copies of this work have been included in many calligraphy model-books, but the one titled *Tingyulou tie* (Listening to the Rain Pavilion model-book), published in the Qing dynasty by the Yunnan collector Zhou Liya (act. 1796–1820), is considered the best version.

A master calligrapher of the Tang dynasty, Chu Suiliang

practiced Wang Xizhi's style. Critics in the Tang dynasty rated Chu's calligraphy as "top minus" (*shang xia pin*).[2] His "Ode of the Withered Tree" was probably in the collection of the Tang dynasty court. During the reign of the Tang emperor Zhongzong, it was awarded to Empress Wu Zetian's nephew Zong Chuke (d. 710), who held various official positions culminating with *zhongshuling*. He had Chu's calligraphy incorporated into a decorative screen. When he invited members of the nobility to a banquet, his guests were so astonished to find such beautiful calligraphy that "they forgot all about the food and music."[3] Throughout the dynasties, countless admirers have left behind their copies of this work by Chu. There is also a copy by the Qianlong emperor himself; it was stored in the Yangxin Dian (Hall of Mental Cultivation).[4] According to the dated signature, Dong Qichang's copy was made when he was seventy-one years old, early in the *bingyin* year (1626). The mood for the entire work is peaceful and relaxed, the brushwork sophisticated, and the techniques refined and friendly.

Dong Qichang's calligraphy was much favored by the Kangxi emperor (r. 1662–1722), who not only collected his works but also personally copied them. *The Shiqu baoji* listed at least a dozen of Kangxi's copies of Dong's works.[5] They were also sought after by Qing courtiers who loved to contend in a show of wealth. For example, Dong Qichang's scroll *In Imitation of Zhang Xu's Langguan Biji (Dong Qichang lin Zhang Xu langguan biji yi zhou)* was acquired by the minister Zhang Zhao (1691–1745) and was later acquired by the Qing court.[6]

This scroll had been in the imperial collection and is affixed with six of Qianlong's seals, as well as those of the Jiaqing and Xuantong emperors. The front face of its jade clip, which was manufactured within the palace, is lightly incised with a simplified cloud design; its back is carved with the inscription "Qianlong yushang, Dong Qichang lin Kushu fu" (appreciated by Qianlong; Dong Qichang's copy of the "Ode of the Withered Tree"). This scroll left the palace when Puyi awarded it to Pujie on January 9, 1923 (the 23rd day of the 11th month, the 14th year of Xuantong).[7] After passing through many hands, it was acquired by the Liaoning Provincial Museum.

WWHC (trans. DHWS)

1. Shen Roujian, ed., *Zhongguo meishu cidian* [Dictionary of Chinese art] (Taipei, Xiongshi meishu chubanshe, 1989), p. 184.
2. Zhang Yanyuan, *Fashu yaolu* [The art of calligraphy], *juan* 3, cited in *Guhua pinlu* [Classified record of ancient paintings], Siku yishu congshu [Art books from the Comprehensive library of the Four Treasuries] (reprint, Shanghai: Shanghai guji chubanshe, 1991), p. 812/148.
3. Ibid., *juan* 3, p. 812/154.
4. *Shiqu baoji xubian* [Treasured boxes of the Stone Channel, continued] (Taipei: Guoli gugong bowuyuan, 1971), p. 2012.
5. See the table of contents (*mulu*) of *Shiqu baoji* [Treasured boxes of the Stone Channel], Siku yishu congshu [Art books from the Comprehensive library of the Four Treasuries] (Shanghai: Shanghai guji chubanse, 1991), *juan* 1, pp. 12–13.
6. *Shiqu baoji xubian*, p. 442. Zhang Zhao (sobriquet, Tianpin Jushi) attained his *jinshi* in the Kangxi period and rose to the post of minister in the Board of Punishments. In calligraphy, he began by studying Dong Qichang; later he practiced the styles of Yan Zhenqing and Mi Fu. His style was simple and vigorous, showing boldness of vision. He painted both ink orchids and ink plum. See Yu Jianhua, ed., *Zhongguo meishujia renming cidian* [Dictionary of Chinese artists] (Shanghai: Shanghai renmin meishu chubanshe, 1985), p. 861.
7. Registered under the serial number Yong 129 in *Gugong yiyi shuji shuhua mulu si zhong* [Four catalogues of dispersed calligraphy and paintings from the imperial palace] (Beijing: Gugong bowuyuan, 1926), p. 18.

13

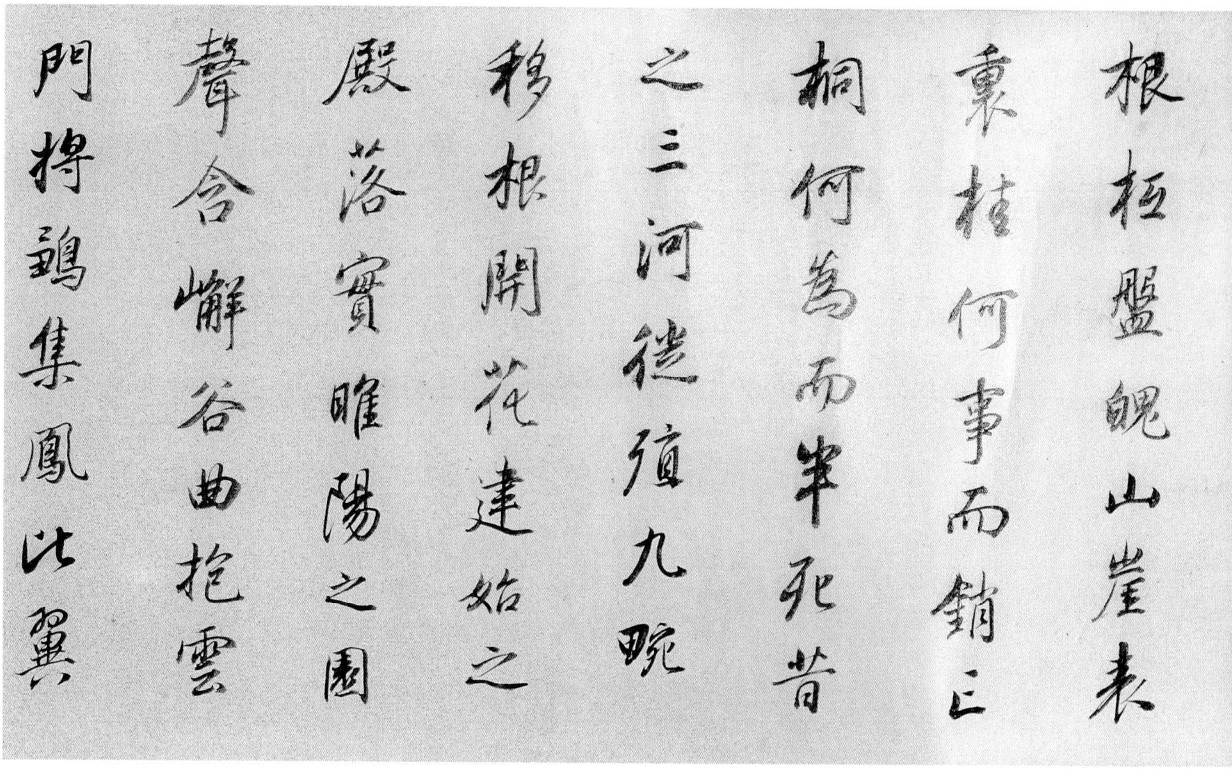
根柢盤魄山崖表
裏桂何事而銷亡
桐何為而半死昔
之三河徙植九畹
移根開花建始之
殿落實睢陽之園
聲含嶰谷曲抱雲
門將鶵集鳳比翼

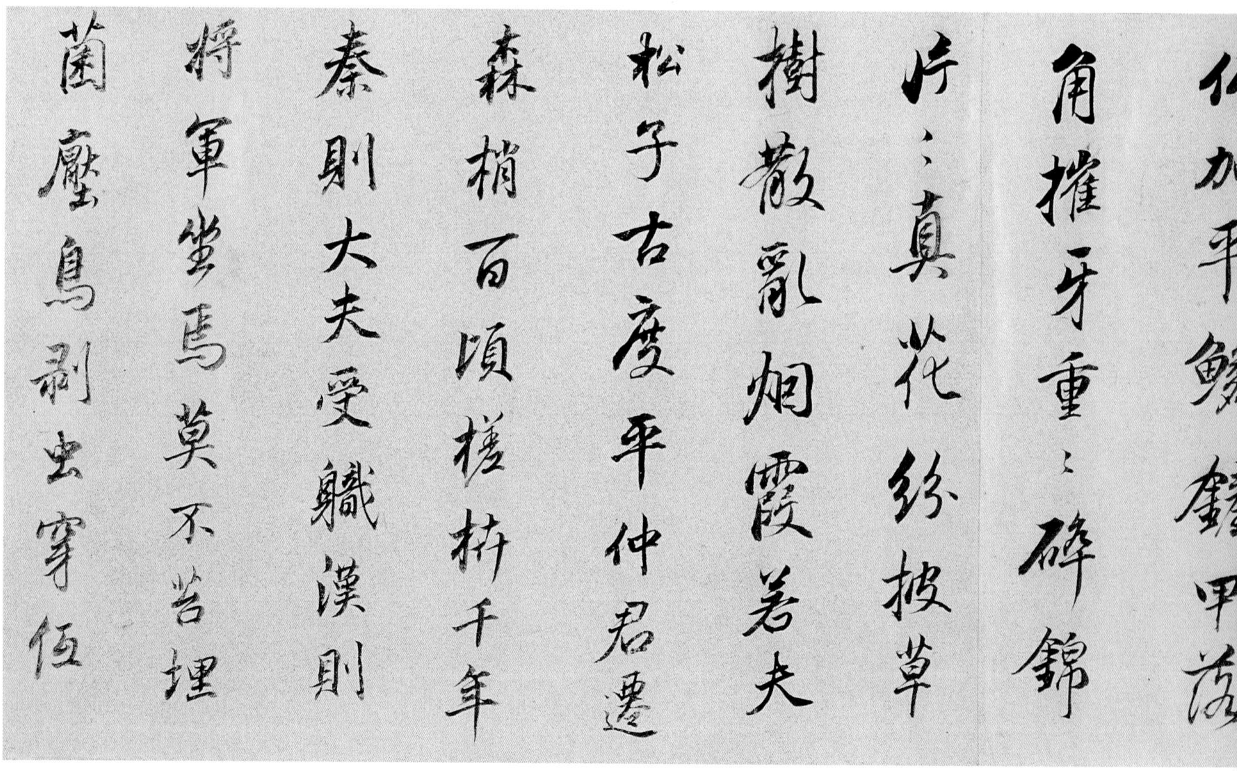
仍加平鏟甲落
角摧牙重重碎錦
片片真花紛披草
樹散亂烟霞若夫
松子古度平仲君遷
森梢百頃槎枿千年
秦則大夫受職漢則
將軍坐焉莫不苔埋
菌壓鳥剝蟲穿

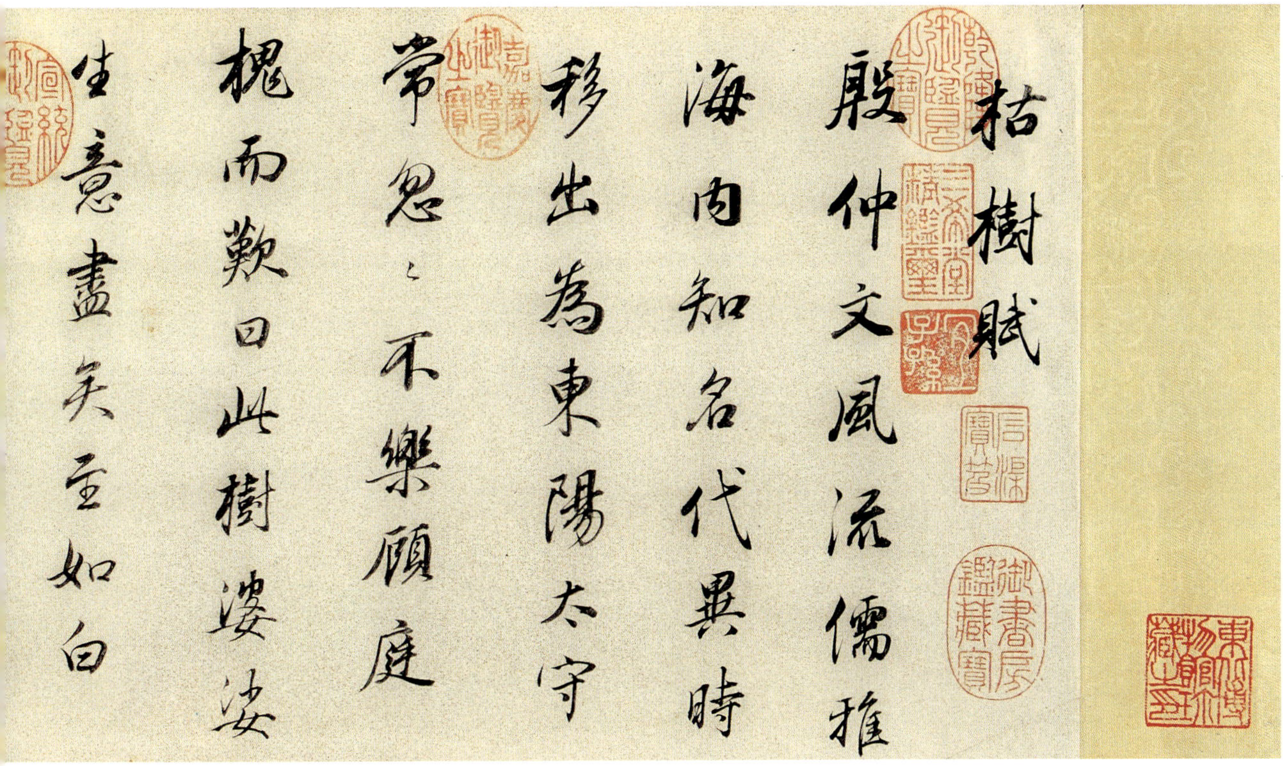
枯樹賦
殷仲文風流儒雅
海內知名代異時
移出為東陽太守
常忽忽不樂顧庭
槐而歎曰此樹婆娑
生意盡矣至如白

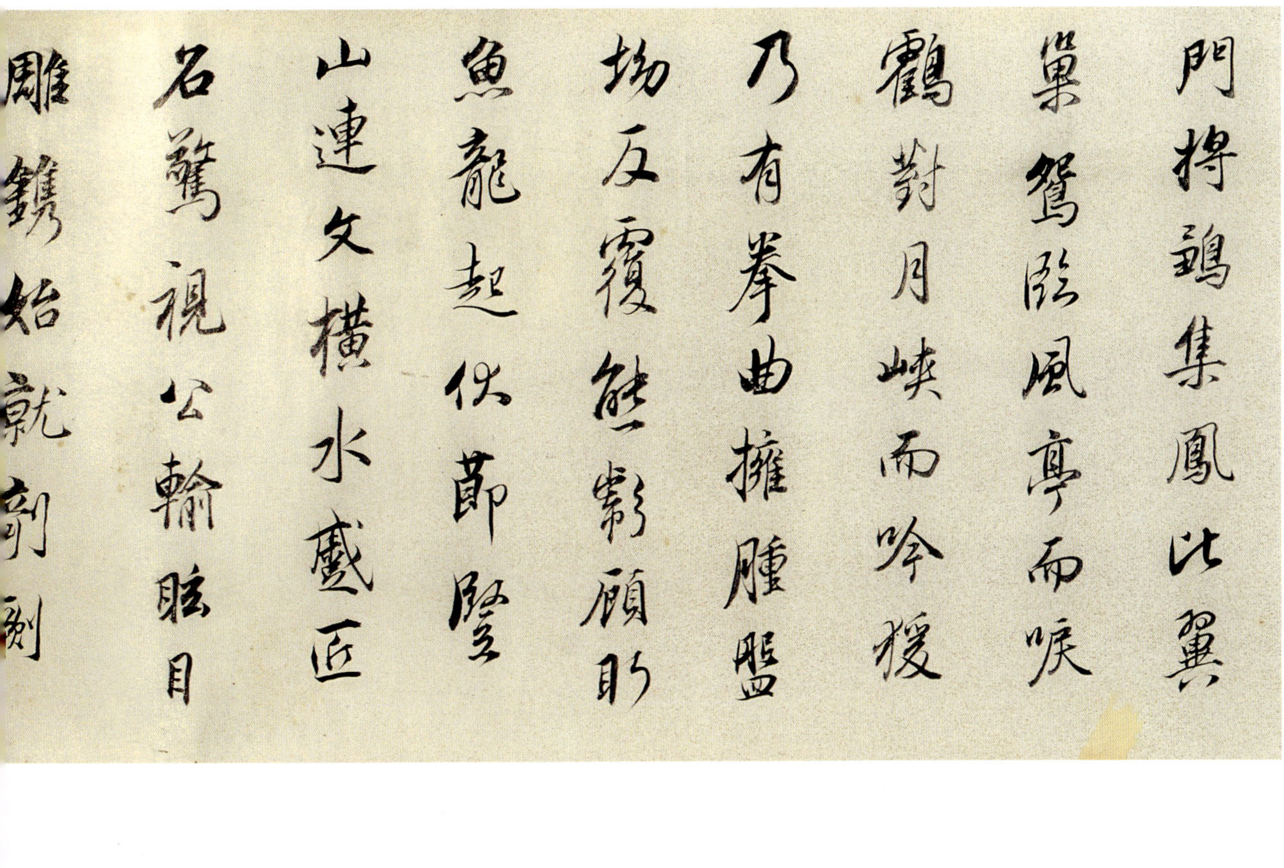
門將鵾集鳳比翼
巢鴛臨風亭而唳
鶴對月峽而吟猨
乃有拳曲擁腫盤
坳反覆熊彪顧盼
魚龍起伏節竪
山連文横水蹙匠
石驚視公輸眩目
雕鐫始就剞劂

13

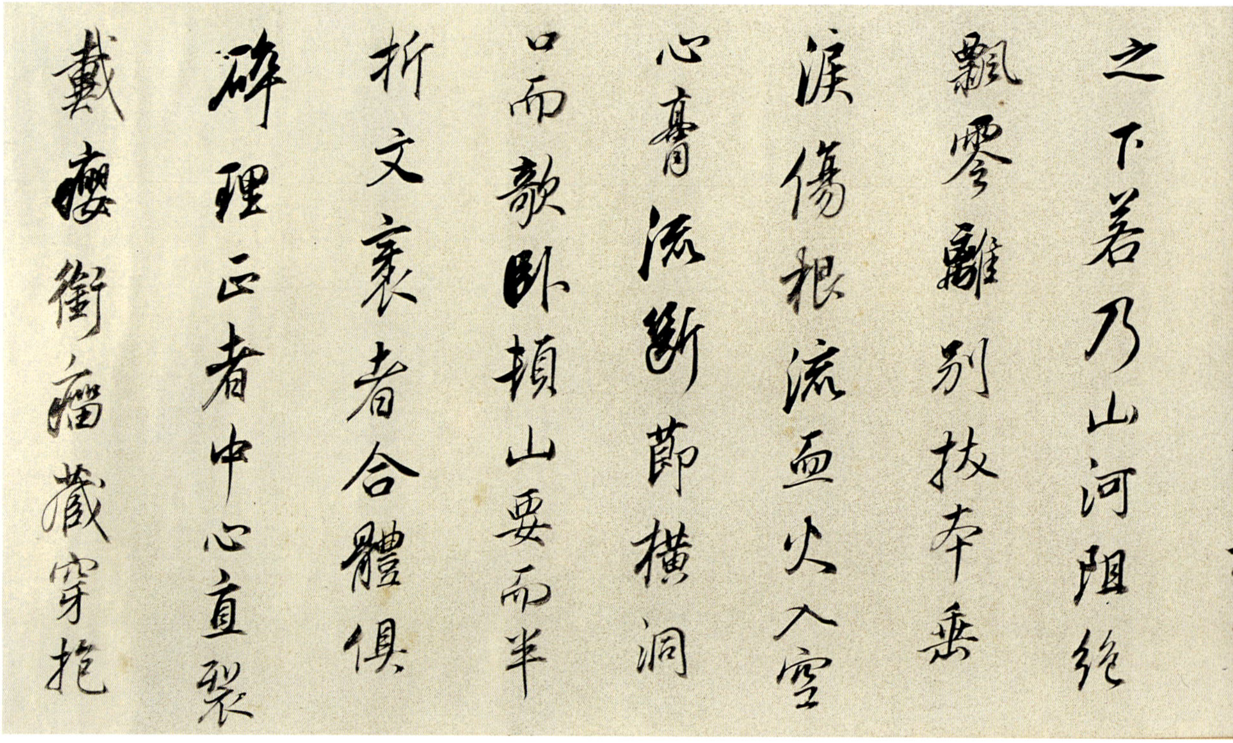
之下若乃山河阻絕
飄零離別拔本垂
淚傷根流血火入空
心膏流斷節橫洞
口而敧臥頓山腰而半
折文衺者合體俱
碎理正者中心直裂
戴癭銜瘤藏穿抱

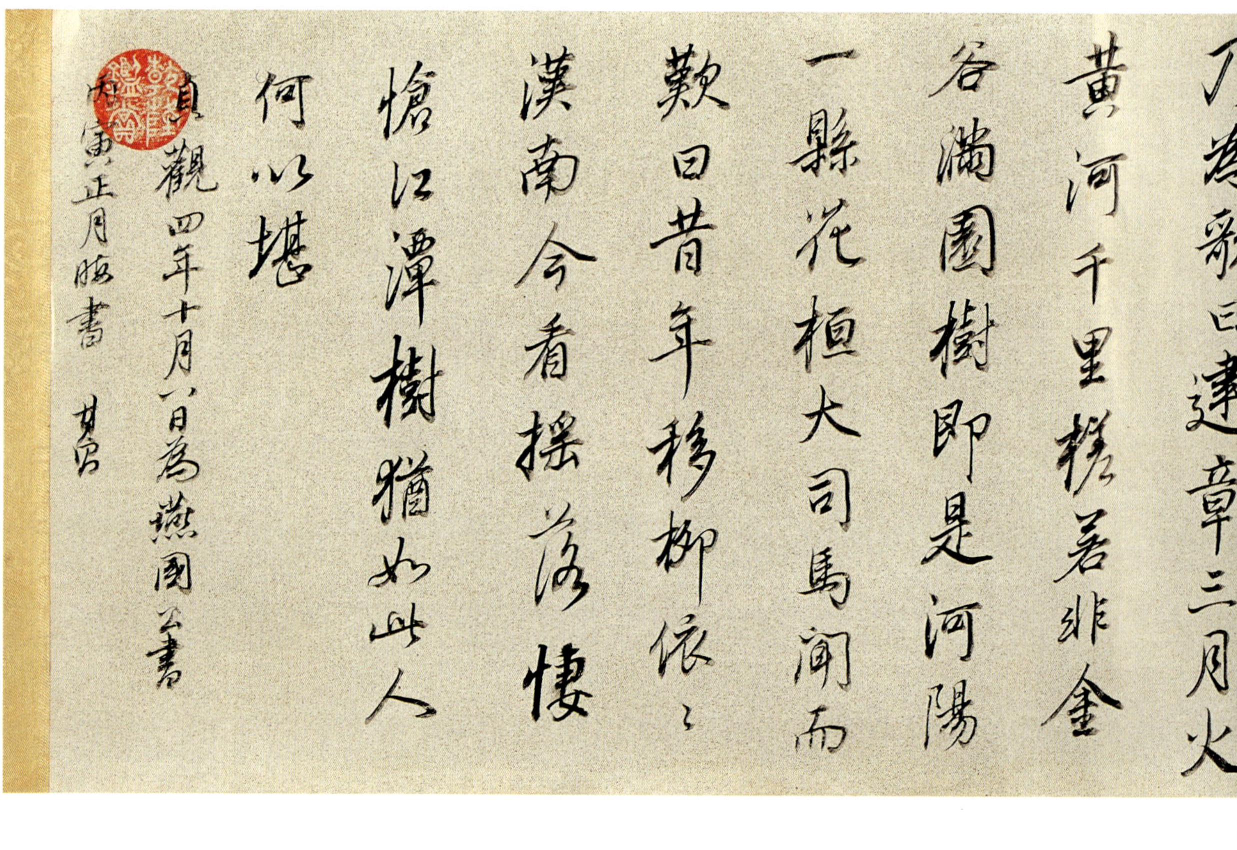
乃為歌曰建章三月火
黃河千里槎若非金
谷滿園樹即是河陽
一縣花桓大司馬聞而
歎曰昔年移柳依依
漢南今看搖落悽
愴江潭樹猶如此人
何以堪
貞觀四年十月八日為燕國公書
丙寅正月臨書 其昌

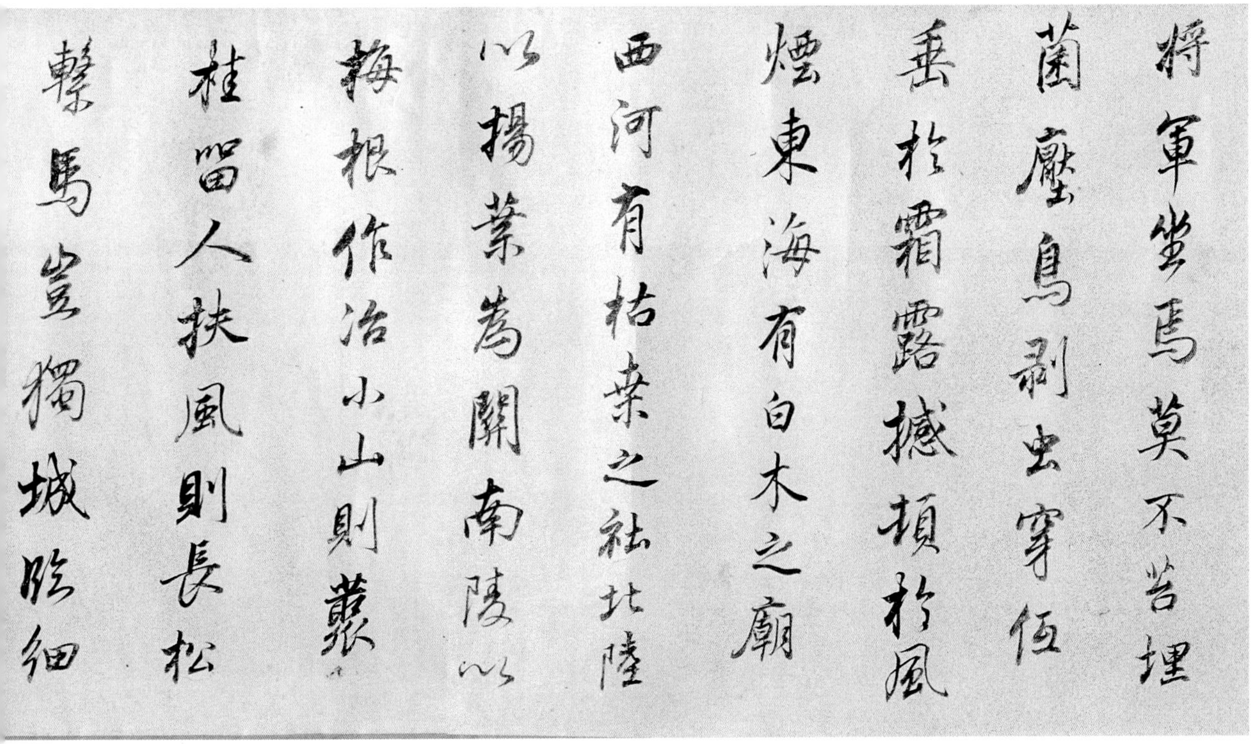
將軍坐馬莫不苔埋
菌壓鳥剝虫穿何
垂於霜露撼頓於風
煙東海有白木之廟
西河有枯桑之社北陸
以楊葉為關南陵以
梅根作冶小山則叢
桂留人扶風則長松
繫馬豈獨城臨細

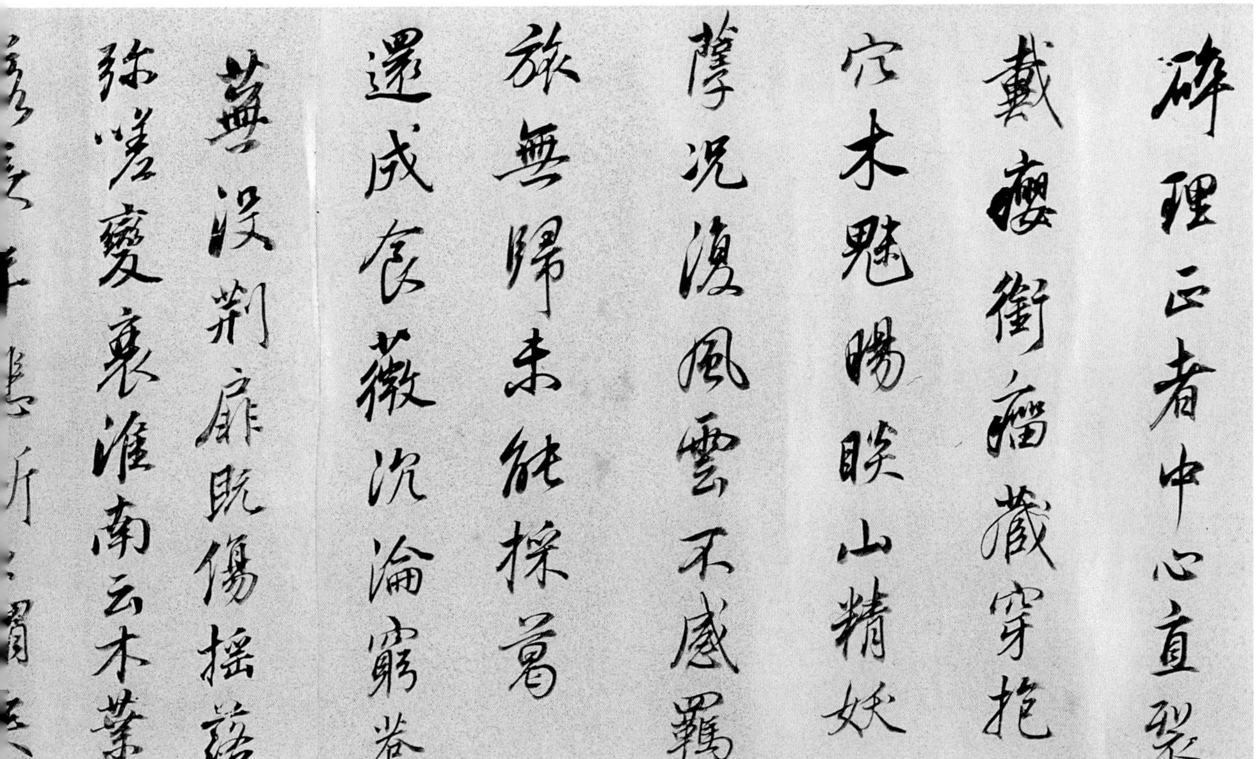
碎理正者中心直裂
戴癭銜瘤藏穿抱
穴木魅睗睒山精妖
孽況復風雲不感羈
旅無歸未能採葛
還成食薇沉淪窮巷
蕪沒荊扉既傷搖落
彌嗟變衰淮南云木葉

董其昌字玄宰，号香光，华亭（今上海松江）人，神宗万历十七年（1589）进士，曾官至礼部尚书。才华俊逸，工书画，精鉴赏，富收藏。其书法先学唐人颜真卿（709－785）、虞世南（558－638），后喜魏晋，转法钟繇（151－230）、王羲之（约303－约361）并参唐代书法家李邕（678－747）、徐浩（703－782）、五代书法家杨凝式（873－954）笔意，自称于率意中得秀色，分行布白，疏宕秀逸，自成一派，与邢侗（1551－1612）、米万钟（1570－1628）、张瑞图（卒于－1644）并称“明末四大家”，对明末清初书坛影响颇巨（注1）。

《枯树赋》为北周诗人庾信（513－581）的名作，其父庾肩吾是南朝萧梁时的名诗人，庾信随父及徐离、徐陵父子出入宫廷，陪太子萧纲（梁简文帝，在位550－551）写过一些绮艳诗，称为“徐庾体”。此诗苍劲悲凉，借当时炙手可热的桓玄（369－404）感树木摇落的诗句，兴起对历史，对时空，对生命无常的感怀。褚遂良的“枯树赋”，题为贞观四年（630）十月八日为燕国公书。书法共存三十九行，四百六十七字，其行气用笔，仿佛亭亭移步，神闲气定，端庄秀润，用笔错落变化，雅丽生动，为多本法帖所收，而以清代云南藏家周立崖（活跃于1796－1820）的“听雨楼帖”所录版本者为最好。褚为唐代名书家，师法王羲之，唐代有人评论书法时，将其书法列为上下品（注2）。褚书“枯树赋”大概后来被收入唐代内宫，中宗时曾赏赐武则天的侄子，官至中书令的宗楚客（卒于710），他拿来装饰屏风，邀请贵族宴赏，与会客人“废食叹美，不复宴乐”（注3）。历来不乏临摹者，乾隆皇帝亦有临本，藏于养心殿（注4）。此卷为董氏临本，据落款，董氏在1626年（丙寅）正月书写，当时董已经七十九岁高龄。通篇书法气势舒展停匀，运笔精敛，法则温雅。

董其昌书法为康熙皇帝所最欣赏，他不但收藏董氏作品，还亲自临摹，《石渠宝笈》所录的，由他御临的董氏书法就有不下十二件（注5）。宫中人臣也竟相收藏比附，如“董其昌临张旭郎官壁记一轴”就曾为尚书张照(1691－1745)收藏，后入清宫收藏（注6）。

此卷曾为皇室收藏，钤有乾隆六玺，并钤有嘉庆和宣统皇帝的鉴藏印。本卷几何纹织锦包首，清宫制玉别子正面有浅刻的简化云纹，背面以隶书体刻有“乾隆御赏。董其昌临枯树赋”。宣统十四年十一月二十三日，由末帝溥仪以赏赐其弟溥杰为名，而流落宫外（注7）。后辗转为辽宁省博物馆收藏。

海蔚蓝

注解：

1. 沈柔坚主编《中国美术辞典》(台湾雄狮美术出版社，1989)，第184页。
2. [唐]张彦远《法书要录》卷三，载四库艺术丛书《古画品录》(上海古籍出版社，1991)，第812/148页。
3. [唐]张彦远《法书要录》卷三，载四库艺术丛书《古画品录》（上海古籍出版社,1991），第812/154页。
4. [清]《石渠宝笈》续编（台湾国立故宫博物院，1971），第2012页。
5. [清]《石渠宝笈》卷一目录，载《四库艺术丛书》（上海古籍出版社，1991），第12－13页。
6. [清]《石渠宝笈续编》，张照，号天瓶居士，康熙时进士，官至刑部尚书，书法出学董其昌，后出入颜、米，气魄浑厚，兼画墨兰墨梅。著《天瓶斋书画题跋》等（台湾国立故宫博物院，1971），第442页。俞剑华《中国美术家人名辞典》（上海人民美术出版社，1996），第861页。
7. 《故宫已佚书籍书画目录四种》此一卷宫中登记号为永字一百二十九号，（故宫博物院，民国十五年版，1926），第18页。

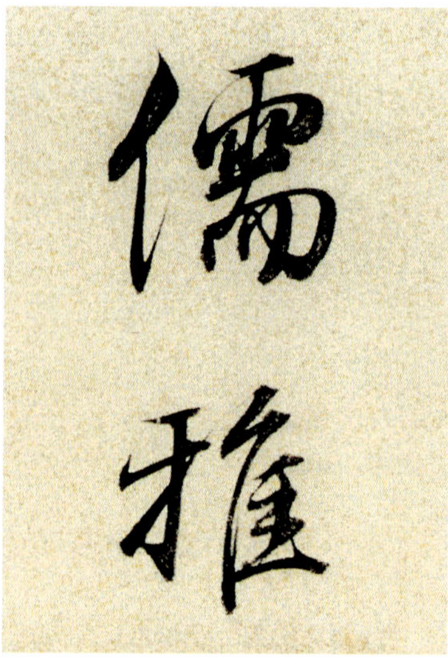

13 (detail 局部)

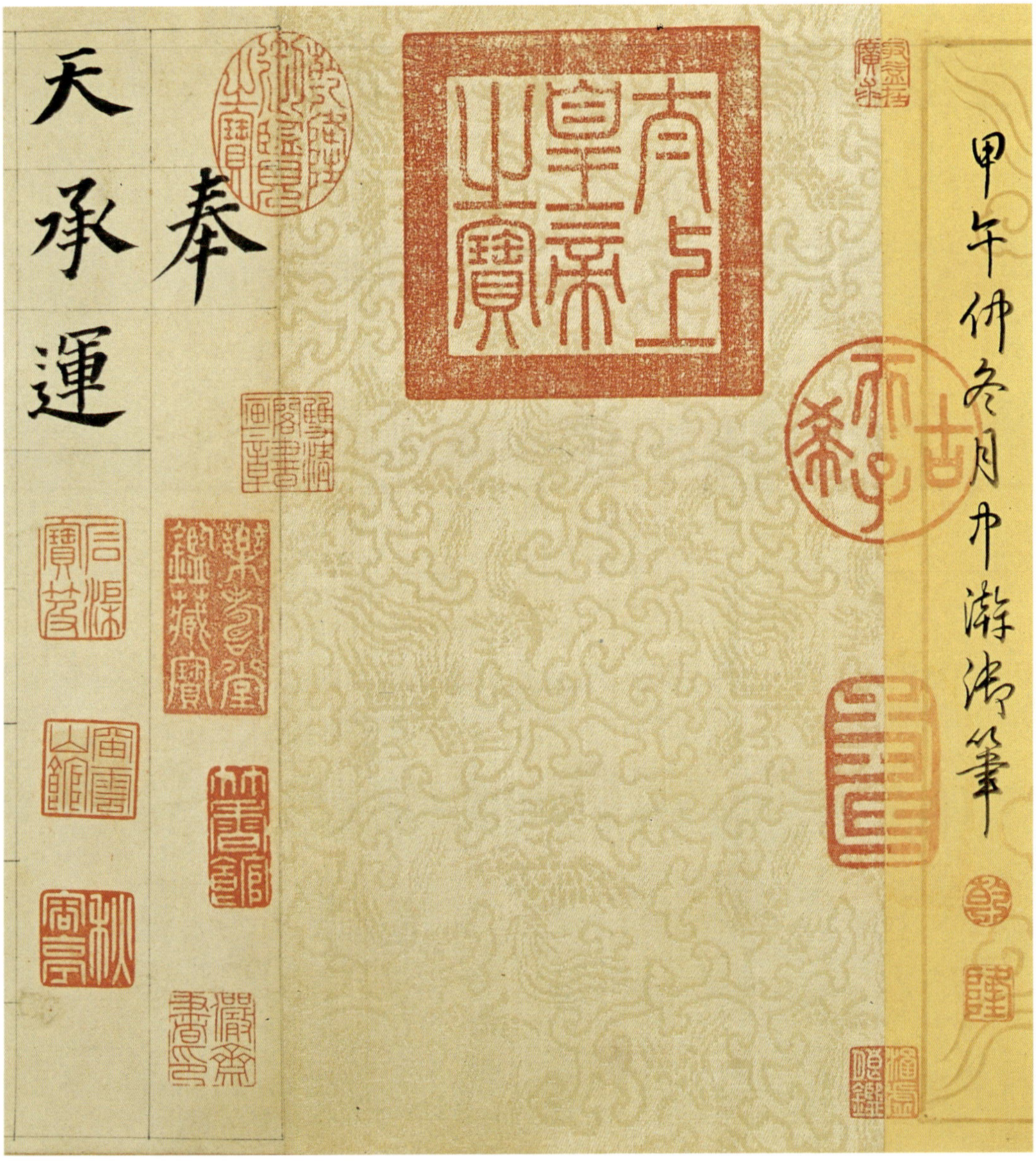

14 (detail 局部)

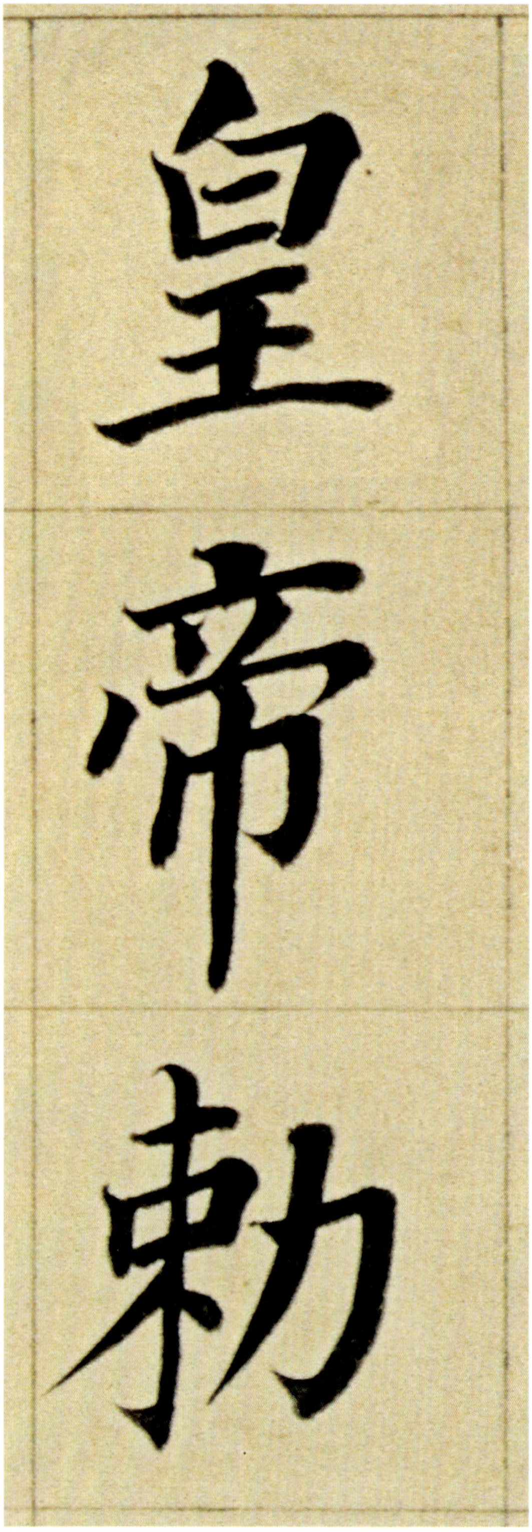

14 (detail 局部)

14
明　　董其昌 自书封敕稿本
手卷，纸本水墨
Dong Qichang (1555–1636)
***Calligraphy after the Imperial Mandates,* 1596**
Handscroll; ink on paper
Calligraphy: 25.7 x 276.4 cm; entire scroll: 26.8 x 827 cm

IMPERIAL SEALS: [Qianlong, r. 1736–95] Qianlong yulan zhibao (oval/relief), Leshoutang jiancangbao (rectangular/intaglio), Shiqu baoji (rectangular/relief), Shiqu dingjian (round/relief), Baoji chongbian (square/intaglio), Ningshougong xuru shiqu baoji (square/relief), Qianlong jianshang (round/intaglio), Sanxitang jingjianxi (square/relief), Yizisun (square/intaglio), Taishang huangdi zhibao (large square/relief), Guxi Tianzi (round/relief), Wufu wudaitang guxi tianzi bao (large square/relief), Shou (rectangular/intaglio), Bazheng maonian zhibao (large square/relief), Quyi zai guangqiu (rectangular/relief), Hanxu langjian (square/intaglio), Shui yue liang chengming (rectangular/relief); [Jiaqing, r. 1796–1820] Jiaqing yulan zhibao (oval/relief); [Xuantong (Puyi), r. 1909–11] Wuyizhai jingjianxi (rectangular/relief), Xuantong yulan zhibao (square/relief)

OTHER SEALS: [Wang Zhuan, 1623–1709] Sanyuguan shuhua yin (rectangular/intaglio); [Liang Ruhong, Qing dynasty] Zhuxiangguan (rectangular/intaglio); [Wang Hongxu, 1645–1723] Hengyun Shanren (square/intaglio), Yanzhai miwan (square/relief), Yanzhai shuyin (square/relief), Liuyun shanguan (square/relief), Qiurongting (square/intaglio; repeated once); [Li Zongwan, 1705–1759] Lanxuetang kaocangyin (rectangular/relief), Shuijing yuexiang zhuxi yanwu (square/intaglio), Kegong jiafa (rectangular/relief), Shuangqingge shuhuazhang (square/relief); [Museum of the Northeast] Dongbei bowuguan zhencang zhiyin (square/relief)

COLOPHON WRITER (SEAL): the Qianlong emperor (Qian-Long [linked seal; round and square/relief])

皇家印鉴：[清乾隆皇帝弘历，在位1736－1795]乾隆御览之宝（朱文椭圆印）、乐寿堂鉴藏宝（白文长方印）、石渠宝笈（朱文长方印）、石渠定鉴（朱文圆印）、宝笈重编（白文方印）、宁寿宫续入石渠宝笈（朱文方印）、乾隆鉴赏（白文圆印）、三希堂精鉴玺（朱文长方印）、宜子孙（白文方印）、太上皇帝之宝（朱文大方印）、古希天子（朱文圆印）、五福五代堂古稀天子宝（朱文大方印）、寿（白文长方印）、八征耄念之宝（朱文大方印）、取益在广求（朱文长方印）、涵虚朗鉴（白文方印）、水月两澂明（朱文长方印）。[清嘉庆皇帝颙琰，在位1796－1820]嘉庆御览之宝（朱文椭圆印）。[清宣统皇帝溥仪，在位1909－1911]无逸斋精鉴玺（朱文长方印）、宣统御览之宝（朱文方印）

其他印鉴：[王撰，1623－1709]三馀馆书画印（白文长方印）。[梁汝鸿，清代人]竹香馆（白文长方印）。[王鸿绪，1645－1723]横云山人（白文方印）、俨斋秘玩（朱文方印）、俨斋书印（朱文方印）、留云山馆（朱文方印）、秋容亭（白文方印）。[励宗万，1705－1759]兰雪堂考藏印（朱文长方印）、水景月香竹溪烟坞（白文方印）、恪恭家法（朱文长方印）、双清阁书画章（朱文方印）。[东北博物馆]东北博物馆珍藏之印（朱文方印）。

题跋者（钤印）：清乾隆皇帝弘历（乾、隆[二朱文连珠一圆一方印]）。

Huating (present-day Shanghai) was Dong Qichang's hometown. At age thirty-five, after passing the metropolitan examination to become a *jinshi*, he was admitted into the court as a *shujishi*, a low-level official. At age forty, he was selected to be the head instructor to the eldest prince. Two years later, Dong Qichang was awarded the two imperial decrees transcribed in this scroll as emblems of his ultimate merit. Having just received orders to travel to Changsha as an envoy to confer the title of Governor of Ji on Zhu Yiluan, one might say that Dong's career was at that time becoming distinguished. Later, he was transferred to serve as assistant education chief of the Hu and Guang region and assistant education officer of Fujian Province. Finally, in 1622 (the 2nd year of Tianqi), he was appointed a minister in the Bureau of Rites in Nanjing, rising to a civil official of the first rank.

Dong Qichang had a tremendous impact on future generations. As an art collector, he amassed the largest collection in the region. He was also an experienced connoisseur and art theorist with independent views. The theory of *Nan-Bei zong*, the "Southern and Northern Schools," that he proposed was to dominate trends in later Chinese painting for centuries. He established the Songjiang School and became a leader in art circles. Dong Qichang's calligraphy is delicate and graceful; the new style was very much favored by the Kangxi emperor (r. 1662–1722) of the Qing dynasty, who established it as a model. Those who practiced his style in the imperial examinations and in drafting official documents had great advantages at the time.

The contents of this scroll are the two imperial decrees issued by the Wanli emperor of the Ming dynasty (r. 1573–1620) on the 24th and 28th day of the 8th month, the 24th year of Wanli's reign (October 16 and 20, 1596). The first one posthumously appoints Dong Hanru to the official position of *wenlinlang*, or "Fellow of Letters," while conferring the honorary title of *ruren* to his deceased wife (née Shen). The great importance placed on the ceremony of issuing such posthumous decrees was to honor their son Dong Qichang, who at that time was serving as compiler and editor at the Hanlin Imperial Academy, for his ability to "introduce the best in learning from a family tradition to the court and make it shine there."

In reality, the first decree was for just an honorary title while the second was for a position that had real administrative power, although the two were supposedly of the same rank. According to the second decree, "Dong Qichang, Compiler and Editor at the Hanlin Imperial Academy, an erudite, incredible talent, and non-ambitiously cultivated scholar…commands the highest esteem and is the pride of the country." As described, he was regarded as the cream of the crop in the country; therefore, the language of the appointment was also loaded with high praise when the decree was issued:

> This is to certify that the title of Fellow of Letters has now been officially bestowed on and appointed to you, with the responsibilities of a keeper for the imperial library.

The reason for his appointment follows: "You have been known to be indifferent to fame or benefit and have been highly recommended by the literati and gentry. Therefore you deserve commendation. Good virtues and integrity are valued. I, the sovereign, have more promotions for you later on."

Next the imperial mandate commends Dong Qichang's wife (née Gong), praising her as a fine woman for her role in assisting her "husband in attaining brilliance and becoming a remarkable figure in history." She was therefore awarded the title of *ruren*. In the two decrees, the Wanli emperor gave Dong Qichang extremely high commendations; thus he and his family received the greatest honors.

Dong Qichang hand copied the decrees using a fine and formal calligraphic presentation known as the "hair-lined format." The entire work looks very neat and precise. However, the expressive quality of Dong's calligraphy is not restrained by such a format. It is executed in a thoroughly free yet delicate artistic style.

The Qianlong emperor inscribed a long colophon for the scroll, saying that the words used in the decrees were too flattering. He related the decrees to the guidelines of recognition for individual merits exercised during the Song dynasty and expressed his views. When the work was remounted, Qianlong's long inscription was placed at the beginning section of the handscroll and several collection seals of the Qing court were placed on it.

HWL (trans. DHWS)

董其昌的家乡在华亭（今属上海市），35岁中进士后，被选在宫中任低级官职庶吉士，40岁时就被选为皇长子的首任讲官，又两年后，董其昌即得到了这两个象征着至高荣誉的诰命，当时，他正奉命持节赴长沙封吉藩朱翊銮，可谓仕途顺达。此后，他又转任湖广提学副史、福建副史等地方官，终在天启二年（1622年）被任命为南京礼部尚书，官居一品。

董其昌对后世产生过巨大影响，他本人是富甲一方的大收藏家，还是具有独特见解的鉴定家和书画艺术理论家，他提出的“南北宗”两大画派的理论，几乎主宰了后来中国绘画艺术的发展方向。他开创了松江画派，本人也成为书画界领袖。董其昌的书法，以清秀、洒脱的格调，开启了一种新的风尚，被清朝的康熙皇帝（1662－1722年）奉为楷模，在科举考卷、官方文件中，凡效仿董其昌的书法者，均大受青睐。

这是明朝万历皇帝（1573－1620年在位）在万历二十四年（1596年）八月二十四日和二十八日所封敕的两个任职诰命。前面的一封，是赐赠给已经死去的生员董汉儒名为“文林郎”的官职，同时赐赠给他也已经死去的妻子沈氏为孺人（注1）。之所以这么郑重地封敕已经死去的董汉儒夫妇，是因为他们的儿子时任翰林院编修的董其昌（1555－1636年）能“绍其家学，以耀于廷”。

实际上，第一个封敕只是赐赠一个名誉上的官职，是荣誉性的封赐。第二个诰命，颁敕的才是实际职务，虽然与前一封是同样的官职，但是，正如诰命中所述：“翰林院编修董其昌，博学闳才，清修彦士……卓然士望，郁为国华”。可以列为国家的菁英人才，所以授新职位时才语气郑重言之：“兹以岁阅，授而阶文林郎。锡之敕命：夫天禄石渠之任”。接着又说明授他该职原因：“尔业以恬淡端悫，推重士林，予寔汝嘉，益贞而操。朕且有后命”。接着，诰命又称赞董其昌的妻子龚氏是优秀的女子，并且因为她内助“尔夫烨然，为时良史”。所以封为孺人。在这两封诰命中，崇祯皇帝对董其昌给予了极高的推崇，董其昌及其家人也由此获得了至高无上的荣耀。

这卷董其昌书写的《封敕》稿本，在书法格式中比较庄重的一种款式“乌丝格”内完成，整幅看起来非常精整。然而，这样的格式并没有束缚住董其昌书法中所具有的灵动的艺术特质，整幅书法贯通在婉转洒丽的格调中。

清代乾隆皇帝在亲笔题写的长篇跋文中，认为诰命中的溢美之词过高，又联及宋代的封赏用人制度，表述了他的见解。清宫在重新装裱时，将乾隆皇帝的长跋放在了卷首的位置，并加盖了多方清宫收藏印。

黄伟利

15
明　　沈贞　　竹炉山房图
立轴, 纸本水墨设色
Shen Zhen (1400–1482)
***The Studio of Zhulu Hut*, 1471**
Hanging scroll; ink and color on paper
35.3 x 105.5 cm

ARTIST'S SEALS: Shen Zhen zhiyin (square/intaglio), Shenshi Zhenji (square/relief), Yifengtang (rectangular/relief), Nanzhai (square/relief)

IMPERIAL SEALS: [Qianlong, r. 1736–95] Qianlong yulan zhibao (oval/relief), Qianlong jianshang (round/intaglio), Shiqu baoji (square/relief), Sanxitang jingjianxi (rectangular/relief), Yizisun (square/intaglio)

COLOPHON WRITER (SEALS): the Qianlong emperor (De jiaqu [square/intaglio], Jixia yiqing [square/intaglio])

画家印鉴：沈贞之印（白文方印）、沈氏贞吉（朱文方印）、怡奉堂（朱文长方印）、南斋（朱文方印）。

皇家印鉴：[清乾隆皇帝弘历，在位1736－1795]乾隆御览之宝（朱文椭圆印）、乾隆鉴赏（白文圆印）、石渠宝笈（朱文方印）、三希堂精鉴玺（朱文长方印）、宜子孙（白文方印）。

题跋者（钤印）：清乾隆皇帝弘历（得佳趣[白文方印]、几暇怡情[白文方印]）。

Shen Zhen was a well-known poet, scholar, and artist in the Jiangnan region during the Ming dynasty. His grandfather, Shen Liang, was a smart businessman who had acquired a lot of farmland and property and an experienced connoisseur of painting and calligraphy, as well as a good friend of the Yuan dynasty master painter Wang Meng. His father, Shen Cheng (1376–1463), served at the imperial court when young but resigned from his post, claiming to be in poor health, and upon returning to his place of birth devoted himself to a reclusive life of reading and study. Shen Zhen's nephew Shen Zhou (1427–1509) pioneered what is famous in the history of Chinese art as the "Wu School." This scroll by Shen Zhen, titled *The Studio of Zhulu Hut* (*Zhulu shanfang tu*), was a precursor to this particular school of painting.

At the top right corner of the painting, Shen Zhen inscribed a colophon that tells the viewer of the motivation behind the creation of this painting: In the early summer of the year *xinmao* during the reign of Chenghua (1471), the artist visited Piling (present-day Changzhou, Jiangsu) where he was hosted and entertained by Master Puzhao; as they enjoyed wine and conversation, Master Puzhao spread out a sheet of rice paper and politely requested a painting from him.

In the painting, the Zhulu studio is peacefully situated in a natural landscape setting with a running stream that winds its way around two huts. The one in the foreground is a study with wide, open windows and clean desks for reading. The hut in the back is set amidst a lush bamboo grove; within the living room there is a pleasant moment of wine toasting between the host and the guest as they sit leisurely across the table from each other. Outside this hut is a stove for preparing tea, which is being attended to by a servant; this is undoubtedly the main focus of this painting. A kind of pure and elegant atmosphere that is evoked by the poetic painting of an artistic concept—such is the aesthetic characteristic that fills the painting titled *The Studio of Zhulu Hut*.

There is very little known about the provenance of this painting before it reached the Qing court. After it became part of the imperial collection, however, this painting was one of the Qianlong emperor's favorites. All six of the seals found on the painting are Qianlong's collection seals, and the emperor has, in addition, personally inscribed a poem on the painting's upper left:

Beneath the stone steps, Hui Spring comes whirling
and gushing.
By a stove in a bamboo grove one sips Zhaozhou's Zen [tea].[1]
Amidst such settings, I have also experienced complete
relaxation.
After three hundred years, this remains an unforgettable tradition.
Imperial inscription in mid-autumn in the *gengchen* [1760] year.

The last two lines of this poem especially emphasize the uninterrupted, three-hundred-year-old tradition of elegant and leisurely living that is represented in this painting.

HWL (trans. DHWS)

Notes

1. Zhaozhou (778–897) was a Chan (Zen) Buddhist monk who was credited with originating a koan, or riddle, about drinking tea.

沈贞（1400－1482年），为明代蜚声江南的诗人和学者、画家。其祖父沈良，善于经商，广置田产，又精于书画鉴赏，与元代大画家王蒙是好朋友。其父亲沈澄（1376－1463年），早年被征召到皇宫中供职，不久称病辞职返乡，潜心读书问学。沈贞的侄子沈周（1427－1509年），开创了在中国美术史上著名的"吴门画派"。沈贞所作《竹炉山房图》轴，就是这一画派的先声之作。

沈贞在画面右上方的自题中，表述了创作此画的意境：成化辛卯（1471年）初夏，他到毗陵（今江苏省常州市），在普照师的竹炉山房受到主人的热情款待，饮谈正兴，普照师铺好宣纸请他作画。画面中，竹炉山房的景致自下而上地展开，所设的前后山房，清泉回绕。前者窗明几净，是主人读书之所。后面的一座山房，建于茂密的竹林中，室内主宾相对，畅饮正欢，屋前有一僮仆，正在火炉旁拂火备茶，此处应是画中的主旨所在。通过诗话般的绘画意境来表达一种清雅的情怀，是充溢在《竹炉山房图》轴中的艺术特点。

此画入清宫以前的收藏状况尚不能知晓。此画在入宫以后，受到乾隆皇帝的特别珍爱，画幅中的六方均是清乾隆收藏印，乾隆皇帝还在画面的左上方亲笔题诗："阶下回回淙惠泉，竹炉小呷赵州禅(注1)。箇中我亦曾清息，为缅流风三百年。庚辰仲秋御题"。诗的后两句中，特别强调这幅画轴中，蕴涵了三百年流传不断的雅逸之风。

黄伟利

注解：

1. 赵州（778－897），是一个禅师，据说最先发明了与饮茶相关的谜语。

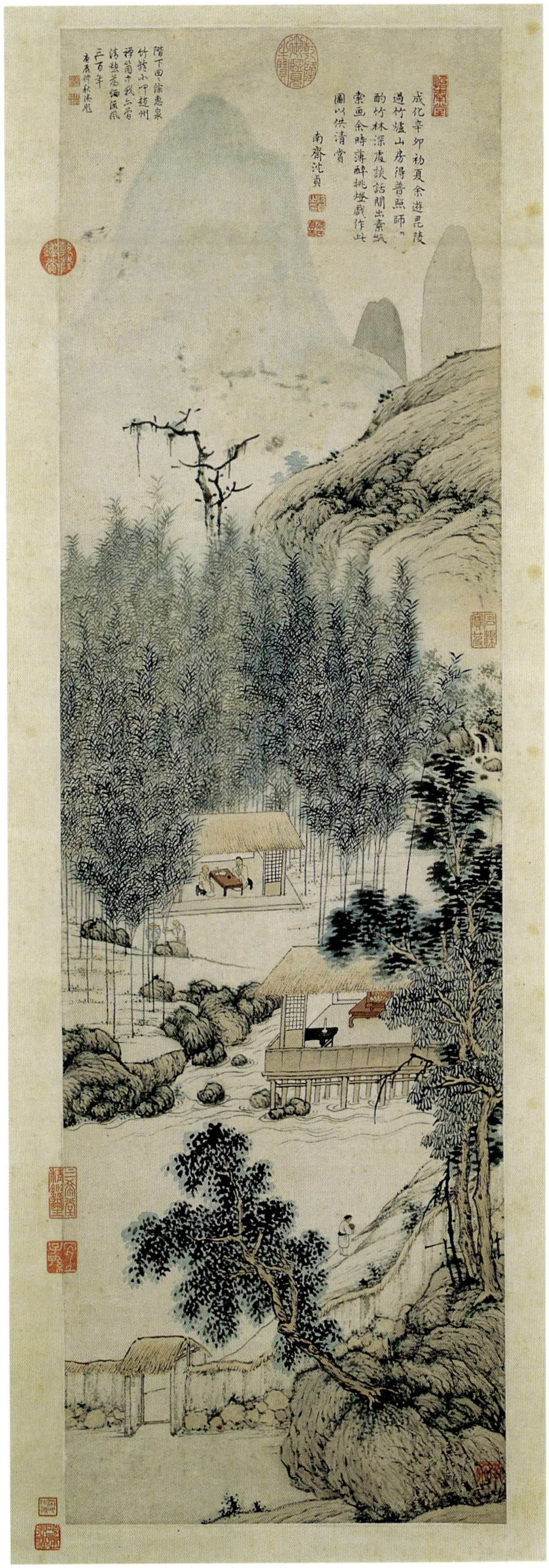

16
明　　董其昌 仿米氏山水书画合璧图
手卷, 纸本水墨
Dong Qichang (1555–1636)
Landscape in the Mi Style, 1620/ 1627

Handscroll; ink on paper
Painting: 28.2 x 119 cm

ARTIST'S SEALS: Huachan (rectangular/relief), Zongbo xueshi (square/intaglio), Dongshi xuanzai (square/intaglio), Taishishi (square/intaglio), Dong Qichang (square/relief)

IMPERIAL SEALS: [Qianlong, r. 1736–95] Qianqinggong jiancangbao (rectangular/relief), Sanxitang jingjianxi (rectangular/relief), Yizisun (square/intaglio), Qianlong yulan zhibao (oval/relief), Qianlong jianshang (round/intaglio), Shiqu baoji (rectangular/relief), Shiqu dingjian (round/relief), Baoji chongbian (square/intaglio); [Jiaqing, r. 1796–1820] Jiaqing yulan zhibao (square/relief); [Xuantong (Puyi), r. 1909–11] Xuantong yulan zhibao (oval/relief), Xuantong jianshang (square/relief), Wuyizhai jingjianxi (rectangular/relief)

OTHER SEALS: [An Qi, 1638–ca. 1744] Guxiang shuwu (rectangular/relief), Yizhou jianshang (square/intaglio), Anshi Yizhou shuhua zhizhang (rectangular/relief), Xinshang (double-gourd/relief), An Yizhou jia zhencang (rectangular/relief), Chaoxian ren (rectangular/intaglio), An Qi zhiyin (square/intaglio); [Museum of the Northeast] Dongbei bowuguan zhencang zhiyin (square/relief)

COLOPHON WRITERS (SEALS): the Qianlong emperor (Congyun [rectangular/relief], Jixia yiqing [square/intaglio], Qianlong chenhan [square/relief])

JADE CLIP INSCRIPTION: Qianlong Yuyong. Dong Qichang shuhua hebi

画家印鉴：画禅（朱文长方印）、宗伯学士（白文方印）、董氏玄宰（白文方印）、太史氏（白文方印）、董其昌（朱文方印）

皇家印鉴：[清乾隆皇帝弘历,在位1736－1795]：乾清宫鉴藏宝（朱文长方印）、三希堂精鉴玺（朱文长方印）、宜子孙（白文方印）、乾隆御览之宝（朱文椭圆印）、乾隆鉴赏（白文圆印）、石渠宝笈（朱文长方印）、石渠定鉴（朱文圆印）、宝笈重编（白文方印）。[清嘉庆皇帝颙琰,在位1796－1820]：嘉庆御览之宝（朱文方印）。[清宣统皇帝溥仪,在位1909－1911]：宣统御览之宝（朱文椭圆印）、宣统鉴赏（朱文方印）、无逸斋精鉴玺（朱文长方印）。

其他印鉴：[安岐, 1638－約1744]：古香书屋（朱文长方印）、仪周鉴赏（白文方印）、安氏仪周书画之章（朱文长方印）、心赏（朱文葫芦印）、安仪周家珍藏（朱文长方印）、朝鲜人（白文长方印）、安岐之印（白文方印）。[东北博物馆]东北博物馆珍藏之印（朱文方印）。

题跋者（钤印）：清乾隆皇帝弘历(丛云[朱文长方印]、几暇怡情[朱文方印]、乾隆宸翰[朱文方印]）。

玉别子镌：乾隆御咏。董其昌书画合璧

Dong Qichang's inscription, dated to the third lunar month (April 16–May 14) of 1627, appears at the end of *Landscape in the Mi Style*. It is an avowedly art historical inscription: "Dong Beiyuan [Dong Yuan] liked to execute misty scenery; as to the transformations of mist and cloud, this is [to be found only in] the Mi [family's] painting. I was awakened to the secrets [Skt., *samadhi*; Ch., *sanmei*] of ink-play by Mi Fu's *White Clouds over the Xiao and Xiang*."[1] For Dong Qichang, the concepts of "misty scenery" (*yanjing*), "transformations of mist and cloud" (*yanyun bianmo*), and "ink play" (*moxi*) were closely tied to the tradition of "scholar painting" (*shirenhua*) from Song times on and remained at the heart of his definition of "painting by men of culture" (*wenrenhua*). Although he says that Dong Yuan (d. 962) liked to paint misty scenery, the very notions of cloudy mountains and ink play were most closely linked with Mi Fu (1051–1107) and his son Mi Youren (1074–1151). Dong Qichang placed similar inscriptions on a number of paintings. He was able to trace the idea of cloudy mountains and ink play back through Dong Yuan in the tenth century to the splashed ink (*pomo*) of Wang Qia (d. 805) and ultimately back to the great Tang poet and painter Wang Wei (701–761), whom he saw as the fountainhead of the tradition of painting by men of culture. In one inscription he stated that Mi Fu was able to correct the errors of painters and that in doing so the Mi family brought about a transformation of the methods of painting.[2]

The Mi family style was a distinctive manner in which mountains were built up through layers of soft, wet horizontal strokes of ink that gave a rich, moist surface to the mountain forms. In this scroll, Dong Qichang employs this type of stroke in the distant mountains girdled with bands of white clouds. The clouds are not painted in; rather Dong leaves areas of the paper in reserve to create the undulating bands of the clouds. In a well-orchestrated composition, he clearly sets out the foreground, middle ground, and far distance at the beginning of the scroll and then plays the foreground off against the bands of clouds and Mi-style mountains. He concludes the composition with a middle-ground passage of landscape: a few trees on a bank by a stream emptying into a lake. In depicting the foreground areas, Dong Qichang does not use the Mi-style dots; rather he uses long, parallel texture strokes—the hemp-skin strokes—associated with Dong Yuan and with Yuan dynasty painters like Huang Gongwang (1269–1354). The foreground passages are particularly close to Huang Gongwang, even including a Y-shaped configuration employed by Huang to suggest the three visible surfaces of a rock. In the early Yuan period, the Mi-family style had been transmitted to Gao Kegong (1248–1310) and in the mid-Ming dynasty to Chen Chun (1483–1544). Each artist had developed the style, and Dong Qichang's explorations of the formal properties of cloudy mountains and ink play with combinations of Mi-style brushwork and brushwork derived from Huang Gongwang were conscious moves in a game played over time with the earlier masters. Dong would sometimes conclude an inscription with the exclamation "It is indeed regrettable that the old masters cannot see my painting!"[3]

Dong Qichang was born in 1555 into a commoner family from what was then the small village of Shanghai.[4] He began his studies at home with his father, a local teacher, and then continued them at the prefectural school in Songjiang. He passed the first level of the examinations but did not place first because his calligraphy was considered poor. This setback started him on a lifelong journey to become a great calligrapher, a goal that he achieved by rigorously studying the Tang masters and the Two Wangs—Wang Xizhi (ca. 303–ca. 361) and his son Wang Xianzhi (344–388). While preparing for the next level of the examinations he tutored in several wealthy households including that of the most important collector of the time, Xiang Yuanbian (1525–1590). This gave him access to many important early works of calligraphy and painting. After several attempts he passed the second level of the examinations in 1588 and went to Beijing to attempt the last examination for the *juren* degree. He passed and was given an appointment to the Hanlin Academy. In 1591, however, he took a leave of absence and did not return to Beijing again until 1594 when he was appointed tutor to the heir apparent. Sensing jealousy on the part of other officials, he once again retired in 1599. He remained at home until 1604 and then took up a provincial appointment. Once again his time in office was short. Local families instigated a riot against him because he was not corruptible, and the government office was burned. Dong Qichang was cleared of responsibility but sought to return home. This he did in 1606, remaining in retirement until 1622. With the ascension of his former pupil to the throne in 1620, he was appointed vice-minister of the Court of Imperial Sacrifices and director of studies at the National University, but the emperor died within a month and Dong did not take up his position until 1622. He rose to be vice-minister of the Ministry of Rites and then chief minister of the Ministry of Rites in Nanjing. This last position was largely ceremonial, but Dong, ever alert to the shifting winds of politics, resigned in 1626, avoiding the political purges carried out by the eunuch Wei Zhongxian. In 1632 he was recalled and served another two years before retiring for good.

It was during his periods out of office that Dong Qichang actively pursued his career as a painter and theorist, becoming perhaps the most pivotal figure in the history of later Chinese painting.[5] Through his paintings and his theoretical writings, he shaped the course of Chinese painting after him. Using an analogy to the history of Chan Buddhism, he separated the history of Chinese landscape painting into two schools, a Northern School and a Southern School. The Northern School was composed of painters who gradually attained enlightenment, that is, professional painters who learned and lived by their craft; the Southern School was made up of those who attained enlightenment suddenly, that is, the scholar-amateur painters who pursued painting as a form of self cultivation. Mi Fu and Mi Youren were important painters in the Southern School lineage stemming from Wang Wei and leading to the great masters of the Yuan dynasty. Dong Qichang's ideas of painter lineages were codified to become the Orthodox tradition of painting during the course of the seventeenth century. Wang Yuanqi (1642–1715; cat. no. 18) was one of the greatest painters in the Orthodox succession.

Landscape in the Mi Style has three seals of the important Qing collector An Qi, who was of Korean descent. His family had been bondservants of the Plain Yellow Banner, and his father, working for the powerful minister Mingju (1635–1708), had amassed a fortune through the salt trade, allowing An Qi to become a connoisseur and collector. He completed a catalogue of his collection in the early 1740s, but this painting is not included. A large portion of his collection was acquired by the Qianlong emperor in 1746, and the emperor inscribed the painting in the following year. Some time before the scroll entered the palace collection, it was mounted together with Dong Qichang's transcription of a poem by the Tang poet Du Fu (712–770) written out in the twelfth month of the *jiwei* year (January of 1620) in the Mi style. In the history of calligraphy,

16

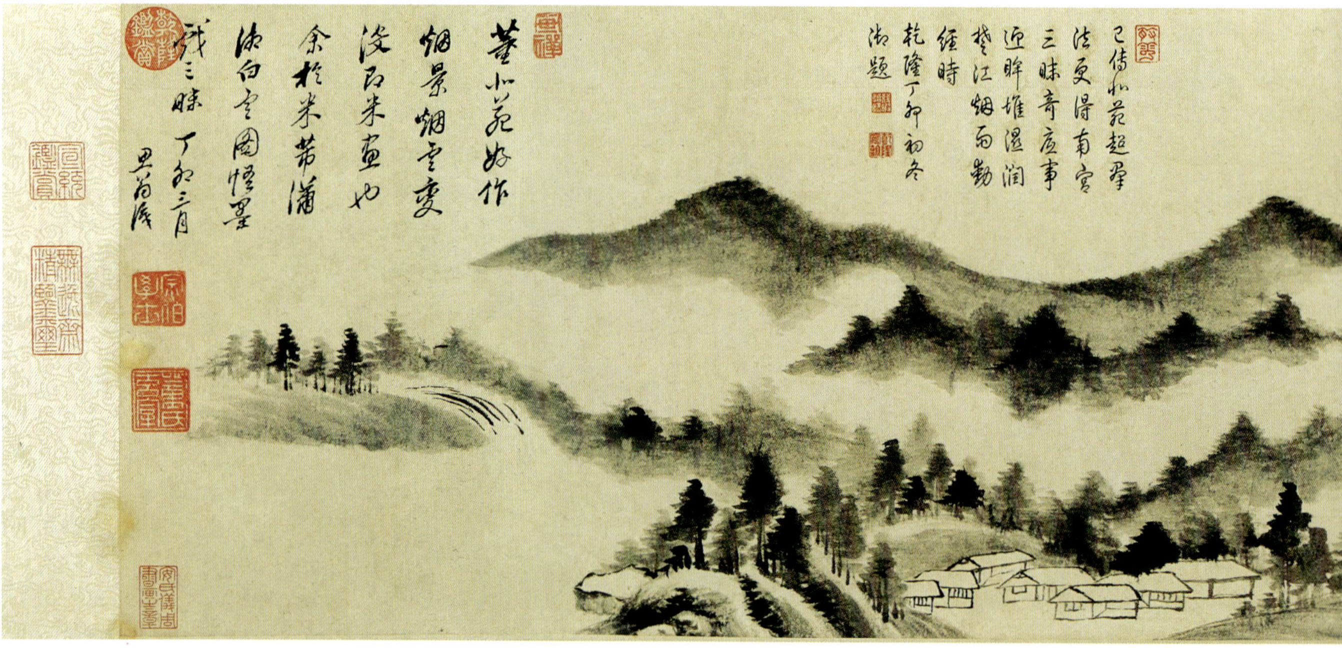

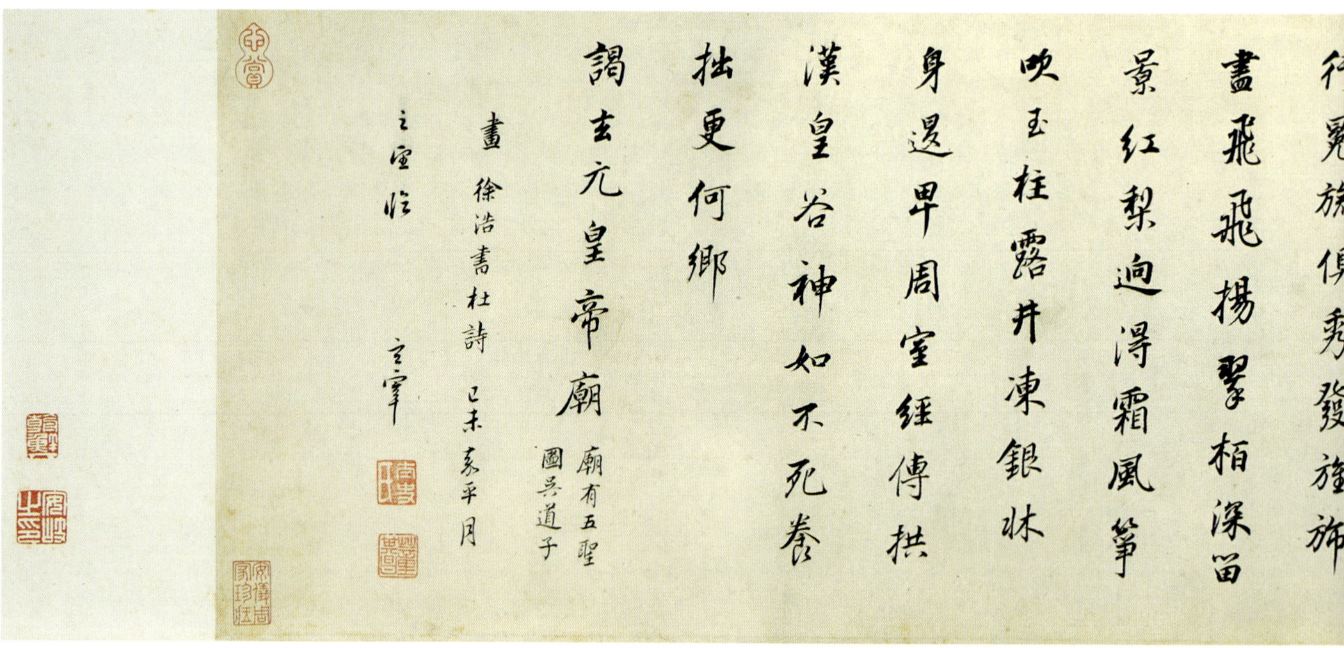
盡飛揚翠柏深留
景紅梨迥得霜風筝
吹玉柱露井凍銀牀
身退卑周室經傳拱
漢皇谷神如不死養
拙更何鄉
謁玄元皇帝廟
廟有五聖圖吳道子
徐浩書杜詩

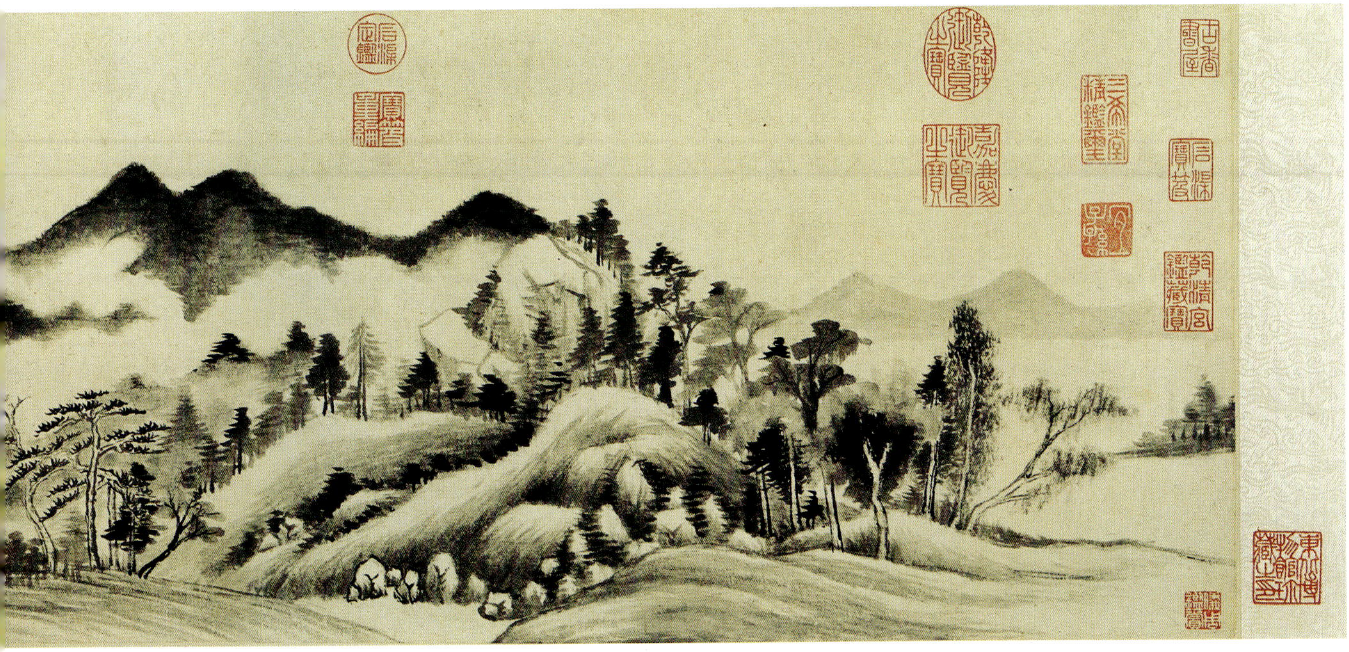

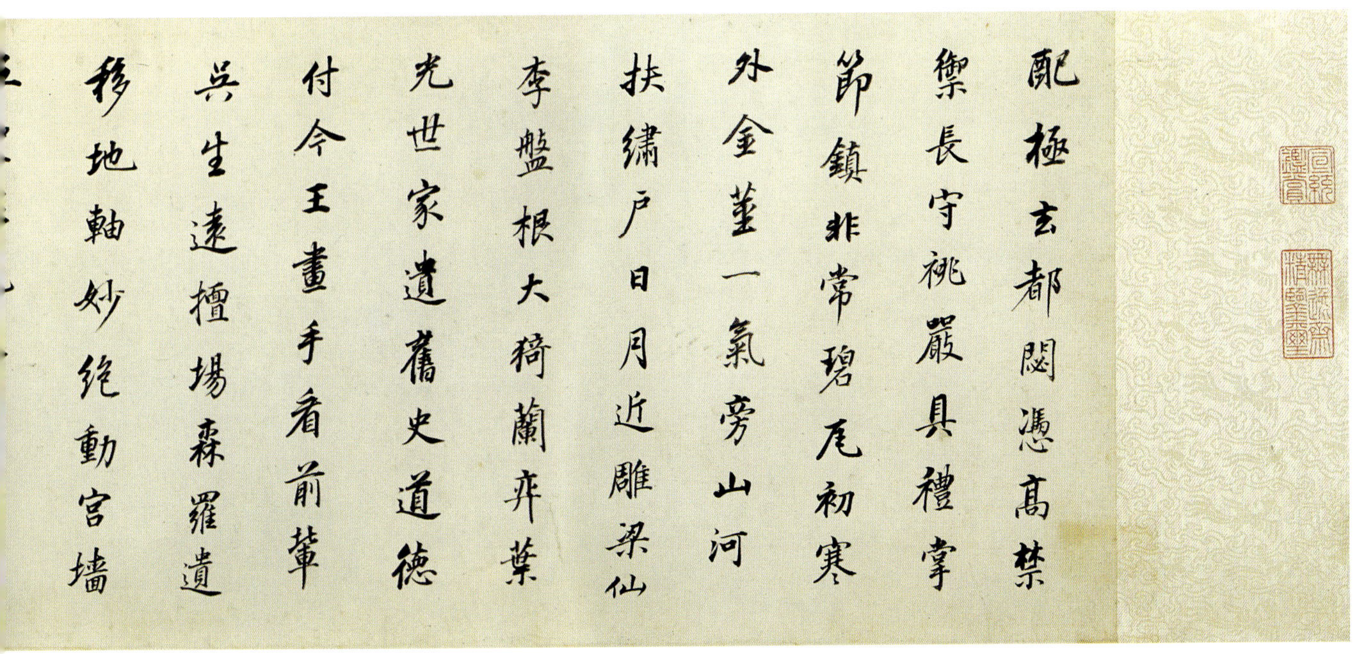
配極玄都閟憑高禁
籞長守祧嚴具禮掌
節鎮非常碧瓦初寒
外金莖一氣旁山河
扶繡戶日月近雕梁仙
李盤根大猗蘭奕葉
光世家遺舊史道德
付今王畫手看前輩
吳生遠擅場森羅遺
移地軸妙絕動宮墻

Mi Fu was one of Dong Qichang's most admired models, and it thus may have seemed only natural to mount the two together. An Qi's seals appear on both the painting and the calligraphy, so the two parts were already together when the scroll left his collection. It is even possible that he had them combined in one handscroll. In addition to a full complement of Qianlong seals, there are seals of the Jiaqing emperor and the Xuantong emperor. Puyi and his brother Pujie (1907–1994) smuggled the scroll out of the palace before 1924, and it was taken to Manchukuo when Puyi became the ruler in 1932.

DAS

Notes

1. This painting and its inscription is recorded in *Shiqu baoji xubian* [Treasured boxes of the Stone Channel, continued] (1793), reprinted in *Midian zhulin Shiqu baoji hebian* [Pearl forest of the Secret Hall and Treasured boxes of the Stone Channel, combined edition], 12 vols. (Shanghai: Shanghai shudian, 1988), vol. 3, pp. 441–42.
2. Dong Qichang, *Huayan* [The Eye of Painting], reprinted in *Mingren huaxue lunzhu*, vol. 12 of *Yishu congbian* [Collection of writings on art], 1st series (Taipei: Shijie shuju, 1962), p. 31.
3. For an example, see Dong's inscription on *River and Mountains on a Clear Autumn Day* in the Cleveland Museum of Art, illustrated in *Eight Dynasties of Chinese Painting: The Collections of the Nelson Gallery-Atkins Museum, Kansas City, and The Cleveland Museum of Art* (Cleveland: Cleveland Museum of Art, 1980), no. 191, pp. 244–46.
4. For biographical information, see Celia Carrington Riely, "Tung Ch'i-ch'ang's Life," in *The Century of Tung Ch'i-ch'ang, 1555–1636*, ed. Wai-kam Ho (Kansas City: The Nelson-Atkins Museum of Art, 1992), vol. 2, pp. 385–457; and Ren Daobin, *Dong Qichang xinian* [Dong Qichang's life year by year] (Beijing: Wenwu chubanshe, 1988).
5. On Dong Qichang's career as a painter and theorist, see Ho, *The Century of Tung Ch'i-ch'ang*, in particular Wai-kam Ho and Dawn Ho Delbanco, "Tung Ch'i-ch'ang's Transcendence of History and Art," pp. 3–41; Wen C. Fong, "Tung Ch'i-ch'ang and Artistic Renewal," pp 43–54; and Xie Zhiliu, "The Ch'an of Painting in Tung Ch'i-ch'ang's Theory," pp. xxxv–xxxvi.

董其昌将题款日期，1627年农历三月，记录于《仿米氏山水》图之后。题款中则以艺术史家之态势，明确的指出："董北苑[董源]好作烟景，烟云变没，即米画也。余于米芾潇湘白云图，悟墨戏三昧……"对董其昌而言，"烟景"、"烟云变没"、"墨戏"均与自宋代以降的士人画有着一脉相承的关系，并始终是董其昌致力追求文人画传统，对艺术最高境界的基本诠释。虽然他曾说董源(卒于962)好描绘烟云，但认为最得云山与墨戏之功的则数米芾(1051－1107)、米友仁(1074－1151)父子。董其昌曾不止一次的在自己的题跋中申述类似的看法。他将云山墨戏的观念追溯到十世纪的董源、继而上溯王洽(卒于805)的泼墨技法、归结至唐朝大诗人与画家王维(701－761)的艺术，认为王维为文人画传统的源头活水。在一个题跋中，他更指出米芾纠正了画家普遍的失误，并因此得以米家山水改革了山水画之技法。

米家云山之法独到之处，在于其山头均以层层松软、湿润的横向皴法点缀，形成一种云雾迷漫的山色。董其昌运用这种皴法描绘远山，并附加白云远岫。然其云岫不施墨色，而将其部分保留，于外围设以淡墨，形成云气氤氲起伏的效果。此画构图精巧，远近层次分明；前景、中景、远景，均设在卷首，之后将近景放在米家法山陵的云雾聚集处，图画卷尾处则介入中景一段之山水 — 溪水之畔几许参差的树木，远处湖水连溪。前景处，董其昌运用的不是米点皴，而用绵长平行走向的披麻皴，借用了董源与元代画家黄公望 (1269－1354)另一种轻灵的笔法。前景一段细节更进一步沿用了黄公望的笔触，为了强调三处山石，还着意加强了一个"Y"字形的山势结构。米家法于元代早期传承到高克恭(1248－1310)，明代中期由陈淳(1483－1544)接续，风格上均有不同的发展。董其昌所探索的云山墨戏实为米家与黄公望笔法的综合结果，其形式则是一种与早期名家长期相抗衡的自觉表现。董曾与题跋中如此感叹："当恨古人不见我也！"

董其昌1555年出生于上海的一个平民人家，早年在家与身为私塾先生的父亲学习，之后在松江县立学校继续求学。他参加会考因书法粗劣而未能名列前茅，深受刺激的董其昌从此毕生发奋钻研书法，并勤奋临摹唐代名家及二王，即王羲之(约303－约361)与其子王献之(344－388)之作，立志自成一家。在准备下一次会试之际，董其昌曾在一些大户人家中担任教席，包括当时最知名的收藏家项元汴(1525－1590)，因此有了一窥早期书画名作之绝佳机会。经过几番尝试，董其昌终于通过了乡试，在1588年到北京准备参加举人资格的会试。获得举人资格后，他得了一个翰林院的职衔。1591年，他却自请去职离京，直到1594年才又重回北京，充任皇太子之講學官。因顾忌同侪之妒嫉，又于1599年再次辞官。董辞官在家，直到1604年受命出任提學副使一职，此次董依然仕途短暂。因拒绝收贿，致使當地鄉民蓄意挑起暴动，将他的提學办公处付之祝融。董其昌虽然无咎，仍于1606年离职还乡，告老在家至1622年。即位伊始的前皇子，待念师徒之过往，在1620年诏董其昌任太常寺少卿，掌國子司業事，旋后出任南京禮部尚書。董之此职衔为一虚悬之礼仪性官职，但董有感于宦海浮沉，于1626年再度辞官，并因此避过了宦官魏忠賢镇压迫害朝中东林党人一劫。1632年，董再度被招入京任职，两年後才卸任，并从此致仕。

辞官期間，董其昌悠遊於山水與書畫之間，成就了他集画家与理论家于一身的艺术生涯，并可称得上是中国绘画史晚期最杰出、影响后世最大的一个人物。他的绘画与理论写作，影响了他身后中国绘画的发展方向。他用佛教禅宗的历史作比拟，将中国山水画分为南北两宗。北宗画家采渐悟之蹊径，以画事为业，并藉以钻研学习；南宗则为文人画家，由顿悟而成家，以书画为自我陶冶之事。米芾、米友仁即为南宗画派之中坚分子，一脉传承从王维至元代各大家之传统。董其昌对画史画风的评断，成为十七世纪清初画界公认的正统派。王原祁(1642－1715;见图录第18号)即是此正统派的重要传承人物之一。

《仿米氏山水》一图中有两方清代名藏家安岐的收藏印。安氏原为朝鲜后裔，其家族原为满清正黄旗之包衣，安之父因为当时权倾一时的相国明珠(1635－1708)工作，以盐业贸易而致富，安岐因此得以成为知名的鉴藏家。安岐于1740年初编辑了一套收藏目录，然此画却未编入其中。1746年间，安岐大部分的收藏为乾隆皇帝收入内府，乾隆并于次年为此画作了题跋。此图卷在被收入内府收藏前，将董其昌1620年1月时以米家书法写就的一首杜甫(712－770)诗作一并装裱入画。在书史中，米芾为董其昌最为赞赏的书家之一，将该诗裱入此仿米之画当是自然之事。而安岐之印各打在图画与题字旁，可见此两件作品在流出安府前，即已如是装裱合一。更可能的是安岐本人，蓄意将此二书画作品装裱在同一图卷中。除了乾隆皇帝全数八方御印，嘉庆、宣统之鉴藏玺亦在其中。溥仪与弟弟溥杰(1907－1994)早在1922年即将此图卷偷运出宫，1932年溥仪称帝时被一并带到伪满洲国。

江文苇（LYC译）

注解：

1. 此画与其题跋收录于《石渠宝笈续编》(1793)，重刊于《秘殿珠林石渠宝笈合编》，12册(上海:上海书店,1988)，第3册，第441－42页。
2. 董其昌，《畫眼》，重刊于《藝術叢編》（台北:台北世界書局，1962）第一集，第12冊，第31页。
3. 有关图例，参见克里夫兰美术馆所藏，董于《江山秋霁》中之题跋。插图见于《八代之中国绘画：尼尔森。阿特金博物馆和克里夫兰艺术博物馆藏珍》(克里夫兰：克里夫兰博物馆，1980年)，第191号图，第244－46页。
4. 有关董其昌生平事迹，见Celia Carrington Riely,〈董其昌的一生〉,收于《董其昌世纪，1555－1636》，何惠鉴（Wai-kam Ho）编(堪萨斯市:The Nelson-Atkins Museum of Art,1992)，第2册，第385－457页;任道斌《董其昌系年》(北京:文物出版社,1988)。
5. 关于董其昌画家与理论家的艺术生涯，见《董其昌世纪，1555－1636》，特别是何惠鉴（Wai-kam Ho）与何晓嘉（Dawn Ho Delbanco）〈Tung Ch'i-ch'ang's Transcendence of History and Art〉，第3－41页；方闻,〈董其昌与艺术的复兴〉，第43－54页;以及谢稚柳,〈董其昌理论之画禅〉，第xxxv－xxxvi页。

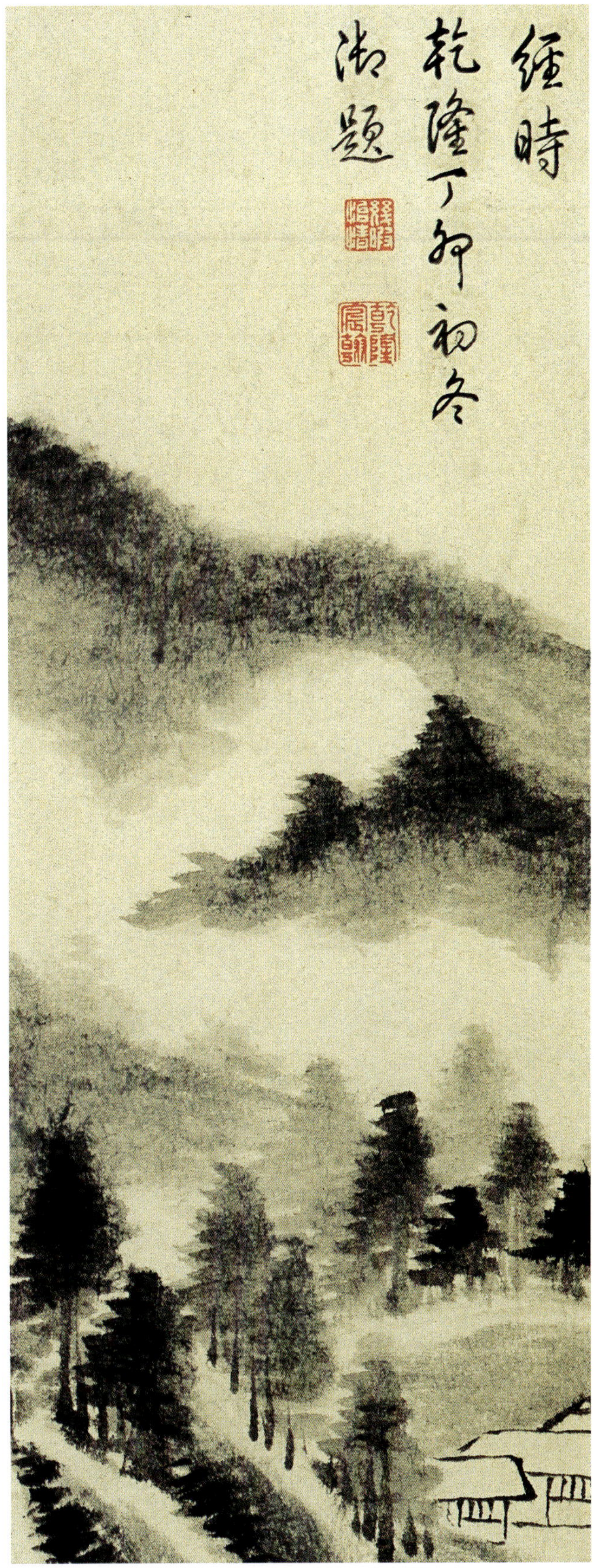

16 (detail 局部)

17
清 弘历 临怀素千字文
手卷，纸本水墨
Hongli (Qianlong emperor, 1711–1799)
Copying Huaisu's "Thousand-Character Essay," 1770

Handscroll; ink on paper
30.3 x 689.3 cm

ARTIST'S SEAL: Guquanzhai (rectangular/relief), Yanlu (rectangular/relief), Zhuizuoqiyi (square/intaglio), Shuiyue liang chengming (rectangular/relief), Moyun (rectangular/intaglio), Chuilu (rectangular/relief), Xinyin jing kanji (round/relief), Jushui yue zaishou (rectangular/intaglio), Miaoyi xie qingbo(rectangular/relief), Ai zhu xue xinxu (rectangular/intaglio).

IMPERIAL SEALS: [Qianlong, r. 1736–95] Qianlong chenhan (square/relief)

OTHER SEALS: [Museum of the Northeast] Dongbei bowuguan zhencang zhiyin (square/relief)

书家印鉴：古泉斋（朱文长方印）、研露（朱文长方印）、追琢其意(白文方印)、水月两征明（朱文长方印）、墨云（白文长方印）、垂露（朱文长方印）、心印静堪寄（朱文圆印）、掬水月在手（白文长方印）、妙意写清波（朱文长方印）、爱竹学心虚（白文长方印）

皇家印鉴：［清乾隆皇帝弘历，在位1736－1796］乾隆宸翰（朱文方印）

其他印鉴：［东北博物馆］东北博物馆珍藏之印（朱文方印）

The fourth emperor of the Qing dynasty, Hongli, took the name Qianlong to designate his reign. A superb ruler with great abilities, the Qianlong emperor was very passionate about the arts. He expanded the flourishing age that began in the Kangxi era (1662–1722), bringing about unprecedented prosperity under Manchu rule. When Chinese calligraphers study works by masters of the past, they routinely make copies. Hongli also routinely practiced the copying of calligraphy masterworks.

Copying Huaisu's "Thousand-Character Essay" is an example of Hongli's attempt to learn and absorb the fine qualities found in Huaisu's (ca. 736–ca. 799) calligraphy.[1] Once part of the Qing court collection, Huaisu's *Thousand-Character Essay* is currently in Japan. This long scroll of a thousand characters was hand-copied by Hongli using Huaisu's original as a model. All the characters are constructed of strokes showing a rounded and full-bodied quality, a marked feature of Hongli's personal calligraphic style. The dexterity in Huaisu's calligraphy, which is executed in slimmer but more vigorous strokes, is also captured here, resulting in a lighter composition with a livelier expression than those found in most of Hongli's works.

HWL (trans. DHWS)

Notes

1. Huaisu was a monk of the Tang dynasty known for his love of wine and calligraphy. Legend has it that he led an untrammeled life, never concerned himself with trifles, and had the tendency to create spontaneously when drunk. His improvisational work is so free and dynamic that the brushwork, with a multitude of unexpected changes, resembles nothing less than a fierce storm yet never departs from aesthetic principles. His brushwork gives the appearance of vigorous movements—flying, leaping, and swinging.

清代的第四个皇帝弘历，年号乾隆，是一位治国能力超强而且富有文艺才情的国君，他继续扩大了康熙（1662－1722年）以来的盛世，使清统治达到了空前繁荣。书法家们在研究古人作品时，通常要亲自临写，弘历也常临写前人的书法名作。

弘历的这卷《临怀素千字文》，就是他为吸收怀素书法的优点，而临写的一个精品长卷（注1)。怀素《草书千字文》，曾入清宫收藏，现藏于日本。弘历就是依据怀素本的本子，临写成了草书千字文大卷。卷中书法，整体形态依然呈现了弘历书法的基本特点，以圆浑见长，但又吸收了怀素书法中瘦劲而灵妙的笔意，致使通篇布局上出现了不同以往的轻盈神采。

黄伟利

注解：

1. 怀素（約736－約799)，是唐代著名的僧人，他的生平以酒和书法而传奇，传说他性情疏放，为人不拘小节，醉酣兴发，则任意挥写，下笔如骤雨疾旋，随手万变，而终不离法度，呈现了飞动跳荡、神彩飞扬的景象。

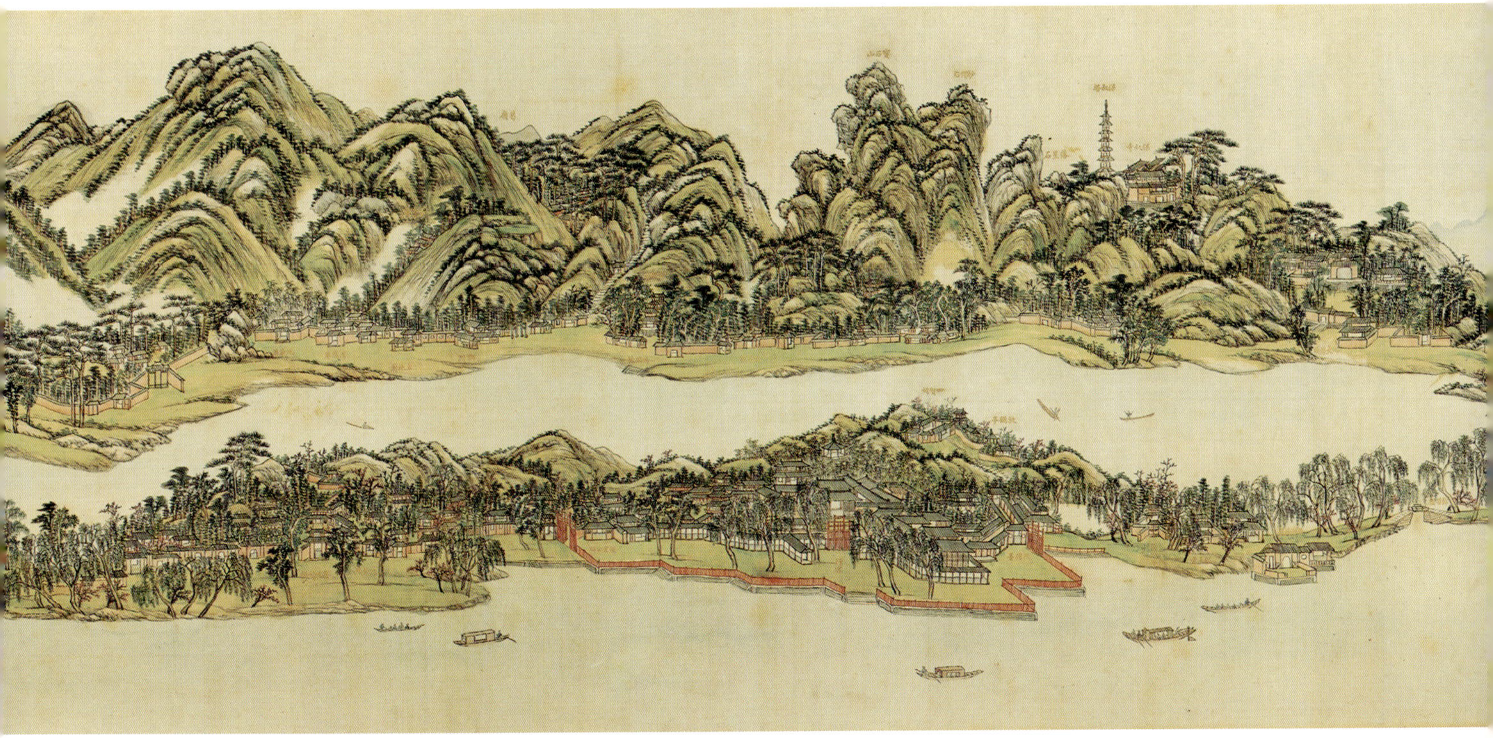

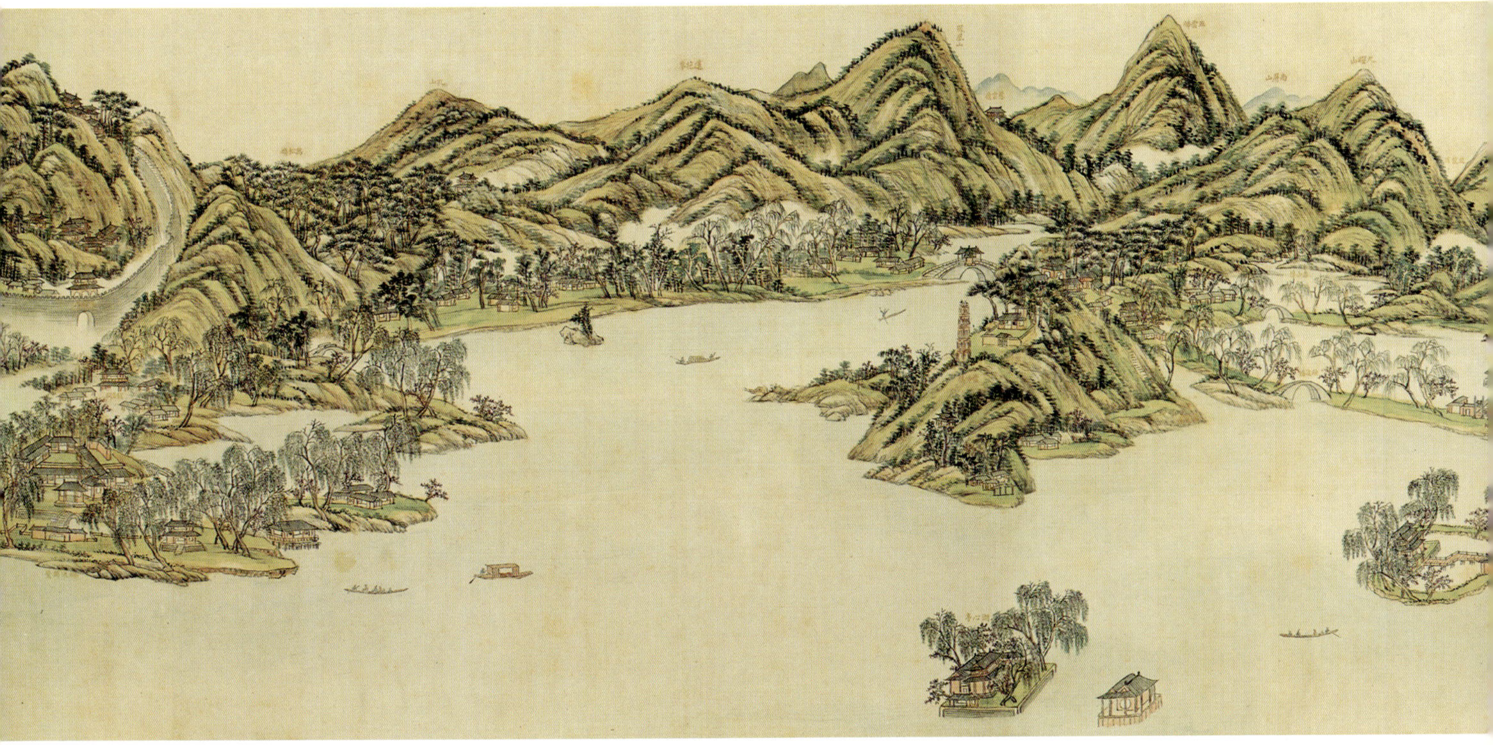

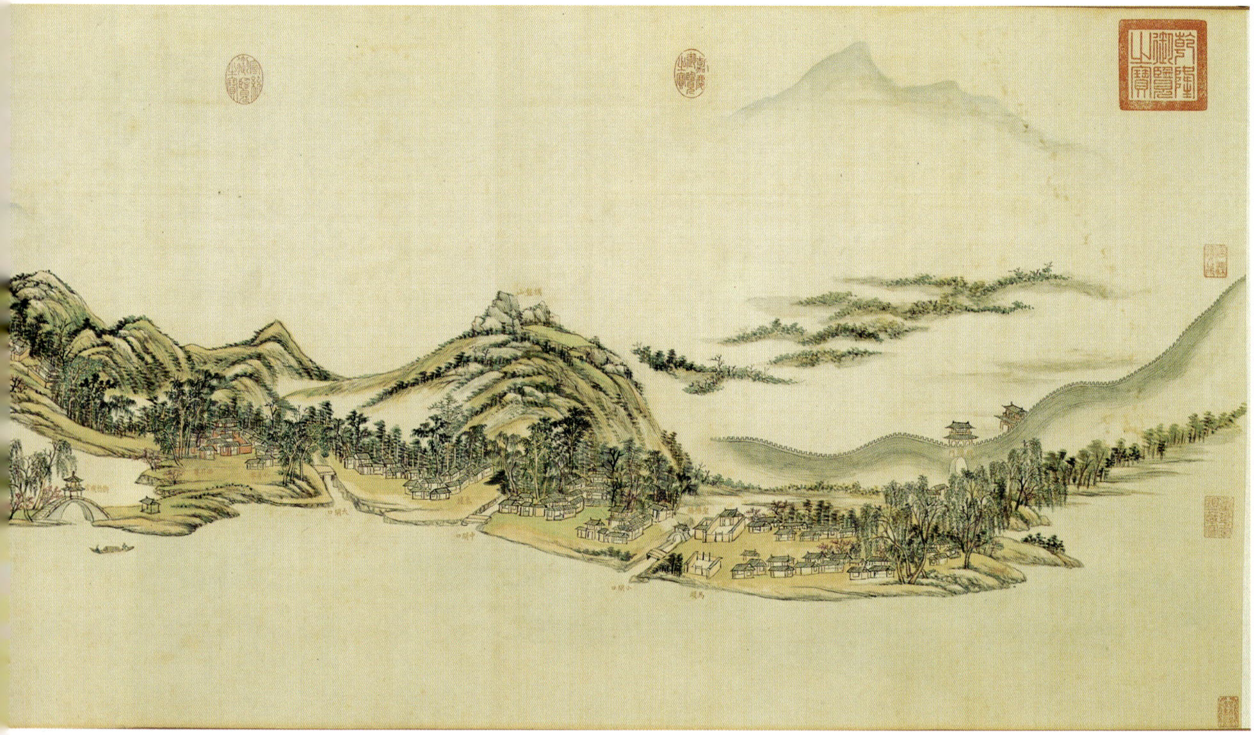

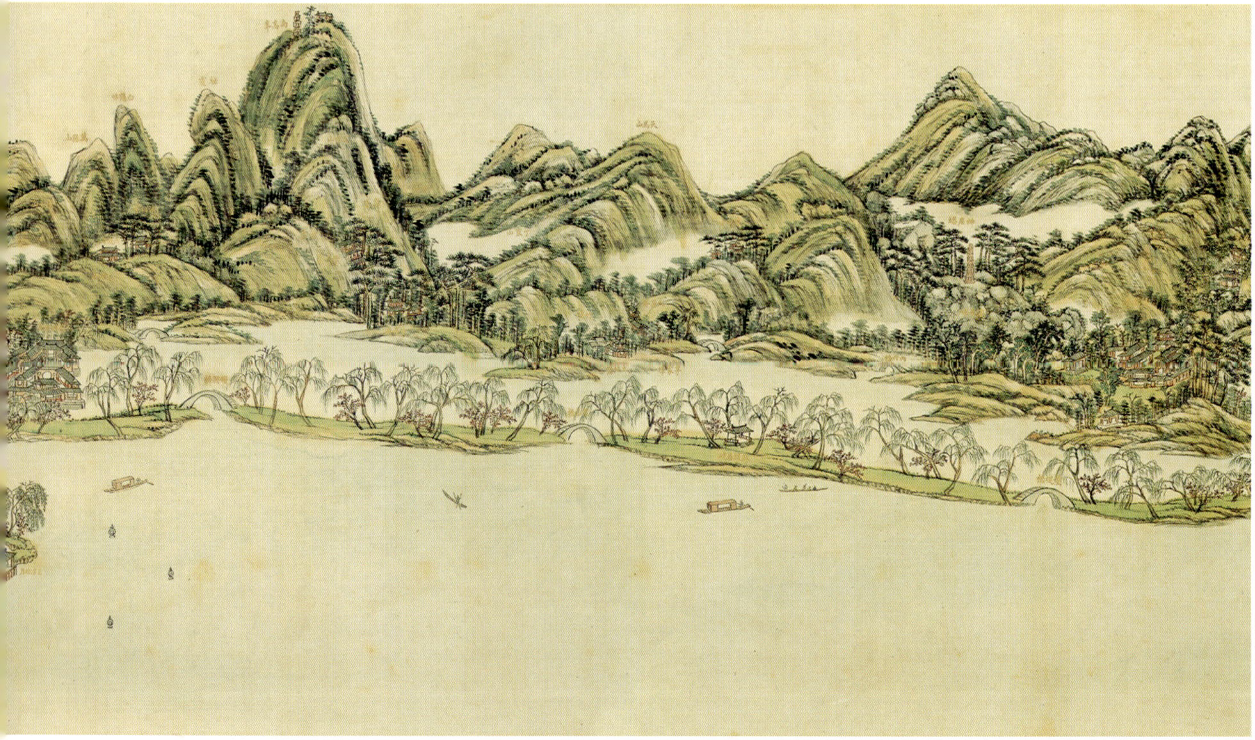

18
清 王原祁 西湖十景图
手卷，绢本水墨设色金书
Wang Yuanqi (1642–1715)
Ten Views of West Lake, after 1699

Handscroll; ink, color, and gold on silk
62 x 652.5 cm

ARTIST'S SEAL: Wang Yuanqi (square/relief and intaglio)
IMPERIAL SEALS: [Qianlong, r. 1736–95] Qianlong yulan zhibao (square/relief), Shiqu baoji (rectangular/relief), Chonghuagong jiancangbao (rectangular/relief), Leshoutang tushuji (rectangular/relief); [Jiaqing, r. 1796–1820] Jiaqing yulan zhibao (oval/relief); [Xuantong (Puyi), r. 1909–11] Xuantong yulan zhibao (oval/relief)

画家印鉴：王原祁（朱白文方印）
皇家印鉴：[清乾隆皇帝弘历，在位1736－1795]：乾隆御览之宝(朱文方印)、石渠宝笈（朱文长方印）、重华宫鉴藏宝（朱文长方印）、乐寿堂图书记（朱文长方印）。[清嘉庆皇帝顒琰，在位1796－1820]：嘉庆御览之宝（朱文椭圆印）。[清宣统皇帝溥仪，在位1909－1911]：宣统御览之宝（朱文椭圆印）

The theme of the Ten Views of West Lake developed in the thirteenth century during the Southern Song dynasty (1127–1279) and is most closely associated with the court painter Ma Lin (ca. 1180–after 1256). After the Song court had settled on Hangzhou as its temporary capital, nearby West Lake, located to the east of the city and surrounded by mountains, became a source of artistic inspiration. Its natural scenic beauty was enhanced by its literary associations; the poet Su Shi (1037–1101), for example, had a government position in Hangzhou and composed numerous poems extolling the beauty of West Lake. During his administration, a dike had been built which became known as "Su Dike." As a program of paintings illustrating the beauty of West Lake, The Ten Views owed much to the Eight Views of Xiao and Xiang, a painting theme that had developed during the eleventh century and was associated with the painter Song Di (ca. 1015–ca. 1080).[1] Wu Zimu's (ca. 1256–after 1334) *Record of the Millet Dream* (*Mengliang lu*), an account of Hangzhou with a preface dated to 1274, records the Ten Views as follows:

> In recent times the ten most spectacular scenes of the four seasons around West Lake and its mountains have been illustrated by painters. These are (1) Spring Dawn at Su Dike, (2) Lotus Breeze at Qu Winery, (3) Autumn Moon Above the Placid Lake, (4) Remnant Snow on Broken Bridge, (5) Listening to the Orioles by the Willow Ripples, (6) Watching Fish at Flower Cove, (7) Sunset on Lifeng Pagoda, (8) Twin Peaks Piercing the Clouds, (9) Evening Bell from Nanping Hill, and (10) Three Stupas and the Reflecting Moon. In spring, flowers and willows compete in beauty, while lotus and pomegranates bloom in summer. In autumn, the fragrance of cassia floats in the air, and in winter, jade-like plums bloom amidst the whirling flakes of auspicious snow. The scenes of the four seasons are ever changing, and these things that gratify the heart and give pleasure proceed endlessly apace.[2]

The Ten Views combined famous scenic spots with the seasons and the time of day. An album by Ye Xiaoyan (act. ca. 1253–58), a follower of the court painter Ma Yuan (act. ca. 1190–1230), the father of Ma Lin, preserves all ten scenes.[3] It had been in the collection of the great early Qing collector Liang Qingbiao (1620–1691) and may well have been known to Wang Yuanqi. Here, however, Wang chooses the handscroll format, and in this choice is probably following the model of the panoramic landscape handscrolls developed by Wang Hui (1632–1717) in the 1690s to illustrate the second southern inspection tour of the Kangxi emperor. Wang Yuanqi would have been very familiar with this project while serving at court; he had met with Wang Hui in Beijing in 1690. An immediate source for his painting, however, may have been a thirteenth-century depiction of West Lake attributed to the Southern Song court painter Li Song (act. ca. 1190–1230) and another handscroll depicting West Lake and Hangzhou also attributed to Li Song.[4] Both scrolls were in private collections, and it is possible that Wang Yuanqi saw one or both of them. His handscroll is like a stretched out version of the first Li Song scroll.

Wang Yuanqi begins his scroll with the Hangzhou city wall and then moves from north to south along the western side of West Lake. The city wall reappears at the end of the scroll. Each spot is identified by characters written in gold ink. It is a topographical panorama executed in a style of landscape derived from the Yuan dynasty painter Huang Gongwang (1269–1354). Wang's juxtapositions of solids and voids and the undulating rhythm of the landscape display his mastery of the principles of landscape painting espoused by Dong Qichang (1555–1636) and his grandfather Wang Shimin (1592–1680). Wang Yuanqi developed these ideas in both his paintings and his writings, often speaking of "dragon veins" (*longmo*), a geomantic term, as an underlying principle in landscape painting.[5]

The composition of the handscroll is continuous, following the topography of West Lake rather than depicting each scene separately as had been common in early paintings of the Eight Views of Xiao and Xiang. Ma Yuan's composition for these eight views, which would have been contemporary with the development of the Ten Views of West Lake, is known only thought a copy by the Qing court painter Dong Bangda (1699–1769).[6] Ma's solution had been to have each scene follow consecutively in the handscroll but to separate each scene from the next. Wang's solution was to follow the topography and not the subject matter of the Ten Views.

Wang Yuanqi, the grandson of the great painter and connoisseur Wang Shimin, was born in 1642, two years before the Manchu conquest of China.[7] He grew up little affected by the conquest under the tutelage of his grandfather, learning to paint and absorbing the teachings transmitted from Dong Qichang. After he earned his *jinshi* degree in 1670, he served as a district magistrate before being appointed a censor and beginning a long career in Beijing. He rose to be chancellor of the Hanlin Academy and, in 1712, was appointed senior vice-president of the Ministry of Revenue, a position that he held until his death in 1715. He served as a *gongfeng*, a sort of talented companion, to the Kangxi emperor, advising him on the palace collection of calligraphy and painting. According to Zhang Geng, writing in 1735, the emperor often went to the South Library, where Wang Yuanqi served, and ordered him to paint landscapes. The emperor bestowed on him a seal reading: "Huatu liuyu ren kan" (Your paintings should be preserved for people to see).[8] In 1705 he was made editor-in-chief of the *Encyclopedic Collection of Writings on Calligraphy and Painting of the Peiwen Studio* (*Peiwenzhai shuhuapu*), which was submitted to the throne in 1708. In celebration of the Kangxi emperor's sixtieth birthday, a long scroll titled *Ten Thousand Years Birthday Celebration Scroll* (*Wanshou tu*) was undertaken. The project was so large that it required the creation of a special Painting Bureau. In 1713 Wang Yuanqi was brought in to supervise the completion of the project, but he died the year before it was finished. The completed scroll was signed by the court painter Leng Mei.

The Kangxi emperor visited the West Lake in 1699, on his third southern inspection tour. At the time, he made some changes in the names of the Ten Views of West Lake and in some place names. These name changes are incorporated into the labels on Wang Yuanqi's scroll, indicating that it was executed after 1699, probably at imperial request in order to record the visit. The *Shiqu baoji* catalogue of the imperial collection, commissioned in 1744, records two handscrolls by Wang Yuanqi depicting West Lake, one in ink monochrome on silk and the other in ink and color on silk with inscriptions in gold ink.[9] The ink-only scroll may have been the preparatory painting for the finished version, which was then executed using color. The present painting has seals of both the Qianlong and Jiaqing emperors and was taken out of the Forbidden City by Puyi and his brother Pujie. It was then taken by Puyi to Changchun when he became ruler of Manchukuo, and after the founding of the People's Republic of China, it entered the collection of the Liaoning Provincial Museum.

DAS

Notes

1. For a discussion of the Ten Views of West Lake and the cultural landscape of West Lake, see Hui-shu Lee, "West Lake and the Mapping of Southern Song Art," in Hui-shu Lee, *Exquisite Moments: West Lake and Southern Song Art* (New York: China Institute Gallery, 2001), pp. 19–59. For the Eight Views of Xiao and Xiang, see Richard M. Barnhart, "Shining Rivers: *Eight Views of the Hsiao and Hsiang* in Sung Painting," in *International Colloquium on Chinese Art History, 1991, Proceedings, Painting and Calligraphy, Part I* (Taipei: National Palace Museum, 1992), pp. 45–95.
2. Translation adapted from Hui-shu Lee, "West Lake and the Mapping of Southern Song Art," p. 32.
3. For documentation and illustration of Ye Xiaoyan's album, see *Gugong shuhua tulu* [Illustrated catalogue of calligraphy and painting in the National Palace Museum], vol. 22 (Taipei: Guoli gugong bowuyuan, 2003), pp. 74–79.
4. The first handscroll is in the Shanghai Museum of Art and the second in the Freer Gallery of Art. For illustrations, see Hui-shu Lee, *Exquisite Moments*, pp. 24–27.
5. See Susan Bush, "Lung-mo, K'ai-ho, and Ch'i-fu: Some Implications of Wang Yuan-ch'i's Three Compositional terms," *Oriental Art* 8, no. 3 (Autumn 1962): 120–22.
6. See *The Jade Studio: Masterpieces of Ming and Qing Painting and Calligraphy from the Wong Nan-p'ing Collection* (New Haven: Yale University Art Gallery, 1993), no. 71, pp. 228–32.
7. For biographical information, see J. C. Yang, "Wang Yüan-ch'i," in *Eminent Chinese of the Ch'ing Period*, ed. Arthur W. Hummel (Washington: United States Government Printing Office, 1944), pp. 844–45.
8. Zhang Geng, *Guochao huazheng lu* (preface dated 1735) [Painters of the (Qing) dynasty], reprinted in *Zhongguo sh-uhua quanshu*, vol. 10 (Shanghai: Shanghai shuhua chubanshe, 1996), pp. 440–41.
9. *Shiqu baoji* [Treasured boxes of the Stone Channel] (1745), reprinted in *Midian zhulin Shiqubaoji hebian* [Pearl forest of the Secret Hall and Treasured boxes of the Stone Channel, combined edition], 12 vols. (Shanghai: Shanghai shudian, 1988), vol. 2, p. 756.

《西湖十景图》此一主题源于十三世纪南宋时期(1127－1279)，且与当时宫廷画家马麟(约1180－1256后)有着密切的关系。南宋定都于西湖边、群山环绕的杭州城东，其都城亦成了文学家与艺术家创作灵感的来源。它秀丽的自然景致，吸引了历代许多文人墨客，苏轼(1037－1101)就是其中之一。在苏州从官时，苏轼作了无数赞赏西湖之美的诗词，而他任职期间所负责督建的堤防，则被后人称为“苏堤”。以自然美景如西湖者成为一绘画主题，起缘于十一世纪画家宋迪(约1015－约1080)的名作《潇湘八景》。吴自牧(约1256－1334后)在他1274年作序的《梦粱录》中，有一则关于《西湖十景》的记载：

> 近者画家称湖山四时景色最奇者有十，曰苏堤春晓，曲（麯）院风荷，平湖秋月，断桥残雪，柳浪闻莺，花港观鱼，雷锋夕照，两峰插云，南屏晚钟，三潭映月。春则花柳争妍，夏则荷榴竞放，秋则桂子飘香，冬则梅花破玉，瑞雪飞瑶。四时之景不同，而赏心乐事者亦与之无穷矣。

该十景之描述包含了西湖胜景景名，以及游览其景区之特定时间与季节。画家叶肖岩(活动于约1253－58)，画风追随宫廷画家马远（活动于约1190－1230；马麟之父）之传统，将其十景一一绘入一套册页中。该册页一直都为清初大收藏家梁清标(1620－1691)所有，并可能为王原祁所熟知。然而，王原祁选择了图卷的形式，并以王翚(1632－1717)于1690年代为康熙皇帝绘制二次南巡图所创的全景山水卷形式为典范。奉为宫廷画师，王原祁对此次南巡之策划定有相当的了解，他与王翚早已于1690年时在北京相识。然王原祁更直接的灵感来源，来自于传为十三世纪南宋宫廷画师李宋(活动于1190－1230)的一幅描写西湖景致，以及另一幅亦传为李宋所画，关于杭州与西湖的图卷。两帙图卷当时均属私人收藏，但王原祁可能于当时已得见此二作。王此卷作品就像是李宋的前一幅西湖图卷，但更加延长之版本。

画卷伊始，王原祁以杭州城墙作为开场，然后将视野从西湖的北面与南面依序延伸，该城墙则在图画结尾再次出现。各个景点均以文字用金墨标示。作品诠释风格承续于元朝画家黄公望(1269－1354)类似地形学之全景山水形式；虚实相间、起伏有致的风景描绘，则显示了画家对董其昌(1555－1636)与祖父王时敏(1592－1680)山水原理之深切掌握。王原祁时而提及“龙脉”一风水学名词，以此为山水画最潜在之根本理念，并将此原则詳盡闡述于自己的绘画与写作当中。

与早先如《潇湘八景》图普偏运用分景布置的不同手法，王原祁此卷的构图，悉从西湖的自然地理形式而相连续。时间上相当于《西湖十景》成型之期，马远式的《八景图》，目前只可从清朝画家董邦达(1699－1769)之摹本一窥究竟。方法上将所有景区连贯在图面上，但每一景则又与其他图景清楚划分，毫无关联。王原祁不以《十景》本身为主题，却采用了依从地理形势的方式处理山水。

王原祁生于1642年，满洲入关前两年，他的成长过程并未因清廷入主中国而受到太大的冲击。王原祁师从祖父、知名画家与鉴赏家王时敏，学习并师法传承董其昌的书画传统。王1670年中进士，不久后被召入内廷，从此开始他在北京几十年的仕途生涯。王后被擢为翰林院学士，并于1712年出任户部左侍郎，直至1715年去世。他也曾担任“供奉”一职，陪侍康熙皇帝，并负责宫中书画收藏之顾问工作。根据张庚于1735年的纪录，康熙时常亲临王原祁之工作处南书房，传谕作山水画。康熙并曾赠王一方印，上刻“画图留与人看”。1705年，王奉任翰林院书画谱馆总裁，主持编纂《佩文斋书画谱》。《画谱》于1708完成，奉承御览。为庆祝康熙六十大寿所绘制的《万寿盛典图》，因作品程序浩大，内廷不但另设了特别画院，并于1713年，擢任王原祁监督完成该画之职。王在画事完成前去世，全画由宫廷画家冷枚完成监制题款。

康熙皇帝于1699年第三次南巡时临幸西湖，并于当时对几个《西湖十景》景点及杭州地名名称加以改动。这些西湖景点后均收入在王原祁图卷的标示中，图中指称该作于1699后完成，显示此图卷为奉敕而作、并以纪录皇帝南巡的历程。清廷皇室于1744年钦定的书画目录《石渠宝笈》中，记载了两幅由王原祁所画描写西湖的图卷。一幅为绢本水墨，一幅为绢本设色，以金墨题款。前者水墨本，应为后作设色成品起稿前的草稿备样。现今世人所知之作盖有乾隆和嘉庆御玺，为溥仪之弟溥杰从紫禁城挟带出宫。此画继由溥仪就位满洲国皇帝时攜至长春，在中国人民共和国成立时，才正式为辽宁省博物馆收为馆藏。

江文苇（LYC译）

注解：

1. 有关西湖十景的讨论与西湖的文化景观，见李慧淑，〈西湖与南宋艺术之概况〉，收于李慧淑，《精致的时刻：西湖与南宋艺术》(纽约：华美协进社中国美术馆，2001)，第19－59页。有关潇湘八景，见班宗华(Richard M. Barnhart)，〈闪耀之河：宋画中的潇湘八景〉，收录于《1991年国际中国艺术文物讨论會：论文集/书画（上）》(台北：国立故宫博物院，1992)，第45－95页。
2. 引用译文，见李慧淑，〈西湖与南宋艺术之概况〉，第32页。
3. 关于叶肖岩册页之记录与图例，见《故宫书画图录》(台北：国立故宫博物院，2003)，第22册，第74－79页。
4. 前图为上海博物馆收藏，后图由佛利尔美术馆所藏。参考图片，见李慧淑，《精致的时刻》，第24－27页。
5. 见Susan Bush，〈龙脉、开合、起伏：王原祁三个构图名称之含义〉，*Oriental Art*（东方美术），第8册，第3期(1962年秋)，第120－22页。
6. 见《玉斋：王南平珍藏明清书画精选》(纽海文：耶鲁大学美术馆，1993)，第71号画，第228－32页。
7. 有关王原祁生平事迹，见 J. C. Yang （或 Yang Rujin），〈王原祁〉，收录于《清代名人传略》，恒慕义（Arthur W. Hummel）编（华盛顿特区：国会图书馆，1943年），第844－45页。
8. 张庚，《国朝画征录》(序言作于1735)，重刊于《中国书画全书》（上海：上海书画出版社，1996)，第10册，第440－41页。
9. 《石渠宝笈》(1745)，重刊于《秘殿珠林石渠宝笈合编》，12册(上海：上海书店，1988)，第2册，第756页。

19

清　　张照　临苏轼杂帖　　卷

手卷，纸本水墨

Zhang Zhao (1691–1745)

***Copying Su Shi's Model Calligraphy,* 1737**

Handscroll; ink on paper

26 x 196.2 cm

ARTIST'S SEALS: Zhang Zhao (square/intaglio), Fahualu (square/relief)

IMPERIAL SEALS: [Qianlong, r. 1736–95] Qianlong yulan zhibao (oval/relief), Ningshougong xuru shiqubaoji (square/relief), Shiqubaoji (rectangular/relief), Leshoutang jiancangbao (rectangular/intaglio), Shiqudingjian (round/relief), Baoji chongbian (square/intaglio), Qianlong jianshang (round/intaglio), Sanxitang jingjianxi (rectangular/relief), Yizisun (square/intaglio); [Jiaqing, r. 1796–1820] Jiaqing yulan zhibao (oval/relief); [Xuantong (Puyi), r. 1909–11] Xuantong yulan zhibao (oval/relief)

画家印鉴：张照（白文方印）、法华庐（朱文方印）

皇家印鉴：[清乾隆皇帝弘历，在位1736－1795]乾隆御览之宝（朱文椭圆印）、宁寿宫续入石渠宝笈（朱文方印）、石渠宝笈（朱文长方印）、乐寿堂鉴藏宝（白文长方印）、石渠定鉴（朱文圆印）、宝笈重编（白文方印）、乾隆鉴赏（白文圆印）、三希堂精鉴玺(朱文长方印)、宜子孙（白文方印）。[清嘉庆皇帝颙琰，在位1796－1820]嘉庆御览之宝（朱文椭圆印）。[清宣统皇帝溥仪，在位1909-1911]宣统御览之宝（朱文椭圆印）。

Typical of the kind of calligraphic style prevalent during the early Qing dynasty, this scroll, titled *Copying Su Shi's Model Calligraphy*, was created by Zhang Zhao in the ninth month of the *dingsi* year (1737) in the Qianlong reign.

A successful candidate at a metropolitan examination in the forty-eighth year of the Kangxi reign (1709), Zhang Zhao attained his *jinshi* when he was only nineteen years old. During the Yongzheng reign (1723–35) he was promoted to minister in the Board of Punishments, a position he held until his death in the tenth year of Qianlong (1745).

Although he lived a brief fifty-five years, Zhang Zhao demonstrated multiple talents. His thorough understanding of the law, versatility in music, comprehensive knowledge of Buddhist classics, and his poetry are all impressive. The most highly acclaimed of all his accomplishments, however, is his calligraphy. A native of Songjiang, as was Dong Qichang, Zhang Zhao was greatly influenced by Dong Qichang in calligraphy. In addition, he absorbed a great deal from the calligraphy of Yan Zhenqing of the Tang dynasty and Mi Fu of the Song dynasty, enabling him to form an open and pleasant style of his own, which is clearly demonstrated in this work.

The signature "Siweng" in the postscript at the end of the scroll provides extra information about this work. Siweng was an alias used frequently by Dong Qichang. The scroll consists of two five-character poems by the outstanding Northern Song dynasty writer, calligrapher, and art theorist Su Shi that Dong Qichang, out of respect for Su, had copied from printed calligraphy model-books. Similarly, out of respect to both Dong and Su, Zhang Zhao carefully copied Dong's work in its entirety.

The many collection seals of the Qing imperial palace placed on this scroll indicate that this scroll by Zhang Zhao was already recognized as an excellent work of art in its own day, worthy of being kept in the imperial collection.

HWL (trans. DHWS)

张照（1691－1745年）作于乾隆丁巳年（1737年）9月的这卷《临苏轼杂帖》，是清代前期书法艺术的一种典型风格。

张照于康熙四十八年（1709年）考中进士，时年仅19岁，雍正年间（1723－1735）就升迁到了刑部尚书的官位，直到乾隆十年（1745年）辞世。尽管张照的寿命仅55岁，却显示了多方面的才能，他精通法律，通晓音乐，精通佛典，擅长作诗，然而，最为世人称道的还是他的书法。张照也是松江人，与董其昌同乡，他的书法深受董其昌影响，他又在唐代颜真卿、宋代米芾的书法中吸取法度，最终形成了属于他自己特有的，在这卷《临苏轼杂帖》行书作品中可清晰地看到一种开朗舒展的格调。

卷后署名“思翁”的跋中，透露出此卷作品的信息：“思翁”是董其昌常用的别号，卷中的内容，是董其昌从法帖中临写北宋杰出文学家、书法家和艺术理论家苏轼的两首五言诗，以此表达他对苏轼的敬意。出于对董其昌以及苏轼的崇敬，张照又将董其昌的原作仔细地临写下来。

卷中钤盖的多方清宫内府藏印，说明张照的这卷作品被认同为那个时代的优秀作品，被皇家保存了下来。

黄伟利

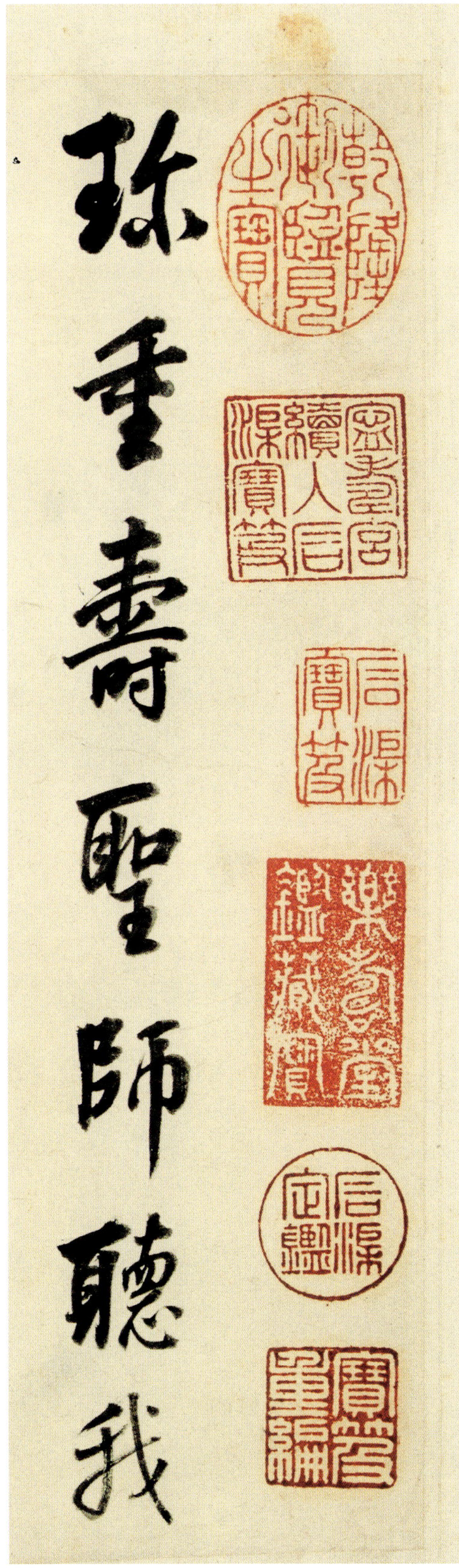

19 (detail 局部)

19

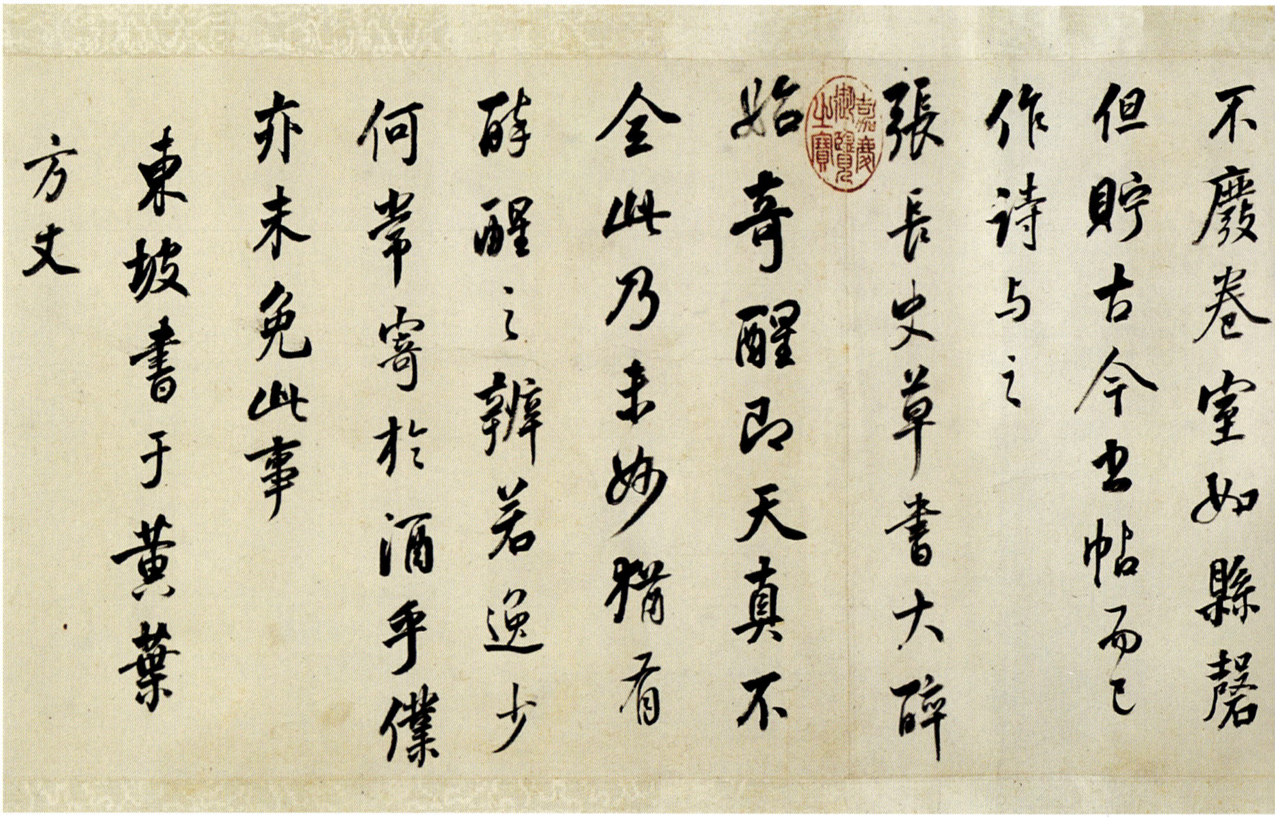
不廢卷室如縣磬
但貯古今書帖而已
作詩與之
張長史草書大醉
始奇醒後天真不
全此乃未妙猶有
醉醒之辨若遂步
何常寄於酒乎僕
亦未免此事
東坡書于黃葉
方丈

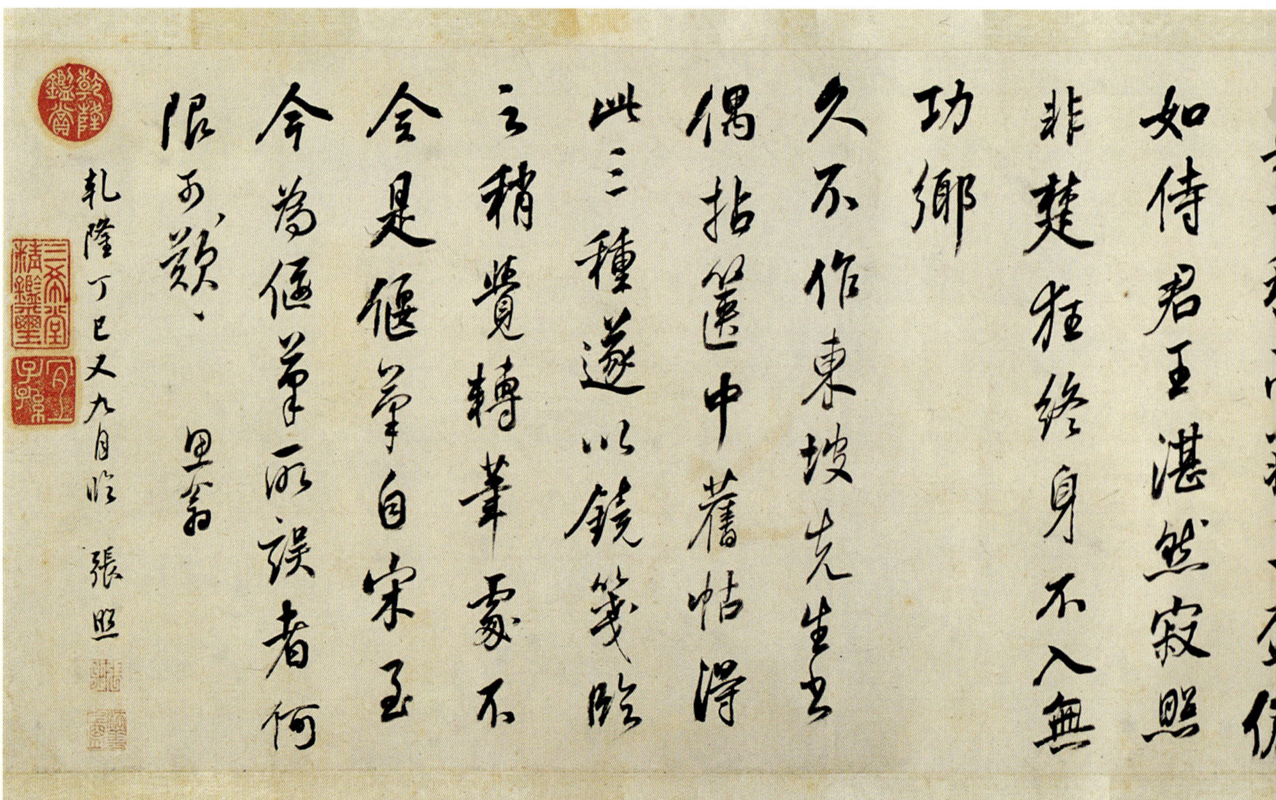
如侍君王湛然寂照
非楚狂終身不入無
功鄉
久不作東坡先生
偶拈篋中舊帖得
此三種遂以鏡箋臨
之稍覺轉筆豪不
全是偃筆自宋至
今為偃筆所誤者何
限耶題、 思翁
乾隆丁巳又九月臨 張照

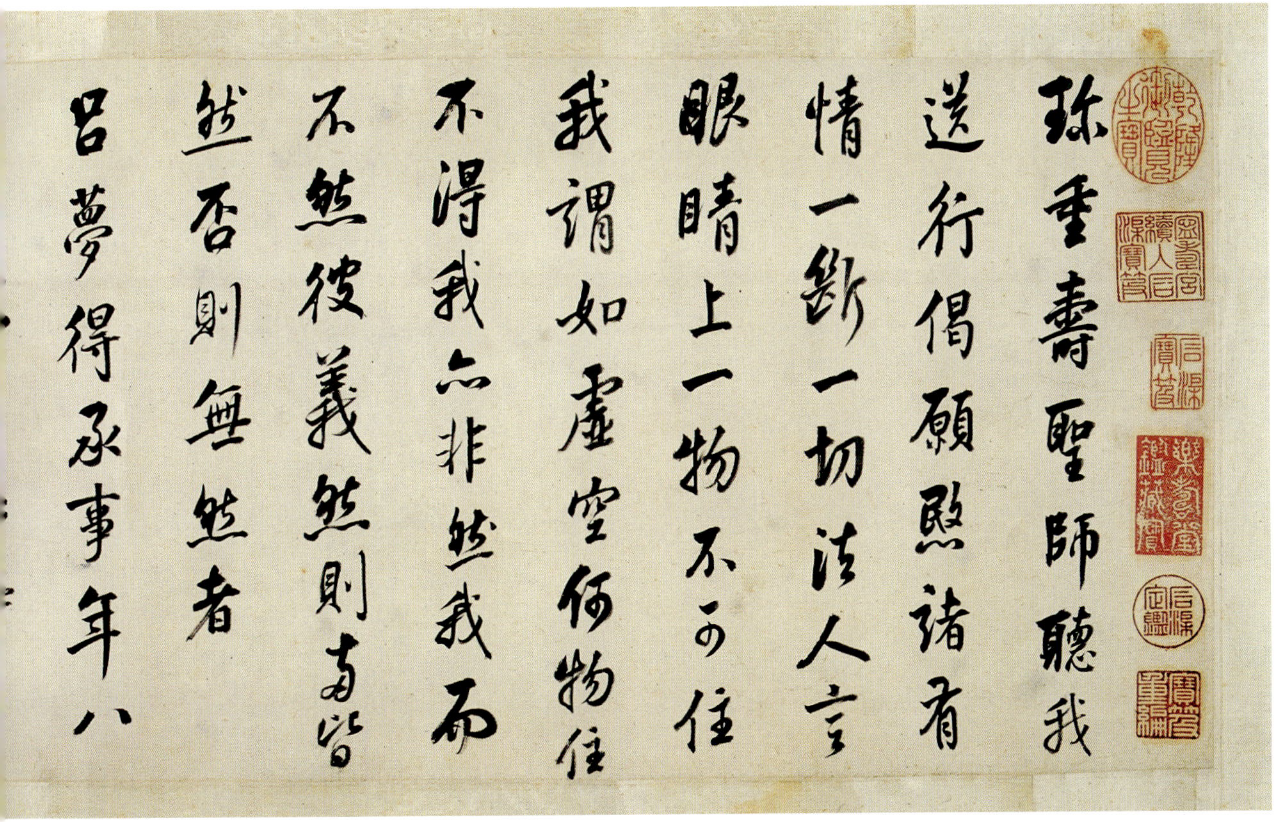
孫重壽聖師聽我
送行偈願慇諸有
情一斷一切法人言
眼睛上一物不可住
我謂如虛空何物住
不得我亦非然我而
不然彼義然則高皆
然否則無然者
呂夢得承事年八

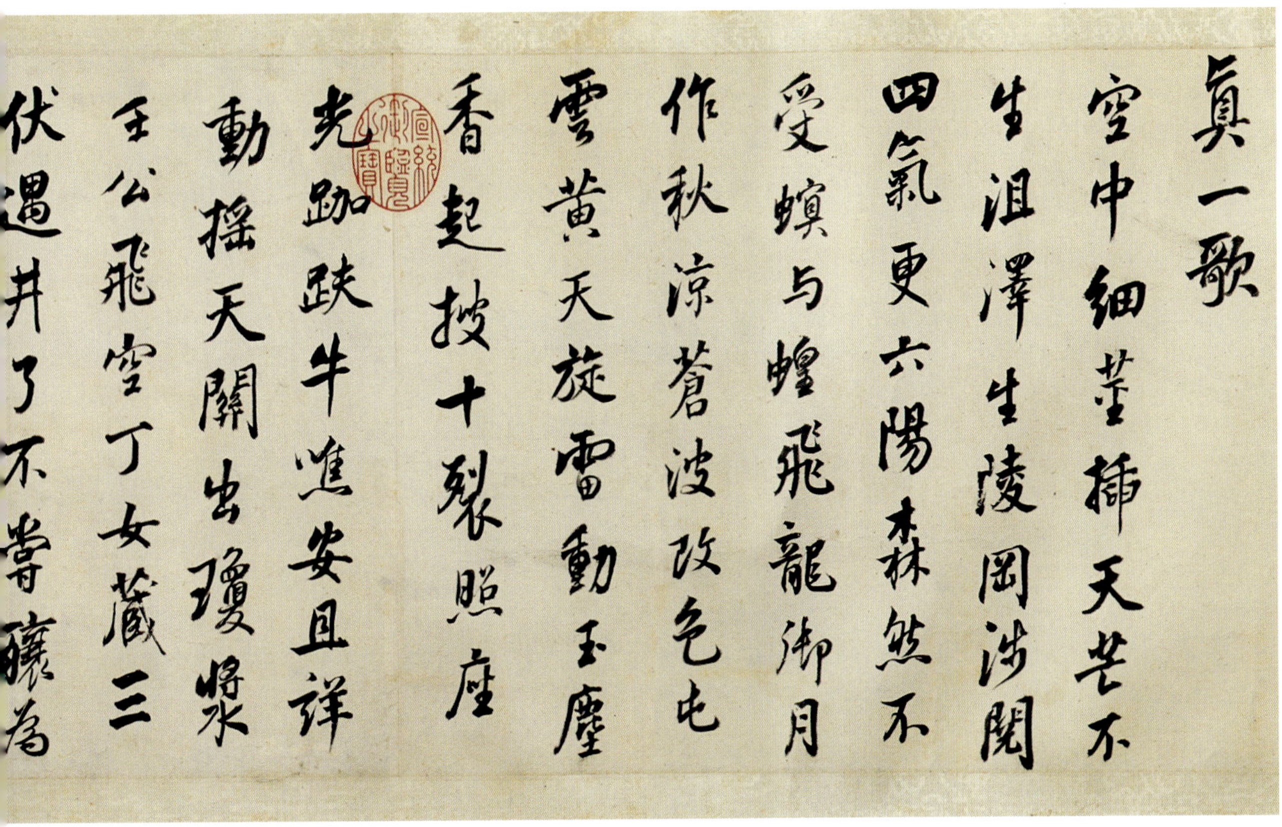
真一歌
空中細莖插天芒不
生沮澤生陵岡涉閱
四氣更六陽森然不
受螟与蝗飛龍御月
作秋涼蒼波改色屯
雲黃天旋雷動玉塵
香起搜十裂照座
光跏趺牛噍安且詳
動搖天關出瓊漿
壬公飛空丁女藏三
伏遇井了不嘗釀為

20
清　　弘旿　　降魔图 卷
手卷，纸本水墨
Hongwu (act. ca. 1736–1820)
Subjugating the Demons
Handscroll; ink on paper
32.9 x 556.6 cm

ARTIST'S SEAL: Chen-Wu (linked seal; square/intaglio)
IMPERIAL SEALS: [Qianlong, r. 1736–95] Wufu wudaitang guxi tianzi bao (large square/relief), Bazheng maonian zhibao (large square/relief), Qianlong yulan zhibao (oval/relief), Qianlong jianshang (round/intaglio) , Wanyou tongchun (square/relief), Yongbi zaixin (square/intaglio), Yinyong chunfengli (square/relief), Jishi duo suoxin (square/intaglio), Midian zhulin (square/relief), Sanxitang jingjianxi (rectangular/relief), Yizisun (square/intaglio), Zhulin sanbian (square/relief); [Jiaqing, r. 1796–1820] Jiaqing yulan zhibao (square/relief), Jiaqing jianshang (round/intaglio); [Xuantong (Puyi), r. 1909–11] Xuantong yulan zhibao (square/relief), Wuyizhai jingjianxi (rectangular/relief)
OTHER SEAL: [Museum of the Northeast] Dongbei bowuguan zhencang zhiyin(square/relief)
JADE CLIP INSCRIPTION: Jiaqing yushang. Hongwu hua jiangmo tu (filled with gold)

画家印鉴：臣、旿（白文连珠方印）
皇家印鉴：[清乾隆皇帝弘历，在位1736－1795]五福五代堂古希天子宝（朱文大方印）、八征耄念之宝（朱文大方印）、乾隆御览之宝（朱文椭圆印）、乾隆鉴赏（白文圆印）、卐有同春（朱文方印）、用笔在心（白文方印）、吟咏春风里（朱文方印）、即事多所欣（白文方印）、秘殿珠林（朱文方印）、三希堂精鉴玺（朱文长方印）、宜子孙（白文方印）、珠林三编（朱文方印）。[清嘉庆皇帝颙琰，在位1796－1820]嘉庆御览之宝（朱文方印）、嘉庆鉴赏（白文圆印）。[清宣统皇帝溥仪，在位1909－1911]宣统御览之宝（朱文方印）、无逸斋精鉴玺（朱文长方印）。
其他印鉴：[东北博物馆]东北博物馆珍藏之印（朱文方印）
玉别子镌：嘉庆御赏。弘旿画降魔图（填金）

Hongwu bore the title of *gushan beizi* (banner prince), used Yaohua Daoren as his sobriquet, and was recognized for his talents in poetry, calligraphy, and painting. This narrative scroll, which brings together the Qing dynasty's multicultural elements, depicts the Buddhist tale of Sakyamuni Buddha's conquest of the demons just before his enlightenment. The artist Hongwu was an imperial family member of the Qianlong era (1736–95).

Arranged in a continuous narrative format, the scroll presents scenes illustrating how demons of all kinds are conquered by Prince Siddhartha, who in the end becomes Sakyamuni Buddha. The beginning section is a demon territory, where Mara, king of the demons, is seen with hair and beard standing on end; he wears a ferocious expression and sits bare-chested on the Vajra Lion Throne. Behind him are the leaders of all kinds of demons, carrying either banners or weapons. Most have a human body and a different animal head, such as that of a monkey, lion, tiger, elephant, donkey, cow, bird, or some other creature. A one-legged, animal-headed demon leader kneels in front of the demon king, giving him a report.

In the next section is a situation where the demons launch an attack on Prince Siddhartha. The army on land advances astride strange-bodied creatures having separately the heads of a lion, tiger, deer, and sheep. A commander standing on a big rock being carried by several lesser demons is crying out. The army from the sky arrives riding on clouds. Among the animal-headed demons are reincarnated deities of ancient India, such as Yaksa, Mahoraga, Raksasa, and other supernatural beings.

The third section captures the moment when Prince Siddhartha gets the demons under his control, the climax of the entire scroll. Here, the demon king orders his troops to surround the Prince; their sharp arrows, however, turn into lotus blossoms, standing for all the weapons that have been directed at him but have changed into flowers . The Prince is seen sitting calmly on the bodhisattva throne under the Bodhi tree, a halo emanating from behind him. His left hand points to the earth. A dignified guard standing next to him with auspicious clouds at his feet represents the great earth, which has come forth to give

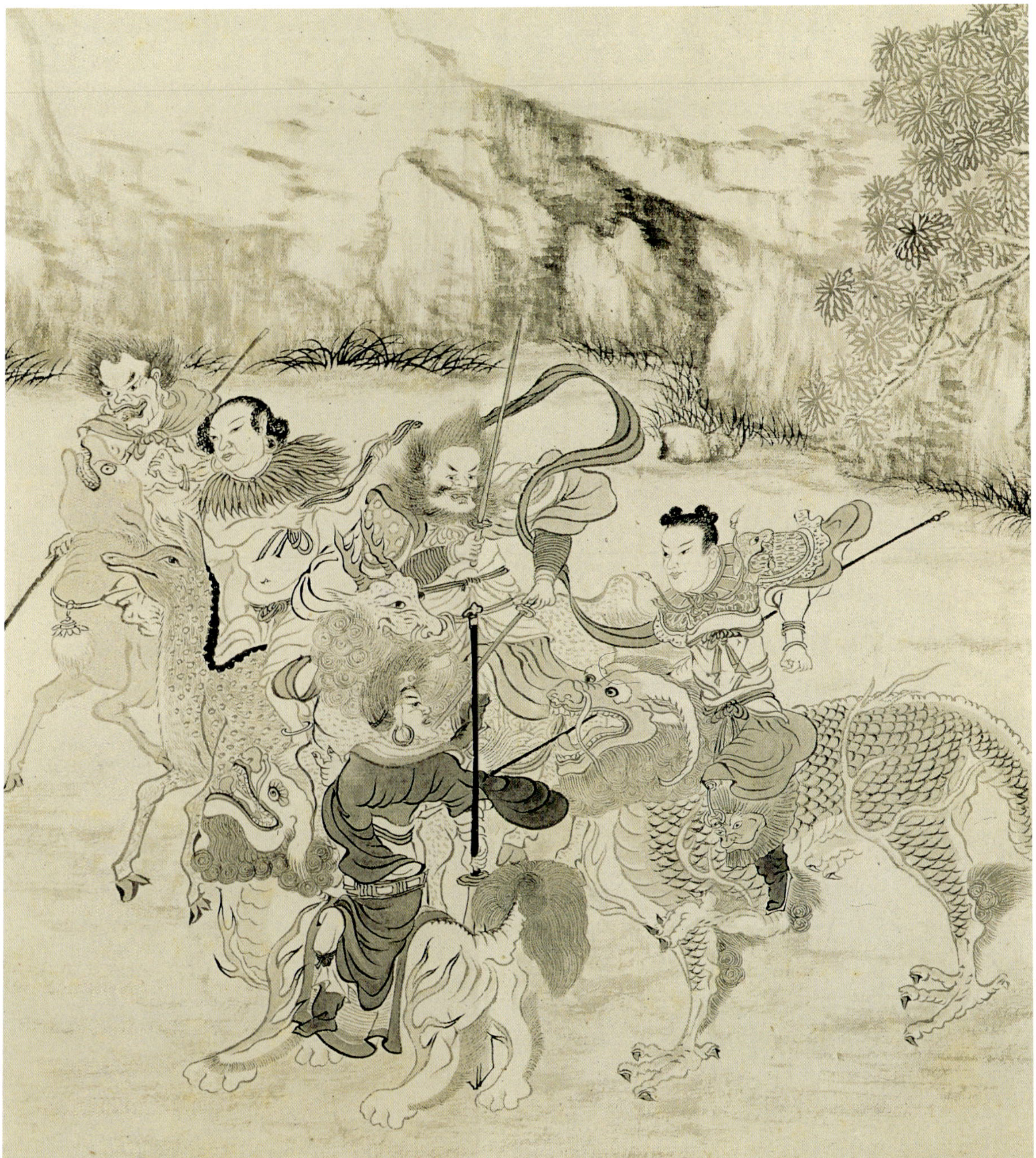

20 (detail 局部)

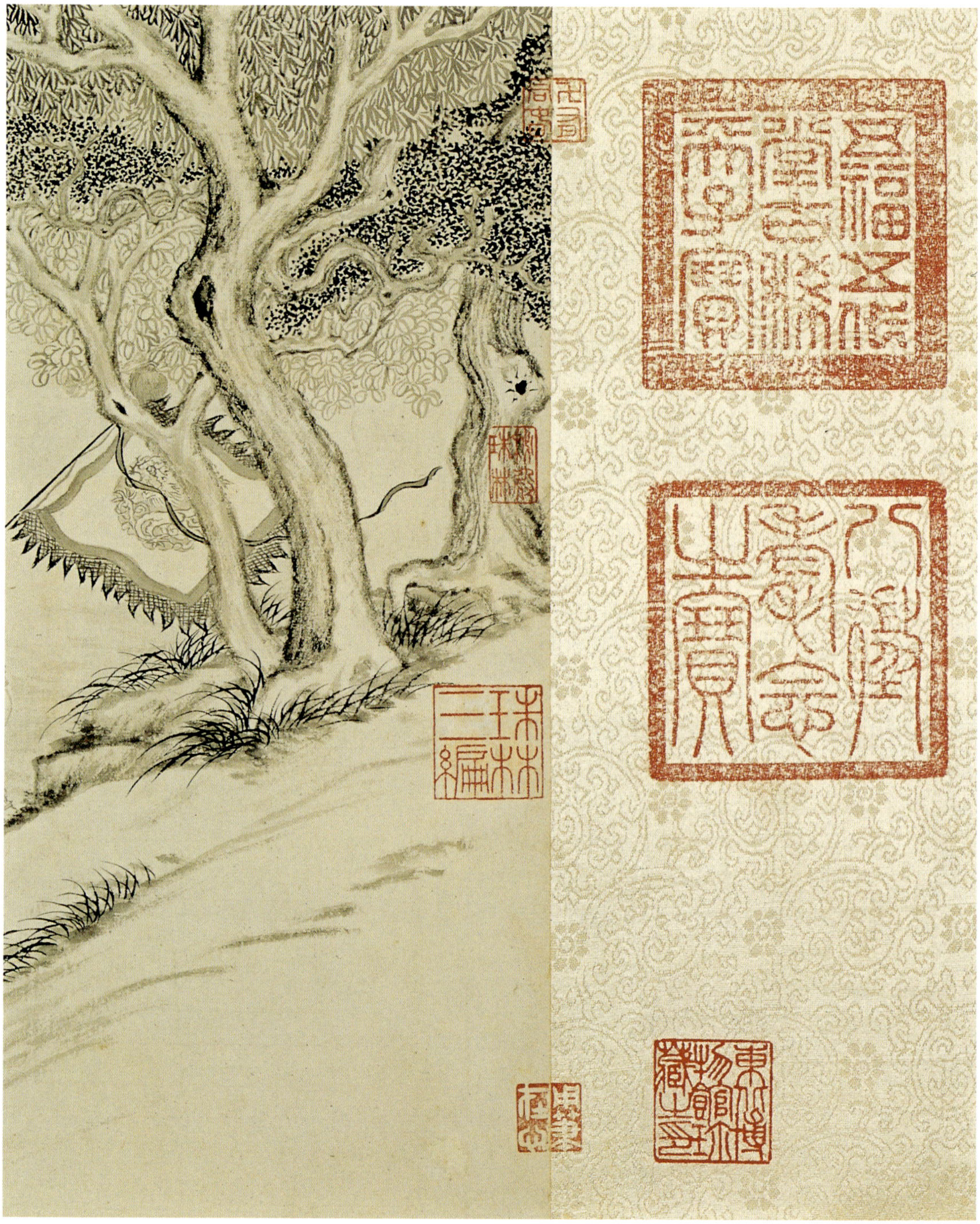

20 (detail 局部)

testimony. In the next scene, the celestial army of the good arrives, and the demons are completely subjugated.

A scene of celebration for Prince Siddhartha's attainment of Buddha-hood through cultivation and practice takes place in the final section. The sky opens up as if to proclaim heaven's joy, and the demons submit themselves to the authority of the Buddha. They hold lotus blossoms, peonies, and Bodhi flowers as Mara, the demon king, leads them in a celebratory procession. Dressed in white, the ancient reigning Buddha arrives from heaven on a white elephant to witness the enlightenment of Prince Siddhartha and his becoming the Sakyamuni Buddha. The ancient Buddha and Sakyamuni greet each other with peonies in hand.

Towards the end, in the lower left corner, the scroll is signed, "humbly painted by your servant Hongwu," a standard format for Qing court painters. Multiple seals of the Qianlong emperor are placed at both ends of the scroll. The mounting format is the same as that of the other artworks of previous dynasties in the Qing court collection. Both factors indicate how much the Qianlong emperor liked this work. This scroll represents the relatively high artistic level achieved by narrative figure paintings of the middle Qing dynasty.

HWL (trans. DHWS)

弘旿,清皇室子弟，封固山贝子，别号瑶华道人，以诗、书、画三绝著称。这卷清乾隆（1736－1795年在位）时代的画家弘旿所作的《降魔图》，是表现佛主释迦牟尼降魔成佛的佛教故事画。

图卷以连环画的形式，展现了悉达多太子降服各路魔军，最终成为佛的情景。首段是魔界，魔王波旬须发倒立、凶面袒胸坐于金刚狮子座，围在他身后的是各路魔头，他们或持各路旗帜，或持各种武器，形象多为猴首、狮首、虎首、象首、驴首、牛首、鸟首等与人身组合成的鬼怪模样，一位兽首魔头单腿跪在魔王的前面，在向他报告。

接下一段，是各路魔将魔兵向悉达多太子进攻，陆上一路的兵将分别骑着狮、虎、鹿、羊头首的怪兽前进，前面的指挥官站在由众小鬼抬起的巨石上呼号着。天上的一路则乘云而来。这些兽首人身的魔众中有“药叉”、“魔候罗迦”、“罗刹”等古印度神祇的化身。

第三段，悉达多太子降服魔怪，也是全图的高潮。魔王率魔军团团围住太子，然而，所有发向他的利箭都变成了莲花。太子稳坐在菩萨座上，背后的菩提树下发出了祥光，他的左手指向大地，站在他身旁的一位相貌端庄之士，脚下有祥气，是大地的代表前来作证。接下来看到，天兵天将乘云而来，魔界被彻底降服。

最后部分，悉达多太子修练成佛，天际开朗，诸魔趋向菩萨之心，并手持莲花、牡丹、菩提等天花，在魔王带领下前来庆贺。身着白衣的古佛乘白象从天宫来，见证悉达多太子成就，古佛与释迦牟尼各持牡丹，恭身同贺。

卷后左下侧：“臣。弘旿敬绘”，落款样式是清代宫廷画家为皇家作画时的标准格式。在画卷的前后，加盖了多方乾隆收藏印，其装裱款式，也与清宫所藏历代书画是一样的装裱规格，由此可见乾隆皇帝珍爱此卷画作，此卷人物故事画中也代表了那个时代较高的艺术水平。

黄伟利

21
清 董邦达 盘山十六景图
手卷，纸本水墨设色
Dong Bangda (1699–1769)
Sixteen Views of Mount Pan
Handscroll; ink and color on paper
41.6 x 586.5 cm

ARTIST SEALS: Chen, Bangda (linked seal; double square/relief)
IMPERIAL SEALS: [Qianlong, r. 1736–95] Sanxitang jingjianxi (rectangular/relief), Yizisun (square/intaglio), Leshoutang jiancangbao (rectangular/intaglio), Ningshougong xuru shiqu baoji (square/relief), Shiqu baoji (rectangular/relief), Shiqu dingjian (round/relief), Baoji chongbian (square/intaglio), Qianlong yulan zhibao (oval/relief), Guxi tianzi (round/relief), Shou (rectangular/intaglio), Qianlong jianshang (round/intaglio); [Jiaqing, r. 1796–1820] Jiaqing yulan zhibao (oval/relief); [Xuantong (Pu Yi), r. 1909–11] Xuantong yulan zhibao (square/relief), Wuyizhai jingjianxi (rectangular/relief)
OTHER SEALS: [Dongbei bowuguan] Dongbei bowuguan zhencang zhiyin (square/relief)
COLOPHON WRITERS (SEALS): Qianlong, r. 1736–95 (Yunxiasi [rectangular/relief], Qianlong chenhan [square/relief], Jixia linchi [square/intaglio]). Liang Shizheng, 1697–1763 (Chen Liang Shizheng [square/intaglio], Zhaozhao ranhan [square/relief]).
JADE CLIP INSCRIPTION: Qianlong yuyong. Dong Bangda hua Jingji shanzhuang shiliujing tu (filled with gold)

画家印鉴：臣、邦达(朱文连珠方印)
皇家印鉴：[清乾隆皇帝弘历，在位1736－1795]三希堂精鉴玺(朱文长方印)、宜子孙(白文方印)、乐寿堂鉴藏宝(白文长方印)、宁寿宫续入石渠宝笈(朱文方印)、石渠宝笈(朱文长方印)、石渠定鉴(朱文圆印)、宝笈重编(白文方印)、乾隆御览之宝(朱文椭圆印)、古希天子(朱文圆印)、寿(白文长方印)、乾隆鉴赏(白文圆印)。[清嘉庆皇帝颙琰，在位1796－1820]嘉庆御览之宝（朱文椭圆印）。[清宣统皇帝溥仪，在位1909－1911]宣统御览之宝（朱文方印）、无逸斋精鉴玺(朱文长方印)。
其他印鉴：[东北博物馆]东北博物馆珍藏之印[朱文方印]
题跋者（钤印）：清乾隆皇帝弘历，在位1736－1795（云霞思[朱文长方印]、乾隆宸翰[朱文方印]、几暇临池[白文方印]。梁诗正，1697－1763（臣梁诗正[白文方印]、朝朝染翰[朱文方印]）。
玉别子镌：乾隆御詠。董邦达画静寄山庄十六景图（填金）。

Dong Bangda (style names, Fucun and Feiwen; sobriquet, Dongshan) was a native of Fuyang, Zhejiang. Starting his career as a *jinshi* degree holder (at the metropolitan level in the imperial exams) and eventually promoted to minister at the Board of Rites, Dong was not only an outstanding literary talent but also a distinguished painter serving the imperial court. His style of landscape is derived from the Yuan dynasty masters and shows effective use of dry brush.

Panshan (Mount Pan) is a famous mountain located between Tianjin and Beijing. Situated twelve kilometers northwest of Jixian city, it covers more than 20 square kilometers in area and reaches a height of 858 meters above sea level. Featuring a wide range of huge boulders and grotesque rocks, Panshan boasts many ancient temples and famous monasteries constructed during various dynasties. In appreciation of the scenic beauty of Panshan, the Qing emperor Qianlong once remarked: "If I had known about Panshan earlier, why would I have traveled all the way south of the Yangtze." He made thirty-two excursions to Panshan and wrote as many as thirteen hundred poems about the site. In the nineteenth year of the Qianlong reign (1754), construction of a travel palace in Panshan was completed at the Jingji Shanzhuang (Peaceful Mountain Resort), and three important officials, Jiang Fu, Wang Youdun, and Dong Bangda, were ordered to compile the *Qin ding Panshan zhi* (Imperial records of Panshan). With their superior literary talents, personal travel experiences in Panshan, and an extensive collection of relevant information, they were able to come up with a book extolling the virtues of the Qianlong emperor and celebrating the great prosperity of the Qing empire as well as the beautiful scenery of Panshan. Completed within the same year that it was commissioned, the book included the following chapters on Panshan: "Ceremonial Places," "Imperial Documents," "Pictorial Images," "Scenic Spots," "Religious Temples," "Temporary Lodgings," "Monks and Priests," "Arts and Literature," and "Local products."

This is the most exquisite of all the Panshan scrolls painted by Dong Bangda. In the painting's broad panoramic

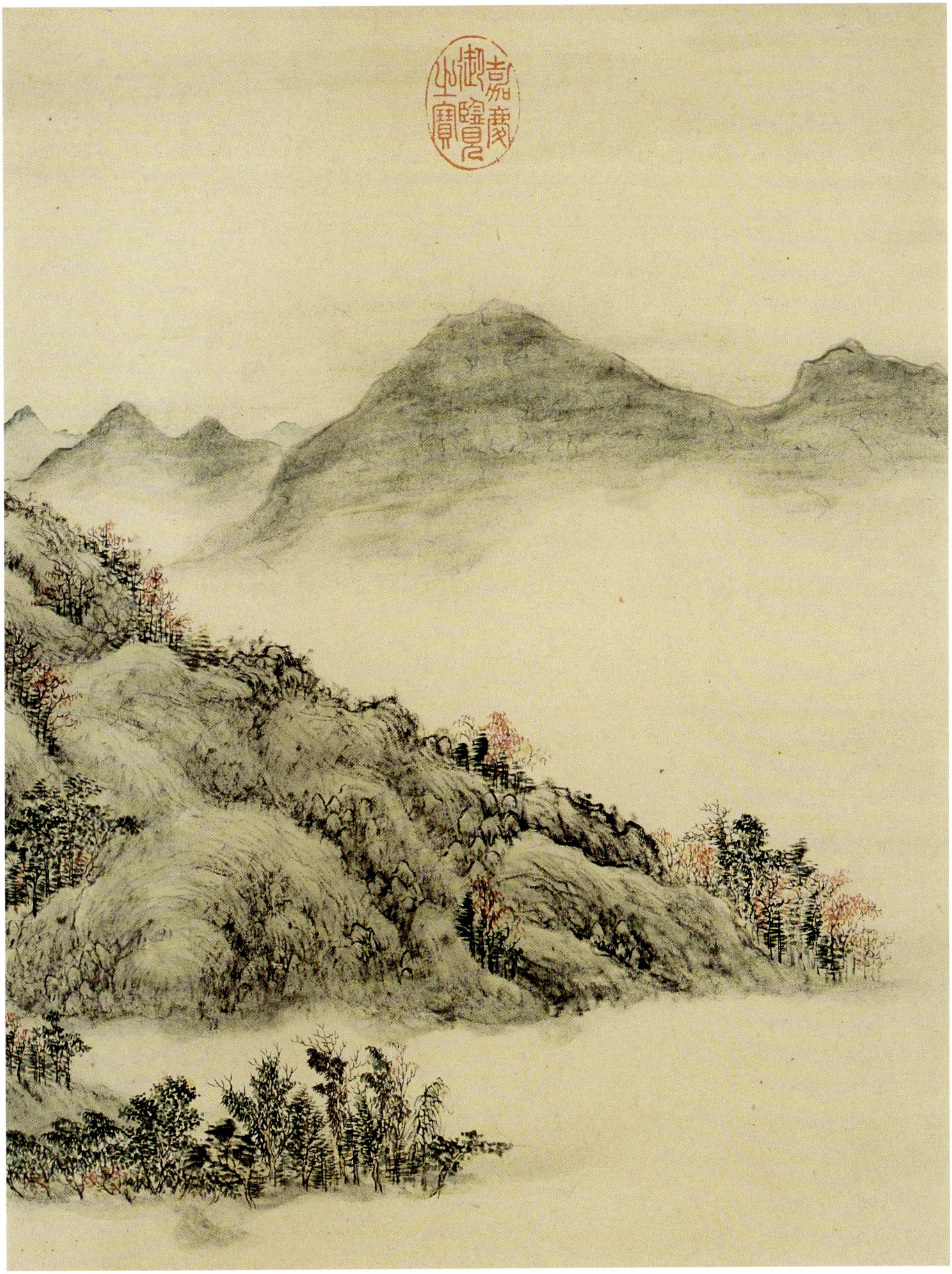

21 (detail 局部)

composition, a full view of Panshan, as well as the individual locations of sixteen scenic spots distributed throughout the mountain, unfolds before our eyes. The distinctive feature of each scenic spot is rendered using the *jiehua* (ruled line) architectural rendering technique. Arranged from beginning to end, the sixteen scenic highlights of Panshan are as follows: (1) Temple of a Thousand Bodhisattvas, (2) Celestial Purity Daoist Temple, (3) Tranquility Mountain Villa, (4) House in Primeval Mists, (5) Pavilion Surrounded by Hibiscus, (6) Ensemble of Pine Whispers, (7) Mirror of Permanent Reflections, (8) Overlapping Green Peaks, (9) Site of Zhenguan Ruins, (10) Purple Umbrella Peak, (11) Cloud Shrouded Temple, (12) Floating Stone Boat, (13) Pan Gu Monastery, (14) Temple of Ten Thousand Pines, (15) Sword Dance Platform, and (16) Heavenly Town Monastery. The name of each scene is separately indicated by the artist in a refined small seal script. He captures in tastefully detailed brushwork the magnificent image of Panshan in the warmth of spring at the height of its flowering.

The Qianlong emperor, who had long been attracted to the beauty of Panshan, was so inspired upon seeing this painting that he wrote the following poem:

Seasons of the year come and go,
The one I love is with flowers in bloom.
Each time it came I had to be elsewhere,
Spending my time in a state of gloom.
Recently I take delight in travel,
Through fields with thinning snow.
Homage to the gods is not missed,
Nor have I missed spring plough.
Trotting along with six bridled horses,
I come just in time for the mountain home.
Things in the hills are looking prettier day by day
Green peaches, pink apricots contend in the brume.
Unique are all pods and stamens, budding and blown.
Celebrate any romance, bitter or sweet has it grown.
It's prime time, I guess, in mid-spring,
Who needs colored banners on tall trees for decoration.
Wishing upon the hills to provide the best of time,
They have proven worthy for me to have come.

Imperial inscription on the recent painting of Panshan in spring. At the end of autumn in the *dingmao* year.

That *dingmao* year was the twelfth year of the Qianlong reign (1747), when the country was stable and prosperous. Qianlong's recollection of his visit to Panshan was marked with joy and excitement, especially now that the turbulent years of the conquests were over. From Qianlong's poem, we can tell that he spent a very pleasant spring there that year, one with lasting memories of happiness. Although it was late in the fall when he wrote the poem, he was thrilled to see the spring scenes in the painting.

The artist's signature is written on the end section of the scroll: "Painted by your servant Dong Bangda," which is followed by his name seal "Chen Dong Bangda" (your servant Dong Bangda). At the end of the scroll is Qianlong's "Imperial Poem of the Sixteen Views of Panshan," exquisitely transcribed in small standard script by Liang Shizheng (1697–1763), a preeminent scholar of the Dong Ge pavilion, and followed by two seals: "Chen Liang Shizheng yin" (Your servant Liang Shizheng) and *Zhaozhao ranhan* (Inking the brush every day in your service).

HWL (trans. DHWS)

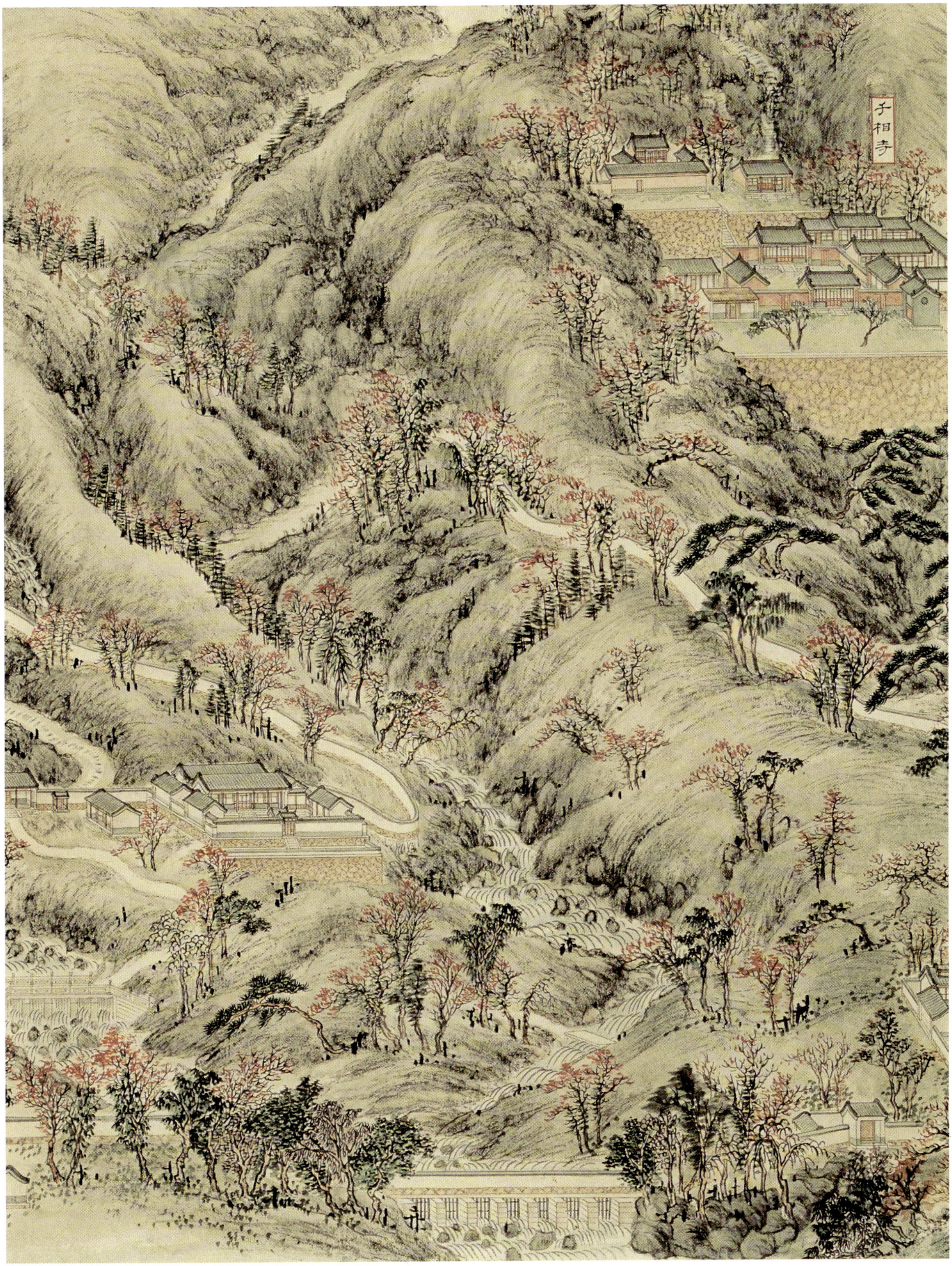

21 (detail 局部)

21

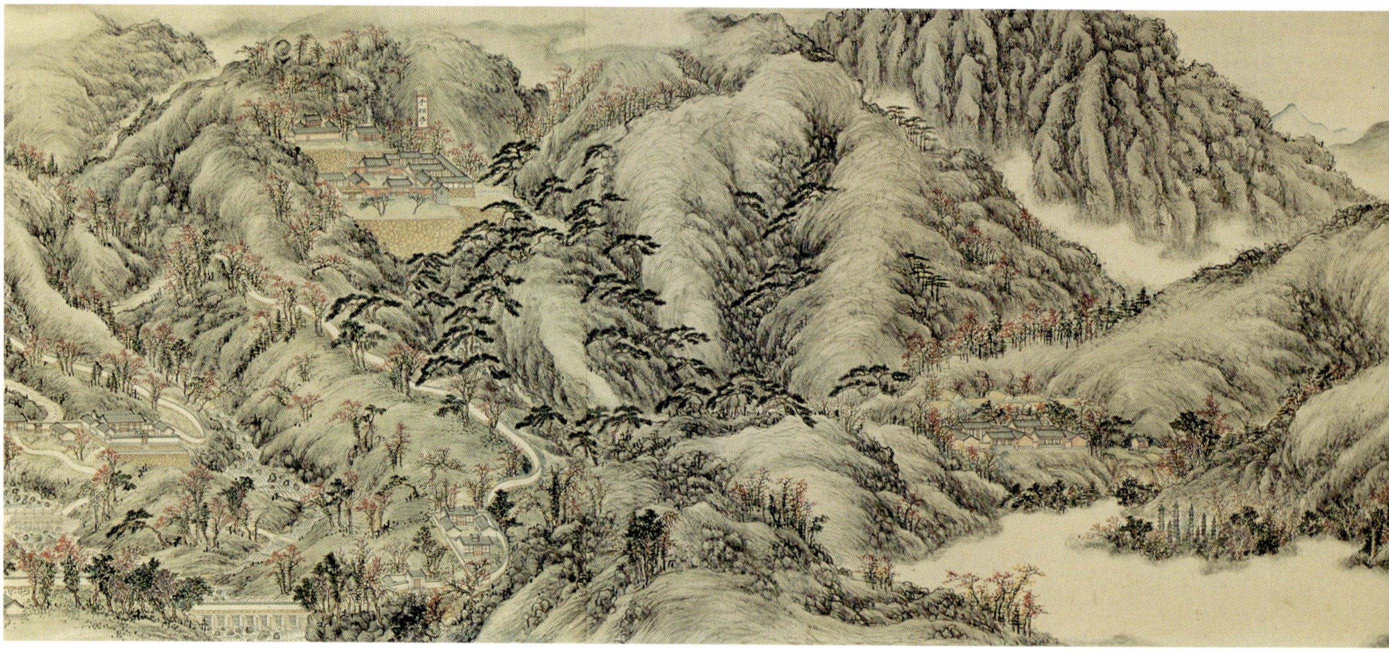

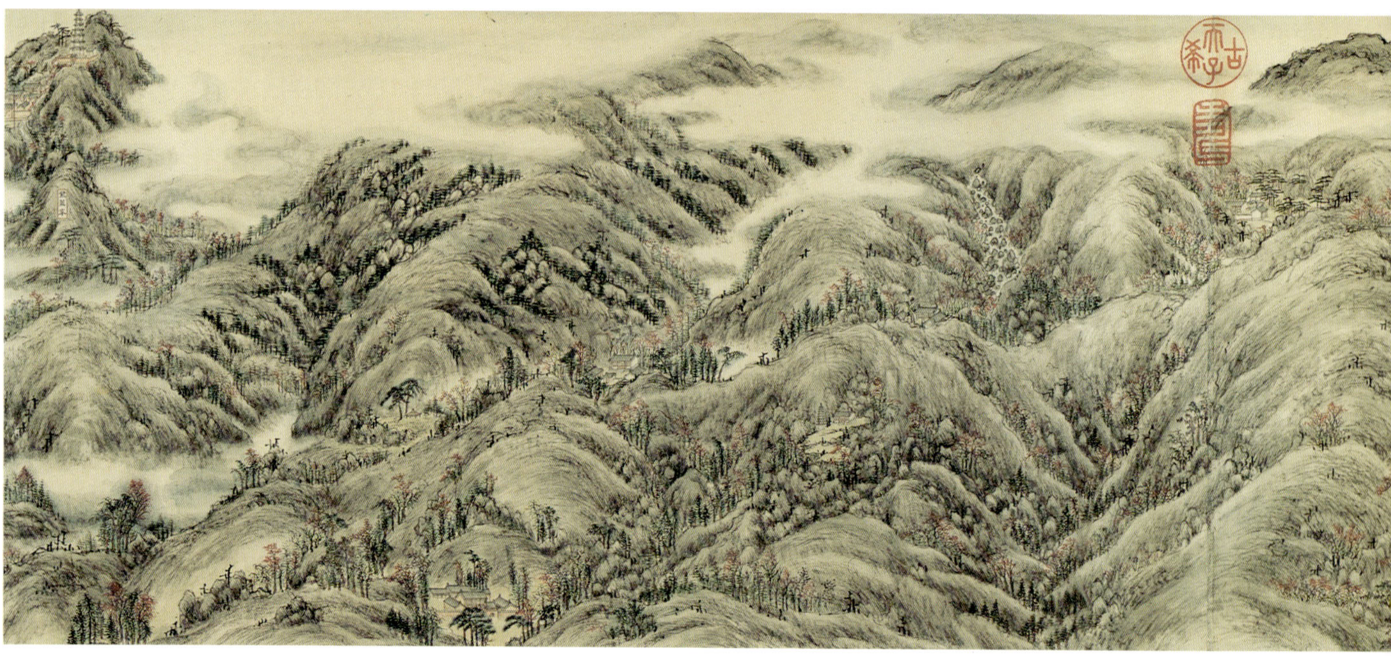

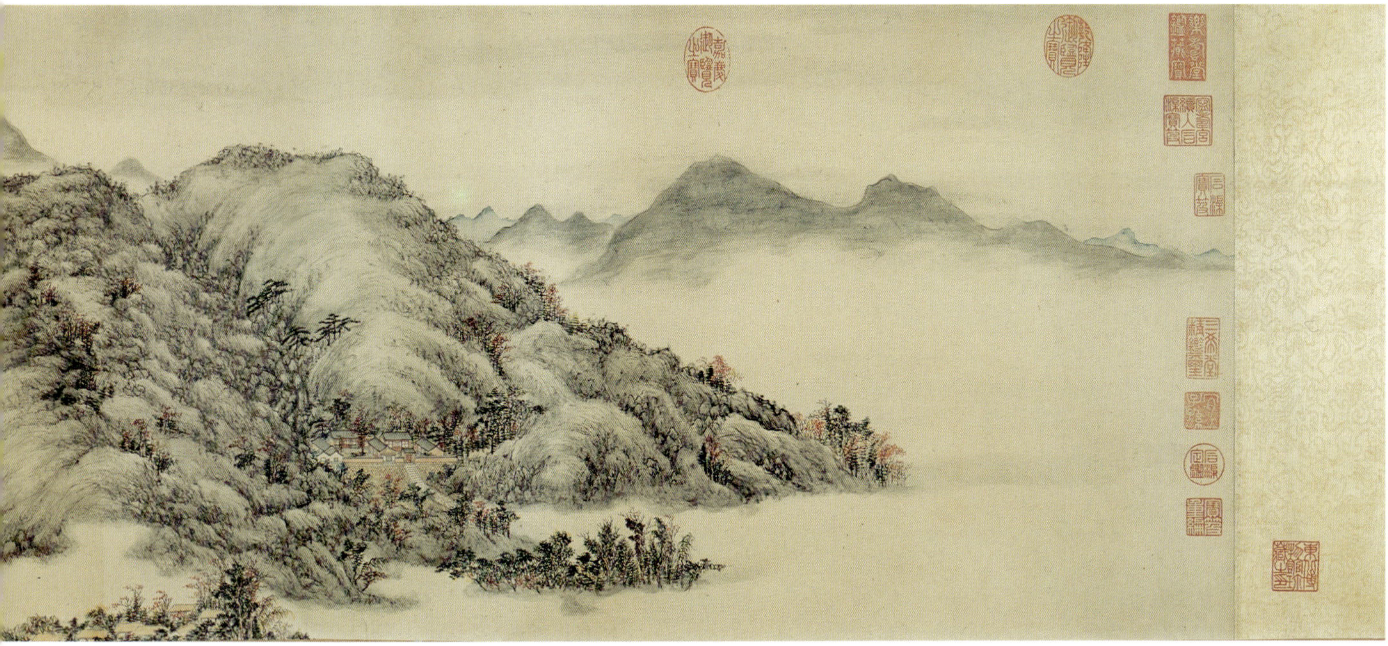

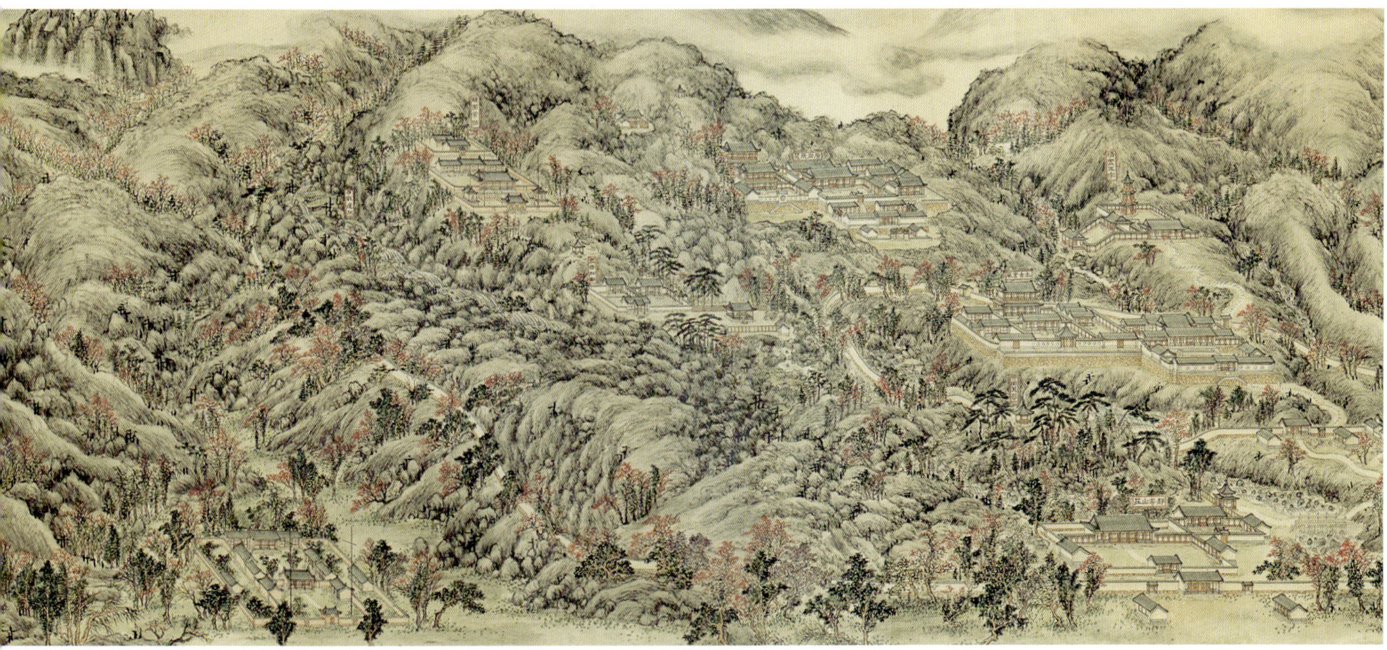

21

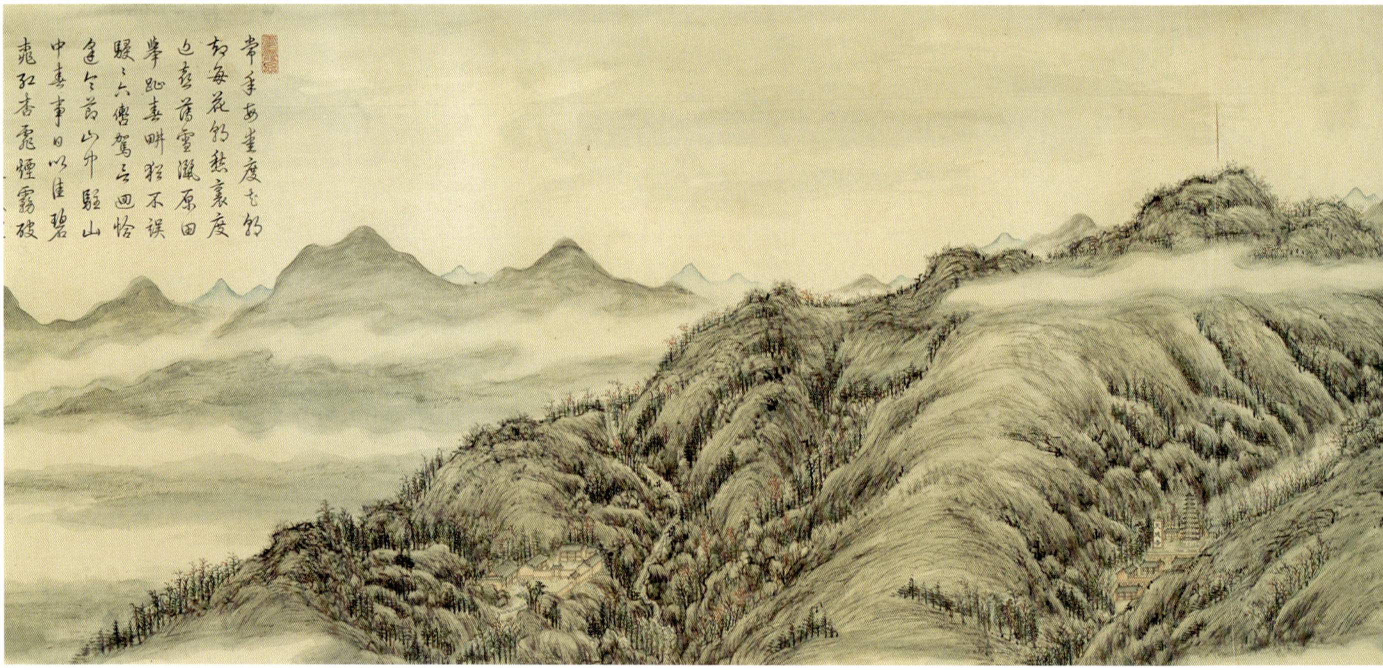

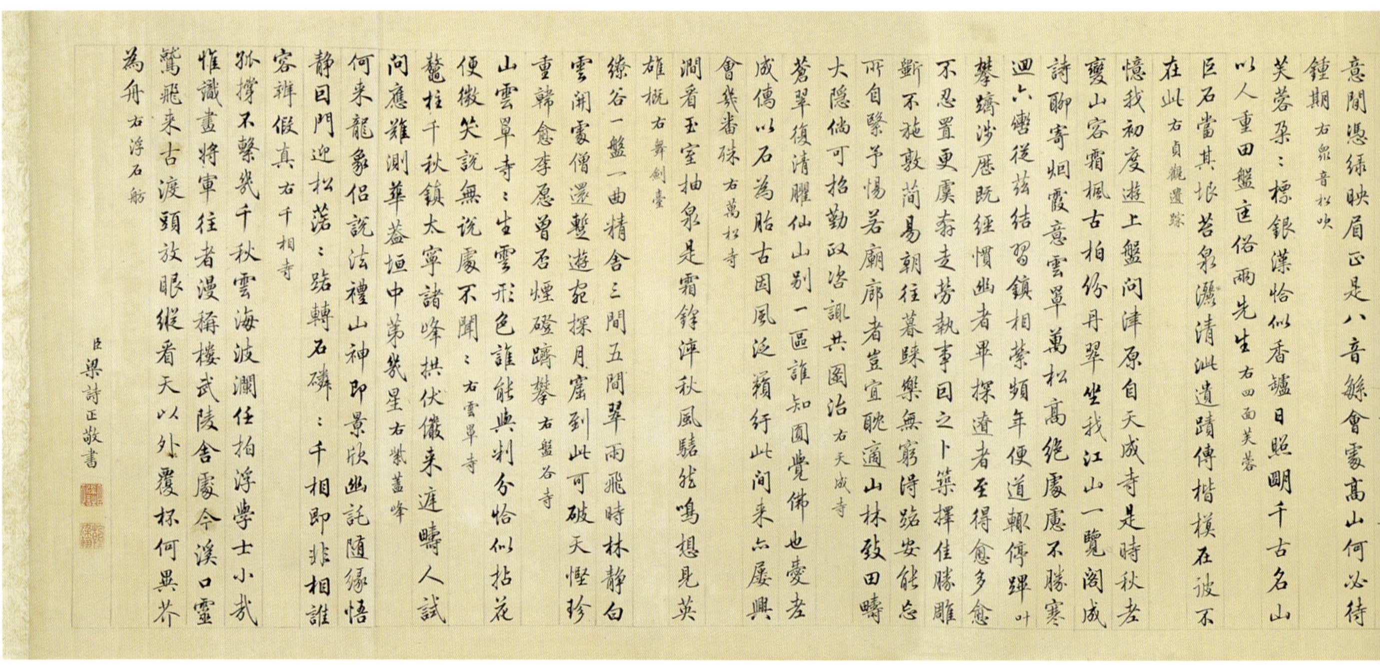
意聞憑綠映眉正是八音繇會處高山何必待
鍾期 右泉音松吹
芙蓉朶朶標銀漢恰似香爐日照明千古名山
以人重田盤匡俗兩先生 右四面芙蓉
巨石當其垠若泉瀨清泚遺蹟傳楷模在彼不
在此 右貞觀遺踪
憶我初度遊上盤問津原自天成寺是時秋老
霽山容霜楓古柏紛丹翠坐我江山一覽閣成
詩聊寄烟霞意雲罩萬松高絕處愿不勝寒
四六鑾從茲結習鎮相縈頻年便道輒停蹕 叶
攀躋涉歷既經慣幽者畢探遺者至得愈多愈
不忍置更虞森走勞執事因之卜築擇佳勝雕
斲不施敦簡易朝往暮睞樂無窮詩貽安能忘
所自繫予惕若廟廊者豈宜耽適山林致田疇
大隱倘可指勤政咨諏共圖治 右天成寺
蒼翠復清臒仙山別一區誰知圓覺佛也愛老
成儒以石為胎古因風泛穎行此間來亦屢興
會幾番殊 右萬松寺
澗看玉室抽泉是霜鋒淬秋風驕猶鳴想見英
雄概 右舞劍臺
繚谷一盤一曲精舍三間五間翠雨飛時林靜白
雲閑處僧還整遊屐探月窟到此可破天慳珍
重韓愈李愿曾否煙磴躋攀 右盤谷寺
山雲罩寺寺生雲形色誰能典刹分恰似拈花
便微笑說無說處不聞聞 右雲罩寺
鼇柱千秋鎮太寧諸峰拱伏儼來庭疇人試
問應難測華蓋垣中第幾星 右紫蓋峰
何來龍象侶說法禮山神即景欣幽託隨緣悟
靜因門迎松落落路轉石磷磷千相即非相誰
容辨假真 右千相寺
孤撐不繫幾千秋雲海波瀾任泊浮學士小哉
惟識畫將軍往者漫稱樓武陵含處今溪口靈
鷲飛來古渡頭放眼縱看天以外覆杯何異芥
為舟 右浮石船
臣梁詩正敬書

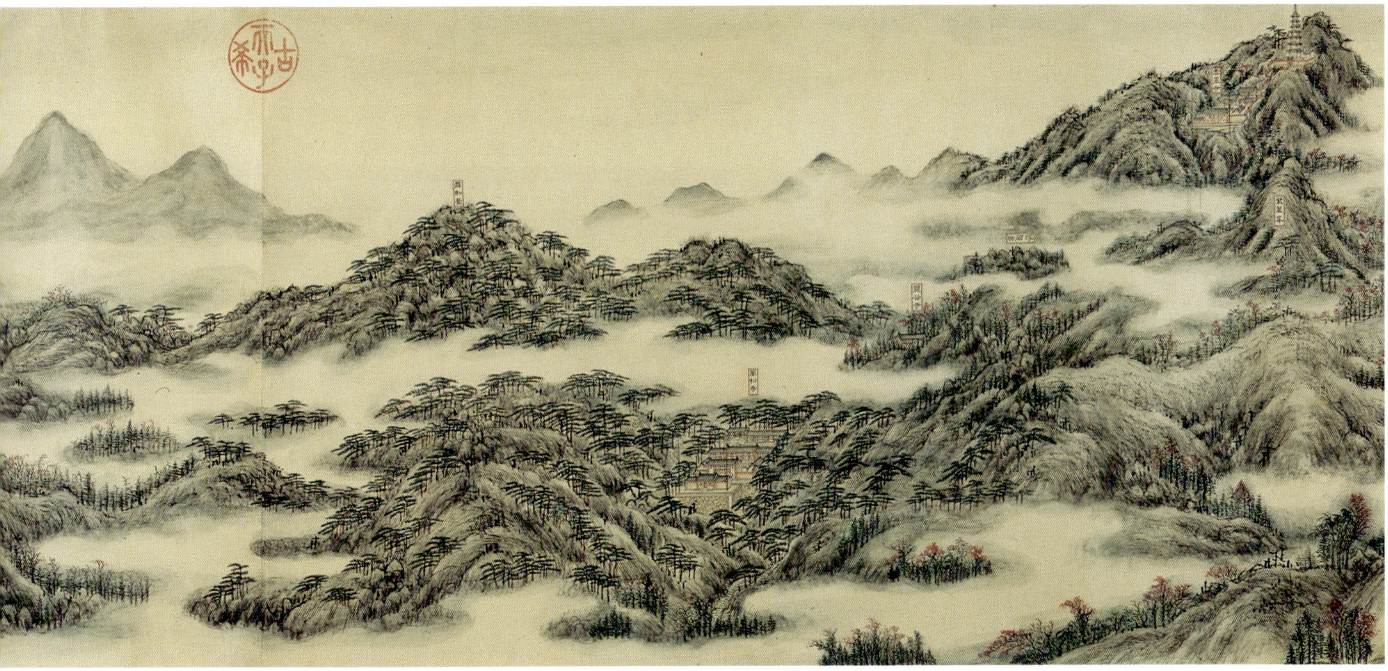

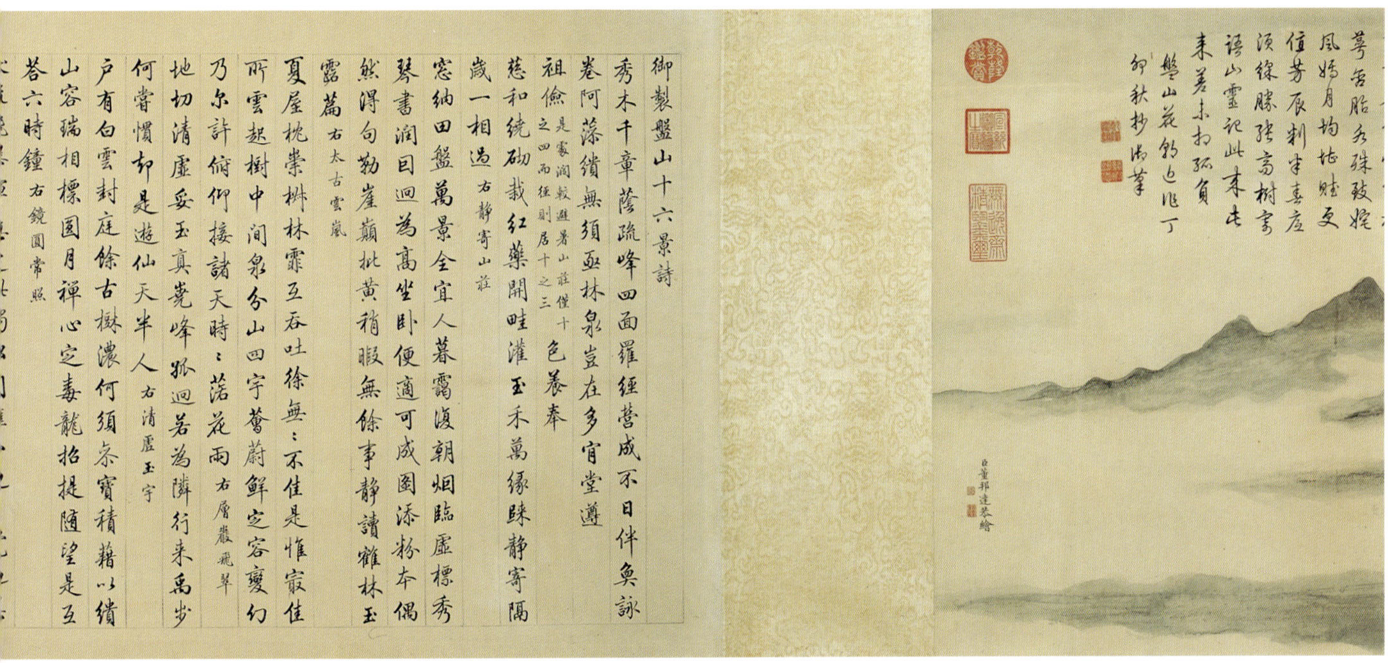
御製盤山十六景詩
秀木千章蔭疏峰四面羅經營成不日佇奐詠
卷阿藻繢無須亟林泉豈在多宜堂遵
祖儉是處潤較避暑山莊僅十之四而經則居十之三色養奉
慈和繞砌栽紅藥開畦灌玉禾萬緣睞靜寄隔
歲一相過 右靜寄山莊
窓納田盤萬景全宜人暮靄復朝烟臨虛標秀
琴書潤曰迴為高坐卧便適可成圖添粉本偶
然得句勒崖巔批黃稍暇無餘事靜讀雜林玉
露篇 右太古雲嵐
夏屋枕崇巒林霏互吞吐徐無〻不佳是惟寂佳
所雲起樹中間泉分山四宇蓊蔚鮮定容變幻
乃爾許俯仰接諸天時〻落花雨 右層巖飛翠
地切清虛妥玉真甍峰狐迴若為隣行來禹步
何嘗慣都是遊仙天半人 右清虛玉宇
戶有白雲封庭餘古樹濃何須尒寶積藉以繢
山容瑞相標圓月禪心定毒龍拈提隨望是互
荅六時鐘 右鏡圓常照

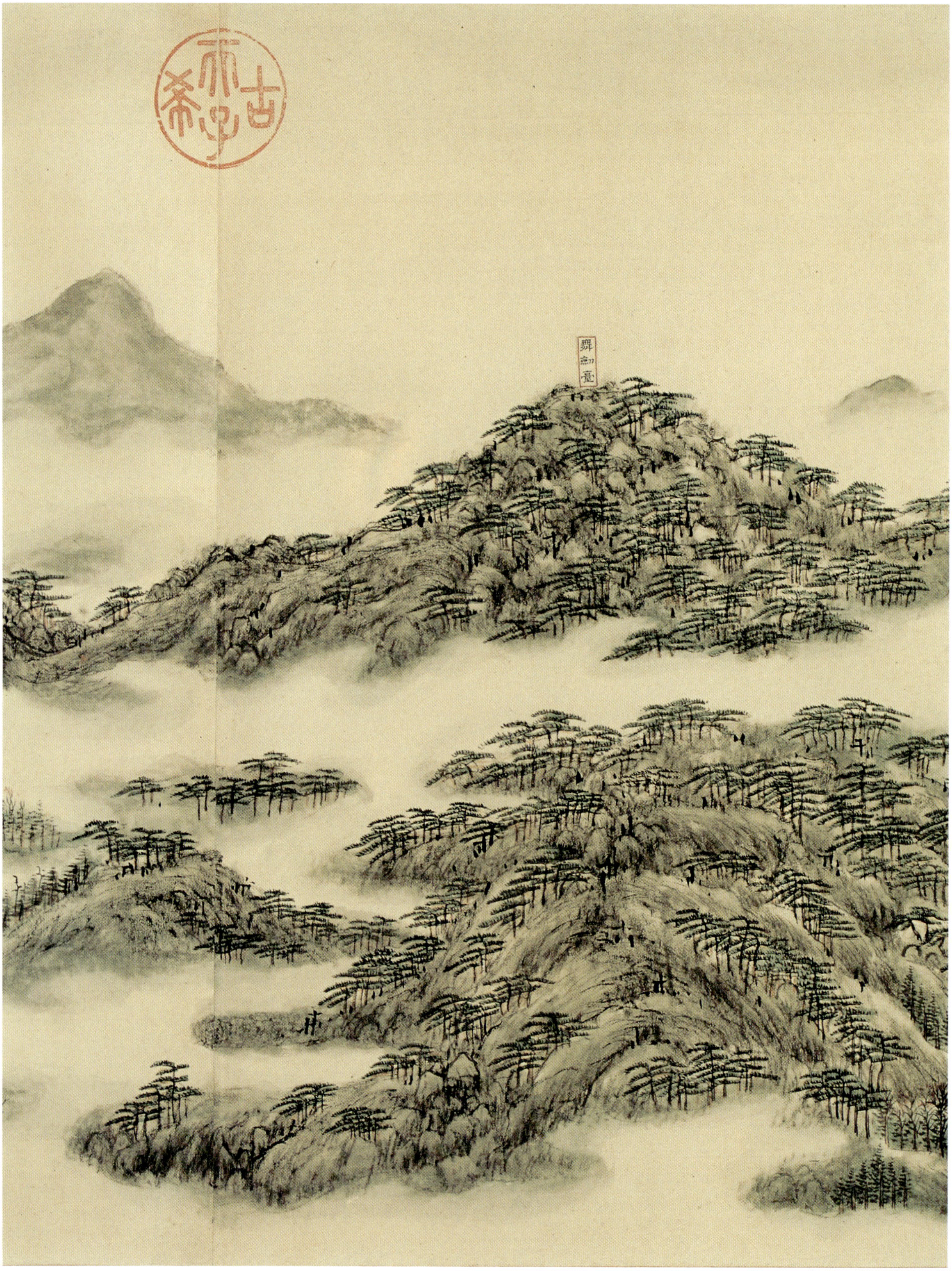

21 (detail 局部)

董邦达，字孚存，一字非闻，号东山，浙江富阳人，进士出身，官至礼部尚书，不仅文采出众，而且还是当时服务于宫庭的杰出画家。其山水取法元人，好用枯笔。

盘山是位于天津与北京之间的一座名山，坐落在蓟县城西北12公里处，面积20多平方公里，最高峰海拔858米。圆浑而怪秀的山石构成了盘山的一大特色，历代在此大兴土木，劈山建寺，留下诸多古刹名寺，清乾隆皇帝尤其钟爱地慨叹到："早知有盘山，何必下江南"，他曾32次驻跸盘山，而咏盘山诗则多达一千三百余首。乾隆十九年（1754年），盘山行宫正式在静寄山庄建成，并命殿宰重臣蒋缚、汪由敦、董邦达三人纂修《钦定盘山志》，诸公本来就具有超群的文艺才华，又亲历盘山实境，广搜博采，当年即以巡典、天章、图考、名胜、寺寓、流寓、方外、艺文、物产等篇章编撰成书，颂乾隆帝功德，歌大清盛世，写盘山美景。

此为董邦达创作的多幅有关盘山的画作中极其精彩的一卷。画面以横向布景的方式，展现了盘山的全貌以及十六个景点分布于山中的各个位置。以界画的技巧，按前后顺序分别描绘了千相寺、清虚玉宇、静寂山庄、太古云岚、四面芙蓉、众音松吹、镜圆常照、层岩飞翠、贞观遗踪、紫益峰、云罩寺、浮石舫、盘古寺、万松寺、舞剑台、天成寺等各景的独特风貌。作者以精美的小楷书分别表明了各景的名称，并以精微灵动的笔致，描绘出了盘山在春暖花开时节的灿烂景象。

迷恋于盘山景色的乾隆皇帝，看见此画，触景生情，欣然题写了他的感怀诗："常年每爱度花朝，却每花朝愁里度。近喜薄雪洒原田，句趾春耕犹不误。骎骎六辔驾言迴，恰逢令节山中驻。山中春事日以佳，碧桃红杏霏烟雾。破萼含胎各殊致，姹风嫣月均堪赋。更值芳辰判半春，底须綵胜张高树。寄语山灵记此来，此来差未相孤负。盘山花朝近作，丁卯秋杪，御笔"。丁卯为乾隆十二年（1747年），此时天下大定，社会呈现繁荣景象，因而，乾隆皇帝在诗中回顾了征战年代的动荡岁月以后，更感到在山中度过花朝节的喜悦与兴奋。尽管在此图上题诗时，已经是这一年的深秋，但是，从乾隆题诗中的叙述可以知道，这一年，他曾在盘山山中过了一个前所未有的且十分快乐的花朝节，而图中生意盎然的春天景象，仍然使他激动不已。

画面尾部有作者自署款为："臣，董邦达恭绘"。钤"臣董邦达印"。卷后，有同时代的东阁大学士梁诗正（1697—1763）以精美的小楷书写的乾隆皇帝所作"御制盘山十六景诗"，钤"臣梁诗正印"、"朝朝染翰"。

黄伟利

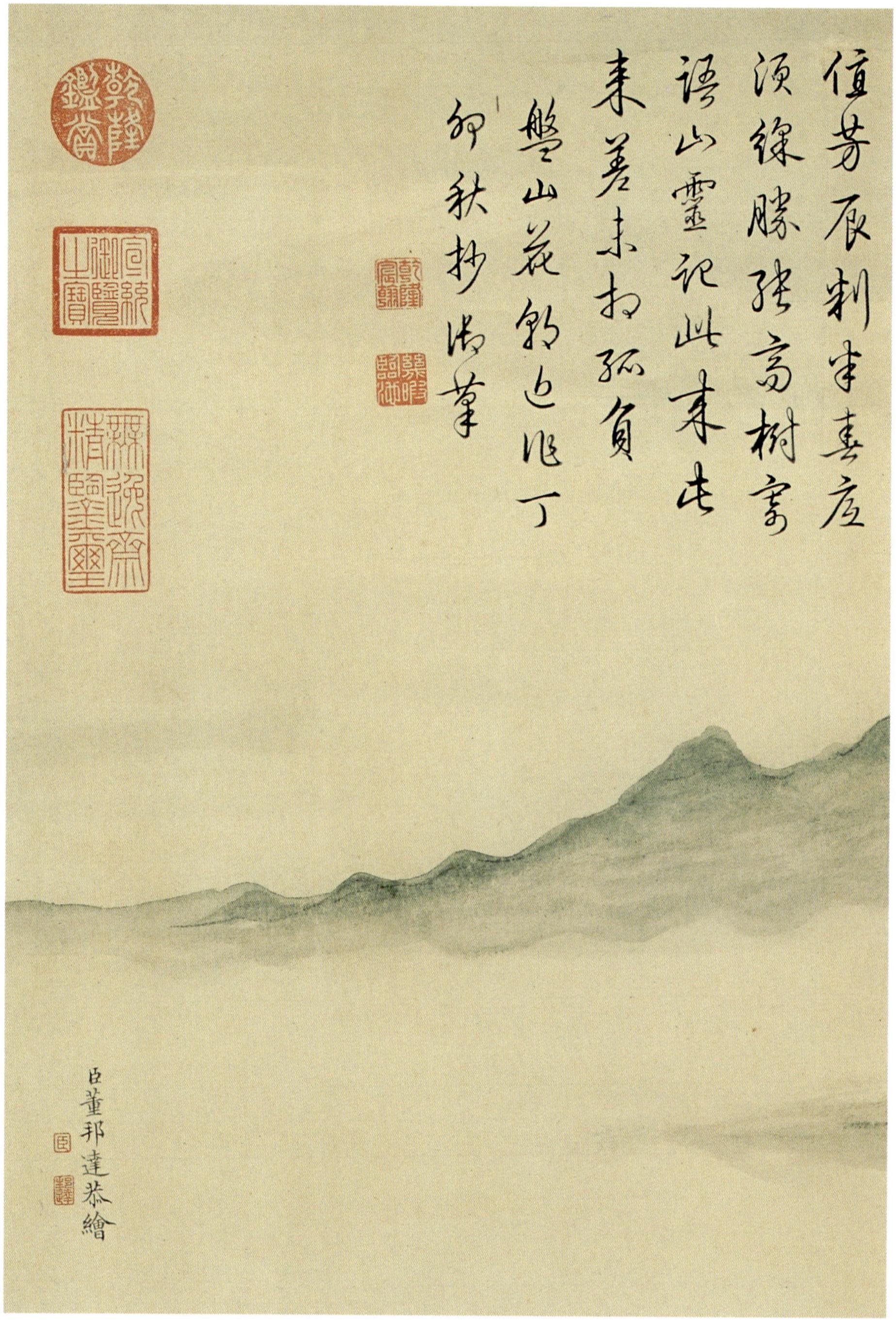

21 (detail 局部)

22
清　　张镐　瀛台赐宴图
手卷，绢本水墨设色界画
Zhang Gao (act. 1736–95)
Imperial Banquet of the Qianlong Emperor at Ying Tai, 1746

Handscroll; ink and color on silk
36.5 x 207.7 cm

ARTIST'S SEALS: Chen (square/intaglio), Gao (square/relief)
IMPERIAL SEALS: [Qianlong, r. 1736–95] Qianqinggong jiancangbao (rectangular/relief), Qianlong yulan zhibao (oval/relief), Qianlong yushang (round/intaglio), Shiqu baoji (rectangular/relief), Shiqu dingjian (round/relief), Baoji chongbian (square/intaglio), Sanxitang jingjianxi (rectangular/relief), Yizisun (square/intaglio); [Jiaqing, r. 1796–1820] Jiaqing yulan zhibao (oval/relief); [Xuantong (Puyi), r. 1909–11] Xuantong yulan zhibao (oval/relief)
OTHER SEALS: [Museum of the Northeast] Dongbei bowuguan zhencang zhiyin (square/relief)
COLOPHON WRITER (SEALS): Ji Huang (Chen Huang [square/intaglio], Bizhan chunyu [square/relief])

画家印鉴：臣（白文方印）、镐（朱文方印）。
皇家印鉴：[清乾隆皇帝弘历，在位1736－1795]乾清宫鉴藏宝（朱文长方印）、乾隆御览之宝（朱文椭圆印）、乾隆御赏（白文圆印）、石渠宝笈（朱文长方印）、石渠定鉴（朱文圆印）、宝笈重编(白文方印)、三希堂精鉴玺(朱文长方印)、宜子孙(白文方印)。[清嘉庆皇帝颙琰，在位1796－1820]嘉庆御览之宝（朱文椭圆印）。[清宣统皇帝溥仪，在位1909－1911]宣统御览之宝（朱文椭圆印）。
其他印鉴：[东北博物馆]东北博物馆珍藏之印（朱文方印）。
题跋者（钤印）：稽璜（臣璜[白文方印]、笔霑春雨[朱文方印]）。

Zhang Gao (courtesy name, Wuqian; sobriquet, Yangxian) was a native of Qiantang, Zhejiang, who served as a court painter during the reign of the Qianlong emperor in the Qing dynasty.

This scroll depicts the scene of an imperial banquet hosted by the Qianlong emperor. On the twenty-seventh day, eleventh year, eighth month of his reign (October 11, 1746), the Qianlong emperor invited 103 guests—princes, dukes and members of the imperial family—to a banquet held at the Fengzeyuan courtyard next to the Ying Tai garden. The next day, on the twenty-eighth, the emperor held another banquet at the same place for ministers of both Manchu and Han origins, staff members of the imperial court, and members of the Hanlin Imperial Academy, a total of 176 guests. After the banquet, the participants went on to the Shuqing Yuan courtyard where the party continued in the form of a poetry contest with "floating cups of wine served along a zigzagging stream." Whoever sat next to a cup that stopped moving had to come up with the next line for the poem.[1] The calligraphy in the concluding section to the left of the painting consists of this collectively improvised poem, which in its entirety had an exhausting number of lines contributed by the more than one hundred participants on that day. The signature reads "painted by your humble servant Zhang Gao."[2]

The Ying Tai setting, with its balconies, platforms, and pavilions, is rendered in the typical *jiehua* (ruled-line) manner, in which orderly and neatly brushed lines are filled in with rich and bright colors. In the painting are some 220 people: some stand in respectful attendance, ceremonially attired with feathered hats; some are carrying stuff around; and some are getting ready for some kind of performance. It appears to be just before the banquet; everything is ready and everyone is waiting for the grand arrival of his majesty the emperor. Typical of paintings documenting events at the Qing court, the style is careful and constrained. Attention to detail is paid throughout the composition.

Court artists were often commissioned by the Qing emperors to create historical paintings. According to records, the Qianlong emperor ordered several hundred works to document the various occasions he had attended and to record his imperial image at different stages of his life.[3] The creation of such a painting usually involved three steps: imperial order, approval of the draft drawing, and the final approval of the painted work. If fidelity to appearance or accuracy to true events were desired, the *huahuaren* (a title used for court painters at the Qing imperial academy) was required to attend the event so as to observe the activities and gather materials through participation before making any drawings. After the drawing was approved by the emperor, the painting would then be allowed to proceed in compliance with any suggestions or requirements the emperor might make during the evaluation process.[4] Because the artists were working under the command of a superior, their signatures had to be carefully worded with "your humble servant" to show the utmost respect. Such a form of signing one's name clearly reveals the court artists' overcautious, extremely deferential attitude.

To the west of the Forbidden City outside the West Gate (Xihuamen) are the West Gardens (Xiyuan), which consist of three huge and interconnecting lakes known as the Celestial Ponds

(Taiyechi) that extend from north to south. Located on the South Lake (Nanhai) of the Center-South Lake Complex (Zhongnanhai) is the Ying Tai garden. Built during the Ming and renovated twice during the Qing dynasty, once in the reign of Shunzhi and then in the reign of Kangxi, the Ying Tai garden and its multi-chambered buildings and pavilions are surrounded by water on three sides. Pagoda trees and weeping willows line its banks and the peaceful walkways from the Xiangluan Ge to the Yingxun Ting pavilions; fantastic garden rocks stand amidst exotic flowers and plants. Such a setting resembles that of Yingzhou, an island known as the "Fairyland Platform" off the coast in the East China Sea, believed to be the dwelling place of the immortals.

The Manchus liked buildings with raised foundations.[5] High, spacious, and exquisite, the Ying Tai garden was a favorite place for emperors and their ladies to hold banquets, appreciate the scenery, escape the heat of summer, and play on ice in the winter. The experience here would often inspire poems, and the Qianlong emperor had left more of these than anybody else, at least several dozens as documented by the *Guochao gongshi* (History of the imperial courts).[6] This is where Qing dynasty emperors often held banquets and threw parties featuring improvisational poetry contests of the type depicted in this scroll. Recorded at the end of the scroll, after the painting, are the *bailiang* style (requiring a rhyming character at the end of each line) verses that were created by the emperor and the participants of that day's gathering.[7] The banquet depicted here was held in celebration of the autumn harvest, so it was only proper for the Qianlong emperor to commence the poetry contest with this initial line: "In celebration of the harvest, gold glittering breeze and nourishing dews have arrived." Ministers and officials of various departments followed suit in the order of their rank; according to records, there were 176 of them. Their poems were then "respectfully calligraphed" by the "humble servant" Ji Huang.[8] The Qianlong emperor regarded this gathering as an event of great importance. To mark the occasion he ordered a book to be made: "*Collection of Relay Poems from the Ying Tai Banquet*, with a preface from his majesty, to be calligraphed by servant and minister Wang Youdun and carved into stone in the eleventh year of the Qianlong reign [1746]."[9] Other works marking the event include Zhang Ying's calligraphy *Verses of the Banquet at the Ying Tai Garden*.

This painting entered the imperial collection immediately after its completion in 1746. Its mounting format is therefore typical of Qing court style. The wrapping section is made of brocade. Impressed on the label is a rectangular seal: "Collection of the Northeast Library." The frontispiece is a light green paper with gold flecks, and the border strips are light yellow twill with a dragon-in-cloud pattern. Both the painting and the end section calligraphy are on silk tabby. Two small seals of the artist Zhang Gao are affixed to the painting section; the rest consists of a complete array of Qianlong's eight collection seals as well as the collection seals of the Jiaqing emperor and the Xuantong emperor. There is also the collection seal of the Museum of the Northeast. Originally stored at the Qianqing Gong (Palace of Heavenly Purity), it left the court when it was awarded by Puyi to his brother Pujie on January 12, 1923 (the 12th day of the 12th month, the 14th year of the Xuantong reign).[10] It was later acquired by the Liaoning Provincial Museum after traveling the same route as Zhu Zhanji's *Ten-Thousand-Year-Old Pine Tree* (cat. no. 3).

WWHC (trans. DHWS)

Notes

1. E'ertai, Zhang Tingyu, et al., *Guochao gongshi* [History of the imperial courts] (Beijing: Beijing guji chubanshe, 1987), pp. 127–28.
2. *Shiqu baoji xubian* [Treasured boxes of the Stone Channel, continued] (Taipei: Guoli gugong bowuyuan, 1971), p. 1036.
3. Yang Boda, *Qingdai huayuan* [The Qing imperial art academy] (Beijing: Zijincheng chubanshe, 1993), p. 49.
4. Ibid., pp. 48–49.
5. Tie Yuqin, *Shenjing huanggong* [The imperial palace in Shenyang] (Beijing: Zijincheng chubanshe, 1987), p. 113. Wan Yi, Wang Shuqing, and Liu Lu, *Qingdai gongting shi* [History of the Qing imperial court] (Tianjin: Baihua wenyi chubanshe, 2004), p. 7, records that in Manchu architecture, blue-green bricks were used. They like to use colorfully glazed roof tiles, reflecting the convention "to delight in green and in living on high platforms."
6. E'ertai, *Guochao gongshi*, pp. 282–84.
7. The Han dynasty emperor Wudi built the Bailiang Tai pavilion, where he and his ministers composed poetry in linked verse with each seven-character line ending in a rhyme. Hence, the style is named *bailiang*. See *Cihai* [Sea of words] (reprint, Shanghai: Shanghai cishu chubanshe, 1985), p. 1288.
8. *Shiqu baoji xubian*, p. 760.
9. E'ertai, *Guochao gongshi*, p. 688.
10. *Gugong yiyi shuji shuhua mulu si zhong* [Four catalogues of dispersed calligraphy and paintings from the imperial palace] (Beijing: Gugong bowuyuan, 1926), p. 26.

张镐字武迁，号仰仙，浙江钱塘人。清乾隆时期宫廷画家。

此图绘于1746年秋，记载了乾隆皇帝在瀛台赐诸臣宴之情景。乾隆十一年八月二十七日，乾隆皇帝在瀛台丰泽园赐宴王公宗室一百三人入宴；次日，八月二十八日，又在瀛台丰泽园赐满汉大臣、翰林等官员一百七十六人，宴毕，至淑清院“曲水流觞”设宝座赋诗（注1），图后的书法纪录了八月二十八日与会者一百多人即兴所赋的诗词。款“臣张镐恭画”（注2）。图中以典型的界画方式表现瀛台的环境，楼阁亭台，用笔整饬，设色富丽，画面中有二百二十余人，或朝服翎帽，恭谨侍立，或捧物行走，或着装待演，似乎是宴前的一切即将就绪，正在等待皇帝御驾的光临。全画仔细收拾，风格拘谨，是典型的清宫记事画作。

这类历史性的画作是清代宫廷画家们常要遵旨绘制的，据记载，乾隆皇帝一生中，便指命画了几百幅各种场合下的御容和记事画作（注3）。其作画程序常常有降旨，审稿，审画三个程序，如果描绘真人真事，则派画画人（清宫廷画院对宫廷画家的称呼）参加活动，体验生活，收集素材，勾勒草稿，经过皇帝审核后，按照皇帝的要求再制作完成（注4）。既为画家尊旨而画，在落款时，也是必须写上“臣”某某，其谨小慎微，毕恭毕敬之态从签名中亦可透露一二。

瀛台在今北京中南海的南海，西华门之西的西苑太液池中，明建，称南台，清顺治康熙年间两次重修。这里亭台楼阁错落，槐柳夹岸，自翔鸾阁至迎薰亭，三面环水，围植奇石花树，宛若蓬莱瀛洲仙境，统名“瀛台”。满人喜高台建筑（注5），高敞而优美的瀛台遂成为帝王后妃宴筵赏景避暑冰戏的游娱之地，不乏歌咏之诗篇，尤以乾隆皇帝为最，据《国朝宫史》记载者，便达数十首(注6)。清代皇帝也常以不同缘由在此宴客赋诗，这幅画便是很好的例子。画心之后，又记录了诗兴勃发的皇帝与与会者仿柏梁体所赋的诗句(注7)。因此次宴会是为了庆祝秋天的农业丰收，故乾隆皇帝先以御制“金风玉露庆西成”一句导吟，接著与宴的各位依各部门及官阶的高低依次联句，据记载者有176人，然后由臣嵇璜（18世纪）“敬书”（注8）。乾隆皇帝对此次盛会非常重视，并命制书籍“瀛台赐宴联句诗帖一部，御制序文，亲书成帙，命尚书臣汪由敦书诗，乾隆十一年勒石”（注9）。其他关于这一盛宴的艺术作品，还有张英的书法“瀛台赐宴赋”。

此画完成后便由宫中收藏，装裱应为典型的清宫装，包首为锦本，题签上有“东北图书馆藏”朱文长方印，引首为淡青洒金笺，隔水为淡黄云龙文绫本，画心和拖尾皆为绢本。由画上的钤印看，除了张镐自己的两枚小印外，其余收藏印为乾隆八玺全，和嘉庆、宣统的鉴赏印玺，并有“东北博物馆珍藏之印”。此画原藏乾清宫，宣统十四年十二月十二日，由末帝溥仪赏赐给其弟溥杰，而流落宫外（注10）。最后为辽宁省博物馆收藏的途径与图录第三号“万年松图卷”相同。

海蔚蓝

注解：

1. [清]鄂尔泰、张廷玉《国朝宫史》（北京古籍出版社, 1987），第127－128页。
2. [清]《石渠宝笈》续编记载（台湾，故宫博物院，1971），第760－764页。
3. 杨伯达《清代院画》（紫禁城出版社, 1993），第49页。
4. 杨伯达《清代院画》“清乾隆朝画院沿革”，（紫禁城出版社，1993），第48－49页。
5. 铁玉钦主编《盛京皇宫》（沈阳故宫博物院编，北京紫禁城出版社，1987），第113页。万依，王树卿《清代宫廷史》记载满人建筑中，用青砖，屋顶喜用琉璃瓦，是“喜绿色喜居高台”的习俗的反映，（天津百花文艺出版社，2004），第7页。
6. [清]鄂尔泰、张廷玉《国朝宫史》（北京古籍出版社, 1987），第282－284页。
7. 参见《辞海》缩印本，汉武帝筑柏梁台，与群臣联句赋诗，句句用韵的七言诗，故名（上海辞书出版社1985），第1288页。
8. [清]《石渠宝笈》续编（台湾国立故宫博物院1971），第760页。
9. [清]鄂尔泰，张廷玉编《国朝宫史》（北京古籍出版社，1987），第688页。
10. 《故宫已佚书籍书画目录四种》（故宫博物院，民国十五年版，1926），第二十六页。

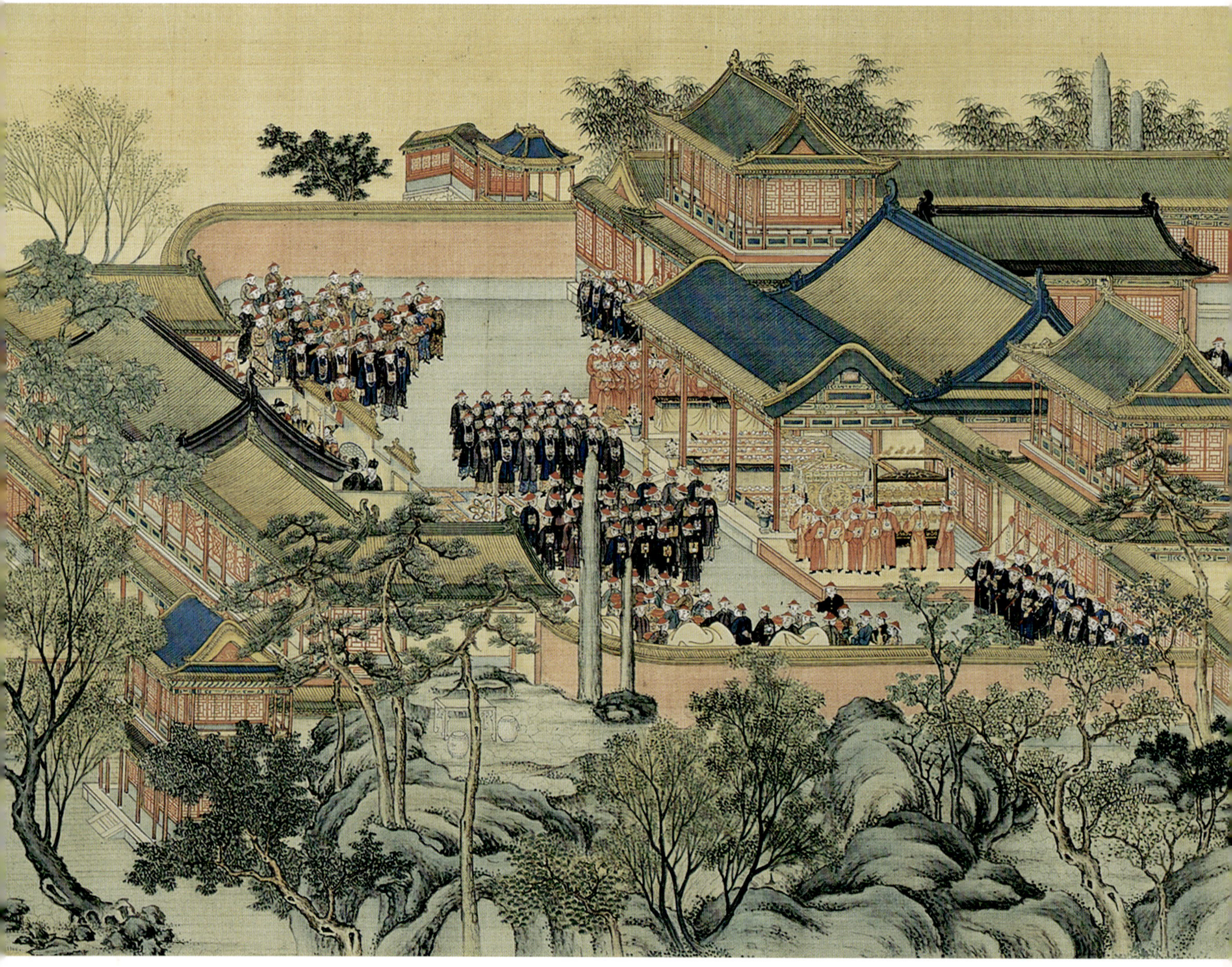

22 (detail 局部)

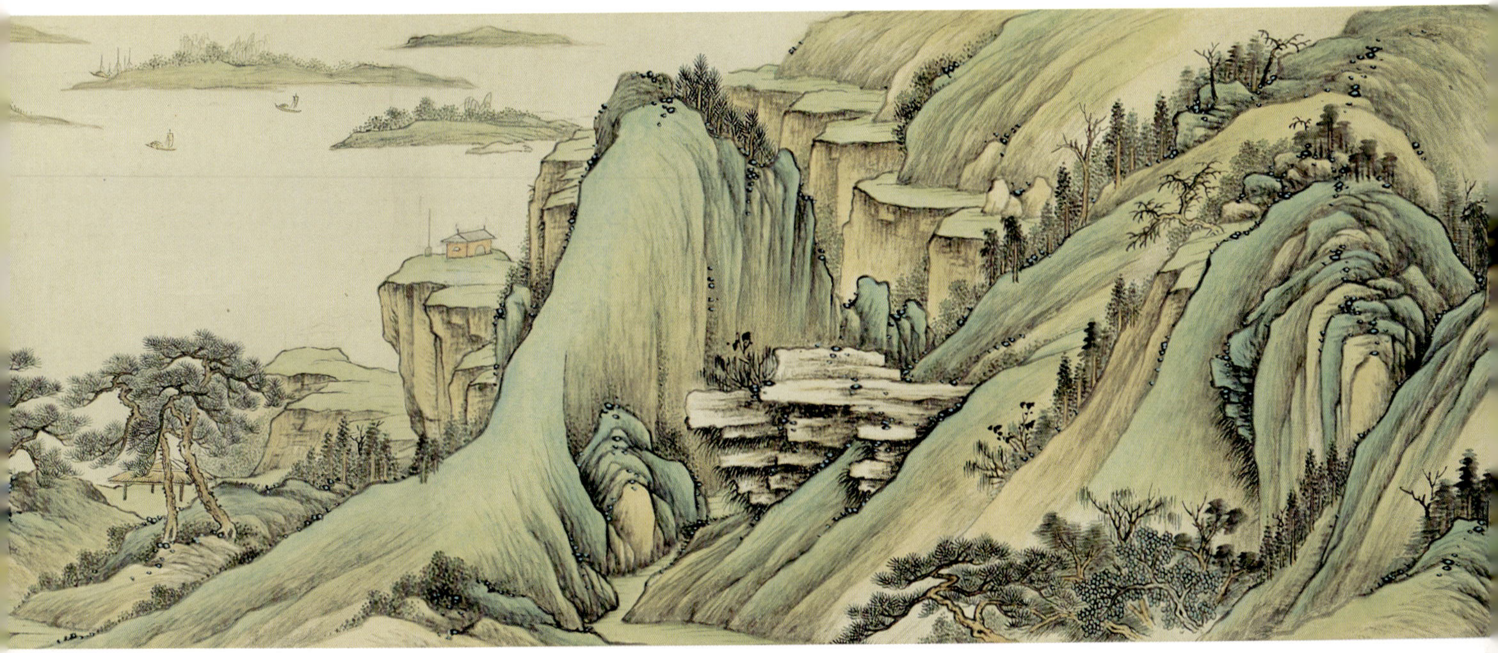

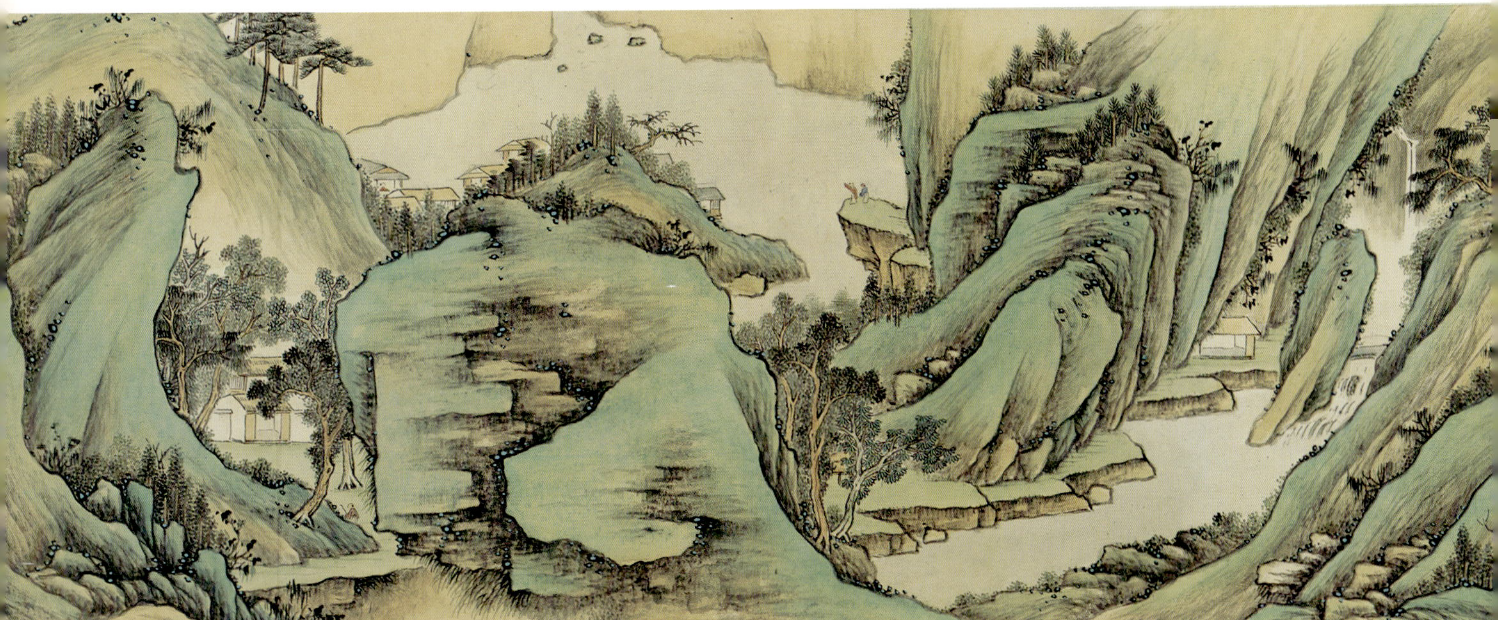

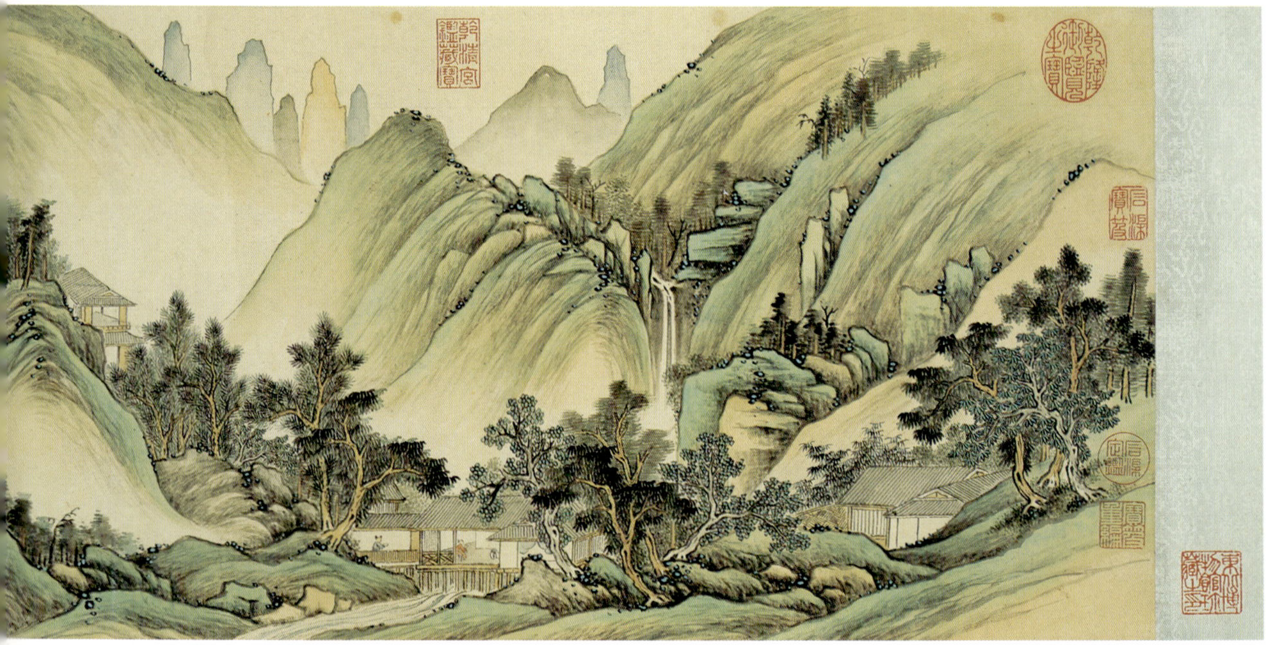

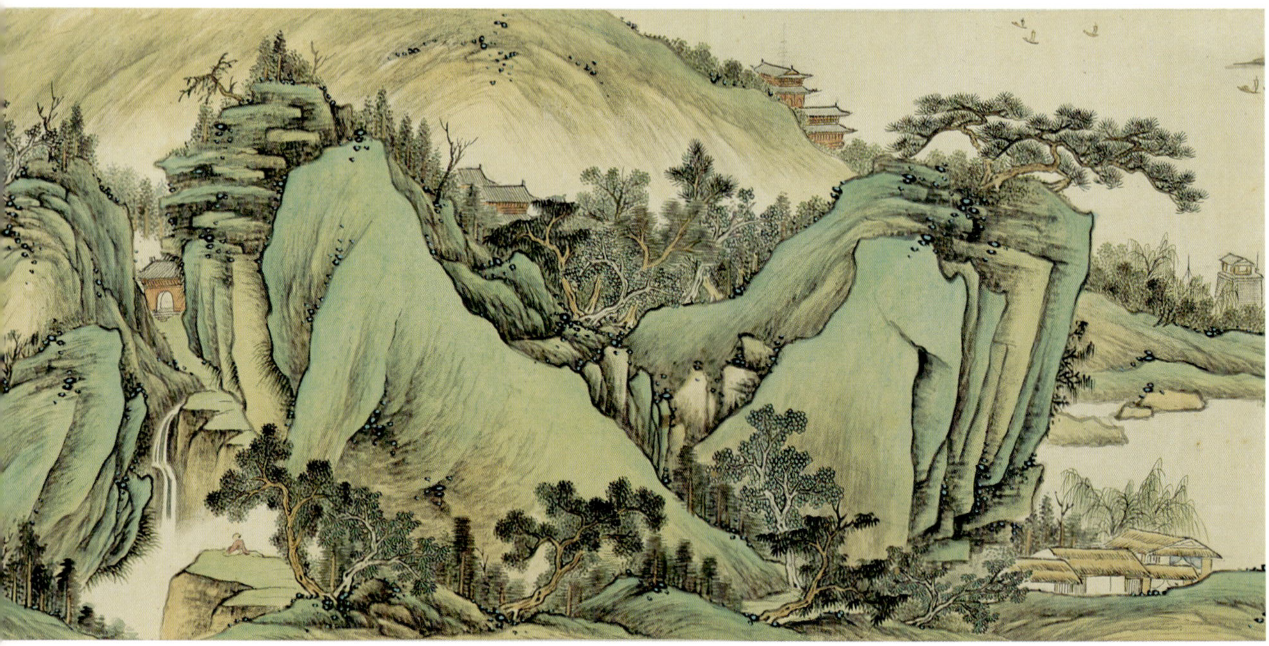

23

清 永瑢 长江帆影图

手卷，纸本水墨设色

Yongrong (1743–1790)

Sailing Boats on the Changjiang (Yangzi River)

Handscroll; ink and color on paper

32.5 x 414.2 cm

ARTIST'S SEALS: Zi chen Yongrong (small square/intaglio), Jinghua (small square/intaglio)

IMPERIAL SEALS: [Qianlong, r. 1736–95] Qianlong yulan zhibao (oval/relief), Shiqu baoji (rectangular/relief), Shiqu dingjian (round/relief), Baoji chongbian (square/intaglio), Qianqinggong jiancangbao (rectangular/relief), Qianlong jianshang (square/intaglio), Sanxitang jingjianxi (rectangular/relief), Yizisun (square/intaglio); [Jiaqing, r. 1796–1820] Jiaqing yulan zhibao (oval/relief); [Xuantong (Puyi), r. 1909–11] Xuantong yulan zhibao (square/relief)

OTHER SEALS: [Museum of the Northeast] Dongbei bowuguan zhencang zhiyin (square/relief)

画家印鉴：子臣永瑢（白文小方印）、敬画（白文小方印）。

皇家印鉴：[清乾隆皇帝弘历，在位1736－1795]乾隆御览之宝（朱文椭圆印）、石渠宝笈（朱文长方印）、石渠定鉴（朱文圆印）、宝笈重编（白文方印）、乾清宫鉴藏宝（朱文长方印）、乾隆鉴赏（白文圆印）、三希堂精鉴玺（朱文长方印）、宜子孙（白文方印）。[清嘉庆皇帝颙琰，在位1796－1820] 嘉庆御览之宝（朱文椭圆印）。[清宣统皇帝溥仪，在位1909－1911]宣统御览之宝（朱文方印）。

其他印鉴：[东北博物馆]东北博物馆珍藏之印（朱文方印）。

The sixth son of Emperor Gaozong (Qianlong) of the Qing dynasty, Yongrong held the title Prince Zhizhuang and adopted the sobriquet Master Jiusi. He was a good calligrapher and an excellent landscape and flower-and-bird painter. His calligraphy is reminiscent of that of Xu Hao of the Tang dynasty. His flowers have a classic but elegant plainness, combining the best of Shaogu (Zhou Zhimian, act. 1573–1620) and Tuojiang (Chen Gua [act. 1547–53], a flower-and-bird painter, son of Chen Chun [Baiyang Shanren]). His landscapes are based on those of Wang Shimin with a hint of Huang Dachi, though less energetic. He was the author of *Jiusitang shichao* (Collection of poems from the Jiusitang Studio).[1]

This scroll depicts a beautiful slice of landscape with a sprawling succession of lush green hills, waterways dotted with sporadic sails in the distance, and ancient temples hidden in mist. Its composition and coloring has been painstakingly executed, the brushwork is flawless, and the texture strokes seem effortless. The signature reads, "Respectfully painted by son and servant Yongrong." There are a complete set of Qianlong's eight collection seals.[2] A great number of Yongrong's works are landscapes. Another of his landscapes, listed in the *Shiqu baoji* under the title *Autumn Temples and Running Streams*, is done with color on *xuande* paper and also has the complete array of Qianlong's eight collection seals. The *Gugong yiyi shuji shuhua mulu si zhong* (Four catalogues of dispersed calligraphy and paintings from the imperial palace) documents other landscapes by Yongrong, including *Green Mountains with Clouds* (*Yunlan qingcui tu*), *Carrying a Qin Zither in a Valley of Blossoming Plums* (*Mei gu xieqin tu*), and the landscape albums which were awarded by Puyi to Pujie after December 13, 1922 (25th day of the 10th month in the 14th year of the Xuantong reign.[3]

As a result of fervent advocacy and persistent personal practice by the Qing emperors, all princes of the imperial family were required from childhood to receive a stringent education in Chinese culture in the imperial study rooms.[4] Therefore, there were no lack of artists and calligraphers among the Manchu princes and princesses. Among the princes of the Qianlong emperor, the fourth son, Prince Yongcheng, was good at painting ink lotus; the eighth son, Yongxuan, produced calligraphy in the style of Zhao Mengfu (1254–1322) and level-distance type landscape paintings; and the eleventh son and younger brother of Yongrong, Prince Yongxing, was an accomplished and influential calligrapher of the Qing dynasty.[5] The crown prince Yongyan, who was to succeed Qianlong as the Jiaqing emperor, was also very refined; not only did he paint ink plums and recite poetry, but he also continued the course set by his father by completing the compilation of the third edition of the *Shiqu baoji*. He also left his seal "Jiaqing yulan zhibao" (Imperial treasure viewed by Jiaqing) on the many works of art that he had viewed.

It is not clear if this painting was done for the artist's own pleasure or was meant to be a gift to his imperial father, but it is evident that it was brought into the Qing court collection soon after it was completed and was stored at the Qianqing Gong (Palace of Heavenly Purity). Aside from the inscription of the artist's name and painting title, the light-yellow, *xuan* paper title strip on the brocade wrapper is affixed with the seal of the Northeast Library collection. On the painting itself, there are many collection seals from the Qianlong to the Xuantong emperors in addition to the artist's signature seals. It was awarded by Puyi to his brother Pujie as a gift on January 2, 1923 (the 16th day of the 11th month, the fourteenth year of Xuantong).[6]

WWHC (trans. DHWS)

Notes

1. Yu Jianhua, ed., *Zhongguo meishujia renming cidian* [Dictionary of Chinese artists] (Shanghai: Shanghai guji chubanshe, 1985), p. 167.
2. Recorded in *Shiqu baoji xubian* [Treasured boxes of the Stone Channel, continued] (Taipei: Guoli gugong bowuyuan, 1971), p. 507.
3. Registered under the serial number *Yong* 9 in *Gugong yiyi shuji shuhua mulu si zhong* [Four catalogues of dispersed calligraphy and paintings from the imperial palace] (Beijing: Gugong bowuyuan , 1926), pp. 8, 19, 20.
4. Zhao Yi, *Yanpu zaji* [Anecdotes to air under the eaves], Qingdai shiliao biji congkan [Notes on Qing dynasty history and events series] (1982; reprint, Beijing: Zhonghua shuju, 1997), *juan* 1, p. 8.
5. Yu Jianhua, *Zhongguo meishujia*, pp. 166–67
6. Registered under the serial number *Chang* 2 in *Gugong yiyi shuji shuhua mulu si zhong*, p. 14.

永瑢为清高宗（乾隆）第六子，封质庄亲王，号“九思主人”，工书法，擅画山水、花卉。书法得唐代徐浩笔意，花卉古淡苍逸，兼有少谷（周之冕，活跃于1573—1620）、沱江（陈栝，白阳山人陈淳之子，善花卉，活跃于1547—1553）之胜。山水由王时敏上窥黄大痴，但气息欠超妙。著有《九思堂诗钞》（注1）。

此卷绘绵延之江山，苍翠欲滴，水波山色，孤帆远影，古寺藏云，一片美丽的国土。构图设色都很精心，用笔娴熟，皴法自如，落款为“子臣永瑢恭画”。钤印二，很小，为“子臣永瑢”，“敬画”。鉴藏宝玺八玺全（注2）。永瑢的山水作品较多见，在《石渠宝笈》同一编中亦记载了其另一幅山水画作“秋寺鸣泉”图，以宣德笺本，设色。鉴藏宝玺亦八玺全。《故宫已佚书籍书画目录四种》也记载了其的“云岚晴翠图”卷，“梅谷携琴图”卷和“山水册页”等，为溥仪于宣统十四年十月二十五日以后陆续赏赐给溥杰（注3）。

由于清帝的身体力行和极力倡导，所有的皇室子弟从小就在上书房接受严格的汉文化教育（注4）。因此皇室子弟能书善画者于清代并不少见，乾隆皇帝的诸王子中，如其第四子永成善墨荷，其第八子永璇，书法如赵孟頫，亦作平远山水，而其第十一子成亲王永瑆，永瑢的弟弟更是清代有造诣和有影响的书法家（注5）。乾隆皇帝的儿子，继承其皇位的颙琰，即嘉庆皇帝也很风雅，不仅会画墨梅吟诗，并继父业，续编清宫书画鉴藏之作《石渠宝笈》三编，并于观赏过的书画上钤有“嘉庆御览之宝”的玺印。

此卷或为王子自作，或以供奉父皇之用虽不得而知，但画成后显然便为内府收藏，储于乾清宫。本卷用天青色的几何纹锦包首，浅黄色的宣纸签条题了画家名字和画题外，并钤“东北图书馆藏”朱文长方印。画心上除了画家的名章外，均为自乾隆皇帝到宣统皇帝的收藏印。宣统十四年十一月十六日为末帝溥仪以赏赐为名，将此画赠送给其弟溥杰（注6）。后为辽宁省博物馆收藏。

海蔚蓝

注解：

1. 俞剑华编《中国美术家人名词典》（上海人民美术出版社，1985），第167页。
2. ［清］《石渠宝笈》续编（台北国立故宫博物院，1971），第570页。
3. 《故宫已佚书籍书画目录四种》（故宫博物院，民国十五年版，1926），第8、19—20页。
4. ［清］赵翼《檐曝杂记》卷一，载《清代史料笔记丛刊》（北京中华书局，1997），第8页。
5. 俞剑华编《中国美术家人名词典》（上海人民美术出版社，1985），第166—167页。
6. 《故宫已佚书籍书画目录四种》，此一卷的宫中登记号为长字二号（故宫博物院，民国十五年版，1926），第十四页。

24
明　　佚名仿仇英　　汉宫春晓图
手卷，绢本水墨淡设色
Anonymous, in imitation of Qiu Ying
Spring in the Han Palace

Ming dynasty (1368–1644)
Handscroll; light ink and color on paper
33.8 x 562 cm

ARTIST'S SEAL: Shizhou (double-gourd/relief)
IMPERIAL SEALS: [Qianlong, r. 1736–95] Qianlong jianshang (round/intaglio), Yangxindian jiancangbao (rectangular/relief), Qianlong yulan zhibao (oval/relief), Sanxitang jingjianxi (rectangular/relief), Yizisun (square/intaglio), Shenpin (linked seal; double square/relief), Jixia jianshang zhixi (square/relief), Shiqu baoji (rectangular/relief), Wufu wudaitang guxi tianzi bao (large square/relief), Bazheng maonian zhibao (large square/relief), Taishang huangdi zhibao (large square/relief); [Jiaqing, r. 1796–1820] Jiaqing yulan zhibao (round/relief); [Xuantong (Puyi), r. 1909–11] Xuantong yulan zhibao (oval/relief), Xuantong jianshang (square/relief), Wuyizhai jingjianxi (rectangular/relief)
OTHER SEALS: [unidentified] Zhangjingzhai zhenwan tushu ji (square/relief); [Museum of the Northeast] Dongbei bowuguan zhencang zhiyin (square/relief)
FRONTISPIECE TITLE (SEALS): Hangong Chunxiao. Qianlong yubi (Hanhao miaoran [oval/relief], Qianlong chenhan [square/relief], Danshu shi suyuan [oval/relief])
COLOPHON WRITERS (SEALS): Gu Bingjun, dates unknown (Gu [round/relief], Bingjun [square/intaglio]; Gao Zhao, ca. early 18th c. (Gao Zhao zhiyin [square/intaglio], Guzhai [square/relief]); Du Shouchang, dates unknown (Du Shouchang yin [square/intaglio], Xiangcao [square/relief])
TITLE STRIP (SEALS): Qiu Ying Hangong chunxiao tu. Neifu shending zhenji shenpin. (Qianlong chenhan [square/relief])

画家印鉴：十洲（朱文葫芦印）
皇家印鉴：[清乾隆皇帝弘历，在位1736－1795]乾隆鉴赏（白文圆印）、养心殿鉴藏宝（朱文长方印）、乾隆御览之宝（朱文椭圆印）、三希堂精鉴玺（朱文长方印）、宜子孙（白文方印）、神品（朱文方形联珠印）、几暇鉴赏之玺（朱文方印）、石渠宝笈（朱文长方印）、五福五代堂古稀天子宝（朱文大方印）、八征耄念之宝（朱文大方印）、太上皇帝之宝（朱文大方印）。[清嘉庆皇帝颙琰，在位1796－1820]嘉庆御览之宝（朱文椭圆印）。[清宣统皇帝溥仪，在位1909－1911]宣统御览之宝（朱文椭圆印）、宣统鉴赏（朱文方印）、无逸斋精鉴玺（朱文长方印）。
其他印鉴：张静斋珍玩图书记（朱文方印）。[东北博物馆]东北博物馆珍藏之印（朱文方印）
引首题额（钤印）：汉宫春晓。乾隆御笔(含毫渺然[朱文椭圆印]、乾隆宸翰[朱文方印]、耽书是宿缘[朱文方印])
题跋者(钤印)：[顾秉均，生卒年不详]顾（朱文圆印）、秉均（白文方印）。[高兆，约18世纪初]高兆之印（白文方印）、固斋（朱文方印）。[杜首昌，生卒年不详]杜首昌印（白文方印）、湘草（朱文方印）。
签条（钤印）：仇英汉宫春晓图。内府审定真迹神品。（乾隆宸翰[朱文方印]）

Inside the imperial palace of the Han dynasty (206 BCE–220 CE), there were many famous buildings and gardens; nevertheless, it was not a happy life for the several thousand women of the inner palace who find themselves waiting indefinitely for a chance to be with the emperor. The despair was best illustrated by the sad story of the Han dynasty consort Zhaojun.[1] Therefore, in classical Chinese literature and art, the Han Palace is synonymous with both the fantastic grandeur of a fairyland and the great sorrow of unfulfilled longings for love. This scroll, titled *Spring in the Han Palace*, by an anonymous Ming dynasty artist working in imitation of Qiu Ying (ca. 1405–1552), depicts the activities of court ladies within splendid imperial palace gardens in spring.

This scroll begins with a fairy-tale like imperial palace garden whose tall buildings, chambers, and balconies are shrouded in mist, corresponding to the floating white clouds in the far distance. The architecture of the palace buildings is rendered in detail with exquisitely worked foundations and zigzagging balustrades. There are gazebos and pavilions on the terrace corners and grotesque rocks amidst lush vegetation and flowers off the balconies. Court ladies looking like fairies are seen at leisure everywhere, attended by their female servants. Some are drinking at banquets, while others are viewing flowers or chatting in gardens. Still others gather on carpets, helping each other in applying makeup. Apparently overcome with boredom, some stay high up in their rooms, heavy-hearted, and others are in pavilions, lost in deep thought.

Crossing to the other side of a subtly indicated wall, we enter the imperial park, which is landscaped with peaceful lakes and forested hills. The buildings by the lakes have courtyards, side rooms, and connecting corridors. The court ladies are seen engaged in all kinds of activities: some play chess in a pavilion; others play string instruments and sing; some boat on the lake; others enjoy a walk in a forest near the lake; some read books in the upper stories of mountain villas; and still others practice dance together. On an open platform, several court ladies resting on a couch admire peacocks with outspread, fanlike tails. On the one hand the women are enjoying their leisurely pastimes, while on the other they are constantly working on their looks and entertainment skills, hoping someday to be singled out by the emperor and enjoy his favor.

Towards the end of the scroll, a group of ladies gather around a swing on the inside of a long corridor. One lady is standing on the swing, while behind her two others help in pushing. They seem to be enjoying the excitement of the swing rising higher and higher. Outside the long corridor, a group of girl servants gather around a wagon decorated with feathers. The mother and child in the wagon are treated extremely respectfully, suggesting that they are blessed by the emperor's favor because the woman has given birth to a child for the imperial family and has now risen to a highly respected position. This is a much dreamed of objective of the court ladies, and so they follow her closely to better their chances of getting close to the emperor. There are indeed tremendous anxieties within the court.

Life as an imperial concubine within the inner palace has been extensively and explicitly described in court ballads of the middle and late Tang dynasty (8th–9th centuries). At the end of the scroll, Gu Bingjun of the Qing dynasty recorded the full text of some of these court ballads in standard script, complementing the illustrations in the painting by recounting the hidden bitterness of the court ladies. Not only did the Qianlong emperor personally inscribe the four characters which read "Spring Comes to Han Palace" on the scroll's frontispiece, he also affixed several collection seals of the Qianlong reign.

HWL (trans. DHWS)

Note

1. An imperial consort who eventually volunteered to marry a khan of the Huns and live beyond the Great Wall.

汉代（前206－公元220年）宫廷中有许多著名的建筑和园林，但在后宫中企盼皇帝宠幸的数千佳丽们的生活却并不幸福，例如汉元帝时有昭君出塞的故事（注1）。于是，在中国古代文艺作品中，汉宫总是与仙境般的辉煌壮观以及幽怨情长的故事联系在一起。这卷明代佚名画家仿仇英技法绘制《汉宫春晓图》，展现的就是春日里众多宫女们在富丽堂皇的皇家宫苑中的活动。

展卷伊始，是仙境般的皇家宫苑，雾霭缭绕的瑶台上，楼阁高耸，与远处飘拂的白云遥遥相对，曲折的镂槛台基精致整齐，转角处亭榭点缀；台外奇石怪异，花繁木青。如仙的宫女分处于各处，在众多女侍们的服侍下，优裕而又闲适，或在楼阁饮宴，或在庭院赏花聊天，或聚于地毯相互妆扮。有人楼上愁，有人亭中思，显得百无聊赖。越过一道隐约可见的院墙，进入了皇家园林，山水幽深，临湖的建筑，或隐于山林之中，或有回廊连成院落。宫女们有的在亭中对棋，有的在楼上抚琴吟歌，有的在湖中荡舟，有的在岸边林中散步，有的在山阁中读书，有的聚集舞蹈。一处露台上，几位宫女们倚坐在床榻上，欣赏孔雀开屏。宫女们一边惬意地度着清闲的时光，一边在不断地美容或练艺，企盼着有朝一日能够得到皇帝的召见和恩宠。

画卷结尾处，长廊内的一群宫女们，正聚集在秋千架旁，一人站立在踏板上，后面两人在助推，她们享受着秋千高高荡起的快感。长廊外的一群宫女，紧紧地簇拥在一辆装饰着羽毛的辇车旁，车上坐着的母子尊贵至极，暗示着这位母亲得到了皇帝的恩宠，因为有了皇家的后代而达到了很尊贵地位，这是宫女梦寐以求的目标，所以她们要紧紧相随，以便得到更多接近皇帝的机会，宫中的忧思可谓深矣！

后宫生活在中晚唐时期（8－9世纪）流行的宫词中，叙述的最为详尽。卷后，清代人顾秉钧楷书录写的唐人宫词七言诗全文，与图绘内容相辅相成，述说了宫女的幽怨。顾秉均并在诗后有跋文，与高兆和杜首昌的跋文一起，均对仇英此卷的娇娆淡雅赞赏有加。乾隆皇帝不仅于画卷前迎（引首）亲笔题写了“汉宫春晓”四字，还亲自为画题签，并钤盖了多方乾隆朝的收藏印。

黄伟利

注解：

1. 王昭君是汉代的宫女，公元前33年，匈奴单于入朝求和亲，昭君自请嫁之，遂远离故乡嫁到长城之外。

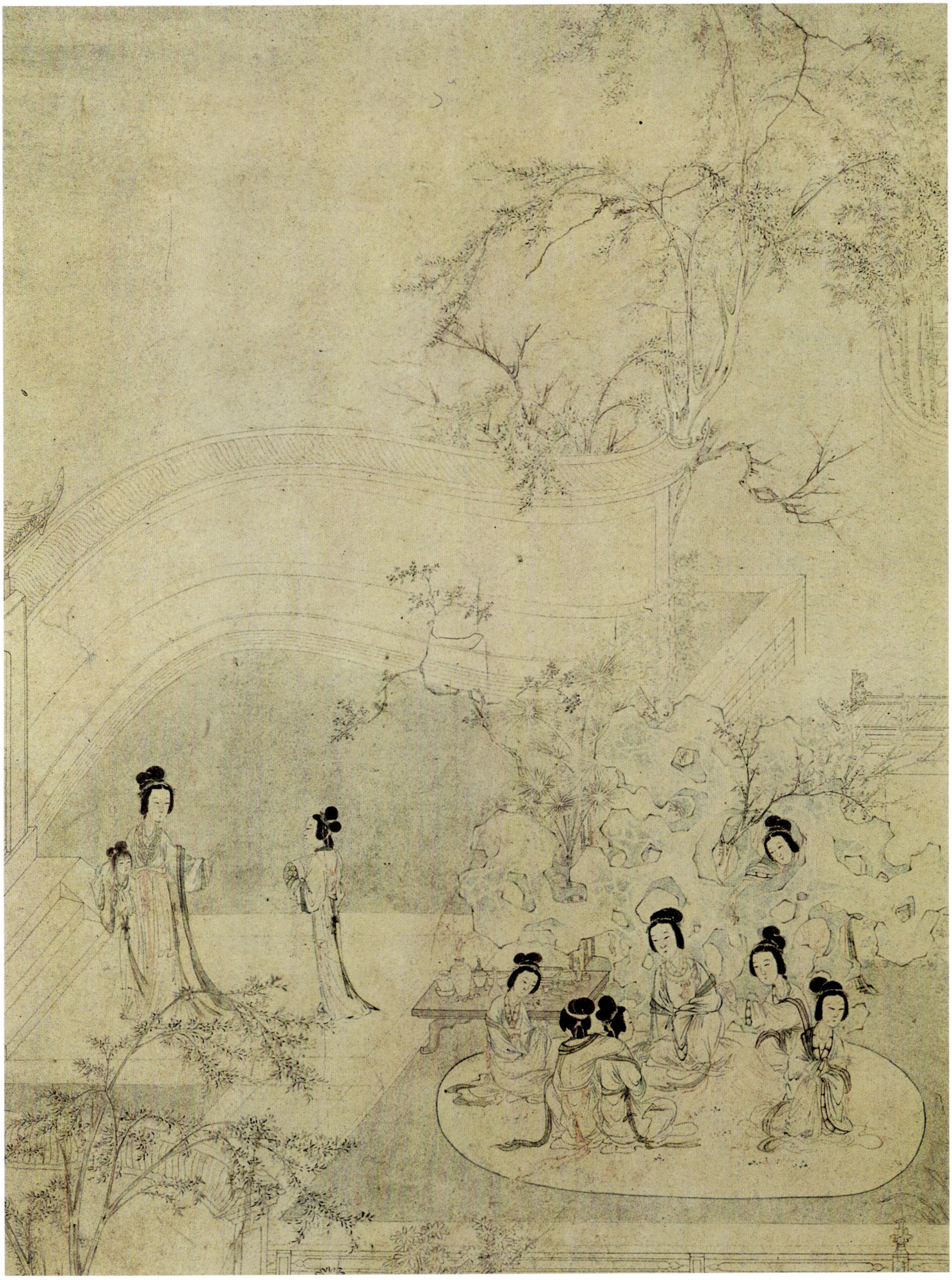

24 (detail 局部)

24

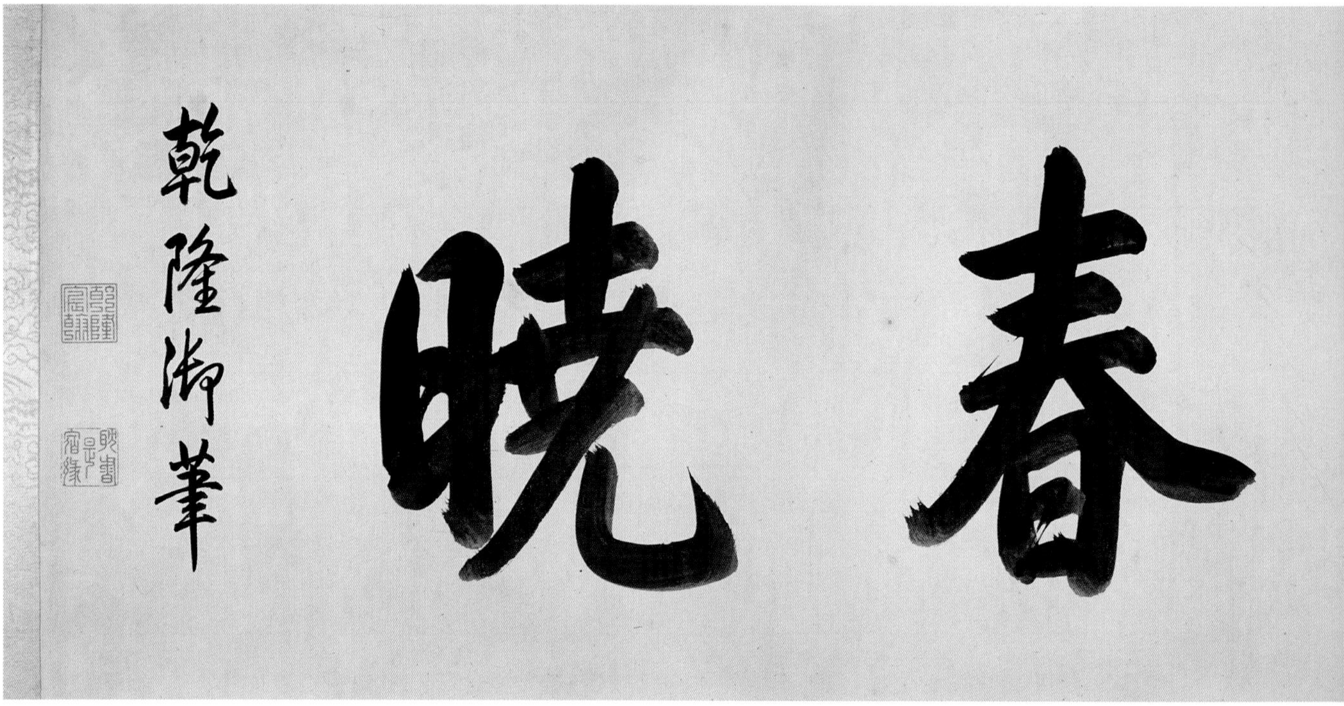

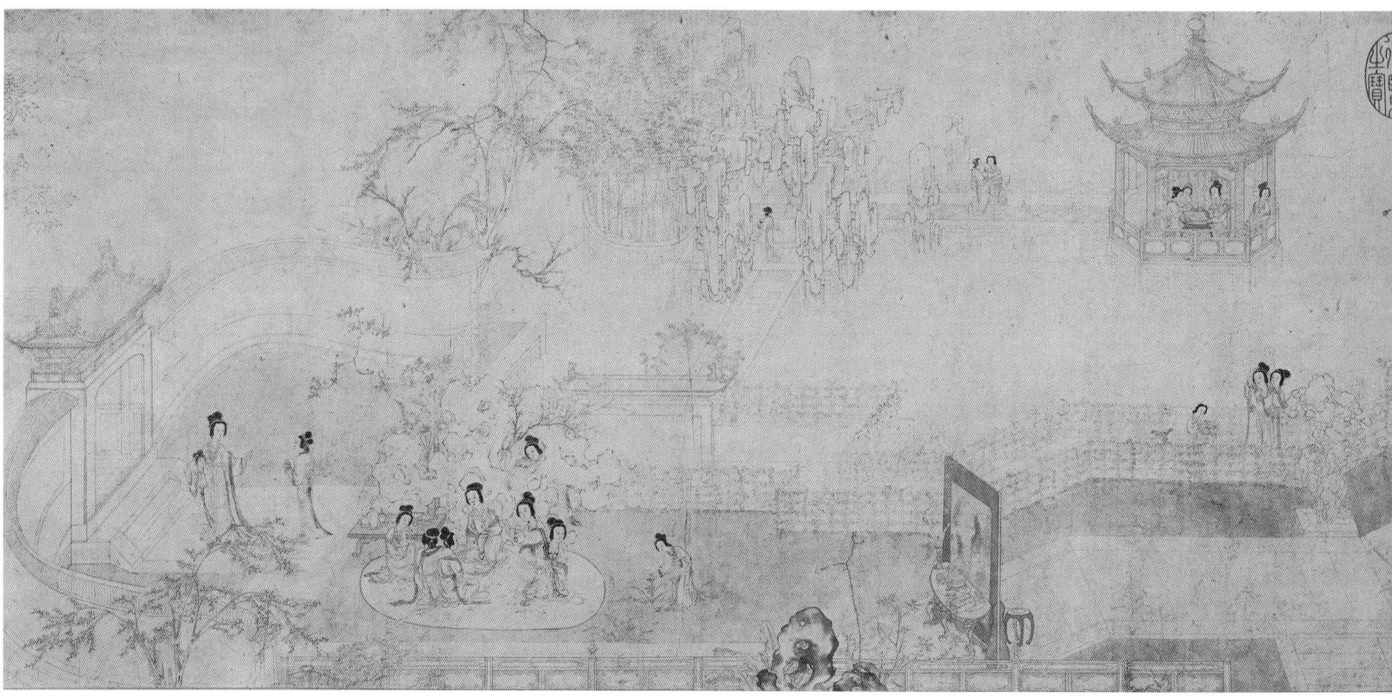

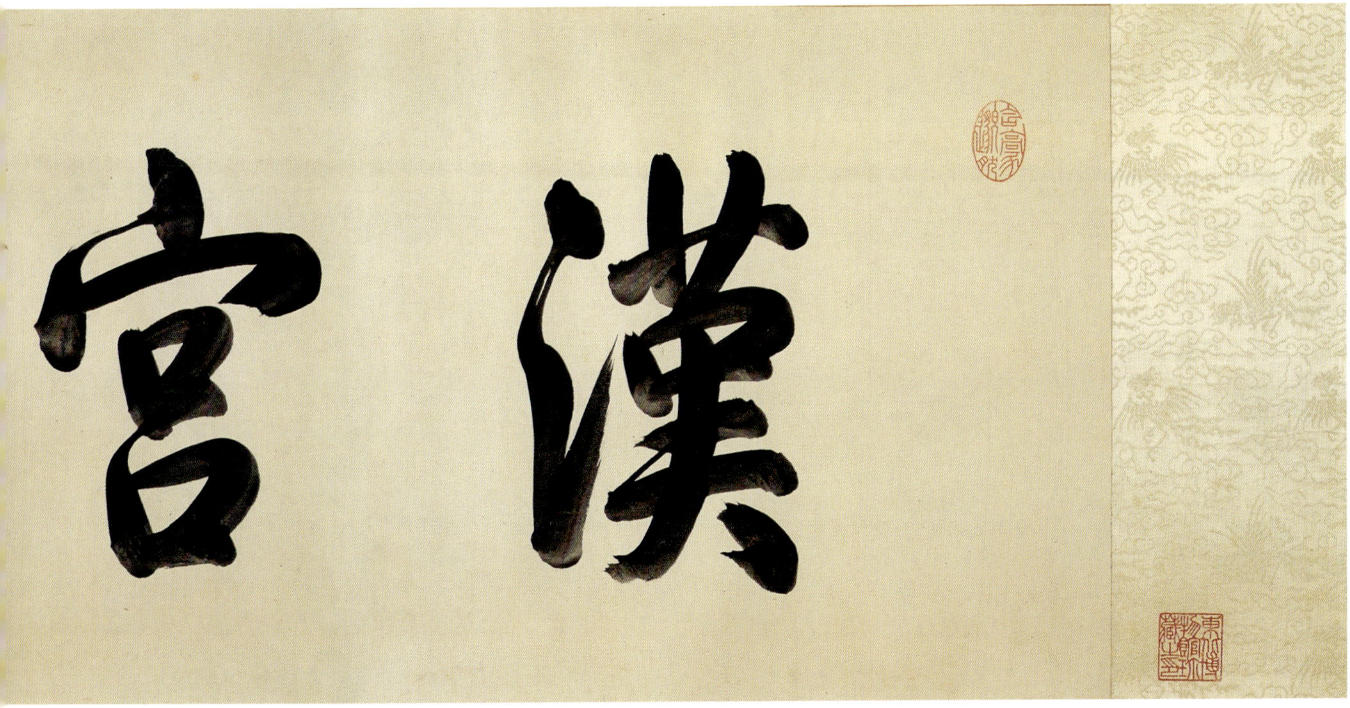
宫
漢

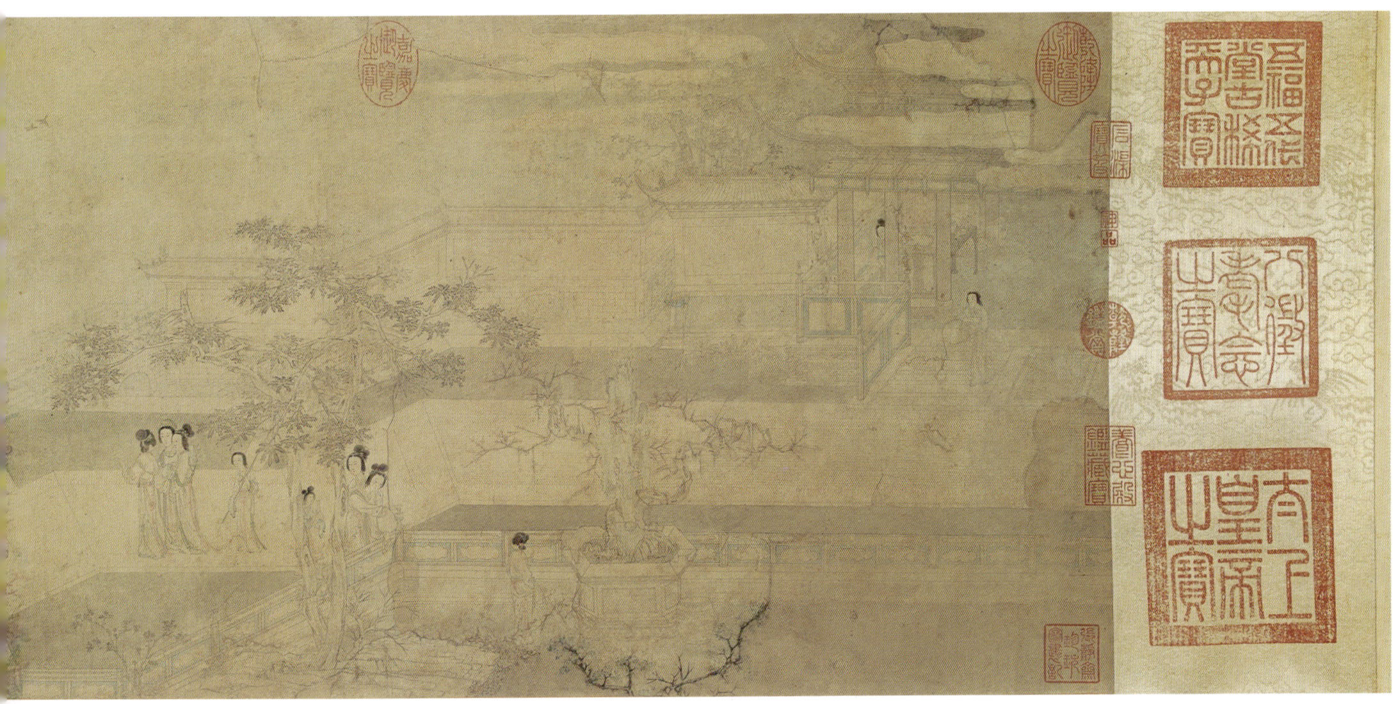

24

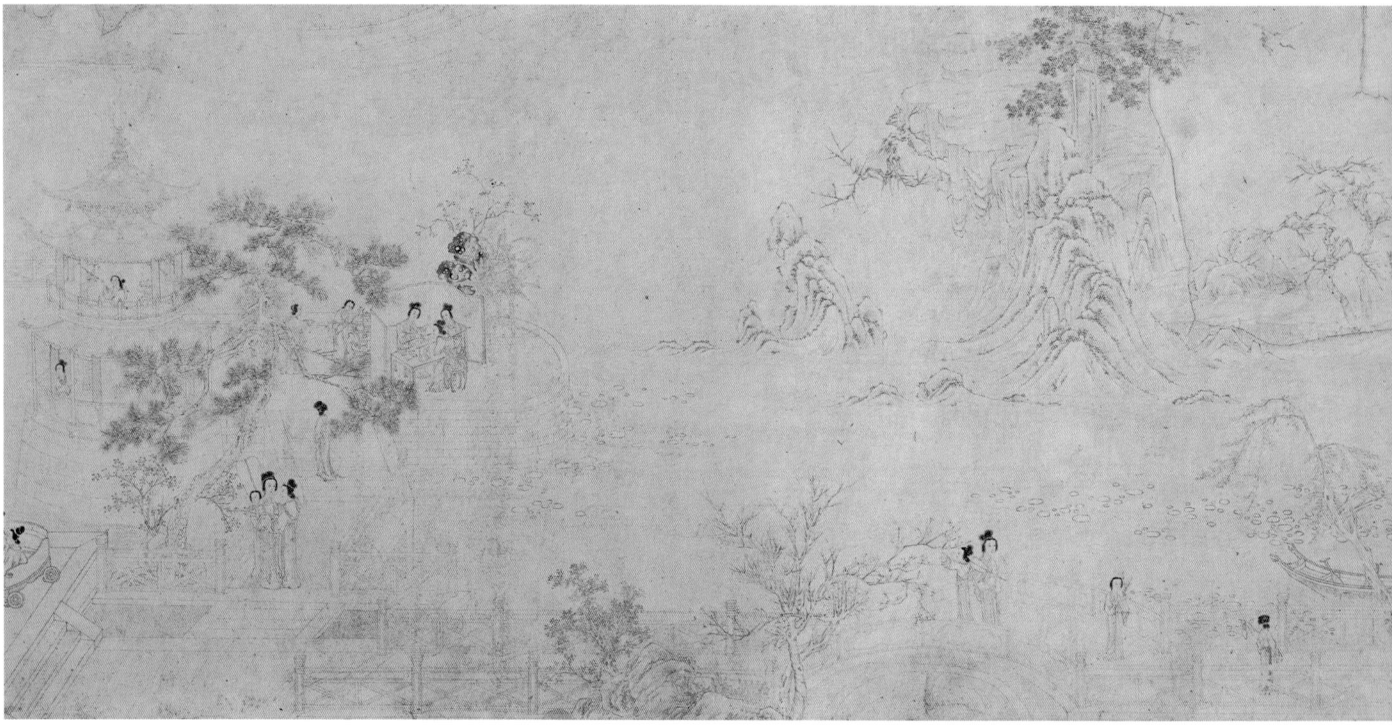

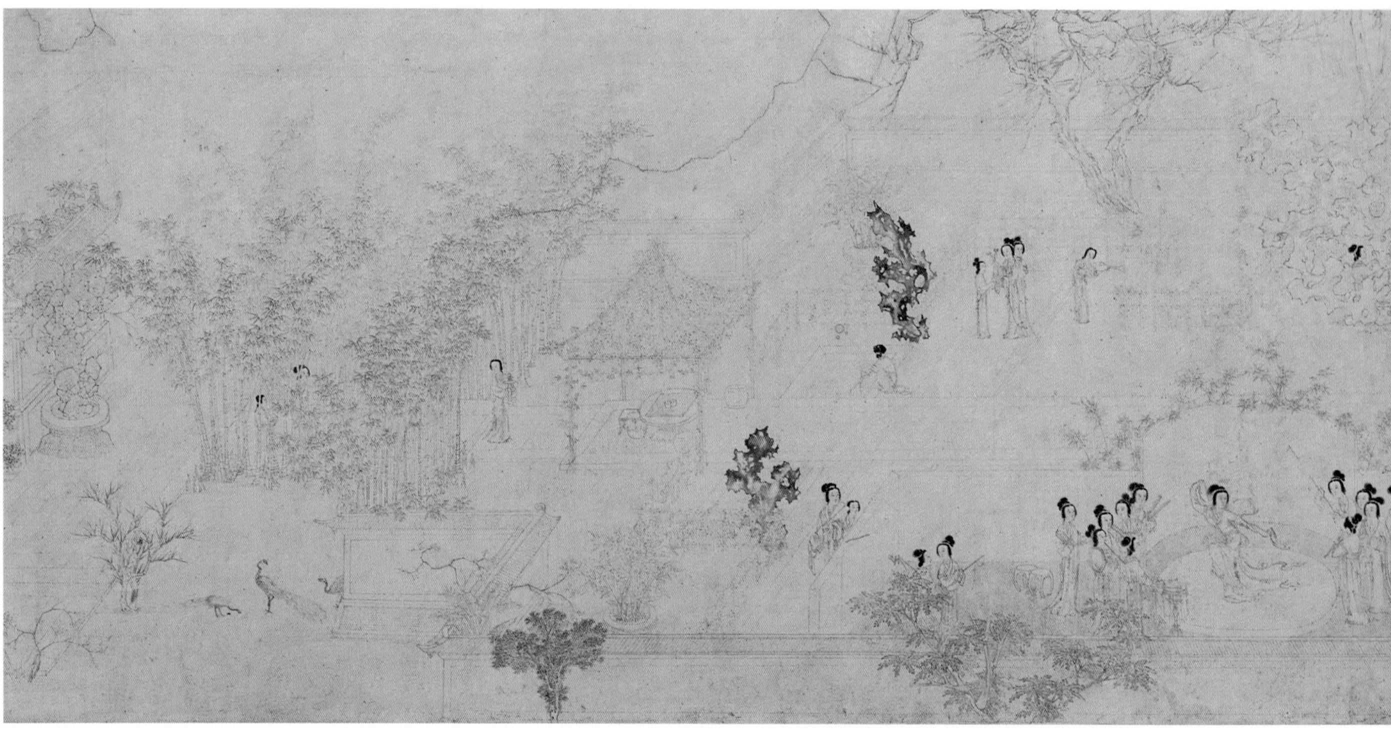

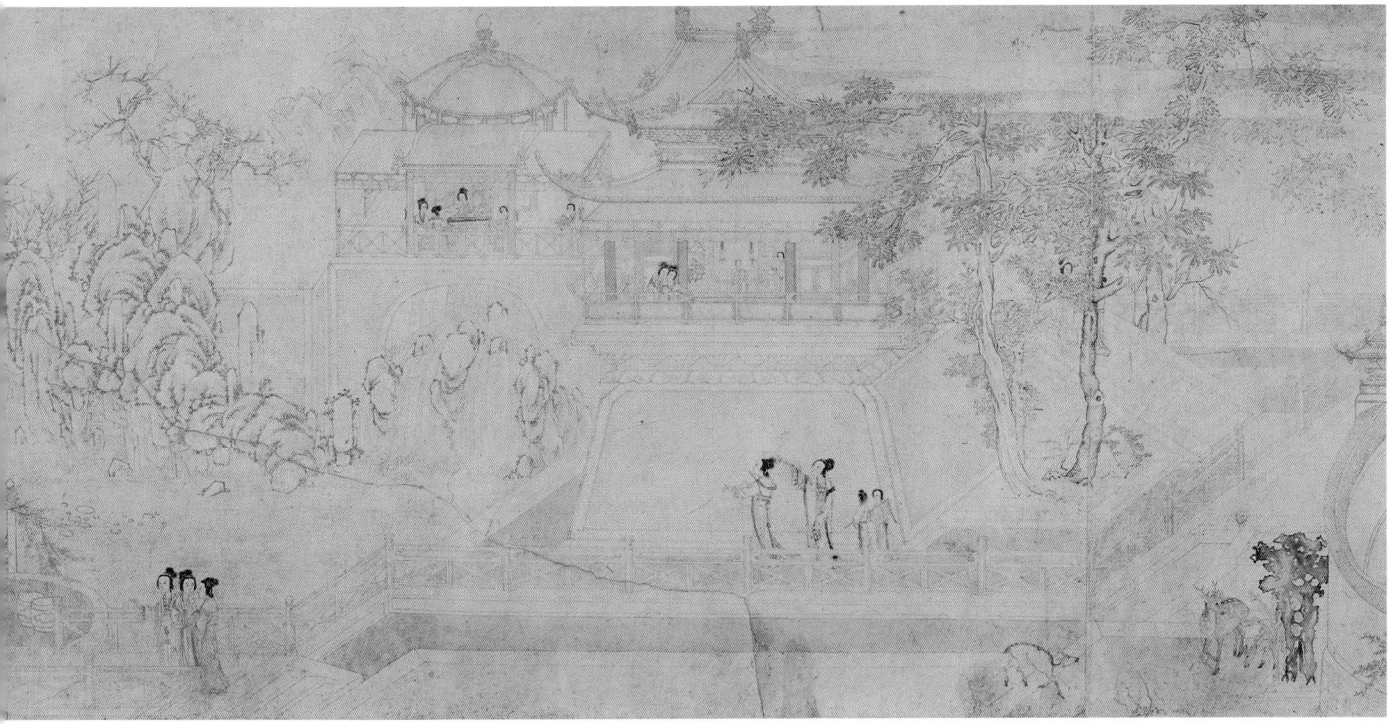

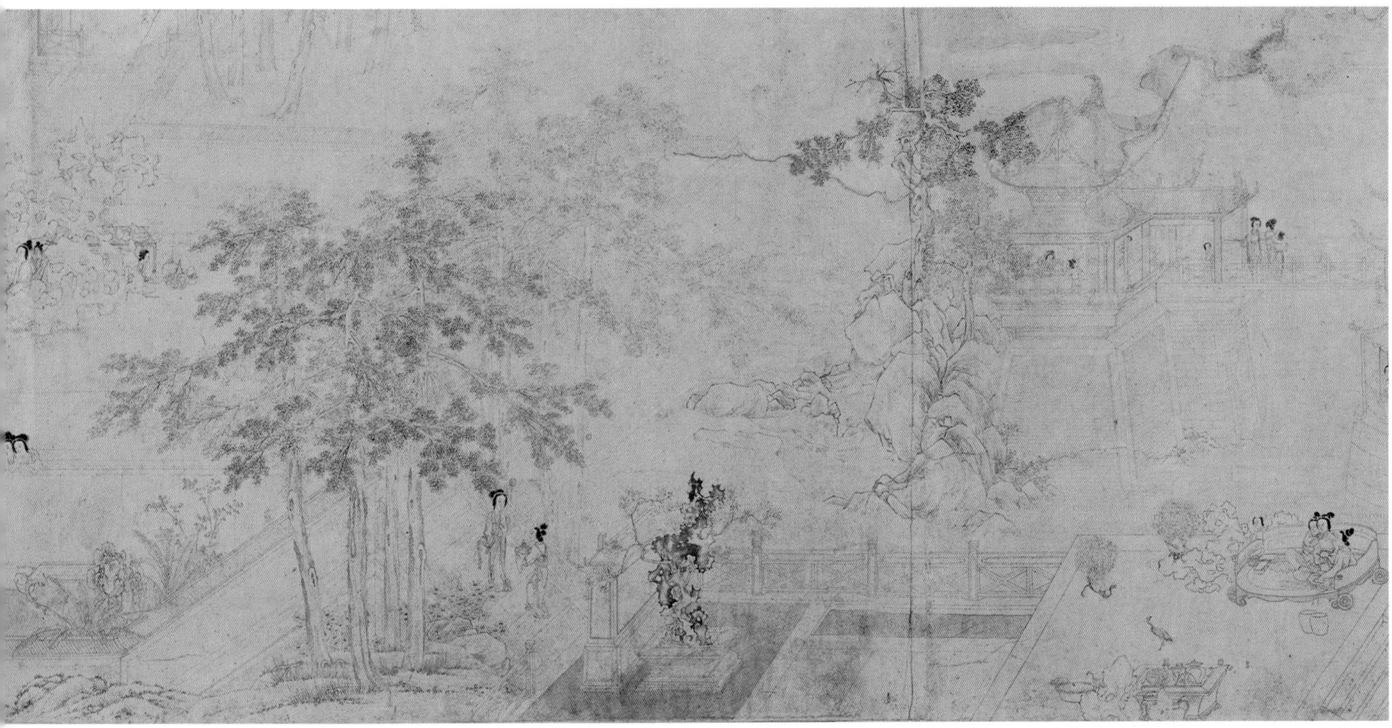

24

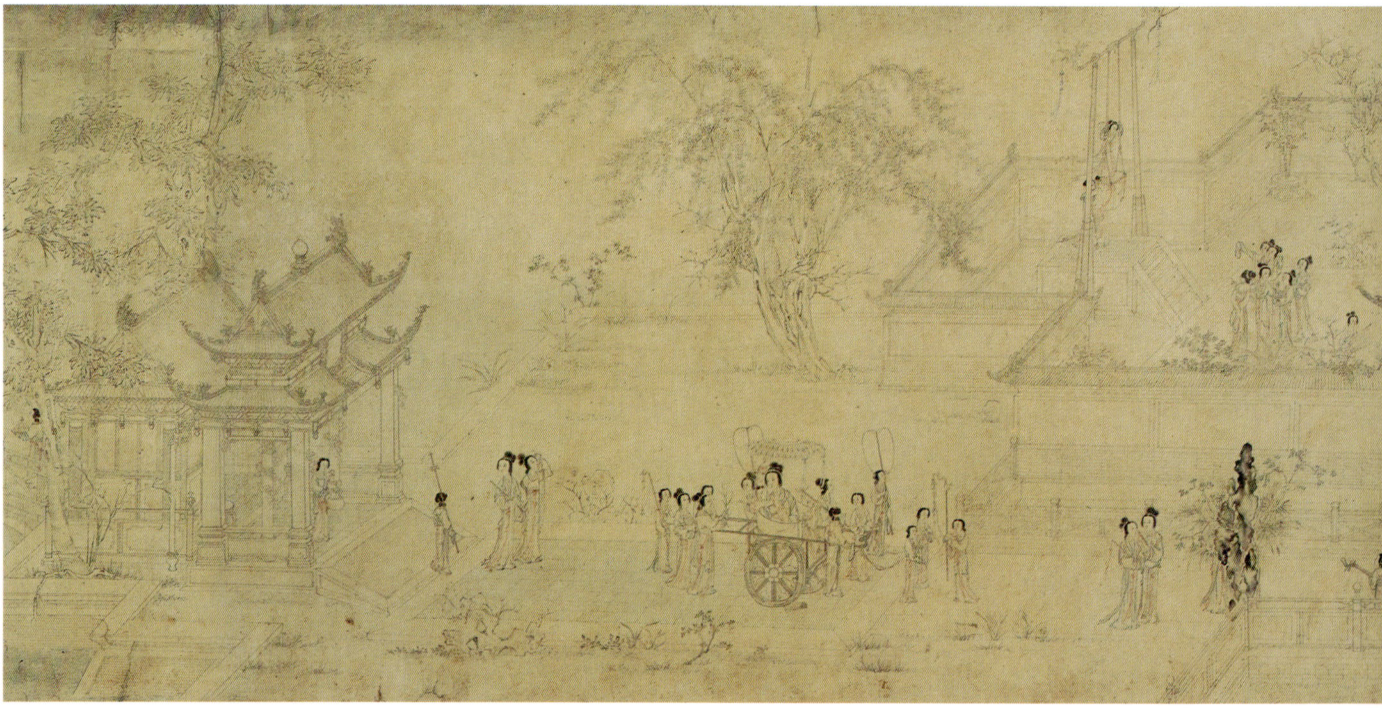

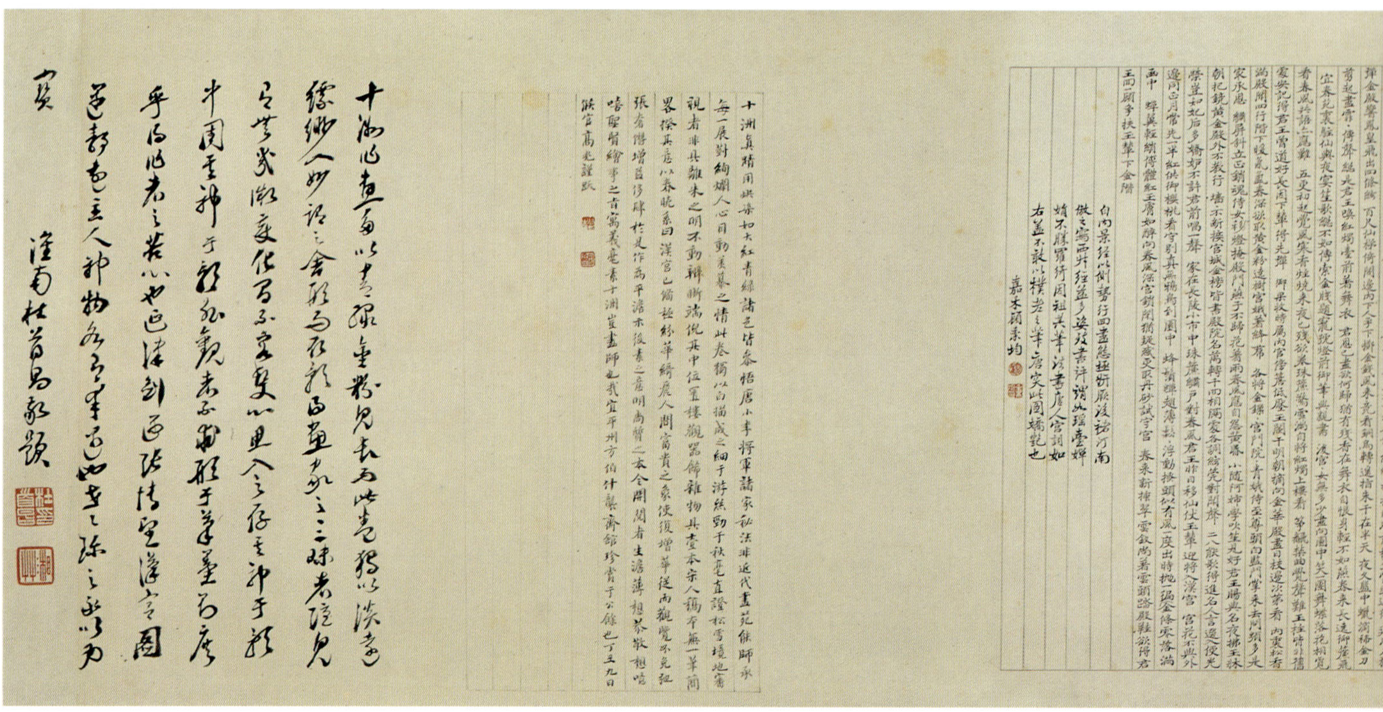

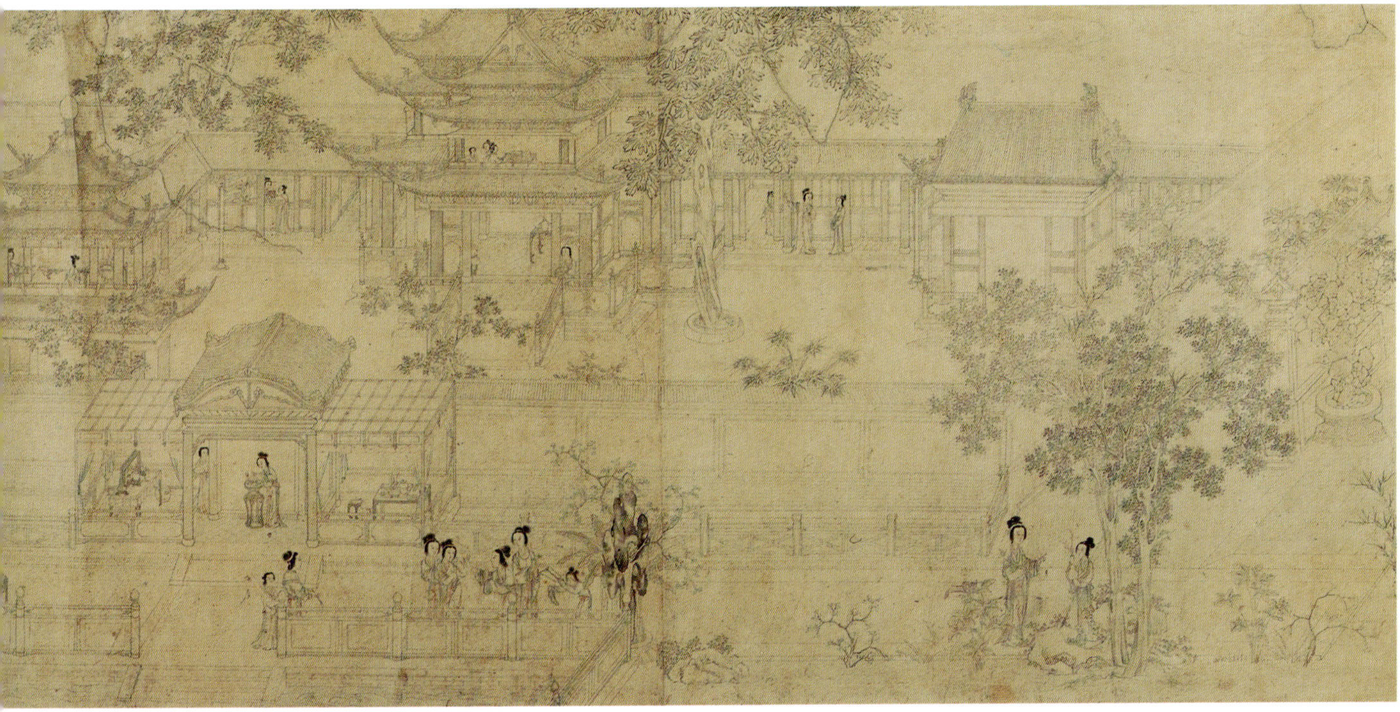

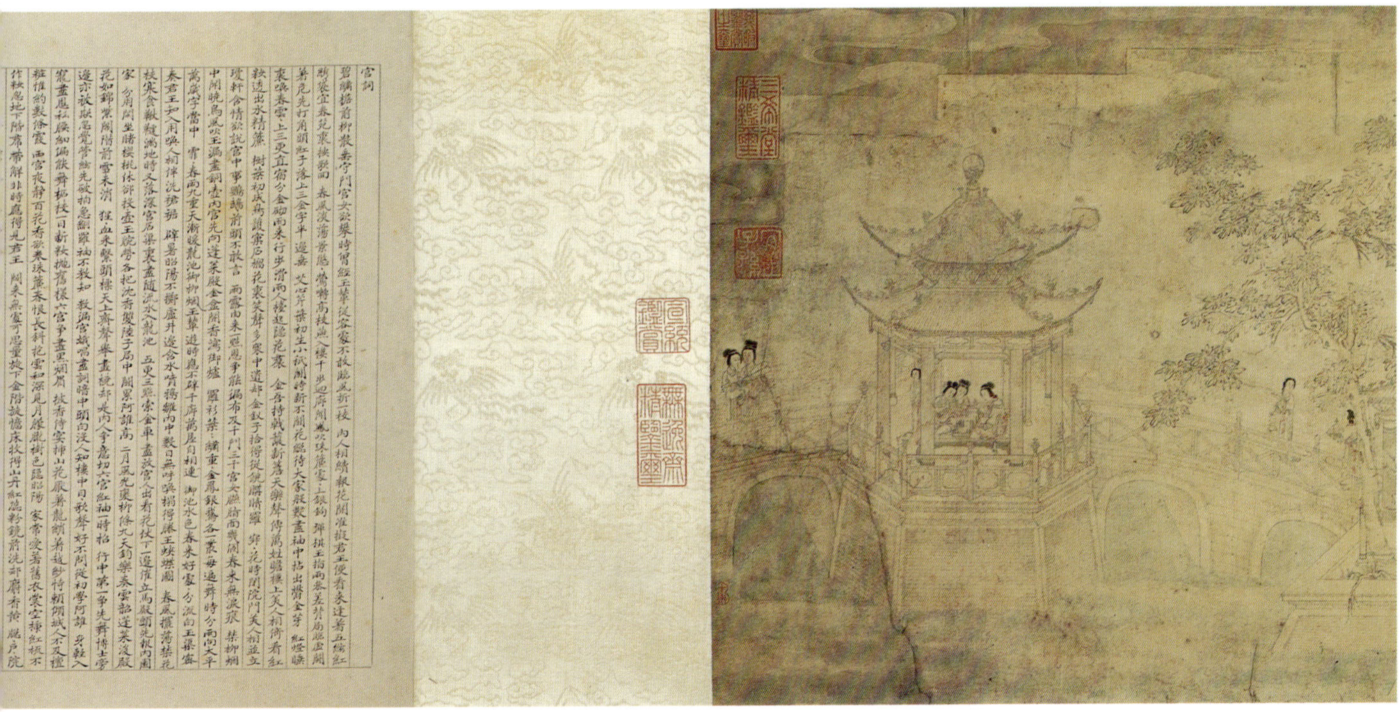

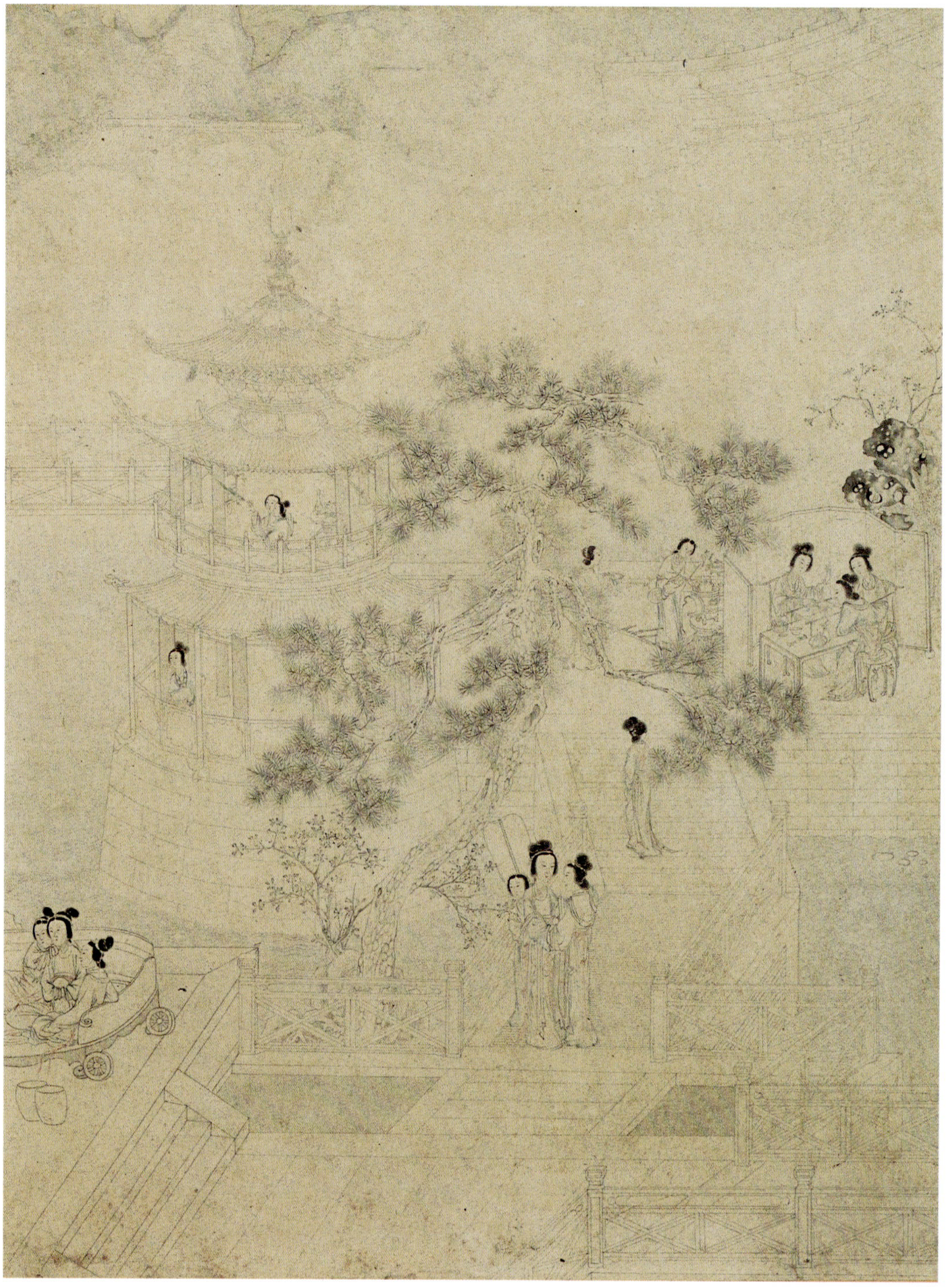

24 (detail 局部)

25

清 张照、梁诗正等奉旨编纂《秘殿竹林·石渠宝笈》
初编（1745），续编（1793），三编（1816）
国立故宫博物院，民国六十年重印本，1971

Three volumes of *Midian zhulin Shiqu baoji*

Chubian (1st ed.) 1745, *xubian* (2nd ed.), 1793; (3rd ed.), 1816

Editors: Zhang Zhao (1691–1745), Liang Shizheng (1697–1763), et al.

Reprint edition: Taipei: National Palace Museum, sixtieth year of Minguo (1971)

26.5 x 19.5 cm

In the last dynasty of China's feudal period, the formation of the imperial painting and calligraphy collection came about because of the advocacy and vigorous initiative of the Kangxi and Qianlong emperors. Under the command of these emperors, the great scholars of the Qing court began a sizeable project to identify and arrange the works, especially between the ninth year of Qianlong (1744) and the twenty-first year of Jiaqing (1816). On three successive occasions within that time, dozens of volumes of the large-scale calligraphy and painting catalogue *Shiqu baoji* (Treasured boxes of the Stone Channel) were compiled. The total number of recorded works of painting and calligraphy in the Qing court collection comes to ten thousand. It includes more than two thousand works of Tang, Song, and Yuan dynasty calligraphy and painting, and more or less about two thousand such works from the Ming dynasty. In addition, there are a considerable quantity of works by the imperial brush and by ministers and artisans. Each time a work was examined for the collection, it was affixed with imperial inspection seals (*jiancangxi*) as a certification. A reprint of the first volume of each edition has been selected for this exhibition to provide a glimpse of the cataloguing system of the Qing imperial collection.

WWHC (trans. DHWS)

清代是中国封建时代的最后一朝，因有康熙和乾隆两位皇帝的重视和大力倡导，形成了中国皇家书画收藏集大成的规模，在皇帝的敕命之下，清宫的大学士们开始了有规模的鉴别整理工作，特别是自乾隆九年始（1744）至嘉庆二十一年（1816），前后共有三次，陆续编成了《石渠宝笈》的大型书画著录数十卷，记载了清宫收藏的总数达上万件的书画作品，其中唐宋元书画两千多件，明代书画约两千件左右，并有相当数量的御笔书画和臣工书画作品，每次的鉴藏工作，均以钤有乾隆皇帝和嘉庆皇帝的鉴藏玺印为证。本次展览中选择了《石渠宝笈》各编重版本的第一集以为例子，籍此略可管窥清代皇家书画著录的概况。

海蔚蓝

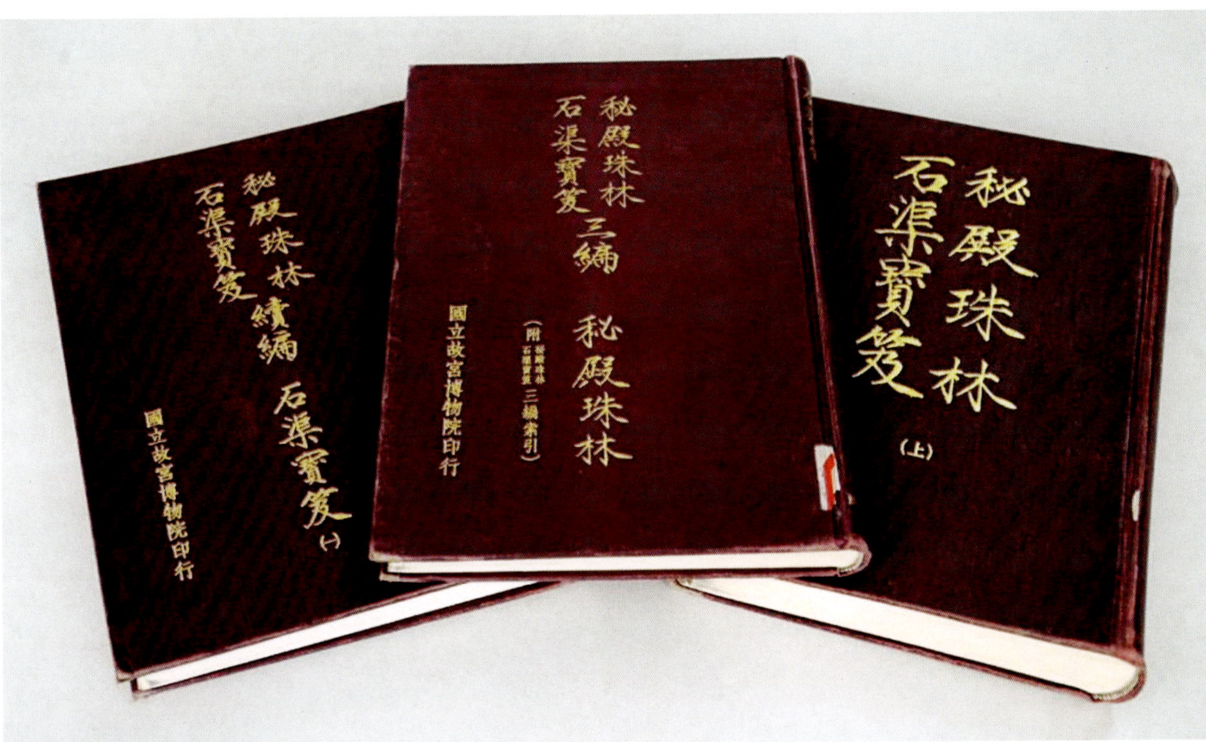

26
故宫已佚书籍书画目录四种
清室善后委员会，
故宫博物院印，
民国十五年版1926
One volume of *Gugong yiyi shuji shuhua mulu si zhong*

Editor: Qingshi shanhou weiyuanhui (Qing Royal Estates Management Committee)
Publisher: [Beijing]: Gugong bowuyuan yin, 1926
26.4 x 15.5 cm

The 1911 Revolution led by Dr. Sun Yat-sen overthrew the Qing ruling house, China's last imperial dynasty. On February 12, 1912, the last emperor, Puyi, announced his abdication, and the Qing dynasty came to an official end. But according to the Articles of Favorable Treatment of the Qing Imperial Family, Puyi was allowed to remain in the Forbidden City as a resident. Surrounded by a group of old loyalists and young diehards, he planned the restoration of a mini-imperial court. Almost daily, for some one hundred days from November 1922 to late January 1923, he robbed the palace of the imperial collection's valuable paintings and calligraphic works under the pretext of awarding gifts to his brother Pujie (1907–1994). This was part of his plan to finance his restoration to the throne. On November 5, 1924, the troops of General Feng Yuxiang drove Puyi out of the Forbidden City, dismantling the foundation of his mini-court. The Articles of Favorable Treatment was dissolved. On November 24, 1924, General Duan Qirui seized control of the Republican government and established the Qing Royal Estates Management Committee (Qing shi shan hou weiyuan) to handle the affairs of the Qing palaces. In the course of making an inventory of the Yangxin Dian palace, this committee discovered, on July 31, 1925, a detailed list of the gifts that Puyi had awarded to Pujie and a list of what Pujie received. The *Gugong yiyi shuji shuhua mulu si zhong* (Catalogue of dispersed calligraphy and paintings from the imperial palace) was compiled on the basis of these lists. In reality, the precious calligraphy and paintings of successive dynasties that were stolen out of the palaces were far from limited to just these works.

WWHC (trans. DHWS)

1911年，由孙中山领导的辛亥革命推翻了中国的最后一代封建王朝清朝，1912年2月，末帝溥仪宣布逊位，清朝正式灭亡，但在民国政府“优待清室条件”的政策中，溥仪仍然得以留居宫中，他在一批遗老遗少的簇拥下，筹划着小朝廷的复辟。宣统十四年，溥仪以赏赐其弟溥杰为名，从九月到十二月中（1922年11月至1923年1月）的一百多天里，几乎每天都将珍贵的皇家收藏的书画盗运出宫，为他的东山再起作财政上的准备。1924年十一月五日，民国政府的冯玉祥部闯入紫禁城，撵走了溥仪，拆了“小朝廷”的台，“优待清室条件”遂无形消失。1924年十一月二十四日，段祺瑞执政的民国政府成立了清室善后委员会来处理清宫事务。1925年七月三十一日，该委员会在查点养心殿藏书画时，发现了溥仪赏赐溥杰的清单，和溥杰收到的清单，便凭此编印了《故宫已佚书籍书画目录》，实际上，溥仪盗运出宫的历代珍贵书画远不止这些。

海蔚蓝

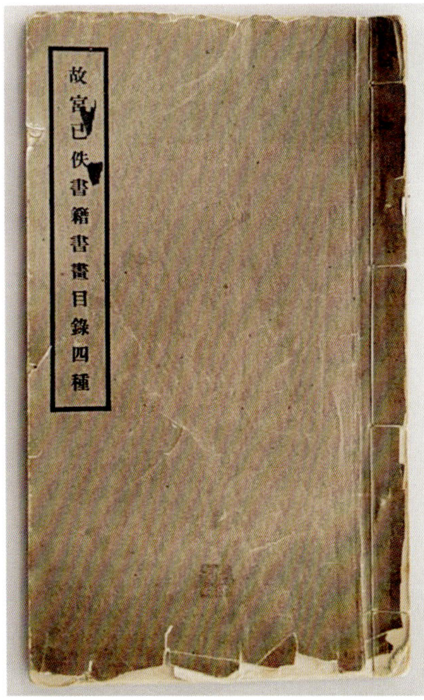

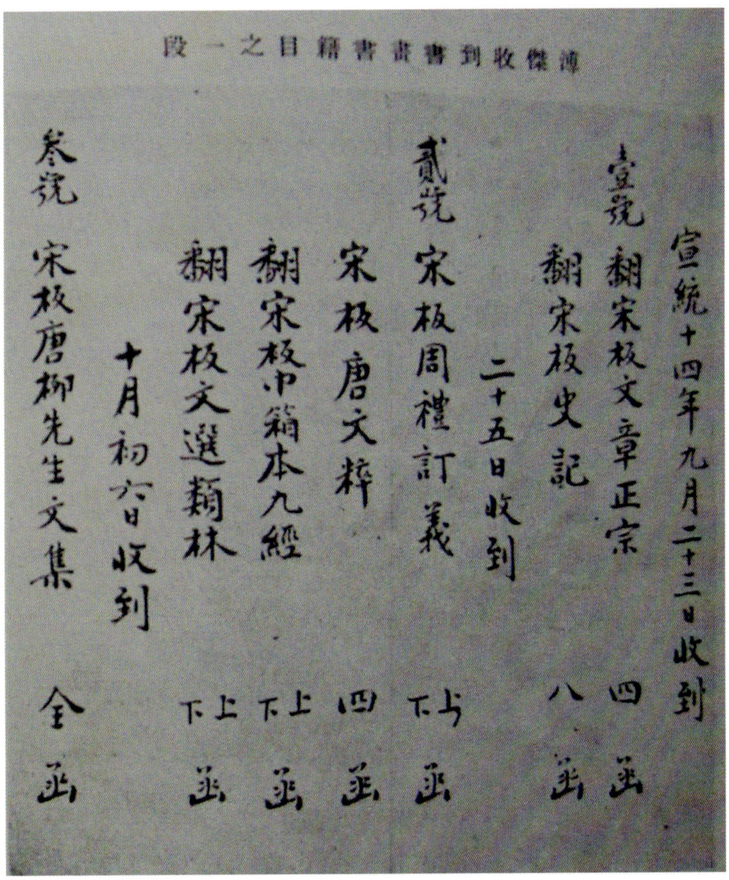

溥傑收到書畫書籍目之一段

宣統十四年九月二十三日收到
壹號 翻宋板文章正宗 四函
翻宋板史記 八函
二十五日收到
貳號 宋板周禮訂義 上下函
宋板唐文粹 四函
翻宋板巾箱本九經 上下函
翻宋板文選類林 上下函
十月初六日收到
叁號 宋板唐柳先生文集 全函

26 (detail 局部)

CATALOGUE II
FLOWER-AND-BIRD PAINTINGS IN THE LIAONING PROVINCIAL MUSEUM

图录第二部分
辽宁省博物馆藏明清花鸟画选

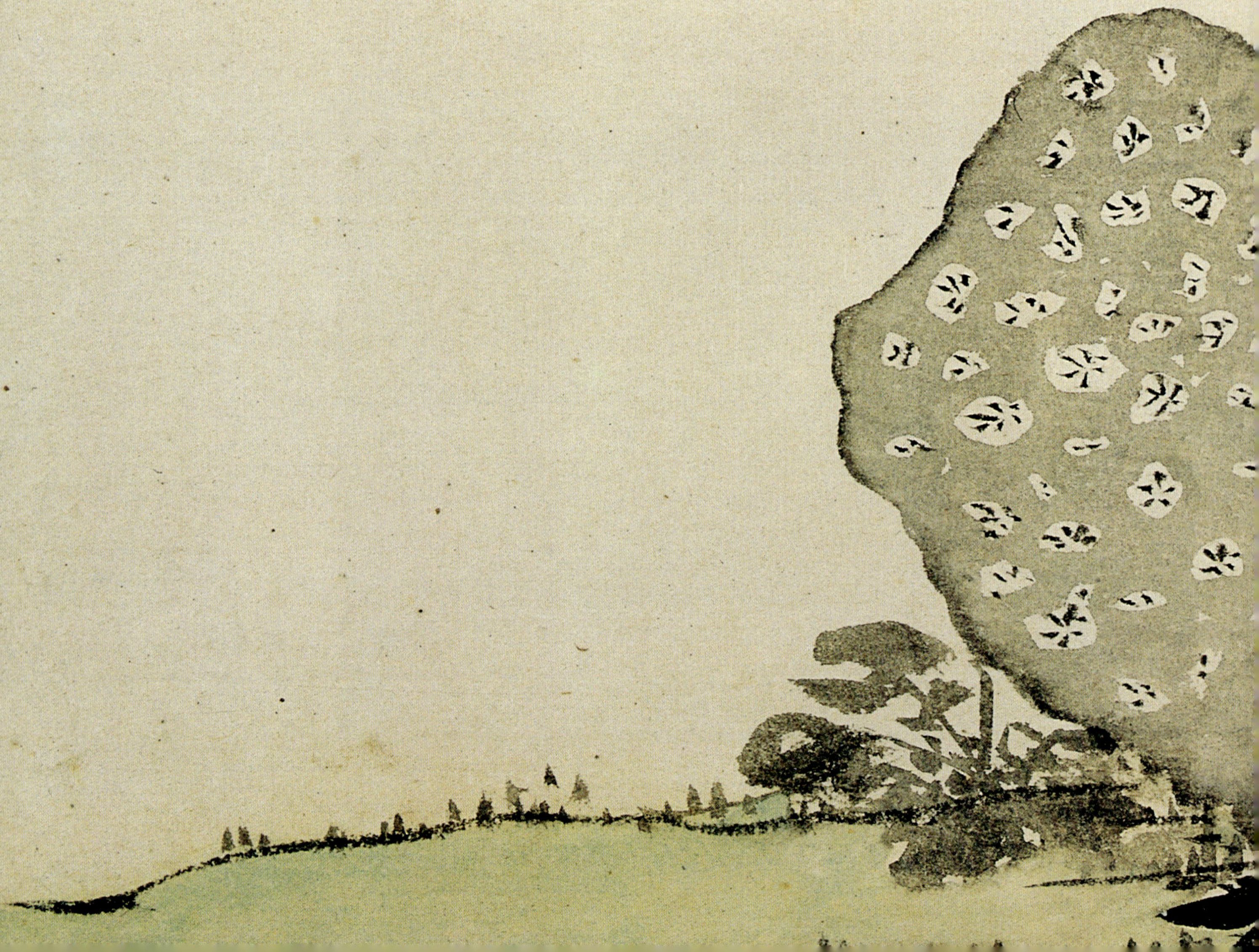

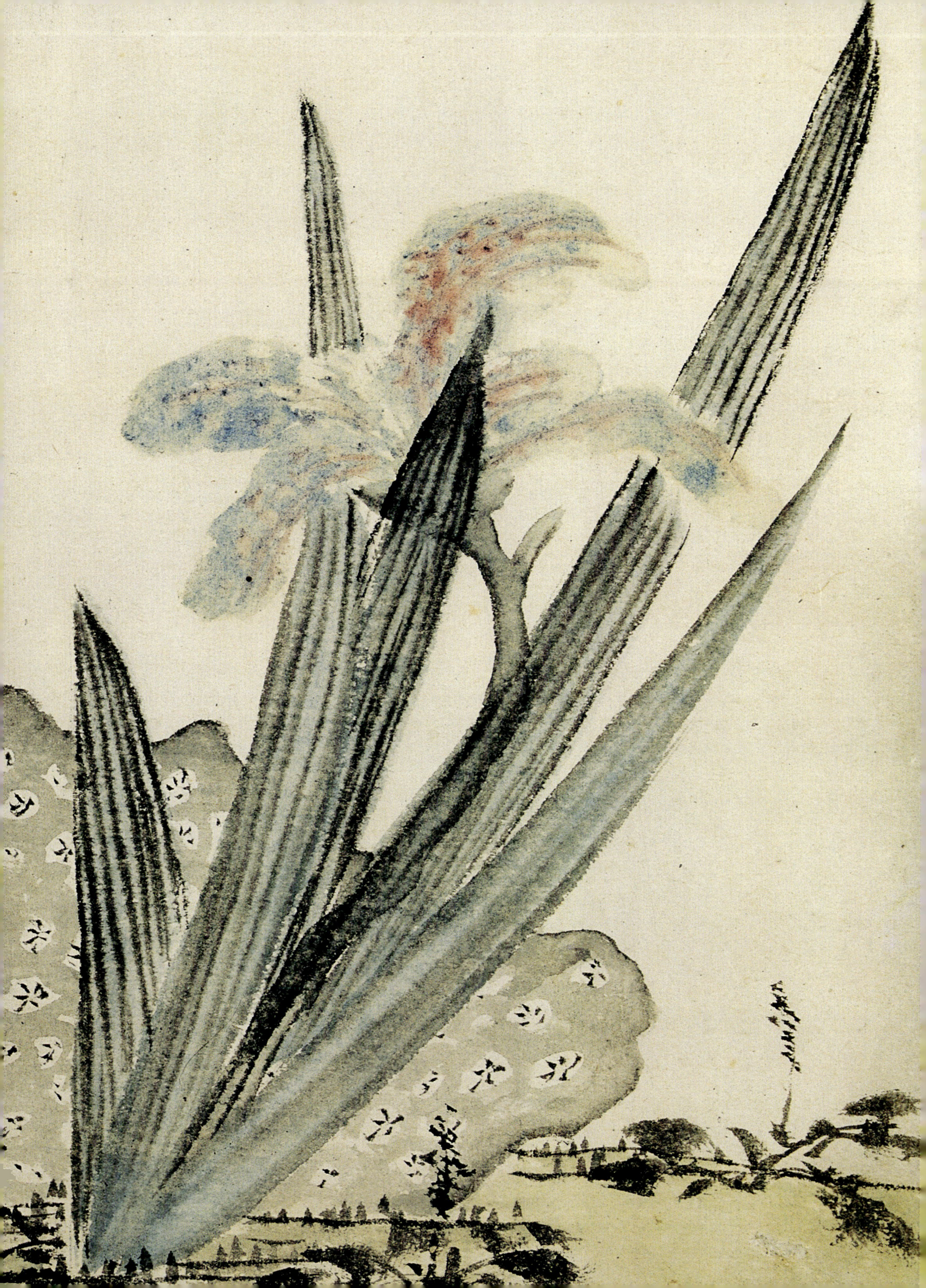

Overleaf: cat. no. 34 (detail leaf e)

Introduction to Chinese Flower-and-Bird Painting

Willow Weilan Hai Chang

Along with figures and landscapes, the flower-and-bird theme is one of the three main genres of Chinese painting. Although one can find images of birds, frogs, deer, cattle, and tigers on Neolithic pottery and rock art, the dragon and phoenix on silk paintings from the Spring and Autumn and Warring States periods of more than two thousand years ago, and images of all types of birds, animals, and plants in Han murals, lacquers, and brick and stone carvings, bird-and-flower painting as a genre originated in the dynamic cultural and flourishing artistic period of the Six Dynasties. Almost no works from this period can be seen today, but from the written record we know that paintings by the Three Masters of the Six Dynasties included this theme: there were Gu Kaizhi's (346–407) *Ducks, Geese, and Water Birds*, Lu Tanwei's (act. 465–72) *Fighting Ducks*, Zhang Sengyou's (act. ca. 500–550) *Fighting Dragons at the Horizontal Spring* and *In Praise of the Plum*. It was said that as late as the Song period, the Xuanhe court possessed a work by the Six Dynasties painter Gu Yewang (519–581) titled *Insects*.[1]

Flowers and birds gradually became a popular subject in the Tang period, and painters specializing in this began to emerge. The early Tang official Xue Ji (649–713) was famous for painting cranes, and Diao Guangyin (ca. 852–ca. 935) and Sun Wei (9th century) excelled at painting rocks, flowers, and bamboo. Outstanding among them was the late Tang court painter Bian Luan (act. 785–804), famous for his realistic peacocks with finely detailed plumage and for his delicate tree branches and flowers. Unlike traditional paintings that depicted an entire scene, his details of flowers and birds brought a new visual perspective, landing him an important position in the history of Tang flower-and-bird painting. At the end of the Tang and the Five Dynasties period, the sumptuous style of flower-and-bird painting of which Huang Quan's (d. 965) work is representative appeared in the artistic center that formed in the Later Shu kingdom (present-day Sichuan). Influenced by Tang art, this style employed precise, solid outlines filled with rich color. In the Southern Tang, another artistic center, an elegant and free style of flower-and-bird painting emerged, represented by Xu Xi (act. 937–42). It employed a *mogu,* or "boneless," (also called *luomo*, or "fallen ink [flower]") technique using primarily ink on a natural background. These two artists directly influenced later ideas about the genre and the two main approaches to Chinese flower-and-bird painting—the *gongbi* style of meticulous outline and strong color (see fig. 1) and the *xieyi* ("capturing the essence" or, literally, "writing the idea") style of spontaneous, freehand ink painting (see fig. 2). Because scholars preferred Xu's *xieyi* style for its expressiveness while the imperial painting academy emphasized the colorful, decorative *gongbi* style, artists would favor either Huang's or Xu's approach, and the two styles competed with one another in popularity. At different times and under the influence of differing tastes, new fusions drove the development of flower-and-bird painting—*xieyi* mixed with *gongbi* technique, or the reverse.

The Northern Song was an important period in the history of the genre. Zhao Chang (act. 1008–1016) was a famous flower-and-bird painter who had a reputation for works that were lifelike and vibrant because he painted from nature. Yi Yuanji (mid-11th century), whose paintings of gibbons elicited marvel, was praised by the great scholar Mi Fu (1051–1107) as only second to the bird-and-flower painter Xu Xi. Scholars' appreciation of Xu's *xieyi* style inspired creativity and new techniques. During Emperor Shenzong's reign in the latter half of the Northern Song, the court painter Cui Bai (act. 1068–1077) was the heir to both Xu and Huang, inventing a delicate, sparse style. His contemporary Ai Xuan was a good colorist with idyllic appeal. Their work was a harbinger of the new flower-and-bird work that emerged during Emperor Huizong's reign (1101–1125). With this emperor at the forefront, observing and painting from nature was emphasized along with an attempt to tap a poetic sentiment. This blending of the techniques and characteristics of both the Xu and Huang styles led to the flower-and-bird art of the painting academy at the late Northern Song and the Southern Song court. While Song scholar-artists such as Su Shi

(1037–1101) were enamored of simple *xieyi* painting, folk artists also practiced a rough, bold style. *Xieyi* and *gongbi* each had its own attraction. This period was the peak for Chinese flower-and-bird painting, which had begun to incorporate certain cultural meanings and aesthetic sentiments. The introduction to flower-and-bird painting in the *Xuanhe huapu* (Xuanhe painting catalogue) clearly points this out: "Woody and herbaceous peonies, pheasants and peacocks must be sumptuous, while pine, bamboo, plum, and chrysanthemum as well as gulls, egrets, geese, and ducks must be serene and at ease. Cranes are dignified; raptors strike. Willow and paulownia are spacious and graceful; pine and cypress are open and upright in the cold. Displayed thus in paintings, they will inspire the viewer. Exceeding nature, they can move the spirit and imagination, like the vista gained upon climbing to a height."[2]

In the Yuan, the flower-and-bird style of the Southern Song painting academy was adopted by non-court painters and disseminated broadly. In addition, under Mongol rule, painters withdrew from the court and lived in seclusion, engaging in scholarly pursuits. This resulted in a revival of *xieyi* painting. Bamboo, plum, and pine became favorite subjects of ink play by scholars. Painters such as Li Kan (1245–1320), Guan Daosheng (1262–1319), and Ke Jiusi (1290–1343) were good at ink bamboo; Wang Mian (1287–1359) was good at ink plum. Expressing their emotions through objects, they imbued these plants with human spirit and earned for them the laudatory title "Three Friends of Winter." From this time, flower-and-bird painting further developed into an enduring form and subject matter that was transmitted to the Ming and Qing periods.

In the Ming, between the Xuande and the Yongle periods, the imperial painting academy continued to expand the Song *gongbi* and Yuan *xieyi* traditions. For example, the famous flower-and-bird painter Bian Wenjin (14th–15th centuries), recognized as a master of *gongbi* and strong color, also used ink with lighter color. Within the Xuande painting academy, Zhu Zhanji (Emperor Xuanzong, 1398–1435) was an outstanding painter of flowers, birds, insects, and fish, rivaling Emperor Huizong of the Song. The court painters Lin Liang (ca. 1416–1480) and Lü Ji (b. 1477) are representative of the flower-and-bird artists of the middle Ming. Lin Liang was noted for crossing between representational and *xieyi* brushwork; he forged the path for Ming *xieyi* flower-and-bird painting. Lü Ji, on the other hand, primarily used *gongbi* but was influenced by the looser, bolder characteristics of the Zhejiang School, which resulted in more vigorous images. Toward the end of the Ming, the ink *xieyi* style dominated, as exemplified by the Wu School painters Shen Zhou (1427–1509), Wen Zhengming (1470–1559) and his disciples, and Chen Chun (Chen Daofu, 1483–1544). They appreciated elegance and emphasized the "scholarly spirit" of painting. The *xieyi* flower-and-bird painting of Chen Daofu, in particular, was relaxed yet disciplined, fluid, and poetic (see cat. no. 28). He had a strong influence on the Ming and Qing flower-and-bird painting. The culmination of this genre emerged with the late Ming artist Xu Wei (1521–1593; see cat. no. 29). His ink botanicals broke all previous rules for composition and strict brush technique, rebelling against them with a free, original spirit. He had "wild grass-script"-like (*kuangcao*) brushwork and a lavish, unrestrained use of ink. With Chen Daofu, he shared the honor as one of the two great flower-and-bird masters known as "Qingteng Baiyang." Their influence found its way into the work of the Qing masters Zhu Da (1626–1705), Shitao (1642–ca. 1718), and the Eight Eccentrics of Yangzhou, and more recent and contemporary painters such as Wu Changsuo (1844–1927), Qi Baishi (1864–1957), and Zhang Daqian (1899–1983). Other late Ming painters like Zhou Zhimian (act. 1573–1620) raised birds and observed their movements. Zhou created a painting style with detailed flowers and loosely rendered leaves. Some scholars of this period followed the Yuan tradition. To be cultivated, painting ink plum, orchid, and bamboo was essential. Xia Chang (1388–1470) was noted for his ink bamboo and Chen Lu (act. 1436–1448) for his ink plum.

At the beginning of the Qing, Yun Shouping (1633–1690), who was especially good at the boneless painting method, created a fresh, new style with bright color. As the leader of the Changzhou School, he influenced later famous flower-and-bird artists such as Jiang Tingxi (1669–1732) and Zou Yigui (1686–1772). The early Qing also included the four monks Zhu Da, Shitao, Hongren, and Kuncan. In particular, Zhu Da (sobriquet, Bada Shanren) painted flowers and birds with almost human qualities. Harboring a Ming loyalist's tragic resentment, he revealed a spirit of resistance in the disdainful expressions of his ink fish and birds. His *xieyi* flower-and-bird painting is unparalleled and spellbinding in power.

In the mid-Qing, the flower-and-bird painting of the Eight Eccentrics of Yangzhou (Jin Nong [1687–1764; see cat. no. 34], Luo Pin [1733–1799], Zheng Xie [1693–1765; see cat. no. 33], Li Shan [b. 1686], Wang Shishen [1686–1759], Li Fangying [1695–1754], Huang Shen [1687–after 1768; see cat. no. 31], and Gao Fenghan [1683–1748; see cat. no. 32]) inherited the free, creative

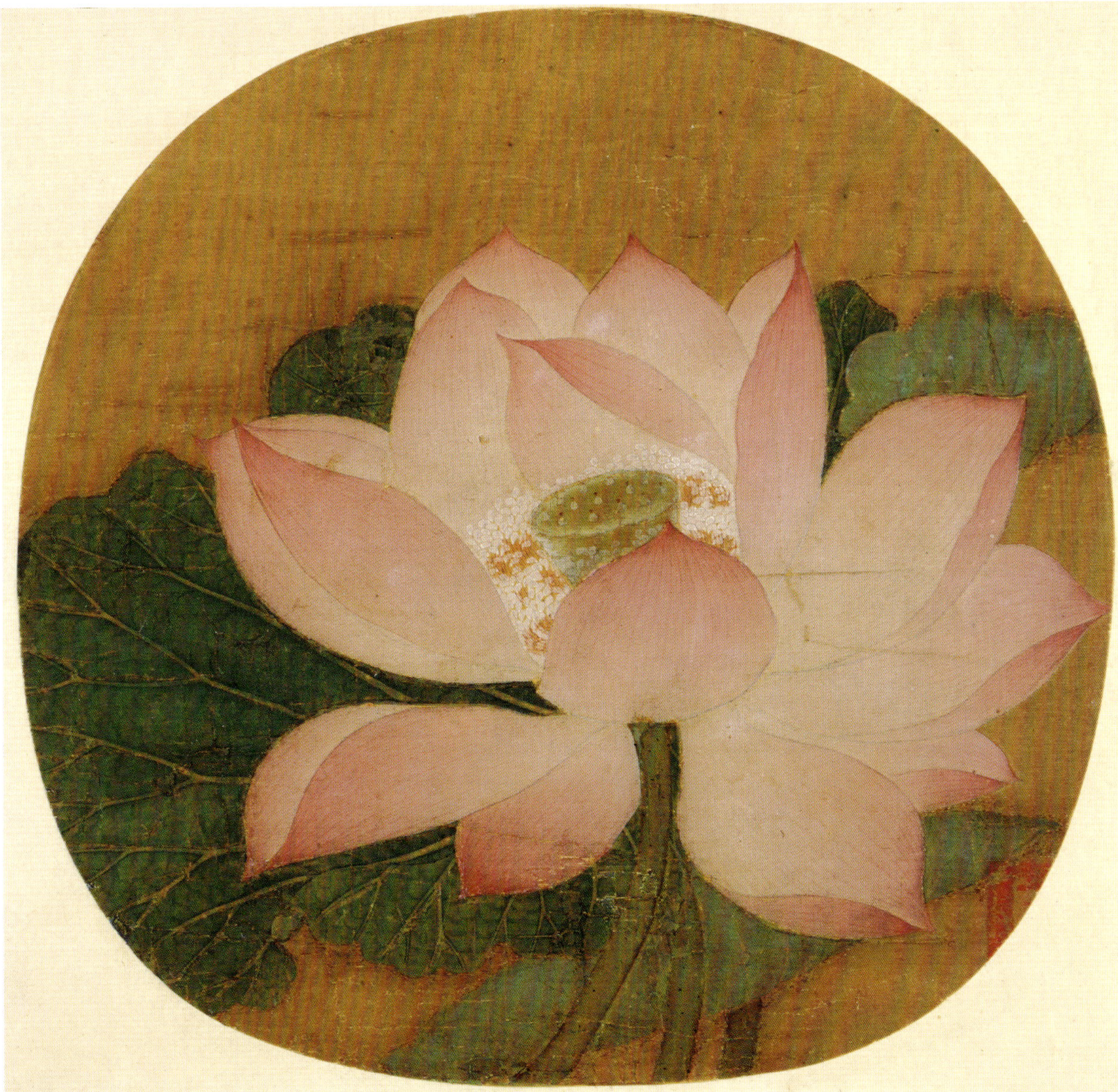

Fig. 1. Anonymous, Lotus Blossom on the Water, Southern Song (1127–1279).
Album leaf. Ink and color on silk. Palace Museum, Beijing
南宋，佚名，出水芙蓉图，绢本设色，北京故宫博物院

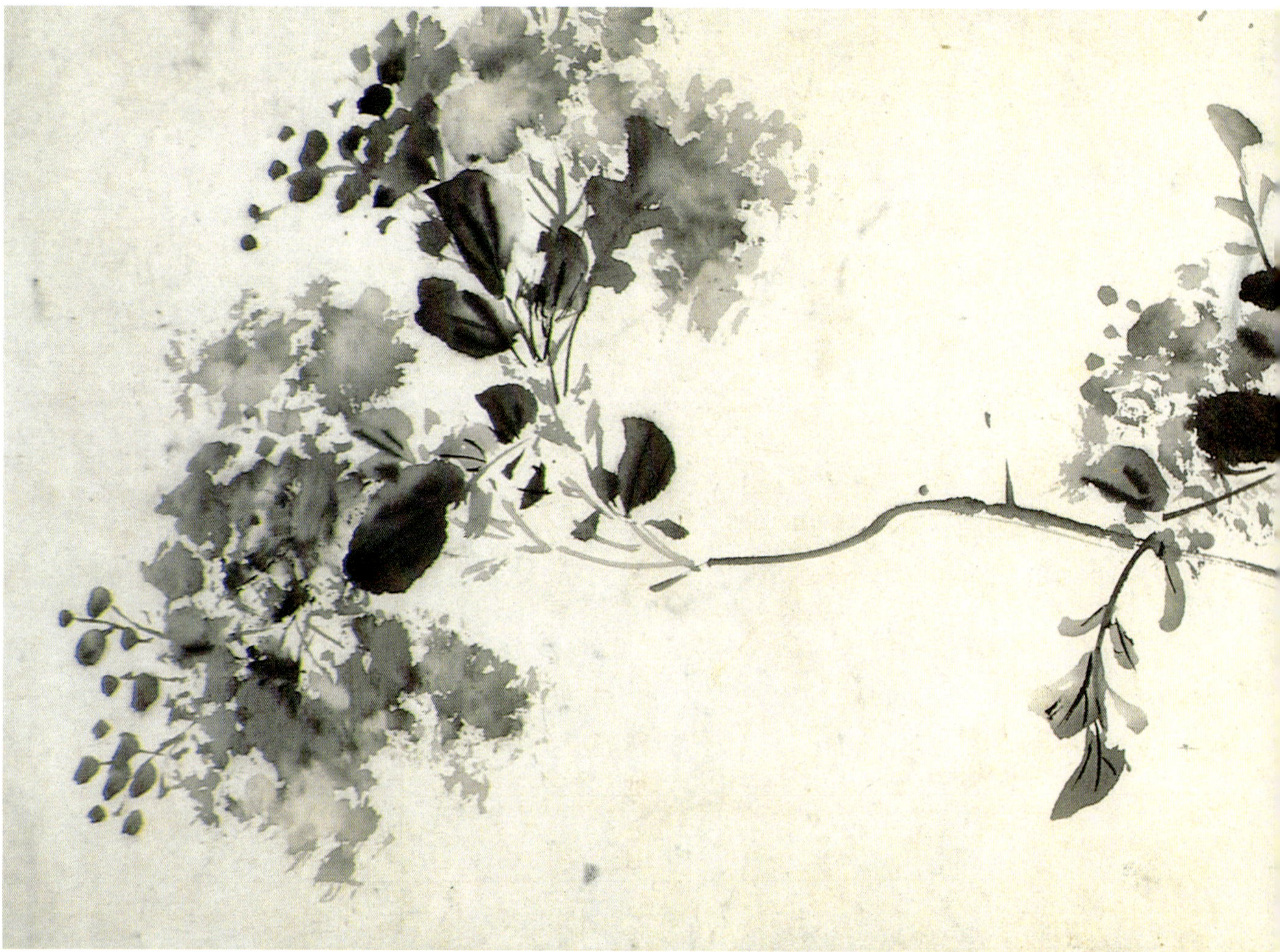

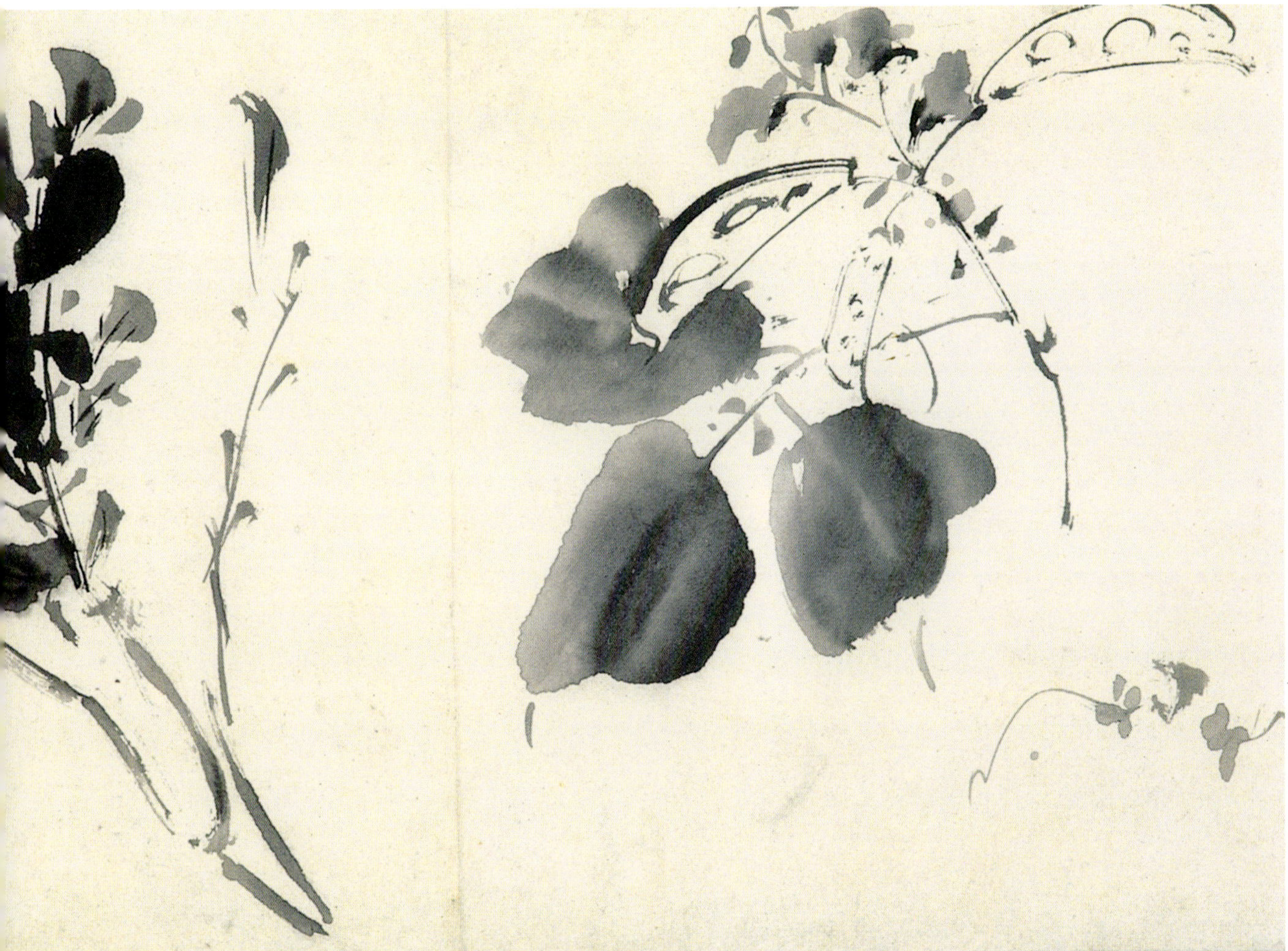

Fig. 2. Xu Wei (1521–1593), Various Flowers. Detail of handscroll. Ink on paper. Nanjing Museum
明，徐渭，杂花图卷（局部），手卷，纸本水墨，南京博物院

spirit of "Qingteng Baiyang" and Bada Shanren. Although they had nothing to do with court painting, their work had a less scholarly flavor because it was commercial. But by focusing on emotions and visual effect, they brought the expressive qualities of *xieyi* together with color that delighted the senses and treated conventional symbolic flower-and-bird motifs in an unorthodox way to produce something new. This made their work accessible to and admired by a large audience. At the same time, Lang Shining (Giuseppe Castiglione, 1688–1766) headed a special school of painters who merged Chinese and Western painting techniques in a rich, decorative style enjoyed by the court.

The painting style of the Eight Eccentrics of Yangzhou, popular with high and low alike, continued until the late Qing. As Shanghai became a commercial port, many artists congregated there and sold paintings for a living, forming the so-called Shanghai School. Their representative artists included Zhao Zhiqian (1829–1884), who painted with epigraphic strokes in a primitive and vigorous style; Ren Yi (Bonian, 1840–1927), whose flower-and-bird art was creative and lively; and Wu Junqing (Wu Changsuo [sobriquet, Fou Lu], 1844–1927), who employed the Stone Drum seal-script (*Shigu wen*) stroke in his paintings, used fresh, bright colors, and had strong, seasoned brushwork. Beginning in the Qing, there had been loyalist painters who immigrated south to Guangdong. There they started the Lingnan School, which included such artists as Zhang Mu (1607–ca. 1687), known for his raptors and horses, and Wu Ruilong (1585–1668), known for his peonies. In the final years of the Qing, the brothers Ju Chao and Ju Lian (1828–1904) invented and developed a special technique called "water spatter" and "powder spatter" which resulted in a vivid new style beloved by the Guangdong people and referred to as the "Ju School." But in an increasingly commercial era, flower-and-bird painting quickly lost a gracious and moral scholarly flavor.

Flower-and-bird art is one of the main genres of Chinese painting. Both *xieyi*, which focused on expressing inner feelings, and *gongbi*, with its decorative use of color, developed on the foundation of observing and recording nature. Although scholars were less accepting of the *gongbi* style, it was passed down through generations in the imperial painting academy. The subject matter was influenced by Chinese cultural ideas, tastes, and customs, ultimately becoming fixed in a few typical subjects that had auspicious meanings.

Subjects included the "Three Friends," the "Four Gentlemen," and the "Five Purities." The Three Friends are pine, bamboo, and plum. In the Tang dynasty, for example, Bi Hong (8th century) and Wei Yan were good at pine trees. From the Five Dynasties to the Northern Song, ink bamboo and ink plum became playful subjects for all the literati, and many of them excelled in it; for example, Wen Tong (1018–1079) and Su Shi (1037–1101) were known for ink bamboo, a monk named Zhong Ren of Sichuan was good at ink plum, and Yang Weizhen (1296–1370) did a painting of an ink pine tree titled *The Winter*. Since then, these three subjects—pine, bamboo, and plum—as a single theme in one picture were called "The Three Friends of Winter." To these, Wu Zhen (1280–1354) of the Yuan added the orchid and called them the "Four Friends." During the Wanli reign, that of the Ming emperor Shenzong (1573–1619), Huang Fengchi edited the *Mei zhu lan ju si pu* (Catalogue of plum, bamboo, orchid, and chrysanthemum). The famous Chen Jiru (1558–1639) called these plants "Four Gentlemen," and the name was used thereafter for this grouping. Later, some variously added pine, narcissus, or scholars' rocks to the group, naming them the "Five Purities" or the "Five Friends." In the Qing, Wang Gai (1654–1710) edited the *Mustard Seed Garden Painting Manual* with systematic summaries and examples of how to paint plum, orchid, bamboo, and chrysanthemum. It became a model for all who studied painting. This type of subject matter was symbolic of a noble and unsullied character, uprightness, perseverance, optimism, and a spirit unafraid of brutality. It encouraged people in how to conduct themselves in society and has been an enduring and popular aspect of Chinese painting.

Translated by Mansheng Wang

1. Yu Jianhua, *Zhongguo meishujia renming cidian* [Dictionary of Chinese artists] (Shanghai: Shanghai renmin meishu chubanshe, 1996), p. 1542.
2. *Xuanhe huapu* [Xuanhe painting catalogue] reprinted in *Huashi* [History of painting], Siku yishu congshu [Art books from the Comprehensive library of the Four Treasuries] (Shanghai: Shanghai guji chubanshe, 1991), pp. 156–57.

中国花鸟画简介

海蔚蓝

中国绘画中，花鸟画是与人物、山水并列的三大画种。虽然几千年前新石器时代的陶器和岩画上已经出现了鸟、蛙、鹿、牛、虎等动物，两千多年前的春秋战国时代的帛画上的龙凤图像，汉代的壁画、漆画、画像石、画像砖上更多见的各种鸟兽花木图形，这些都会与后来的花鸟画有关，但花鸟画的作为一个画种的萌芽，约始自人文荟萃、艺术勃发的伟大的六朝时代，虽然几乎没有传世的作品可见了，但在文献记载中，被称为“六朝三杰”的顾恺之（346－407）绘有“凫雁水鸟图”，陆探微（活跃于465－472）绘有“斗鸭图”，张僧繇（南朝梁时人）绘有“ 横泉斗龙图”，“咏梅图”等，据说到宋代，宣和御府还藏有六朝时擅长草虫的画家顾野王（519－581）的作品，“草虫图”（注1）。

花鸟画大约在唐代才慢慢地成为流行的画题，专门的花鸟画家也渐渐出现，初唐时的宰相薛稷（649－713）以画鹤闻名；刁光胤（约852－935）、孙位（9世纪）善湖石花竹等。 尤其是晚唐的宫廷画家边鸾（活跃于785－804）以画孔雀闻名，其花鸟画姿态逼真，尤善于画千变万化的鸟羽，和精美的折枝花，一反传统的全景入图法，别开花鸟画的新视角， 在唐代花鸟史上占有重要的地位。唐末五代，在当时艺术中心的四川的后蜀，出现了以黄筌（卒于965）为代表的富贵体花鸟画，在唐代大画面的影响下，以严正骨法的描线，加富丽色彩的“勾勒填彩法”，浓艳细密；而在另一艺术中心的江南南唐，以徐熙（活跃于937－942)为代表的野逸体的花鸟画，在自然的背景中，以水墨为主的“没骨画法”（又称“落墨”法），轻秀天然。这两者直接影响了日后中国花鸟画的理念和相关的两种主要表现手法，即工笔（图一）重彩和写意（图二）水墨，并由于中国文人推崇易于抒发胸臆的徐氏的写意画，皇家画院则重工笔重彩的装饰手法，故而或为黄氏，或为徐氏，两种手法或受宠爱，或遭落寞，或在不同的时间和不同欣赏品味的影响下，有所融合衍变，产生新的以写带工，或以工带写等手法推动着花鸟画的发展。

北宋是中国花鸟画史上的重要时期，在十世纪的北宋中期， 出现了一位著名的花鸟画家赵昌（活跃于1008－1016），他的画直接来自写生而活龙活现，故有“写生赵昌”的美誉。继起的易元吉（活跃于11世纪中叶），以他存世的《猿猴图》为世所惊叹，在十一世纪的花鸟画坛，他被大文人米芾（1051－1107）赞为徐熙之后的第一人。文人们对徐氏野逸风格的赞赏，引起了画界在创作理念和手法上的改革，自北宋后半期神宗朝的宫廷画家崔白（活跃于1068－1077）继承徐黄二体，别创清淡疏秀之格，同时代的艾宣则擅傅色晕淡，尤长野趣，他们的努力，逐渐将有明显黄氏装饰风格的写生画，融入徐氏没骨的墨法，是为徽宗朝新花鸟画风格形成的前声。徽宗朝的花鸟画，在皇帝赵佶（1082－1135）的亲自带领之下，注重观察写生，又试图发掘诗意情趣，基于写实的基础，而采用徐熙花鸟画的画法，将花鸟置于一个自然的背景之中，手法上也吸收黄徐二氏的特点而通融变化，以细致的线描晕彩见长，形成了北宋末年到南宋朝的院体花鸟画。而宋代的文人，如苏轼（1037－1101）等则醉心于简淡的水墨写意之作， 同时，民间画工也有粗放苍劲的风格。因此，水墨、工笔各领风骚，形成了中国花鸟画的鼎盛时期。并且，开始通过花鸟画来表现一定的文化寓意和审美情趣。《宣和画谱》的“花鸟画绪论”便明确指出：“花之于牡丹、芍药，禽之于鸾凤、孔翠，必使之富贵，而松竹梅菊，鸥鹭雁鹜，必见之幽闲，至于鹤迹轩昂，鹰隼之击搏，杨柳梧桐之扶疏风流，乔松古柏之岁寒磊落，展张于图绘，有以其起人之意者，率能夺造化而移精神遐想，若登临览物之有得也”（注2）。

元代的花鸟画，一方面是南宋院体画的风格为在野的画家们所采用而推广，另外，在异族统治下，画家纷纷隐居山林，追求自然天趣的文人理念和鉴赏品味，导致了清淡写意水墨花卉的兴起，墨竹、墨梅、墨松，成为文人们墨戏中喜爱的题材，如李珩（1245－1320）、管道升（1262－1319）、柯九思（1290－1343）皆善墨竹，王冕（1287－1359）善墨梅。并借物抒情，赋予了这些植物以人格的精神和魅力，有所谓“松竹梅岁寒三友”的美称。花鸟画自此，除了手法上延续或融汇黄氏徐氏的或为工笔重彩，或为写意的路数外，并在内涵上广延伸展，使许多花鸟画富有寓意，赋予文化性的象征符号，并形成了许多经久不衰的构图和题材，而流行于明清时代。

明代从永乐到宣德年间，宫廷画院花鸟画继承着宋代工笔着彩的院体画，并有大的发展，也受到元代水墨画法的影响，如著名的花鸟画家边文进（14－15 世纪）兼擅工笔重彩和水墨淡色，有黄氏体花鸟画妙手之称，也能仿宋院体画。宣宗朝的宣德画院，首当其冲的宣宗皇帝朱瞻基（1398－1435）就以自己出色的花鸟虫鱼，可与宋徽宗媲美，在他麾下，有商喜（1426－1435）以善画虎著名。明代中期的花鸟画，一是以宫廷画家林良（约1416－1480）和吕纪（生于1477）为代表的院体，尤其是林良以其介于“写形”与“写意”之间的笔法，善写水墨花鸟虫鱼，开启了明代水墨写意花鸟的先河；而以工笔重彩笔法为主的吕纪，撷取浙派粗放的风格，形成具有特色的生气勃勃的花鸟画。明代中晚期，则以水墨写意的花鸟画为主，以沈周（1427－1509）、文征明（1470－1559）及其弟子陈淳（道复，1483－1544）为代表的“吴门派”，真正开启了文人水墨写意的花鸟画，崇尚秀雅，强调绘画要有“士气”。尤其是陈道复的写意花鸟，虽放纵但不恣肆，灵动而富文趣，对明清以来的花鸟画影响极大。及至明代晚期，出现了集花鸟画之大成的徐渭（1521－1593），其水墨花卉，打破了老一套的构图法和严肃的笔法，代之以充满叛逆的自由独创的精神，狂草般的笔法，恣肆淋漓，无拘无束，而以“青藤白阳”的美誉与陈道复共享花鸟大家的盛名。其深远影响延至清代的朱耷（1624－1705）、石涛（1642－约1718）、扬州八怪和近代的吴昌硕（1844－1927）、齐白石（1864－1957）、张大千（1899－1983）等。明末其他著名的花鸟画家如周之冕（16至17世纪），家饲禽鸟，以观动态，创造了钩花点叶的笔法，乃钩染点簇，兼工带写，其画作为时人争购，并有“夏卿一个竹，西凉十锭金”之谚。终明一代，文人们也继承元代之风，水墨梅兰竹成为文人必修的雅事，著名者如夏昶（1388－1470）之墨竹，陈录（活跃于1436－1448）的墨梅等。

清代初年，以没骨画法见长的恽寿平（1633－1690），创造出色彩鲜明、笔墨简洁的清新画风，引领了“常州画派”，影响了之后的著名花鸟画家如蒋廷锡（1669－1732）、邹一桂（1686－1772）等。清初另有以四僧为主（朱耷、石涛、弘仁和萧云从）的“野逸派”，尤其是号为八大山人的朱耷（1626－1705），其拟人化的花鸟，是他满怀明代遗民的悲愤情怀，淋漓尽致地将叛逆和不羁的精神，通过他睥睨一切的墨鱼墨鸟达到了飘逸高超的极致，其大写意的花鸟画，将主观意志的表现张力扩大到一个前所未有的境地，而具有摄人心魄的强烈个性。

清代中期以金农（1687－1764）、罗聘（1733－1799）、郑燮（1693－1765）、李鱓（十八世纪中叶）、汪士慎（十八世纪中叶）、李方膺（1695－1754）、黄慎（1687－1768后）和高凤翰（1683－1748）为名的扬州八怪的花鸟画，则沿袭着“青藤白阳”，和八大山人以来的自由创作的精神，肆意于花鸟画的创作和表达，并由于他们作品的商业和市场效应，虽然不与宫廷绘画合流，但文人画的气味有所减少，却重视感觉和绘画的效果，融表达性的写意和愉悦感官的彩墨，以及有寓意的花鸟造型为一体，而标新立异，产生一种新的，能为更多人欣赏的美感。同时以朗世宁（Giuseppe Castiglione,1688－1766）为首的中西合璧的独特画派， 也以富于装饰意味的花鸟画取悦宫廷。

由扬州八怪创造的这种新的雅俗共赏的以写意和着彩为主的新花鸟画，流风沿续到清代后期，随着上海成为一个热闹的商埠，许多画家蛰居于此卖画为生，而形成了所谓的“海上画派”，代表者如赵之谦（1829－1884）以金石书法入画，风格古拙雄浑，任颐（伯年1840－1895）花鸟富有创意，兼工带写，生机活泼；吴俊卿（吴昌硕，号缶庐1844－1927）以石古文篆法入画，色泽鲜亮，笔力老辣雄厚。自清代以来，在广东也有遗民画家南下，开始了岭南绘画的高潮，如善画鹰马的张穆（1607－约1687），善画牡丹的伍瑞隆（1585－1668）等， 到清代末年，则有居巢、居廉（1828－1904）兄弟为首的花鸟画家，发明和发展了一种特殊的技法，称之为“撞水、撞粉”之法，形成鲜活艳丽、明亮清新的画风，而为粤人珍爱，有“居派”之称。但清代的这些花鸟画，在逐渐商业化的历史时期，很快地便失去了文人超逸清高的品味，都具有迎合世俗的特色。

花鸟画作为中国绘画的一大画种，在观察自然，写生写实的基础上，发展出既可借写意而畅心怀的水墨，也可凭着彩以资装饰的工笔，虽然工笔重彩的画法曾为文人们所不屑，但在宫廷院派中代代相传，其富丽堂皇的装饰效果兀然有她的独到之处。而花鸟画的题材，自宋元以来，不断地从中国文化的观念、欣赏和习俗中，凝炼出一些经典的主题，在中国文化背景中产生的吉祥寓意，更使中国的花鸟画富有特色和无穷的回味，历经千年而传承绵延。

在花鸟画的题材中，最高雅者，如“三友”、“四君子”、“五清”。“三友”者，松竹梅也。唐代就有画松石的画家，如毕宏（8世纪）、韦偃（8世纪）有“双松图”。五代以后文献中不断记载有画“墨竹”“墨梅”的画家，到北宋后期盛行，在文人的墨戏中成为一种重要的形式，文同（1018－1079）、苏轼（1037－1101）均以墨竹名，蜀僧仲仁（北宋）以墨梅名，杨维祯（1296－1370）有“岁寒图”的墨松图，以后松、竹、梅被誉为“岁寒三友”，而出现以此为标志的特定构图。元代吴镇（1280－1354）在三友之外，加画兰花，名“四友图”。沿至明代，神宗万历（1573－1619）间，黄凤池辑《梅竹兰菊四谱》，明代最著名的隐士文人陈继儒（1558－1639）称之为“四君”，后名为“四君子”。在梅竹兰菊之外，后人如加上松树，或水仙，或奇石，便合称“五清”或“五友”。清代王概编《芥子园画传》第三集，即梅、兰、竹、菊四谱，对这些花卉的绘法有系统的总结和示范，成为所有学画者的范本。这类题材，借物比兴，象征高洁的品格和正直、坚忍、乐观以及不畏强暴的精神，是对所有人为人处世的鼓励，而为历代画家喜爱，经久不衰。

注解：

1. 俞剑华《中国美术家辞典》第1542 页，上海人民美术出版社1996。
2. 《宣和画谱》第156－157页，载四库艺术丛书《画史》，上海古籍出版社1991。

27
明　杜大成　花卉草虫 / 杜堇　竹林七贤图
手卷，纸本水墨
Du Dacheng (act. 1465–1505) and Du Jin (act. 1465–1505)
Insects and Grass / Seven Sages in the Bamboo Grove

Handscroll; ink on paper, (entire scroll) 35 x 611.3 cm

A. *Insects and Grass*, by Du Dacheng

28.6 x 44.8 cm

ARTIST'S SEALS: Yun'a jingshe (square/intaglio), Bi tan qiu yue (square/ relief)

OTHER SEALS: [Luo Zhenyu, 1866–1940] Luo Zhenyu yin (square/intaglio); Liu jiu xueren dizi (square/relief); [unidentified] Kuiyi (square/relief); [Chen Jide, 19th century] Qianli baomi (rectangular/relief); [Museum of the Northeast] Dongbei bowuguan zhencang zhiyin (square/relief)

COLOPHON WRITERS (SEALS): by Chen Jide (Jide [square/intaglio]); Lu Shou (Chen Shou [square/intaglio]), Yizi nanzhong [square/intaglio]); Pan Jin (Chen Jin [square/intaglio], Baizhai [square/relief])

杜大成　花卉草虫图

画家印鉴：云阿精舍（白文方印）、碧潭秋月（朱文方印）。

其他印鉴：[罗振玉，1866-1940]罗振玉印（白文方印）；六九学人弟子（朱文方印）；亏一（朱文方印）；[陈骥德，19世纪]千里宝秘（朱文长方印）；[东北博物馆]东北博物馆珍藏之印（朱文方印）。

题跋者(钤印)：[陈骥德]骥德（白文方印）。[陆售]臣售（白文方印）、一字南仲（白文方印）。[潘锦]臣锦（白文方印）、白斋（朱文方印）。

B. *Seven Sages in the Bamboo Grove*, by Du Jin

28.7 x 149.1 cm

ARTIST'S SEAL: Chengju (square/intaglio)

OTHER SEAL: [Chen Jide] Liangzhai shen ding (square/relief)

COLOPHON WRITERS (SEALS): Zhou Huan (Dahu Juren [square/relief], Zhou Huan zhiyin [square/intaglio]); Chen Jide (Jide qianli [square/intaglio and relief], Liangzhai [rectangular/relief])

杜堇　竹林七贤图

画家印鉴：柽居（白文方印）

其他印鉴：[陈骥德]良斋审定（朱文方印）

题跋者（钤印）：[周寰]大瓠居士（朱文方印）、周寰之印（白文方印）；[陈骥德]骥德千里（半白半朱方印）、良斋（朱文长方印）

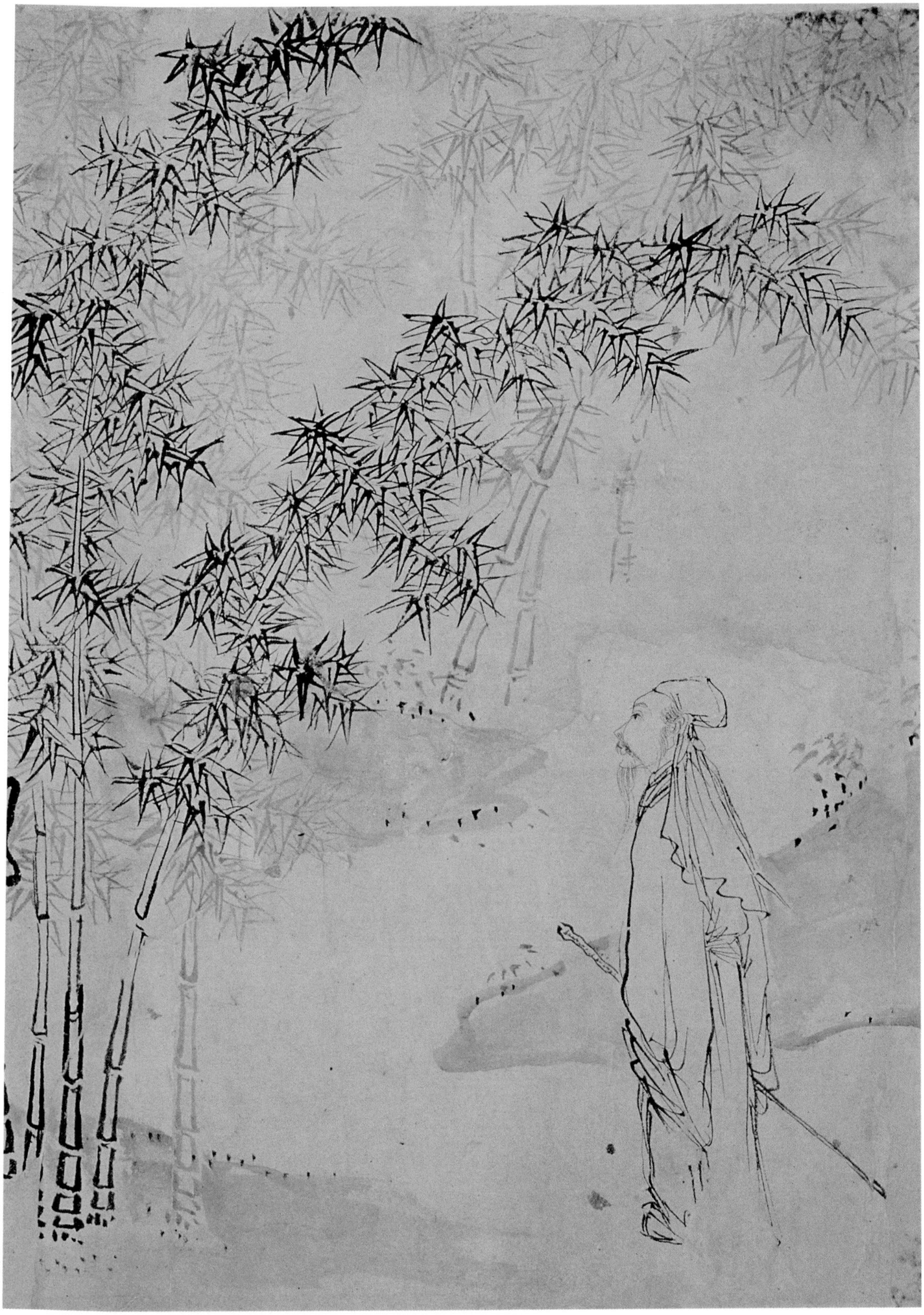

27 (detail 局部)

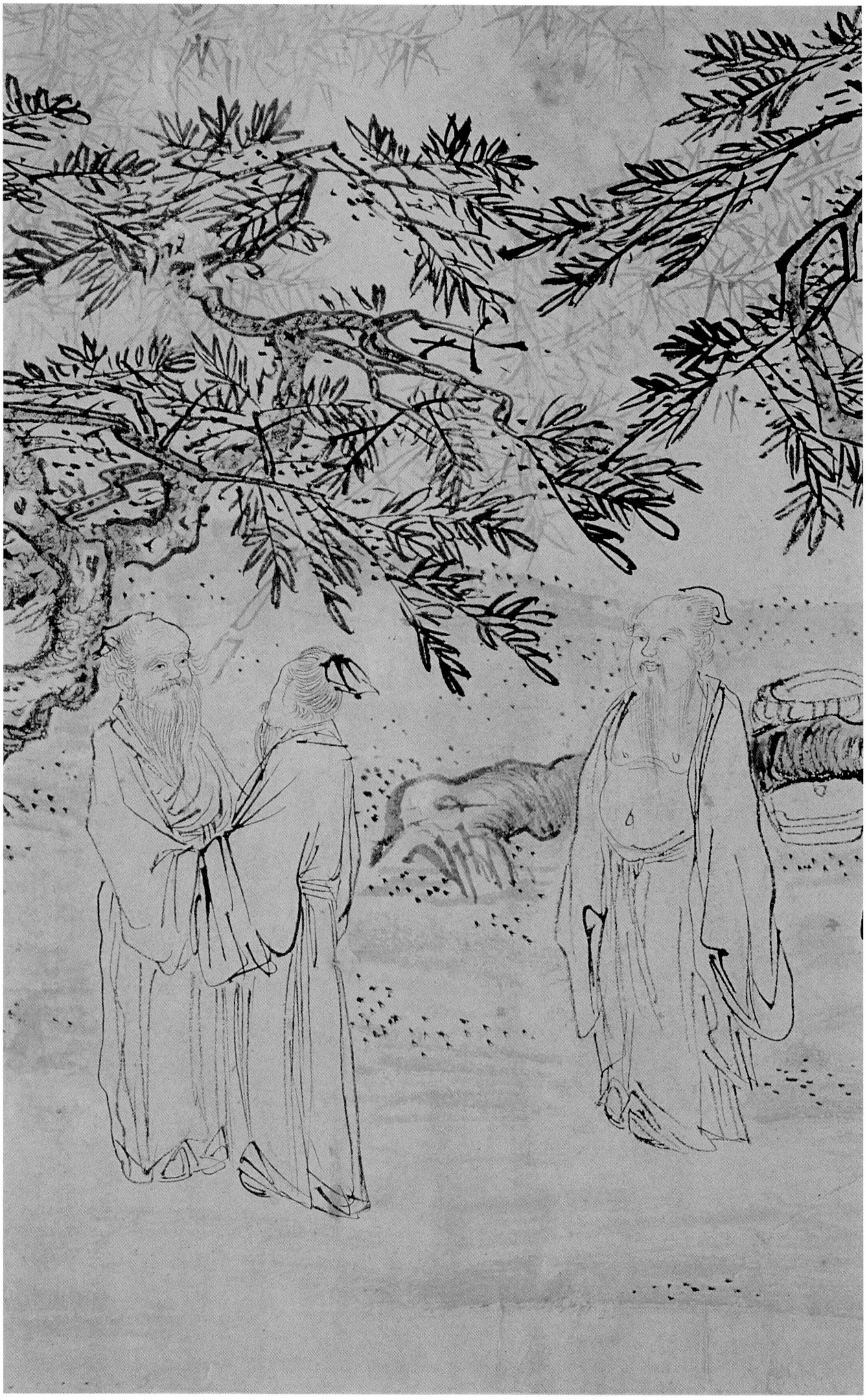

27 (detail 局部)

Du Dacheng (courtesy name, Runxiu; sobriquet, Shankuang sheng) was a native of Nanjing, Jiangsu. He was a skilled musician and good at painting botanical subjects, especially insects. In this painting he uses ink economically, painting only a loose fanlike cluster of orchid leaves and crooked, thorny stems among which are crickets, bees, and a butterfly. Although the brushwork is simple and fine, the work is full of life and a natural, quiet atmosphere. A masterpiece of insect painting, it is a typical example of the "spare ink" (*ximo*) aesthetic. The signature "Shankuang" appears on the upper left, under which is a square seal with the characters "Yun'a jingshe" (Cloud Retreat) and a square seal with the characters "bitan qiuyue" (azure pond autumn moon). Within the mounting on either side of the painting are colophons in running script by Chen Jide, Lu Shou, and Pan Jin. Seals of collectors indicate that the painting was owned by Chen Jide and Luo Zhenyu. It later entered the Dongbei Museum, now known as the Liaoning Museum.

Du Jin (original surname Lu; courtesy name, Junan) was a native of Dantu, Jiangsu. He used the sobriquets Chengju and Gukuang, and he also called himself Qingxia Tingzhang. During the Chenghua reign, following his failure in the *jinshi* examination, he turned his focus to painting. He excelled at landscapes, people, flowers and birds, and architectural subjects. At the time, he was considered the best at outline drawing in ink (*baimiao*).

The Seven Sages of the Bamboo Grove were recluses of the Jin period. They were not swayed by popular fashion or controlled by the imperial court and were fond of drinking. These seven independent spirits were very talented. They were admired by Chinese intellectuals throughout history and have been a painting subject for many generations. Amidst bamboo, pines, and rocks, the seven are depicted in a casual manner—sitting, standing, holding a staff, playing musical instruments, and drinking wine. This painting employs the outline technique. It is an outstanding work, confirming that Du Jin was a true heir of the Song dynasty *baimiao* master Li Longmian. At the end of the painting is Du Jin's seal "Chengju." The mounting at the end of the painting has a running script colophon by Zhou Huan and the end of the handscroll has a colophon by Chen Jide.

From the colophons we can see that these two paintings were in the collection of Chen Jide. Because both painters were surnamed Du and had sobriquets containing the character *kuang* (crazy) and the paintings were both outstanding, Chen mounted them on a single handscroll as "two matchless works of the Du family."

WWHC (trans. MSW)

杜大成字允修，号山狂生，江苏南京人，工音律，善花卉，尤擅草虫。此卷草虫用墨不多，仅有一丛疏落舒展的兰草，间杂刺枝横斜的荆棘，其间有螳螂、蜜蜂和蝴蝶，或踏登草叶，或飞舞空中，然而笔墨精炼，意趣横生，充满自然清幽的灵气，是草虫画出神彩的佳作，可以作为中国画审美观念中“惜墨”之作的典型例子。画心左上方署款“山狂”，下钤画家两印。前后隔水处分别有陈骥德、陆售和潘锦的行书题跋。从收藏印来看，此画曾为陈骥德、罗振玉收藏，后入东北博物馆即现在的辽宁省博物馆。

杜堇，本姓陆，字惧南，号柽居，古狂，自称青霞亭长， 江苏丹徒人。成化中举进士不第，遂致力绘画，山水人物花鸟界画，无不精妙，时称白描第一手。竹林七贤是晋代的高士，不俯仰时流，不受皇家左右，而借酒畅怀，独抒性灵的七位富有才情的人，历来为中国知识分子所推崇为榜样。以此为题材的绘画历代均有人为之，并为人所爱。此画纯用白描双钩法，在竹林松石间，描绘了七贤或坐，或立，或曳杖，或弹阮，或品酒，各各洒脱不羁的风姿，出神入化，得中国白描大师宋代李龙眠的真传。画后有杜堇“柽居”的白文方形印章款。后隔水有周寰行书题跋，拖尾有陈骥德题跋。

从陈氏的题跋来看，杜大成的草虫图和杜堇的竹林七贤图都曾在陈氏的收藏中，陈以两人皆姓“杜”，且杜大成号“山狂”，杜堇号“古狂”，其画皆精妙出神，因而将两位“狂”人的画作合成一卷，“以为杜家双绝”。

海蔚蓝

28
明　　陈淳　萱茂栀香图
立轴，纸本水墨
Chen Chun (1483–1544)
Blossoming Flowers and Rock
Hanging scroll; ink on paper
58.8 x 127 cm

ARTIST'S SEAL: Fufushi (square/intaglio), Baiyang Shanren (square/intaglio)
COLOPHON WRITER (SEALS): Wen Zhengming, 1470–1559 (Wen Zhengming yin [square/intaglio], Zhengzhong [square/intaglio])

画家印鉴：复父氏（白文方印）、白阳山人（白文方印）
题跋者（钤印）：［文征明］文征明印（白文方印）、征仲（朱文方印）

Chen Chun (courtesy name, Daofu; sobriquet, Baiyan Shanren) was a native of Suzhou, Jiangsu Province, and a student of the Wu School founder Wen Zhengming. Building on the foundation of the rigorous approach inherited from his teacher, he gradually developed his own bold and unrestrained style. He used his courtesy name (*zi*) Daofu to sign this painting, which has the flavor of early summer. A strange, upright, finely wrought Taihu rock stands on a slope with a gardenia shrub in full bloom. The blossoms and leafy branches sway in a breeze. Several clusters of tawny daylilies are situated below and to the side of the rock; orchids grow on the slope. The flourishing fragrance that fills the garden is set off by a refined tranquility. On the upper right is a poetic inscription in Wen Zhengming's running script, which captures the ambience of the entire scene: "In June's hot and steamy drowsiness, a clear fragrance assails me. Worries forgotten, I understand. It is a companion in my loneliness."

HWL (trans. MSW)

陈淳（1483—1544），字道復，号白阳山人，江苏苏州人。陈淳是吴门画派鼻祖文征明的门生，他的绘画风格在继承乃师功力严谨的基础上，逐渐形成了属于自己的奔放纵逸格调。此作以其字“道復”署款，画面表现了初夏的气息，奇兀玲珑的太湖石傲立于坡上，盛开的栀子花从太湖石上绽放而出，花与枝叶随风飘曳；几丛萱花在太湖石下侧，坡石旁生长的兰草，以清雅幽艳衬托着满园的花香华滋。画面右上方文征明的行书五言题诗，清晰地点明了全图的意境：“六月炎蒸困，清香自袭人。忘忧偏会意，留伴寂寥身”。

黄伟利

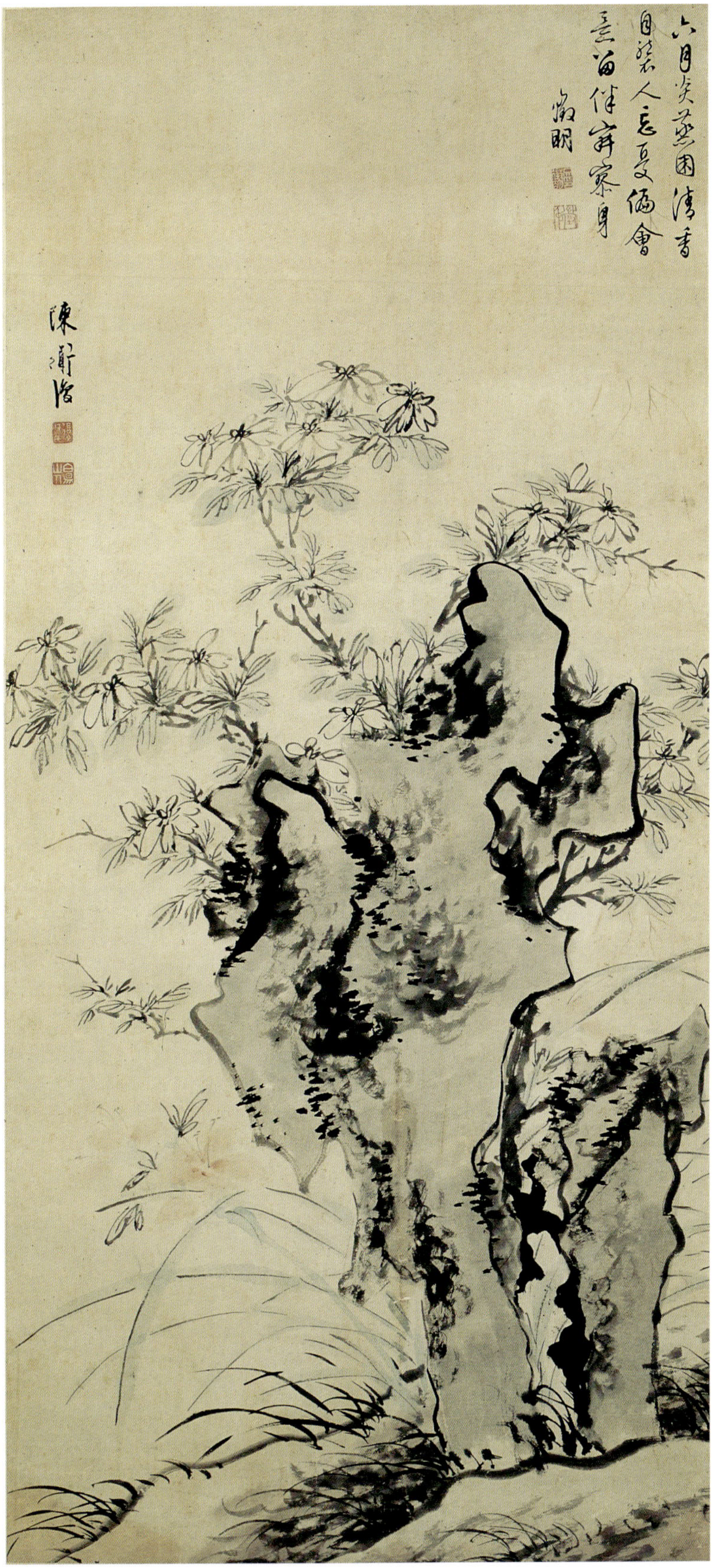

29
明　徐渭　水墨菊花
立轴，纸本水墨
Xu Wei (1521–1593)
Chrysanthemums

Hanging scroll; ink on paper
44.6 x 90.2 cm

ARTIST'S SEALS: Xu Wei zhiyin (square/relief), Wenchang (square/intaglio)
OTHER SEALS: [Unidentified] Qinghuitang yin (square/intaglio), Zishan miwan (square/relief), Lu runzhi cang (rectangular/relief), Shanghai Xu Zishan shoucang shuhua jinshi shuji yin (square/relief)

画家印鉴：徐渭之印（朱文方印）、文长（白文方印）
其他印鉴：清晖堂印（白文方印），紫珊秘玩（朱文方印），陆润之藏（朱文长方印），上海徐紫珊收藏书画金石书籍印（朱文方印）

Xu Wei (courtesy name, Wenqing, later changed to Wenchang) had various sobriquets including Tianchi and Qingteng Laoren and was a native of Shaoxing, Zhejiang. He was a multi-talented artist with unique styles in literature, calligraphy, and painting. In his middle age, he was recruited as an assistant to the Zhejiang circuit inspector Hu Zongxian. Because he was implicated in a conflict within official circles, he made repeated abortive suicide attempts, after which he became mentally unstable and was imprisoned for killing his wife. As a result of his many misfortunes, his calligraphy and painting expressed a wild, uncontrolled style for which he became noteworthy. This work, signed with his sobriquet Tianchi, depicts a tall, erect stem of chrysanthemums growing beside bamboo, rocks, and grasses, all freely executed with an ink-laden brush. On the upper right he inscribed a poem expressing his feelings: "My life is like a boat stranded in the sea. I close the door and do not comb my hair for months. As butterflies idly come and go along the eastern fence, I pass the autumn viewing and painting chrysanthemums."

HWL (trans. MSW)

徐渭（1521－1592），字文清，更字文长，号天池、青藤老人等，浙江绍兴人。

徐渭是一位具有文学、书法、绘画多方面才艺而且风格独具的艺术家，他在中年时代被闽督（浙江巡抚）胡世宗（宗宪）招入幕中，因宦场争斗而受到牵连，屡次自杀未遂后精神错乱，竟因误杀妻子而入狱。多舛的人生境遇，连同他在书法、绘画作品中所表现的那种狂放不羁的艺术风格，构成了他突出的艺术特点。此幅作品以他的号"天池"署款，钤有画家两印。淋漓的水墨画一株傲挺的菊花，旁饰竹石草丛，皆以狂放的笔致和淋漓的水墨挥就。画面右上方自题诗中，道出了他的心境："身世浑如泊海舟，关门累月不梳头。东篱蝴蝶闲来往，看写黄花过一秋"。

黄伟利

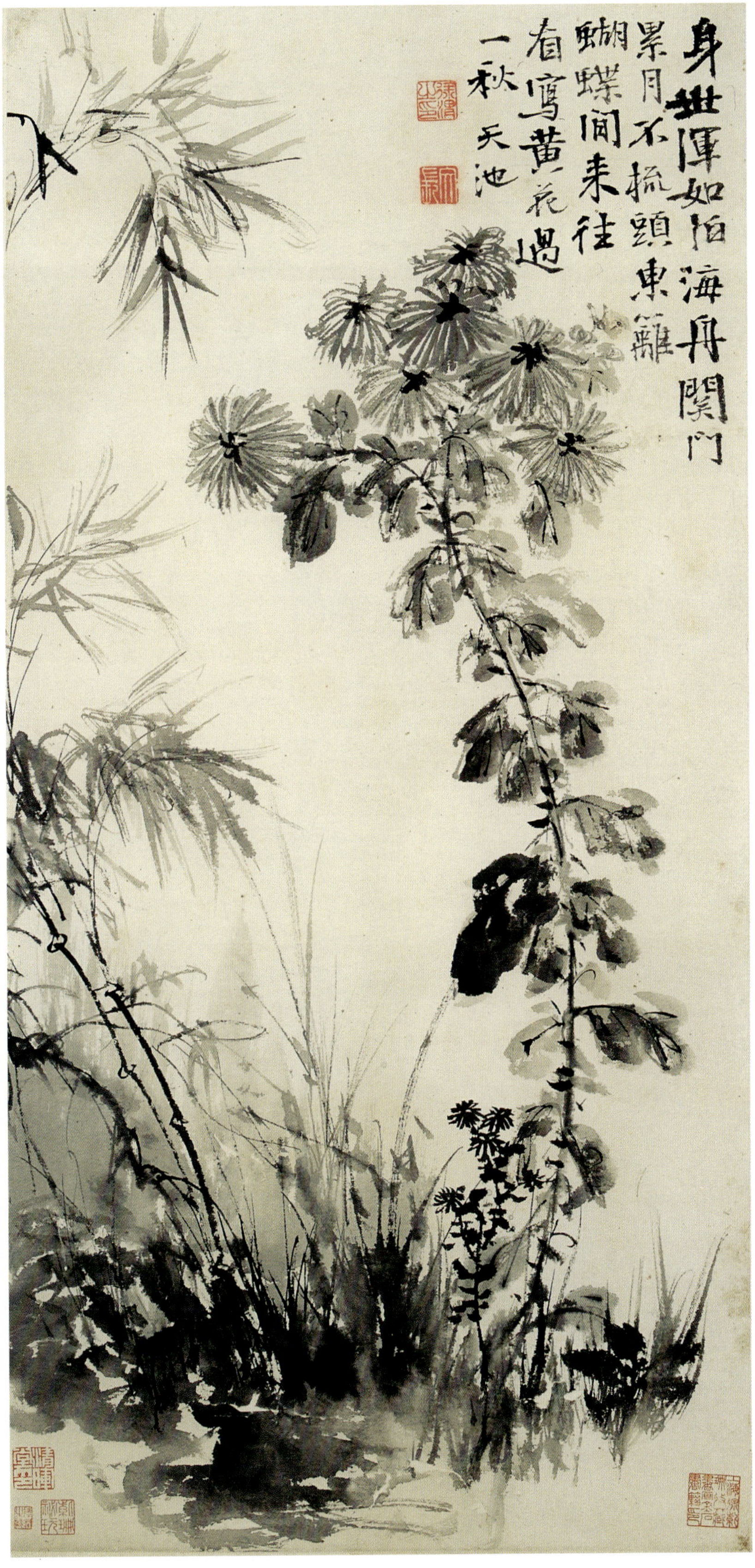
身世渾如泊海舟關門
累月不梳頭東籬
蝴蝶閒来往
看寫黃花過
一秋 天池

30
明　佚名　锦鸡图
立轴，绢本设色
Anonymous
Ming dynasty (1368–1644)
Golden Pheasant
Hanging scroll; color on silk
93 x 99.5 cm

This painting is done by an anonymous Ming dynasty artist in the imperial court style. Rich colors and fine brush technique are used to depict birds and flowers in a natural setting. A male and female pheasant move at ease among the blooms; in the painting's lower left two small birds search for food amidst the plants. One can almost hear the bird calls in this secluded scene. Around the rocks grow white okra, maroon peony, and mountain chrysanthemums of varied hues, vying for attention. The subjects are realistically depicted with strong skill and artistic technique. This painting has no signatures or seals.

HWL (trans. MSW)

此为明代无名氏所作的一幅具有皇家格调的画作，画面以浓丽的色彩和精整工致的笔法，表现了鸟语花香的自然景象：一雄一雌两只雉鸡和谐相伴地活动在繁花似锦的自然环境中，一派悠然自得；两只翠鸟在左下方花草丛中跳跃觅食，有如闻见空谷中的鸣叫声；围绕玲珑石间，白色的秋葵、紫红的牡丹以及各色山菊含苞怒放、争奇斗艳，具有很强的写实功力与艺术技巧。此图无款识和钤印。

黄伟利

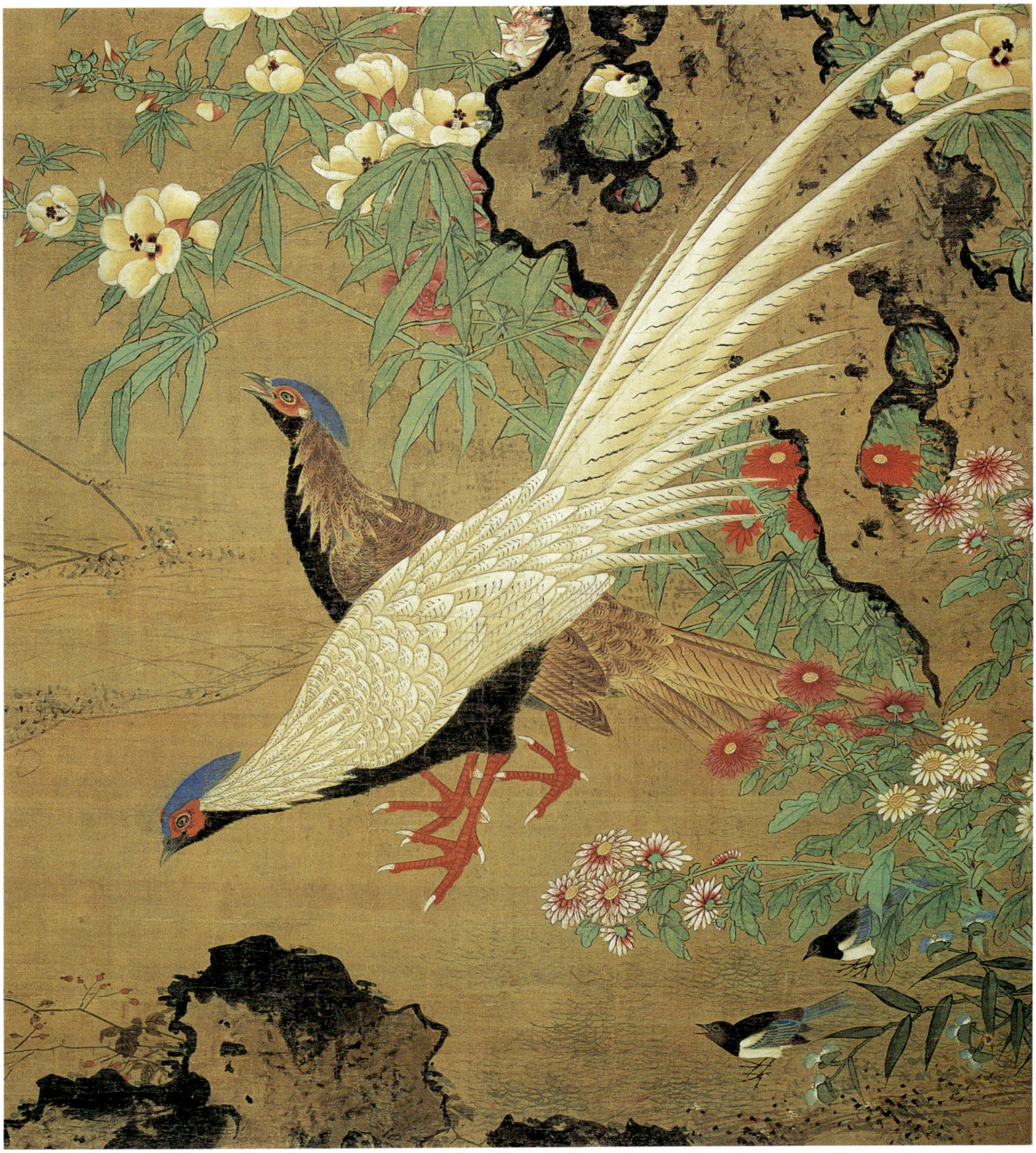

31
清 黄慎 柳荫双鹭图
立轴，纸本水墨
Huang Shen (1687–after 1768)
Two White Egrets under the Willow Tree

Hanging scroll; ink on paper
62.5 x 138.5 cm

ARTIST'S SEALS: Yingpiao (square/intaglio), Donghai Buyi (square/intaglio)

画家印鉴：瘿瓢（白文方印），东海布衣（白文方印）

Huang Shen (courtesy name, Gongshou; sobriquet, Yingpiao) was a native of Ninghua, Fujian, who resided in Yangzhou and sold paintings for a living. He was one of the Eight Eccentrics of Yangzhou. Born into a poor family, he boarded at an old temple where he studied poetry writing and calligraphy in his early years. At that time, he also studied painting with the famous figure painter Shang Guanzhou. He employed a distinctive brush technique, using a bold, simple style to depict figures, birds, and flowers from popular stories. This work, signed with his sobriquet Yingpiao, uses free brushstrokes to paint a weeping willow on a bank and two egrets in the water searching for food. The aged trunk done in rough strokes and leaves floating in the breeze are paired with simply rendered yet lifelike birds. A poem in grass script is inscribed on the painting's upper left: "Light mist moves across a blue haze of mountains, willow and high building beside a wide road. At loose ends in the spring light, I spy fluttering egrets. One stab shatters the sky in the water."

HWL (trans. MSW)

黄慎（1687－1768后），字恭寿，号瘿瓢，福建宁化人，寓居扬州以鬻画为生，为“扬州八怪”之一。黄慎出身贫寒之家，早年寄宿在古寺中学习作诗与书法，又从当时著名的人物画家上官周学画。他以自己别具一格的笔法入画，以豪放、凝练的画风表现民间喜闻乐见的人物或花鸟，趣味横生。此作以其号“瘿瓢”署款，画面以洒脱的笔法画出了岸边的垂柳和一对在水边觅食的鹭鸶，柳干苍浑，柳叶飘逸，与笔墨简洁而神情毕现的鹭鸶相映成趣。画面左上方的草书自题诗表达了画面的意境：“青山淡抹走轻烟，杨柳高楼大道边。闲杀春光看振鹭，一拳撑破水中天”。

黄伟利

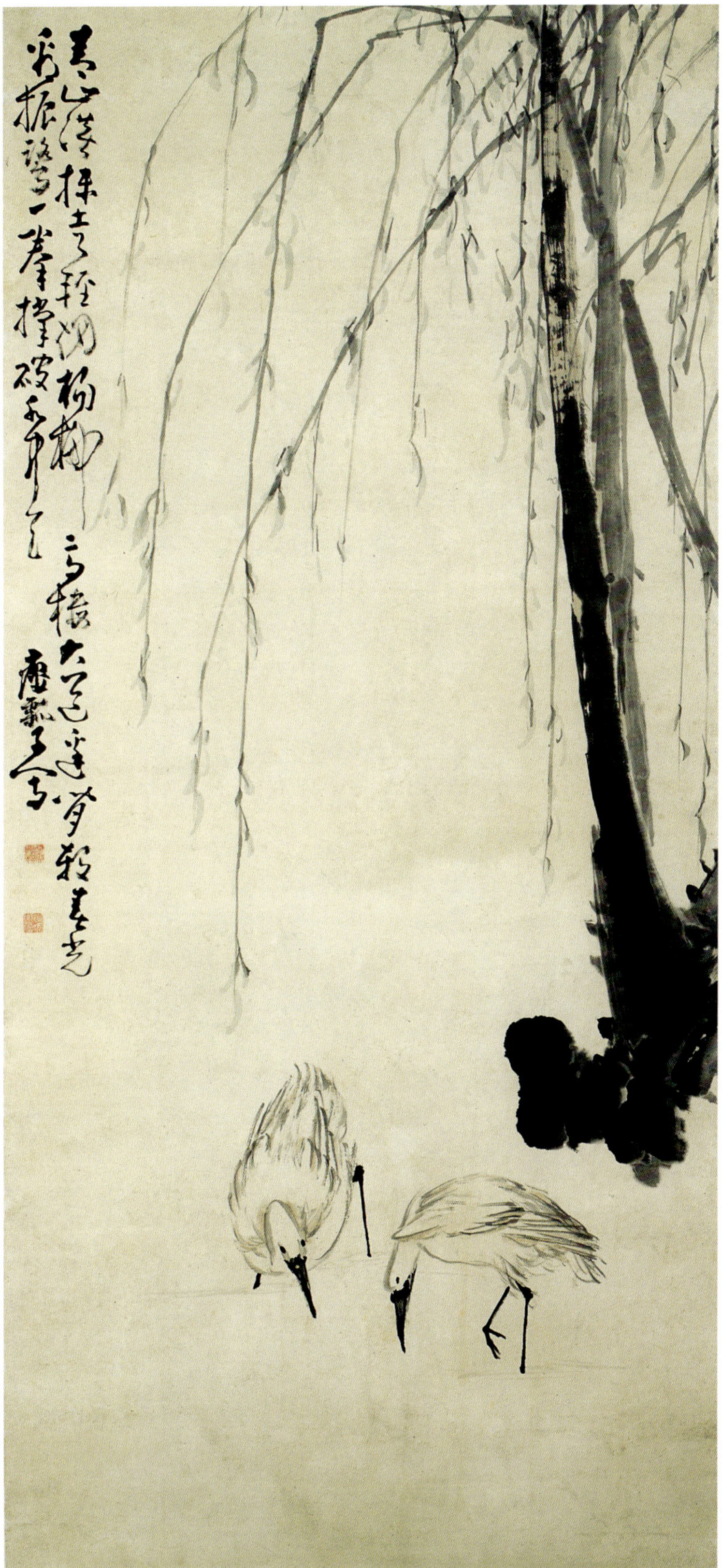

32
清　　高凤翰　设色牡丹图
立轴，纸本水墨设色
Gao Fenghan (1683–1748)
Peonies, 1726

Hanging scroll; ink and color on paper
62.5 x 138.5 cm

ARTIST'S SEALS: Feng-Han (linked seal; double square/relief), Nanfu Shanren (square/intaglio)
OTHER SEALS: [Li Zuoxian; *juren*, 1828] Li Zuoxian shoucang shuhua zhiyin (square/intaglio); [Liang Dingfen, 1859–1919] Shuangxi jingshe (square/relief)

画家印鉴：凤、翰（朱文联珠方印）、南阜山人（白文方印）
其他印鉴：[李佐贤]李佐贤收藏书画之印（白文方印）；
[梁鼎芬]双溪精舍（朱文方印）

Gao Fenghan (courtesy name, Xiyuan) used the sobriquets Nancun and, later in life, Nanfu. He was a native of Jiaozhou, Shandong, and became an official early in life, having served as the county [magistrate] of Huizhou, Jixi. After resigning from this position, he lived in Yangzhou and became known for his writing and painting. His attainments in calligraphy and painting, which had a marked character, were considerable. His grass script, with its full and robust brush technique, was superb. He was especially good at flower-and-bird painting. He had solid skills but was not restrained by convention. The relaxed tenor of his work had natural appeal. According to the long inscription on the painting, in the spring of the *yisi* year, i.e., third year of Yongzheng's reign (1725), Gao Fenghan saw peonies blooming in Li Xueshi's garden in Haiqu (present-day Rizhao, Shandong) and was inspired to write a seven-character *shi* poem. In the following year, he painted this work for a Mr. Mao, a fellow Shandong native, and inscribed the poem in running script. The poem, the calligraphy, and the painting together form a perfect composition.

HWL (trans. MSW)

高凤翰（1683－1748），字西园，号南村，晚号南阜，山东胶州人。早年为官，曾任徽州绩溪知县，辞官后寓居扬州，以诗文书画知名，在书法、绘画方面均有高超的造诣，并具鲜明的个性。书法以草书为胜，笔法圆劲；尤为擅长花鸟画，功力深厚而不拘成法，气韵纵逸而得天趣。据此画上长跋述，高凤翰在乙巳年，即康熙三年（1725）的春天于海曲（今山东省日照市）李学士宅中看到牡丹花开时，触景生情而得此七言诗。次年，又为同乡山东安丘人卯君兄（史进）追图其意，并以行书体书全诗于画上。此图以诗书画完美结合的形式，生动而超然地体现了牡丹绽放的逸趣，并为后人题为“富贵图”。

黄伟利

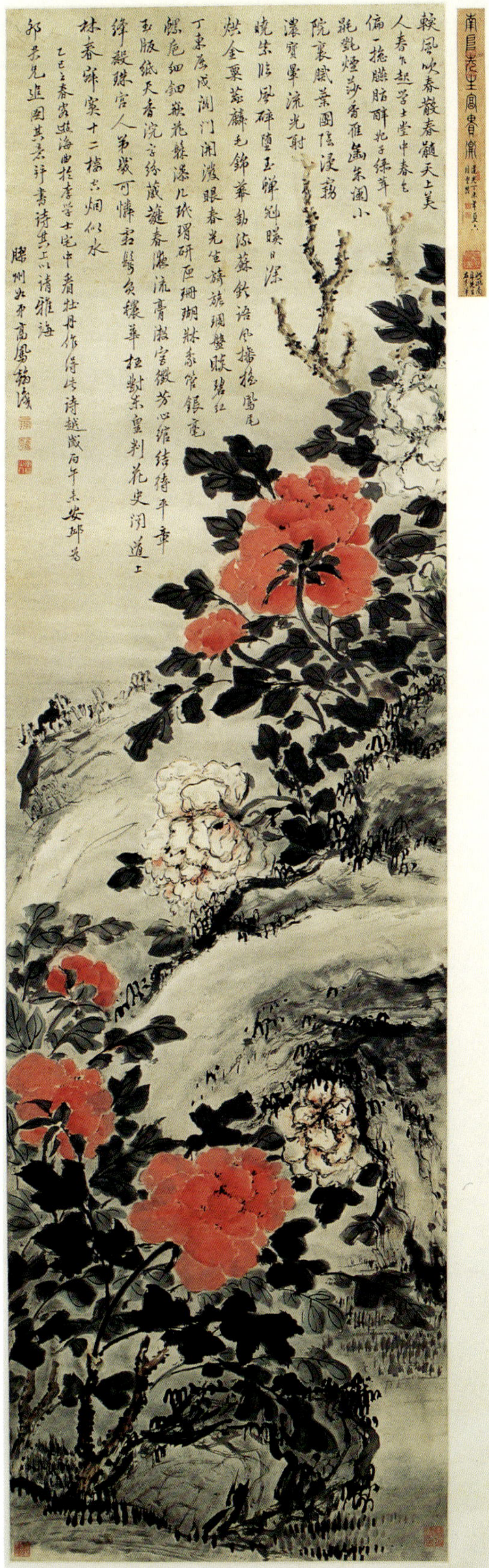

33
清　　郑燮　　幽兰图
立轴，纸本水墨
Zheng Xie (1693–1765)
Orchid
Hanging scroll; ink on paper
51 x 121.1 cm

ARTIST'S SEALS: Zheng Xie zhiyin (square/intaglio), Ershi nian qian jiu Banqiao (square/relief)
OTHER SEAL: [Yao Youqing, dates unknown] Quantang Yao Youqing zhencang shuhua zhiyin (square/relief)
COLOPHON WRITER (SEALS): Deng Bangshu, 1868–1939 (Biweng [square/intaglio], Shisi shiguan [square/ relief])

画家印鉴：郑燮之印（白文方印）、二十年前旧板桥（朱文方印）
其他印鉴：[姚又卿]泉塘姚又卿珍藏书画之印（朱文方印）
题跋者（钤印）：[邓邦述，1868–1939] 碧翁（白文方印）、世四史官（朱文方印）

Zheng Xie (courtesy name, Ke Rou; sobriquet, Banqiao) was a native of Xinghua, Jiangsu. He lived in Yangzhou and was one of the Eight Eccentrics of Yangzhou. In the inaugural year of Qianlong's reign (1736), Zheng Xie passed the examination for the *jinshi* degree, after which he spent twelve years as the [head] (*xianling*) of Fan and Wei counties in Shandong. He was an upright official but was dismissed after taking the blame for aiding famine victims by opening the granaries. He then moved to Yangzhou in order to make his living as a calligrapher and painter and became famous. He was fond of drink and easygoing. His poetry, calligraphy, and painting all had individuality and showed a rejection of popular taste. He did not use current idiom in his verse. Good at painting botanical subjects and rocks, he was especially known for orchid and bamboo. In calligraphy, he mixed standard and clerical scripts together, and called it "six and a half" (*liufenban*) style. This work displays orchids growing amidst a group of rocks. The leaves, painted loosely and easily with a wet brush, spread out in all directions. On the right side is a seven-character *shi* poem expressing his feelings: "Once past the blue mountain, another mountain. A secluded orchid hidden away, the road winding. Who can enter into the kingdom of many fragrances? Just allow me, the bookworm, half a room."

HWL (trans. MSW)

郑燮（1693—1765），字克柔，号板桥，江苏兴化人，寓居扬州，为"扬州八怪"之一。郑燮在乾隆元年（1736）考中进士，曾先后在山东范县、潍县任县令达十二年之久，却两袖清寒，而因开仓赈济遭遇大饥荒的灾民而被诬罢官，遂移居扬州以书画为生，名声大震。郑燮性嗜酒，为人疏放不羁，诗、书、画皆具个性，脱尽时习。其诗词不作熟语，画擅花卉木石，尤长于兰竹，书法楷书与隶书体参而和之，自称六分半体。此图以生长在丛石间的兰花，纷披穿插，姿态酣畅淋漓。右侧以行书自书七言律诗直抒胸臆："转过青山又一山，幽兰藏躲路迴环。众香国里谁能到，容我书獃屋半间"。

黄伟利

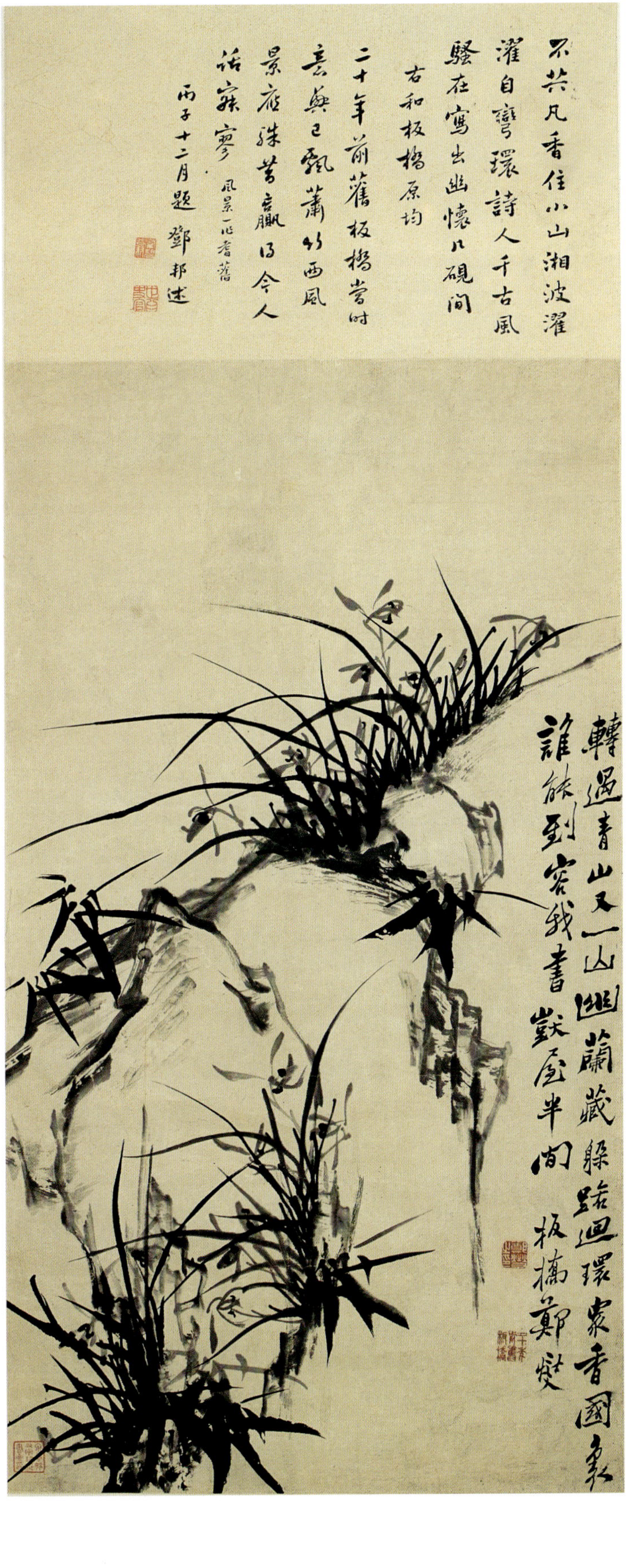
轉過青山又一山
幽蘭藏躲路迴環
衆香國裏
誰能到
容我書獃屋半間
板橋鄭燮

34
清　　金农　　花卉
册页八开，纸本水墨设色
Jin Nong (1687–1764)
Album of Flowers and Plants
Album of 8 leaves; ink and color on paper
30.3 x 24.2 cm

ARTIST'S SEALS: Guquan (coin-shaped/relief), Jin Jijin yin (square/intaglio), Nong (square/intaglio), Shou-Men (linked seal; double square/relief)

画家印鉴：古泉（朱文古钱印）、金吉金印（白文方印）、农（白文方印）、寿、门（朱文联珠方印）

Jin Nong (courtesy name, Shou Men) used the sobriquets Dongxin, Sinong, Jijin, Xiye Jushi, and others. A native of Hangzhou, Zhejiang, he lived in Yangzhou and was one of the Eight Eccentrics of Yangzhou. He was a scholar with an interest in antiquities; he had a rich collection and was a connoisseur of inscriptions on bronzes and stone. His calligraphy was an amalgam of standard and clerical scripts, which he called "lacquer" style. He began to paint at the age of fifty-three and excelled at botanical subjects. His use of the brush was distinctive and held in high esteem. This album contains eight leaves separately depicting red bamboo, iris, loquat, calamus, magnolia, orchid, banana tree, and narcissus. Each has a unique calligraphic or poetic inscription. The iris inscription (leaf a), for example, reads, "Wild flowers and small grasses; the Shen family garden has this scenery." The poetic inscription on the calamus (leaf f) reads, "Five years, ten years, I boast of my gardening skills. White stones, clear springs become a family. Don't be surprised that the calamus has no flowers. It only blooms when it meets a soul mate [intimate friend]." Each leaf is signed with one of his many sobriquets and has different seals. This album, done when Jin Nong was seventy-five, is rich in content and displays the artistic character and accomplishments in poetry, calligraphy, and painting of Jin Nong's late years.

HWL (trans. MSW)

金农（1687—1764），字寿门，号冬心，又号司农、吉金、昔耶居士等，浙江杭州人，流寓扬州，为“扬州八怪”之一。金农博学好古，富藏金石，精于鉴赏，书法在楷书与隶书之间变化，自称漆书，53岁开始作画，尤擅长花卉，落笔奇崛，颇受推崇。此花卉册共为八开，分别画朱竹图、蝴蝶兰图、枇杷图、菖蒲图、玉兰花图、兰花图、芭蕉图和水仙图，每开皆有其独具特点的书法题辞或诗题，如在蝴蝶兰图中题道：“野花小草，沈家园内有此风景”，如在菖蒲图中题诗道：“五年十年种法夸，白石清泉自一家。莫讶菖蒲花罕见，不逢知己不开花”。各幅的落款亦自署有多种称谓及不同的钤印。此金农七十五岁时所作花卉册，以较为丰富的内容，反映了金农晚年时诗书画的艺术特点与成就。

黄伟利

34 (leaf a)

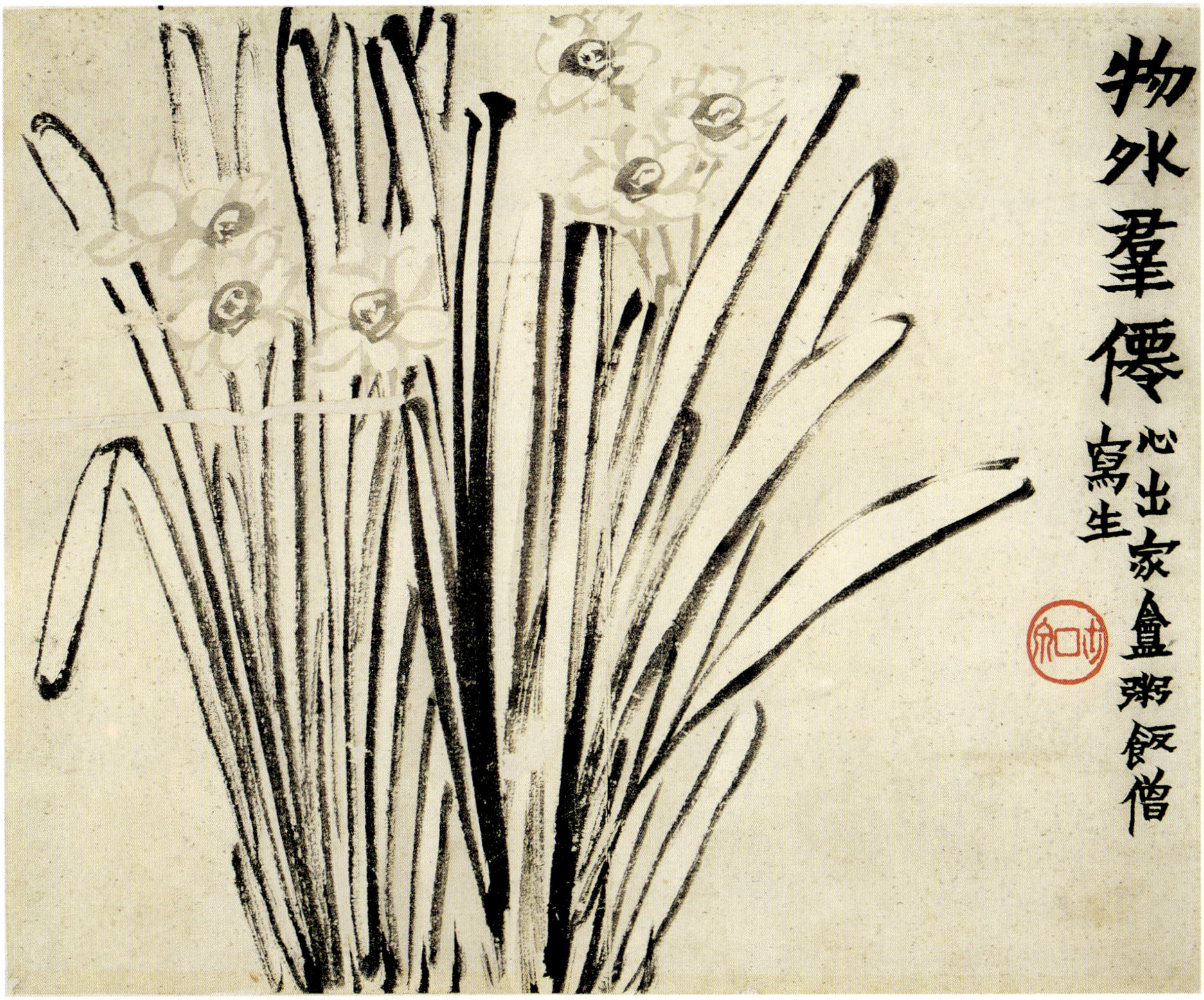

34 (leaf b)

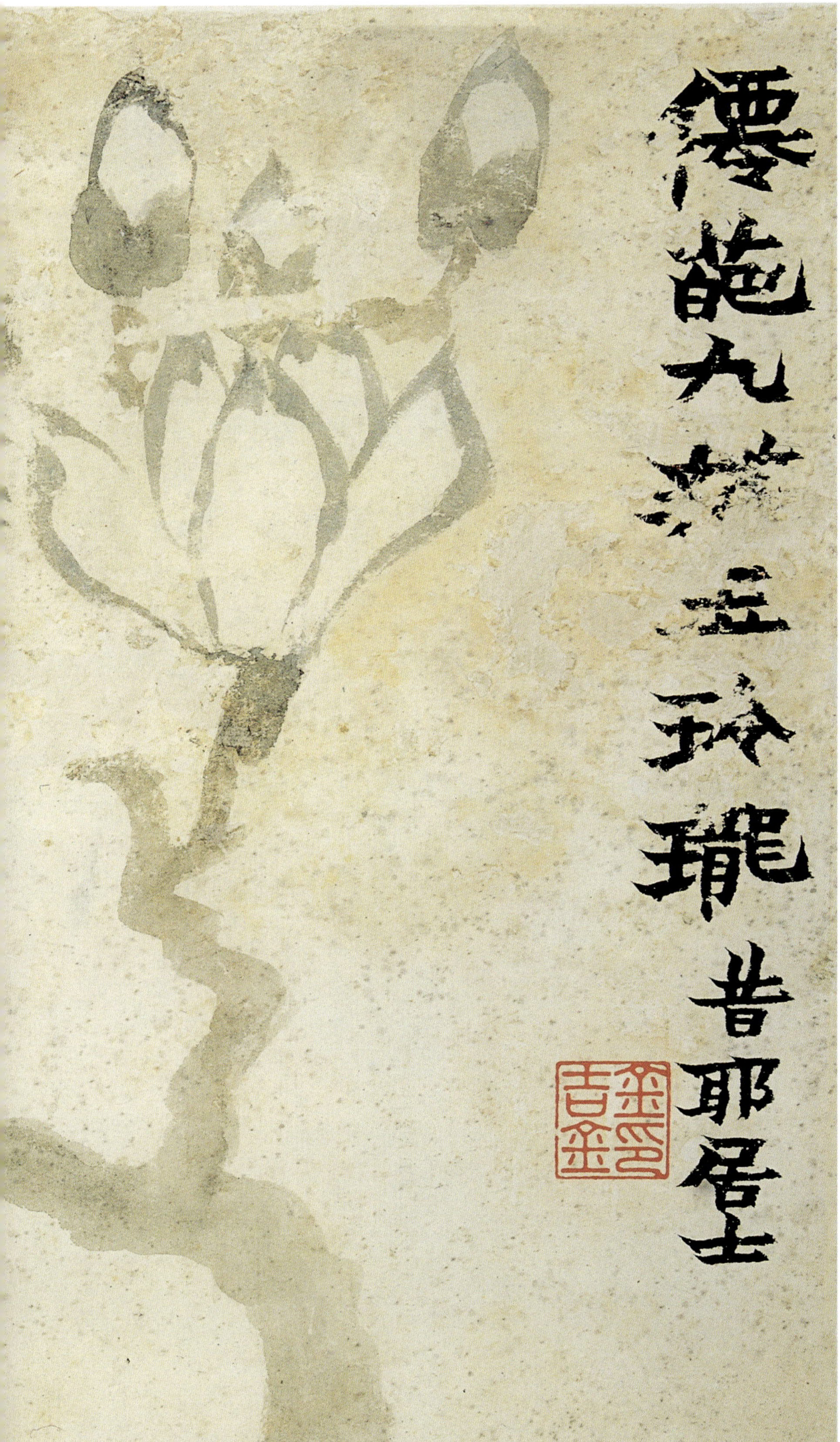
優鉢九莖玉玲瓏
普耶居士

34 (leaf c)

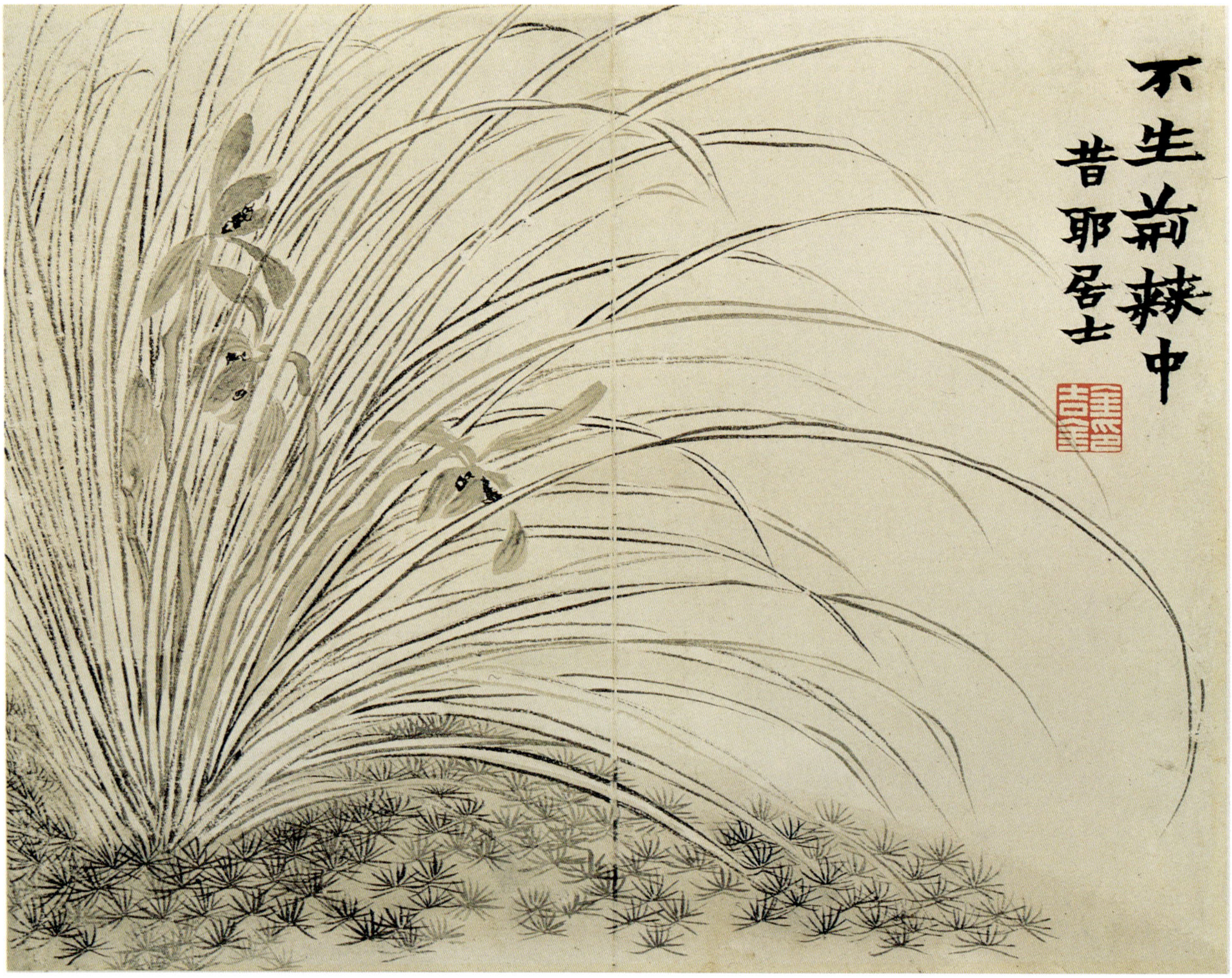

34 (leaf d)

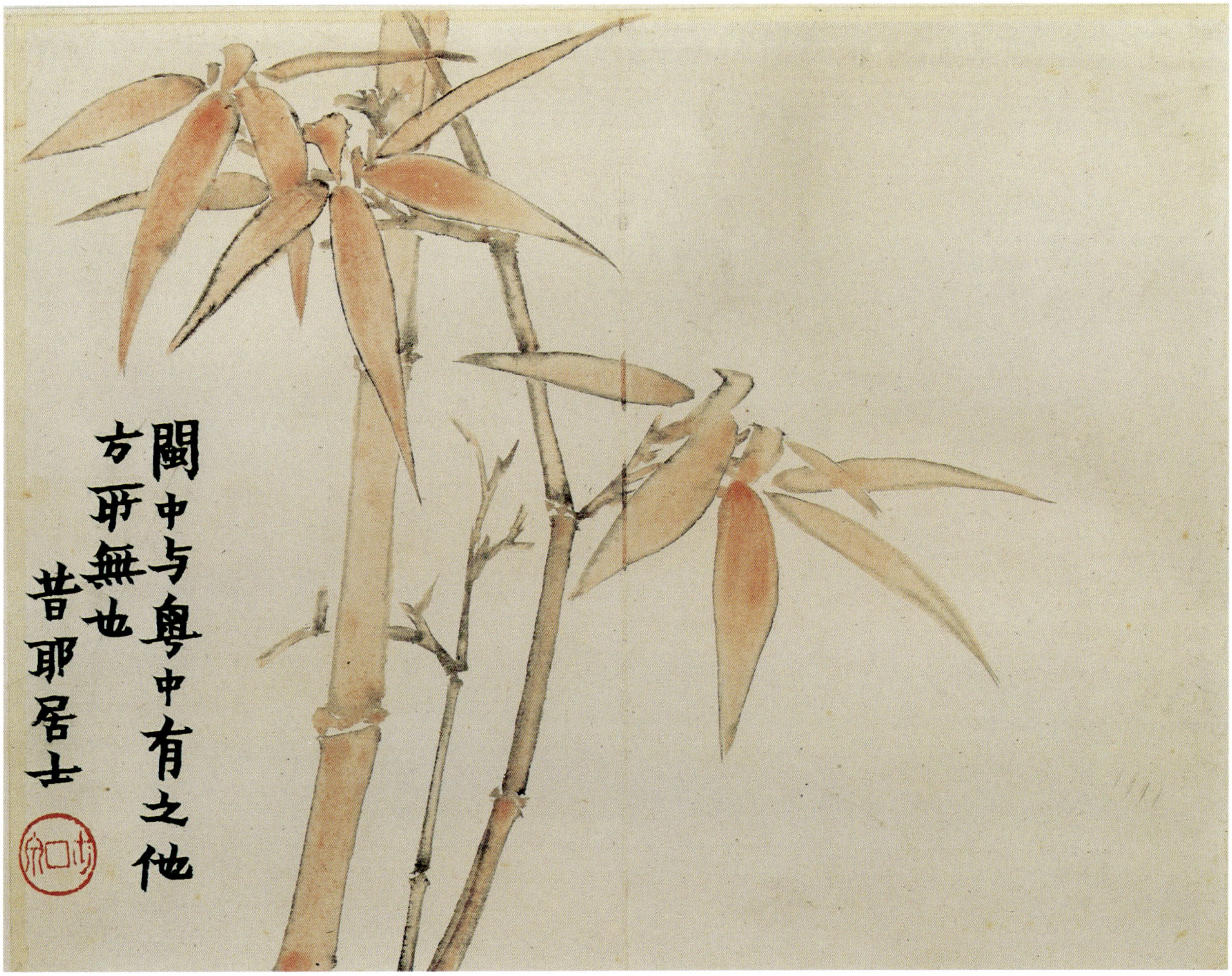

34 (leaf e)

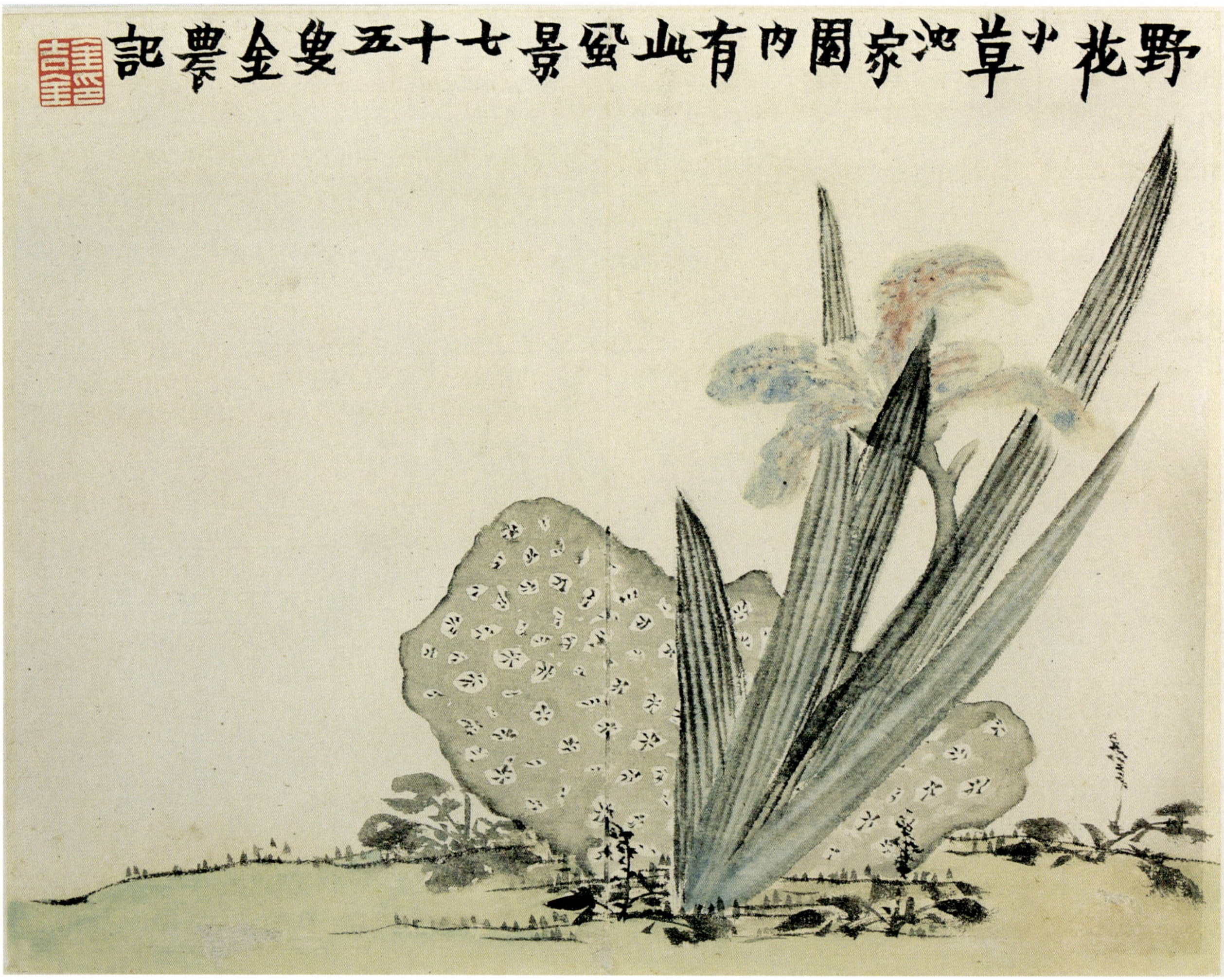

34 (leaf f)

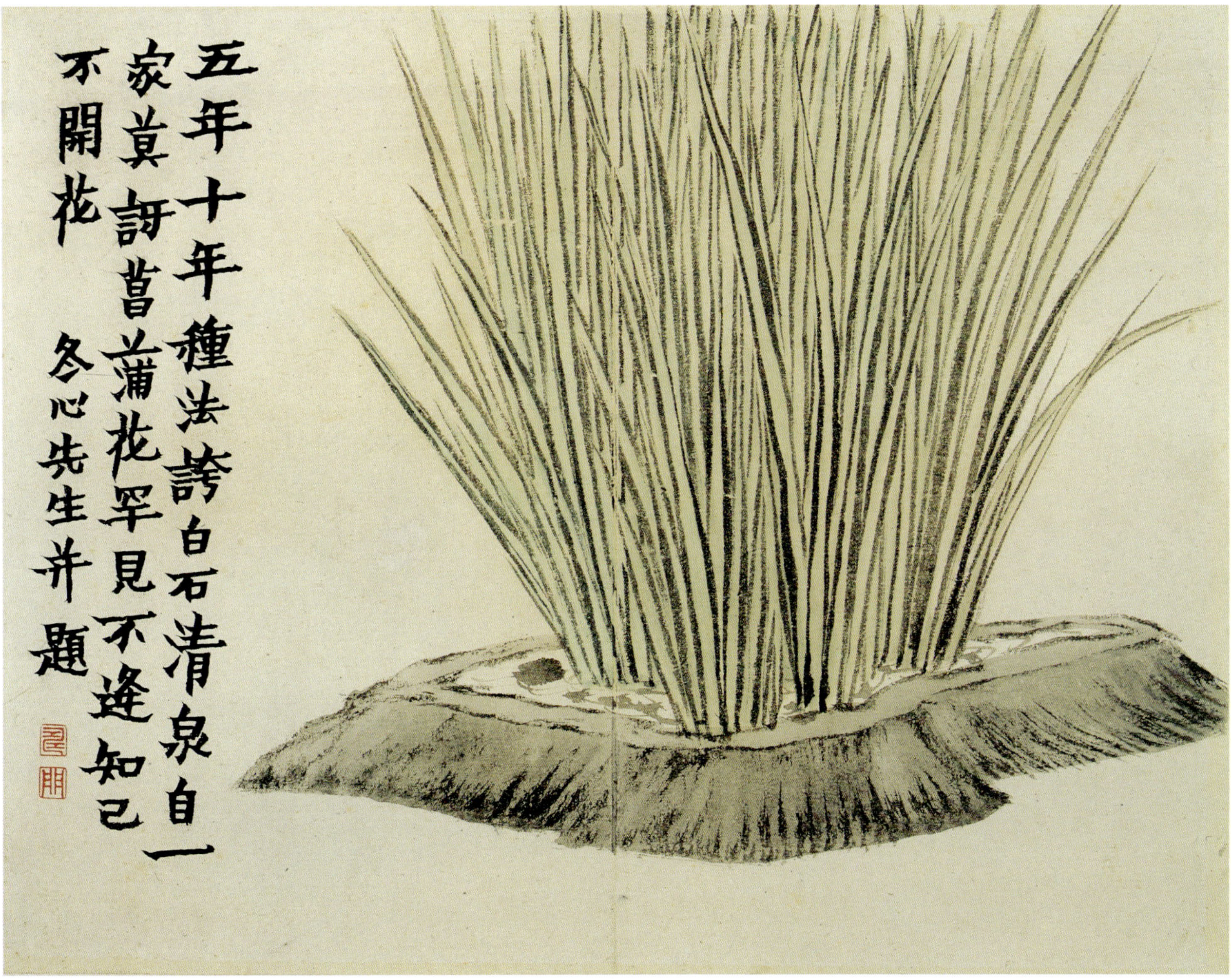

34 (leaf g)

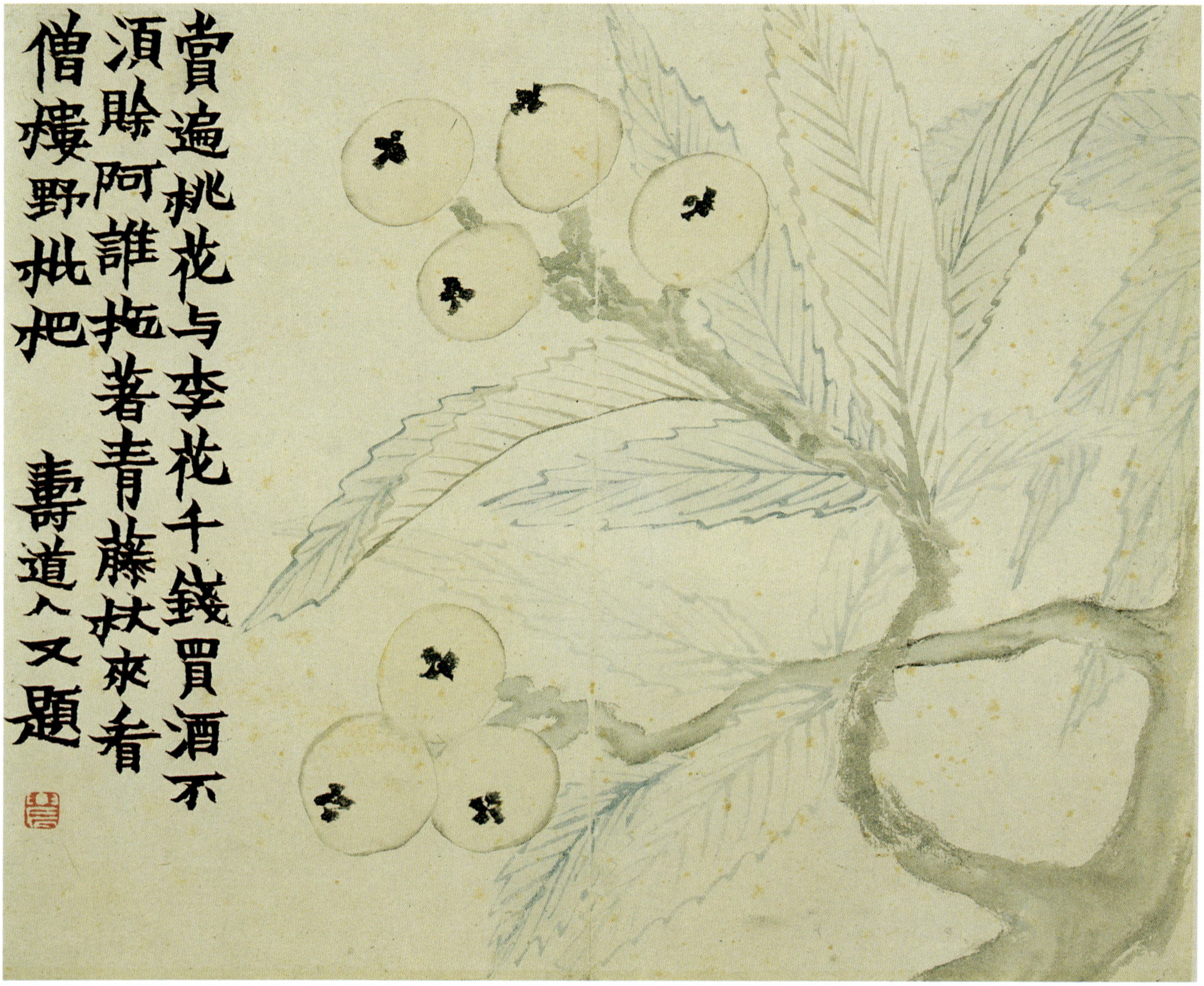

34 (leaf h)

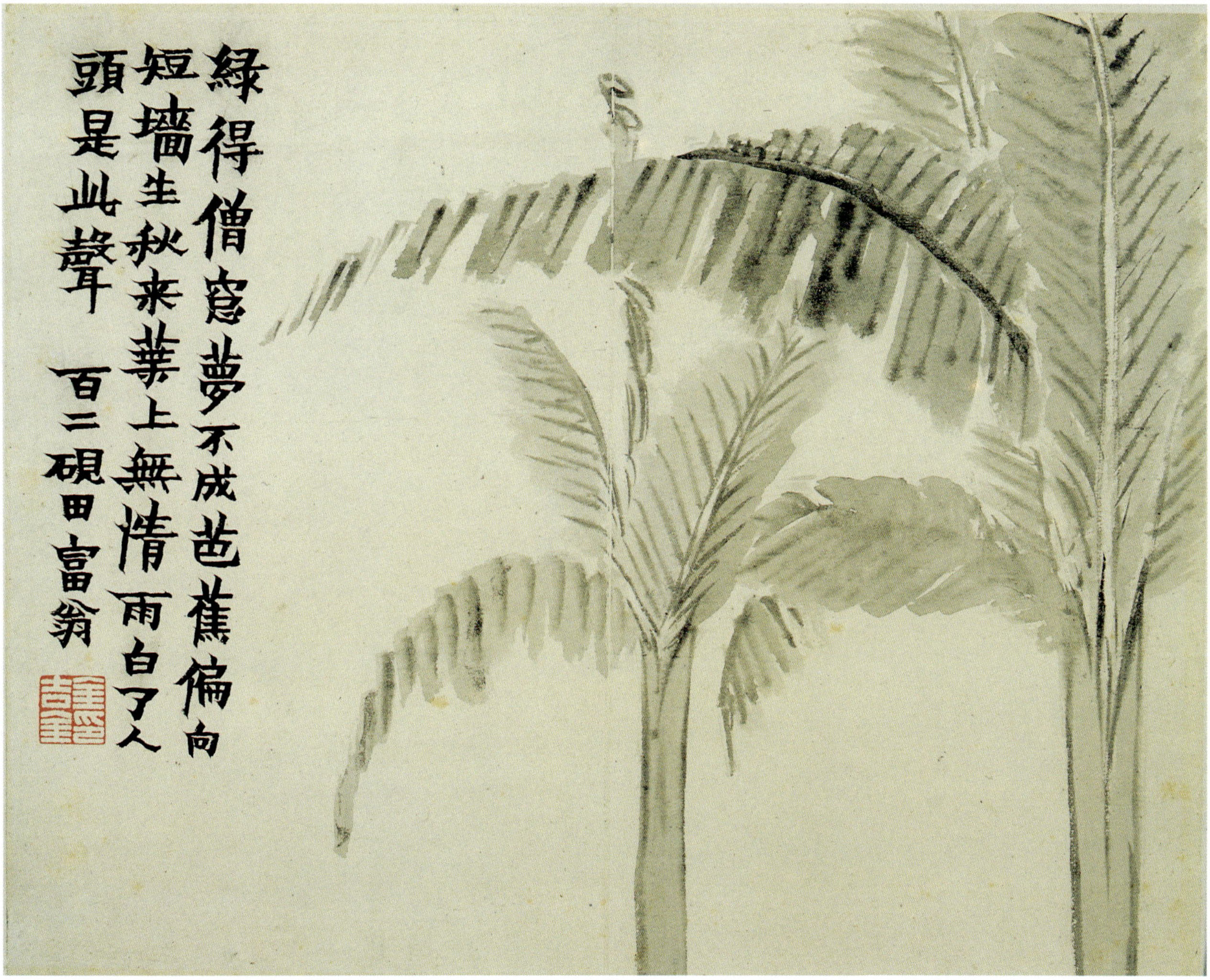

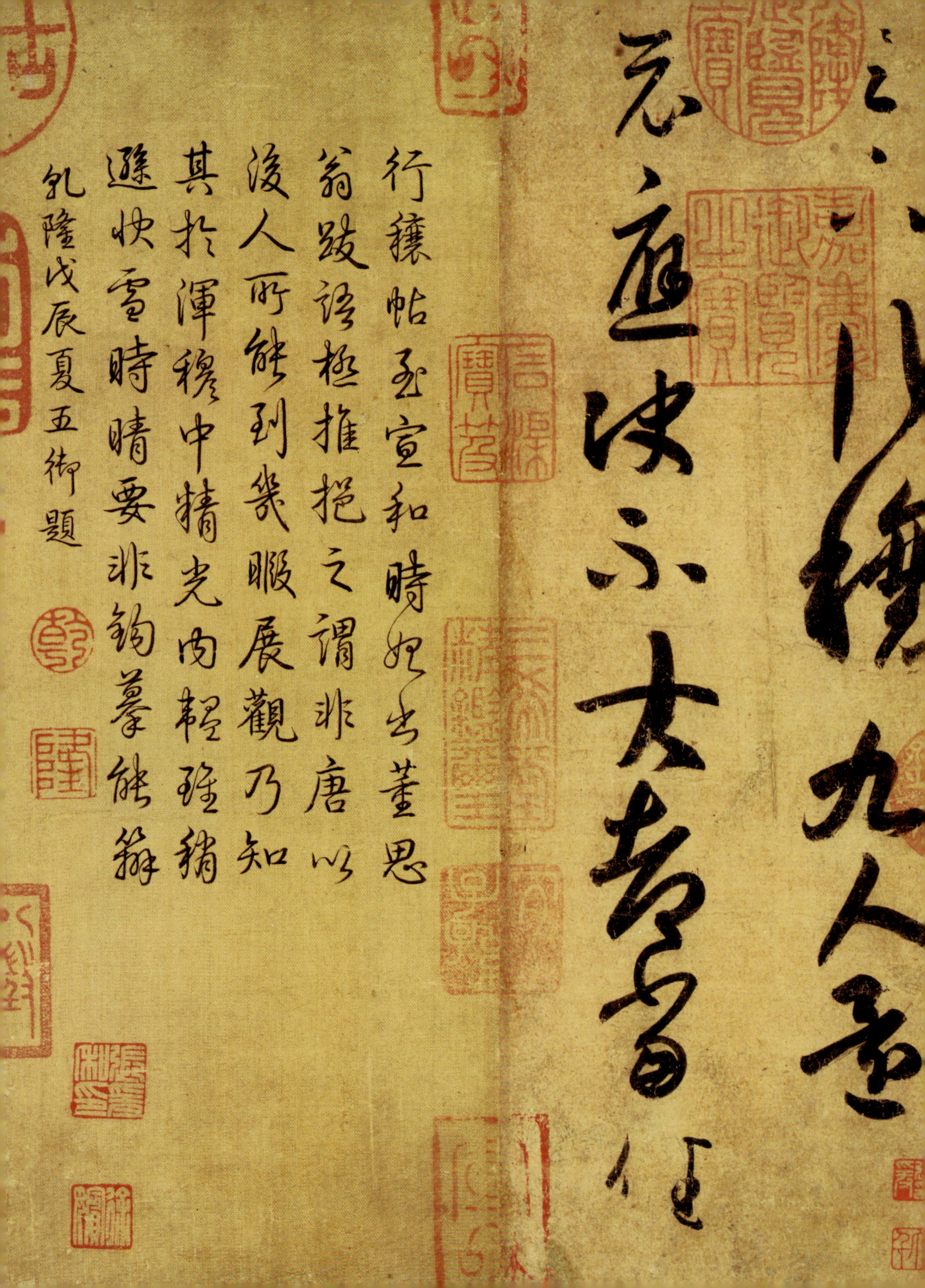
行穰帖至宣和時始出董思
翁跋語極推挹之謂非唐以
後人所能到幾暇展觀乃知
其於渾穆中精光內韞殆猶
遜快雪時晴要非鉤摹能辦
乾隆戊辰夏五御題

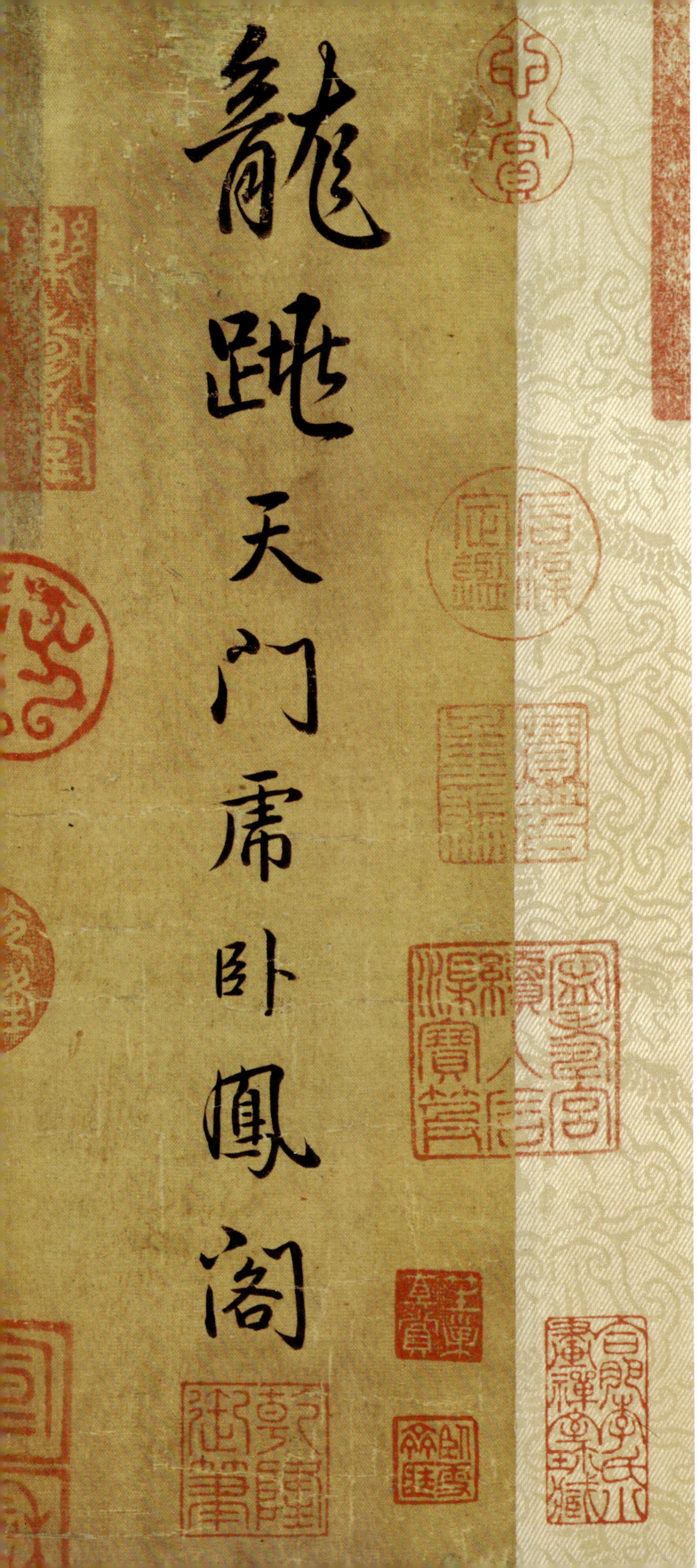

The Imperial Collection in American Museums

美国博物馆藏

中国皇家书画收藏简介

Detail of PUAM (1). Photo: Bruce M. White

Strangers in a Strange Land
From the Qing Palaces
to the Princeton University Art Museum

Cary Y. Liu

The Destination

The history of Princeton's Asian collection starts at the very beginning of the Princeton University Art Museum and Department of Art and Archaeology in the 1880s.[1] Chinese and Japanese art were included in the founding collection of ceramics, which was given on the condition that a "proper museum" and a "department of art instruction" be established. During the museum directorships of Allan Marquand from 1882 to 1922 and Frank Jewett Mather Jr. from 1922 to 1946, interest in the arts of Asia focused primarily on Japanese art. This stemmed from the era's fascination with the Japanese decorative arts displayed at several major exhibitions, including the nearby 1876 Philadelphia Centennial and the 1893 World's Columbian Exposition in Chicago.[2]

The Mather years saw a growing interest in Chinese art with the appointment of George Rowley in 1927 as the first curator of Far Eastern art. Although he received his graduate training at Princeton in medieval and Renaissance art history, Rowley developed a passion for Chinese art. He joined the faculty at Princeton in 1925, where he became "the mainstay of Far Eastern studies" until 1962, and traveled to Beijing in the mid-1930s.[3]

With the growing appreciation of Chinese painting in the 1930s and 1940s, Princeton became the repository of two major loan collections—that of Frederick Peterson and of DuBois Schanck Morris—which served as the nucleus for instruction and research and for future collection growth. Not a connoisseur, Dr. Frederick Peterson bought "what he liked" and assembled a collection of about 250 paintings, drawings, and prints, which was catalogued in 1930 by the sinologist Berthold Laufer and was originally promised to Princeton. In 1941 Rowley selected about forty Ming and Qing paintings from the Peterson Collection for Princeton,[4] and the remainder of the collection was divided among educational institutions at Amherst, Bowdoin, Dartmouth, and Williams in order to advance interest in the field of Chinese painting.

Supplementing the Peterson Collection at Princeton were over five hundred paintings accumulated by DuBois Schanck Morris, Class of 1893. Morris served as a Presbyterian minister and missionary in China for thirty years and lived through the tumultuous 1911 revolution, which ended imperial rule in China. In 1928, he returned to the United States with a large collection of Chinese paintings, which had reportedly been assembled for the purpose of educating young Chinese about their own cultural heritage. Stored on loan at Princeton, the Morris Collection became an invaluable teaching asset.

The 1935 International Exhibition of Chinese Art, London, gathered nearly four thousand Chinese works of art from fourteen nations. The exhibition centered on eight hundred paintings, calligraphies, bronzes, pottery, porcelain, jades, textiles, sculpture, and other works selected, with the support of the Chinese government, from the former Qing imperial palace collections.[5] In this unprecedented display, Chinese art of high quality, reflecting Chinese aesthetic values, was placed on view for the first time in the West. The long belittled fields of sculpture, painting, and calligraphy came to the fore, and critical discernment and appreciation of Chinese art rose to new heights. Selected for display in the London exhibition were two paintings from the Morris Collection: Li Gongnian's (act. ca. 1120) *Wintry Night Landscape* (acc. no. y1946-191) and the anonymous *Ducks Playing in the Shade of a Willow* (acc. no. y1947-8).[6]

At about this time events in Asia forced their way onto the world scene. With the outbreak of World War II, Asian art and culture could no longer be viewed as mere exotica—something different seen from "that kaleidoscopic vision of the tourist or of the mediocre spectator"—but needed to be perceived as "diversity, the knowledge that something is other than one's self" even if

The author would like to acknowledge the invaluable assistance received from Wu Xiaojin and Sinead Kehoe in reading Japanese language sources for this essay. My gratitude also goes to Bruce M. White, whose photography on many of my projects has always been spot on.

colored by subjective cultural, societal, and political overtones and bias.[7] During the war years, Japanese art was actually removed to storage in many galleries across the United States for fear of vandalism, and attention shifted to the arts of China.

After the war, Morris formally presented his collection at the Princeton University Bicentennial Conferences on Far Eastern Culture and Society, organized by Rowley in 1947.[8] In conjunction with this gift, Rowley published his influential *Principles of Chinese Painting with Illustrations from the DuBois Schanck Morris Collection* (Princeton, 1947), in which he attempted to use Chinese aesthetic values and principles to examine the uniqueness of Chinese art. Participants at these landmark conferences included leading art historians—among them Archibald G. Wenley, director of the Freer Gallery of Art, and Liang Sicheng, director of the Institute of Architectural Research at Qinghua University—and the foremost sinologists of the day, including John K. Fairbank, Department of History, Harvard University, and J. J. L. Duyvendak, University of Leiden. The study and collecting of Asian art, archaeology, and architecture had now become inseparable from any consideration of Asian society and culture as a whole.

Organized to accompany the bicentennial conferences were five exhibitions: fifty paintings from the Morris Collection, ritual bronze vessels, Rowley's collected rubbings taken from engraved stones with figural representations,[9] rare books from the National Beijing Library (temporarily stored at the Library of Congress during the war), and photographs of sculpture and architecture provided by Liang Sicheng. A calligraphy exhibition from China was also planned, but it had run into difficulties. In Rowley's own estimation, "Although these five exhibitions could not compete in interest or quality with the unique International Exhibition in London in 1935, nevertheless they represented a very creditable attempt to cover the major problems in the field of Chinese art history."[10]

After the 1947 bicentennial conferences and exhibitions, the academic discipline of Asian art and cultural study developed around two pairings of a research center with an academic department: the Asian collections in the Princeton University Art Museum with the Department of Art and Archaeology and the East Asian Library (including the Gest Oriental Library) with the Department of Oriental Studies (present-day Department of East Asian Studies). The museum's Asian collection became indispensable in the teaching of Asian art by Rowley and later by his student Wen Fong, who joined the faculty in 1958. Complementing the close teaching relationship between Museum and Department was a similar co-dependence between the East Asian Library[11] and the instruction of Chinese and Japanese studies in the Department of Oriental Studies. In 1961, these two complementary pairs were united through the inauguration of the Interdepartmental Program in East Asian Studies and the concurrent establishment of the Program of Chinese and Japanese Art and Archaeology. The close coordination between the two programs allowed students of Asian art to receive training in art history coupled with sinological instruction in the fields of history, literature, languages, and religion. This balanced approach combining stylistic analysis with sinology, object with text, and art with culture has led one observer to comment on the emergence of a "Princeton School" in the field of Asian art history.[12]

The close association between the Museum and East Asian Library has also led to joint exhibitions, such as *Calligraphy and the East Asian Book* in the spring of 1989.[13] Among the Chinese rare books at Princeton are some of the earliest materials that belonged to the former imperial collection. The first painting from the Qing imperial collection to enter the Museum—*Eight Fragrant Summer Flowers* by the Qianlong emperor (r. 1736–95)—was among about forty-five paintings in the Arthur M. Sackler Collection donated during the late 1960s and early 1970s. Later gifts of Chinese calligraphy and painting masterpieces from the Edward L. Elliott family, especially from his son John B. Elliott, brought another eleven works from the Qing palace collections, many of which number among the following "travelers."[14]

The Travelers

The arts of calligraphy and painting played a formative role in Chinese civilization, where the past was venerated as a source of cultural authority and legitimacy. Because written characters and graphic forms transmit the legacy of the past, there is a personal and public reverence for these arts, which can be said to reflect images of the cultivated mind at work. More than instruments for the representation of worldly phenomena and ideas, calligraphy and painting are acts of presentation that can express through form and style the feelings and disposition of the artist; they have the power to embody the forces of nature and to mirror dynastic and cosmological harmony. It is no small wonder that after conducting state affairs emperors and empresses practiced calligraphy and painting as "leisurely activities" (*xian shi*) and amassed vast collections of these "useless things" (*wu yi*). It is partly in this context that the building of the Qing imperial art collections may be understood as "assembling worlds"—an exercise in "cultural imagining."[15]

The calligraphy and painting recorded in sequential editions of the Qing imperial catalogue *Shiqu baoji* (Treasured boxes of the Stone Channel Pavilion) captures such an imagined assembly of a visual world. Because the catalogue was never fully completed, it now only groups the art by their storage location; but one wonders if the original intention had not been to establish a taxonomy for a visual ordering of the world. Such an ordering parallels the archival hierarchy imagined in other Qing imperial catalogues, including that of the imperial library, the *Siku quanshu* (Comprehensive library of the four treasuries), which represented the sum of knowledge bestowed from heaven—a ritual symbol of the Qing dynasty's legitimacy and ability to rule.[16] Collections, particularly imperial collections, formed taxonomic sets in which individual components were mutually associated, and each component and their groupings held special meaning for the royal collector.[17]

It is sometimes difficult, almost sacrilegious, to imagine separating collected pieces away from their assembled world—in this case the Qing imperial collection. It may sometimes be even harder to comprehend how such pieces might travel to strange lands to be assembled into new collections for new audiences. The question then is sometimes raised as to whether "foreigners" (Chinese or non-Chinese) outside the "assembled world" of Qing imperial collecting can ever fully appreciate these travelers that have gone astray. This question is somewhat ironic since most of the holdings in the Qing palace collection were originally created in very different circumstances, and their transmission from collector to collector may best be understood as a continual journey.[18]

The separation of particular art works from the Qing imperial collections has been commonly assumed to be the result of (1) the damage to and looting of the Yuanming Yuan imperial garden-palace (*ligong xing huangjia yuanlin*)[19] by British and French troops in 1860; (2) the Boxer Rebellion, from 1898 to 1901; (3) clandestine removal and the 1923 destruction by dishonest or disgruntled eunuchs; (4) works sold or taken by the last emperor, Puyi (1906–1967), to Tianjin and Changchun, the capital of the Manchukuo puppet regime (in present-day Jilin Province), or (5) the shipment to Taiwan in 1948 of selected works in about four thousand crates to form the core collection of the National Palace Museum, Taipei.[20] This is only a small selection from the entire range of myriad circumstances that befell items detached from the former palace collections, and we must exercise care not to be guided by general assumptions and expectations. As Yang Renkai's research demonstrates, we are only beginning to understand the complexities of how particular pieces came to leave the palace collections.[21] For example, recent studies have also shown that items from the imperial collection were regularly bestowed or loaned as royal favors since the nineteenth century, and some of these items eventually found their way into the market. In addition, besides the Qing palace collections in Beijing, the outcome of former palace collections housed at the Shenyang imperial palaces in Liaoning Province, at the Imperial Summer Villa (*Bishu shanzhuang*) at Rehe (in present-day Hebei Province), at various imperial travel residences and gardens, and at Buddhist and Confucian temples and institutions under imperial sponsorship all need to be carefully examined on an item by item basis.

General expectations can prove deceiving. A case in point is the presumed 1860 destruction of the Yuanming Yuan garden-palace by Anglo-French forces. Using photographic documentation, Régine Thiriez has shown that while enormous damage was indeed inflicted on the garden-palace, concurrent and subsequent decay, scavenging, and vandalism by the local population continued for decades, matching the initial damage.[22] The question raised here is this: Which art works were taken by European forces and which were taken or sold by local opportunists? It is possible to speculate that Europeans primarily seized paintings and artifacts as curios to take home, ignoring arcane calligraphy. It is also possible that the British and French troops did not discriminate in their plunder, but later auctioned off or disposed of what they did not want to keep.[23] Among scrolls (particularly calligraphy) that made their way into the Chinese market during this period, including Wang Xizhi's *Ritual to Pray for Good Harvest* (see below), it is conceivable that some came out of the Yuanming Yuan through indiscriminate seizure by the British or French armies or through native Chinese aware of the artifacts' cultural value. It is also possible that many scrolls were illicitly removed from the Beijing palaces and princely residences during this period when the emperor was away from the capital.[24] Once on the market, the paths traveled were as numerous as the number of travelers.

(1)
王羲之 行穰帖 唐双钩填墨
Wang Xizhi (ca. 303–ca. 361)
***Ritual to Pray for Good Harvest* (*Xingrang tie*)**
Handscroll; Tang dynasty tracing copy,
ink on *yinghuang* paper
Letter 24.4 x 8.9 cm, overall 30.0 x 372.0 cm
Princeton University Art Museum. Bequest of
John B. Elliott, Class of 1951
(1998-140.1 [scroll], -140.2 [fabric wrapper])

Active during the Eastern Jin (317–420), the calligrapher Wang Xizhi developed new forms of running (*xingshu*) and cursive (*caoshu*) script that transformed calligraphy into a personally expressive medium. Although Wang wrote many types of texts that came to be prized as works of art, the personal letter was the format in which the new expressive flexibility of calligraphy was most fully realized. Collectors valued these letters not for their literary content, but for the excellence of the calligraphy in which they were written. Owing to the now obscure references they contain, many of Wang's letters are no longer fully intelligible. In *Ritual to Pray for Good Harvest*, Wang appears to refer to a ritual sacrifice conducted by a friend and inquires about the political intentions of this person's followers.

This tracing copy of the letter preserves only the first half of Wang's original text and probably dates from the early Tang dynasty.[25] It remains one step removed from the original artifact. Yet because no authentic work by Wang survives, this copy was highly prized by later collectors, including emperors whose numerous inscriptions and seals surround the remaining two columns of cursive-script characters. The earliest mention of the full letter is found in *Fashu yaolu* (Essential records on models of calligraphy), by the late Tang dynasty scholar Zhang Yanyuan.[26] After this letter fragment entered the Northern Song imperial collection, six palace seals were added, and Emperor Huizong (r. 1101–1125) personally wrote an inscription in faint gold ink on a title strip at the upper right corner of the letter. With the fall of the Northern Song, the scroll found a home in the Jin dynasty, and a copy was reportedly engraved and included as a rubbing in Wang Tingjun's (1151–1202) *Xuexitang tie* (Model calligraphies from the Xuexi Tang hall).[27] In the Ming dynasty, *Ritual* passed through the hands of the collector and artist Xiang Yuanbian (1525–1590);[28] Han Shineng (d. 1598), the Hanlin Academy teacher of Dong Qichang (1555–1636);[29] and the official and artist Dong Qichang; then returned to Han Fengxi, the son of Han Shineng; and finally entered the collections of Wu Ting (act. 1575–1625)[30] and Zhou Minzhong.[31] The scroll was included in Wu Ting's *Yuqingzhai fatie* (Model calligraphies from the Yuqing Studio) rubbing anthology issued in 1614. Also produced was a late-Ming forgery, which may actually be a Qing copy made for the production of the imperial calligraphy model-book *Sanxitang fatie* (Model calligraphies of the Hall of Three Rarities).[32]

In the Qing, the scholar and official Sun Chengze (1593–1675) viewed the scroll and wrote a note to its owner. This note was later attached to the scroll when it was in the collection of An Qi (1683–ca. 1744), who still owned *Ritual* in 1744. Since *Ritual* was not included when the *Shiqu baoji chubian* (first edition) was produced between 1744 and 1745, it most likely had not yet entered the palace collection. The scroll was included in the *Sanxitang fatie* imperial rubbing anthology, which was produced between 1747 and 1750. At the very latest, the scroll entered the imperial collection by 1748, the date of two colophons on the scroll by the Qianlong emperor. Subsequently, the *Shiqu baoji xubian* (second edition, 1793) notes that *Ritual* was stored in the Forbidden City's Ningshou Gong hall,[33] and a collector's seal of the Jiaqing emperor (r. 1796–1820) indicates that it was still in the palace during his reign.

The next mention of *Ritual to Pray for Good Harvest* is in 1862 when it surfaces outside the palace in the hands of Investigating Censer (*jiancha yushi*) Zeng Xiejun (*zi* [courtesy name]: Shengchao),[34] who openly added two seals on the scroll. In a July 9, 1865 diary entry, Weng Tonghe (1830–1904) notes hearing that the scroll was in Beijing's Liulichang market.[35] From these dates, it is possible to surmise that the scroll was removed from the imperial collection during the turmoil associated with the 1860 burning of the Yuanming Yuan garden-palace by Anglo-French armies. This is the view of Nishijima Shin-ichi, whose assessment relies on the seal carver Wang Zhuangwei (writing in 1970). Nishijima suspects Wang learned that *Ritual* was looted from the Yuanming Yuan through his close friendship with Zhang Daqian (1899–1983), who acquired the scroll in 1957.[36] But how would Zhang have known? While such speculation may ultimately prove correct, until there is firm evidence that the scroll came out of the Yuanming Yuan, or at least was moved there before 1860, it is best to ponder alternatives. For example, if the scroll had remained in the Forbidden City, it may have been surreptitiously removed some time before 1862 or given earlier as a gift to a royal family member or minister, who later sold it. To my knowledge, European troops did not enter or occupy the Forbidden City at

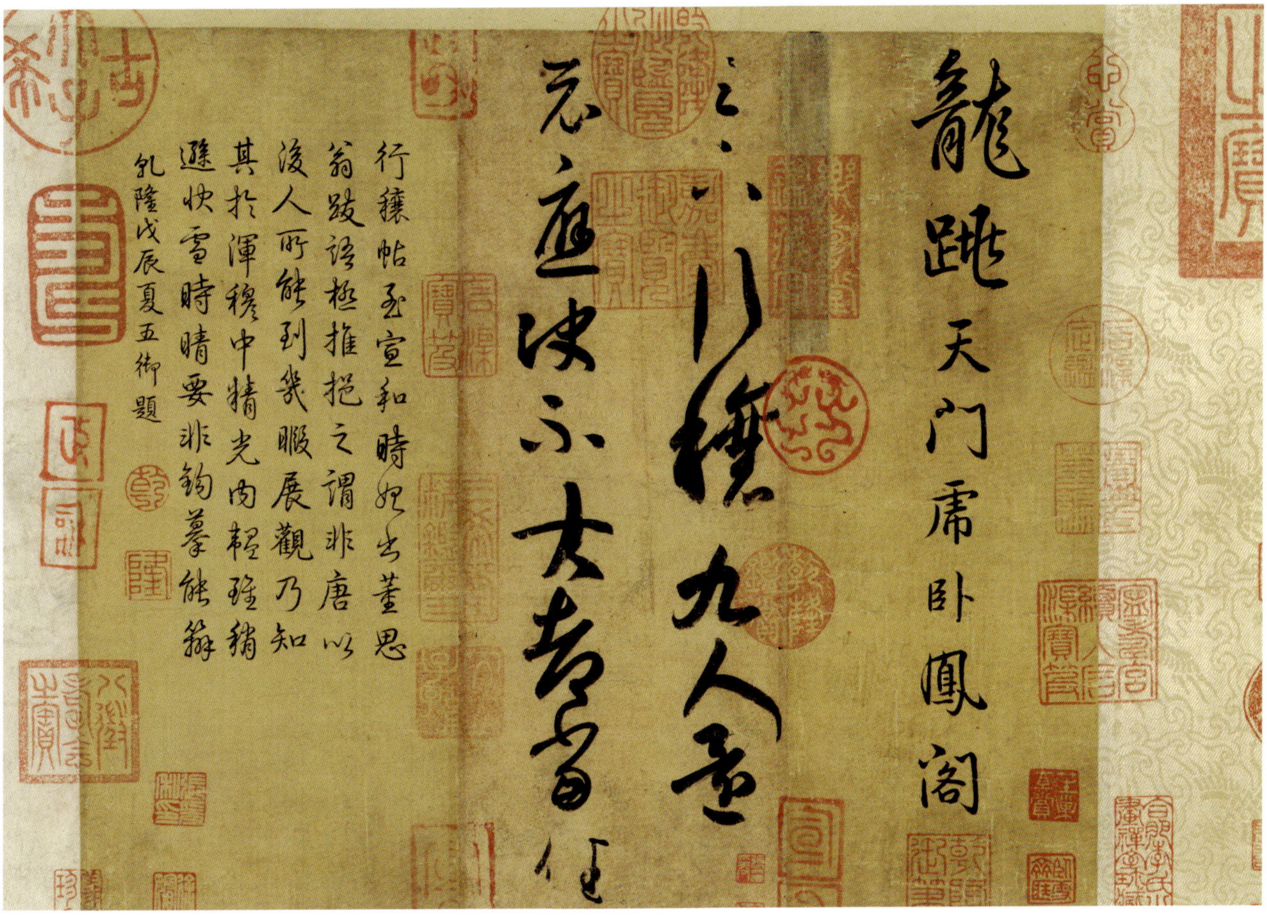

PUAM (1). Section (局部). Photo: Bruce M. White

this time.[37] As a piece of arcane calligraphy, it is unlikely *Ritual* would have been purloined by Western soldiers unless by accident; consequently, that the scroll surfaced in 1862 in the possession of Investigating Censer Zeng Xiejun, who openly impressed his seals on the scroll, suggests the possibility that the scroll may have left the palace collection as a gift.

Ritual to Pray for Good Harvest may then have passed through the possession, or inspection, of Jing Hengyi(?) (1877–1938), whose seals appear on the scroll.[38] Afterwards the scroll was owned by the Shanghai branch of the prominent Li family from Hefei. The seal of Li Jingbian (1876–1940; born to a concubine of the statesman Li Hongzhang) appears on the scroll and indicates that it was his acquisition. Following his death, his son Li Guochao sold the family's Shanghai real estate and moved to Hong Kong.[39] According to Zhang Daqian's 1957 colophon on the scroll, Cheng Ke'an (20th century; seals appear on the scroll) introduced him to the Li family of the Xiaohua Chanshi studio, from whom he purchased the scroll that winter for US$10,000. Zhang was in Tokyo for medical treatment of his eyes at the time, and his close friend in Hong Kong, the editor Gao Lingmei (20th century), made a special trip (*zhuan cheng*) there to bring *Ritual*.[40] The connoisseur Zhang Heng (1915–1963) examined the scroll some time before 1961, documenting its condition in detail.[41] Collotype reproductions of the scroll were made in 1962 by the publishing company Benridō (in Kyoto) and distributed by Bungadō (in Tokyo). Zhang Daqian then sold the scroll to "some Japanese collector" for the equivalent of about US$20,000.[42] At some point during its stay in Japan, the scroll spent half a year in the household of the calligrapher Nishigawa Yasushi (1902–1989), who published an article about *Ritual* in 1963.[43] By 1970 the scroll had entered John Elliott's collection through the Japanese rare book dealer Eda Yūji, the owner of Bungadō. Placed on anonymous loan at the Princeton University Art Museum, the scroll was remounted in the 1980s at the Asian art conservation studio of the Metropolitan Museum of Art and found a permanent home at Princeton in 1998.

(2)
赵孟頫 赵氏一门合札
Zhao Mengfu (1254–1322) et al.
Collected Letters of the Zhao Mengfu Family
Six letters mounted as a handscroll; ink on paper
a. Zhao Mengfu
Letter to Zhongfeng Mingben, 1321
29.5 x 50.2 cm
b. Zhao Mengfu
Letter to Shu Jibo, after 1310
27.7 x 49.6 cm
c. Guan Daosheng (1262–1319; wife), author
Zhao Mengfu, calligrapher
Letter to a Relative, after 1310
29.0 x 49.7 cm
d. Zhao Yong (1290–ca. 1362; son)
Letter to Gao Su, after 1330
32.6 x 61.8 cm
e. Zhao Yong
Letter to Gao Su, after 1330
30.0 x 51.9 cm
f. Zhao Youxi (act. late 13th–early 14th century; daughter)
Letter to Qiang Wenshi, 1319
28.3 x 42.4 cm
Princeton University Art Museum. Bequest of John B. Elliott, Class of 1951 (1998-54 a–f)

The *Collected Letters* by Zhao Mengfu family members were executed in the calligraphy style developed by Zhao through his study of Wang Xizhi. In the first letter, Zhao expresses gratitude to the Chan monk Zhongfeng Mingben (1263–1323) for having arranged services on the death anniversary of his wife Guan Daosheng. The funeral arrangements are the topic of the sixth letter, possibly the only surviving example of calligraphy from the couple's eldest daughter, Zhao Youxi, to her husband. Guan Daosheng's signature appears on the third letter, but it is thought to have been written on her behalf, without her knowledge, by Zhao Mengfu;[44] it congratulates a female relative on the homecoming of a son who had achieved official rank. The letters of the second son, Zhao Yong, offer apologies to a friend. In one letter, after being late with a painting commission, Zhao Yong asks an acquaintance to put in a good word for him with his high-ranking father.[45]

The six letters bear different sets of collector seals, including those of Xiang Yuanbian, Liang Qingbiao (1620–1691), and the Qianlong, Jiaqing, and Xuantong (r. 1909–1911) emperors. Only the seals of Liang Qingbiao appear on all six, suggesting the letters were probably all first mounted into this handscroll when they were in Liang's possession. Because the scroll is recorded in the imperial catalogue *Shiqu baoji chubian*, it must have entered the Qing imperial collection by 1745; it is listed as being stored in the Forbidden City's Yushu Fang.[46] The seal of the Xuantong emperor indicates that the scroll remained in the palace collection until the fall of dynasty. By the time the last emperor, Puyi, left the Forbidden City in 1924, he had arranged to take many works, including *Collected Letters*, along with him eventually to Tianjin and then in 1932 to Changchun, where they were deposited in the Xiaobai Lou (Small White House).[47] With Japan's defeat, Puyi departed Changchun in August 1945 with selected treasures. Subsequently, many of the remaining treasures sealed in the Xiaobai Lou were illicitly appropriated by soldiers and opportunists.[48] *Collected Letters* was probably among these prizes and, according to Yang Renkai, found its way to the Changchun dealer Li Zhifu, who sold it to Jin Bosheng and Jin Yunqing, the owners of the Lunchizhai gallery in Beijing.[49] The Jins, who handled at least twenty-seven of these "northeast goods" (*dongbei huo*), in turn sold the scroll to the Shanghai collector Tan Jing (1911–1991), who later took the scroll to Hong Kong.[50] John Elliott had acquired this scroll by 1970, when he first placed it on loan at the Princeton University Art Museum.

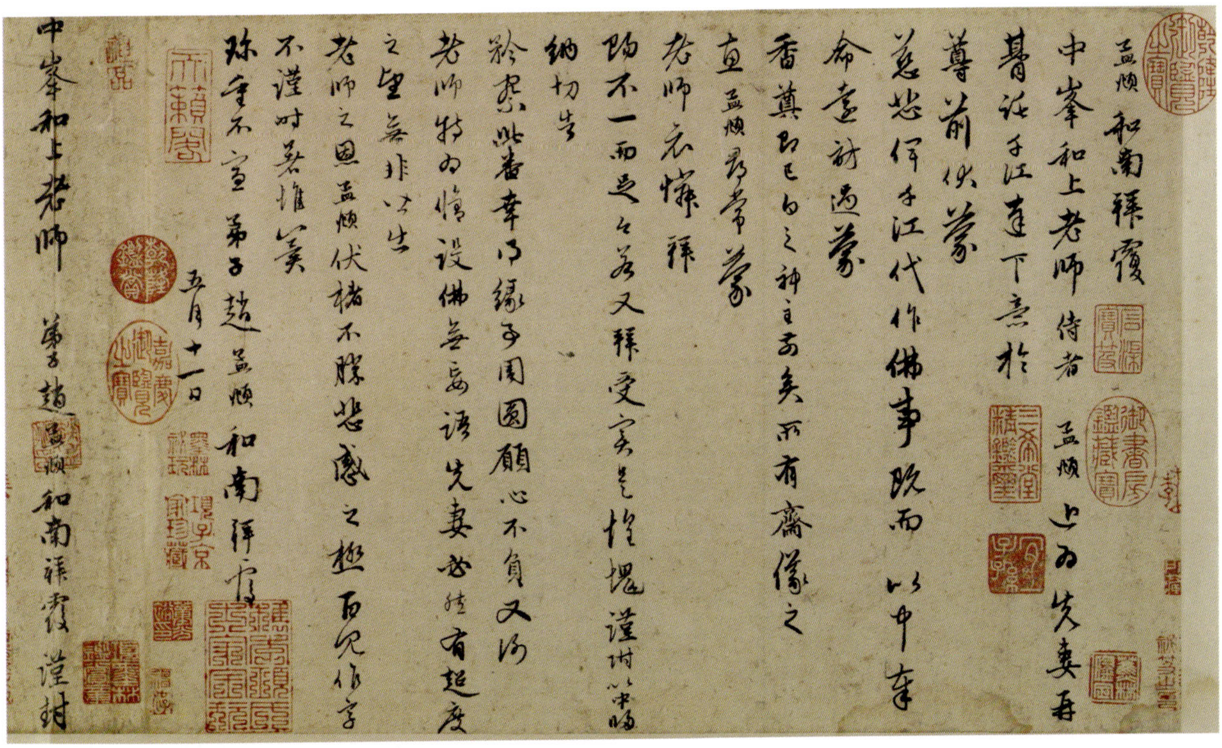

PUAM (2). Section (局部), letter 札 a: Zhao Mengfu 赵孟頫, *Letter to Zhongfeng Mingben* 与中峰明本 (1321), 29.5 x 50.2 cm. Photo: Bruce M. White

(3)
柯九思 上京宫词
Ke Jiusi (1290–1343)
***Shangjing Palace Poems*, ca. 1331–38**
Handscroll; ink on paper
30.5 x 53.0 cm
Princeton University Art Museum. Bequest of John B. Elliott, Class of 1951 (1998-55)

Ke Jiusi came from a family of scholar officials. At the Yuan capital, Dadu (present-day Beijing), he rose to prominence during the reign of Emperor Wenzong (r. 1328–32), who founded the Hall of Literature (Kuizhang Ge), a palace institution devoted to preserving Chinese artistic and literary culture. Ke served as a connoisseur of calligraphy and artistic advisor in the Hall, and he composed "Palace Poems" while in office. After Ke Jiusi retired to southern China, he transcribed five of these poems in this calligraphy for the Buddhist monk Wuyan.[51] The imagery of virtuous rulers and imperial rituals in this scroll, written in small-standard (*xiaokai*) script, recalls his days as a favored member of Wenzong's court.[52]

It is difficult to reconstruct the collection history of this scroll and to determine when, or if, it entered and exited the Qing imperial collection. Collector and viewer seals on the scroll include those of Xiang Yuanbian, Wu Zhaonan (Ming dynasty), Nian Gengyao (d. 1726), Chen Maoben (*zi*: Jixun; *juren* degree, 1792), Chen Yiben (late 18th–early19th century), Wu Zuoyu(?), Jin Chuansheng (act. Daoguang reign, 1821–50), Liu Dingzhen (20th century),[53] Tan Jing (1911–1991), Zhang Heng (1915–1963), and several that are unidentified. The scroll also has colophons by Liu Yong (1719–1804), dated 1787; Weng Fanggang (1733–1818), undated; Tiebao (1752–1824), dated 1789; Chen Chongben (*jinshi* degree, 1775), dated 1790, which notes that the calligraphy had been cut and mounted as an album; Chen Maoben (who remounted the album leaves as a handscroll), dated 1794; and Wang Wenzhi (1730–1802), dated 1800. During the Ming period, the scroll was in Xiang Yuanbian's collection and was apparently owned or viewed by Wu Zhaonan. During the Qing, it apparently passed though the

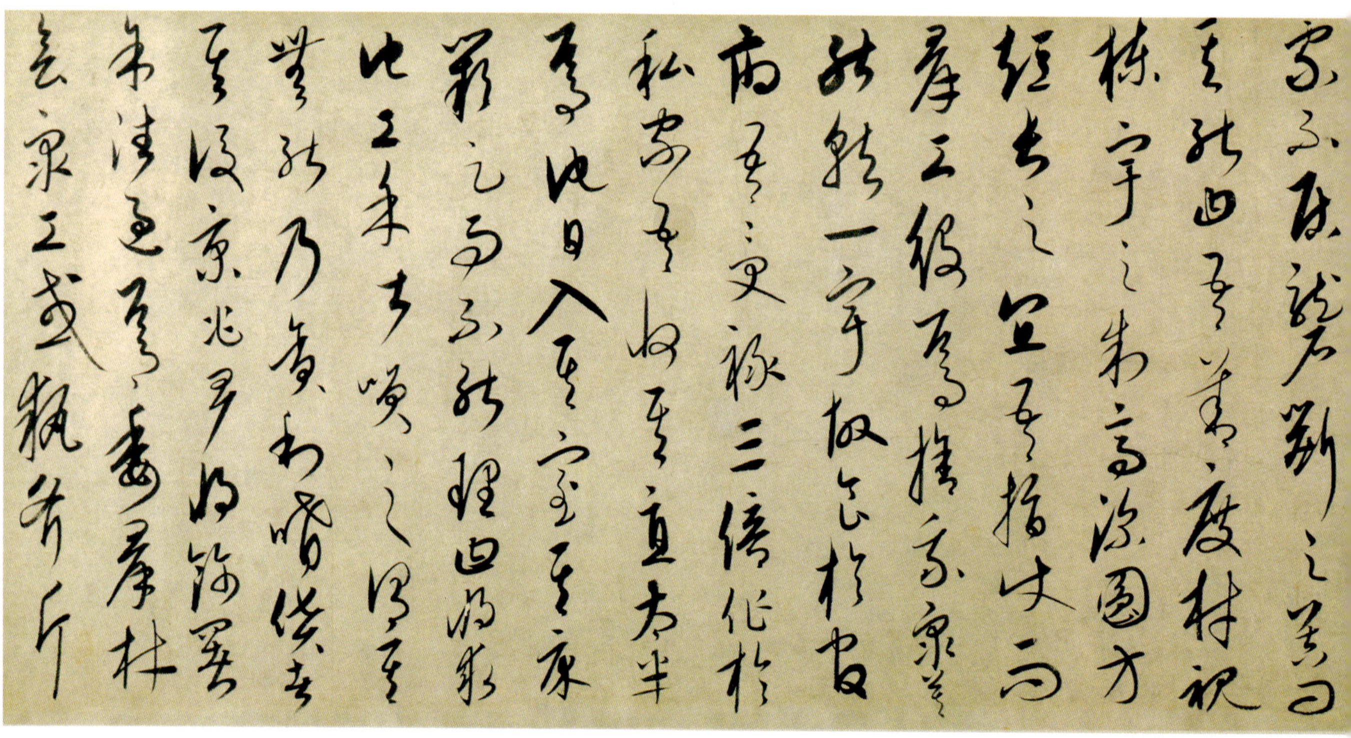

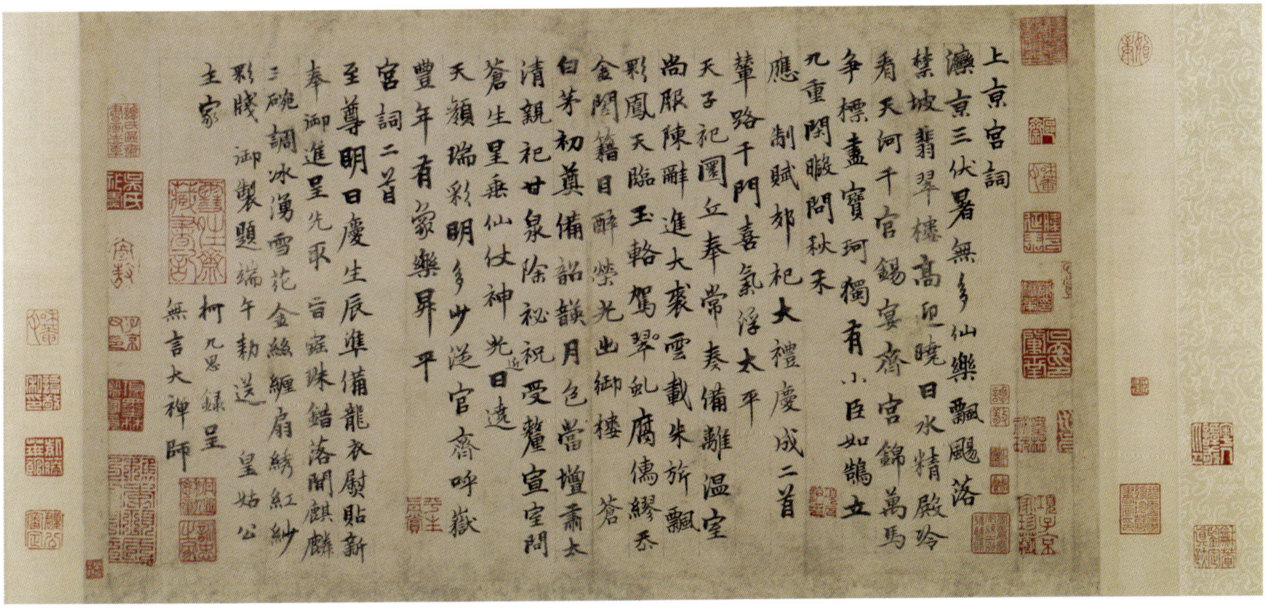

hands of Nian Gengyao, Liu Yong, Weng Fanggang, Tiebao, the three Chen brothers (Chen Chongben, Chen Maoben, and Chen Yiben), and Wang Wenzhi in 1800. The scroll was still in private hands when Jin Chuansheng added his seals during the Daoguang reign. According to Yang Renkai this handscroll, and similarly Kangli Naonao's (1295–1345) *Biography of a Carpenter* (*Ziren zhuan*, fig. 1),[54] entered the Qing palaces, but there are no imperial seals and no listing in the *Shiqu baoji sanbian* (third edition, 1817).[55] It is possible that *Shangjing Palace Poems* entered the palace after the *Shiqu baoji sanbian*'s compilation and after the addition of Jin Chuansheng's seals. The phoenix-and-cloud patterned silk damask mounted before and after the calligraphy resembles Qing palace mounting and may indicate that the scroll was indeed part of the imperial collection during the second half of the nineteenth century. Although the still unidentified seals make it hard to know the scroll's history in the nineteenth and early twentieth century, it is likely that Tan Jing acquired it in the late 1940s and brought it with him to Hong Kong. The connoisseur Zhang Heng possibly viewed the scroll at about this time. The scroll was acquired by John Elliott and first placed on loan at the Princeton University Art Museum in 1970.[56]

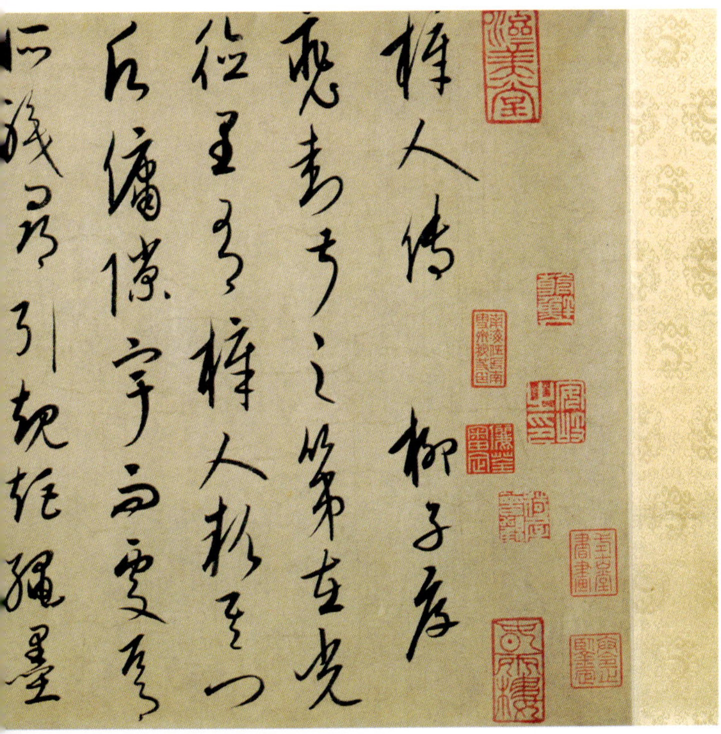

▲ PUAM (3). Section (局部). Photo: Bruce M. White

◄ Fig. 1. Kangli Naonao 康里夒夒 (1295–1345), *Biography of a Carpenter* (*Ziren zhuan*) 梓人传, 1331. Section (局部). Handscroll; ink on paper, 27.8 x 281.0 cm. Princeton University Art Museum. Gift of John B. Elliott, Class of 1951, in honor of Lucy L. Lo (y1985-11). Photo: Bruce M. White

(4)
俞和　临乐毅论
Yu He (1307–1382)
***Essay on Yue Yi*, 1360**
Handscroll; ink on paper
24.7 x 68.5 cm
Princeton University Art Museum. Bequest of
John B. Elliott, Class of 1951 (1998-76)

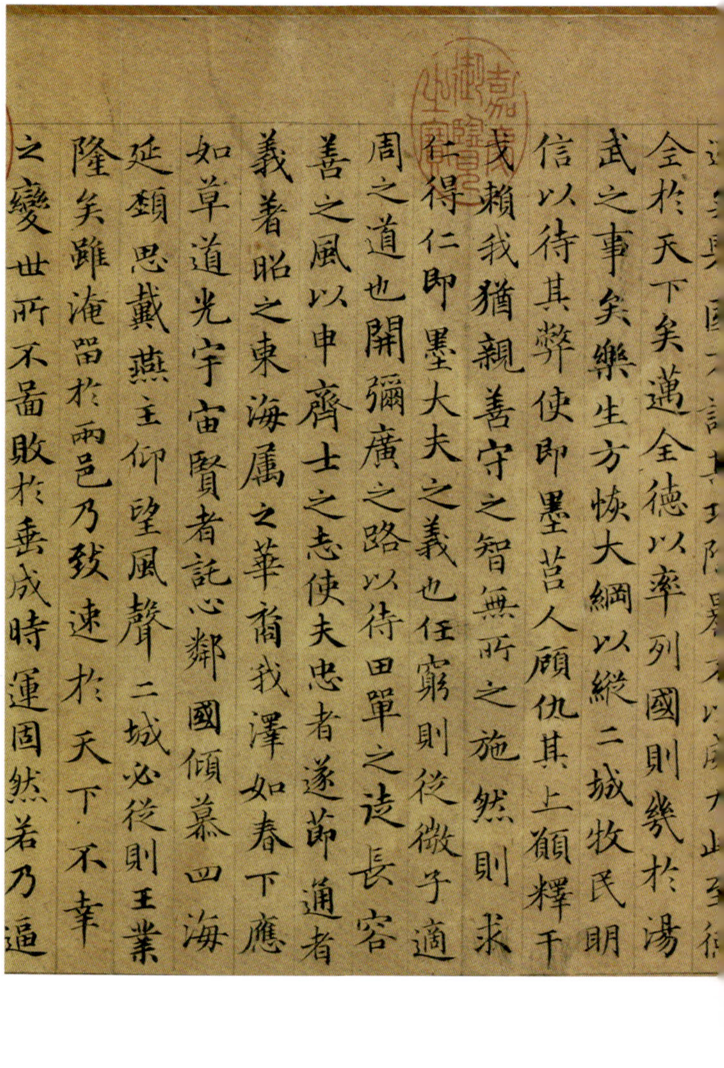

The "Essay on Yue Yi," composed by Xiahou Xuan (209–254), discusses the virtues of the Warring States period (ca. 470–221 BCE) general Yue Yi. Yu He's *Essay on Yue Yi* is based on a model of small-standard-script calligraphy attributed to Wang Xizhi. Personalized with greater liveliness and fluidity of the brushed characters, Yu He's style appears to have also been influenced by the small-standard script of Zhao Mengfu, whose calligraphy he also studied.[57]

The scroll has several collector and viewer seals, including those of Xiang Yuanbian, Gu Congde (late Ming–early Qing dynasty), Geng Zhaozhong (1640–1686), Wu Kuntian (Qing dynasty), the Qianlong emperor, Jiaqing emperor, Xuantong emperor, and a few that are unidentified. In addition there are two colophons by Wen Congjian (1574–1648), dated 1631, and one by Nian Gengyao (d. 1726). The scroll was recorded in the *Shiqu baoji chubian* as being stored in the Forbidden City's Yangxin Dian hall, indicating that it had entered the imperial collection by 1745. The *Shiqu baoji* entry documents all the non-imperial seals and colophons on the scroll, but for some reason it omits Nian Gengyao's pre-1726 colophon.[58]

Essay on Yue Yi left the palace collection with Puyi and traveled to Changchun. According to Yang Renkai, after World War II *Essay* went into the hands of the dealer Chang Boxiang of Changchun, who sold it to Mu Panchen of Beijing; later, while in the possession of Zhang Dingchen, it was taken to Hong Kong.[59] John Elliott had acquired the scroll by 1970, when he first placed it on loan to the Princeton University Art Museum.

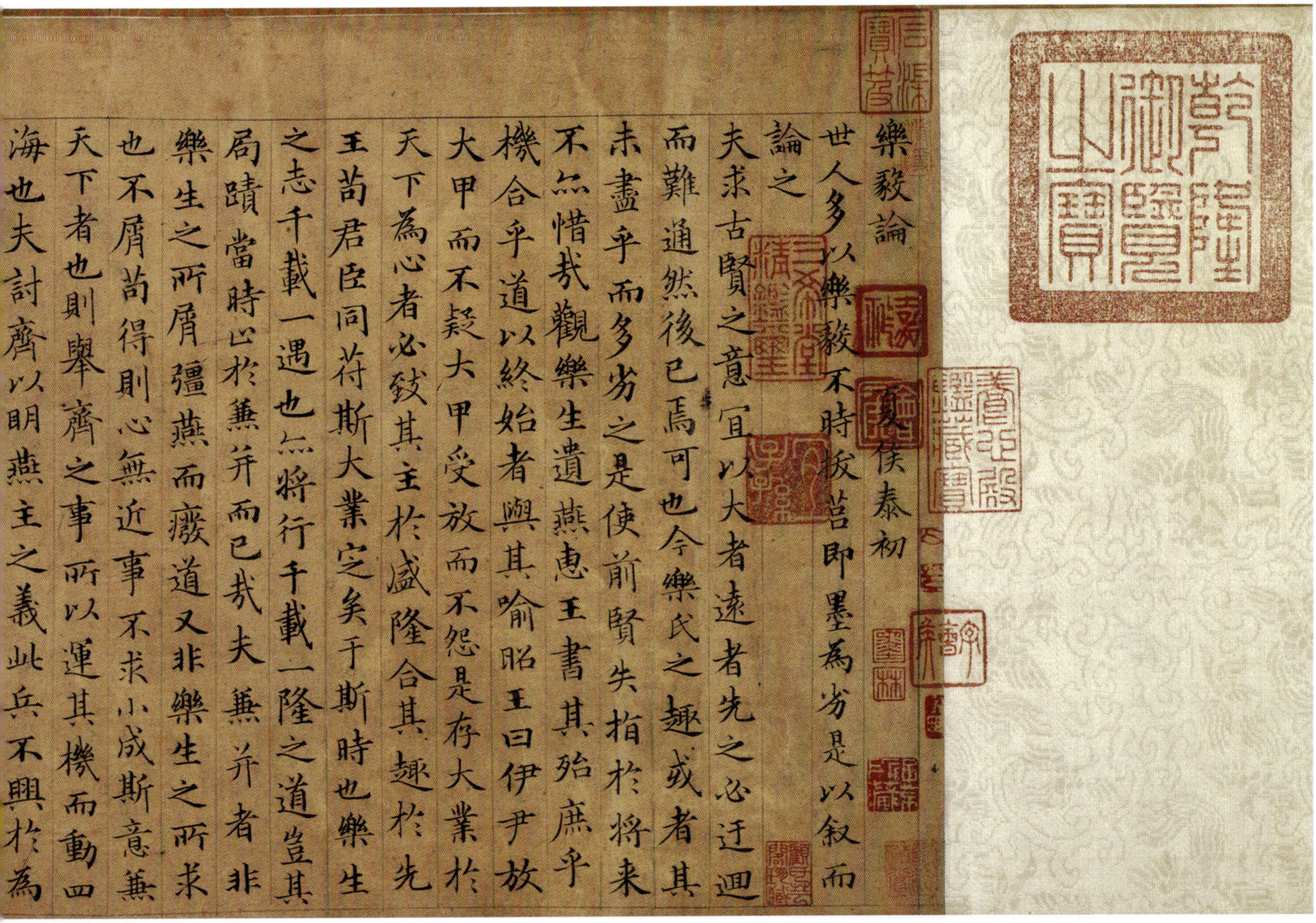

PUAM (4). Section(局部). Photo: Bruce M. White

(5)
传宋克　陶潜诗并画竹石小景
Song Ke (1327–1387), attributed to
"Tao Qian's Poems" and *"Bamboo and Rocks,"* 1370

Handscroll; ink on paper
Calligraphy 25.9 x 627.9 cm; painting 25.9 x 151.0 cm
Princeton University Art Museum. Bequest of John B. Elliott, Class of 1951 (1998-106)

Song Ke was one of the leading calligraphers of the late Yuan and early Ming. Following Zhao Mengfu in his study and practice of calligraphy, he blended standard (*kaishu*), running, and draft-cursive (*zhangcao*) scripts. This handscroll combines Song Ke's transcription of twenty-eight poems by Tao Qian (Tao Yuanming; 365–427), three artist's inscriptions (each dated 1370), and an ink painting of bamboo and rocks.[60] Collector and viewer seals include those of Zhou Zhaolü (Ming dynasty?), Gu Yuntao (Ming dynasty?),[61] Wu Bing (d. 1646), Bian Yongyu (1645–1712), the Qianlong emperor, Jiaqing emperor, and Xuantong emperor, Song Bangyi (dates unknown), and some that have yet to be identified.

The authenticity of this scroll, which was in the Qing imperial collection, has been questioned. In Bian Yongyu's painting and calligraphy catalogue, *Shigutang shuhua huikao*, the text of the copied poems and artist's inscriptions are transcribed, and the seals are also documented.[62] The seals in the calligraphy section of the present scroll agree with Bian's record up to the paper joint with the painting. In the painting section, several seals—including those of Gu Yuntao and Wu Bing—that should have been recorded are not; many of these same seals are found on the calligraphy section and their presence recorded by Bian. So why are they absent from his painting description? In addition, some repeated seals found in both painting and calligraphy sections appear slightly different when compared.

There are also problems in the numerical notation of the paper sheets in the scroll. There are two sets of numbers. One group (1–5) marks the original, longer sheets of paper and is noted in faint ink at the bottom left corner of each sheet; for example, "1" is to be found below the second "Shigutang" joint seal. The second set of numbers (1–8) corresponds to each appearance of the "Shigutang" joint seal and was likely added when the scroll was remounted in Bian Yongyu's collection. These numbers are located in the bottom right corner of each recut sheet. For example, "1" is found on the bottom right corner at the beginning of the scroll, and the subsequent

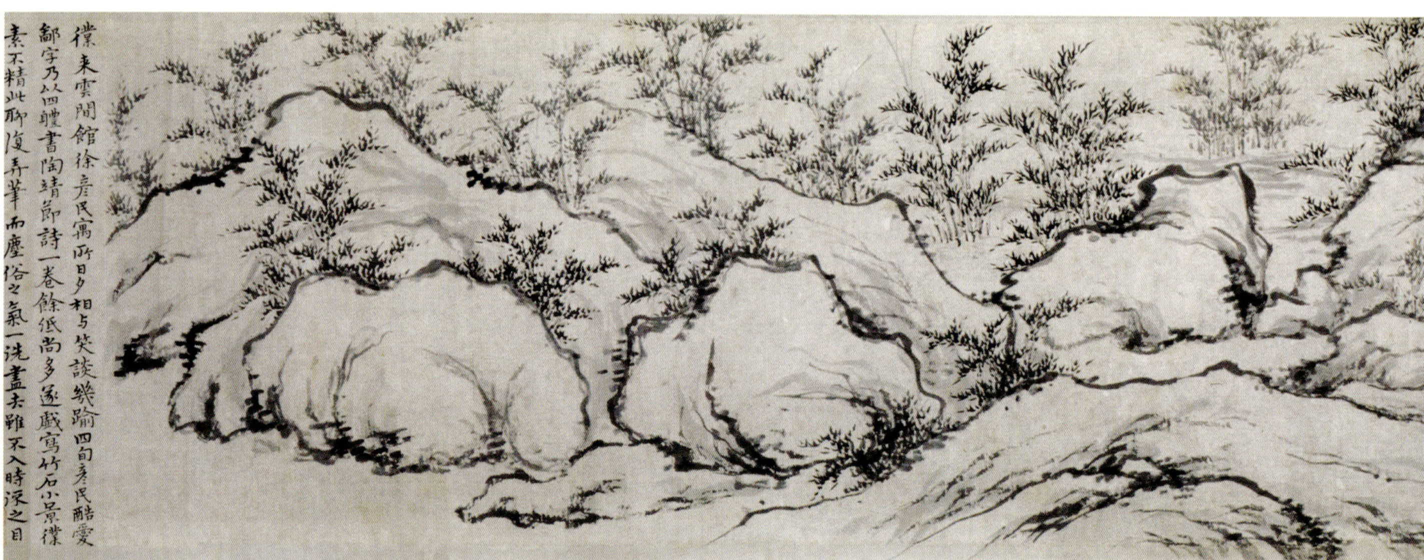

numbers are found below each joint seal. The only exception occurs on the last sheet—the painting section—from which both sets of numbers are missing. A possible explanation is that the end section was cut off, and the present painting may be a later copy spliced onto the original calligraphy. There is some speculation that this painting may actually be a retouched underlayer copy of the original. Such an underlayer, separated from the original top layer during remounting, may not have retained traces of sheet numbers lightly inked on the surface.[63]

This handscroll needs to be examined alongside another version with forty-eight poems and without Qing imperial seals that is now in the collection of the Palace Museum, Beijing. According to Xiao Yanyi, the calligraphy on both scrolls is by the same hand, but not that of Song Ke. As for the painting, in Xiao's judgment the Beijing work is superior; however, through comparison with other Song Ke paintings that are accepted as authentic, Xiao concludes that both the Beijing and Princeton paintings are copies done by different hands. He speculates that Qian Bo (*jinshi*, 1445), a student of Song Ke, brushed several copies of the calligraphy in Song Ke's style, some complete, some incomplete. However, since Qian Bo was not a painter, he had to enlist different painters to execute the scene of bamboo and rocks.[64]

Regardless of the handscroll's attribution to Song Ke or a later copyist, it is this scroll that had entered the Qing imperial collection by 1745, when it was recorded in the *Shiqu baoji chubian* as being stored in the Forbidden City's Yushu Fang hall.[65] Remaining in the palace after the Xuantong era, Puyi removed the scroll as a gift to Pujie on January 8, 1923 (ed.: converted to Gregorian).[66] After World War II it was sold by the wife of the Guomindang official Duan Kewen,[67] and the scroll likely made its way to Hong Kong, where it was published in *A Garland of Chinese Painting* (1967).[68] John Elliott had acquired the scroll by 1973, when it was placed on loan at the Princeton University Art Museum.

PUAM (5). Section (局部), *Bamboo and Rocks* 竹石小景.
Photo: Bruce M. White

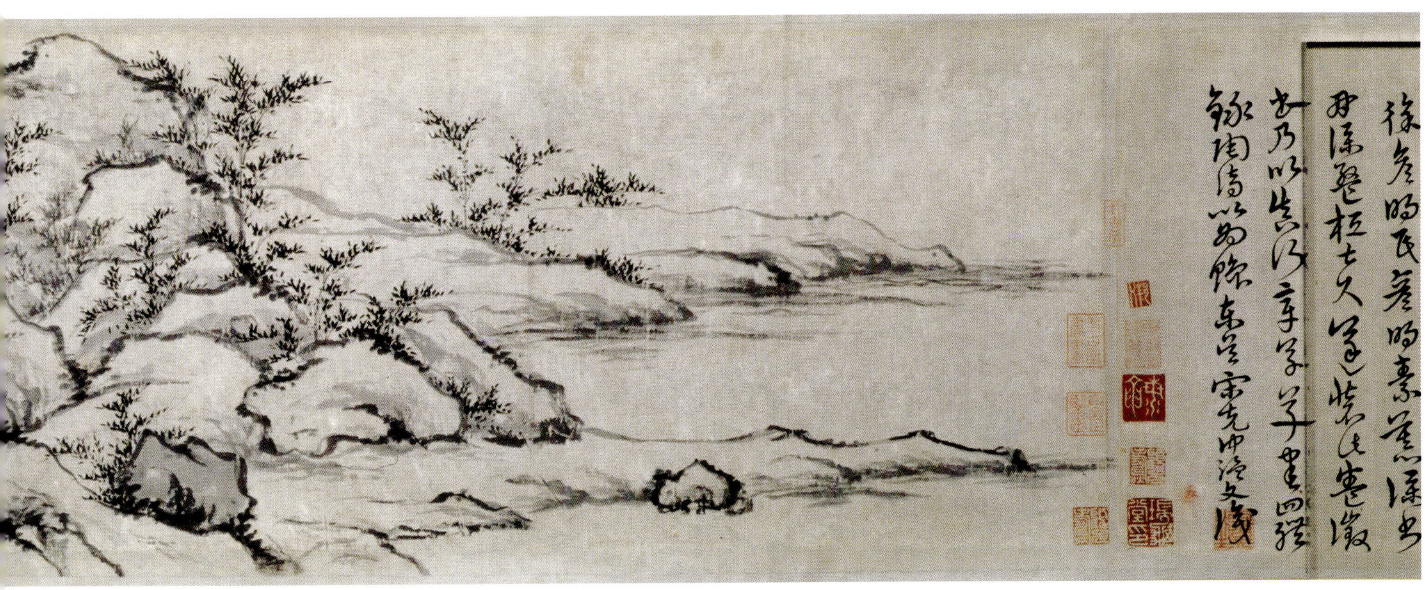

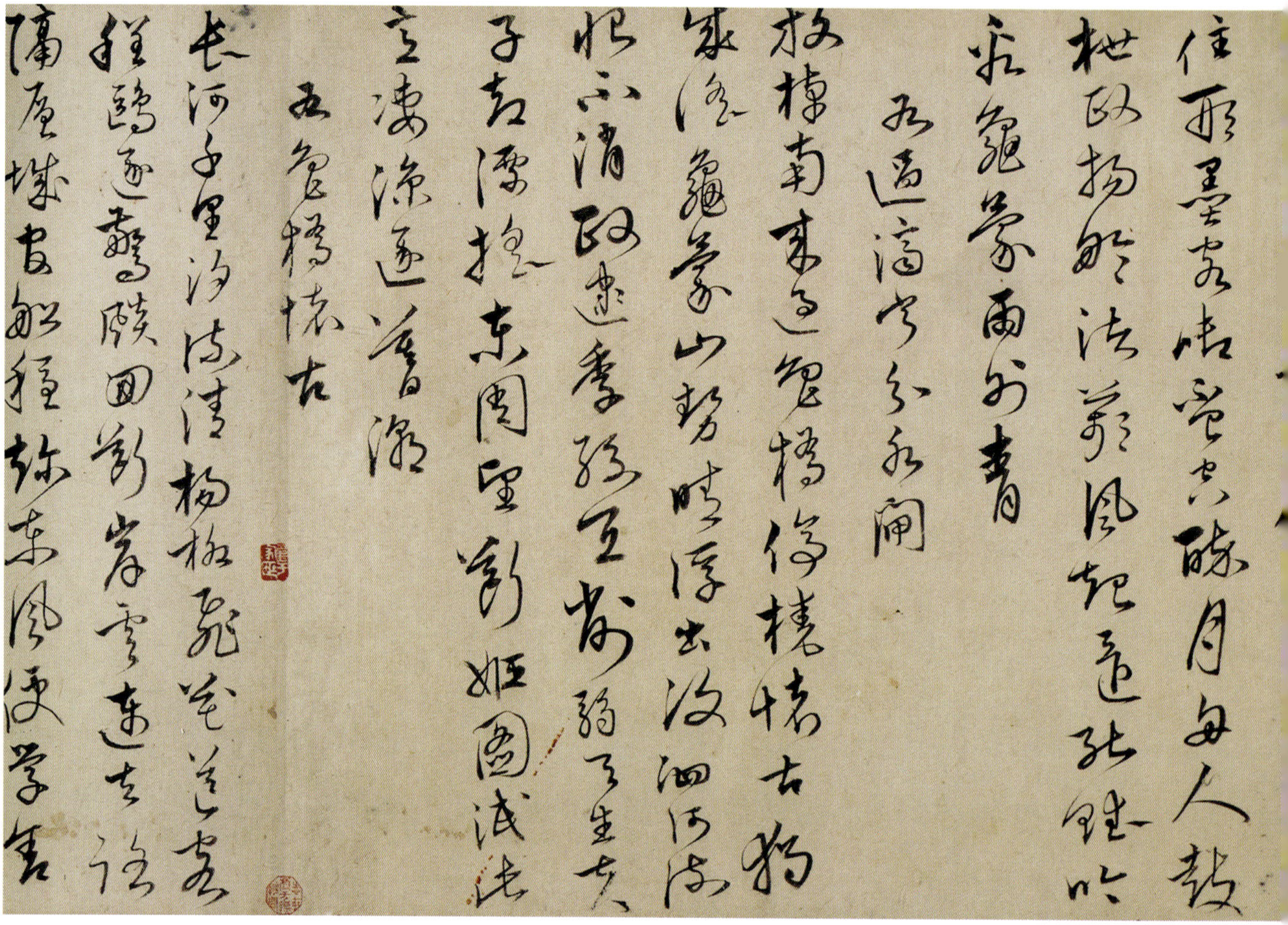

(6)
沈粲和沈度 诗书
Shen Can (1379–1453) and Shen Du (1357–1434)
Collected Poems
Handscroll; ink on paper
Shen Can, 28.0 x 152.4 cm; Shen Du, 25.9 x 86.1 cm
Princeton University Art Museum. Bequest of
John B. Elliott, Class of 1951 (1998-57)

The brothers Shen Du and Shen Can served at court and excelled in calligraphy, prose, and poetry. Song Ke, whose work they owned, influenced their calligraphy; together they became known as the Three Songs of the early Ming. While the younger Shen Can was known for writing in cursive script, this is a rare example of Shen Du's ability in this form. The brothers also developed a distinctive standard-script style known as the Chancellery (*Taige ti*) or Academy (*Guange ti*) style, which was used in imperial documents.[69]

In the first section, writing in a draft cursive, Shen Can transcribed eight poems he composed on his 1426 return from Beijing to his home in Songjiang. In the following section, writing in both draft cursive and standard script, Shen Du transcribed a preface and seven poems (the fifth written twice, once in cursive and once in standard script) by the Southern Song philosopher Zhu Xi (1130–1200).[70] The differing paper heights in each section, as well as the lack of any textual relationship, indicates that the brothers probably did not collaborate on this scroll. Instead, some later collector most likely remounted these two sections together.

Collector and viewer seals on the scroll include those of Zhu Zhichi (Ming dynasty), Zhang Yingtian (Qing dynasty), and the Qianlong, Jiaqing, and Xuantong emperors. The official, painter, and calligrapher Zhang Zhao (1691–1745) added two colophons. In the first, he notes that the scroll had once been owned by Zhu Zhichi and Gao Shiqi (1645–1703). Zhang also

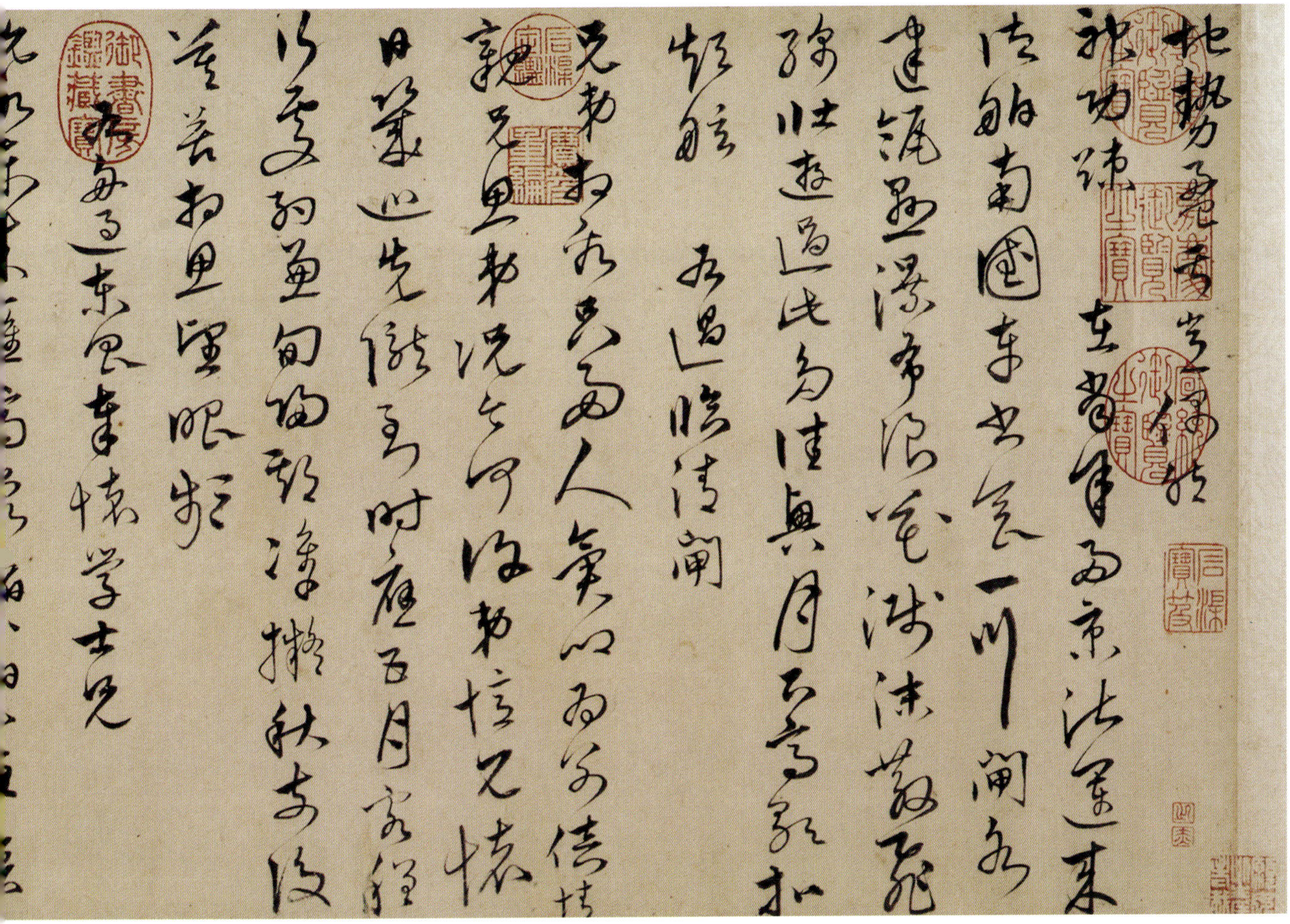

PUAM (6). Section (局部), Calligraphy by Shen Can 沈粲之诗书.
Photo: Bruce M. White

points out that in Shen Du's transcription of the preface, the character for the number of poems had first been replaced by "eight" (*ba*), which was then erased and left blank. He also suspects that Shen's signature "Du" after the seventh poem was added, suggesting the scroll had once included additional poems from the original set of twenty, and that a dealer may have cut them off to create a separate work. In the second colophon, dated 1738, Zhang Zhao comments that the scroll had been in his family for three reign periods. The scroll had then found its way into the Qing imperial collection by 1793, when it was recorded in the *Shiqu baoji xubian*.[71] After remaining in the palace beyond the end of the Xuantong reign, Puyi removed the scroll as a gift to Pujie on January 4, 1923 (ed.: converted to Gregorian).[72] The scroll likely traveled to Changchun with Puyi and entered the market after World War II. John Elliott had acquired the scroll by 1970, when it was placed on loan at the Princeton University Art Museum.[73]

(7)
佚名 梨花山雀
Anonymous (14th century)
Pear Blossoms and Bird
Hanging scroll; ink and color on paper
91.5 x 30.7 cm
Princeton University Art Museum. Bequest of John B. Elliott, Class of 1951 (1998-108)

In the imperial catalogue *Shiqu baoji chubian* (1745), *Pear Blossoms and Bird* is recorded as a painting by the master Huang Quan (903–968), whose spurious signature is hidden in the tree branch along the lower right.[74] Recent scholarship now attributes this scroll to a fourteenth-century follower from southern China working in the Qian Xuan (ca. 1235–after 1300) style. The painting's composition exemplifies the genre of early flower-and-bird painting: a single bird on a flowering branch. Here, the painter is particularly interested in color, patterns, and surface texture employed with a sense of decoration.

The earliest collector seals on the painting belong to the Ming dynasty connoisseur Xiang Yuanbian. After entering the Qing imperial collection, the scroll is recorded in the *Shiqu baoji chubian* as being stored inside the Forbidden City's Yangxin Dian hall. The *Shiqu baoji* description records a "poetry hall" (*shitang*) header with an eleven-character inscription by Dong Qichang, which is now missing. Chen Rentao (1906–1968) speculates that this inscription was either later removed because it was considered spurious or was lost.[75] The *Shiqu baoji* entry does mention the title-slip inscription by the Qianlong emperor, now mounted at the painting's upper right. However, it does not record the emperor's 1758 inscription on the painting nor the spurious Huang Quan signature, nor does it mention several imperial seals of the Qianlong, Jiaqing, and Xuantong emperors. This is probably because these elements were all added after the *Shiqu baoji* entry. The imperial seals indicate the painting remained in the palace collection until the Xuantong reign at the very end of the dynasty. After leaving the palace, the painting had found its way into the collection of Chen Rentao by 1956, when it was included in three of Chen's publications.[76] John Elliott had acquired the painting by 1978, when it was placed on loan at the Princeton University Art Museum.

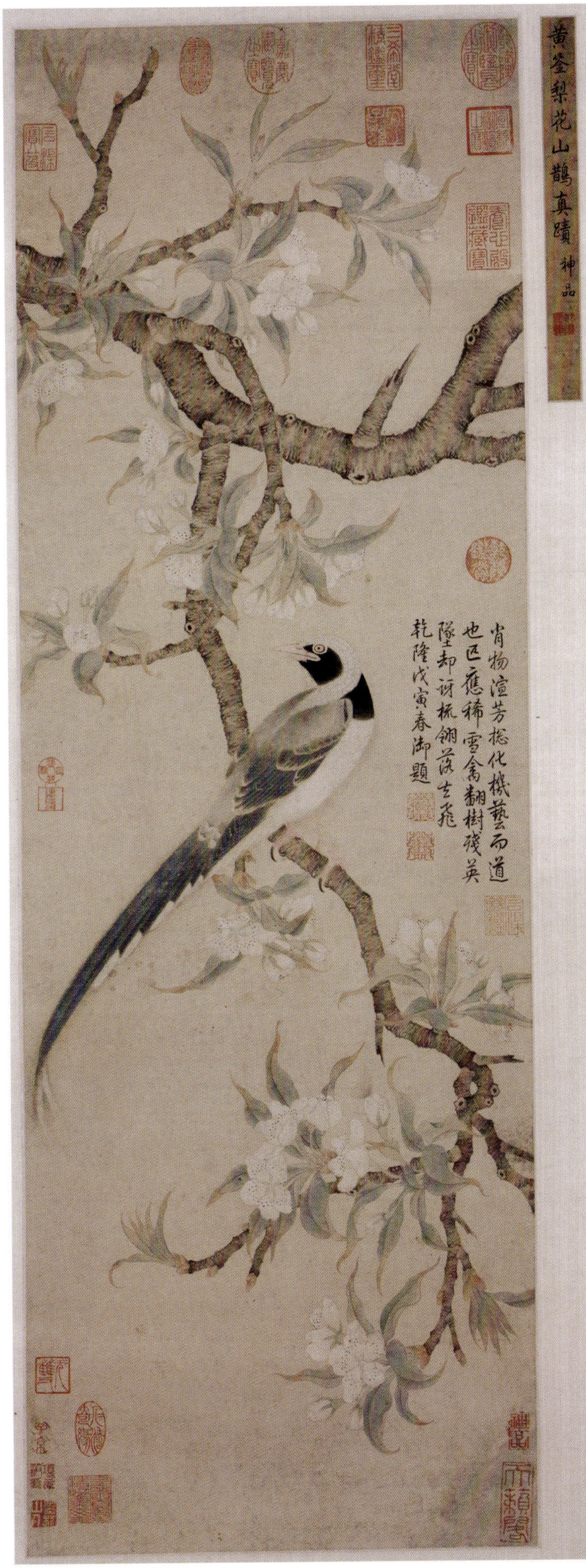

PUAM (7) Photo: Bruce M. White

(8)
清乾隆皇帝弘历 夏卉八香图
Qianlong emperor (Hongli, 1711–1799; r. 1736–95)
***Eight Fragrant Summer Flowers*, 1759**
Handscroll; ink on paper
28.3 x 98.0 cm; frontispiece: 28.4 x 72.6 cm
Princeton University Art Museum. The Arthur M. Sackler Collection (y1968-225)

Beginning with a love for flower-and-bird painting, the Qianlong emperor learned to paint at age nineteen. Here, after a summer stroll through a garden after rain, the emperor is inspired to paint and compose poems for eight fragrant summer flowers. He paints with deliberate yet tremulous lines and graded wash over a faint charcoal sketch, adopting a style associated with the amateurism of literati painting. Like the emperor, many high officials, such as Zou Yigui (1686–1772) and Jiang Tingxi (1669–1732), also painted bird and flower themes. That they were painted by ministers and emperors cannot be overlooked. The painting of flowers recreates the act of gardening and may allude to a passage in the *Analects*: when Confucius was asked how to garden, he deferred to a humble gardener. Like a gardener correctly naming and ordering plants in a garden, a virtuous ruler similarly had to recognize that each individual has his own role and place. The painting of flowers, fruits, or vegetables, therefore, may have been meant to represent an act of humility and virtue.[77]

The *Shiqu baoji xubian* (1793) records that this scroll was stored in the Ying Tai pavilion of the Western Garden (Xi Yuan).[78] The original palace mounting is preserved along with a

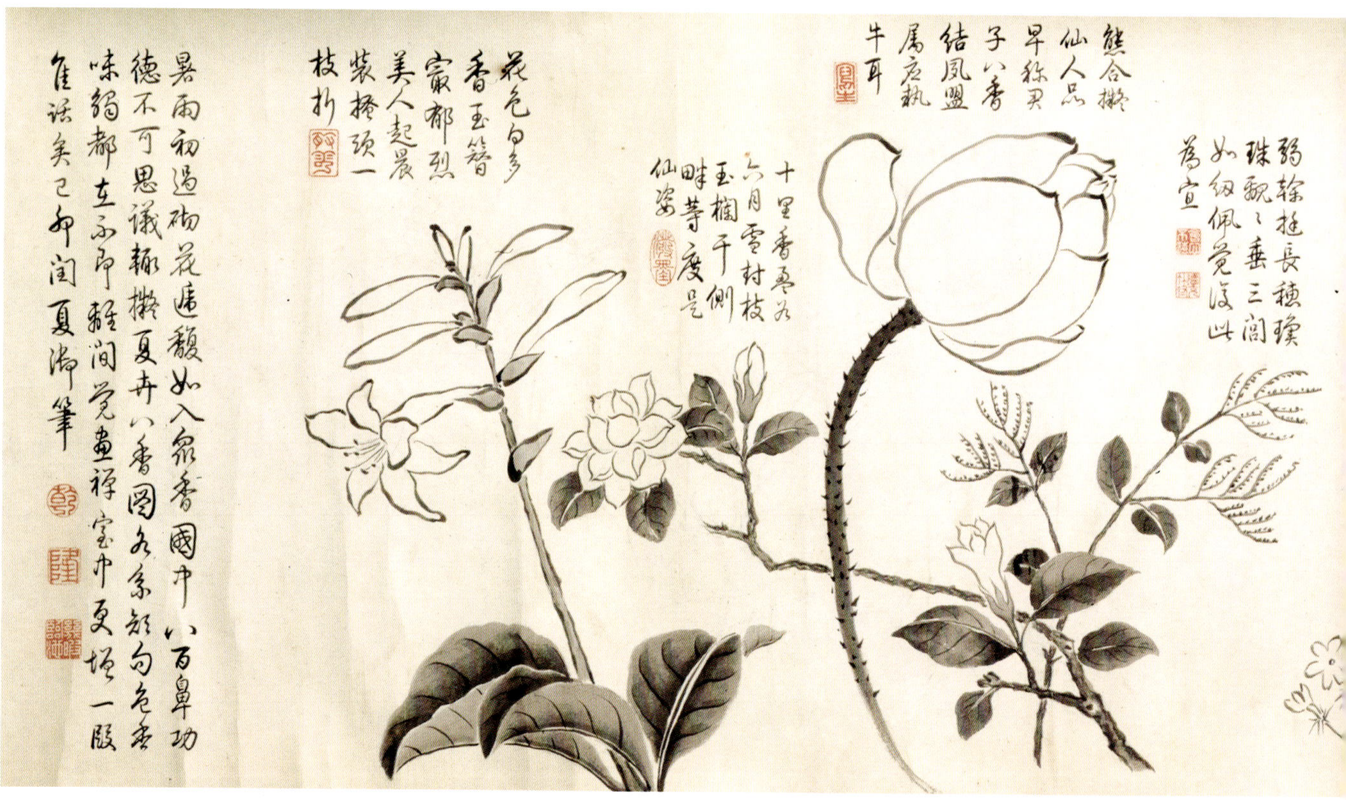

jade clasp with the carved and gilt title inscription "Eight Fragrant Summer Flowers" and a frontispiece with four running-script characters brushed by the Qianlong emperor. There are nineteen imperial seals of the Qianlong emperor on the scroll. No other collectors' seals or colophons are found, leaving little information about how it left the palace and where it had traveled before being acquired from the New York dealer Frank Caro by the Princeton University Art Museum.

PUAM (8). Photo: Bruce M. White

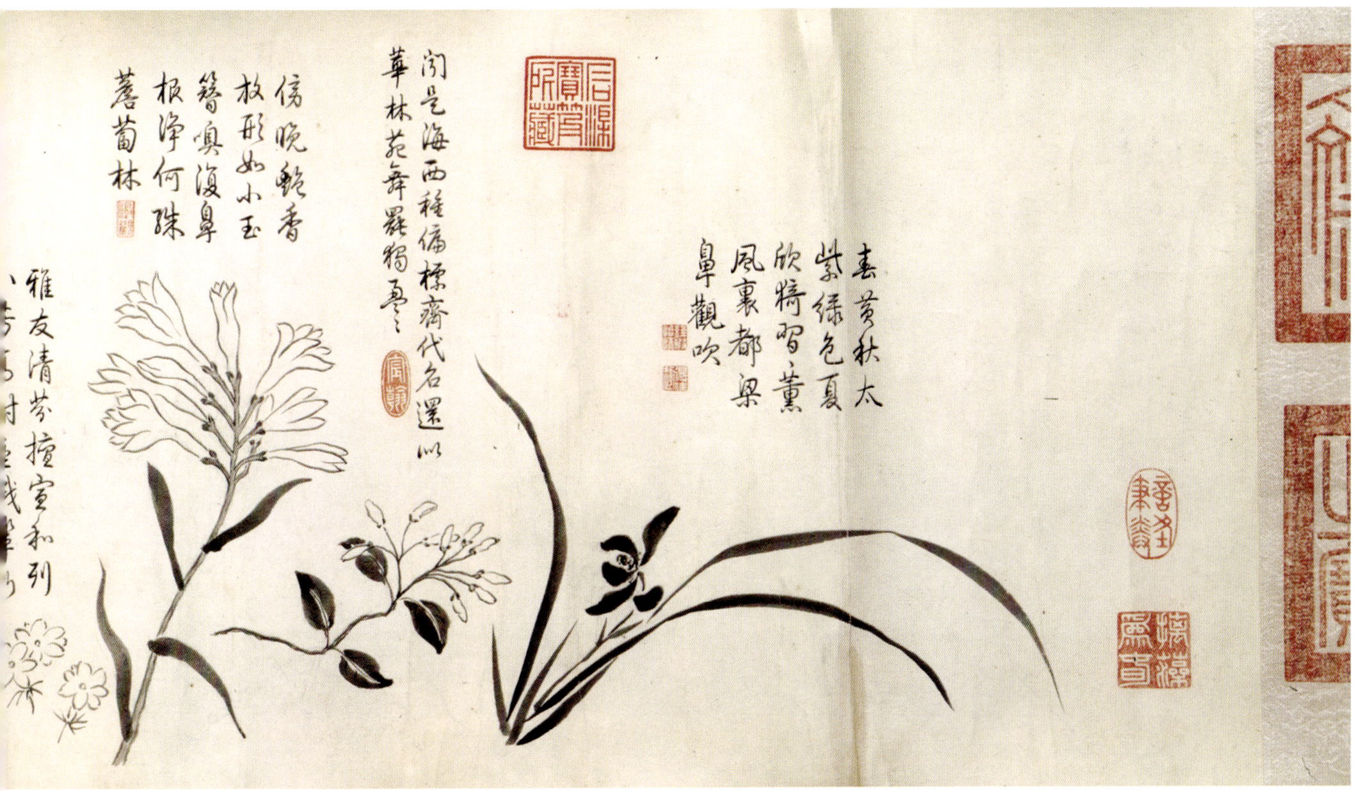

Coda

It is remarkable and indeed fortunate that the above works of art and others from the Qing imperial collection have found a home so far away from their country of origin.[79] Almost all were acquired outside China proper during the height of the Cultural Revolution, when appreciation for such "useless things" in China and abroad was relatively limited. It is largely through a familiarity over time and the growing global influence of Asian culture that Chinese art now is less and less viewed as mere exotica. However, such "strangers in a strange land" should also never expect to be "grokked" (to achieve complete intuitive understanding) by their new audiences.[80] Still it is the awareness of such "eternally incomprehensible" things, recognized on whatever level, that permits an appreciation of an aesthetics of "diversity, the knowledge that something is other than one's self."[81]

Notes

1. For the history of Asian art at the museum, this section draws from the author's "Asian Art Collection: From Exotica to Art and History," *Record of The Art Museum, Princeton University* 55, nos. 1–2 (1996): 125–34.
2. The use of such exhibitions as cultural diplomacy is discussed in Warren Cohen, *East Asian Art and American Culture: A Study in International Relations* (New York: Columbia University Press, 1992). At the Philadelphia Centennial, Japanese and Chinese art were shown as crafts in the Industrial Hall.
3. Wen Fong, "George Rowley, 1893–1962," *Artibus Asiae* 25, nos. 2–3 (1962): 195–96.
4. Berthold Laufer, *Catalogue of a Collection of Chinese Paintings in the Possession of Dr. Frederick Peterson* (New York: privately printed, 1930). For more on the Princeton group, see George Rowley, "The Peterson Collection," *Record of The Museum of Historic Art, Princeton University* 1, no. 1 (1942): 3–7.
5. For the 1935 London exhibition, see *The Chinese Exhibition: A Commemorative Catalogue of the International Exhibition of Chinese Art, Royal Academy of Arts, November 1935–March 1936* (London: Faber and Faber, [1935?]) and *Illustrated Catalogue of Chinese Government Exhibits for the International Exhibition of Chinese Art in London*, 4 vols. (Shanghai: Shangwu yinshuguan, 1936). For more on international exhibitions of Palace Museum materials, see Susan Naquin, "The Forbidden City Goes Abroad: Qing History and the Foreign Exhibitions of the Palace Museum, 1974–2004," *T'oung Pao* 90, no. 4 (2004): 341–97.
6. See "The Dubois S. Morris Collection of Chinese Paintings," *Bulletin of the Memorial Art Gallery, Rochester, New York* 3, no. 1 (1930): 9–10. For more on the two Morris collection paintings shown in the 1935 London exhibition, see *The Chinese Exhibition*, cat. nos. 1115, 1322; George Rowley, *Principles of Chinese Painting with Illustrations from the DuBois Schanck Morris Collection* (Princeton: Princeton University Press, 1947), cat. nos. 24, 43.
7. For the cited passages, see Victor Segalen, *Essay on Exoticism: An Aesthetics of Diversity*, trans. and ed. Yaël Rachel Schlick (Durham: Duke University Press, 2002), pp. 20–21, 19, respectively. See this entire collection of unfinished essay fragments for Segalen's understanding of "exoticism" as the recognition of diversity and "eternal incomprehensibility" (ibid., p. 21).
8. For more on the Morris Collection, see George Rowley, "The Morris Collection of Chinese Paintings," *Record of the Museum of Historic Art, Princeton University* 6, nos. 1–2 (1947): 2–3, and the first edition of his *Principles of Chinese Painting*. For the 1947 conferences, see *Far Eastern Culture and Society*, Princeton University Bicentennial Conferences, ser. 2, conference 7 (Princeton: Princeton University, [1947]).
9. The rubbings were given to Princeton in the period from 1957 to 1958 and were originally intended to illustrate Rowley's "Chinese Figure Painting." Regrettably this manuscript was never completed.
10. *Far Eastern Culture and Society*, pp. 3–4.

11. The Gest Collection (presently part of Princeton University's East Asian Library) was founded in 1926 at McGill University and was moved to Princeton in 1937. For the library's history and collection, see Hu Shih, "The Gest Oriental Library at Princeton University," *Princeton University Library Chronicle* 15, no. 3 (1954): 113–41.

12. Warren Cohen, *East Asian Art*, pp. 155, 185–86.

13. See Frederick W. Mote et al., *Calligraphy and the East Asian Book*, special catalogue issue of *The Gest Library Journal* 2, no. 2 (1988). Also see Sören Edgren, *The Traditional Chinese Book: Form and Function*, exhibition brochure (Princeton: The Art Museum, Princeton University, 1995).

14. For more on the Elliott collections, see Wen C. Fong et al., *Images of the Mind: Selections from the Edward L. Elliott Family and John B. Elliott Collections of Chinese Calligraphy and Painting at The Art Museum, Princeton University* (Princeton: The Art Museum, Princeton University, 1984). For the John Elliott gifts, see also Robert E. Harrist, Jr., Wen C. Fong et al., *The Embodied Image: Chinese Calligraphy from the John B. Elliott Collection*, ed. Dora C. Y. Ching, Robert E. Harrist Jr., and Cary Y. Liu (Princeton: The Art Museum, Princeton University, 1999); *Umi o watatta Chūgoku no sho: Eriotto korekushon to Sō Gen no meiseki / The Embodied Image: Chinese Calligraphy from the John B. Elliott Collection*, ed. Ōsaka Shiritsu Bijutsukan (Tokyo: Yomiuri Shinbunsha, 2003).

15 . For a detailed examination of collecting "useless things" as a means "to assemble a world," see Wai-yee Li, "The Collector, the Connoisseur, and Late-Ming Sensibility," *T'oung Pao* 81, nos. 4–5 (1995): 275–86. Also see Cary Y. Liu, "The *Admonitions Scroll* in the Context of Ming Aesthetics and Collecting: Material Artefact, Cultural Biography, and Cultural Imagining," in *Gu Kaizi and the Admonitions Scroll*, ed. Shane McCausland (London: The British Museum Press with the Percival David Foundation, 2003), pp. 257–59.

16. Cary Y. Liu, "The Ch'ing Dynasty Wen-yüan-ko Imperial Library: Architecture and the Ordering of Knowledge" (PhD diss., Princeton University, June 1997).

17. For the special significance of certain painting and calligraphy groupings in the Qing palace collection, see Zhang Hongxing, "The Nineteenth-Century Provenance of the *Admonitions* Scroll: A Hypothesis," in *Gu Kaizhi and the Admonitions Scroll*, pp. 277–87.

18. Besides geographic travel, there is also the distance of time to consider. See David Lowenthal, *The Past is a Foreign Country* (Cambridge: Cambridge University Press, 1985).

19. This term may have been first coined in Zhou Weiquan, "Bishu Shanzhuang yu Yihe Yuan" [Retreat for Escaping the Summer Heat and the Summer Palace], reprinted in *Zhongguo jianzhu shi lunwen xuanji* [Selected essays on Chinese architectural history] (Taipei: Mingwen shuju, 1983), vol. 2, p. 434.

20. See Chang Lin-sheng, "The National Palace Museum: A History of the Collection," in Wen C. Fong and James C. Y. Watt et al., *Possessing the Past: Treasures from the National Palace Museum, Taipei* (New York: The Metropolitan Museum of Art; Taipei: National Palace Museum, 1996), pp. 3–4, 24.

21. Yang Renkai, *Guobao chenfu lu—Gugong sanyi shuhua jianwen kaolue* [Record of the vicissitudes of national treasures: A brief account of what is known of the calligraphy and paintings dispersed from the former palaces] (Shanghai: Renmin meishu chubanshe, 1991).

22. Régine Thiriez, *Barbarian Lens: Western Photographers of the Qianlong Emperor's European Palaces* ([Amsterdam]: Gordon and Breach Publishers, 1998), pp. 62–64.

23. The British army held a two-day public auction of property confiscated by officers from the Yuanming Yuan. Chinese buyers participated in the auction and the proceeds were divided as prize money among the army. See Lieut.-Colonel G. J. Wolseley, *Narrative of the War with China in 1860* (1862; reprint, Wilmington: Scholarly Resources, Inc., 1972), pp. 238–42; General Sir Hope Grant, *Incidents in the China War of 1860*, comp. Henry Knollys (Edinburgh: William Blackwood and Sons, 1875), pp. 191–94. Nishijima Shin-ichi, "Meihin no Ryūten" [Treasures outside of China], in *Umi o watatta Chūgoku no sho*, p. 284, cites Robert Swinhoe, *Narrative of the North China Campaign of 1860* (London: Smith, Elder and Co., 1861), in noting Chinese participation.

24. The Xianfeng emperor (r. 1851–61) had retreated to the Imperial Summer Villa at Rehe.

25. For a recent study on the collecting history of this scroll, see Yang Yuanzheng, "Junjia liang hang shier zi, qiya yehou sanwan qian—Pulinsidun daxue yishu bowuguan cang 'Xingrang tie' liuchuan kaolue" [The Tang tracing copy of Wang Xizhi's calligraphy *Ritual to Pray for Good Harvest*: A study of its provenance], *Gugong bowuyuan yuankan* [Palace Museum journal], gen. no. 135 (2008.1): 6–23. (I would like to acknowledge Yang's excellent scholarship produced while he was a visiting scholar at Princeton University and his willingness to share his draft manuscript.) Also see Shen C. Y. Fu et al., *Traces of the Brush: Studies in Chinese Calligraphy* (New Haven: Yale University Press, 1977), pp. 5–8, 241–43, and Robert E. Harrist, Jr., "A Letter from Wang Hsi-chih and the Culture of Chinese Calligraphy," in Harrist and Fong, *The Embodied Image*, pp. 241–59.

26. Zhang Yanyuan, *Fashu yaolu* [Essentials of calligraphy], in *Zhongguo shuhua quanshu* [Comprehensive collection of Chinese calligraphy and painting] (Shanghai: Shanghai shuhua chubanshe, 1992–1999), vol. 1, p. 110. The *Xuanliang tie* rubbing, known by its first two characters, is purportedly the missing part of *Ritual*; included in several rubbing anthologies, a version from Dong Qichang's *Xihongtang fatie* [Model calligraphies from the Hall of Playing Geese] (1603) compilation is reproduced in Harrist and Fong, *Embodied Image*, p. 246, fig. 5.

27. The *Xuexitang tie* no longer survives. The inclusion of the *Xingrang tie* is reported in Feng Fang, *Tongxue shucheng*, in *Zhongguo shuhua quanshu* (see note 26), vol. 3, p. 860.

28. Xiang Yuanbian wrote a colophon for *Ritual* that became detached before this scroll entered the Qing palaces. See Yang Yuanzheng, "Junjia," p. 9.

29. On the relationship between Han Shineng and Dong Qichang in viewing and collecting art, see Celia Carrington Riely, "Tung Ch'i-ch'ang's Life (1555–1636)," in *The Century of Tung Ch'i-ch'ang 1555–1636*, ed. Wai-kam Ho (Kansas City: The Nelson-Atkins Museum of Art, 1992), vol. 2, pp. 397–400.

30. For the best study of Wu Ting and his collecting activities, see Ma Tailai [Ma Tai-loi], "Mingdai wenwu dagu Wu Ting shilue" [The case of Wu Ting, a Ming dynasty connoisseur and merchant], *Gugong xueshu jikan* [National Palace Museum research quarterly] 23, no. 1 (2005): 397–411.

31. Textual evidence indicates that Zhou Minzhong owned this scroll; see Yang Yuanzheng, "Junjia," p. 15.

32. For more on the copy in the National Palace Museum, Taipei, (1) as a forgery, see Shen Fu, *Traces of the Brush*, p. 8, or (2) as a production copy for the *Sanxitang fatie*, see Yang Yuanzheng, "Junjia," p. 17.

33. *Shiqu baoji xubian* [Treasured boxes of the Stone Channel Pavilion, part 2], comp. Wang Jie et al. (7 vol. facsimile reprint, Taipei: National Palace Museum, 1971), vol. 5, pp. 2599–600.

34. Yang Yuanzheng, "Junjia," pp. 18–19, notes that the scroll is recorded on the first page of *juan* 1 in Zeng Xiejun, *Renxu xiaoxia ji* [Record about passing the summer of 1862], and is also recorded to have been seen in Zong Yuanhan (1834–1897), *Xian yu suo jian lu* [Record of what was seen after the flames], *juan* 3, p. 19. Also see *Lidai zhulu fashu mu* [Records of model calligraphy through the ages], ed. Zhu Jiajin (Beijing: Zijincheng chubanshe, 1997), p. 52.

35. Weng Tonghe, *Weng Tonghe riji* [Diary of Wen Tonghe] (1925; Beijing: Zhonghua shuju, 1989), vol. 1, p. 403. He does not seem to have actually seen the scroll.

36. Nishijima Shin-ichi, "Meihin no Ryūten" (see note 23), p. 283. The scroll is discussed in Wang Zhuangwei, *Shufa congtan* [Collected notes on calligraphy] (Taipei: Zhonghua congshu bianshen weiyuanhui, 1965), pp. 165–67, pl. 22; however, there is no mention of it coming out of the Yuanming Yuan or the Qing palaces.

37. There is no mention of the European armies ever entering the Forbidden City in either Wolseley, *Narrative of the War with China in 1860*, or Grant, *Incidents in the China War of 1860*. John Finlay (personal communication by e-mail, September 11, 2007) notes, "as far as I can tell there was no looting in Beijing at that time. (My source is Michael Mann, *China, 1860* [Salisbury: Michael Russell Publishing, 1989]: '...In October, the British and French did occupy part of Beijing, specifically the Anding Gate...and marched up to the "Hall of Audience on the south side of the city" to sign the treaty' [Mann, p. 154])."

38. For the biography of Jing Hengyi, see Yao Hui and Huang Jianguo, "Dianjiao houji" [Collator's postface] (pp. 1–2) appended to Jing Hengyi, *Jing Hengyi riji* [Diary of Jing Hengyi] (Hangzhou: Zhejiang guji chubanshe, 1984); *Minguo renwu da cidian* [Biographical dictionary of the Republican period] (Yangzhou: Hebei renmin chubanshe, 1991), p. 1302. For the tentative reading of the seal as that of Jing Hengyi, see Shen Fu, *Traces of the Brush*, p. 241.

39. Yang Yuanzheng, "Junjia," p.19.

40. Li Yongqiao, *Zhang Daqian nianpu* [Chronology of Zhang Daqian's life] (Chengdu: Sichuan sheng shehui kexueyuan chubanshe, 1987), pp. 312–13, records that Zhang was in Tokyo and Gao Lingmei came from Hong Kong to see him at the end of the year.

41. Zhang Heng, *Muyanzhai shuhua jianshang biji* [Notes on the connoisseurship of painting and calligraphy from the Muyan Studio], vol.: *Shufa er* [Calligraphy 2] (1961; Beijing: Wenwu chubanshe, 2000), pp. 1–8. Zhang Heng must have examined the scroll between the end of 1957 and 1961; he documents the condition of the scroll (including Zhang Daqian's colophons and seals) before its 1980s remounting.

42. Zhu Xingzhai, *Yiyuan tan wang* [Reminiscences on art] (Hong Kong: Shanghai shuju, 1964), p. 264–65. The 1962 collotype reproduction records the condition of the scroll before its remounting in the 1980s and includes all of Zhang Daqian's colophons and seals presently seen on the scroll; John Elliott also acquired the collotype (now in the Princeton University Art Museum, acc. no. 1998-50a).

43. Nishikawa Yasushi, "Shinjutsu no Gyōjō-jō" [The newly discovered *Xingrang tie*], *Shohin* [Calligraphy], no. 142 (1963): 2–39. Also see Nishijima Shin-ichi, "Meihin no Ryūten" (see note 23), p. 287.

44. For more on Zhao Mengfu serving as a ghost calligrapher for his wife, see Jiang Yihan, "Zhao shi yimen he zha yanjiu" [Research on "Collected letters of the Zhao Mengfu family"], *Gugong jikan* [National Palace Museum quarterly] 11, no. 4 (1977): 35, and Harrist and Fong, *Embodied Image*, p. 126. Also see Wang Lianqi, "Zhao Mengfu wei qi daibi" [Zhao Mengfu ghost writes for his wife], *Zijincheng* [Forbidden City] gen. no. 23, no. 1 (1984): 42–43. Out of the six letters, this is the only one to be included in the *Sanxitang fatie* [Model calligraphies of the Hall of Three Rarities] (1750; reprint, Harbin: Heilongjiang renmin chubanshe, 1984), vol. 2, pp. 1618–21.

45. For studies on this scroll, see Jiang Yihan, "Zhao shi yimen he zha yanjiu," pp. 23–50, pls. 1–12, English abstract, pp. 33–37; Nakata Yūjirō and Fu Shen, eds., *Ō-Bei shūzō Chūgoku hōsho meisekishū* [Masterpieces of Chinese calligraphy in American and European collections] (Tokyo: Chūōkōron-sha, 1981–83), vol. 3, pp. 145–48, pls. 44–49; Harrist and Fong, *Embodied Image*, pp. 126–28, cat. no. 12; *Umi o watatta Chūgoku no sho*, cat. no. 13; and Yang Renkai, *Guobao chenfu lu*, pp. 196, 543.

46. *Shiqu baoji chubian* [Treasured boxes of the Stone Channel Pavilion, part 1], comp. by Zhang Zhao (submitted in 1745; 2 vol. facsimile reprint, Taipei: National Palace Museum, 1971), pp. 923–924.

47. *Collected Letters* is listed as a gift to Pujie on January 7, 1923 in *Gugong yiyi shuhua mulu san zhong* [Three catalogues of lost calligraphy and paintings from the former palaces] (Beijing: Gugong bowuyuan, 1931), p. 17a. For more on works leaving the Forbidden City and being taken to Tianjin and Changchun, see Yang Renkai, *Guobao chenfu lu*, passim, and on the Xiaobai Lou, see ibid., pp. 63–66, 88–93.

48. Yang Renkai, *Guobao chenfu lu*, pp. 381–411.

49. For more on Li Zhifu's activities, see Yang Renkai, *Guobao chenfu lu*, pp. 406–407, 543; on "northwest goods," see ibid., passim, especially pp. 276–379; on Lunchizhai, see Nishijima Shin-ichi, "Meihin no Ryūten" (see note 23), p. 286.

50. Yang Renkai, *Guobao chenfu lu*, p. 543. Chen Rentao, annot., *Gugong yiyi shuhua mu jiaozhu* [Annotated catalogue of lost calligraphy and paintings from the former palaces] (Hong Kong: Tongying gongsi, 1956), p. 55a, notes that this scroll was with Tan Jing in Hong Kong.

51. Identified as Guang Xuan (another *ming*, Zhina); see Shen Fu, *Traces of the Brush*, p. 256 n4.

52. For more on this scroll, see Shen Fu, *Traces of the Brush*, pp. 142, 255–56; and Fu, *Ō-Bei shūzō Chūgoku hōsho meisekishū*, vol. 4, pp. 137–38, pls. 1–5; Harrist and Fong, *Embodied Image*, pp. 132–35, cat. no. 14; and *Umi o watatta Chūgoku no sho*, cat. no. 15.

53. In Shen Fu, *Traces of the Brush*, p. 256, this seal is identified as that of Liu Dingzhi, a contemporary mounter.

54. Princeton University Art Museum, acc. no. y1985-11. For more on *Biography*, see Shen Fu, *Traces of the Brush*, pp. 86–87, 256–57; Nakata and Fu, *Ō-Bei shūzō Chūgoku hōsho meisekishū*, vol. 3, pp. 155–56, pls. 72–78; Harrist and Fong, *Embodied Image*, pp. 136–37, cat. no. 15; and *Umi o watatta Chūgoku no sho*, cat. no. 16.

55. Yang Renkai, *Guobao chenfu lu*, p. 545, notes that this scroll is listed in the *Shiqu baoji* (I have not succeeded in confirming this) but was omitted from the *Gugong yiyi shuhua mulu*.

56. Two seals, including a square intaglio seal reading "Zitenghua guan" on the silk mounting have been attributed to Zhang Heng. See Shen Fu, *Traces of the Brush*, p. 256; however, this scroll is not recorded in Zhang's *Muyanzhai shuhua jianshang biji*.

57. For more on this scroll, see Nakata and Fu, *Ō-Bei shūzō Chūgoku hōsho meisekishū*, vol. 4, pp. 153–54, pl. 40; Harrist and Fong, *Embodied Image*, pp. 138–39, cat. no. 16; and *Umi o watatta Chūgoku no sho*, cat. no. 17.

58. *Shiqu baoji chubian*, p. 537.

59. Yang Renkai, *Guobao chenfu lu*, pp. 544–45. For more on Chang Boxiang, see ibid., pp. 387–89. Cf. Chen Rentao, *Gugong yiyi shuhua mu jiaozhu*, p. 55b.

60. For more on this scroll, see Fong, *Images of the Mind*, pp. 292–301, cat. no. 12, and Xiao Yanyi, "Song Ke shu Tao shi bing hua zhu shi xiao jing liang ben bianwei" [Judging the authenticity of two copies of Song Ke's *Tao Qian's Poems* and *Bamboo and Rocks*], *Gugong bowuyuan yuankan* (1985.1): 48–52.

61. Although Gu Yuntao is unidentified, the positions of his seals indicate that he predates Wu Bing. Xiao Yanyi, "Song Ke bianwei," p. 49, also dates Zhou Zhaolü, Wu Bing, and Gu Yuntao before Bian Yongyu.

62. Bian Yongyu, *Shigutang shuhua huikao* [Collected studies on calligraphy and painting in the Shigutang collection] (Mijunlou [1921] ed.; 4 vol. facsim. reprod., Taipei: Zhengzhong shuju, 1958), vol. 2, *juan* 23, pp. 336–40. The seals are not included in the *Siku quanshu* edition.

63. The ragged edges on three sides of this painting support the possibility that it may be an underlayer copy. Another possible retouched underlayer painting is Ni Zan's *Distant Music, Wind, and Moonlight* (Princeton University Art Museum, acc. no. y1968-227); see Cary Y. Liu, "Seeing Double: Copies and Copying in the Arts of China," *Orientations* 32, no. 3 (2001): 154.

64. Xiao Yanyi, "Song Ke bianwei," pp. 48–52. Another factor to be considered is that three colophons at the end of the Beijing scroll appear to be authentic. The first colophon notes that the work transcribed forty-four poems and was executed on twenty sheets of paper. The Beijing scroll, however, has forty-eight poems on sixteen sheets. This may indicate that the colophons were originally attached to another scroll.

65. *Shiqu baoji chubian*, p. 1088.

66. *Gugong yiyi shuhua mulu san zhong*, p. 17a.

67. Yang Renkai, *Guobao chenfu lu*, p. 560.

68. *A Garland of Chinese Painting*, comp. Wang Shijie et al. (Hong Kong: CAFA Company Limited, 1967), vol. 2, no. 37.

69. For more on this handscroll, see Shen Fu, *Traces of the Brush*, pp. 90, 106–7, 143, 174, 260–61; Nakata and Fu, *Ō-Bei shūzō Chūgoku hōsho meisekishū*, vol. 4, pp. 163–65. pls. 68–74; Mote, *Calligraphy and the East Asian Book*, pp. 118, 120 (illus.), 121–22, 132 n13–16; Harrist and Fong, *Embodied Image*, pp. 148–49, cat. no. 19; and *Umi o watatta Chūgoku no sho*, cat. no. 20.

70. The preface and poems belong to "Zhai ju ganxing," a set of twenty poems, which can be found in *Zhu Xi quanji* [Comprehensive works of Zhu Xi] (Taipei: Wenguang tushu gongsi, 1963), vol. 1, *juan* 4, pp. 7a–9b.

71. *Shiqu baoji xubian*, pp. 2051–54.

72. *Gugong yiyi shuhua mulu san zhong*, p. 14b.

73. A handwritten note without source in the museum files indicates that Xu Siqian and Zhang Heng viewed this scroll at the [Qu?] Zhai studio on New Year's Eve, 1946. (Unconfirmed.)

74. *Shiqu baoji chubian*, pp. 641. For more on this painting, see Chen Rentao, *Jingui cang hua ji* [Record of paintings from the Jingui collection] (2 vols., Hong Kong: Tongying gongsi, 1956), vol. 1, no. 1 (color plate); Chen Rentao, *Jingui cang hua pingshi* [Critical notes on paintings from the Jingui collection] (Hong Kong: Tongying gongsi, 1956), vol. 1, pp. 1–2; Richard M. Barnhart, *Peach Blossom Spring* (New York: The Metropolitan Museum of Art, 1983), pp. 43, 46–47, 131, cat. no. 14; and Fong, *Images of the Mind*, pp. 288, cat. no. 8.

75. Chen Rentao, *Jingui cang hua pingshi*, p. 2.

76. See note 74, above. Also listed in Chen Rentao, *Gugong yiyi shuhua mu jiaozhu*, p. 42a.

77. Cary Y. Liu, *Chinese Flower Painting: Reflections of Glory, Virtue, and Humility*, exhibition brochure (Princeton: The Art Museum, Princeton University, 1996). *The Analects*, trans. D. C. Lau (1979; paperback ed., Hong Kong: The Chinese University Press, 1983), bk. 13, pp. 122–23. This gardening analogy may be related to an *Analects* passage imploring a study of the *Shijing* (*Book of Odes*) in part to learn the proper names of plants and animals (ibid., bk. 17, p. 175).

For a detailed analysis of this painting, see Marilyn and Shen Fu, *Studies in Connoisseurship: Chinese Paintings from The Arthur M. Sackler Collections in New York, Princeton, and Washington D.C.* (Princeton: Trustees of Princeton University, 1973), pp. 328–33, cat. no. 37.

78. The *Shiqu baoji xubian* entry transcribes the "Kanyun" seal as "Congyun." It also omits mention of the large "Taishang huangdi zhi bao" seal on the mounting between the frontispiece and painting and does not record the paired seals "Qian" "Long" after the epilogue. The entry also locates the "Shiqu baoji suo cang" seal on the mounting between the frontispiece and painting, but it is actually stamped along the upper edge of the painting.

79. Other pieces in the Princeton University Art Museum, authentic or attributed, that may have formerly come from the Qing palaces include Kangli Naonao, *Biography of a Carpenter* (acc. no. y1985-11); Dong Qichang (1555–1636), attributed to, *Calligraphy in the Styles of the Four Song Masters* (*Fang Su Huang Mi Cai xingshu*) (acc. no. 1998-114); and Chen Ruyan (act. 14th century), attributed to, *Streams and Mountains* (*Xi shan qing shuang tu*) (acc. no. 1998-789).

80. The fictional Martian word "grok" (now in the *Oxford English Dictionary*) was invented in Robert A. Heinlein, *Stranger in a Strange Land* (1961), where it is defined as: "to understand so thoroughly that the observer becomes a part of the observed—to merge, blend, intermarry, lose identity in group experience. It means almost everything that we mean by religion, philosophy, and science—and it means as little to us (because we are from Earth) as color means to a blind man."

81. For more on the aesthetics of diversity, see Segalen, *Essay on Exoticism.*

流落异乡为异客
从清宫到普林斯顿大学艺术馆（摘要）

刘怡玮

书画艺术在中华文明的长期发展过程中起着十分重要的作用，中华书画艺术有重渊源，讲传承的特点。古人佳作、前人业绩皆凭文字图象得以传世，所以善书画者和世人一样，对这两种据说是能反映一个人学养的艺术形式十分敬重。中国书画，意在象外，不但能表现作者的个性和情怀，而且宣泄作者的感悟，流露出天地乾坤之气、江山社稷之和。难怪在处理朝政之余，帝王们也将书画当作“闲事”时而习之，还大量收藏这些所谓“无益”之物。在这样的前提下，清廷建立了内府收藏，欲“集古今之大全”以发思古之幽，或者说进行“文化漫游”，也就不足为奇了。

清宫御览藏品目录《石渠寶笈》及其续编几乎囊括了所有传世书画，可谓洋洋大观。由于编纂工作始终没有完结，至今只能以藏品的储藏位置分类。面对这批数量浩瀚的珍品人们不禁要问，撰修宝笈的真正意图也许并不在于对作品进行分类编目。清朝其它的钦定典籍荟要也是按照类似的方式编纂的，如集古今学识之大全的《四庫全書》。修书，旨在标榜清朝统治乃授命于天，以确立其合法性。这类藏品，尤其是皇室秘笈，皆自成体系编成纲目，分目内的诸件往往相互关连，对皇家收藏者有某种特殊的意义。

原本完美无缺的大全或集成，如清宫的收藏，怎么可能会被残忍地拆散？更神奇的是，这些失散了的作品是怎样漂洋过海后竟然会在异国重逢，汇聚成新的规模，呈现在他乡的观众面前？然而对许多离群的作品来说问题往往就在于出宫以后，流落天涯，不熟悉清宫秘藏的“外人”（包括中国人和洋人）是否能够了解并珍惜它们所代表的价值。这个问题说来有点教人哭笑不得，因为大部分原属清宫内阁的藏画散失前后曾经诸多藏家之手，它们转辗迁徙，可谓各有各的经历。

导致清宫内阁书画散佚的大致原因如下：

（1）1860年英法联军对离宫型皇家园林圆明园的掳掠和破坏，

（2）1898年至1901年间的义和团运动，

（3）宫中偷盗和1923年太监闹宫作乱，

（4）部分作品被末代皇帝溥仪(1906 - 1967)变卖并携带到天津及伪满洲国首都长春（今吉林省），

（5）大约有四千箱左右的文物被选送装箱于己于1948年运往台湾，构成现今台北故宫博物院的主要收藏。

综上所述，只是原清宫文物史上较为人瞩目的几次较大的流失的大致情况，而每件文物的具体流失过程和细节千差万别，决不可一概而论，否则易生误导。据杨仁恺研究，某些文物出宫的具细过程错综复杂之极，其中之前因后果如今才初露端倪。近来的研究表明，十九世纪以来宫中所藏文物常被当作皇上赏识臣下的奖品，或御赐、或供借阅赏玩。有些文物就这样神不知鬼不觉地流入了市场。除了北京清廷皇宫内的文物以外，原藏于辽宁沈阳故宫、热河的夏令行宫“避暑山庄”（今河北省）、各地行宫及皇家园林、寺院孔庙等的文物不计其数，应逐件逐项分别进行调查研究。

想当然的看法容易产生谬误，比方说1860年英法联军捣毁圆明园事件。瑞洁•瑟列慈（Régine Thiriez）通过照相图片纪实向人们显示，这场浩劫确实造成严重破坏，但随即而来的损毁、当地人对劫后残余的搜寻洗劫和蓄意破坏持续了数十年之久，其损害程度比先前那场劫难有过之而无不及。这儿的问题是：被欧洲人掳走的究竟是哪些作品，而被当地人趁机拿走并盗卖掉的又是哪些作品？是否可以这样猜测：欧洲人攫取的并要当战利品带回家的只是绘画作品和其它文物，但对于不知为何物的书法他们根本就不予理睬。也有可能英法军队在掳掠时是不分青红皂白的，待到后来才将他们自己不想留住的东西拍卖或扔掉。可想而知，这个时期流入中国市场上的卷轴（尤其是书法作品）其中就有一些是由英法军队不分情由抢出圆明园的藏品，另外一些是由懂得其文化价值的中国人弄到市场上去的，再者就是当年赏赐给皇亲国戚和达官显贵的礼物。在此期间皇帝曾从京城出走，所以许多原收藏在内宫和亲王府第的作品因而被非法盗出去也很有可能。而这些作品一旦流落到市面上，其遭遇便会是五花八门、应有尽有，最后汇聚到普林斯顿艺术馆的每件作品各有各的路径。

自1880年代普林斯顿艺术馆和艺术和考古系成立伊始，普林斯顿的亚洲藏品收藏就开始了。艺术馆的亚洲藏品对亚洲艺术教学是不可或缺的。东亚图书馆和东亚系相互依赖，使对中国和日本的研究教学工作相得益彰。这两个项目之间的紧密协调使得学亚洲艺术的学生能得到艺术史方面的训练以及汉学中包括历史、文学、语言和宗教等内容。

普林斯顿艺术馆跟东亚图书馆之间的紧密配合也促成了多次联合展出。普林斯顿所藏中国善本图书有相当一部分就是原清宫旧藏之古本。后获中国书画中有十一件原属清宫藏品，其中包括本文要讨论的下列作品：

- 王羲之（约303－约361）《行穰帖》唐双钩填墨
- 赵孟頫（1254－1322）《赵氏一门合札》
- 柯九思（1290－1343）《上京宫词》
- 俞和（1307－1382）《临乐毅论》
- 宋克（1327－1387）《陶潜诗并画竹石小景》
- 沈粲（1379－1453）和沈度（1357－1434）之《诗书》
- 佚名（14世纪）《梨花山雀》
- 清乾隆皇帝弘历(1736－95在位)《夏卉八香图》

这些清宫旧藏之物竟能在如此遥远的异国他乡安家落户，实属奇妙，亦乃大幸！这批藏品几乎全都是文革期间在海外征收到的，正值这些“无用之物”在海内外皆很少有人问津之时。随着不断了解和亚洲文化在全球范围内影响日盛，中国艺术至今才渐渐脱离被人们仅仅视为稀奇古怪之形式的观念。不过对这些“流落异乡为异客”来说，要指望新的观众们能完完全全地了解它们恐怕是永远不可能的事。然而，正因为意识到世上还有这般“永远无法让人彻底理解”之物，人们才有可能去欣赏“……多元化，即懂得什么是有别于自己的东西……”

（沈慧伟译）

Qianlong in Our Eyes
A Study of Evolving Taste at the Museum of Fine Arts, Boston

Joseph Scheier-Dolberg

There is a fever for all things Qianlong, all things Qing, in the world of Chinese art at the moment. This phenomenon is reflected in the museum world, where exhibitions of major scale—the Royal Academy's "China: The Three Emperors" of 2006 and The Field Museum's "Splendors of China's Forbidden City" of 2004 are two recent examples—have introduced large audiences to the Qing court and its material culture. The growing focus on Qianlong is further manifest within the Academy, where the cultural production of the high Qing period has in recent years received increased attention in the forms of symposia, doctoral dissertations, and scholarly publications.[1] The market for art objects reflects Qianlong fever perhaps most intensely: luxury goods from the Qing imperial workshops routinely fetch record prices at auction,[2] and items that were used personally by the Qianlong emperor create frenzies of excitement when offered for sale.[3] Paintings and calligraphy of the Qing imperial court are increasingly well received, while classical paintings of demonstrable art historical value find their appeal bolstered significantly by imperial provenance.[4] Indeed, the name Qianlong is ubiquitous, and his aesthetics and imperial cultural apparatus are, at least for the moment, decidedly triumphant.

It is interesting to note, in light of this current climate, that our predecessors in the field of Chinese art studies in the West did not all share such a hearty appetite for the Qing court's aesthetic contributions or for its system of collecting and cataloguing paintings and calligraphy. Some exhibited a distinctly disinterested—if not chilly—view towards Qianlong court culture, with charges of decadence and imperial excess being leveled more often than those of brilliance and scholarly accomplishment.[5] Whereas Qianlong strikes a victorious pose at the outset of the twenty-first century, his was a hangdog stance at the dawn of the twentieth.

The current exhibition at the China Institute, in which Qianlong's superlative collection takes center stage, offers an apt opportunity to take stock of the road we have traveled to today's deep appreciation for this emperor and his culture machine. As one of the oldest and richest collections of Chinese painting in the West, the Museum of Fine Arts, Boston (MFA) offers a particularly interesting case study in this regard. Several important paintings from the MFA's collection bear basic evidence of ownership by the Qianlong emperor, and, in the case of a few, Qianlong left quite a bit more by which we may remember him. How the curators who acquired and cared for these objects on behalf of the Museum viewed their imperial legacy has much to tell us about how Qianlong was received during the formative period of the great public art collections in the West. Acknowledging from the outset that it would not be possible in this limited space to cover all relevant paintings in the collection, I will treat three works in detail—key pieces that have something to tell us about Qianlong's reception in Boston during the twentieth century. Our story begins in the late nineteenth century, before the fall of the Qing dynasty, just as America's major museum collections began to be formed.

Collecting Chinese Paintings in Boston: The Early Period

Though the MFA began to accumulate important works of Chinese art very early—before the turn of the twentieth century—many of these were in the media of ceramics and sculpture rather than paintings; those painting masterpieces that did land in Boston before 1900 came through Japan.[6] It was not until 1905, when Okakura Kakuzō (1862–1913) arrived in Boston to lead the MFA's collection and documentation of Asian art, that a concerted and systematic effort to build the collection's Chinese holdings was undertaken. Okakura brought ample resources to the job: impressive language skills, a discerning eye, broad curatorial knowledge, and an abiding belief that to acquire great works of Asian art one had to shop in Asia. Okakura's first trip to Asia to acquire works for the MFA, taken in 1906, resulted in some very fine paintings being added to the collection, among them a Yuan painting of peonies, a

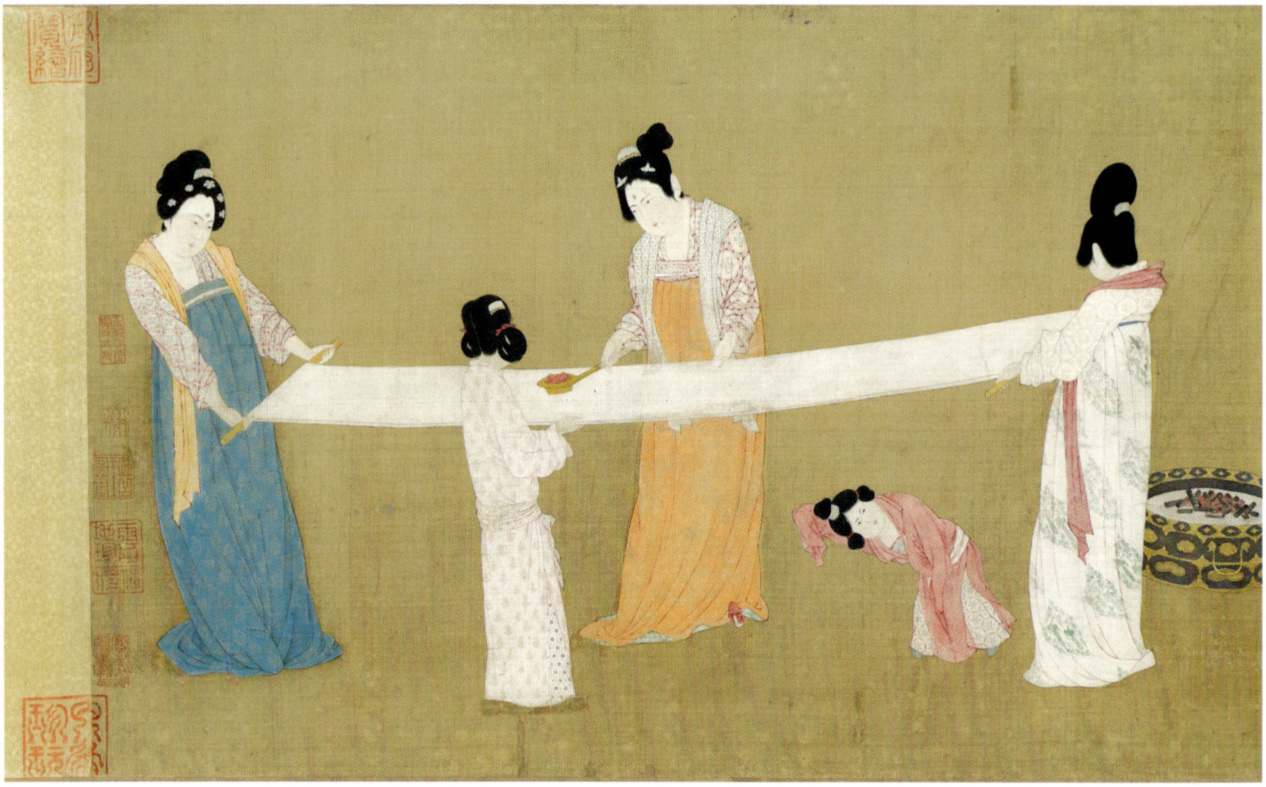

Fig. 1. Attributed to Emperor Huizong 传宋徽宗 (r. 1101–1125), *Court Ladies Preparing Newly Woven Silk* 摹张萱捣练图卷, early 12th century. Section of a handscroll (手卷局部). Ink, color, and gold on silk. Special Chinese and Japanese Fund. Museum of Fine Arts, Boston (MFA 12.886). Photograph © 2008 Museum of Fine Arts, Boston

landscape attributed to the early Ming painter Xu Ben (1335–1380), and an impressive set of twelve hanging scrolls by the Qing painter Yuan Yao (act. ca. 1739–88).[7] These paintings, along with others he acquired during the first few years of his curatorship, formed a core group of worthy works; alongside the already first-rate holdings in Japanese painting, these initial purchases made the MFA's collection of East Asian paintings preeminent in the nation at the close of the first decade of the twentieth century. In these early years, no paintings of Qing imperial provenance were purchased by the Museum.

The MFA might have gone on collecting Chinese paintings at the same deliberate rate if not for the parallel rise of a private collection that was slated to become public—that of the Detroit railroad tycoon Charles Lang Freer (1854–1919). In late 1911 a group of MFA patrons traveled to Detroit to view Freer's collection. Accustomed as they were to assuming Boston's preeminence in Asian art collecting, the group was shocked to find how much, and how well, Freer had purchased in the area of Chinese painting on his recent trips to Asia. On January 19, 1912, the Museum's president Gardiner M. Lane (1859–1914) wrote to Okakura, who was then in Japan, to say: "Recently I have heard so much about Mr. Freer's collection from Mrs. Sears and others that I have become a little envious and wish that we had as much as he seems to have of Chinese art."[8] MFA director Arthur Fairbanks (1864–1944) echoed Lane's sentiment in a letter of his own on March 6, 1912:

> As you will see from the enclosed letter, Mr. Freer's Chinese paintings have stirred up the envy e.g. of Dr. [Denman Waldo] Ross…This is not limited to Chinese paintings, but you should know that it is Freer's paintings that have been attracting attention.[9]

Freer apparently went on to goad the MFA, "saying that he has opportunities for securing fine paintings which are open only to him."[10] These letters from Fairbanks and Lane, dripping with wounded Bostonian pride, preserve the seeds of one of the greatest periods of acquisition for the MFA's Chinese collection, for they spurred the MFA's leaders into immediate action.

Eager to compete with Freer—and to show him that the MFA had its own exclusive buying prospects in China—Lane and Fairbanks aggressively raised acquisition funds to ensure that Okakura not miss any opportunities while in Asia. Their profound faith in Okakura's abilities notwithstanding, they must have been overjoyed at the cache of treasures their curator shipped to the Museum early in the summer of 1912 after a one-month trip to China. Okakura himself sounds more than a little triumphant, writing "In paintings we were very fortunate to obtain specimens of the first grade which will place our Chinese paintings at once on the highest level";[11] taken in light of his bosses' anxieties about Freer, it is obvious that "the highest level" here means "a level higher than Freer." Okakura goes on to cite an impressive list of acquisitions: Emperor Huizong's (r. 1101–1125) *Court Ladies Preparing Newly Woven Silk* (fig. 1), an album of important Song and Yuan fan paintings, and Qiu Ying's (ca. 1494–ca. 1552) *Harp Player in a Pavilion* were just a few of the works acquired for the MFA on this trip.[12]

It is interesting to note that Okakura bought no paintings of Qing imperial provenance during his month in China, especially given the fact that he was seeking the very best and was armed with a not-insignificant amount of Bostonian money.[13] This is likely due in part to coincidence, as the princely collectors that Okakura did most of his buying from were often rich in paintings and calligraphy received as gifts from the imperial collections, and he certainly had opportunities to buy such works. It may, though, also reflect Okakura's savvy as a buyer. Okakura knew that local dealers were only too ready to give foreign buyers what they expected to find—paintings with Qing imperial seals bleeding out from the palace and princely collections—and so he seems to have exercised particular restraint when it came to such objects. In a 1913 article, Okakura offered this caution:

> Already collectors in the West must have found, to their cost, many spurious objects of Japanese art bearing the Tokugawa crest or purporting to come from the collections of famous daimios and temples, and it is likewise probable that for some years to come the world will be flooded with Chinese Imperial pieces of dubious nature.[14]

In light of the foregoing (prescient) statement, it seems that paintings of Qing imperial provenance were not a particular desideratum on this trip for Okakura, if for no other reason than the prevalence of forged works on the market.[15]

The Nine Dragons

It was not until five years later, in 1917, that the MFA made its first purchase of an important painting from the Qing imperial collections: the *Nine Dragons* handscroll (fig. 2) by Chen Rong (act. first half 13th century).[16] This Southern Song masterwork—the preeminent Chinese dragon painting in existence—was the breakthrough acquisition for Okakura's successor, John Ellerton Lodge (1878–1942), who had assumed the reins of the department after his mentor's untimely death in 1913. Lodge had continued to buy Chinese paintings in the wake of Okakura's death—primarily through Okakura's agent in China, Hayasaki Kokichi (1874–1956)—but until 1917, he had failed to make a purchase of signal importance. In the *Nine Dragons*, Lodge found his *Court Ladies Preparing Newly Woven Silk*: an iconic painting that would be recognized by his senior colleagues in the MFA as a work of genius and would help to solidify the Boston Museum's reputation as a leader in Asian art collecting.

It is easy to recognize why the *Nine Dragons* made such an impact upon its arrival in Boston. A handscroll of monumental proportions and first-rate execution, the *Nine Dragons* impresses immediately. The painting, which bears the date of 1244, is strikingly well-preserved for such a large early work on paper. A dramatic display of different brush techniques, the *Nine Dragons* employs calligraphic strokes to describe horns and claws, fine linework to render hair, bravura brushwork to suggest the dragon's primordial warrens, and delicate shading to give form to the mythical beasts. There are even some highly unorthodox techniques in evidence: in spots, it seems that Chen Rong may have applied ink as if he were creating a rubbing, using a pounce bag to ensure even but dry coverage on the paper; in other places, the artist splattered ink onto the page in a wild fashion. Through all these methods and with an uncanny knack for imbuing his fabled subjects with life, the artist managed to create an image at once supernatural and sympathetic. Chen Rong inscribed his painting twice in a vigorous calligraphic style—once in 1244 at the time of its execution and once several years later upon seeing it again—making it a work of impressive completeness.

Breathless, Curator Lodge described *Nine Dragons* to Director Fairbanks in this way:

> The dragon scroll I consider one of the ultimate masterpieces of Chinese painting...I cannot, however, better express my own opinion of the picture and of the Museum's duty in regard to it, than by quoting what Dr. [William Sturgis] Bigelow wrote me

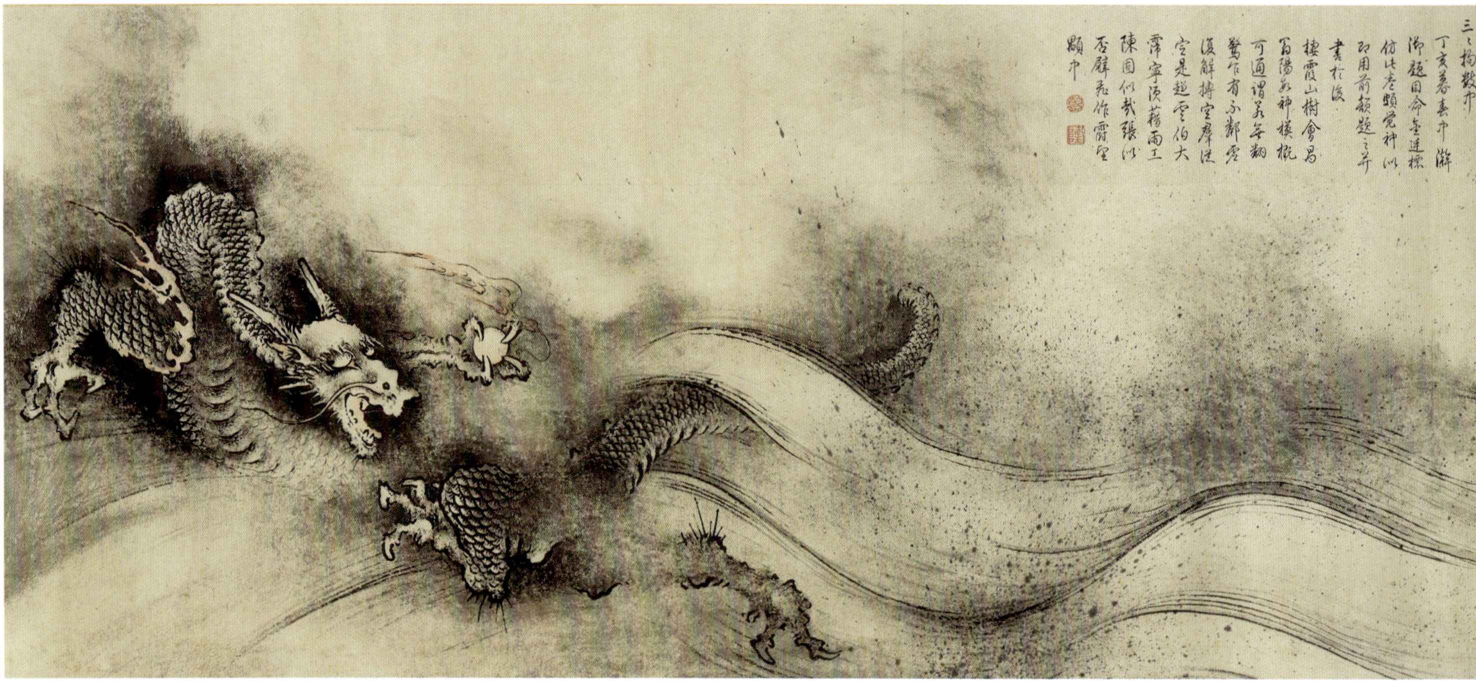

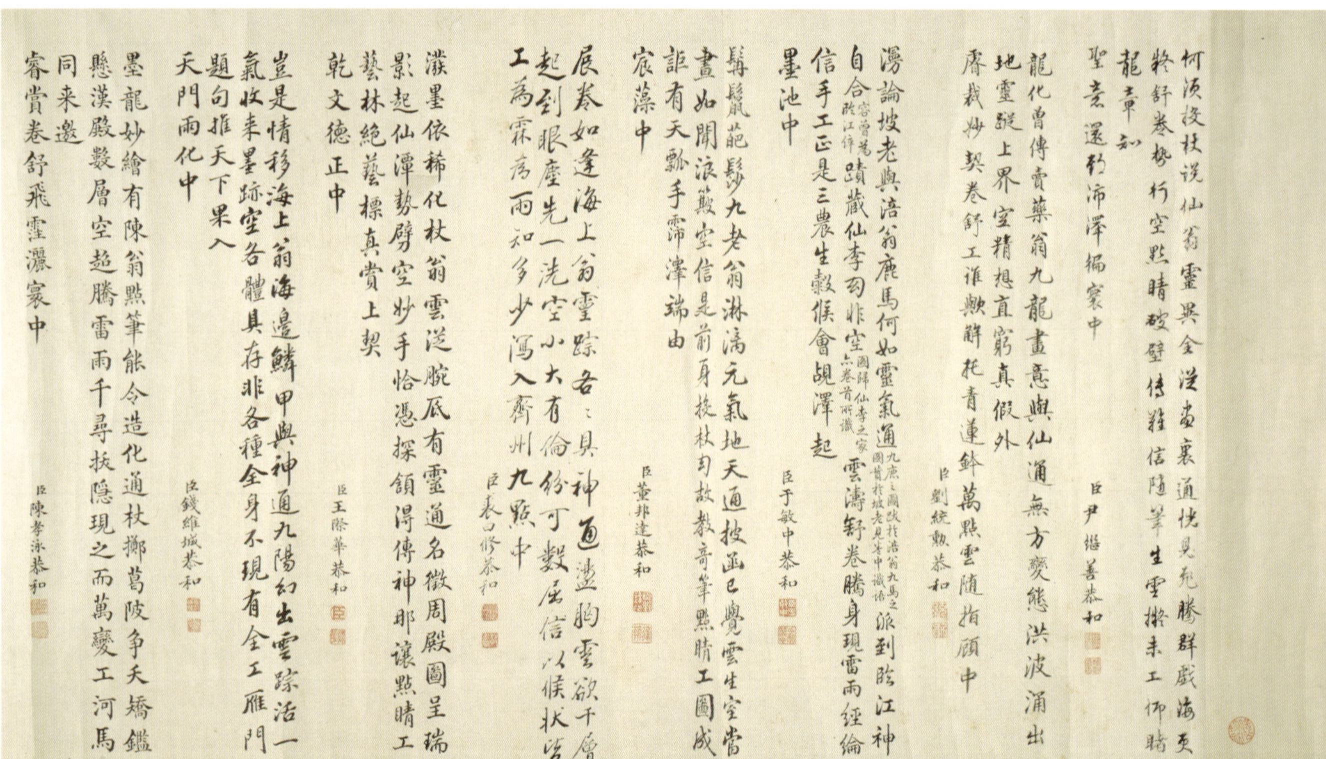

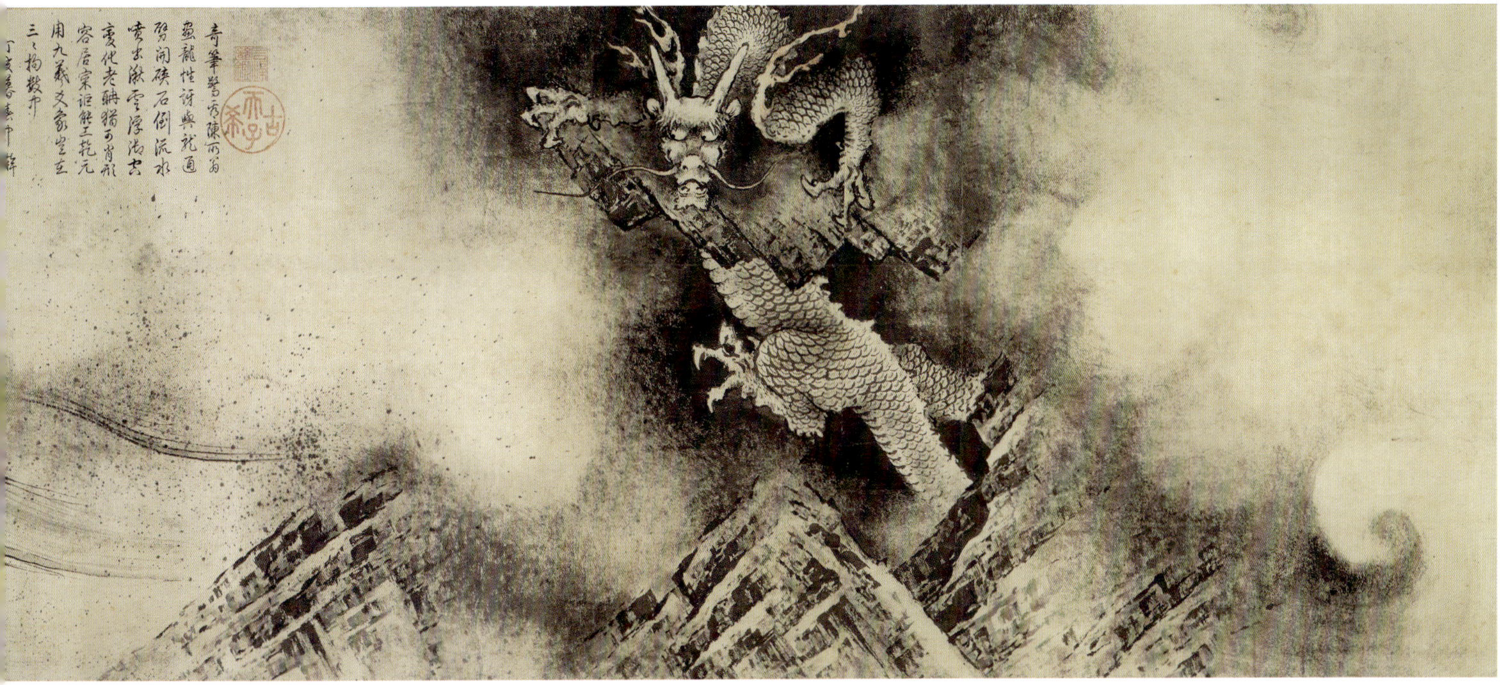

Fig. 2. Chen Rong 陈容, *Nine Dragons* 九龙图卷, 1244. Section of a handscroll (手卷局部). Ink and traces of red color on paper. Francis Gardner Curtis Fund. Museum of Fine Arts, Boston (MFA 17.1697). Photograph © 2008 Museum of Fine Arts, Boston

Fig. 3. Colophons by various senior officials of the Qianlong court 清乾隆朝诸官宦之题跋, from *Nine Dragons* 九龙图卷, by Chen Rong 陈容, 1244. Section of a handscroll (手卷局部). Ink and traces of red color on paper. Francis Gardner Curtis Fund. Maria Antoinette Evans Fund. Museum of Fine Arts, Boston (MFA 17.1697). Photograph © 2008 Museum of Fine Arts, Boston

> concerning it. He said: "As for the (dragon) roll, it is a thing to judge other things by, not to compare with them. The price is not a matter to be considered. Such a thing is a bargain at any price."[17]

Viewing the *Nine Dragons* today, we are, as Lodge was, struck by its brilliance. But beyond what it has to teach us about Southern Song dragon painting and about Chen Rong in particular, we are also struck by what it has to teach us about its most distinguished former owner, the Qianlong emperor, and his uniquely engaged imperial collecting apparatus. It is clear that the emperor treasured this work. He not only wrote two colophons directly on the painting's surface, but he also invited eight of his most senior court officials to rhyme his verse in colophons of their own (fig. 3). As further signs of devotion, Qianlong had the painting copied at least three times by important court painters.[18] These acts of veneration demonstrate the great extent to which Qianlong's massive collection was a dynamic, living entity; the objects within remained constant sources of engagement and inspiration at court. Notably, Lodge did not discuss any of this when recommending the painting to his director. He touches on the imperial legacy only in passing, by way of a conservation note: "the painting was executed for an Emperor and has since then belonged exclusively to Emperors, whose appreciation of its quality accounts, doubtless, for its perfect condition."[19] What would certainly be a major point of interest were the painting to appear on the market today was, for Lodge, but a casual side-note—a telling clue as to the Qianlong emperor's status among Western collectors in 1917.[20]

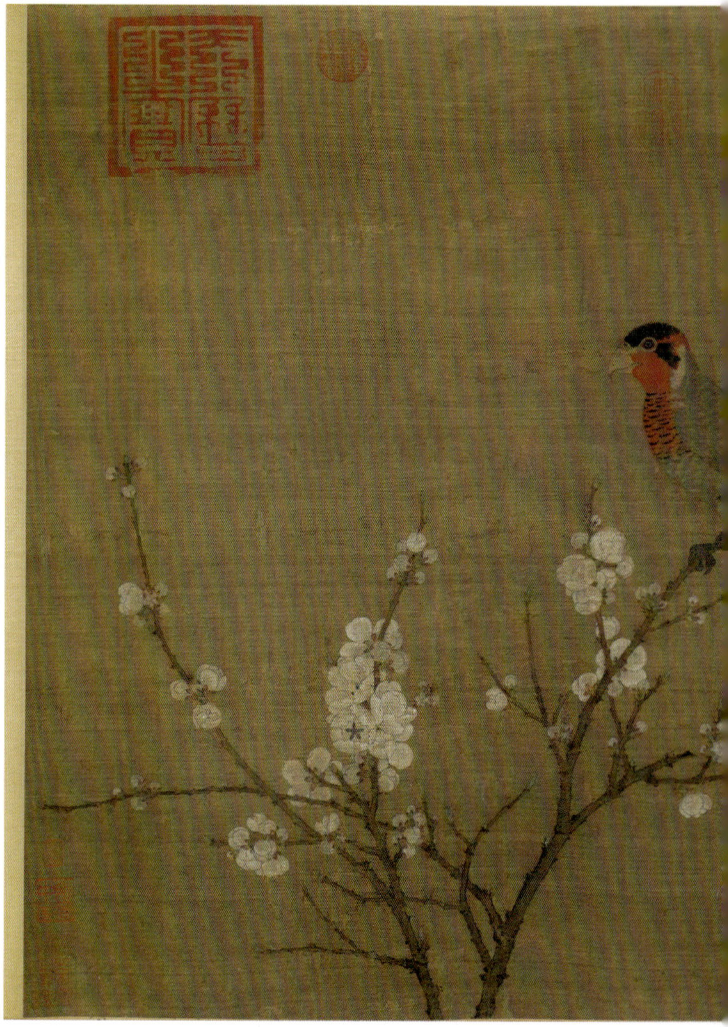

The Five-colored Parakeet on a Blossoming Apricot Tree

In 1931 John Lodge stepped down as curator at the MFA and assumed full-time duties as curator at the Freer Gallery. He was replaced at the MFA by his protégé Kojiro Tomita (1890–1976), who two years later made his own signature Chinese painting acquisition: Emperor Huizong's *Five-colored Parakeet on a Blossoming Apricot Tree* (fig. 4), another work once housed in Qianlong's collection.[21] A striking combination of text and image and one of the earliest surviving combinations of poetry, calligraphy, and painting, *Parakeet* instantly took its place alongside *Court Ladies* and the *Nine Dragons* as an icon of Chinese art in Boston.

The *Five-colored Parakeet* takes the form of a short but very tall handscroll. The scroll opens with a long inscription, beginning in prose and ending in verse, written in Huizong's unique "slender gold script" (*shoujinshu*), so known for its piercingly sharp, clean edges. Though damaged, the vestiges of Huizong's signature and sign-manual can be discerned to the left of his poem. After the inscription is an image of a bird of variegated plumage, shown in profile, sitting on the branch of a flowering fruit tree in mid-bloom. Framed against an empty background, the bird and flowers make for an image of strikingly stark beauty, executed with a realism that has a decidedly documentary flavor.[22] Unlike the *Nine Dragons*, *Parakeet* bears no inscriptive content from Qianlong's hand. The painting does bear the customary series of six seals that accompany all paintings considered to be "superior grade" (*shang deng*) in the Qing imperial catalogue *Shiqu baoji* (Treasured boxes of the Stone Channel).[23] Surprisingly, the painting does not bear any of the grand jubilee seal impressions that Qianlong used in his later years, seals that by virtue of their often prominent positioning on important works of art have become synonymous with Qianlong's collection.[24] It is clear from *Parakeet's* designation as "superior grade" that the Qianlong emperor considered this painting an authentic example of Huizong's hand and therefore an item to be treasured; we have no evidence, however, that among Qianlong's many important paintings, this one held particular significance for him.

Tomita does not appear to have been any more taken with *Parakeet's* Qing provenance than was Lodge with that of *Nine Dragons*. In the *MFA Bulletin*, Tomita simply lists Qianlong's among the "collections in which the scroll was treasured"; he does mention, though, that "since its execution about eight hundred years ago, the scroll has enjoyed the favor of emperors and statesmen of China until recently."[25] The avenue of inquiry ends there, with Tomita showing apparent disinterest in how this painting—executed by an emperor-aesthete in the twelfth century—might have functioned at the court of an emperor-

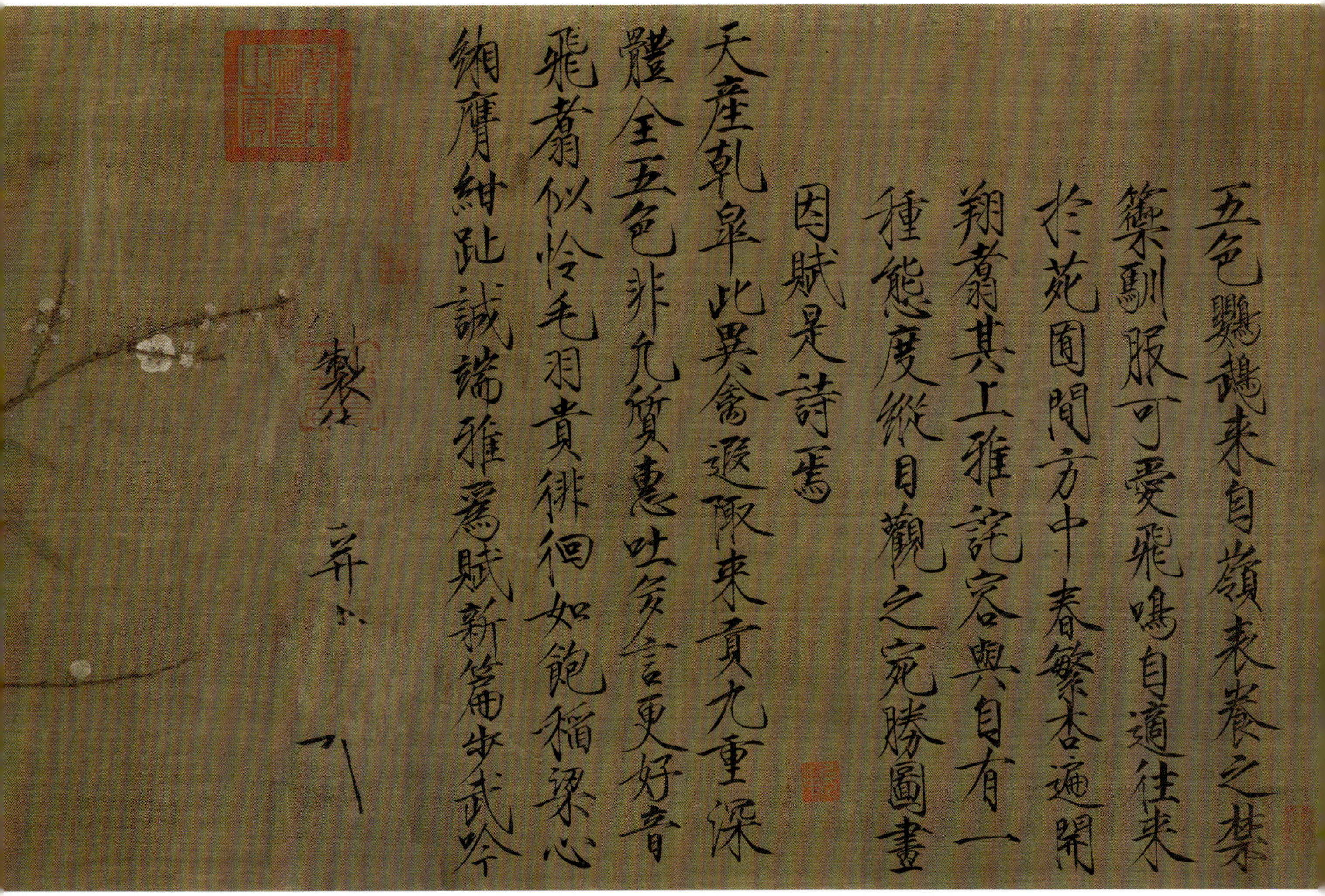

Fig. 4. Emperor Huizong 宋徽宗 (r. 1101–1125), Five-colored Parakeet on a *Blossoming Apricot Tree* 五色鹦鹉图卷, early 12th century. Section of a handscroll (手卷局部). Ink and color on silk. Maria Antoinette Evans Fund. Museum of Fine Arts, Boston (MFA 33.364). Photograph © 2008 Museum of Fine Arts, Boston

aesthete of the eighteenth century. Like Lodge before him, Tomita is silent on *Parakeet's* most distinguished and engaged prior owner, a sign that in 1933 neither the lure of the imperial touch nor an interest in the Qianlong emperor's collecting practices were particularly pronounced at the MFA.

Illustrations to Six Texts from the Xiaoya Section of the Book Of Odes

In 1951 Tomita acquired the *Illustrations to Six Texts from the Xiaoya Section of the Book of Odes* (fig. 5), another painting with ties to emperors of more than one dynasty; the *Xiaoya* handscroll was born under Emperor Gaozong (r. 1127–62) of the Southern Song and rehabilitated under the Qianlong emperor some six hundred years later. Featuring verses from the *Book of Odes* (*Shijing*) interspersed with images, this long handscroll is the result of a large-scale imperial project initiated under Gaozong to show the emperor's veneration for the *Book of Odes* and, by extension, the principles of righteous governance laid out therein.[26] As Julia Murray has pointed out in her exhaustive study of the extant *Odes* scrolls, Gaozong was at particular pains to show his respect for Confucian ruling structures, having entirely subverted them in order to assume the role of sovereign himself.[27]

The *Xiaoya* handscroll and the other *Odes* paintings commissioned by Gaozong became an obsession for Qianlong, who recognized their importance and sought to reunite the set in his own collection. Qianlong went so far as to name a building for this set of paintings—the Hall for Learning from the Odes (Xueshi Tang)—and to have corresponding seals carved for impression on the authentic *Odes* scrolls; even for an emperor given to venerating art objects in his collection, these scrolls clearly were invested with particular significance.[28] Qianlong's involvement with the scrolls went far beyond adoration, though. Through intensive study and side-by-side comparison, he assessed the authenticity of each of the seventeen scrolls in his possession and ranked its importance. For each of those he deemed genuine, he added a frontispiece and colophon, along with the aforementioned Hall for Learning from the Odes seals (fig. 6). In the case of the Boston scroll, Qianlong apparently was the first to ascribe the calligraphy to Gaozong. Indeed, Qianlong's imprint upon scholarship about the *Odes* scrolls is impressive and undeniable.

We may note with interest, then, that Qianlong assumes a greater role in the Museum's own scholarship about the *Xiaoya* scroll. In a 1952 article in the *MFA Bulletin*, Tomita devotes a great deal of space—particularly in comparison to the above treatments of *Nine Dragons* and *Five-colored Parakeet*—to engaging with the legacy left by Qianlong's imperial research apparatus.[29] Tomita offers a complete translation of Qianlong's colophon and notes that, while scholars of the Qianlong era must have had their reasons for categorically ascribing the calligraphy to Gaozong, not enough comparative material existed in the United States in 1952 to make such a strong attribution. Tomita's willingness to engage with Qianlong here may not have been born so much out of a newfound interest in the emperor. Rather, it may have more to do with the guise in which Qianlong appears on the *Odes* scroll: that of the diligent scholar of Chinese paintings. Qianlong's relationship to the *Xiaoya* scroll was different than his relationship to the *Nine Dragons*; his colophon on the *Xiaoya* scroll not only venerates, but it also adds to the scholarly discourse in a way that Tomita could relate to and engage with. (By comparison, Qianlong's relationship to the *Nine Dragons* seems more spectacle and imperial prerogative.)[30] Beyond the emperor's contributions to scholarship on the painting in question, however, Tomita expresses the same studied indifference toward Qianlong and his collection that he did in the case of the *Five-colored Parakeet*. Nowhere does he hype the important role that this painting played at the Qianlong court, nor does he express an interest in how Qianlong might have used these paintings—or the building that he named for them—as tools in a state culture apparatus. In

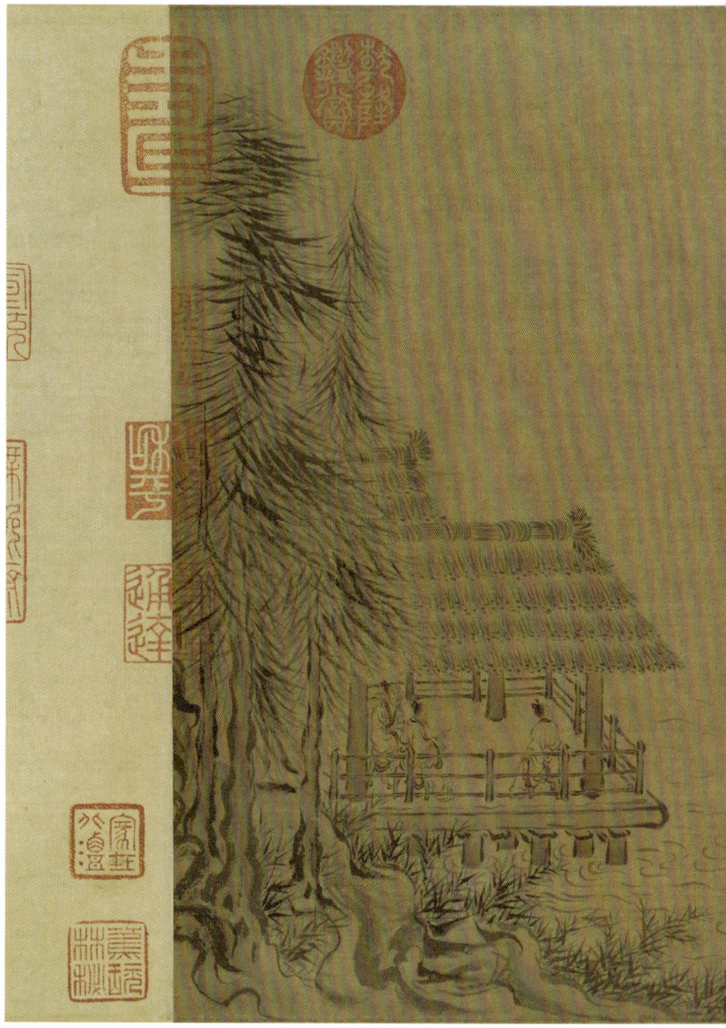

▲ Fig. 5. Attributed to Ma Hezhi (12th century) and Emperor Gaozong (r. 1127–1162) 传宋高宗(书)、马和之(画), *Illustrations to Six Texts from the Xiaoya Section of the Book of Odes* 小雅南有嘉鱼篇书画卷, 12th century. Section of a handscroll (手卷局部). Ink and color on silk. Marshall H. Gould Fund. Museum of Fine Arts, Boston (MFA 51.698). Photograph © 2008 Museum of Fine Arts, Boston

Fig. 6. The Qianlong emperor (r. 1736–96) 清乾隆皇帝弘历, ▶ colophon, with large seal impression reading "Hall for Learning from the Odes" 题跋与"学诗堂"大印, to *Illustrations to Six Texts from the Xiaoya Section of the Book of Odes* 小雅南有嘉鱼篇书画卷, attributed to Ma Hezhi (12th century) and Emperor Gaozong (r. 1127–1162) 传宋高宗(书)、马和之(画). Section of a handscroll (手卷局部). Ink and color on silk. Marshall H. Gould Fund. Museum of Fine Arts, Boston (MFA 51.698). Photograph © 2008 Museum of Fine Arts, Boston

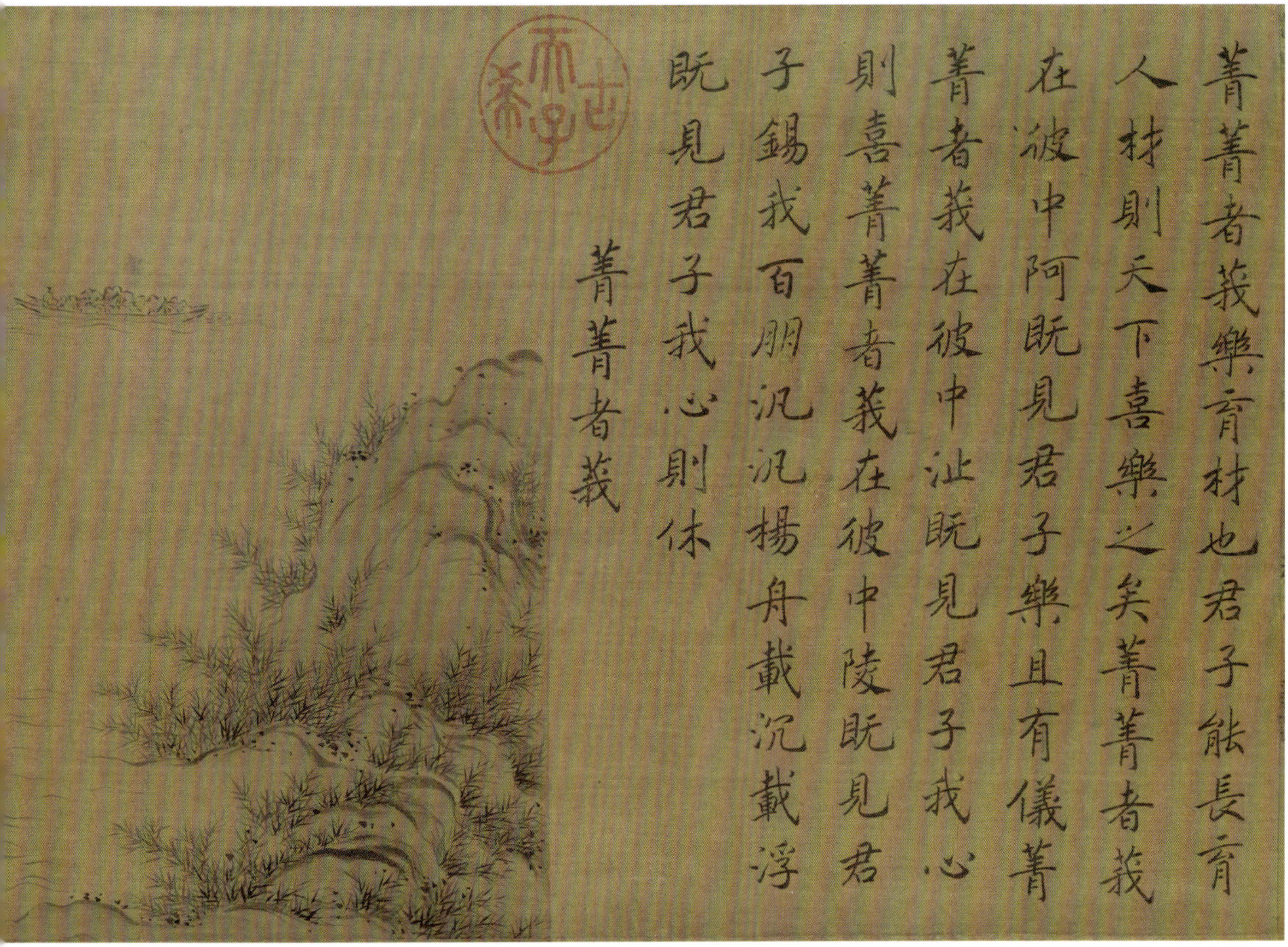
菁菁者莪樂育材也君子能長育
人材則天下喜樂之矣菁菁者莪
在彼中阿既見君子樂且有儀菁
菁者莪在彼中沚既見君子我心
則喜菁菁者莪在彼中陵既見君
子錫我百朋汎汎楊舟載沉載浮
既見君子我心則休
菁菁者莪

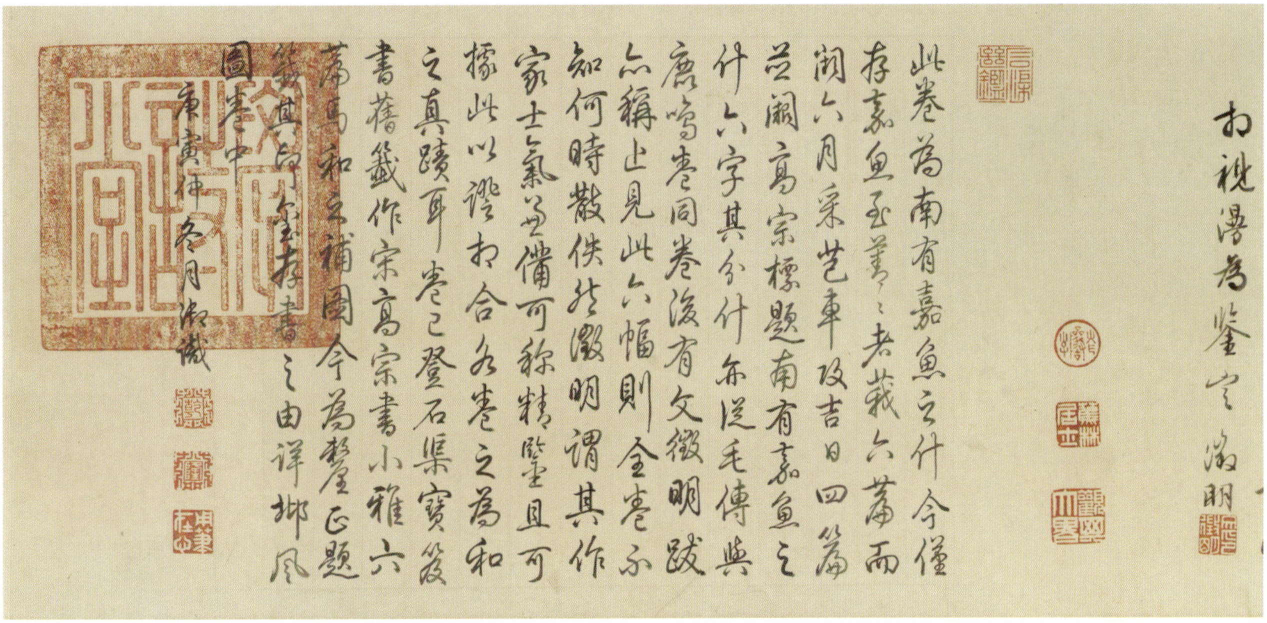

this, Tomita's seems representative of scholarly attitudes toward Qianlong in the early 1950s. We may reflect with some pride at the progress that has been made since then in the realm of scholarship, progress that has enabled us to take stock of Qianlong's unique role in stewarding, and studying, so many of China's greatest cultural treasures during the eighteenth century.

Qianlong at the MFA: A Case of Evolving Tastes

The Qianlong emperor's cultural legacy has perhaps been overdue its current appreciation. No one collected more or better in the realm of Chinese paintings and calligraphy—to say nothing of works in other media—and no emperor did more to cultivate and support his own vision of beauty during his time on the throne. (Only Huizong merits a worthy debate.) As the preceding discussion has sought to suggest, however, the emperor's legacy has not always seemed an obviously compelling subject of study in its own right; the case of the MFA suggests that Qianlong and the abundant evidence of his imperial collecting practice were regarded with a sort of bemused indifference for a good part of the twentieth century. The recent intense focus on Qianlong—and the Qing court in general—has thankfully led us to a richer understanding of this once-dismissed area of inquiry. The current exhibition by the China Institute adds admirably to this growing body of knowledge by introducing the unique and underappreciated role of the Liaoning Provincial Museum in this story. The recent advances in scholarship also point up the significant work that remains to be done, though, and this brief essay, which only scratches the surface of the MFA's relevant holdings, is fittingly more of a starting point for discussion than a conclusion.[31] It is my hope nonetheless that a recognition of the long road of evolving tastes traveled by our predecessors will lead us not only to redouble our efforts to understand Qianlong and Qing court culture as deeply as possible, but also to shine light on today's understudied and underappreciated areas of inquiry—those that occupy the dark corners once reserved for the Qianlong emperor.

Notes

1. "Court Culture in Qing China," a symposium at the School of Oriental and African Studies, University of London (March 4 and 5, 2006), accompanying the exhibition "China: The Three Emperors"; Cary Y. Liu, "The Ch'ing Dynasty Wen-yüan-ko Imperial Library: Architecture and the Ordering of Knowledge" (PhD diss., Princeton University, 1997); Patricia Berger, *Empire of Emptiness* (Honolulu: University of Hawaii Press, 2003); and Feng Mingzhu, ed., *Qianlong Huangdi de wenhua daye / Emperor Ch'ien-lung's Grand Cultural Enterprise* (Taipei: Guoli gugong bowuyuan, 2002) are a few recent examples.
2. One need look no further than the most recent auction cycle for record prices on Qing court luxury goods. See, for instance, the "Imperial Beijing Enamel Glass Brushpot" sold at Christie's Hong Kong on November 27, 2007, for more than US$8 million. Christie's Hong Kong, *Important Chinese Ceramics and Works of Art* (Autumn 2007), lot 1665.
3. A white jade seal carved to commemorate the Qianlong emperor's abdication from the throne was sold at Christie's Hong Kong on November 27, 2007, for more than US$5 million. See Christie's Hong Kong, *Important Chinese Ceramics and Works of Art* (Autumn 2007), lot 1861.
4. A recent comment by C. M. Ma, Senior Consultant, Christie's Chinese Paintings Department, is telling in this regard: "As the interest in Chinese Classical paintings and calligraphy increases among collectors in Greater China and Asia, there is steady growth in this category…In particular, works that have Imperial affiliations excite a high level of interest." Auction review, *The Asian Art Newspaper*, January 2008, p. 21.
5. Raphael Petrucci, *Chinese Painters: A Critical Study* (New York: Brentano's, 1920), pp. 131–35; R. L. Hobson's 1927 introduction in a revised edition of his *Chinese Art* (New York: Macmillan, 1952), pp. 17–18; and Chiang Yee, *The Chinese Eye: An Interpretation of Chinese Painting* (London: Methuen and Co., 1936), pp. 137–38 offer representative examples.
6. The seminal acquisition of Chinese paintings for the MFA was a selection of ten works from a set of one hundred *luohan* paintings from the collection of the Daitokuji monastery in Kyoto, Japan. For a thorough account of their provenance, acquisition, and reception by the MFA, see Gregory P. Levine, "Rakan in America: Travels of the Daitokuji *Five Hundred Luohan*," in *Moving Objects: Time, Space, and Context* (Tokyo: National Research Institute for Cultural Properties, 2004), pp. 96–109.
7. Respectively, MFA 06.1899, 08.87, and 08.93–08.104.
8. Gardiner M. Lane to Okakura Kakuzō, January 19, 1912. Museum Archives, Museum of Fine Arts, Boston (hereafter cited as MFAA).
9. Arthur Fairbanks to Okakura Kakuzō, March 6, 1912. MFAA.
10. Ibid.
11. Okakura Kakuzō to Arthur Fairbanks, May 16, 1912. MFAA.
12. MFA 12.886, 12.888–12.901, and 12.887, respectively. A full account of Okakura's acquisitions can be seen in Okakura Kakuzō, "Exhibition of Recent Acquisitions in Chinese and Japanese Art," *Museum of Fine Arts Bulletin* 10, no. 60 (December 1912): 46–58.
13. Okakura did, however, buy paintings of Song, Jin, Yuan, and Ming imperial provenance on this trip. *Court Ladies* is believed to have begun life in the hands of Emperor Huizong himself, after which it passed into the hands of Emperor Zhangzong (r. 1190–1208) of the Jin dynasty. *A Grand Dragon Boat* (MFA 12.899), one of the leaves included in the

album of Song and Yuan masters, bears a Yuan imperial seal. *Budai* (MFA 12.883) bears the seal of the Ming empress Xiaosu (1430–1504).

14. Okakura, "Exhibition," p. 50.
15. There are only two works that may be taken as exceptions. In 1914 two paintings were accessioned into the collection bearing full suites of Qianlong seals: a painting of water buffaloes and herd-boys (MFA 14.49) and a dragon painting (MFA 14.50). They belong to a group of paintings Okakura seems to have expressed interest in while in China in 1912; his relative and agent in China, Hayasaki Kokichi (1874–1956), saw these purchases through and shipped them to the MFA after Okakura's death. These paintings, the only works of purported Qing imperial provenance to have been accessioned as a result of the 1912 buying spree, support Okakura's caution: the Qianlong seals on 14.49 are dubious while those on 14.50 are obviously spurious.
16. The best and most thorough exploration of this painting is in Hsien-chi Tseng, "A Study of the Nine Dragons Scroll," *Archives of the Chinese Art Society of America* 11 (1957): 17–39.
17. John Ellerton Lodge to Arthur Fairbanks, June 7, 1917. Museum of Fine Arts, Boston, Art of Asia, Oceania and Africa Archives (hereafter cited as MFA AAOA Archives).
18. In his 1767 colophon, Qianlong mentions having commissioned a copy from Jin Tingbiao (active at court ca. 1757–67); he commissioned another copy by Yang Dazhang in 1790. A miniature copy was also made, likely by Zhang Ruoai (1713– 1746), which now resides in the MFA (1971.324). This tiny painting, a skillfully rendered "pocket edition," is quintessentially Qianlong: the monumental rendered as monumentally cute. For more, see Chou Ju-hsi and Claudia Brown, *The Elegant Brush: Chinese Painting Under the Qianlong Emperor 1735–1795* (Phoenix: Phoenix Art Museum, 1985), p. 73.
19. Lodge to Fairbanks, June 7, 1917. MFA AAOA Archives. It is not entirely clear how Lodge formed this mistaken first impression of an unbroken imperial provenance for *Nine Dragons*.
20. Lodge's disinterest in Qianlong's devotion to the *Dragons* scroll is echoed in Zeng Xianqi's (Hsien-chi Tseng) otherwise thorough 1957 study of the painting and its colophons. Zeng translates and annotates in painstaking detail all inscriptive content on the scroll except for the colophons by Qianlong and his ministers, which he only mentions. For Zeng in 1957, it seems, these Qing court colophons were not an important part of the story of the *Dragons*. See Tseng, "A Study of the Nine Dragons Scroll."
21. Like the *Nine Dragons, Parakeet* bears the seals of Prince Gong (1833–1898). It is likely that both paintings left the palace collection in the form of gifts to this eminent prince. For more on the phenomenon of imperial use of ancient paintings and calligraphy as gifts to officials and princes during the 19th century, see Yang Renkai, *Guobao chenfu lu* [The loss and recovery of national treasures] (Shenyang: Liaohai chubanshe, 1999), pp. 31–34.
22. Maggie Bickford's explorations of paintings by Huizong and his workshops elucidate the motivations behind this documentary approach to painting, which she has called a "curiously impersonal palace style." See Maggie Bickford, "Emperor Huizong and the Aesthetic of Agency," *Archives of Asian Art* 53 (2002–2003): 77–79.
23. For a thorough discussion of Qianlong's collecting and cataloguing apparatus, including his use of seals to denote specific documentary information, see Gerald Holzwarth, "The Qianlong Emperor as Art Patron and the Formation of the Collections of the Palace Museum, Beijing," in *China: The Three Emperors 1662– 1795* (London: Royal Academy of Arts, 2005), pp. 41–53.
24. The absence of jubilee seals is particularly surprising given that the painting bears seals of the Jiaqing emperor, indicating that it remained in the palace through Qianlong's later years and into the Jiaqing reign period (1796–1820).
25. Kojiro Tomita, "The Five-colored Parakeet By Hui Tsung (1082–1135)," *Museum of Fine Arts Bulletin* 31 (October 1933): 79.
26. How direct a result of Gaozong's original commission this scroll is has long been a subject of debate. See Julia K. Murray's review of related scholarship in her *Ma Hezhi and the Illustration of the "Book of Odes"* (Cambridge: Cambridge University Press, 1993), p. 195. Current scholarly consensus seems to rest very close to Tomita's 1952 appraisal of the work, perhaps uncharacteristically conservative for its day: the paintings and calligraphy may be generally attributed to Ma Hezhi and Gaozong respectively, but they are more likely to be later Southern Song versions by followers of these masters. See Kojiro Tomita, "Scroll of Six Odes from Mao Shih," *Museum of Fine Arts Bulletin* 50, no. 281 (October 1952): 48–49.
27. Murray, *Ma Hezhi*, pp. 10–21.
28. Qianlong seems to have sited the importance of the *Odes* scrolls in their images of ancient society. Murray points out that in his own writings on the subject, Qianlong slights both the scrolls' artistic importance and their role in Emperor Gaozong's system of governance and public perception, choosing instead to focus on what they had to teach about antiquity. See Murray, *Ma Hezhi*, pp. 153–54. It is also clear, however, that Qianlong sought to vie with Gaozong in his devotion to antiquity through his rehabilitation and veneration of the *Odes* scrolls—in Murray's words, "Qianlong regarded Gaozong as both a role model and a competitor." Murray, *Ma Hezhi*, p. 150.
29. Tomita, "Scroll of Six Odes," p. 46.
30. Gerald Holzwarth frames a typology for understanding these two different categories of Qianlong's colophons. See Holzwarth, "The Qianlong Emperor," pp. 45–47.
31. Regrettably, I have been unable to cover a number of other interesting paintings in the MFA with Qing imperial provenance due to space limitations. In the future, a more comprehensive treatment of the collection's holdings would include Zhao Lingrang (late 11th–early 12th century), *Whiling Away the Summer by a Lakeshore Retreat*, dated 1100, ink and color on silk (MFA 57.724); Lu Zhi (1496–1576), *View of Lake Shi*, dated 1558, ink and light color on paper (MFA 48.1245); Xiang Shengmo (1597– 1658), *An Untrammeled Immortal and Soughing Pines*, dated 1628–29, ink on paper (MFA 55.928); Dong Bangda (1699–1769), *Mount Lu*, ink and color on paper (MFA 1973.90); Yan Hongzi (act. 18th century), *Daoist Deities of Water, Earth, and Heaven*, ink on paper (MFA 57.685–687); Qian Weicheng (1720–1776), *Profusion of Flowers*, ink and color on paper (MFA 56.257), along with several paintings that feature possibly spurious Qianlong seals. For images of these works and the others mentioned in this study, please visit the Museum website: www.mfa.org/collections.

我们眼中的乾隆

对波士顿美术馆鉴赏趣味转化的研究（摘要）

史耀华

眼下的中国艺术界有一股乾隆热，这种热忱反映在各大博物馆的展览、学术著作及其艺术市场本身。在目前的气候状况下，值得一提的是在西方研究中国艺术的前辈们，对于乾隆朝内府的艺术贡献，及其系统性地对历代绘画书法的收集和整理编目，并非都怀着同样强烈的好感。对于乾隆朝的宫廷文化，他们表现的如果不是冷漠置之，便是毫无兴趣，乃至指责其腐败挥霍，远胜于称赞它的宏伟业绩和学术成就。

目前在华美协进社中国美术馆的展览，以乾隆收藏的书画精品为核心，为我们提供了一个恰当的机会，来回顾对乾隆皇帝及其他文翰机构的热衷，达到象今天这样的程度所走过的历程。作为在西方最早开始收藏中国绘画，而且拥有最丰富藏品的机构之一的波士顿美术馆，在某种意义上为我们提供了一个特别有趣的研究范例。在这篇短文里，我集中对三幅比较重要的作品进行分析，来探讨二十世纪以来，波士顿艺术博物馆是如何接纳清宫廷藏品的。

迄于二十世纪初期，波士顿艺术博物馆已经奠定了它在美国及国际范围内亚洲艺术研究的重要地位。1906年，冈仓覚三（Okakura Kakuzō 1862–1913）受聘来到波士顿任职文物保管顾问， 凡有机会，他便不断地将出色的中国画添加入馆藏品中。不过直到1911年，的波士顿美术馆才被促使进入积极的行动。在那一年里，一群的波士顿美术馆的资助人去底特律访问了查里斯。郎。佛利尔（Charles Lang Freer），惊讶地看到其中国绘画的收藏，似乎已超过了的波士顿美术馆的藏品。他们立刻提高了资助金额。并将这项专款传给在日本的冈仓覚三，用来购买中国画的代表性作品，试图使波士顿超出佛利尔，重振往日的雄风。冈仓覚三没有让人失望。在中国逗留一个月后，携归宋徽宗的“捣练图卷”（12.866），仇英的“弹箜篌图轴”（12.887），以及其他数件珍品。有意思的是在此次大采购中，冈仓覚三并没有购买任何清宫廷藏品。根据冈仓覚三自己所述，当时盖有乾隆帝假印章的画品充斥了市场。似乎是为此原因这位博识的文物保管人故意避免了清宫廷的藏品。

1917年，波士顿美术馆购进了它的第一幅清宫藏的重要作品：陈容的“九龙图卷”。笔法精湛的巨幅手卷“九龙图”，立刻引起了世人的注目。在传世的署名陈容（活跃于十三世纪）— 这位最杰出的画龙高手的作品里，它是最为可靠的。购买了此件佳作的保管人约翰。艾勒顿。喀吉（John Ellerton Lodge，1878–1942），在滔滔不绝地称赞其在绘画中的重要性，以及在它上面的早期题跋的同时，却对它来自宫廷收藏的问题只字不提。不论是在他已发表的文章中，还是其存档的信函里，都没有谈论以前的所属。甚至于不管是乾隆皇帝的亲笔长跋，还是其大臣们的八段题字，皆无法使喀吉发表任何评价。这个在今天的市场上最能惹人心动的因素，对喀吉来说，却几乎不值得一提。由此可见，1917年期间的乾隆皇帝在西方收藏家的心目中处于何等的地位。

1933年，喀吉的继任富田幸次郎（Kojiro Tomita 1890–1976）带到波士顿美术馆又一幅清宫廷藏品中的杰作 — 徽宗的“五色鹦鹉图卷”。此图卷不仅是北宋花鸟画之杰出范本，而且附有徽宗“瘦金体”的一首长诗题跋。它立即被推崇为波士顿美术馆标志性的收藏。富田幸次郎既没有讨论“五色鹦鹉图卷”曾经清宫廷收藏的问题，也没有对这件被一位十二世纪的皇帝艺术家绘制，可能在十八世纪的另一位皇帝艺术家的宫廷里有着的独特用途表示出任何的兴趣。显而易见，1933年间，无论是出于帝王亲笔，还是曾经被乾隆帝收藏，在波士顿美术馆里都不会引起特别的兴趣和注意。

为六段诗经所绘的手卷画 —“小雅南有嘉鱼篇书画卷”传为马和之画，宋高宗书法，于1951年收入波士顿美术馆的藏品中。象“五色鹦鹉图卷”一样，“小雅”手卷与数代的帝王有关。乾隆皇帝学术性的题跋，卷首，及印章，包括特别为这套画而篆刻的“学诗堂” 印，皆表明它曾经属于乾隆拥有。在一篇向波士顿观众介绍此画的文章里，我们看到富田幸次郎采取了不同的态度，大篇幅地叙及乾隆皇帝。鉴于乾隆之于“九龙图卷”和 “五色鹦鹉图卷”更多的是敬慕之意；对“诗经图卷”则是以学者式的方式

Detail of fig. 2. 图二之部分 ▶

分析，为此而得到了象富田幸次郎这样的现代学者的认同。乾隆收集了当时可以找到的所有相关作品及资料，详细比较和考证其来源出处及可靠性。正由于上述原因，富田幸次郎似乎在此对乾隆帝另眼相看，在对此画的历史背景的叙述中，给乾隆以比较突出的位置。

本文对三幅绘画的讨论，虽然不够全面，然而也足以说明一个已往的事实，那就是近一百年间乾隆皇帝的形象在我们的眼里是如何变化的。今天的学术界，人们对这位独特的皇帝系统性收藏和编目历代艺术品，鼓励和促进宫廷艺术的发展有着强烈的兴趣。但是，并非从来如此，回望我们所走过的长路，对乾隆皇帝的探索和理解赏识能达到今天这样的程度，便可能有希望使人认识到其他的，迄今为止仍然被我们忽略的研究课题，那曾经属于乾隆帝的无人问津的寂寞角落。

（王满晟译）

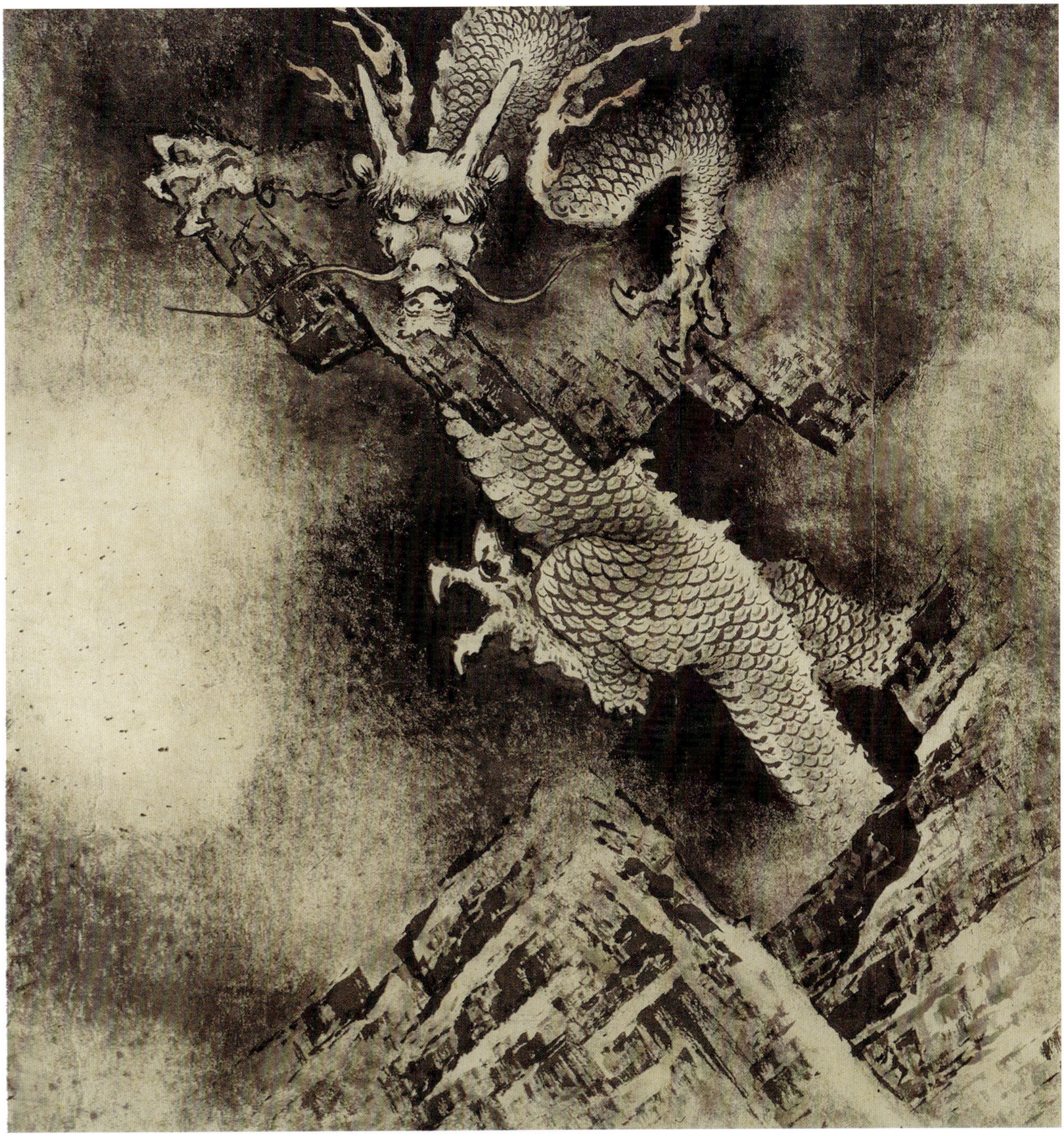

Appendix A
清宫常用书画鉴藏印
Qing Imperial Appreciation Seals for Calligraphy and Painting

乾隆皇帝弘历(在位1736－1795) / Qianlong emperor (Hongli; r. 1736–1795)

Qianlong yulan zhibao 乾隆御览之宝	oval/relief 朱文椭圆印	4.2 × 3.4 cm
Qianlong yulan zhibao 乾隆御览之宝	square/relief 朱文方印	8 × 8
Qianlong yushang zhibao 乾隆御赏之宝	square/relief 朱文方印	2.5 × 2.5
Qianlong jianshang 乾隆鉴赏	circle/intaglio 白文圆印	(diam.) 2.7 直径: 2.7
Shiqu baoji 石渠宝笈	rectangular/relief 朱文长方印	2.8 × 2
Yizisun 宜子孙	square/intaglio 白文方印	2.5 × 2.4
Sanxitang jingjianxi 三希堂精鉴玺	rectangular/relief 朱文长方印	4 × 2.2
Shiqu dingjian 石渠定鉴	round/relief 朱文圆印	(diam.) 2.7 直径: 2.7
Baoji chongbian 宝笈重编	square/intaglio 白文方印	2.4 × 2.4
Midian xinbian 秘殿新编	round/relief 朱文圆印	(diam.) 2 直径: 2
Zhulin chongding 珠林重定	square/intaglio 白文方印	1.9 × 2.1
Midian zhulin 秘殿珠林	rectangular/relief 朱文长方印	2 × 1.2
Qian-Long 乾、隆	linked circle-square/relief 朱文连珠圆方印	(diam.) 1.1 [Qian]; 1.2 × 1.2 [Long] 直径：［乾］1.1、 ［隆］1.2 × 1.2
Qian-Long 乾、隆	linked circle-square/relief 朱文连珠圆方印	(diam.) 3.1 [Qian]; 3.1 × 3.1 [Long] 直径：［乾］3.1、 ［隆］3.1 × 3.1
Wufu wudaitang guxi tianzi bao 五福五代堂古稀天子宝	square/relief 朱文方印	9.7 × 9.7
Guxi tianzi 古希天子	round/relief 朱文圆印	(diam.) 4.5 直径: 4.5
Bazheng maonian zhibao 八征耄念之宝	square/relief 朱文方印	10 × 10

Taishang huangdi 太上皇帝	square/relief 朱文方印	7.2 × 7.2
Taishang huangdi zhibao 太上皇帝之宝	square/relief 朱文方印	9.6 × 9.7; (border) 1 边宽: 1
Qianlong chenhan 乾隆宸翰	square/relief 朱文方印	3.5 × 3.5
Qianlong chenhan 乾隆宸翰	square/relief 朱文方印	1.4 × 1.4
Yangxindian jiancangbao 养心殿鉴藏宝	rectangular/relief 朱文长方印	4 × 2.7
Yushufang jiancangbao 御书房鉴藏宝	oval/relief 朱文椭圆印	4.45 × 2.9
Qianqinggong bao 乾清宫宝	square/relief 朱文方印	8.4 × 8.4
Qianqinggong jiancangbao 乾清宫鉴藏宝	rectangular/relief 朱文长方印	3.5 × 2.8
Chonghuagong jiancangbao 重华宫鉴藏宝	rectangular/relief 朱文长方印	2.6 × 3.65
Leshoutang jiancangbao 乐寿堂鉴藏宝	rectangular/intaglio 白文长方印	4.4 × 2.5
Ningshougong xuru shiqu baoji 宁寿宫续入石渠宝笈	square/relief 朱文方印	3.3 × 3.3
Danshu shi suyuan 耽书是宿缘	square/relief 朱文方印	2.8 × 2.8
Jixia yiqing 几暇怡情	square/intaglio 白文方印	0.8 × 0.8
Dejiaqu 得佳趣	square/intaglio 白文方印	0.8 × 0.8
Yongbi zaixin 用笔在心	square/intaglio 白文方印	1.9 × 1.75
Yuyi yuwu 寓意于物	square/relief 朱文方印	1.7 × 1.7
Jixia jianshang zhixi 几暇鉴赏之玺	square/relief 朱文方印	2 × 2
Shou 寿	rectangular/intaglio 白文长方印	4.3 × 2.7
Quyi zai guangqiu 取益在广求	rectangular/relief 朱文长方印	1.6 × 1.3
Hanxu langjian 涵虚朗鉴	square/intaglio 白文方印	1.6 × 1.6
Shuiyue liang chengming 水月两徵明	rectangular/relief 朱文长方印	2.6 × 1.3
Yunxiasi 云霞思	rectangular/relief 朱文长方印	2.4 × 1

Jixia linchi 几暇临池	square/intaglio 白文方印	1.4 × 1.4
Qinxue haowen 勤学好问	square/intaglio 白文方印	3.6 × 3.6
Zhuizhu qiyi 追逐其意	rectangular/relief 朱文长方印	1.7 × 1.4
Yanlu 研露	rectangular/relief 朱文长方印	2.4 × 1.5
Jushui yue zaishou 掬水月在手	rectangular/intaglio 白文长方印	1.6 × 1.2
Moyun 墨云	rectangular/intaglio 白文长方印	2 × 1.4

嘉庆皇帝颙琰（在位1796－1820）/ Jiaqing emperor (Yongyan; r. 1796–1820)

Jiaqing yulan zhibao 嘉庆御览之宝	oval/relief 朱文椭圆印	4.8 × 3.1 cm
Jiaqing yulan zhibao 嘉庆御览之宝	square/relief 朱文方印	3.6 × 3.6
Jiaqing jianshang 嘉庆鉴赏	round/intaglio 白文圆印	(diam.) 3.2 直径: 3.2

宣统皇帝溥仪（在位1909－1911）/ Xuantong emperor (Puyi; r. 1909–1911)

Xuantong yulan zhibao 宣统御览之宝	square/relief 朱文方印	2.9 × 2.9 cm
Xuantong yulan zhibao 宣统御览之宝	oval/relief 朱文椭圆印	3.4 × 4.3
Xuantong jianshang 宣统鉴赏	square/relief 朱文方印	2.6 × 2.6
Wuyizhai jingjianxi 无逸斋精鉴玺	rectangular/relief 朱文长方印	4.9 × 2.4

乾隆皇帝鉴赏书画钤印的一般规律：

1744年《石渠宝笈》第一次鉴定御藏书画，于入《石渠》者钤有“乾隆御览之宝”、“石渠宝笈”、“乾隆鉴赏”、“三希堂精鉴玺”、“宜子孙”，是为五玺，并加钤贮藏宫殿印记，是为六玺。1791年《石渠宝笈》第二次鉴定，除原来的六玺之外，又加钤“石渠重编”、“石渠定鉴”诸玺，即所谓的八玺。如系宗教作品，则钤“珠林新编”诸印。大约在乾隆皇帝后期，又在观赏的书画上随时补钤“五福五代堂古稀天子宝”、“八徵耄念之宝”、“古希天子”的大玺。

Qianlong's Use of Appreciation Seals on Painting and Calligraphy

In 1744, when the paintings and calligraphy of the imperial collection were first authenticated and compiled into the *Shiqu baoji* (Treasured boxes of the Stone Channel) catalogue, the selected works of art were generally affixed with the “five imperial seals”—“Qianlong yulan zhibao” (treasure viewed by the Qianlong emperor), “Shiqu baoji,” “Qianlong jianshang” (appreciated by Qianlong), “Sanxitang jingjianxi” (meticulous inspection seal of the Studio of the Three Rare Treasures), and “yizisun” (suitable for sons and grandsons)— and usually an additional seal to indicate the storage location, thus making a total of six imperial seals. When the second *Shiqu baoji* catalogue was compiled in 1791, the two seals “Shiqu chongbian” (second compilation of the *Shiqu*) and “Shiqu dingjian” (continued evaluation of the *Shiqu*) were added to the previous six, constituting what is called the “eight imperial seals.” A religious work of art would usually be affixed with the “Zhulin xinbian” (new compilation of the *Midian zhulin*) seal. Late in his reign, the Qianlong emperor would probably spontaneously place “wufu wudaitang guxi tianzi bao” (five generations of progeny in one lifetime, treasure of the septuagenarian Son of Heaven), “bazheng maonian zhibao” (treasure commemorating the advanced age of eighty), and “guxi Tianzi” (the septuagenarian Son of Heaven) seals on whatever work of art he was reviewing.

海蔚蓝据《石渠随笔》、黄伟利有关钤印的说明、辽宁省博物馆保管部同仁的协助和观摩书画的纪录编辑，仅供参考。

This reference list, which incorporates information from Huang Weili's note on the use of appreciation seals, has been compiled by Willow Weilan Hai Chang based on what can be observed on the works of art and what has been recorded in the *Shiqu suibi*, and has been verified by colleagues at the Liaoning Provincial Museum.

a

b

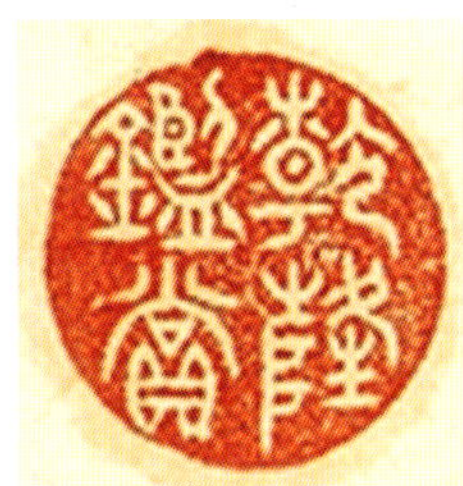
c

d

e

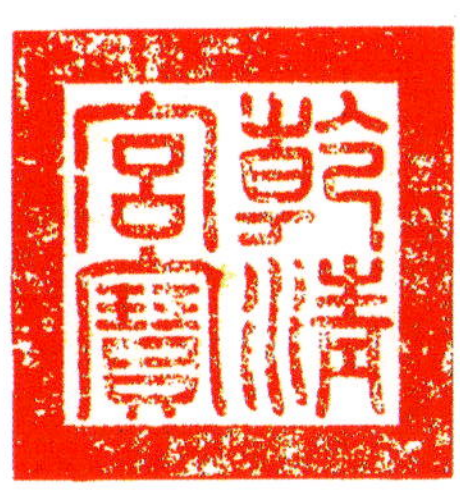
f

g

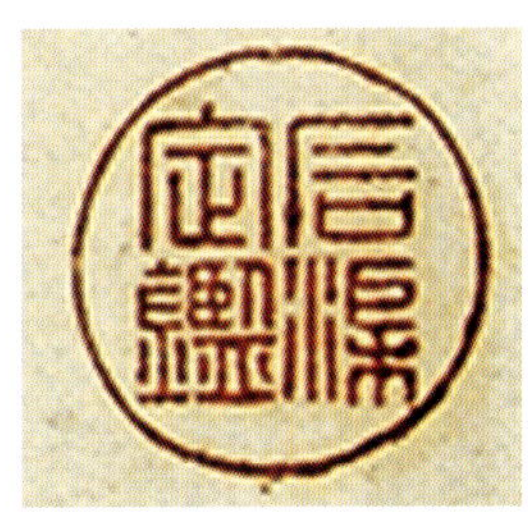
h

Seal impressions: (a) Qianlong yulan zhibao; (b) Shiqu baoji; (c) Qianlong jianshang; (d) Sanxitang jingjianxi; (e) Yizisun; (f) Qianqinggong bao; (g) Shiqu chongbian; (h) Shiqu dingjian

Appendix B
展品的文学资料选辑
Literary Citations from Selected Works

陶渊明　归去来辞
（见图录第4号）

归去来兮！田园将芜胡不归？既自以心为形役，奚惆怅而独悲？悟已往之不谏，知来者之可追；实迷途其未远，觉今是而昨非。

舟摇摇以轻飏，风飘飘而吹衣。问征夫以前路，恨晨光之熹微。乃瞻衡宇，栽欣载奔。童仆欢迎，稚子候门。三径就荒，松菊尤存。携幼入室，有酒盈樽。引壶觞以自酌，眄庭柯以怡颜。倚南窗以寄傲，审容膝之易安。园日涉以成趣，门虽设而常关。策扶老以流憩，时翘首而遐观。云无心以出〔山由〕，鸟倦飞而知还。景翳翳以将入，抚孤松而盘桓。

归去来兮，请息交以绝游。世与我而相遗，复驾言兮焉求？悦亲戚之情话，乐琴书以消忧。农人告余以春兮，将有事乎西畴。或命巾车，或〔木卓〕孤舟。既窈窕以寻壑，亦崎岖而经丘。木欣欣以向荣，泉涓涓而始流。羡万物之得时，感吾生之行休。

已矣乎！寓形宇内复几时？何不委心任去留？胡为惶惶欲何之？富贵非吾愿，帝乡不可期。怀良辰以孤往，或执杖而耘耔。登东坳以舒啸，临清流而赋诗。聊乘化以归尽，乐夫天命复奚疑？

Coming Home
Tao Qian (365–427)
(see cat. no. 4)

To get out of this and go back home!
My fields and garden will be overgrown with weeds—I must go back.
It was my own doing that made my mind my body's slave
Why should I go on in melancholy and lonely grief?

I realize that there's no remedying the past
But I know that there's hope in the future.
After all I have not gone far on the wrong road
And I am aware that what I do today is right, yesterday wrong.
My boat rocks in the gentle breeze
Flap, flap, the wind blows my gown;
I ask a passerby about the road ahead,
Grudging the dimness of the light at dawn.
Then I catch sight of my cottage—Filled with joy I run.

The servant boy comes to welcome me
　　My little son waits at the door.
The three paths are almost obliterated
　　But pines and chrysanthemums are still here.
Leading the children by the hand, I enter my house
　　Where there is a bottle filled with wine.
I draw the bottle to me and pour myself a cup;
Seeing the trees in the courtyard brings joy to my face.
I lean on the south window and let my pride expand,
I consider how easy it is to be content with a little space.

Every day I stroll in the garden for pleasure,
Although there is a gate, it is always shut.
Cane in hand I walk and rest,
Occasionally raising my head to gaze into the distance.
The clouds aimlessly rise from the peaks,
The birds, weary of flying, know it is time to come home.
As the sun's rays grow dim and disappear from view
I walk around a lonely pine tree, stroking it.

Back home again!
May my friendships be broken off and my wanderings come to an end.
The world and I shall have nothing more to do with one another.
If I were again to go abroad, what should I seek?
Here I enjoy honest conversation with my family
And take pleasure in books and cither to dispel my worries.

The farmers tell me that now spring is here
There will be work to do in the west fields.
Sometimes I call for a covered cart,
Sometimes I row a lonely boat,
Following a deep gully through the still water
Or crossing the hill on a rugged path.
The trees put forth luxuriant foliage,
The spring begins to flow in a trickle.
I admire the seasonableness of nature
And am moved to think that my life will come to its close.
    It is all over—
So little time are we granted human form in the world!
Let us then follow the inclinations of the heart:
Where would we go that we are so agitated?
I have no desire for riches
And no expectation of Heaven.

Rather on some fine morning to walk alone
Now planting my staff to take up a hoe,
Or climbing the east hill and whistling long
Or composing verses beside the clear stream:
So I manage to accept my lot until the ultimate homecoming.
Rejoicing in Heaven's command, what is there to doubt?

杜甫 饮中八仙歌
（见图录第9号）

知章骑马似乘船，眼花落井水底眠。
汝阳三斗始朝天，道逢曲车口流涎，恨不移封向酒泉。
左相日兴费万钱，饮如长鲸吸百川，衔杯乐圣称避贤。
宗之潇洒美少年，举觞白眼望青天，皎如玉树临风前。
苏晋长斋绣佛前，醉中往往爱逃禅。
李白一斗诗百篇，长安市上酒家眠。天子呼来不上船，
自言臣是酒中仙。
张旭三杯草圣传，脱帽露顶王公前，挥毫落纸如云烟。
焦遂五斗方卓然，高谈阔论惊四筵。

Translated under the title "Song of the Eight Immortals of the Wine Cup" by Jonathan Chaves, Professor of Chinese, Department of East Asian Languages and Literatures of The George Washington University

Eight Drunken Immortals
Du Fu (712–770)
(see cat. no. 9)

Zhizhang rides his horse
as if he were swaying in a boat:
Blurry-eyed, he falls into a well
and falls asleep there in the water.

Prince Ruyang must have three quarts
before he appears in court,
And if he encounters a vintner's cart
he starts to salivate,
Wishing he could be re-enfeoffed
in the Province of Wine-Stream!

The Minister of the Left's daily exhilaration
costs ten thousand cash:
He drinks like a gigantic whale
imbibing a hundred streams!
Cup to lips, he loves the "Sage"
but will decline the "Worthy."

Zongzhi is a free spirit,
a really handsome youth—
He lifts his goblet, and rolls the whites of his eyes
up to azure heaven above,
As brilliant as a tree of jade
that leans into the wind.

Su Jin undertakes long fasting times
before embroidered Buddhas:
When he gets drunk, he yearns to withdraw
into Zen meditation!

Li Bai writes a hundred poems
for every quart he drinks;
Then goes to sleep right in the wine-shops
there in Ch'ang-an town!
The Emperor summons him; he refuses
to get into the boat,
Himself proclaiming, "I your subject
am really an Immortal of Wine!"

Zhang Xu drinks just three cups
and shows why he's called the "Sage of Cursive Script:"
He casts off his cap, exposing his pate
right in front of princes!
He twirls his brush, drops it to the paper,
producing cloud and mist!

Jiao Sui requires five quarts
before he perks right up,
And brings forth noble discourse and heroic debate,
amazing all the guests!

陶渊明　桃花源记

（见图录第12号）

晋太元中，武陵人，捕鱼为业，缘溪行，忘路之远近，忽逢桃花林。夹岸数百步，中无杂树，芳草鲜美，落英缤纷。渔人甚异之。复前行，欲穷其林。林尽水源，便得一山。山有小口，彷佛若有光。便舍船，从口入。初极狭，才通人；复行数十步，豁然开朗。土地平旷，屋舍俨然。有良田美池桑竹之属，阡陌交通，鸡犬相闻。其中往来种作，男女衣著，悉如外人；黄发垂髫，并怡然自乐。见渔人，乃大惊，问所从来，具答之。便要还家，设酒杀鸡作食。村中闻有此人，咸来问讯。自云先世避秦时乱，率妻子邑人来此绝境，不复出焉；遂与外人间隔。问今是何世，乃不知有汉，无论魏晋。此人一一为具言所闻，皆叹惋。余人各复延至其家，皆出酒食。停数日，辞去。此中人语云：“不足为外人道也”。

既出，得其船，便扶向路，处处志之。及郡下，诣太守，说如此。太守即遣人随其往，寻向所志，遂迷不复得路。南阳刘子骥，高尚士也，闻之，欣然规往。未果，寻病终。后遂无问津者。

Peach Blossom Spring

Tao Qian (365–427)

(see cat. no. 12)

During the reign-period Taiyuan (326–97) of the Jin dynasty there lived in Wuling a certain fisherman. One day, as he followed the course of a stream, he became unconscious of the distance he had traveled. All at once he came upon a grove of blossoming peach trees which lined either bank for hundreds of paces. No tree of any other kind stood amongst them, but there were fragrant flowers, delicate and lovely to the eye, and the air was filled with drifting peachbloom.

The fisherman, marveling, passed on to discover where the grove would end. It ended at a spring; and then there came a hill. In the side of the hill was a small opening which seemed to promise a gleam of light. The fisherman left his boat and entered the opening. It was almost too cramped at first to afford him passage; but when he had taken a few dozen steps he emerged into the open light of a day. He faced a spread of level land. Imposing buildings stood among rich fields and pleasant ponds all set with mulberry and willow. Linking paths led everywhere, and the fowls and dogs of one farm could be heard from the next. People were coming and going and working in the fields. Both the men and the women dressed in exactly the same manner as people outside; white-haired elders and tufted children alike were cheerful and contented.

Some, noticing the fisherman, started in great surprise and asked him where he had come from. He told them his story. They then invited him to their home, where they set out wine and killed chickens for a feast. When news of his coming spread through the village everyone came in to question him. For their part they told how their forefathers, fleeing from the troubles of the age of Qin, had come with their wives and neighbors to this isolated place, never to leave it. From that time on they had been cut off from the outside world. They asked what age was this: they had never even heard of the Han, let alone its successors the Wei and the Jin. The fisherman answered each of their questions in full, and they sighed and wondered at what he had to tell. The rest all invited him to their homes in turn, and in each house food and wine were set before him. It was only after a stay of several days that he took his leave.

"Do not speak of us to the people outside," they said. But when he had regained his boat and was retracing his original route, he marked it at point after point; and on reaching the prefecture he sought audience of the prefect and told him of all these things. The prefect immediately dispatched officers to go back with the fisherman. He hunted for the marks he had made, but grew confused and never found the way again.

The learned and virtuous hermit Liu Ziji heard the story and went off elated to find the place. But he had no success, and died at length of a sickness. Since that time there have been no further "seekers of the ford."

庾信 枯树赋

（见图录第13号）

殷仲文风流儒雅，海内知名；
世异时移，出为东阳太守；
常忽忽不乐，顾庭槐而叹曰：

此树婆娑，生意尽矣。
至如白鹿贞松，青牛文梓；
根抵盘魄，山崖表里。
桂何事而销亡，桐何为而半死？
昔之三河徙植，九畹移根；
开花建始之殿，落实睢阳之园。
声含嶰谷，曲抱《云门》；
将雏集凤，比翼巢鸳。
临风亭而唳鹤，对月峡而吟猿。
乃有拳曲拥肿，盘坳反覆；
熊彪顾盼，鱼龙起伏；
节竖山连，文横水蹙。
匠石惊视，公输眩目。
雕镌始就，剞劂仍加；
平鳞铲甲，落角摧牙；
重重碎锦，片片真花；
纷披草树，散乱烟霞。
若夫松子古度平仲君迁，森梢百顷，搓枿千年
秦则大夫受职，汉则将军坐焉。
莫不苔埋菌压，鸟剥虫穿；
或低垂于霜露，或撼顿于风烟。
东海有白木之庙，
西河有枯桑之社，
北陆以杨叶为关，
南陵以梅根作冶。
小山则丛桂留人，扶风则长松系马。
岂独城临细柳之上，塞落桃林之下。
若乃山河阻绝，飘零离别；
拔本垂泪，伤根沥血。
火入空心，膏流断节。
横洞口而敧卧，顿山腰而半折，
文斜者百围冰碎，理正者千寻瓦裂。
载瘿衔瘤，藏穿抱穴，木魅睒睗，山精妖孽。
况复风云不感，羁旅无归；
未能采葛，还成食薇；
沉沦穷巷，芜没荆扉，既伤摇落，弥嗟变衰。
《淮南子》云“木叶落，长年悲”，斯之谓矣。

乃歌曰：
建章三月火，黄河万里槎；
若非金谷满园树，即是河阳一县花。

桓大司马闻而叹曰：
昔年种柳，依依汉南；
今看摇落，凄怆江潭；
树犹如此，人何以堪！

Ode of the Withered Tree

Yu Xin (513–581)

(see cat. no. 13)

Yin Zhongwen was a free spirit and a man of learning, whose fame was known the whole world over.
When the times changed, he went forth to serve as Governor of Dongyang.
But always he was unhappy and ill at ease. He gazed at the locust tree in the courtyard and, sighing, he said:
'This tree is withering away: the life in it is gone.'
Trees like the pure pines in White Deer Pass or the striped *zi* tree that became a grey ox—
their roots may hump and coil around the folds of a mountain slope;
but why does the cassia waste away and perish [as Han Wudi lamented when he lost Lady Li], why then is the *wutong* half dead [as described in the *Qifa*]?
Once transplanting succeeded in the Three River Provinces [when the altar tree of the house of Han flourished again for Guangwudi, Liu Bei of the Shu-Han Kingdom, and Liu Yu of the Song]; and roots were shifted in the nine acres [as in the *Li Sao*].
Such trees blossomed by [Cao Cao's] Jianshi Palace, and their fruits fell in the gardens of Suiyang [of Prince Xiao of Liang].
Within them lay the music of Xie Valley [where the Yellow Emperor sent his musician Li Ling to get bamboo for pipes]; and of song they contain the "Gates of Cloud" [of the Yellow Emperor].
There trees are roosts for the 'phoenix with its brood' [song title], and provide nests for the pair of ducks that shares a single wing [showing their conjugal devotion].
When they hang over wind-swept pavilions, the cranes cry out; when they face moonlit gorges, they bring gibbons to moan.
Then there are those which are gnarled, knotty, pocked, inverted,
where bears and tigers turn heads and look, where fish and dragons rise and sink,
upright, knobbed like capitals, mountain-linked; cross-grained and crinkling like waters.
Carver Shi is startled to see such as these; the craftsman Gongshu Ban's eyes are dazzled.
First the carving out is done; then curved awls and scrollers are applied.
They level scales and scrape shells flat, fell horns and break off tusks,
layer after layer of shattered brocade, petal after petal of true flowers,
grass and trees spreading in profusion, mists and red clouds scattering in confusion.
Then there are trees like the pine, pomegranate, ginko, and persimmon [mentioned together in Zuo Si's "Fu on the Capital of Wu"]
whose dense tops spread over a hundred acres, and sprouts from whose stumps last a thousand years.
In Qin one of these was appointed as a minister [when Qin Shihuang enfeoffed a tree that sheltered him from a storm], and in Han a general sat under one [Fen Yi, the "General of the Big Tree"].
But they all become buried in moss, weighed down by growths, pared by the birds, bored into by worms,

and some hang low with the frost and dew, some are shaken and ruined by winds and mists.
East by the sea was a temple for a white tree, and an altar for a barren mulberry lay in the western reaches of the Yellow River;
and in the northland they made a gate of willow leaves, and at South Ridge made a foundry among plum roots;
in Xiaoshan['s poem, "the Summons to the Recluse," in the *Chuci*] groves of cassia could make one linger, while in the "Ballad of Fufeng" Liu Kun tied his horse to a tall pine—
do you think such famous trees are found only where the walls [of Chang'an] look down on Thinwillow Camp, or where the passes sink behind Peach Forest [in the capital region]?
But when they are separated [from their native soil] by mountains and rivers, or are leaf-stripped in parting,
their torn up roots may cause tears to be shed, or their wounded radicals may ooze blood;
fire will enter their hollow trunks [pun: "heart"], and sap flow from their broken joints [pun: "resolution"].
They lie slanting, stretched across the mouths of caves; or are broken in half, collapsed across the waists of mountains.
Those of slanting stripes ice-shatter their hundred-span girths; the straight-grained tile-split their thousand yard heights.
Knob-covered, filled with swellings, pierced in hidden places, holes within,
there tree goblins flicker, and mountain demons cast their spells.
Worse still that the winds and thunder no longer stir them, and that their one-time lodgers never return.
No more can one 'gather dolichoes' there [as in *Shi* 72, interpreted to mean that even while one is away a short while 'gathering dolichoes,' one is slandered in court; i.e. Yin Zhongwen and I need not worry about our reputations at home because we're not returning]; but one can still eat the bracken [as did Bo Yi and Shu Qi, the loyal recluses who refused to serve a usurping state].
They lie sunken away in some narrow lane or drowned in weeds by a thatch door.
Once I was pained by the falling of leaves from such trees; now I sigh even more for their dying.
The *Huainanzi* says: 'When leaves fall from the trees, old men grieve.' This is what I am talking about.

Hence my song:
They are the fire that lasted three months at Jianzhang Palace,
they are the log going thousands of miles on the Yellow River:
they might have been the trees that once filled [Shi Chong's] garden of Golden Valley—
and if not, then surely they were a whole county of blossomers in Heyang [the peach trees planted by Pan Yue].

The Grand Marshal, Huan Wen, heard of this and sighed, saying:
'Once a long time ago I planted willows, and Hannan swayed with their pliant branches;
now I see them as they lose their leaves, and the pools of the Yangzi become a sad sight.
If it is so even with trees, how can one bear it thinking of man?'

Modified from Stephen Owen's translation under the title "Fu on the Barren Tree," in his "Deadwood: The Barren Tree from Yü Hsin to Han Yü," *Chinese Literature: Essays, Articles, Reviews (CLEAR)* 1, no. 2 (July 1979): 157–60.

Selected Bibliography
参考书目提要

Full references for the sources used in this publication can be found in both the Chinese and English notes following the essays and catalogue entries. This abbreviated list contains frequently used sources and publications of general interest for the readers of English.

各篇中英文稿的注解均附有详细的参考书目，此提要仅列出为英文读者所常用者。

Acker, William R. B. *Some T'ang and Pre-T'ang Texts on Chinese Painting.* Leiden: E. J. Brill, 1954.

An Qi. *Moyuan huiguan.* Preface dated 1742. In vol. 10 of *Zhongguo shuhua quanshu* [Complete writings on Chinese calligraphy and painting]. Shanghai: Shanghai shuhua chubanshe, 1996.

Barnhart, Richard M. *Painters of the Great Ming: The Imperial Court and the Zhe School.* Dallas: Dallas Museum of Art, 1993.

———. *Peach Blossom Spring.* New York: The Metropolitan Museum of Art, 1983.

———. "Shining Rivers: *Eight Views of the Hsiao and Hsiang* in Sung Painting." In *International Colloquium on Chinese Art History, 1991, Proceedings, Painting and Calligraphy, Part I*, pp. 45–95. Taipei: National Palace Museum, 1992.

Berger, Patricia. *Empire of Emptiness.* Honolulu: University of Hawaii Press, 2003.

Bian Yongyu. *Shigutang shuhua huikao* [Collected studies on calligraphy and painting in the Shigutang collection]. Facsim. reprod. of Mijunlou (1921) ed. 4 vols. Taipei: Zhengzhong shuju, 1958.

Bickford, Maggie. "Emperor Huizong and the Aesthetic of Agency." *Archives of Asian Art* 53 (2002–2003): 71–104.

Bush, Susan. "Lung-mo, K'ai-ho, and Ch'i-fu: Some Implications of Wang Yuan-ch'i's Three Compositional terms." *Oriental Art* 8, no. 3 (Autumn 1962): 120–22.

Chang Lin-sheng. "The National Palace Museum: A History of the Collection." In Fong and Watt, *Possessing the Past*, pp. 3–25.

Chang, Chin-sung. "Mountains and Rivers, Pure and Splendid: Wang Hui (1632–1717) and the Making of Landscape Panoramas in Early Qing China." PhD diss., Yale University, 2004.

Chang, K. C. *Art, Myth, and Ritual: The Path to Political Authority in Ancient China.* Cambridge, MA: Harvard University Press, 1983.

Chaves, Jonathan. *The Chinese Painter as Poet.* New York: China Institute Gallery, 2000.

Chen Jiru. *Ni gu lu* [Fondness for antiquities]. In vol. 1 of *Meishu congshu* [Fine art series], edited by Huang Binhong and Deng Shi. Reprint, Nanjing: Jiangsu guji chubanshe, 1997.

Chen Rentao, ed. *Gugong yiyi shuhua mu jiaozhu* [Annotated catalogue of lost calligraphy and paintings from the former palaces]. Hong Kong: Tongying gongsi, 1956.

———. *Jingui cang hua ji* [Record of paintings from the Jingui collection]. 2 vols. Hong Kong: Tongying gongsi, 1956.

———. *Jingui cang hua pingshi* [Critical notes on paintings from the Jingui collection]. Hong Kong: Tongying gongsi, 1956.

China: The Three Emperors, 1662–1795. See Rawski, Evelyn S., and Jessica Rawson.

The Chinese Exhibition: A Commemorative Catalogue of the International Exhibition of Chinese Art, Royal Academy of Arts, November 1935–March 1936. London: Faber and Faber, [1935?].

Chou, Ju-hsi, and Claudia Brown, eds. *Chinese Painting under the Qianlong Emperor.* Phoebus 8, no. 1. Tempe, AZ: Arizona State University, 1988.

———. *The Elegant Brush: Chinese Painting Under the Qianlong Emperor, 1735–1795.* Phoenix: Phoenix Art Museum, 1985.

Clapp, Anne de Coursey. *The Painting of T'ang Yin.* Chicago: The University of Chicago Press, 1991.

———. *Wen Cheng-ming: The Ming Artist and Antiquity.* Ascona: Artibus Asiae Publishers, 1975.

Clunas, Craig. *Elegant Debts: The Social Art of Wen Zhengming, 1470–1559.* Honolulu: University of Hawaii Press, 2004.

Cohen, Warren. *East Asian Art and American Culture: A Study in International Relations.* New York: Columbia University Press, 1992.

Crossley, Pamela Kyle. *The Translucent Mirror: History and Identity in Qing Imperial Ideology.* Berkeley and Los Angeles: University of California Press, 1999.

Deng Chun. *Hua ji* [Painting sequel]. In *Huashi* [The history of painting]. Siku yishu congshu [Art books from the Comprehensive library of the Four Treasuries]. Shanghai: Shanghai guji chubanshe, 1991.

Dong Qichang. *Huayan* [The Eye of Painting]. In *Mingren huaxue lunzhu*, vol. 12 of *Yishu congbian* [Collection of writings on art], 1st series. Taipei: Shijie shuju, 1962.

———. *Gudong shisan shuo* [Thirteen topics on antiques]. In vol. 2 of *Meishu congshu* [Fine art series], edited by Huang Binhong and Deng Shi. Reprint, Nanjing: Jiangsu guji chubanshe, 1997.

"The Dubois S. Morris Collection of Chinese Paintings." *Bulletin of the Memorial Art Gallery, Rochester, New York* 3, no. 1 (1930): 9–10.

E'ertai, Zhang Tingyu, et al. *Guochao gongshi* [History of the imperial courts]. 2 vols. Beijing: Beijing guji chubanshe, 1987.

Edgren, Sören. *The Traditional Chinese Book: Form and Function.* Princeton: The Art Museum, Princeton University, 1995. Exhibition brochure.

Edwards, Richard. *The Art of Wen Cheng-ming (1470–1559).* Ann Arbor: University of Michigan, 1976.

———. *The Field of Stones: A Study of the Art of Shen Chou (1427–1509).* Washington, D.C.: Smithsonian Institution, 1962.

Eight Dynasties of Chinese Painting: The Collections of the Nelson Gallery-Atkins Museum, Kansas City, and The Cleveland Museum of Art. Cleveland: Cleveland Museum of Art, 1980.

Elliott, Jeannette Shambaugh, and David Shambaugh. *The Odyssey of China's Imperial Art Treasures.* Seattle and London: University of Washington Press, 2005.

Elman, Benjamin A. *From Philosophy to Philology: Intellectual and Social Aspects of Change in Late Imperial China.* Cambridge, MA: Council on East Asian Studies, Harvard University, 1984.

Feng Mingzhu, ed. *Qianlong Huangdi de wenhua daye / Emperor Ch'ien-lung's Grand Cultural Enterprise.* Taipei: Guoli gugong bowuyuan, 2002.

Fong, Wen C. "George Rowley, 1893–1962." *Artibus Asiae* 25, nos. 2–3 (1962): 195–96.

———. "Tung Ch'i-ch'ang and Artistic Renewal." In *The Century of Tung Ch'i-ch'ang, 1555–1636*, edited by Wai-kam Ho, vol. 2, pp. 43–54. Kansas City: The Nelson-Atkins Museum of Art, 1992.

Fong, Wen C., and James C. Y. Watt, ed. *Possessing the Past: Treasures from the National Palace Museum, Taipei.* New York: The Metropolitan Museum of Art, 1996.

Fong, Wen C., et al. *Images of the Mind: Selections from the Edward L. Elliott Family and John B. Elliott Collections of Chinese Calligraphy and Painting at The Art Museum, Princeton University.* Princeton: The Art Museum, Princeton University, 1984.

Fu, Marilyn, and Shen Fu. *Studies in Connoisseurship: Chinese Paintings from The Arthur M. Sackler Collections in New York, Princeton, and Washington D. C.* Princeton: Trustees of Princeton University, 1973.

Fu, Shen C. Y [Fu Shen]. "Princess Sengge Ragi: Collector of Painting and Calligraphy." In Weidner, *Flowering in the Shadows*, pp. 55–80.

———. *Traces of the Brush: Studies in Chinese Calligraphy.* In collaboration with Marilyn W. Fu, Mary G. Neill, and Mary Jane Clark. New Haven: Yale University Press, 1977.

———. *Yuandai huangshi shuhua shoucang shilue* [Brief history of the Yuan dynasty imperial collection], Taipei: Guoli gugong bowuyuan, 1981.

Gao Shiji. *Jiangcun shuhua mu* [Catalogue of calligraphy and painting at Riverside Village]. In vol. 7 of *Zhongguo shuhua quanshu* [Complete series of Chinese calligraphy and painting], edited by Lu Fusheng. Shanghai: Shanghai shuhua chubanshe, 1994.

Gengzi xiaoxia ji [Gengzi summer pastime]. Siku yishu congshu [Art books from the Comprehensive library of the Four Treasuries]. Shanghai: Shanghai guji chubanshe, 1991.

Goodrich, L. Carrington, ed. *Dictionary of Ming Biography.* New York: Columbia University Press, 1976.

———. *The Literary Inquisition of Ch'ien-lung.* Baltimore, MD: Waverly Press, 1935.

Grant, James Hope. *Incidents in the China War of 1860.* Compiled by Henry Knollys. Edinburgh: William Blackwood and Sons, 1875.

Gu Kaizhi and the Admonitions Scroll. See McCausland, Shane.

Gugong shuhua tulu [Illustrated catalogue of calligraphy and painting in the National Palace Museum]. 22 vols. Taipei: National Palace Museum, 1989–2003.

Gugong yiyi shuhua mulu san zhong [Three catalogues of lost calligraphy and paintings from the former palaces]. Beijing: Gugong bowuyuan, 1931.

Gugong yiyi shuji shuhua mulu si zhong [Four catalogues of dispersed calligraphy and paintings from the imperial palace]. [Beijing]: Gugong bowuyan, 1926.

Guhua pinlu [Classified record of ancient paintings]. Siku yishu congshu [Art books from the Comprehensive library of the Four Treasuries]. Reprint, Shanghai: Shanghai guji chubanshe, 1991.

Guo Ruoxu. *Tuhua jianwen zhi* [Experiences in painting]. In *Guhua pinlu* [Classification of ancient painters]. Siku yishu congshu [Art books from the Comprehensive library of the Four Treasuries]. Shanghai: Shanghai guji chubanshe, 1991.

Guy, R. Kent. *The Emperor's Four Treasuries: Scholars and the State in the late Ch'ien-lung Era.* Cambridge, MA: Harvard University Press, 1987.

Harrist, Robert E., Jr. "A Letter from Wang Hsi-chih and the Culture of Chinese Calligraphy." In Harrist and Fong, *The Embodied Image*, pp. 241–59.

Harrist, Robert E., Jr., and Wen C. Fong. *The Embodied Image: Chinese Calligraphy from the John B. Elliott Collection.* With contributions by Qianshen Bai, Dora C. Y. Ching, Chuan-hsing Ho, Cary Y. Liu, Amy McNair, Zhixin Sun, and Jay Xu. Princeton: The Art Museum, Princeton University, 1999.

Hearn, Maxwell K. "Document and Portrait: the Southern Tour Paintings of Kangxi and Qianlong." In *Chinese Painting under the Qianlong Emperor*, edited by Ju-hsi Chou and Claudia Brown, pp. 91–131. Phoebus 8, no. 1. Tempe, AZ: Arizona State University, 1988.

Ho, Chuimei, and Bennet Bronson. *Splendors of China's Forbidden City: The Glorious Reign of Emperor Qianlong*. London: Merril; Chicago: The Field Museum, 2004.

Ho, Wai-kam, ed. *The Century of Tung Ch'i-ch'ang, 1555–1636*. Kansas City: The Nelson-Atkins Museum of Art, 1992.

Ho, Wai-kam, and Dawn Ho Delbanco. "Tung Ch'i-ch'ang's Transcendence of History and Art." In *The Century of Tung Ch'i-ch'ang, 1555–1636*, edited by Wai-kam Ho, vol. 2, pp. 3–41. Kansas City: The Nelson-Atkins Museum of Art, 1992.

Holzwarth, Gerald. "The Qianlong Emperor as Patron and the Formation of the Collections of the Palace Museum, Beijing." In Rawski and Rawson, *China: The Three Emperors*, pp. 41–53

Hu Jing. *Xi Qing zhaji* [Notes from the Western Clarity retreat]. Beijing: Laixunge, 1934.

Hu Shih. "The Gest Oriental Library at Princeton University." *Princeton University Library Chronicle* 15, no. 3 (1954): 113–41.

Huang Binhong and Deng Shi, ed. *Meishu congshu* [Fine art series]. 3 vols. Reprint, Nanjing: Jiangsu guji chubanshe, 1997.

Hummel, Arthur W., ed. *Eminent Chinese of the Ch'ing Period*. Washington: U. S. Government Printing Office, 1943.

Illustrated Catalogue of Chinese Government Exhibits for the International Exhibition of Chinese Art in London. 4 vols. Shanghai: Shangwu yinshuguan, 1936.

Ishida, Hou-mei Sung [Song Houmei]. "Early Ming Painters in Nanking and the Formation of the Wu School." *Ars Orientalis* 17 (1989): 73–115.

———. "From the Min-Che Tradition to the Che School (Part 2), Predecessors of the Che School: Hsieh Huan and Tai Chin." *Gugong xueshu jikan* [Palace Museum research quarterly] 7, no. 1 (1989): 1–15.

———. "Mingchu huajia Wang Fu de yinju yu Zhuchalu zhuangzhi niandai kao" [An investigation into the chronology for the early Ming painter Wang Fu's retirement and his Bamboo Tea Stove]. *Gugong xueshu jikan* [Palace Museum research quarterly] 2, no. 3 (1985): 13–27.

The Jade Studio: Masterpieces of Ming and Qing Painting and Calligraphy from the Wong Nan-p'ing Collection. New Haven: Yale University Art Gallery, 1993.

Jiang Chenying. *Zhanyuan tiba* [Inscriptions noted at Zhanyuan garden]. In vol. 7 of *Zhongguo shuhua quanshu* [Complete series of Chinese calligraphy and painting], edited by Lu Fusheng. Shanghai: Shanghai shuhua chubanshe, 1994.

Jiang Yihan. "Zhao shi yimen he zha yanjiu" [Research on "Collected letters of the Zhao Mengfu family"]. *Gugong jikan* [National Palace Museum quarterly] 11, no. 4 (1977): 23–50. English abstract, pp. 33–37.

Jiang Zhaoshen. *Guanyu Tang Yin de yanjiu* [Research concerning Tang Yin]. Taipei: Guoli Gugong bowuyuan, 1976.

Jiang Zhaoshen. *Wen Zhengming yu Suzhou huatan* [Wen Zhengming and painting in Suzhou]. Taipei: Guoli Gugong bowuyuan, 1977.

Jing Hengyi. *Jing Hengyi riji* [Diary of Jing Hengyi]. Hangzhou: Zhejiang guji chubanshe, 1984.

Jinshu [Book of Jin]. 3 vols. Ershisishi [The twenty-four chronicles], nos. 14–16. Beijing: Zhonghua shuju, 1995.

Johnston, Reginald F. *Twilight in the Forbidden City*. New York: D. Appleton-Century Company, 1934.

Kahn, Harold L. *Monarchy in the Emperor's Eyes: Image and Reality in the Ch'ien-lung Reign*. Cambridge, MA: Harvard University Press, 1971.

Kohara Hironobu. "The Qianlong Emperor's Skill in the Connoisseurship of Chinese Painting." In Chou and Brown, *Chinese Painting Under the Qianlong Emperor*, pp. 56–73.

Krahl, Regina. "The Kangxi Emperor: Horseman, Man of Letters, Man of Science." In Rawski and Rawson, *China: The Three Emperors*, pp. 208–39.

———. "The Yongzheng Emperor: Art Collector and Patron." In Rawski and Rawson, *China: The Three Emperors*, pp. 240–69.

Lai, T. C. *T'ang Yin: Poet/Painter, 1470–1524*. Hong Kong: Kelly and Walsh, 1971.

Laufer, Berthold. *Catalogue of a Collection of Chinese Paintings in the Possession of Dr. Frederick Peterson*. New York: privately printed, 1930.

Lawton, Thomas. "The Mo-yuan hui-kuan by An Ch'i." In *Qingzhu Jiang Fucong xiansheng qishisui lunwenji* [Symposium in honor of Dr. Chiang Fu-tsung on his seventieth birthday], pp. 13–35. Taipei: Gugong bowuyuan, 1969.

———. "Notes on Keng Chao-chung." In Watt, *The Translation of Art*, pp. 144–51.

Ledderose, Lothar. "Some Observations on the Imperial Art Collection in China." *Transactions of the Oriental Ceramic Society* 43 (1978/79): 33–46.

Lee, Hui-shu. *Exquisite Moments: West Lake and Southern Song Art*. New York: China Institute Gallery, 2001.

Lee, Sherman E., and Wai-kam Ho. "The Nature and Significance of the Collection of Liang Ch'ing-piao." In *Zhongyang yanjiu yuan guoji Hanxue huiyi lunwenji* [International Conference on Sinology], pp. 102–57. Taipei: Zhongyang yanjiu yuan, 1981.

Levine, Gregory P. "Rakan in America: Travels of the Daitokuji *Five Hundred Luohan*." In *Moving Objects: Time, Space, and Context*. Tokyo: National Research Institute for Cultural Properties, 2004.

Li Yongqiao. *Zhang Daqian nianpu* [Chronology of Zhang Daqian's life]. Chengdu: Sichuan sheng shehui kexueyuan chubanshe, 1987.

Li, Chu-tsing, ed. *Artists and Patrons: Some Social and Economic Aspects of Chinese Painting*. Lawrence, KS: Kress Foundation Department of Art History, University of Kansas, 1989.

———. "Recent History of the Palace Collection." *Archives of the Chinese Art Society of America* 12 (1958): 61–75.

Li, Wai-yee. "The Collector, the Connoisseur, and Late-Ming Sensibility." *T'oung Pao* 81, nos. 4–5 (1995): 275–86.

Liangshu [Book of Liang]. Ershisishi [The twenty four chronicles], no. 21. Beijing: Zhonghua shuju, 1995

Liscomb, Kathlyn. "Wang Fu's Contribution to a New Painting Style in the Ming Dynasty." *Artibus Asiae* 48, no. 1/2 (1987): 39–78.

Liu Gangji. *Wen Zhengming*. Changchun: Jilin meishu chubanshe, 1996.

Liu Jiuan. "Wumen huajia zhi biehaotu jianding julie" [Distinguishing examples of byname pictures by painters of the Wu School]. In *Wumen huapai yanjiu* [Research on Wu School painting], pp. 35–46. Beijing: Zijincheng chubanshe, 1993.

Liu, Cary Y. "The *Admonitions Scroll* in the Context of Ming Aesthetics and Collecting: Material Artefact, Cultural Biography, and Cultural Imagining." In McCausland, *Gu Kaizi and the Admonitions Scroll*, pp. 257–59.

———. "Asian Art Collection: From Exotica to Art and History." *Record of The Art Museum, Princeton University* 55, nos. 1–2 (1996): 125–34.

———. *Chinese Flower Painting: Reflections of Glory, Virtue, and Humility*. Princeton: The Art Museum, Princeton University, 1996. Exhibition brochure.

———. "The Ch'ing Dynasty Wen-yüan-ko Imperial Library: Architecture and the Ordering of Knowledge." PhD diss., Princeton University, June 1997.

———. "Seeing Double: Copies and Copying in the Arts of China." *Orientations* 32, no. 3 (2001): 154.

Liuru Jushi huapu [Collection of paintings by Liuru Jushi]. In vol. 2 of *Meishu congshu* [Fine art series], edited by Huang Binhong and Deng Shi. Reprint, Nanjing: Jiangsu guji chubanshe, 1997.

Lovell, Hin-cheung. *An Annotated Bibliography of Chinese Painting Catalogues and Related Texts*. Ann Arbor: Center for Chinese Studies, The University of Michigan, 1973.

Ma Tailai [Ma Tai-loi]. "Mingdai wenwu dagu Wu Ting shilue" [The case of Wu Ting, a Ming dynasty connoisseur and merchant]. *Gugong xueshu jikan* [National Palace Museum research quarterly] 23, no. 1 (2005): 397–411.

McCausland, Shane, ed. *Gu Kaizi and the Admonitions Scroll: Ideals of Etiquette, Art and Empire from Early China*. London: The British Museum Press with the Percival David Foundation, 2003.

Meishu congshu [Fine art series]. See Huang Binhong and Deng Shi.

Mi Fu. *Shu shi* [History of calligraphy]. In vol. 1 of *Meishu congshu* [Fine art series], edited by Huang Binhong and Deng Shi. Reprint, Nanjing: Jiangsu guji chubanshe, 1997.

Midian zhulin Shiqu baoji hebian [Pearl forest of the Secret Hall (and) Treasured boxes of the Stone Channel (Pavilion)]. 12 vols. 1745. Reprint, Shanghai: Shanghai shuju, 1988.

Ming shi. 28 vols. Beijing: Zhonghua shuju, 1974.

Ming shilu [Veritable record of the Ming]. Hand-copied manuscript. [Nanjing]: Jiangsu Library of Sinology, n. d.

Minguo renwu da cidian [Biographical dictionary of the Republican period]. Yangzhou: Hebei renmin chubanshe, 1991.

Mote, Frederick W., and Hung-lam Chu. *Calligraphy and the East Asian Book*. Special catalogue issue of *The Gest Library Journal* 2, no. 2 (1988). Boston: Shambhala; New York: Random House, 1989.

Murray, Julia K. *Ma Hezhi and the Illustration of the "Book of Odes."* Cambridge: Cambridge University Press, 1993.

Nakata Yūjirō and Fu Shen, eds. *Ō Bei shūzō Chūgoku hōsho meisekishū* [Masterpieces of Chinese calligraphy in American and European collections]. 4 vols. Tokyo: Chūōkōron-sha, 1981–83.

Naquin, Susan. "The Forbidden City Goes Abroad: Qing History and the Foreign Exhibitions of the Palace Museum, 1974–2004." *T'oung Pao* 90, no. 4 (2004): 341–97.

Nie Chongzheng. "Qing Dynasty Court Painting." In Rawski and Rawson, *China: The Three Emperors*, pp. 76–115.

———, ed. *Qingdai gongting huihua* [Qing dynasty court painting]. Shanghai: Shanghai kexue jishu chubanshe, 1999.

Nishikawa Yasushi. "Shinjutsu no Gyōjō-jō" [The newly discovered *Xingrang tie*]. *Shohin* [Calligraphy], no. 142 (1963): 2–39.

Okakura, Kakuzō. "Exhibition of Recent Acquisitions in Chinese and Japanese Art." *Museum of Fine Arts Bulletin* 10, no. 60 (December 1912): 46–58.

Pan Tianshou. *Lidai huajia pingzhuan* [Biographies and commentaries on painters of successive dynasties]. Reprint, Hong Kong: Zhonghua shu ju, 1986.

Pei Xiaoyuan. *Zhenguan gong si huashi* [History of paintings in imperial and private collections]. In vol. 1 of *Meishu congshu* [Fine art series], edited by Huang Binhong and Deng Shi. Reprint, Nanjing: Jiangsu guji chubanshe, 1997.

Peiwenzhai shuhua pu [Calligraphy and painting compendium of the Peiwen Studio]. 5 vols. Beijing: Zhongguo shudian, 1984.

Petrucci, Raphael. *Chinese Painters: A Critical Study*. New York: Brentano's, 1920.

Puyi. *From Emperor to Citizen: The Autobiography of Aisin-Gioro Pu Yi*. Translated with new general and chapter introductions by W. J. F. Jenner. Oxford: Oxford University Press, 1987.

Qi Gong. "Dong Yuan *Longsu jiaomin tu*" [Dong Yuan's painting of "Residents of the Capital City"]. *Meishu jia* [Artist], no. 5 (1978): 50–51.

Qianlong huangdi de wenhua daye/Emperor Ch'ien-lung's Grand Cultural Enterprise. Taipei: Guoli gugong bowuyuan, 2002.

Qing Gui and Dong Gao. *Guochao gong shi zheng xubian* [Official version of the history of the Qing imperial court]. 5 vols. In Zhongguo shixue congshu [Collected works of Chinese historiography]. Taipei: Mingu wushinian dongfang xuehui, 1961.

Rawski, Evelyn S. "The 'Prosperous Age': China in the Kangxi, Yongzheng, and Qianlong Reigns." In Rawski and Rawson, *China: The Three Emperors*, pp. 22–40.

Rawski, Evelyn S., and Jessica Rawson, eds. *China: The Three Emperors, 1662–1795.* London: Royal Academy of Arts, 2005.

Rawson, Jessica. "The Qianlong Emperor: Virtue and the Possession of Antiquity." In Rawski and Rawson, *China: The Three Emperors*, pp. 270–305.

Ren Daobin. *Dong Qichang xinian* [Dong Qichang's life year by year]. Beijing: Wenwu chubanshe, 1988.

Riely, Celia Carrington. "Tung Ch'i-ch'ang's Life (1555–1636)." In *The Century of Tung Ch'i-ch'ang 1555–1636*, edited by Wai-kam Ho, vol. 2, pp. 387–457. Kansas City: The Nelson-Atkins Museum of Art, 1992.

Rogers, Mary Ann. "Visions of Grandeur: The Life and Art of Dai Jin." In Richard M. Barnhart, *Painters of the Great Ming: The Imperial Court and the Zhe School*, pp. 127–94. Dallas: Dallas Museum of Art, 1993.

Rowley, George. "The Morris Collection of Chinese Paintings." *Record of the Museum of Historic Art, Princeton University* 6, nos. 1–2 (1947): 2–3.

———. "The Peterson Collection." *Record of The Museum of Historic Art, Princeton University* 1, no. 1 (1942): 3–7.

———. *Principles of Chinese Painting with Illustrations from the DuBois Schanck Morris Collection.* Princeton: Princeton University Press, 1947.

Ruan Yuan. *Shiqu suibi* [Notes on the Stone Channel]. In *Biji xiaoshuo daguan* [Compendium of notes and novels]. Yangzhou: Jiangsu Guangling guji keying chubanshe, 1984.

Sanxitang fatie [Model calligraphies of the Hall of Three Rarities]. 1750. Reprint, Harbin: Heilongjiang renmin chubanshe, 1984.

Segalen, Victor. *Essay on Exoticism: An Aesthetics of Diversity.* Translated and edited by Yaël Rachel Schlick. Durham: Duke University Press, 2002.

Sensabaugh, David Ake. "A Few Rocks Can Stir the Emotions: Chinese Gardens and Scholars." *Orientations* 31, no. 1 (Jan. 2000): 32–39.

———. "Guests at Jade Mountain: Aspects of Patronage in Fourteenth-Century K'un-shan." In *Artists and Patrons: Some Social and Economic Aspects of Chinese Painting*, edited by Chu-tsing Li, pp. 93–100. Lawrence, KS: Kress Foundation Department of Art History, 1989.

Shan Guoqiang. "Dai Jin zuopin shixu kao" [An investigation into the chronological sequence of Dai Jin's works]. *Gugong bowuyuan yuankan* [Palace Museum Bulletin], no. 4 (1993): 11–36.

Shen Kuo. *Yuankan Mengxi bitan* [Dream Pool essays, Yuan printing]. Beijing: Wenwu chubanshe, 1975.

Shi Shouqian [Shih Shou-chien]. "Zhepai huafeng yu guizu pinwei" [The style of the Zhe school and aristocratic taste]. In *Fengge yu shibian: Zhongguo huihuashi lun* [Style and social change: Essays on the history of Chinese painting], pp. 181–228. Taipei: Yunchen wenhua, 1996.

Shiqu baoji chubian [Treasured boxes of the Stone Channel Pavilion, part 1]. Compiled by Zhang Zhao. Submitted in 1745. 2 vols. Facsimile reprint, Taipei: National Palace Museum, 1971.

Shiqu baoji xubian [Treasured boxes of the Stone Channel Pavilion, part 2]. Compiled by Wang Jie et al. 7 vols. Facsimile reprint, Taipei: National Palace Museum, 1971.

Sirén, Osvald. *Chinese Painting: Leading Masters and Principles.* 7 vols. New York: The Ronald Press, 1958.

Song Gaozong. *Siling hanmo zhi* [Siling discussions on ink calligraphy]. In *Guhua pinlu* [Classification of ancient painters]. Siku yishu congshu [Art books from the Comprehensive library of the Four Treasuries]. Shanghai: Shanghai guji chubanshe, 1991.

Song Houmei. See Ishida, Hou-mei Sung.

Song Huizong. *Xuanhe lunhua zaping* [Xuanhe art critiques]. In vol. 3 of *Meishu congshu* [Fine art series], edited by Huang Binhong and Deng Shi. Reprint, Nanjing: Jiangsu guji chubanshe, 1997.

Spence, Jonathan D. *Emperor of China: Self-Portrait of K'ang-hsi.* New York: Knopf, 1974.

———. *Treason by the Book.* New York: Viking Penguin, 2001.

Sun Chengze. *Gengzi xiaoxia ji* [Notes to idle away the summer of the *gengzi* year]. 1660. Reprint, Taipei: Hanhua, 1971.

Tao Zongyi. *Shushi huiyao* [Concise history of calligraphy]. Siku quanshu zhenben shiji [Precious editions from the Comprehensive library of the Four Treasuries, tenth collection], no. 166–68, edited by Wang Yunwu. Taipei: Wenshizhe chubanshe, 1974.

Thiriez, Régine. *Barbarian Lens: Western Photographers of the Qianlong Emperor's European Palaces.* [Amsterdam]: Gordon and Breach Publishers, 1998.

Tie Yuqin. *Shenjing huanggong* [The imperial palace in Shenyang]. Beijing: Zijincheng chubanshe, 1987.

Tomita, Kojiro. "The Five-colored Parakeet By Hui Tsung (1082–1135)." *Museum of Fine Arts Bulletin* 31 (October 1933): 75–79.

———. "Scroll of Six Odes from Mao Shih." *Museum of Fine Arts Bulletin* 50, no. 281 (October 1952): 41–49.

Tseng, Hsien-chi. "A Study of the Nine Dragons Scroll." *Archives of the Chinese Art Society of America* 11 (1957): 17–39.

Umi o watatta Chūgoku no sho: Eriotto korekushon to Sō Gen no meiseki / The Embodied Image: Chinese Calligraphy from the John B. Elliott Collection. Edited by Ōsaka Shiritsu Bijutsukan. Tokyo: Yomiuri Shinbunsha, 2003.

Wakeman, Frederick, Jr. *The Great Enterprise: The Manchu Reconstruction of Imperial Order in Seventeenth-Century China.* Berkeley: University of California Press, 1985.

Wan Yi, Wang Shuqing, and Liu Lu. *Qingdai gongting shi* [History of the Qing imperial court]. Tianjin: Baihua wenyi chubanshe, 2004.

Wang Ao et al., ed. *Gusu zhi* [Gazetteer of Suzhou Prefecture]. 1506. Zhongguo shixue congshu [Collected works of Chinese historiography]. Taipei: Taiwan Xuesheng shuju, 1965.

Wang Lianqi. "Zhao Mengfu wei qi daibi [Zhao Mengfu ghost writes for his wife]." *Zijincheng* [Forbidden City] gen. no. 23, no. 1 (1984): 42–43.

Wang Yuxian. *Huishi beikao* [Reference for painting]. In *Gengzi xiaoxia ji* [Gengzi summer pastime]. Siku yishu congshu [Art books from the Comprehensive library of the Four Treasuries]. Shanghai: Shanghai guji chubanshe, 1991.

Wang Zhuangwei. *Shufa congtan* [Collected notes on calligraphy]. Taipei: Zhonghua congshu bianshen weiyuanhui, 1965.

Watt, James C. Y., ed. *The Translation of Art: Essays on Chinese Painting and Poetry.* Renditions Special Art Issue. Hong Kong: Center for Translation Projects, The Chinese University of Hong Kong, 1976.

Weidner, Marsha. "Aspects of Painting and Patronage at the Mongol Court, 1260–1368." In Li, *Artists and Patrons*, pp. 37–59.

———, ed. *Flowering in the Shadows: Women in the History of Chinese and Japanese Painting.* Honolulu: University of Hawaii Press, 1990.

Weng Tonghe. *Weng Tonghe riji* [Diary of Wen Tonghe]. 1925. Beijing: Zhonghua shuju, 1989.

Wolseley, G. J. *Narrative of the War with China in 1860.* 1862. Reprint, Wilmington: Scholarly Resources, Inc., 1972.

Wu Hung. "Emperor's Masquerade—'Costume Portraits' of Yongzheng and Qianlong." *Orientations* 26, no. 7 (July/August 1995): 25–41.

Wu Sheng. *Daguanlu.* Preface 1712. In *Yishu shangjian xuanzhen* [Selected writings on art appreciation]. Taipei: Hanhua, 1970.

Wu Xiu. *Qingxiaguan lunhua jueju* [Qingxiaguan collection of quatrains on painting]. In vol. 2 of *Meishu congshu* [Fine art series], edited by Huang Binhong and Deng Shi. Reprint, Nanjing: Jiangsu guji chubanshe, 1997.

Xi'an beilin bowuguan [Introduction to the Xi'an Forest of Stelae]. Xi'an: Shaanxi renmin chubanshe, 2000.

Xiao Yanyi. "Song Ke shu Tao shi bing hua zhu shi xiao jing liang ben bianwei" [Judging the authenticity of two copies of Song Ke's *Tao Qian's Poems* and *Bamboo and Rocks*]. *Gugong bowuyuan yuankan* (1985.1): 48–52.

Xie Wei. *Zhongguo huaxue zhuzuo kaolu* [Catalogue of writings on Chinese painting]. Shanghai: Shanghai shuhua chubanshe, 1998.

Xie Zhiliu. "The Ch'an of Painting in Tung Ch'i-ch'ang's Theory." In *The Century of Tung Ch'i-ch'ang, 1555–1636*, edited by Wai-kam Ho, vol. 2, pp. xxxv–xxxvi. Kansas City: The Nelson-Atkins Museum of Art, 1992.

Xing Yongfu and Shi Liwu, ed. *Qinggong Rehe dang'an* [Qing imperial archives at Jehol]. National Archives Series. Beijing: Zhongguo dangan chubanshe, 2003.

Xu Qin. *Ming hua lu* [Ming dynasty paintings]. In vol. 1 of *Meishu congshu* [Fine art series], edited by Huang Binhong and Deng Shi. Reprint, Nanjing: Jiangsu guji chubanshe, 1997.

Xuanhe huapu [Xuanhe painting catalogue]. Reprinted in *Huashi* [History of painting]. Siku yishu quanshu [Art books from the Comprehensive library of the Four Treasuries]. Shanghai: Shanghai guji chubanshe, 1991.

Yang Boda. *Qingdai huayuan* [The Qing imperial art academy]. Beijing: Zijincheng chubanshe, 1993.

Yang Renkai. *Guobao chenfu lu—Gugong sanyi shuhua jianwen kaolue* [Record of the vicissitudes of national treasures: A brief account of what is known of the calligraphy and paintings dispersed from the former palaces]. Shanghai: Renmin meishu chubanshe, 1991.

———, ed. *Liaoningsheng bowuguan cang shuhua zhulu: Huihua juan* [Writings on paintings and calligraphic works in the collection of the Liaoning Provincial Museum: Volume on art]. Shenyang: Liaoning meishu chubanse, 1999.

———, ed. *Liaoningsheng bowuguan cang shuhua zhulu: Shufa juan* [Writings on paintings and calligraphic works in the collection of the Liaoning Provincial Museum: Volume on calligraphy]. Shenyang: Liaoning meishu chubanse, 1999.

Yang Wangxiu. *Zhongxing guange chucang tuhua ji* [Record of the paintings stored in the Zhongxing Guange hall]. In vol. 3 of *Meishu congshu* [Fine art series], edited by Huang Binhong and Deng Shi. Reprint, Nanjing: Jiangsu guji chubanshe, 1997.

Yang Yuanzheng. "Junjia liang hang shier zi, qiya yehou sanwan qian—Pulinsidun daxue yishu bowuguan cang 'Xingrang tie' liuchuan kaolue" [The Tang tracing copy of Wang Xizhi's calligraphy *Ritual to Pray for Good Harvest*: A study of its provenance]. *Gugong bowuyuan yuankan* [Palace Museum journal], gen. no. 135 (2008.1): 6–23.

Yee, Chiang. *The Chinese Eye: An Interpretation of Chinese Painting.* London: Methuen and Co., 1936.

Yoshida Haruki. "Guanyu Huqiushan tu zhi wojian" [My view concerning pictures of Tiger Hill]. In *Wumen huapai yanjiu* [Research on Wu School painting], pp. 65–75. Beijing: Zijincheng chubanshe, 1993.

Yu Jianhua. *Wang Fu.* Shanghai: Shanghai renmin meishu chubanshe, 1961.

———, ed. *Zhongguo meishujia renming cidian* [Dictionary of Chinese artists]. Shanghai: Shanghai renmin meishu chubanshe, 1996.

Yuan Jue. *Qing Rong ji* [Collection of writings by Qing Rong]. In *Sibu congkan chubian suoben* [Concise edition of the first compilation of the Four sections of literature]. Shanghai: Shangwu yinshuguan, 1928.

Zhang Geng. *Guochao huazheng lu* [Painters of the (Qing) dynasty]. Preface dated 1735. In *Zhongguo shuhua quanshu*, vol. 10, pp. 423–59. Shanghai: Shanghai shuhua chubanshe, 1996.

Zhang Heng. *Muyanzhai shuhua jianshang biji* [Notes on the connoisseurship of painting and calligraphy from the Muyan Studio]. Vol.: *Shufa er* [Calligraphy 2]. 1961. Beijing: Wenwu chubanshe, 2000.

Zhang Hongxing. "The Nineteenth-Century Provenance of the *Admonitions* Scroll: A Hypothesis." In McCausland, *Gu Kaizhi and the Admonitions Scroll*, pp. 277–87.

———. *The Qianlong Emperor: Treasures from the Forbidden City.* Edinburgh: National Museums of Scotland, 2002.

Zhang Yanyuan. *Fashu yaolu* [Essentials of calligraphy]. Reprinted in *Guhua pinlu* [Classification of ancient painters]. Siku yishu congshu [Art books from the Comprehensive library of the Four Treasuries]. Shanghai: Shanghai guji chubanshe, 1991.

———. *Lidai minghua ji* [Record of famous painters of successive dynasties]. Reprinted in *Guhua pinlu* [Classification of ancient painters]. Siku yishu congshu [Art books from the Comprehensive library of the Four Treasuries]. Shanghai: Shanghai guji chubanshe, 1991.

Zhang Yingwen. *Qing mi cang* [Pure and arcane collecting]. In vol. 1 of *Meishu congshu* [Fine art series], edited by Huang Binhong and Deng Shi. Reprint, Nanjing: Jiangsu guji chubanshe, 1997.

Zhao Yi. *Yanpu zaji* [Anecdotes to air under the eaves]. Qingdai shiliao biji congkan [Notes on Qing dynasty history and events series]. 1982. Reprint, Beijing: Zhonghua shuju, 1997.

Zheng Bingshan. *Shen Shitian* [Shen Shitian (Zhou)]. Shanghai: Shanghai renmin meishu chubanshe, 1958.

Zhongguo jianzhu shi lunwen xuanji [Selected essays on Chinese architectural history]. 2 vols. Taipei: Mingwen shuju, 1983.

Zhongguo shuhua quanshu [Comprehensive collection of Chinese calligraphy and painting]. 14 vols. Shanghai: Shanghai shuhua chubanshe, 1992–1999.

Zhou Mi. *Qidong yeyu* [Unofficial anecdotes from Eastern Qi]. Congshu jicheng chubian [Collection of serialized books, first compilation], no. 2779–82. Beijing: Zhonghua shuju, 1985.

———. *Yunyan guoyan lu* [Private collections viewed]. Congshu jicheng chubian [Collection of serialized books, first compilation], no. 1553. Beijing: Zhonghua shuju, 1985.

Zhu Jiajin, ed. *Lidai zhulu fashu mu* [Records of model calligraphy through the ages]. Beijing: Zijincheng chubanshe, 1997.

Zhu Jingxuan. *Tangchao minghua lu* [Masterpieces of the Tang dynasty]. In vol. 2 of *Meishu congshu* [Fine art series], edited by Huang Binhong and Deng Shi. Reprint, Nanjing: Jiangsu guji chubanshe, 1997.

Zhu Xi quanji [Comprehensive works of Zhu Xi]. Taipei: Wenguang tushu gongsi, 1963.

Zhu Xingzhai. *Yiyuan tan wang* [Reminiscences on art]. Hong Kong: Shanghai shuju, 1964.

China Institute Gallery Exhibitions: 1966–2008

** 1. SELECTIONS OF CHINESE ART FROM PRIVATE COLLECTIONS IN THE METROPOLITAN AREA
November 15, 1966–February 15, 1967
Curator: Mrs. Gilbert Katz

** 2. ART STYLES OF ANCIENT SHANG
April 5–June 11, 1967
Curator: Jean Young

** 3. ANIMALS AND BIRDS IN CHINESE ART
October 25, 1967–January 28, 1968
Curator: Fong Chow

** 4. GARDENS IN CHINESE ART
March 21–May 26, 1968
Curator: Wan-go H.C. Weng

** 5. CHINESE JADE THROUGH THE CENTURIES
October 24, 1968–January 26, 1969
Curator: Joan M. Hartman

** 6. FOREIGNERS IN ANCIENT CHINESE ART
March 27–May 25, 1969
Curator: Ezekiel Schloss

** 7. CHINESE PAINTED ENAMELS
October 23, 1969–February 1, 1970
Curator: J.A. Lloyd Hyde

**8. ALBUM LEAVES FROM THE SUNG AND YUAN DYNASTIES
March 26–May 30, 1970
Curator: C.C. Wang

** 9. MING PORCELAINS: A RETROSPECTIVE
October 29, 1970–January 31, 1971
Curator: Suzanne G. Valenstein

**10. CHINESE SILK TAPESTRY: K'O-SSU
March 24–May 27, 1971
Curator: Jean Mailey

** 11. EARLY CHINESE GOLD AND SILVER
October 21, 1971–January 30, 1972
Curator: Dr. Paul Singer

** 12. DRAGONS IN CHINESE ART
March 23–May 28, 1972
Curator: Hugo Munsterberg

** 13. WINTRY FORESTS, OLD TREES: SOME LANDSCAPE THEMES IN CHINESE PAINTING
October 26, 1972–January 28, 1973
Curator: Richard Barnhart

** 14. CERAMICS IN THE LIAO DYNASTY: NORTH AND SOUTH OF THE GREAT WALL
March 15–May 28, 1973
Curator: Yutaka Mino

** 15. CHINA TRADE PORCELAIN: A STUDY IN DOUBLE REFLECTIONS
October 25, 1973–January 27, 1974
Curator: Claire le Corbeiller

** 16. TANTRIC BUDDHIST ART
March 14–May 24, 1974
Curator: Eleanor Olson

** 17. FRIENDS OF WEN CHENG-MING: A VIEW FROM THE CRAWFORD COLLECTION
October 24, 1974–January 26, 1975
Curators: Marc F. Wilson and Kwan S. Wong

** 18. ANCIENT CHINESE JADES FROM THE BUFFALO MUSEUM OF SCIENCE
April 3–June 15, 1975
Curator: Joan M. Hartman

** 19. ART OF THE SIX DYNASTIES: CENTURIES OF CHANGE AND INNOVATION
October 29, 1975–February 1, 1976
Curator: Annette L. Juliano

** 20. CHINA'S INFLUENCE ON AMERICAN CULTURE IN THE 18TH AND 19TH CENTURIES
April 8 –June 13, 1976
Curators: Henry Trubner and William Jay Rathburn
(Exhibition traveled to the Seattle Art Museum, October 7–November 28, 1976.)

21. CHINESE FOLK ART IN AMERICAN COLLECTIONS: EARLY 15TH THROUGH 20TH CENTURIES
October 27, 1976–January 30, 1977
Curator: Tseng Yu-Ho Ecke

** 22. EARLY CHINESE MINIATURES
March 16–May 29, 1977
Curator: Dr. Paul Singer

** 23. I-HSING WARE
October 28, 1977–January 29, 1978
Curator: Terese Tse Bartholomew
(Exhibition traveled to the Nelson Gallery of Art, Kansas City, February 19–May 21, 1978, and the Asian Art Museum of San Francisco, June 16–September 21, 1978.)

**24. EMBROIDERY OF IMPERIAL CHINA
March 17–May 28, 1978
Curator: Jean Mailey

** 25. ORIGINS OF CHINESE CERAMICS
October 25, 1978–January 28, 1979
Curator: Clarence F. Shangraw

** 26. ART OF THE HAN
March 14–May 27, 1979
Curator: Ezekiel Schloss

27. TREASURES FROM THE METROPOLITAN MUSEUM OF ART
October 25–November 25, 1979
Curator: Clarence F. Shangraw

** 28. CHINESE ART FROM THE NEWARK MUSEUM
March 19–May 25, 1980
Curators: Valrae Reynolds and Yen Fen Pei

29. CHINESE PORCELAINS IN EUROPEAN MOUNTS
October 22, 1980–January 25, 1981
Curator: Sir Francis Watson

* 30. FREEDOM OF CLAY AND BRUSH THROUGH SEVEN CENTURIES IN NORTHERN CHINA: TZ'U-CHOU TYPE WARES 960–1600 A.D.
March 16–May 24, 1981
Curator: Yutaka Mino
(Exhibition originated at Indianapolis Museum of Art.)

**31. THE ART OF CHINESE KNOTTING
July 29–September 21, 1981
Curator: Hsia-Sheng Chen

**32. MASTERPIECES OF SUNG AND YUAN DYNASTY CALLIGRAPHY FROM THE JOHN M. CRAWFORD JR. COLLECTION
October 21, 1981–January 31, 1982
Curator: Kwan S. Wong, assisted by Stephen Addiss
(Exhibition traveled to the Spencer Museum, University of Kansas, March 14–April 18, 1982.)

33. THE COMMUNION OF SCHOLARS: CHINESE ART AT YALE
March 20–May 30, 1982
Curator: Mary Gardner Neill
(Exhibition traveled to the Museum of Fine Arts, Houston, June 22–August 22, 1982, and the Yale Art Gallery, New Haven, October 5, 1982–April 17, 1983.)

* 34. CHINA FROM WITHIN
November 4–December 12, 1982
A Smithsonian Institution Travelling Services Exhibition, organized by the International Photography Society in cooperation with the China Exhibition Agency, Beijing, and the Chinese Embassy, Washington, DC

**35. BAMBOO CARVING OF CHINA
March 18–May 29, 1983
Curators: Wang Shixiang and Wan-go H.C. Weng
(Exhibition traveled to The Nelson-Atkins Museum of Art, Kansas City, July 24–September 11, 1983, and the Asian Art Museum of San Francisco, October 3, 1983–January 15, 1984.)

36. CHINESE CERAMICS OF THE TRANSITIONAL PERIOD: 1620–1683
October 21, 1983–January 29, 1984
Curator: Stephen Little
(Exhibition traveled to the Kimbell Art Museum, Fort Worth, May 26–August 26, 1984.)

* 37. MASTERPIECES OF CHINESE EXPORT PORCELAIN AND RELATED DECORATIVE ARTS FROM THE MOTTAHEDEH COLLECTION
February 10–March 7, 1984
U.S.–China 200 Bicentennial Exhibition, organized by Anita Christy

**38. CHINESE TRADITIONAL ARCHITECTURE
April 6–June 10, 1984
Curator: Nancy Shatzman Steinhardt
(A permanent travelling exhibition of China Institute. Shown at Allegheny College, Meadeville, PA, March 28–April 19, 1985; Marlboro College, Marlboro, VT, September 11–October 31, 1985; State University of New York, Binghamton, January 7–February 27, 1986.)

** 39. CHINESE RARE BOOKS IN AMERICAN COLLECTIONS
October 20, 1984–January 29, 1985
Curator: Soren Edgren

40. THE SUMPTUOUS BASKET: CHINESE LACQUER WITH BASKETRY PANELS
March 20– June 3, 1985
Curator: James C.Y. Watt

** 41. KERNELS OF ENERGY, BONES OF EARTH: THE ROCK IN CHINESE ART
October 26, 1985–January 26, 1986
Curator: John Hay

* 42. PUPPETRY OF CHINA
April 19–June 29, 1986
Curator: Roberta Helmer Stalberg
Organized by the Center for Puppetry Arts, Atlanta

43. SELECTIONS OF CHINESE ART FROM PRIVATE COLLECTIONS
October 18, 1986–January 4, 1987
Exhibition celebrating the 60th Anniversary of China Institute and the 20th Anniversary of China Institute Gallery, organized by James C.Y. Watt and Annette L. Juliano.

* 44. 1987 NEW YEAR EXHIBITION

* 45. CHINESE FOLK ART
April 4–May 30, 1987
Curator: Nancy Zeng Berliner

** 46. RICHLY WOVEN TRADITIONS: COSTUMES OF THE MIAO OF SOUTHWEST CHINA AND BEYOND
October 22, 1987–January 4, 1988
Curator: Theresa Reilly

* 47. 1988 NEW YEAR EXHIBITION
February 4–February 24, 1988

** 48. RITUAL AND POWER: JADES OF ANCIENT CHINA
April 23–June 19, 1988
Curator: Elizabeth Childs-Johnson

** 49. STORIES FROM CHINA'S PAST
September 17–November 12, 1988
Curator: The Chinese Culture Center of San Francisco

* 50. 1989 NEW YEAR EXHIBITION: LANTERNS
January 28–February 25, 1989

* 51. MIND LANDSCAPES: THE PAINTINGS OF C.C. WANG
April 3–May 27, 1989
Curator: Jerome Silbergeld

**52. CHINA BETWEEN REVOLUTIONS: PHOTOGRAPHY BY SIDNEY D. GAMBLE, 1917–1927
June 29–September 9, 1989
Curator: The Sidney D. Gamble Foundation for China Studies and China Institute in America

* 53. VIEWS FROM JADE TERRACE:
CHINESE WOMEN ARTISTS, 1300–1912
October 5–December 2, 1989
Organized by Indianapolis Museum of Art

* 54. 1990 NEW YEAR EXHIBITION:
THE CHINESE EARTH–VIEWS OF NATURE
January–March 1990
Curator: Anita Christy

55. CLEAR AS CRYSTAL, RED AS FLAME:
LATER CHINESE GLASS
April 21–June 16, 1990
Curator: Claudia Brown and Donald Robiner

56. THE ECCENTRIC PAINTERS OF YANGZHOU
October 20–December 15, 1990
Curator: Vito Giacalone

* 57. 1991 NEW YEAR EXHIBITION:
CHILDREN IN CHINESE ART
January 26–March 2, 1991
Organized under the auspices of the China Institute Women's Association

**58. ANCIENT CHINESE BRONZE ART:
CASTING THE PRECIOUS SACRAL VESSEL
April 20–June 15, 1991
Curator: W. Thomas Chase

59. EARLY CHINESE CERAMICS FROM
NEW YORK STATE MUSEUMS
October 19–December 14, 1991
Curator: Martie W. Young

60. TREASURES OF THE LAST EMPEROR:
SELECTIONS FROM THE PALACE MUSEUM, BEIJING
February 1–March 7, 1992
Curator: Lawrence Wu

**61. LAMAS, PRINCES AND BRIGANDS:
PHOTOGRAPHS BY JOSEPH ROCK OF THE
TIBETAN BORDERLANDS OF CHINA
April 15–July 31, 1992
Curator: Michael Aris

** 62. WORD AS IMAGE:
THE ART OF CHINESE SEAL ENGRAVING
October 21–December 12, 1992
Curator: Jason C. Kuo

63. A YEAR OF GOOD FORTUNE:
LEGENDS OF THE ROOSTER AND
TRADITIONS OF THE CHINESE NEW YEAR
January 19–March 6, 1993
Curator: Willow Weilan Hai

* 64. DISCARDING THE BRUSH:
GAO QIPEI, 1660–1734
April 17–June 12, 1993
Curator: Klass Ruitenbeek
Organized by the Rijksmuseum Amsterdam

**65. AS YOU WISH: SYMBOL AND MEANING ON
CHINESE PORCELAINS FROM THE TAFT MUSEUM
October 23–January 15, 1994
Curator: David T. Johnson

* 66. SENDING AWAY THE OLD,
WELCOMING THE NEW
February 5–March 5, 1994
Curator: Karen Kane

* 67. CAPTURING A WORLD:
CHINA AND ITS PEOPLE–
PHOTOGRAPHY BY JOHN THOMSON
March 26–June 11, 1994
Curator: organized by the British Council, catalog by the British Council

* 68. AT THE DRAGON COURT:
CHINESE EMBROIDERED MANDARIN
SQUARES FROM THE SCHUYLER V.R.
CAMMANN COLLECTION
October 20–December 22, 1994
Brochure from similar show which took place at Yale Univ. Art Gallery
Curator: John Finlay

**69. ANIMALS OF THE CHINESE ZODIAC:
CELEBRATING CHINESE NEW YEAR
January 20–March 4, 1995
Curator: Willow Weilan Hai

70. CHINESE PORCELAINS OF THE
SEVENTEENTH CENTURY: LANDSCAPES,
SCHOLARS' MOTIFS AND NARRATIVES
April 22–August 5, 1995
Curator: Julia B. Curtis

71. ABSTRACTION AND EXPRESSION IN
CHINESE CALLIGRAPHY
October 14–December 21, 1995
Curator: H. Christopher Luce
(Exhibition traveled to the Seattle Art Museum, Washington, November 21, 1996 to March 23, 1997.)

* 72. CALLIGRAPHY AS LIVING ART:
SELECTIONS FROM THE JILL SACKLER
CHINESE CALLIGRAPHY COMPETITION
Feburary 3–March 9, 1996
Curator: Willow Weilan Hai, in conjunction with the A. M. Sackler Foundation, Washington, D.C.

* 73. HARE'S FUR, TORTOISESHELL AND
PARTRIDGE FEATHERS CHINESE BROWN-AND BLACK-GLAZED CERAMICS, 400–1400
April 20–July 6, 1996
Curator: Robert Mowry
Organized by the Harvard University Art Museum, Massachusetts

74. THE LIFE OF A PATRON: ZHOU LIANGGONG
(1612–1672) AND THE PAINTERS OF
SEVENTEENTH-CENTURY CHINA
October 23–December 21, 1996
Curator: Hongnam Kim

*75. ADORNMENT FOR ETERNITY:
STATUS AND RANK IN CHINESE ORNAMENT
February 6-July 14, 1997
Curators: Julia White and Emma Bunker
Organized by the Denver Art Museum

76. POWER AND VIRTUE:
THE HORSE IN CHINESE ART
September 11 - December 13, 1997
Curator: Robert E. Harrist, Jr.

*77. SCENT OF INK: THE ROY AND MARILYN PAPP COLLECTION OF CHINESE ART
February 5 – June 20, 1998
Curator: Claudia Brown
Organized by the Phoenix Art Museum

*78. CHINESE SNUFF BOTTLES FROM THE PAMELA R.
LESSING FRIEDMAN COLLECTION
September 16 – December 13, 1998
Organized by the Asian Art Coordinating Council

79. A LITERATI LIFE IN THE TWENTIETH CENTURY: WANG FANGYU—ARTIST, SCHOLAR, CONNOISSEUR
February 11-June 20, 1999
Curator: H. Christopher Luce

80. THE RESONANCE OF THE QIN IN EAST ASIAN ART
September 17-December 12, 1999
Curator: Stephen Addiss

*81. THE STORY OF RED: CELEBRATE THE CHINESE NEW YEAR IN 2000
January 12 - February 11, 2000
Curator: Willow Weilan Hai Chang

82. DAWN OF THE YELLOW EARTH: ANCIENT CHINESE CERAMICS FROM THE MEIYINTANG COLLECTION
March 21-June 18, 2000
Curator: Regina Krahl

83. THE CHINESE PAINTER AS POET
September 14-December 20, 2000
Curator: Jonathan Chaves

*84. LIVING HERITAGE: VERNACULAR ENVIRONMENT IN CHINA
January 25-June 10, 2001
Curator: Kai-yin Lo
Re-organized by the China Institute Gallery

85. EXQUISITE MOMENTS: WEST LAKE & SOUTHERN SONG ART
September 25-December 9, 2001
Curator: Hui-shu Lee

*86. CIRCLES OF REFLECTION: THE CARTER COLLECTION OF CHINESE BRONZE MIRRORS
February 7-June 2, 2002
Curator: Ju-hsi Chou
Organized by the Cleveland Museum of Art

87. BLANC DE CHINE: DIVINE IMAGES IN PORCELAIN
September 19–December 7, 2002
Curator: John Ayers

*88. WEAVING CHINA'S PAST: THE AMY S. CLAGUE COLLECTION OF CHINESE TEXTILES
January 30–June 7, 2003
Curator: Claudia Brown
Organized by the Phoenix Art Museum

89. PASSION FOR THE MOUNTAINS: 17TH CENTURY LANDSCAPE PAINTINGS FROM THE NANJING MUSEUM
September 18 – December 20, 2003
Curator: Willow Weilan Hai Chang

*90. GOLD AND JADE: IMPERIAL JEWELRY OF THE MING DYNASTY FROM THE NANJING MUNICIPAL MUSEUM
February 12 – June 5, 2004
Re-organized by the China Institute Gallery in collaboration with the Nanjing Municipal Museum

*91. THE SCHOLAR AS COLLECTOR: CHINESE ART AT YALE
September 3 – December 11, 2004
Curator: David Ake Sensabaugh
Organized by the Yale University Art Gallery

92. PROVIDING FOR THE AFTERLIFE: "BRILLIANT ARTIFACTS" FROM SHANDONG
February 3 – June 4, 2005
Curators: Susan L. Beningson and Cary Y. Liu
Organized by the China Institute Gallery in collaboration with the Shandong Provincial Museum

*93. MASTERPIECES OF CHINESE LACQUER FROM THE MIKE HEALY COLLECTION
September 16 – December 3, 2005
Curator: Julia M. White
Organized by the Honolulu Academy of Arts

94. TRADE TASTE & TRANSFORMATION: JINGDEZHEN PORCELAIN FOR JAPAN, 1620 – 1645
February 2, 2006 – June 10, 2006
Curator: Julia B. Curtis
Organized by the China Institute Gallery
(Exhibition traveled to the Honolulu Academy of Arts, Honolulu, July 19, 2006 – October 8, 2006)

*95. THE BEAUTY OF CHINESE GARDENS
June 28 – August 12, 2006
Organized by the China Institute Gallery

96. SHU: REINVENTING BOOKS IN CONTEMPORARY CHINESE ART
Part I: September 28 – November 11, 2006
Part II: December 13 – February 24, 2007
Curator: Wu Hung
Organized by the China Institute Gallery
(Exhibition traveling to Seattle Asian Art Museum, August 9 – December 2, 2007 and Honolulu Academy of Arts June 25 – August 24, 2008)

*97. TEA, WINE AND POETRY: THE ART OF DRINKING VESSELS THE INTERNATIONAL ASIAN ART FAIR, NEW YORK
March 23 – March 28, 2007
Organized by the China Institute Gallery

*98. TEA, WINE AND POETRY: QING DYNASTY LITERATI AND THEIR DRINKING VESSELS
March 24 – June 16, 2007
Curators: Guo Ruoyu, Soong Shu Kong
Organized by the University Museum and Art Gallery, The University of Hong Kong

99. BUDDHIST SCULPTURE FROM CHINA: SELECTIONS FROM XI'AN BEILIN MUSEUM FIFTH THROUGH NINTH CENTURIES
September 20 – December 8, 2007
Curator: Annette L. Juliano

* 100. ENCHANTED STORIES: CHINESE SHADOW THEATER IN SHAANXI
January 31 – May 11, 2008
Curators: Chen Shanqiao, Li Hongjun and Zhao Nong
Organized by the China Institute Gallery in collaboration with Shaanxi Provincial Art Gallery

*101. BEIJING 2008: A PHOTOGRAPHIC JOURNEY
June 12 – August 17, 2008
A special exhibition organized by the China Institute Gallery and the Beijing Archive Bureau

For information on the availability of these titles and others, please contact China Institute in America at (212) 744-8181
* No catalogue or exhibition catalogue published by another institution
** Catalogue out of print

FRIENDS OF THE GALLERY

Patrons
Anla Cheng and Mark Kingdon
Argie and Oscar Tang

Leaders
Jane DeBevoise and Paul Calello
John R. and Lynne W. Doss
Robert T. and Kay F. Gow
Alice King
Abel and Sophia Sheng

Sponsors
Susan L. Beningson
Mrs. Christopher C.Y. Chen
John R. and Julia B. Curtis
Dr. Richard and Ruth Dickes
Agnes Gund and Daniel Shapiro
Margro R. Long
Mechlin and Valery Moore
Robert Rosenkranz and Alexandra Munroe
Martha Sutherland
Mary J. Wallach
Charlotte C. Weber
Marie-Hélène Weill
Mrs. Henry H. Weldon
Wan-go H.C. Weng
Robert P. and Barbara Youngman

Friends
Robert M. Beningson
Berwald Oriental Art
William M. Carey
Young Yang Chung
Richard M. and Peggy Danziger
Bruce B. and Ruth Stricker Dayton
Elizabeth Strong De Cuevas
Giuseppe Eskenazi
Michael E. and Winnie Feng
Hart and Nancy B. Fessenden
Ta Chun Hsu
Karen K. Hsu
Carolyn Hsu-Balcer and René Balcer
Annette L. Juliano and Joseph L. Geneve
Virginia A. Kamsky
William W. Karatz
Younghee Kim-Wait and Jarrett F. Wait

Angela H. King
James J. and Helen D. Lally
John M. Leger and Sophie Orloff
William E. and Helen Y. Little
Robert W. and Virginia Riggs Lyons
Warren A. Mackey
Clare Tweedy McMorris and Howard McMorris, III
Gerald M. Meistrell
Robert E. and Joyce H. Mims
Veronica Ogden
William N. Raiford
Theresa M. Reilly
James and Joanne Quan Reynolds
Jeannette N. Rider
Howard and Mary Ann Rogers
Diane H. Schafer and Jeffrey A. Stein
Peter W. Scheinman and Barbara Giordano
Stuart Skalka
Mei Wu Stanton
Charles J. Tanenbaum
Patricia P. Tang
Theow-Huang Tow
Shao F. and Cheryl L. Wang
Laura B. Whitman and Thomas Danziger
Yvonne L. C. and Frederick Wong
Denis C. and Kathleen Yang
Laurie and David Y. Ying

GALLERY COMMITTEE

Virginia Kamsky, Chair
Agnes Gund, Vice-Chair
Yvonne L.C. Wong, Vice-Chair

Susan L. Beningson
Claudia Brown
John R. Curtis, Jr.
Robert E. Harrist, Jr.
Maxwell K. Hearn
Annette L. Juliano
Diane H. Schafer
David Ake Sensabaugh
Jerome Silbergeld
Marie-Hélène Weill
I. Peter Wolff

GALLERY STAFF

Willow Weilan Hai Chang, Director
Sara Tam, Registrar
Caroline Antonelli, Assistant

DOCENTS

Larry Chang
Viviane Chen
Yue Ma
Roberta Nitka
Myoungsook "Mia" Park
Chin-ni Tzou
Pamela Frances Yap

VOLUNTEERS

Ann Dillon
Jackie Handel
Maximilian Kempf
Mary McFadden
Pamela May
Clelia Rotella
Irene Sommerfield
Anna-Rose Tykulsker
Jennifer Wang
Gloria Young